Marriage as a Covenant

Biblical Studies Library

Marriage as a Covenant

Biblical Law and Ethics
as Developed from Malachi

Gordon P. Hugenberger

Baker Books

A Division of Baker Book House Co
Grand Rapids, Michigan 49516

© 1994 by E. J. Brill, Leiden, The Netherlands

Published by Baker Books
a division of Baker Book House Company
P.O. Box 6287, Grand Rapids, MI 49516-6287

First cloth edition published 1994 by E. J. Brill as volume 52 in Supplements to Vetus Testamentum.

First paperback edition published 1998 by Baker Books.

Printed in the United States of America

Library of Congress Cataloging-in-Publication Data is on file at the Library of Congress, Washington, D.C.

ISBN: 0-8010-2192-8

For information about academic books, resources for Christian leaders, and all new releases available from Baker Book House, visit our web site: http://www.bakerbooks.com

FOR JANIE,
חברתי ואשת בריתי

CONTENTS

ACKNOWLEDGEMENTS

It is a very pleasant duty to express here my sincere thanks to my thesis supervisor, Dr. G.J. Wenham, for his patience, careful guidance, and many helpful suggestions over the course of the production of the dissertation which was the precursor of the present work. Beyond this specific help, he has provided a model of meticulous, productive, and relevant scholarship, which I can only hope to emulate.

I am grateful also to the Rev. Canon A.C.J. Phillips for his help as my outside supervisor, offering many valuable comments and encouragement when needed.

Numerous improvements in the present revision owe their existence to the perspicacity of Dr. A. Lemaire, who very generously provided detailed suggestions and constructive criticism in his capacity as a series editor for Supplements to *Vetus Testamentum*.

Thanks are also due to Brian A. Smith, my Teaching Fellow, for his help in the tedious work of indexing the footnotes of chapters six through eight.

While my indebtedness to the community of scholarship is cheerfully acknowledged throughout this work, at almost every turn I am aware of a more personal debt to the scholarly example, academic interests, and encouragement of my colleagues in the Biblical Studies Division at Gordon-Conwell Theological Seminary and especially of two former teachers, Prof. M.G. Kline also of Gordon-Conwell Theological Seminary and Prof. W.G. Lambert of Birmingham University.

It would be impossible to register adequately my sense of gratitude to each of my brothers and sisters at the Orthodox Congregational Church of Lanesville. Without the original prompting of Edwin B. Cobb I would never have dared to undertake this work. Without the subsequent willingness of the church to grant me the necessary time to do this research, as well as their on-going prayer, constant encouragements (especially from Richard N. Gray, who also preached in my stead one year), and financial support, the work would never have been completed.

As for my family, and especially Janie, who also provided indispensable editorial assistance, I know that I can never repay them for their love and support.

Naturally, in spite of the substantial help I have received, I bear full responsibility for the views expressed and the remaining defects of this work.

ABBREVIATIONS

The abbreviations for biblical books and Apocrypha follow the conventions of *JBL* 107 (1988) 584.

AASOR	The Annual of the American Schools of Oriental Research (1920-)
AB	The Anchor Bible, ed. W.F. Albright and D.N. Freedman, *et al.*
ABL	R.F. Harper, *Assyrian and Babylonian Letters*, 14 vols. (1892-1914)
AfO	*Archiv für Orientforschung*
AHw	W. von Soden, *Akkadisches Handwörterbuch* (1959-1985)
AJSL	*American Journal of Semitic Languages and Literature*
AL	W.L. Moran, *The Amarna Letters* (1992)
AnBib	Analecta biblica
ANEP	*Ancient Near Eastern Pictures*, Second Edition with Supplement, ed. J.B. Pritchard (1969)
ANET	*Ancient Near Eastern Texts Relating to the Old Testament*, Third Edition with Supplement, ed. J.B. Pritchard (1969)
AnOr	Analecta orientalia, Rome (1931-)
AOAT	Alter Orient und Altes Testament, ed. K. Bergerhof, M. Dietrich, and O. Loretz
ARN	*Altbabylonische Rechtsurkunden aus Nippur*, M. Çiğ, H. Kizilyay, F.R. Kraus (1952)
ASV	*The Holy Bible containing the Old and New Testaments. Newly Edited by the American Revision Committee, A.D. 1901, Standard Edition* (1901)
AT	Alte Testament
AT	D.J. Wiseman, *The Alalakh Tablets* (1953)
ATD	Das Alte Testament Deutsch, ed. V. Herntrich and A. Weiser; for more recent volumes, O. Kaiser and L. Perlitt (1949-)
AUSS	*Andrews University Seminary Studies*
AV	Authorized Version (Bible)
BA	*Biblical Archaeologist*
BAR	*Biblical Archaeology Review*
BASOR	*Bulletin of the American Schools of Oriental Research*

Bauer-Leander   H. Bauer and P. Leander, *Historische Grammatik der hebräischen Sprache des Alten Testamentes* (1922)

BDB   F. Brown, S.R. Driver, C.A. Briggs, *A Hebrew and English Lexicon of the Old Testament* (1907)

BE   *The Babylonian Expedition of the University of Pennsylvania, Series A: Cuneiform Texts,* Philadelphia (1893-1911), München (1913-14)

BHS   *Biblia Hebraica Stuttgartensia,* ed. K. Elliger and W. Rudolph (1983)

BibOr   Biblica et orientalia

BKAT   Biblischer Kommentar: Altes Testament, ed. M. Noth, S. Herrmann, and H.W. Wolff (1955-)

Blass and Debrunner
                  F. Blass and A. Debrunner, *A Greek Grammar of the New Testament and Other Early Christian Literature,* trans. and revised by R. W. Funk (1961)

BO   *Bibliotheca orientalis*

BOT   De Boeken van het Oude Testament, ed. A. van den Born, J. van Dodewaard, W. Grossouw, and J. van der Ploeg

Brockelmann   C. Brockelmann, *Hebräische Syntax* (1956)

BWANT   Beiträge zur Wissenschaft vom Alten und Neuen Testament

BZAW   Beihefte zur Zeitschrift für die alttestamentliche Wissenschaft

CAD   *The Assyrian Dictionary of the Oriental Institute of the University of Chicago,* ed. J.A. Brinkman, M. Civil, I.J. Gelb, B. Landsberger, A.L. Oppenheim, and E. Reiner (1956-)

CAH   *Cambridge Ancient History*

CBC   The Cambridge Bible Commentary on the New English Bible, ed. P.R. Ackroyd, *et al.*

CBQ   *Catholic Biblical Quarterly*

CD   Damascus Document or Zadokite Fragment

CH   Laws of Hammurabi

COT   Commentaar op het Oude Testament, ed. G.C. Aalders, W.H. Gispen, and N. Ridderbos

Cowley   A.E. Cowley, *Aramaic Papyri of the Fifth Century B.C. Edited with Translation and Notes* (1923)

CT   *Cuneiform Texts from Babylonian Tablets, etc., in the British Museum,* 52 vols. (1896-)

D   Deuteronomic Source

DJD   Discoveries in the Judaean Desert of Jordan, ed. P. Benoit, J.T. Milik, and R. de Vaux (1955-)

E   Elohist Source

EA	J.A. Knudtzon, O. Weber, and E. Ebeling, *Die El-Amarna-Tafeln*, 2 vols. (1915)
ET	English translation
Even-Shoshan	*A New Concordance of the Old Testament Using the Hebrew and Aramaic Text*, ed. A. Even-Shoshan (1983)
EvT	*Evangelische Theologie*
ExpTim	*Expository Times*
FRLANT	Forschungen zur Religion und Literatur des Alten und Neuen Testaments
Fs	Festschrift
GAG	W. von Soden, *Grundriss der Akkadischen Grammatik* (1969)
Gesenius	*Gesenius' Hebrew and Chaldee Lexicon*, trans. S.P. Tregelles (1949)
GKC	*Gesenius' Hebrew Grammar*, second edition, ed. E. Kautzsch, trans. A.E. Cowley (1910)
H	The Holiness Code, i.e., Leviticus 17-26. Alternatively, in the context of a marriage document, H represents the husband's name
HAT	Handbuch zum Alten Testament, ed. O. Eissfeldt (1937-)
Hermeneia	Hermeneia — A Critical and Historical Commentary on the Bible, ed. F.M. Cross Jr., *et al.*
HL	Hittite Laws
Holladay	W.L. Holladay, *A Concise Hebrew and Aramaic Lexicon of the Old Testament* (1971)
Huehnergard	J. Huehnergard, "Five Tablets From the Vicinity of Emar" (1983)
HSM	Harvard Semitic Monograph
HSS	Harvard Semitic Series, 24 vols.
HSSt	Harvard Semitic Studies
HTR	*Harvard Theological Review*
HUCA	*Hebrew Union College Annual*
HKAT	Handkommentar zum Alten Testament, ed. W. Nowack
ICC	The International Critical Commentary, ed. S.R. Driver, A. Plummer, C.A. Briggs (1895-1951); ed. J.A. Emerton and C.E.B. Cranfield (1975-)
IDB	*Interpreter's Dictionary of the Bible*, ed. G.A. Buttrick, *et al.*
IDBSup	Supplement volume to *Interpreter's Dictionary of the Bible*, ed. K. Crim, *et al.* (1976)
IEJ	*Israel Exploration Journal*
ISBE	*The International Standard Bible Encyclopedia, Revised*, ed. G.W. Bromiley, *et al.* (1979-1988)
J	Yahwist Source

JANESCU	*Journal of the Ancient Near Eastern Society of Columbia University*
JAOS	*Journal of the American Oriental Society*
Jastrow	M. Jastrow, *A Dictionary of the Targumim, the Talmud Babli and Yerushalmi, and the Midrashic Literature* (1903)
JB	The Jerusalem Bible (1966)
JBL	*The Journal of Biblical Literature*
JCS	*Journal of Cuneiform Studies*
JETS	*Journal of the Evangelical Theological Society*
JJS	*Journal of Jewish Studies*
JNES	*Journal of Near Eastern Studies*
JNSL	*Journal of Northwest Semitic Languages*
Joüon	P. Joüon, *Grammaire de l'hébreu biblique*, 2nd ed. (1923)
JSJ	*Journal for the Study of Judaism in the Persian, Hellenistic and Roman Period*
JSOT	*Journal for the Study of the Old Testament*
JSOTSup	Journal for the Study of the Old Testament - Supplement Series
JSS	*Journal of Semitic Studies*
JTS	*Journal of Theological Studies*
KAJ	*Keilschrifttexte aus Assur juristischen Inhalts*, ed. E. Ebeling (1927)
KAT	Kommentar zum Alten Testament, ed. E. Sellin, and later, J. Herrmann (1913-); ed. W. Rudolph, K. Elliger, and F. Hesse (1962-)
KB	L. Koehler and W. Baumgartner, *Hebräisches und aramäisches Lexicon zum Alten Testament*, 3e Aufl. (1967, 1974, 1983, 1990)
Keel	O. Keel, *The Symbolism of the Biblical World. Ancient Near Eastern Iconography and the Book of Psalms* (1978)
Kraeling	E. Kraeling, *The Brooklyn Museum Aramaic Papyri. New Documents of the Fifth Century B.C. from the Jewish Colony of Elephantine* (1953)
Lambdin	T.O. Lambdin, *Introduction to Biblical Hebrew* (1971)
LB	Late Babylonian (cir. 625 B.C.-75 A.D.)
LE	Laws of Eshnunna
LI	Laws of Lipit-Ishtar
LU	Laws of Ur-Nammu
LXX	Septuagint (when particular MSS are cited this is based on J. Ziegler, ed., *Duodecim Prophetae. Septuaginta, Vetus Testamentum Graecum, Auctoritate Academiae Scientiarum Gottingensis editum* [1984]. Otherwise, the LXX is taken from The SuperGreek Old Testament

© 1986 P.B. Payne, based on *Septuaginta id est Vetus Testamentum graece iuxta LXX interpretes*, ed. Alfred Rahlfs [1935])

LXX$^\aleph$	Codex Sinaiticus (fourth century A.D.)
LXX$^{\aleph*}$	Codex Sinaiticus, the original hand (fourth century A.D.)
LXX$^{\aleph1}$	Codex Sinaiticus, the first corrector (fourth -sixth century A.D.)
LXX$^{\aleph2}$	Codex Sinaiticus, the second corrector (seventh century A.D.)
LXX^A	Codex Alexandrinus (fifth century A.D.)
LXX^B	Codex Vaticanus (fourth century A.D.)
LXX$^{B\text{-}\aleph*\text{-}68}$	The use of a dash in listing LXX MSS, as in LXX$^{B\text{-}\aleph*\text{-}68}$, implies that the listed MSS form a family group
LXX$^{\text{Chr. III221}}$	Sermons of Chrysostom (344-407 A.D.)
LXX^{Const}	Apostolic Constitutions (380 A.D.)
LXX$^\Gamma$	Codex Cryptoferratensis (eighth century A.D.)
LXX^L	Lucianic Recension of LXX MSS
LXX^Q	Codex Marchalianus (sixth century A.D.)
LXX^V	Codex Venetus (eighth century A.D.)
LXX^W	The Freer Greek MS (third century A.D.), reproduced in H.A. Sanders and C. Schmidt, *The Minor Prophets in the Freer Collection and The Berlin Fragment of Genesis* (1927)
LXX^{68}	a fifteenth century A.D. cursive MS in Venice, Biblioteca San Marco
LXX^{86}	a ninth century A.D. cursive MS in Rome, Vatican Library, Barberini
MA	Middle Assyrian (cir. 1500-1000 B.C.)
MAL	Middle Assyrian Laws
MB	Middle Babylonian (cir. 1600-1000 B.C.)
MSL	Materialien zum sumerischen Lexikon, B. Landsberger, *et al.*(1937-)
MSS	Manuscripts
MT	Masoretic Text, as found in *BHS* (generally as reproduced in *MacHebrew Scriptures* © 1987-1988 P.B. Payne or ThePerfectWORD™ 2.0)
Mur	P. Benoit, J.T. Milik, and R. de Vaux, *Les Grottes de Murabba'ât*, DJD, II (1961)
NA	Neo-Assyrian (cir. 1000-600 B.C.)
NAB	The New American Bible (1970)
NB	Neo-Babylonian (cir. 1000-625 B.C.)
NBL	Neo-Babylonian Laws
NCB	New Century Bible, ed. R.E. Clements and M. Black
NEB	New English Bible
NF	Neue Folge

NICOT	The New International Commentary on the Old Testament, ed. E.J. Young (1965) and R.K. Harrison (1962-)
NIV	New International Version (generally as reproduced in ThePerfectWORD™ 2.0, or *The Holy Bible, New International Version* [London: Hodder and Stoughton, 1979])
NovT	*Novum Testamentum*
NJPS	*Tanakh, a new translation of the Holy Scriptures according to the traditional Hebrew text* (1985) = the new Jewish Publication Society translation
NS	New Series
OA	Old Assyrian (cir. 1950-1750 B.C.)
OB	Old Babylonian (cir. 1950-1600 B.C.)
OT	Old Testament
OTA	*Old Testament Abstracts*
OTL	Old Testament Library, ed. P. Ackroyd, *et al.*
OTS	*Oudtestamentische Studiën*
P	Priestly Source
PN	some proper noun (typically used in the translation of Akkadian texts)
POT	De Prediking van het Oude Testament, ed. A. van Selms, A.S. van der Woude, and C. van Leeuwen
PRU	*Le palais royal d'Ugarit*, ed. C. Schaeffer
Porten-Yardeni	B. Porten and A. Yardeni, *Textbook of Aramaic Documents From Ancient Egypt, Volume 2: Contracts* (1989)
RA	*Revue d'assyriologie et d'archéologie orientale*
RB	*Revue biblique*
*RGG*³	*Die Religion in Geschichte und Gegenwart*, 3e Aufl. (1957-65), ed. K. Galling
RLA	*Reallexikon der Assyriologie und Vorderasiatischen Archäologie*, Bände 1-2, ed. E. Ebeling and B. Meisser (1932-38), for Bände 3-, ed. E. Ebeling and E. Weidner (1957-)
Roth	M.T. Roth, *Babylonian Marriage Agreements: 7th - 3rd Centuries B.C* (1989)
RS	Ras Shamra (field numbers of tablets)
RSP	*Ras Shamra Parallels. The Texts from Ugarit and the Hebrew Bible*, ed. L.R. Fisher, *et al.*, I, *AnOr* 49 (1972); II, *AnOr* 50 (1975)
RSV	Revised Standard Version (generally as reproduced in ThePerfectWORD™ 2.0)
RV	*The Holy Bible. The Revised Version* (1885)
SBLDS	The Society of Biblical Literature Dissertation Series

SBLMS   The Society of Biblical Literature Monograph Series, R.A. Kraft, ed. (1967-1972); L. Keck, ed. (1973-)
SL   Sumerian Laws
Strassmaier, *Liverpool*
               J.N. Strassmaier, *Die babylonischen Inschriften im Museum zu Liverpool, Actes du 6e Congrès International des Orientalistes, II, Section Sémitique (1)* (1885)
StrB   H.L. Strack and P. Billerbeck, *Kommentar zum Neuen Testament aus Talmud und Midrasch* (1922-61)
SVT   Supplements to *Vetus Testamentum*
TB   *Tyndale Bulletin*
TDNT   *Theological Dictionary of the New Testament*, English ed. (1964-74), ed. G. Kittel and G. Friedrich
TDOT   *Theological Dictionary of the Old Testament*, English revised ed. (1977-), ed. G.J. Botterweck and H. Ringgren
THAT   *Theologisches Handwörterbuch zum Alten Testament*, ed. E. Jenni and C. Westermann (1984)
TIM   A. Al-Zeebari, *Texts in the Iraq Museum* (1964)
TOTC   Tyndale Old Testament Commentaries, ed. D.J. Wiseman (1964-)
TRE   *Theologische Realenzyklopädie*, ed. G. Krause and G. Müller
TWOT   *Theological Wordbook of the Old Testament*, 2 vols., ed. R.L. Harris, G.L. Archer Jr., and B.K. Waltke (1980)
UET   *Ur Excavations, Texts*, 10 vols. (1934-66)
UT   C.H. Gordon, *Ugaritic Textbook* (1965)
UT   Ugaritic texts as listed in C.H. Gordon, *Ugaritic Textbook* (1965)
VAT   tablets in the collections of the Staatliche Museen, Berlin (Tafelsignaturen der Vorderasiatischen Abteilung der Berliner Museen)
VS   *Vorderasiatische Schriftdenkmäler der königlichen Museen zu Berlin*, 7 vols. (1907-1916)
vs.   verse
vss.   verses
VT   *Vetus Testamentum*
Vulgate   *Biblia Sacra Iuxta Vulgatam Versionem*, ed. R. Weber, *et al.* (1983)
W   In the context of a marriage document, W represents the wife's name
Waltke and O'Connor
               Bruce K. Waltke, and M. O'Connor, *An Introduction to Biblical Hebrew Syntax* (1990)

WBC	Word Biblical Commentary, ed. D.A. Hubbard, G.W. Barker, and J.D.W. Watts
Williams, *Syntax*	R.J. Williams, *Hebrew Syntax: An Outline*, 2nd ed. (1976)
WMANT	Wissenschaftliche Monographien zum Alten und Neuen Testament
WTJ	*Westminster Theological Journal*
YOS	Yale Oriental Series, Babylonian Texts, 12 vols. (1915-1978)
ZAW	*Zeitschrift für die alttestamentliche Wissenschaft*
ZDMG	*Zeitschrift der Deutschen Morgenländischen Gesellschaft*

ABBREVIATIONS OF CITED ORDERS AND TRACTATES IN MISHNAIC AND RELATED LITERATURE

Ber.	*Berakot*
B. Meṣ.	*Baba. Meṣi'a*
B. Qam.	*Baba Qamma*
Gen. Rab.	*Genesis Rabbah*
Giṭ.	*Giṭṭin*
Ketub.	*Ketubot*
Nid.	*Niddah*
Pe'a	*Pe'a*
Soṭa	*Soṭa*
Šeb.	*Šebi'it*
Qidd.	*Qiddušin*
Yebam.	*Yebamot*

To distinguish tractates by the same name in the Mishnah, Tosefta, and Talmuds, the following prefixes are employed:

b.	Babylonian Talmud
m.	Mishnah
t.	Tosefta
y.	Jerusalem Talmud

CONVENTIONS

Unless otherwise marked, English translations of biblical texts are either taken from the RSV or are the author's. Unless otherwise marked, translations of Akkadian texts are either taken from *ANET* or are the author's. Normalization of Akkadian texts differs from the conventions of *AHw* mainly in one respect: Here, a macron is used to indicate tone long vowels ($\bar{v}$); a circumflex marks vowels assumed to have experienced compensatory lengthening (vC > v̂); and a tilde marks vowels assumed to have been lengthened due to contraction (vCv > ṽ).

When reference is made to Dutch individuals whose surnames include *van*, *de*, *den*, and *der*, standard Dutch practice regarding capitalization will be followed. As a result, these particles, or the first in a series of these particles, will be capitalized when an individual's forename, initials, or title are not included (hence, A.S. van der Woude, but Van der Woude).

Statistics of word uses throughout the dissertation which are unattributed derive, in general, from either Even-Shoshan or from computer searches conducted by the writer utilizing The PerfectWORD™, version 2.0, with complete RSV, NIV, and *BHS* text modules produced and marketed by Star Software, Inc., Casselberry, Florida (1988) for use on an Apple™ brand Macintosh™ computer.

INTRODUCTION

1. SURVEY OF RECENT SCHOLARSHIP ON MARRIAGE IN THE OLD TESTAMENT

The twentieth century has witnessed a proliferation of studies which deal comprehensively with the subject of marriage in the Old Testament: M. Burrows (1938),[1] L.M. Epstein (1942),[2] E. Neufeld (1944),[3] D.R. Mace (1953),[4] R. Patai (1959),[5] W. Plautz (1959),[6] B. Maarsingh (1963),[7] S.F. Bigger (1974),[8] and A. Tosato (1982).[9] Besides these full-scale works, the following briefer studies deserve mention as having exerted a profound influence: R. de Vaux (1958)[10] and Z.W. Falk (1964).[11]

After such a list it may seem that there is little left to be said on this topic. On closer inspection, what emerges from this survey is the fact that while much attention has been focused on legal, historical, comparative (both diachronic and synchronic), and sociological concerns, the relationship between biblical marriage law and covenantal concepts has been left largely unresolved and, much of the time, virtually ignored.

Of course, in one sense this reticence concerning the covenantal nature of marriage is not at all surprising. While this century has witnessed a profusion of research into the nature and administration of covenants within both the Old Testament and the ancient Near East, the result of this massive scholarly enterprise, seemingly, has been to render the biblical concept of "covenant [בְּרִית]" forbiddingly problematic.[12] Given this state of affairs,

---

[1] The Basis of Israelite Marriage.

[2] Marriage Laws in Bible and Talmud.

[3] Ancient Hebrew Marriage Laws — With special references to General Semitic Laws and Customs.

[4] Hebrew Marriage: A Sociological Study.

[5] Sex and Family in the Bible and in the Middle East (Garden City, NY: Doubleday 1959), published the following year in London under the title Family, Love and the Bible.

[6] "Die Frau in Familie und Ehe. Ein Beitrag zum Problem ihrer Stellung im Alten Testament," Ph.D. diss., Kiel Univ.

[7] Het Huwelijk in Het Oude Testament.

[8] "Hebrew Marriage and Family in the Old Testament Period. A Perspective from the Standpoint of Social History and Social Anthropology," Ph.D. diss., University of Manchester.

[9] Il matrimonio israelitico. Una theoria generale.

[10] Les Institutions de L'Ancien Testament, 1 (Paris: Les Editions du Cerf, 1958), later translated as Ancient Israel, Vol. 1, Social Institutions (1961) 24-38.

[11] Hebrew Law in Biblical Times. An Introduction.

[12] For a useful summary of this research cf. D.R. Hillers, Covenant: The History of a Biblical Idea (1969); D.J. McCarthy, Old Testament Covenant (1972); idem, Treaty and Covenant. A Study in Form in the Ancient Oriental Documents and in the Old Testament, 2nd ed. (1981); and E.W. Nicholson, God and His People. Covenant and Theology in the

there would appear to be little to commend the burdensome task of seeking to apply such controversial results.

2. THE NEED FOR A STUDY OF THE COVENANTAL NATURE OF MARRIAGE IN THE OLD TESTAMENT

Nevertheless, at least three considerations make desirable an attempt at a more rigorous examination of the possible covenantal aspects of marriage in the Old Testament.

2.1 The importance of the topic

First of all, regardless of whether firm conclusions are within our present reach, the topic has a potential importance which is simply too great to ignore.[13] It is possible that such a study may suggest new solutions to some of the remaining difficulties in understanding the biblical ethics and practice of marriage (e.g. the precise role of the "bride-price," the dissolubility of marriage, the legal status of premarital sexual union, etc.). Whether or not this proves to be the case, there is a reciprocal benefit from a study of the possible covenantal aspects of marriage which may allow the modern reader to appreciate more fully the breadth of the biblical concept of covenant, freeing it from an excessively political (treaty-document) or cultic orientation.

2.2 The contradictory results of those who support the identification of marriage as a covenant

Second, while a number of scholars have sought to apply covenantal concepts to marriage in the Old Testament,[14] leaving an initial impression of a mounting consensus, a closer comparison reveals that this has been done with strikingly dissimilar and even contradictory results. So, for example, there is confusion over who are the "covenant partners" within marriage. O.J. Baab explicitly identifies the partners as the families of the bride and groom.[15] S.L. McKenzie and H.N. Wallace, on the other hand, offer a slight modification with their claim that the covenant was generally between the husband (not his

---

Old Testament (1986).

Here, and throughout our discussion, we shall follow the convention of rendering every occurrence of בְּרִית with the English term "covenant." This is done merely for convenience and without prejudice to the meaning of בְּרִית. For a recent defence of the relative suitability of "covenant" as a translation for בְּרִית, cf. E.W. Nicholson, *God and His People*, 105f. See also Chapter 6 below for an examination of the meaning of בְּרִית.

[13] Cf. D.J. McCarthy, *Treaty and Covenant* (1981) ix.

[14] While often this is done somewhat incidentally, the following have offered extended attempts along this line: P.F. Palmer, "Christian Marriage: Contract or Covenant?" (1972); G.R. Dunstan, "The Marriage Covenant" (1975); D.J. Atkinson, *To Have and to Hold. The Marriage Covenant and the Discipline of Divorce* (1979); J.B. Job, *The Covenant of Marriage* (1981); and R.S. Westcott, "The Concept of *berît* with Regard to Marriage in the Old Testament" (1985).

[15] "Marriage" (1962) 284.

family) and his father-in-law or brother-in-law.[16] Yet a third view is suggested by D.J. Atkinson, who appears to view the husband and wife as the covenant partners within marriage.[17]

Similarly there is confusion over what it is that "ratifies" the covenant of marriage. M. Burrows considers that the delivery of a bridal gift sealed the marriage covenant.[18] P.F. Palmer, on the other hand, considers sexual union to have been the ratifying act,[19] while D.J. Atkinson appears to agree with G.R. Dunstan in speaking of a "vow of consent" between the bride and the groom.[20] Finally, J.B. Job suggests that the marriage covenant was ratified with blood, either from circumcision, as in Exod. 4:24-26, or from the stained garment of Deut. 22:15.[21]

Further disagreement exists as to what constitutes covenant breaking. D.J. Atkinson writes, "If marriage is understood in covenant terms, then the possibility of divorce must be discussed as the possibility of breaking covenant."[22] Others would argue that it is not divorce which "breaks" the covenant, but only sexual infidelity. P.F. Palmer, on the other hand, claims that precisely unlike contracts, covenants are inherently "inviolable"[23] and "unbreakable."[24]

It is possible that some of these apparent disagreements in applying a covenantal model to marriage are no more than terminological.[25] If this is so, one could wish for greater precision in the use of terms which have acquired rather precise technical meanings elsewhere in the scholarly discussion of covenant. Not all the disagreement, however, seems so amenable to semantic clarification. The simple fact is that such discordant results do not commend the initial assumption that marriage in the Old Testament was in fact covenantal, and hence, in their own way, these results demand a more

---

[16] "Covenant Themes in Malachi" (1983) 553. So also W.E. Barnes, *Haggai, Zechariah and Malachi* (1934) 124.

[17] *To Have and to Hold*, chapter 3.

[18] *The Basis of Israelite Marriage*, 21.

[19] "Christian Marriage," 655. Palmer is speaking here not so much of marriage in the OT as of Christian marriage.

[20] G.R. Dunstan, "The Marriage Covenant," 247f.; and D.J. Atkinson, *To Have and to Hold*, 75.

Here as elsewhere Dunstan is considering either the New Testament view of marriage or a theology of marriage, not its OT practice.

[21] *The Covenant of Marriage*, 9f.

[22] *To Have and to Hold*, 91.

[23] "Christian Marriage," 618. But cf. p. 619.

[24] *Ibid.*, 639.

[25] Cf., e.g., P.F. Palmer who develops his concept of "covenant" as much from the evidence of *foedus* (ecclesiastical Latin) as from בְּרִית (Biblical Hebrew). Palmer writes "covenants are not broken; they are violated when there is a breach of faith on the part of either or both of the covenanters" ("Christian Marriage," 619). Whatever may be the evidence for this assertion from ecclesiastical Latin, in terms of Hebrew usage covenants may be both violated and dissolved — with both of these concepts expressed by the same underlying Hebrew expression which is customarily rendered "broken" in most English versions (Hiphil of פרר + בְּרִית). Cf., e.g., Gen. 17:14; Lev. 26:44; Deut. 31:20; 1 Kgs. 15:19 (cf. F.B. Knutson, "Political and Foreign Affairs," *RSP*, II, 111f.); Isa. 24:5; 33:8; Jer. 11:10; 14:21; 31:32; 33:20ff.; Ezek. 16:59; 17:15ff.; 44:7; and Zech. 11:10f. Cf. also D.J. McCarthy, *Old Testament Covenant*, 4f.

meticulous study of the underlying evidence for this assumption.

2.3 Arguments against identifying marriage as a covenant

Finally, and most importantly, a number of scholars have recently challenged not only particular applications of covenantal concepts to marriage, but also the long-standing underlying assumption that marriage itself was covenantal within the Old Testament. The following is a summary of the principal arguments which have been advanced against marriage being viewed as a covenant.

Arguments based on a more precise definition of "covenant [בְּרִית]"

In the past, all too often the defence of marriage as "covenantal" in the Old Testament proceeded from the now discredited notion that "covenant [בְּרִית]" is essentially a synonym for "relationship."[26] It is now recognized that the *sine qua non* of "covenant [בְּרִית]" in its normal sense appears to be its ratifying oath, whether this was verbal or symbolic (a so-called "oath sign").[27] According to J. Milgrom and others, however, there is no evidence for the existence of any such oath in the case of marriage. Milgrom observes, "though countless marriage contracts and laws from [the] ancient Near East are known, not a single one to my knowledge stipulates an oath."[28] Milgrom counters specific arguments which might imply that an oath did accompany marriage either in Israel or elsewhere in the ancient Near East. For example, the fact that ancient Near Eastern laws so frequently allow an injured husband to mitigate or waive the death penalty against an adulterer itself implies, according to Milgrom, that adultery did not entail the breach of an oath.[29] Milgrom further notes that the oath mentioned in Gen. 31:50ff. prohibits Jacob from contracting any future marriage, but does not regulate his long-existing marriages to Rachel and Leah.[30]

P.F. Palmer argues against the identification of marriage in the Old Testament as a covenant because he likewise begins with a more precise definition of "covenant." Although we cited Palmer in our earlier discussion

---

[26] So, for example, D.J. Atkinson begins his defence of the covenantal nature of marriage with the claim that "all human relations can be expressed in covenantal terms..." (*To Have and to Hold*, 71). If the meaning of the term "covenantal" is to be derived from an examination of בְּרִית, this is simply not the case. E.W. Nicholson points out an analogous error among those who exaggerate the early evidence for identifying Yahweh's relation to Israel in terms of "covenant" by an overly facile identification of "covenant" with "relationship" (*God and His People*, p. 20 and *passim*).

[27] This point is widely acknowledged and is made, for example, by J. Barr, "Some Semantic Notes on the Covenant," 23-38, esp. p. 32. See our further discussion in Chapter 6 below.

[28] *Cult and Conscience. The Asham and the Priestly Doctrine of Repentance* (1976) 134.

[29] *Ibid.* 134, where he cites CH §129, MAL A §§14-16, and HL §§192f. Milgrom is not explicit that he would draw this implication from the evidence he cites.

[30] Although Milgrom discusses this example at some length, with the implication that it is erroneously used to buttress the theory of covenantal marriage, he does not cite any scholar who has made the mistake he alleges.

as generally supportive of the notion that marriage was covenantal in the Old Testament, in fact Palmer holds that this was the case only in terms of the prophetic vision held out most explicitly by Malachi. Because Palmer construes "covenant" as necessarily entailing an exclusive and indissoluble bond (over against a "contract"), he concludes: "In a society where polygamy and divorce were sanctioned by Mosaic law, where the wife was regarded as the property of the husband and adultery a violation of the rights of the Hebrew male, where fecundity was still the overriding concern, it would be unreal to speak of Jewish marriage as a covenant either of love or of fidelity."[31] It is crucial to note that Palmer does not base his conclusion on the all-too-familiar discrepancy between theory and practice, but rather on the striking discrepancy which he alleges existed between the Mosaic legal corpus and the later prophetic reform.

Arguments based on the prophetic blending of images where God is alternatively depicted as being both in covenant with His people and married to them
While most scholars who defend marriage as a covenant consider the force of the prophetic allusions to Yahweh's marriage covenant with Israel to be almost self-evident,[32] J. Milgrom's counter argument appears as a *tour de force* — he simply notes that in such cases "the term *bryt* ... is a literary usage and carries no legal force."[33] Specifically, with reference to Ezek. 16:8,[34] Milgrom objects that the oath mentioned in this text "is taken by God whereas it should have been expected of the bride, Israel, for it is the bride, not the husband, who is subject to the laws of adultery." Milgrom adds that there is a similar anomaly with respect to the charge of infidelity in Mal. 2:14.

M. Greenberg agrees with Milgrom and explains the origin of the oath mentioned in Ezek. 16:8 not as a reflection of marital practice, but as a fusion of the literal divine oath to the patriarchs promising the land of Canaan to their descendants and "the solemn declaration of mutual obligation connected with the Exodus and covenant with the people."[35] In other words, although Ezek. 16:8 mentions "swearing" and "covenant" in connection with the marriage metaphor, in this case the underlying referent has intruded into the metaphor and so implies nothing with respect to literal marriage.[36]

---

[31] "Christian Marriage," 621. Cf. also pp. 619, 639.
[32] Cf., e.g., D.J. Atkinson, *To Have and to Hold*, 71-73; and P.F. Palmer, "Christian Marriage," 619-621. The following passages are typically included in this discussion: Hos. 1-3, Isa. 54:5-8, Jer. 3:1ff., and Ezekiel 16.
[33] *Cult and Conscience*, 134.
[34] "When I passed by you again and looked upon you, behold, you were at the age for love; and I spread my skirt over you, and covered your nakedness: I swore to you [וָאֶשָּׁבַע לָךְ] and entered into a covenant with you [וָאָבוֹא בִּבְרִית אֹתָךְ], says the Lord GOD, and you became mine."
[35] *Ezekiel 1-20* (1983) 278.
[36] So also J. Herrmann, *Ezechiel* (1924); B.M. Vellas, *Israelite Marriage* (1956) 24; P. Kalluveettil, *Declaration and Covenant* (1982) 79; and M. Malul, "Adoption of Foundlings in the Bible and Mesopotamian Documents. A Study of Some Legal Metaphors in Ezekiel 16:1-7" (1990) 126, n. 112.

Arguments based on the notable absence of any text (biblical or extra-biblical) which explicitly identifies marriage as a "covenant [בְּרִית or διαθήκη]"

Of course, the mere absence of a term, such as "covenant," need not exclude the thing signified.[37] For example, although the term "covenant" appears only infrequently in the prophets, nevertheless a number of scholars have argued that the prophetic books may presuppose covenant "as an invisible framework."[38] Similarly, it has been remarked that "covenant" nowhere appears in the "covenant with David" as recorded in 2 Samuel 7, and yet this arrangement is so identified in 2 Sam. 23:5 and particularly Psalm 89 (where בְּרִית is found no less than four times).[39] Not surprisingly G.E. Mendenhall observes there are "numerous references to covenants and covenant relationships where this term does not occur."[40]

Nevertheless, it is notable that the term "covenant [בְּרִית or διαθήκη]" is nowhere applied to marriage at 5th century B.C. Elephantine or during the intertestamental period (e.g., Tobit 7), nor is it to be found in the New Testament. Finally, although W.A. Heth and G.J. Wenham, for example, infer a marriage covenant between Adam and Eve, the term "covenant [בְּרִית]" is also conspicuously absent in this paradigmatic marriage.[41]

Traditionally, three passages have been cited as exceptions to this rule, because they seem explicitly to identify marriage as a covenant. We have already noted that the first of these, Ezek. 16:8, on closer examination may not prove what is being alleged because of its use of marriage as a metaphor.

The second text, Prov. 2:17, is likewise problematic, as M. Greenberg notes.[42] The RSV renders this verse about the adulteress: "who forsakes the companion of her youth and forgets the covenant of her God." While it is possible that the covenant mentioned is an individual covenant of marriage between the woman and her husband, many scholars consider it to be equally possible and perhaps more probable that the covenant is the one she shares with all Israelites and their God.[43] In the same vein, some scholars have suggested that "the companion of her youth" is to be understood as referring

---

[37] M. Silva makes a similar point and offers as one example the lack of the term "hypocrisy" in Isa. 1:10-15 (*Biblical Words and their Meaning* [1983] 26ff.).

[38] So writes D.R. Hillers, *Covenant: The History of a Biblical Idea* (1969) 123f. Cf. J. Limburg, "The Root *ryb* and the Prophetic Lawsuit Speeches" (1969) 291ff. For a different assessment of the prophets, cf., *inter alia*, E.W. Nicholson, *God and His People*, 114ff., following L. Perlitt.

In the same regard, cf. F.C. Fensham's discussion directed against Wellhausen concerning "covenant" in the Former Prophets ("Covenant, Alliance," [1980] 330).

[39] Cf. Psalm 132 (I am grateful to N. Kiuchi for pointing out this example). M. Weinfeld uses this comparison to establish the synonymy of חֶסֶד and בְּרִית ("בְּרִית *bᵉrîth*," 270). Cf. T.E. McComiskey, *The Covenants of Promise*, 59.

[40] "Covenant" (1962) 715. Cf. P. Kalluveettil, *Declaration and Covenant*, 3, n. 12.

[41] *Jesus and Divorce*, 100-103.

[42] *Ezekiel 1-20*, 278.

[43] So, H.W. Wolff, *Anthropology of the Old Testament* (1974) 168, citing E. Kutsch, *Verheissung und Gesetz* (1973) 134ff. Wolff nevertheless accepts the evidence of Mal. 2:14 and Ezek. 16:8 as referring to the covenant of marriage.

not to her husband but to her Lord.

The third text, Mal. 2:14, is perhaps the chief pillar of the traditional identification of marriage in the Old Testament as a covenant.[44]   The following is a summary of the reasons currently being advanced for rejecting the traditional exegesis of this passage, which is apparently assumed by the RSV: "... Because the LORD was witness to the covenant [עַל כִּי־יְהוָה הֵעִיד] between you and the wife of your youth [בֵּינְךָ וּבֵין אֵשֶׁת נְעוּרֶיךָ], to whom you have been faithless [אֲשֶׁר אַתָּה בָּגַדְתָּה בָּהּ], though she is your companion [וְהִיא חֲבֶרְתְּךָ] and your wife by covenant [וְאֵשֶׁת בְּרִיתֶךָ]."   First, it is argued by some that the covenant mentioned in Mal. 2:14 cannot refer to a literal marriage because in a literal marriage the partners to the marriage agreement are the groom (or his parents) and the bride's father (or her brother), not the bride and groom as is implied here.[45]   Second, because the Old Testament considers that "it is the bride, not the husband, who is subject to the laws of adultery," J. Milgrom, for example, insists that Mal. 2:14 cannot be referring to a literal marriage since it suggests that "the husband rather than the bride violates the covenant."[46]   Third, most commentators relate Malachi to the period either just before or contemporaneous with Ezra.[47]   If Mal. 2:10-16 is taken to refer to literal marriage and divorce, however, then a contradiction is introduced between the "I hate divorce" of Mal. 2:16 and the program of enforced divorce mentioned in Ezra 10.[48]   Fourth, if Malachi is as indebted to Deuteronomic ideas as is widely believed,[49] then on a literal marriage interpretation Malachi unaccountably departs from that dependency by seeming to contradict the provision of divorce presupposed in Deut. 24:1-4.

For these reasons and especially because of its claimed suitability to the larger context of Malachi, B. Vawter, for example, has reiterated a view originally set forth by C.C. Torrey. Vawter argues that the divorce which Yahweh hates is not the dissolution of literal marriages, but the repudiation of "the covenant of our fathers" (vs. 10), which is expressed figuratively as "the wife of your youth" (vs. 14).[50]

It has long been recognized that the primary interpretative problem of Mal. 2:10-16 is whether to understand this text as referring to a literal marriage or to a symbolic marriage (whether to God, to the covenant, or to the priesthood).[51] Unhappily, any resolution of this problem largely depends

---

[44] P.F. Palmer appears to consider it to be the only explicit such identification ("Christian Marriage," 619-21).

[45] A. Isaksson broadens this criticism by asserting that the OT concept of covenant was incompatible with the meaning of marriage at this time (*Marriage and Ministry in the New Temple* [1965] 27-34).

[46] *Cult and Conscience*, 134.

[47] See the discussion in Chapter 1.

[48] Thus the passage is interpreted by L. Kruse-Blinkenberg, "The Pesitta [sic] of the Book of Malachi" (1966) 103-104.

[49] Cf., e.g., J. Swetnam, "Malachi 1:11 An Interpretation" (1969) 203, and W.J. Dumbrell, "Malachi and the Ezra-Nehemiah Reforms," 42.

[50] "The Biblical Theology of Divorce" (1967) 232; C.C. Torrey, "The Prophecy of Malachi" (1898).

[51] A symbolic view has been supported by C.C. Torrey, "The Prophecy of Malachi"

on the interpretation of a number of exceedingly obscure phrases or passages including: "the daughter of a foreign god" (2:11),[52] "you cover the Lord's altar with tears" (2:13),[53] and the even more problematic 2:15, which has been called "one of the most difficult verses in the OT."[54] Unless and until these complex interpretative problems are resolved, however, appeal cannot be made to Malachi as supportive of covenantal marriage.

It is the purpose of the present study to take these crucial verses in Malachi as our point of departure for a much needed reassessment of the possible covenantal nature of marriage within the Old Testament. Before doing so, however, we must first consider two major impediments which seem to prohibit such an investigation.

3. PROBLEMS WITH THIS STUDY

3.1 Controversies surrounding "covenant"

Already allusion has been made to the problematic nature of "covenant" within current Old Testament scholarship. Certainly, if there is no agreement on the meaning and nature of a covenant there is not much point in going beyond such a foundational problem to contemplate the possible interrelation of Old Testament marriage law and covenantal concepts.[55]

(1898); H. Winckler, "Maleachi" (1901) 531-9; A.C. Welch, *Post-Exilic Judaism* (1935); I.G. Matthews, "Haggai, Malachi" (1935); F.F. Hvidberg, *Weeping and Laughter in the Old Testament* (1962); A. Isaksson, *Marriage and Ministry in the New Temple* (1965) 27-34; B. Vawter, "The Biblical Theology of Divorce" (1967); G.W. Ahlström, *Joel and the Temple Cult of Jerusalem* (1971); J. Milgrom, *Cult and Conscience* (1976); M. Greenberg, *Ezekiel 1-20* (1983); G.S. Ogden, "The Use of Figurative Language in Malachi 2:10-16" (1988); and J.M. O'Brien, *Priest and Levite in Malachi* (1990).

Favouring the literal view are, among others, G.A. Smith, *The Books of the Twelve Prophets* (1899); A. von Bulmerincq, "Die Mischehen im B. Maleachi" (1926); *idem, Der Prophet Maleachi, Vol. 2: Kommentar zum Buche des Propheten Maleachi* (1932) 289; J.M. Myers, *The World of the Restoration* (1968); T. Chary, *Aggée – Zacharie – Malachie* (1969) 259; E. Kutsch, *Verheissung und Gesetz* (1973) 93f.; S. Schreiner, "Mischehen-Ehebruch-Ehescheidung: Betrachtungen zu Mal 2 10-16" (1979) 207-28; R.L. Smith, *Micah-Malachi* (1984); P.A. Verhoef, *The Books of Haggai and Malachi* (1987).

As will be discussed in Chapter 2, an alternative approach accepts a reference to literal marriage in Mal. 2:10-16, but nevertheless denies that Mal. 2:14 identifies marriage as a covenant. On this approach, the mentioned covenant refers to Israel's covenant with Yahweh, identifying this wife as a fellow-Israelite. Cf., e.g., *ad loc.*, K. Marti, *Das Dodekapropheton* (1904); W. Nowack, *Das kleinen Propheten* (1922); E. Sellin, *Das Zwölfprophetenbuch* (1929-30); and B.M. Vellas, *Israelite Marriage* (1956) 24. B. Glazier-McDonald similarly identifies the covenant in 2:14 with that mentioned in 2:10, but nevertheless supports an identification of marriage as a covenant in Ezek. 16:8 and Prov. 2:17 *(Malachi* [1987] 101f.).

[52] Considered by A.C. Welch to be unparalleled as a description of a non-Jewish woman *(Post-Exilic Judaism*, 120).

[53] F.F. Hvidberg *(Weeping and Laughter*, 120.) and A. Isaksson *(Marriage and Ministry*, 31-32) relate this to ritual mourning, which they feel points to a distinctly cultic interpretation for the בְּרִית.

[54] A.S. van der Woude, *Haggai Maleachi* (1982) 121.

[55] For example, some scholars, such as E. Kutsch *(Verheissung und Gesetz* [1973] and "Gesetz und Gnade. Probleme des alttestamentlichen Bundesbegriff" [1967] 18-35), deny

It should be noted, however, that the areas most plagued with uncertainty are unlikely to affect the proposed investigation into the possible identification of marriage as a covenant. This is so, for example, with the centuries-old controversy surrounding a posited "covenant of works" and "covenant of grace" associated with "federal theology."[56] This also applies to the biblical-theological discussion regarding "covenant" as a possible "centre" for Old Testament theology, if indeed there is a "centre."[57] It is likewise the case with the biblical-theological question concerning the interrelation of the various covenants within the Old Testament and between the testaments.[58]

Beyond these more theological questions, there are also several historical and/or sociological questions regarding "covenant" that remain problematic: Is the concept of a covenant between God and Israel a unique feature of the religion of Israel over against her neighbours?[59] What was the precise role of covenant in the formation of Israel?[60] What was the precise interrelation between covenant and cult?[61] Perhaps the foundational historical question which plagues much of the discussion of "covenant" concerns the antiquity of the concept of "covenant" within Israel[62] and

---

that בְּרִית can mean "covenant." See Chapter 6 below for a discussion of Kutsch and an examination of the meaning of the term בְּרִית.

[56] Cf. P.A. Lillback, "Covenant" (1988); W.W. Benton Jr., "Federal Theology: Review for Revision" (1985) 180-204; and J.H. Hughes and F. Prussner, *Old Testament Theology* (1985) 19.

[57] Of course, the most notable example of such a theology is that of W. Eichrodt, *Theologie des Alten Testaments*, I Leipzig (1933), II (1935), III (1939); ET: *Theology of the Old Testament*, I (1961), II (1967).
For the present debate concerning the problem of a "centre" in OT theology, cf. G.F. Hasel, "The Problem of the Center in the Old Testament" (1974); *idem, Old Testament Theology. Basic Issues in the Current Debate* (1975) 77-103; J.H. Hughes and F. Prussner, *Old Testament Theology* (1985) 257ff.; and H.G. Reventlow, *Problems of Old Testament Theology in the Twentieth Century* (1985) 125-133.

[58] Cf., e.g., R.E. Clements, *Abraham and David* (1967); F.C. Prussner, "The Covenant of David and the Problem of Unity in Old Testament Theology" (1968) 17-41; F.C. Fensham, "The Covenant as Giving Expression to the Relationship between Old Testament and New Testament" (1971); M.G. Kline, *The Structure of Biblical Authority* (1975) 145 and *passim*; R.T. Beckwith, "The Unity and Diversity of God's Covenants" (1987); and I.H. Marshall, "Some Observations on the Covenant in the New Testament" (1990).

[59] K. Baltzer claims that Israel's covenantal relationship to her God is unparalleled in antiquity (*The Covenant Formulary*, 90, n. 4), while F.C. Fensham says it is well-attested ("Covenant, Alliance," 328).

[60] Here attention is particularly focused on M. Noth's hypothesis of an ancient Israelite amphictyony. Cf. M. Noth, *Das System der zwölf Stämme Israels* (1930); *idem, The History of Israel* (1960) 53-109; and the discussion in J. Bright, *A History of Israel* (1981) 162ff.

[61] Cf. S. Mowinckel, who considers the renewal of the covenant in a New Year festival (Tabernacles) to have been a central feature of Israel's cultus (*The Psalms in Israel's Worship* [1962]). Cf. the discussion in D.J. McCarthy, *Old Testament Covenant*, 6f.

[62] Considered not to be particularly old by G. Fohrer, "Altes Testament - 'Amphiktyonie' und 'Bund'?" (1966) 801-16, 893-904; L. Perlitt, *Bundestheologie im Alten Testament* (1969); and more recently E.W. Nicholson, *God and His People*.
Supporting the antiquity of the covenantal concept within the OT are W. Eichrodt, "Prophet and Covenant" (1970); T.C. Vriezen, "The Exegesis of Exodus 24:9-11" (1972); J.

whether there is evidence for any significant development of this concept within the Old Testament.[63]

Related to these historical questions, and in many respects overshadowing all of the preceding debates, is the attempt over the past four decades to assess and relate to the Old Testament the treaty form(s) and terminology exhibited in numerous Hittite Treaties, the Treaties of Esarhaddon, the Aramaean Sefire Treaty inscriptions, along with a number of more fragmentary treaties and some indirect evidence from Mari and Amarna.[64] Since the early studies of G.E. Mendenhall[65] and K. Baltzer,[66] the debate has raged over the possible presence either of individual elements or of the whole of the "treaty document" literary genre within various texts of the Old Testament including: the Decalogue;[67] Deuteronomy, either in whole[68] or in part;[69] Joshua 23;[70] Joshua 24;[71] and 1 Sam. 11:14-12:25.[72]

Halbe, *Das Privilegrecht Jahwes. Ex 34, 10-26* (1975); D.J. McCarthy, *Treaty and Covenant* (1981); and J. Day, "Pre-Deuteronomic Allusions to the Covenant in Hosea and Psalm LXXVIII" (1986) 1-12. Cf. also H.G. Reventlow, *Problems of OT Theology in the Twentieth Century*, 127.

For a summary of this controversy, cf. D.L. Magnetti, "The Oath in the Old Testament in the Light of Related Terms and in the Legal and Covenantal Context of the Ancient Near East," 110f.

[63] Cf., e.g., J. Begrich, who argues against the radical development posited by J. Wellhausen ("Berit. Ein Beitrag zur Erfassung einer alttestamentlichen Denkform" [1944]).

[64] For a recent survey of the fifty-seven currently extant treaties with their publication data, cf. J.H. Walton, *Ancient Israelite Literature in its Cultural Context* (1989) 95-107.

[65] *Law and Covenant in Israel and the Ancient Near East* (1955) [= *BA* 17 (1954) 26-46, 50-76].

[66] *The Covenant Formulary in Old Testament, Jewish, and Early Christian Writings* [from *Das Bundesformular*, 2nd. rev. ed., 1964] (1971). The first edition of Baltzer's work was published in 1960.

[67] Cf., e.g., G.E. Mendenhall, *Law and Covenant* (1955); M.G. Kline, "The Two Tables of the Covenant" (1963); K.A. Kitchen, *Ancient Orient and Old Testament* (1966) 90-102; and A. Phillips, *Ancient Israel's Criminal Law. A New Approach to the Decalogue* (1970). More recently Phillips has reversed his earlier position ("The Decalogue - Ancient Israel's Criminal Law" [1983]). Cf. also D.J. McCarthy, *Treaty and Covenant* (1981) 158-60, 249ff.; and F.B. Knutson, "Literary Genres in *PRU* IV," *RSP*, II, 175-77.

[68] So, e.g., M.G. Kline, *Treaty of the Great King* (1963); K.A. Kitchen, *Ancient Orient and Old Testament* (1966) 96-102; M. Weinfeld, *Deuteronomy and the Deuteronomic School* (1972); and P.C. Craigie, *The Book of Deuteronomy* (1976).

[69] Typically chapters 5-26, 28 (cf. K. Baltzer, *The Covenant Formulary*, 45f.; D.J. McCarthy, *Treaty and Covenant* [1981] 158f.; F.B. Knutson, "Literary Genres in *PRU* IV," *RSP*, II, 165f.). Elements of the treaty form are commonly seen combined in various subsections of Deuteronomy including: Deut. 1:1-4:40 (K. Baltzer, *op. cit.*, 41-43 vs. D.J. McCarthy, *op. cit.*, 188-194; cf. F.B. Knutson, "Literary Genres in *PRU* IV," *RSP*, II, 167ff.); Deuteronomy 4 (cf. M.G. Kline, *Treaty of the Great King*, 136f.); Deuteronomy 5 (D.J. McCarthy, *op. cit.*, 159f.; F.B. Knutson, *RSP*, II, 163f.); and Deut. 28:69-30:20 (K. Baltzer, *op. cit.*, 44-5; F.B. Knutson, *RSP*, II, 168-71).

[70] Cf. F.B. Knutson, "Literary Genres in *PRU* IV," *RSP*, II, 174f.

[71] G.E. Mendenhall acknowledges that while Joshua 24 follows the treaty schema, as a narrative it is not itself the text of a treaty. Cf. also K.A. Kitchen, *Ancient Orient and Old Testament* (1966) 96ff.; H.B. Huffmon, "The Exodus, Sinai and the Credo" (1965) 104, n. 16.

[72] Cf. D.J. McCarthy, *Treaty and Covenant* [1981] 141f.; F.B. Knutson, "Literary Genres in *PRU* IV," *RSP*, II, 171-3; and, especially, J.R. Vannoy, *Covenant Renewal at Gilgal* (1978).

One aspect of this debate in applying the treaty form to biblical texts is the need stressed by some scholars to give greater attention to the treaty versus covenant distinction. Perhaps of even greater significance, there appears to be an increasing awareness of the variety of treaty forms and by-forms with which comparisons should be sought.[73] The more important varieties include: suzerainty (or vassal) treaties, parity treaties, patron treaties, promissory (or grant) treaties, and perhaps still other types;[74] as well as related by-forms including the law collections, the covenant "lawsuit", and the treaty-like *kudurru* stones.[75]

3.2 Method of approach

The method of approach for the present study: the deeper consensus on which we wish to build

Happily for our purpose, much of the present day confusion concerning "covenant" (particularly regarding issues of theology and literary genre) has little bearing on the question whether marriage in the Old Testament was viewed in covenantal terms. What is necessary, however, for us to begin our investigation is an awareness of the major elements which typically comprise a covenant in order that we might have a reasonable idea of what to look for. Fortunately, there is a substantial scholarly consensus as to what these elements are.

Anticipating here some of the conclusions of Chapter 6, we may offer the following working definition for "covenant [בְּרִית]": A covenant, in its normal sense, is an elected, as opposed to natural, relationship of obligation under oath.[76] Supportive of this emphasis on an elected, as opposed to natural, relationship, D.J. McCarthy remarks that covenant was "the means the ancient world took to extend relationships beyond the natural unity by blood."[77]

While few scholars would wish to follow N. Lohfink in identifying בְּרִית with oath,[78] the indispensability of an oath for ratifying a covenant

---

[73] So D. J. McCarthy, *Treaty and Covenant* [1981]. Cf. also F.B. Knutson, "Literary Genres in *PRU* IV," *RSP*, II, 160; and R.P. Gordon, *1 and 2 Samuel*, 76.

[74] Cf. G.E. Mendenhall, "Covenant Forms in Israelite Tradition" (1954). Cf. also M. Weinfeld, "The Covenant of Grant in the OT and in the Ancient Near East" (1970).

[75] H.B. Huffmon, "The Covenant Lawsuit in the Prophets" (1959); G.E. Wright, "The Lawsuit of God" (1962); B. Gemser, *The rîb- or Controversy-Pattern in Hebrew Mentality* (1955). Cf. E.W. Nicholson, *God and His People*, 63f.

[76] Cf. also M.G. Kline, who defines בְּרִית as a "sanction-sealed commitment to maintain a particular relationship or follow a stipulated course of action. In general, then a covenant may be defined as a relationship under sanctions" (*By Oath Consigned*, 16).

Similar also is the definition offered by G.E. Mendenhall, "A solemn promise made binding by an oath, which may be either a verbal formula or a symbolic oath" ("Covenant," 714). Cf. also M. Newman, "Review of E. Kutsch, *Verheissung und Gesetz*" (1975) 120; and W. Dyrness, *Themes in Old Testament Theology* (1979) 113.

[77] *Treaty and Covenant* (1963) 175. P. Kalluveettil notes "Covenant is relational, in one way or other it creates unity, community" (*Declaration and Covenant*, 51). Not all would agree. M.G. Kline offers a more general definition (see the previous footnote), which includes either a relationship or a stipulated course of action.

[78] *Die Landverheissung als Eid*, 101-13.

commands a widespread scholarly consensus. We may note the statement of G.M. Tucker: "the covenant formula was based on the oath pattern and the contract was not."[79] Likewise M. Weinfeld states "*berith* as a commitment has to be confirmed by an oath.... The oath gives the obligation its binding validity...."[80] Hence D.J. McCarthy concludes that the basic idea of a covenant is "a union based on an oath."[81] Accordingly, the lack of an oath in marriage, if it proves to be the case as Milgrom argues, indeed would appear to prohibit marriage from being identified as a "covenant."

A normative versus a descriptive study

Finally, it is important to clarify that we are not seeking to elucidate the actual practice of marriage in ancient Israel (the concern of historical anthropology) — which, no doubt, often fell short of the prophetic ideal.[82] Ours is rather a study of that ideal: a study of Old Testament canonical ethics. In particular, we shall attempt to establish that Malachi, along with several other biblical authors, identified marriage as a covenant and that the implications of such a theory of marriage are not contradicted by other biblical texts, even where the term "covenant" does not happen to appear.

---

[79] "Covenant Forms and Contract Forms" (1965). So also D.J. McCarthy, *Old Testament Covenant*, 34.

[80] "בְּרִית *berîth*," 256.

[81] *Treaty and Covenant* (1981) 141. Supportive of this same observation are K.A. Kitchen (who stresses the invariable presence of sanctions and a ratifying oath even when not explicitly mentioned in the covenant document), E. Gerstenberger (cf. F.B. Knutson, "Literary Genres in *PRU* IV," *RSP*, II, 158), J. Barr ("Some Semantic Notes on the Covenant," esp. p. 32), and E.W. Nicholson (*God and His People*, 103).

[82] A similar disparity between marital ideal and practice is true for all societies according to B.K. Malinowski (as cited by S.F. Bigger, "Hebrew Marriage and Family in the Old Testament Period," vi).

As an analogy, one may compare the OT's teaching regarding monotheism and the apparent rampant polytheism suggested in much of the OT's apologetic and independently attested in archaeology. The admitted presence of the latter in no way diminishes either the validity or the importance of a study of the former.

CHAPTER ONE

THE INTERPRETATIVE CONTEXT OF MALACHI 2:10-16

As indicated in the Introduction, Mal. 2:14 is perhaps the chief pillar of the traditional identification of marriage in the Old Testament as a covenant: "You ask, 'Why does he not?' Because the LORD was witness between you and the wife of your youth, to whom you have been faithless, though she is your companion and your wife by covenant [וְאֵשֶׁת בְּרִיתֶךָ]." Serious objections to this identification, however, have been raised by a number of scholars who prefer a reference to a figurative marriage, whether between Israel and Yahweh (I.G. Matthews, F.F. Hvidberg, A. Isaksson, and others); or between Israel and the covenant (C.C. Torrey, B. Vawter); or between the priests of Malachi's day and the original priestly community (G.S. Ogden).[1]

Even among scholars who accept a reference to a literal marriage in Mal. 2:10-16, some have argued that the covenant mentioned in the expression וְאֵשֶׁת בְּרִיתֶךָ [lit., "and the wife of your covenant"] has nothing to do with the marital relationship as such, but merely designates the wife as a member of the same covenant community as her husband. In other words, "covenant" in this context refers to Israel's covenant with God, not to a marital covenant between the husband and his wife.[2]

The arguments used to support these two distinct interpretative options overlap at significant points, and so for convenience it will be useful to consider them together. In the next chapter we shall focus on arguments

---

[1] In addition to J. Milgrom, who holds that ברית in Mal. 2:14 is used only as a "literary metaphor" (*Cult and Conscience*, 133ff.), a symbolic view has been supported by C.C. Torrey, "The Prophecy of 'Malachi'" (1898); H. Winckler, "Maleachi" (1901); A.C. Welch, *Post-Exilic Judaism* (1935); I.G. Matthews, "Haggai, Malachi" (1935); F.F. Hvidberg, *Weeping and Laughter in the Old Testament* (1962) 120-123; A. Isaksson, *Marriage and Ministry in the New Temple* (1965) 27-34; B. Vawter, "The Biblical Theology of Divorce" (1967); G.W. Ahlström, *Joel and the Temple Cult of Jerusalem* (1971); M. Greenberg, *Ezekiel 1-20* (1983); G.S. Ogden, "The Use of Figurative Language in Malachi 2:10-16" (1988); and J.M. O'Brien, *Priest and Levite in Malachi* (1990).

[2] Cf., e.g., K. Marti, *Das Dodekapropheton* (1904); O. Isopescul, *Der Prophet Malachias* (1908); W. Nowack, *Das kleinen Propheten* (1922); E. Sellin, *Das Zwölfprophetenbuch* (1929-30); B.M. Vellas, *Israelite Marriage* (1956) 24; A.S. van der Woude, "Malachi's Struggle for a Pure Community" (1986) 68f.; W. Rudolph, *Haggai, Sacharja 1-8, Sacharja 9-14, Maleachi* (1976); *idem*, "Zu Mal 2 10-16" (1981); A. Tosato "Il ripudio: delitto e pena (Mal 2,10-16)" (1978) 552, n 19 and p. 553; and B. Glazier-McDonald, although Glazier-McDonald accepts an identification of marriage as a covenant in Ezek. 16:8 and Prov. 2:17 (*Malachi* [1987] 101f.).

Some interpreters seem to view בְּרִית in 2:14 as a reference primarily to Yahweh's covenant with Israel, but secondarily to the marriage covenant. Cf., e.g., T.V. Moore, *A Commentary on Haggai and Malachi* (1856) 134; and A.R. Fausset, *A Commentary, Critical and Explanatory on the Old and New Testaments* (1887) 738.

which rest mainly on evidence adduced from within the book of Malachi itself. Before doing so, however, it will be useful to consider certain matters of introduction to the book of Malachi as a whole in an effort to set our discussion of Mal. 2:14 within a proper interpretative context. In this first chapter, therefore, we propose to consider briefly the date of Malachi; the book's relationship to Ezra, Nehemiah, and the pentateuchal sources; and finally the overall arrangement of the book itself.

1. THE DATE OF MALACHI

Unlike most of the other prophetic books, the book of Malachi offers no explicit indication of the date of its composition. It mentions no datable event nor any contemporary ruler.[3] Moreover, the prophet himself, if "Malachi [מַלְאָכִי]" is even to be regarded as a proper noun,[4] is nowhere else mentioned — not in Ezra, who mentions Haggai and Zechariah (5:1; 6:14); nor even in Josephus, who mentions most of the major characters of the period.[5] Nevertheless, there appears to be a scholarly consensus that the book of Malachi was composed at some point within the Persian period (515 - 330

---

[3] It is uncertain whether the mentioned demise of Edom in 1:2-5 should be related to the campaigns of Nabonidus or, as is more generally thought, to the gradual displacement of the Edomites by the Nabataeans and their relocation in southern Judah. Other historical references, such as to the supposed depredations by Arab tribes following the Babylonian downfall, appear less likely. Cf., e.g., J.G. Baldwin, *Haggai, Zechariah, Malachi* (1972) 223; P.A. Verhoef, *The Books of Haggai and Malachi* (1987) 203-204; and especially B. Glazier-McDonald, *Malachi* (1987) 34-41. Glazier-McDonald suggests that the Nabataeans may have wreaked their devastation less by military means than by the effects of their grazing herds, destroying previously arable land. Cf. also P.C. Hammond, *The Nabataeans* (1973) 13; and J.I. Lawlor, *The Nabataeans in Historical Perspective* (1974). If the reference is to the displacement by the Nabataeans, unfortunately this cannot be dated with any certainty. For a useful survey of Edom during the Persian period cf. A. Lemaire, "Populations et territoires de la Palestine à l'époque perse," *Transeuphratène* 3 (1990) 31-74, esp. 45-54.

Alternatively, it is possible that no particular historical event is intended in Mal. 1:2-5, but that Edom is cited merely as a representative enemy. Cf., e.g., C.C. Torrey, "The Edomites in Southern Judah" (1898) 20; R.A. Mason, *The Books of Haggai, Zechariah, and Malachi* (1977) 141; P.R. Ackroyd, "The History of Israel in the Exilic and Post-Exilic Periods" (1979) 332; and R.J. Coggins, *Haggai, Zechariah, Malachi* (1987) 75.

[4] In favour of an identification of Malachi [מַלְאָכִי] as a proper noun, as it is understood by the Peshitta, Theodotion, Symmachus, and the Vulgate, with 3:1 offering a word-play on the prophet's name, cf., e.g., J.G. Baldwin, *Haggai, Zechariah, Malachi* (1972) 211-213; W. Rudolph, *Haggai, Sacharja 1-8, Sacharja 9-14, Maleachi* (1976) 247f.; B.S. Childs, *Introduction to the Old Testament as Scripture* (1979) 493f.; and P.A. Verhoef, *The Books of Haggai and Malachi* (1987) 154-156.

If the meaning of מַלְאָכִי is felt to be unacceptable, it is possible that it is a hypocorism for מַלְאָכִיהוּ, "messenger of Yahweh," on an analogy with עֹבַדְיָ (1 Chr. 6:44 — cf. עַבְדִיאֵל in 1 Chr. 5:15 and עֹבַדְיָה in Jer. 36:26) and בְּקִי (Num. 34:22; Ezra 7:14 — cf. בְּקִיָּהוּ in 1 Chr. 25:4, 13).

[5] *Antiquities* 11, iv, i-v, 8. Malachi is mentioned, however, in the second century A.D. book 2 Esdras.

B.C.) and, more particularly, at a time roughly contemporaneous with the ministries of Ezra and Nehemiah in the mid-fifth century B.C.[6]

The following arguments have been adduced in support of this approximate dating of Malachi:

1) The canonical placement of Malachi at the end of the Minor Prophets, which in part reflects a chronological arrangement, offers some confirmation for a post-exilic date.[7]

2) The mention of "your governor [לְפֶחָתֶךְ]," an Akkadian loanword,[8] in 1:8 is thought to point to the Persian period — especially since Judah was not administered by "governors" in the pre-exilic period. See, for example, the use of פֶּחָה as a designation for Zerubbabel in Hag. 1:1, 14; 2:2, 21 and for Nehemiah in Neh. 5:14, 15, 18; 12:26.[9]

3) Malachi presupposes the existence of the temple (1:10; 3:1, 8) and so is to be dated after its erection in 516/515 B.C.

4) The problem of hypocritical formalism and apathy which Malachi addresses (1:6-14; 2:1-9; 3:6-12) suggests a period of decline from the standard of temple worship which is thought to have attended the ministries of Haggai and Zechariah.[10]

5) Many of the sins reproved by Malachi are those addressed by Ezra and Nehemiah, suggesting that these were roughly contemporaneous. See, for example, the issue of corruption of the priesthood (Mal. 1:6-2:9; Neh. 13:4-9, 30); mixed marriage (Mal. 2:10f.; Ezra 9-10; Neh. 10:31 [ET 30]; 13:1-3, 23-27); abuse of the disadvantaged (Mal. 3:5; Neh. 5:1-5); and the failure to pay tithes, etc. (Mal. 3:8; Neh. 10:33-40 [ET 32-39]; 13:10-13).[11]

6) The allusion to Mal. 3:24 [ET 4:6] in Sir. 48:10 and the mention of "the twelve prophets" in 49:10 imply that the book could not be later than 180 B.C. This refutes the view of H. Winckler, for example, who dates Malachi to the period of Antiochus.[12]

In addition to the more general parallels between Malachi and Ezra and Nehemiah enumerated above, we may suggest several further parallels specifically between Nehemiah and Mal. 2:10-16. In particular, the mention of godly children in Mal. 2:15 may explain or be compared to Nehemiah's emphasis on the unholy children born of interfaith marriages (Neh. 13:24).

---

[6] Cf., e.g., S.R. Driver, *The Minor Prophets* (1906) 287-93; W.H. Schmidt, *Introduction to the Old Testament* (1984) 281; and R.L. Smith, *Micah – Malachi* (1984) 298-299.

[7] On the approximate chronological order of the minor prophets, cf. R. Rendtorff, *The Old Testament* (1985) 215f. G.M. Tucker argues that this order is also supported by the opening formulae ("Prophetic Superscriptions and the Growth of a Canon" [1977]).

[8] Cf. KB, 872; *AHw* 120a Nr. 18 *[bēl pīḫāti / pāḫāti]*.

[9] Although פֶּחָה often refers to a Persian appointee, it can have a more general reference. Cf., e.g., 1 Kgs. 10:15; 20:24; 2 Kgs. 18:24; Isa. 36:9; Jer. 51:23, 28, 57; Ezek. 23:6, 23; and 2 Chr. 9:14.

[10] So, e.g., P.A. Verhoef, *The Books of Haggai and Malachi*, 157.

[11] These points of contact are so impressive that J. Blenkinsopp wonders if the "messenger of the covenant" in Mal. 3:1 may be Nehemiah (*Ezra – Nehemiah, A Commentary* [1988] 365f.)!

[12] So R.L. Smith, *Micah – Malachi*, 299.

Second, in addition to the parallel between Neh. 13:29 and the corrupted covenant of Levi in Mal. 2:4, 8 (which is unrelated to marital offences), there is a further parallel between Neh. 13:29 and the profaning of "the covenant of our fathers" in Mal. 2:10, which is the result of a marital offence. Finally, Nehemiah's imprecation in 13:25, 29 and his remedy of excommunication in 13:28 may both be compared to Mal. 2:12, where Malachi's curse implies excommunication.[13]

Given the meagre state of the available evidence, however, attempts at greater precision in dating Malachi are bound to be speculative. Nevertheless, scholars have sought to date Malachi more exactly based mainly on two lines of argumentation. The first approach attempts to correlate Malachi's ministry with that of Ezra and Nehemiah. The second approach, which can be complementary to the first, seeks evidence in Malachi for dependence on Deuteronomic and/or Priestly material.

1.1 Malachi in relation to Ezra and Nehemiah

The attempt to correlate Malachi's ministry with that of Ezra and Nehemiah is complicated by the uncertainty regarding the relative chronology of Ezra and Nehemiah.[14] The traditional view, still held by a majority of scholars, considers that Ezra preceded Nehemiah and arrived in Jerusalem about 458 B.C. Nehemiah came for his first term about 445 B.C., worked together with Ezra for a period of 12 years, and returned to Susa about 433 B.C. After an unknown period away, Nehemiah returned for a second visit to Jerusalem, also of unknown duration. An alternative chronology argues that Nehemiah's ministry preceded that of Ezra.

With respect to the more precise attempts to date Malachi, there are five possible views: 1) Malachi precedes Nehemiah and probably also Ezra;[15] 2) Malachi precedes Nehemiah, but perhaps not Ezra;[16] 3) Malachi coincides with Nehemiah's ministry;[17] 4) Malachi ministered between Nehemiah's two

---

[13] Cf. F.C. Fensham, *Ezra and Nehemiah*, 267f.

[14] Cf., e.g., H.H. Rowley, "The Chronological Order of Ezra and Nehemiah" (1948). For a defence of the traditional order, cf. E.M. Yamauchi, "The reverse order of Ezra/Nehemiah reconsidered" (1980) 7-13; and H.G.M. Williamson, "The Chronological Order of Ezra and Nehemiah," in *Ezra, Nehemiah* (1985) xxxix-xliv.

[15] B.S. Childs considers this view to be held by a majority of critical scholars (*Introduction to the Old Testament as Scripture*, 489). Cf., e.g., D.K. Marti (1904); B. Stade (1905); A. van Hoonacker (1908); W. Nowack (1922); A. von Bulmerincq (1926 — Bulmerincq suggests that Malachi was Ezra's assistant and that Ezra was none other than the מַלְאַךְ הַבְּרִית in 3:1); L.H. Brockington, "Malachi" (1962) 656; W. Neil, "Malachi" (1962) 229; O. Eissfeldt, *Old Testament: An Introduction* (1965) 442f.; R.K. Harrison, *Introduction to the Old Testament* (1969) 960f.; J.G. Baldwin, *Haggai, Zechariah, Malachi* (1972) 213; and W.J. Dumbrell, "Malachi and the Ezra-Nehemiah Reforms" (1976).

[16] Cf., e.g., J.T. Marshall, "The Theology of Malachi" (1896) 16f.; G.A. Smith, *The Book of the Twelve Prophets* II (1899) 337f.; and W.C. Kaiser Jr., *Malachi. God's Unchanging Love* (1984) 15-17.

[17] Cf., e.g., H. Cowles, *The Minor Prophets* (1867) 383f., 392 [Cowles considers that the "second time" in Mal. 2:13 "means ye have a second time relapsed into this great sin; the first time being that great apostasy from which they were reclaimed under Ezra. (See Ezra 9)"]; J. Packard, *The Book of Malachi* (1876) 3; C.F. Keil, *The Twelve Minor*

visits to Jerusalem;[18] and 5) Malachi follows both Ezra and Nehemiah.[19] Unfortunately, the arguments which have been advanced for each of these alternatives appear inconclusive.

Concerning the evidence of Mal. 2:10-16 in relation to Ezra and Nehemiah, we need to consider only one argument which has been advanced: namely that Malachi should be dated after Ezra on the assumption that Malachi's repudiation of divorce in 2:16 is the result of the bitter experience of Ezra's enforced program of divorce.[20] However, on closer examination it appears that Malachi shares Ezra's abhorrence of mixed marriage (Mal. 2:10-12) and condemns it in the strongest possible terms as infidelity [בגד], as a profanation of both the covenant of our fathers [חִלֵּל בְּרִית אֲבֹתֵינוּ] and of Yahweh's holiness/sanctuary [חִלֵּל יְהוּדָה קֹדֶשׁ יְהוָה], and also as an abomination [וְתוֹעֵבָה]. In this light, regardless of how the curse in Mal. 2:12 is to be interpreted, it is doubtful that Malachi would have countenanced any lesser remedy than the dissolution of these marriages for so grave an offence. On the other hand, whatever the relation between 2:10-12 and 2:13-16, most scholars assume that 2:14-15 implies that the divorces which Malachi condemns in 2:16 are divorces of Jewish rather than pagan wives, and therefore Malachi's condemnation of divorce appears unrelated to the enforced divorces of Ezra's day.[21]

Although the evidence does not allow us to be sure whether Malachi preceded, followed, or was a contemporary of Ezra and Nehemiah, that he preached in the same general period is assured; this is significant for the interpretation of the text.

Prophets, II (1868); W.H. Lowe, "Malachi" (n.d.) 597f.; and C. von Orelli, *The Twelve Minor Prophets* (1893).

[18] Cf. especially P.A. Verhoef, *The Books of Haggai and Malachi*, 158. Cf. also A.F. Kirkpatrick, *The Doctrine of the Prophets* (1907) 500-502; and R.L. Alden, "Malachi" (1985) 701f. (though cf. p. 703).

[19] T.T. Perowne, *Malachi* (1908) 10; and G.V. Smith, "Malachi" (1986) 227.

Arguing for a fourth century B.C. date are F. Hitzig, *Die zwölf kleinen Propheten* (1881), and I.G. Matthews, "Haggai, Malachi," viii-x.

Arguing for a third century B.C. date is O. Holtzmann ("Der Prophet Maleachi und der Ursprung des Pharisäerbundes" [1931]), and for a second century B.C. date is H.H. Spoer ("Some New Considerations towards the Dating of the Book of Malachi" [1908] 179f.) — the latter, based on the contradiction between Malachi and Ezra on the subject of divorce.

[20] Cf., e.g., L. Kruse-Blinkenberg, "The Pesitta [*sic*] of the Book of Malachi" (1966) 103f. Likewise H.H. Spoer considers the contradiction between Malachi and Ezra on the subject of divorce to support dating Malachi well after Ezra. He dates Malachi about 150 B.C. ("Some New Considerations towards the Dating of the Book of Malachi" [1908] 179f.). Alternatively, G.V. Smith argues that Malachi's stance against the divorce of Israelite wives was a necessary corrective to an assumed illegitimate extension of Ezra and Nehemiah's prior permission for the divorce of foreign wives ("Malachi" [1986] 227).

[21] Cf. also the fuller discussion of Mal. 2:16 in Chapter 3 below.

1.2 Malachi in relation to Dtr and especially P

We turn now to the second line of argumentation, which attempts a more precise dating of Malachi based on its dependence on Deuteronomic and/or Priestly material.

In 445 B.C. the "law" accepted by the people of Israel in Neh. 8:13-18 and 10:33-40 [ET 32-39] (cf. also Ezra 7:12, 25-26) clearly included the Priestly legislation of the Pentateuch and, according to most scholars, was identical with our present Pentateuch, or nearly so.[22] This has been used to prove a late dating for the P source and a corresponding earlier date for Malachi, prior to 445 B.C. Accordingly, scholars have often stressed the evidence for "Deuteronomic" influence in Malachi over against a supposed lack of evidence for any influence from the "Priestly Code."[23]

Perhaps the clearest example of Deuteronomic influence may be seen in Malachi's understanding of the right of Levites to serve at the altar, rather than reserving this prerogative for the priests (the exclusive right of priests in this regard has been considered by most scholars since J. Wellhausen, including J. Milgrom, to be a distinguishing characteristic of P).[24] More exactly, Malachi does not distinguish clearly between "priests [כֹּהֲנִים]" (1:6; 2:1) or "priest [כֹּהֵן]" (2:7) and "Levites [בְּנֵי לֵוִי]" (3:3) or "Levi [לֵוִי]" (2:4, 8).[25]

Other possible examples of Deuteronomic influence include Malachi's mention of a male animal for sacrifice in Mal. 1:14, where the Priestly Code permits either male or female animals. Also Malachi joins the heave-offering [תְּרוּמָה] with the tithe [מַעֲשֵׂר] as does Deuteronomy, while the Priestly Code separates them, assigning the heave-offering to the priests rather than the Levites.[26]

On the other hand, with respect to other aspects of tithing Malachi seems to anticipate the insistence of the Priestly Code that all tithes are to be paid in Jerusalem, where they are to be stored, while Deuteronomy has the triennial tithe paid to the Levites and poor in their city gates, where they are to be eaten. Aware of this slight departure from the provisions of

---

[22] Cf. "The Identification of the Book of the Law" in H.G.M. Williamson, *Ezra, Nehemiah*, xxxvii-xxxix. Cf. also S. Japhet, "Law and 'the Law' in Ezra-Nehemiah" (1988).

[23] E.g., cf. O. Eissfeldt, *The Old Testament: An Introduction*, 443; and C. Stuhlmueller, "Malachi" (1970) 398f. Stuhlmueller lists the following allusions to Deuteronomy: Mal. 1:9 with Deut. 10:17; Mal. 1:12 with Deut. 7:8; Mal. 2:1, 4; 3:3 with Deut. 18:1; Mal. 2:6 with Deut. 33:10; Mal. 3:22 with Deut. 4:10. Cf. also B. Glazier-McDonald, *Malachi*, p. 73, n. 126.

[24] Cf., e.g., E. Rivkin, "Aaron, Aaronides," 1-3.

[25] While this assumed synonymy of "priests" and "Levites" in Malachi has been challenged by K. Elliger (*Maleachi*, 189), it has been carefully argued by J.M. O'Brien (*Priest and Levite in Malachi* [1990] 143f., and *passim*). Cf. also G.S. Ogden and R.R. Deutsch, *A Commentary on the Books of Joel and Malachi*, 93.

[26] For a more complete listing of Deuteronomic words and phrases within Malachi, cf. A. von Bulmerincq, *Der Prophet Maleachi*, I., 436f.

Deuteronomy, J. Wellhausen and J.M.P. Smith considered Malachi to be a kind of "missing link" between D and P.[27]

More recent scholars, however, have challenged Wellhausen's views concerning the literary nature and supposed lateness of P,[28] and many would now question the earlier conviction that Malachi was unaware of Pentateuchal material assigned to P.[29] For example, it has often been noted that Malachi does not use the distinctive Deuteronomic expression הַכֹּהֲנִים הַלְוִיִּם, "the Levitical priests," when speaking of the priests, while, at the same time, it may be questioned whether Malachi's designation for the priests as "sons of Levi" necessarily proves his ignorance of the Priestly Code. Refuting Wellhausen's oversimplification of the evolution of Israel's religious development, B. Glazier-McDonald has argued that a division in clerical orders long preceded Malachi and that Malachi's stress on the Levitical descent of the priests merely accords with post-exilic practice.[30] In addition, the "covenant with Levi" is more likely intended as a reference to Num. 25:12f. than to Deut. 33:10 or Jer. 33:20.[31] Furthermore, Glazier-McDonald notes that Malachi's treatment of the תְּרוּמָה (which she renders "levy, contribution") actually accords quite well with the provisions of Num. 18:26f.[32] Moreover, with respect to his treatment of tithes, "Malachi's presuppositions are best met by the provisions found in the Priestly Code, cf. Lev 27:30f and Num 18:21-31."[33] Additional evidence of dependence on the Priestly Code has been argued by M. Fishbane, who demonstrates how Mal. 1:6-2:9 offers an artfully crafted aggadic exegesis of Num. 6:23-27.[34]

---

[27] J.M.P. Smith, *Malachi*, 7-9.

[28] Among those who consider the P material to be the result of editorial activity, rather than a literary source, are F.M. Cross Jr., *Canaanite Myth and Hebrew Epic* (1973), and R. Rendtorff, *The Old Testament. An Introduction* (1985).

Among those who have argued for the antiquity of P, including the suggestion that the P source may well antedate J, are S.R. Külling, *Zur Datierung der "Genesis-P-Stücke," namentlich des Kapitels Genesis 17* (1964); G.A. Rendsburg, "Late Biblical Hebrew and the Date of P" (1980); *idem,* "A New Look at the Pentateuchal HWᵓ" (1982); *idem, The Redaction of Genesis* (1986); A. Hurvitz, "The Evidence of Language in Dating the Priestly Code; A Linguistic Study in Technical Idioms and Terminology" (1974); *idem, A Linguistic Study of the Relationship between the Priestly Source and the Book of Ezekiel: A New Approach to an Old Problem* (1982); *idem,* "The Language of the Priestly Source and its Historical Setting - the Case for an Early Date" (1983); Z. Zevit, "Converging Lines of Evidence Bearing on the Date of P" (1982); J.G. McConville, "Priests and Levites in Ezekiel: A crux in the interpretation of Israel's History" (1983) 3-31; M. Weinfeld, "Social and Cultic Institutions in the Priestly Source against their Ancient Near Eastern Background" (1983) 95-129; and G.J. Wenham, *Genesis 1-15* (1987) xxxi-xlv.

[29] Cf. especially E.M. Meyers, "Priestly Language in the Book of Malachi" (1986); B. Glazier-McDonald, *Malachi* (1987) 73-80 and *passim*; J.M. O'Brien, "Torah and Prophets: Malachi and the Date of the Priestly Code" (1988) and *idem, Priest and Levite in Malachi* (1990).

[30] *Malachi*, 76ff. Cf. also W. Rudolph, *Haggai, Sacharja 1-8, Sacharja 9-14, Maleachi*, 267.

[31] So, according to B. Glazier-McDonald, *Malachi*, 77-80.

[32] *Ibid.*, 190, which erroneously cites "Num 26:26f."

[33] *Ibid.*

[34] *Biblical Interpretation in Ancient Israel* (1985) 332-334. This particular argument has been challenged by J.M. O'Brien on the grounds that the priestly blessing may predate

Summarizing her study of Malachi's relation to the Priestly Code, J.M. O'Brien notes simply that Malachi appears to be aware of both P and D, although it does not follow either rigorously.[35] Putting this observation somewhat differently, rather than hypothesizing an on-going "Deuteronomic School" or "Priestly School" with their divergent traditions possibly influencing Malachi, it appears more plausible to assume with D.L. Petersen that Malachi merely adduced motifs which are paralleled in earlier Deuteronomic or Priestly literature or, even better, that Malachi made textual allusions to the already written and received Torah, as it existed in his day.[36]

Although there is uncertainty among scholars concerning the originality of Mal. 3:22 [ET 4:4],[37] the expression, "the law of Moses, my servant [תּוֹרַת מֹשֶׁה עַבְדִּי], the decrees and laws I gave him at Horeb for all Israel," appears as a plausible instance of synecdoche intended to encompass the Pentateuch as a whole, even though large portions of the Pentateuch do not present themselves as having been received at Horeb.[38]

2. CANONICAL CONTEXT[39]

Accordingly, although the evidence is insufficient to support a precise dating of Malachi, it is apparent that its post-exilic origin permits it to be heir to a substantial body of received scripture and that this "canonical context" may

---

P ("Torah and Prophets: Malachi and the Date of the Priestly Code" [1988]). Fishbane's conclusions, however, are supported by, *inter alia*, E.M. Meyers, "Priestly Language," 225.

[35] J.M. O'Brien, "Torah and Prophets: Malachi and the Date of the Priestly Code" (1988), and *idem, Priest and Levite in Malachi* (1990).

[36] In comments made during the Israelite Prophetic Literature Section, Annual Meeting of the Society of Biblical Literature, Chicago, IL, November 20, 1988.

[37] Denying the originality of Mal. 3:22 [ET 4:4] are K. Elliger (1956), W. Rudolph (1976), R.A. Mason (1977), A. Deissler (1981), A.S. van der Woude (1982), R.L. Smith (1984), and R.J. Coggins (1987), *inter alios*.

Favouring the originality of Mal. 3:22 [ET 4:4] are W. Nowack (1922), E. Sellin (1929), G. Smit (1934), A. von Bulmerincq (1926), H. Junker (1938), D. Deden (1953), J. Ridderbos (1968), H. Frey (1963), J.G. Baldwin (1972), S. Schreiner (1979), P.A. Verhoef (1972; 1987), B. Glazier-McDonald (1987), and J.M. O'Brien (1990). W. Nowack, E. Sellin, G. Smit, and D. Deden, however, consider 3:23-24 [ET 4:5-6] to be secondary.

Perhaps the most objective evidence for the secondary nature of 3:22-24 [ET 4:4-6] is found in the LXX, which reverses the order of the appendices, placing the Moses appendix after the Elijah appendix. S.L. McKenzie and H.N. Wallace see in this an evidence that the appendices "were not completely fixed in form at the time of the separation of the traditions to which the MT and the LXX belong" ("Covenant Themes in Malachi," 560 n. 34). It is possible, however, that the LXX was motivated by the same concern which led to the later rabbinic practice of repeating 3:22 [ET 4:4] after 3:24 [ET 4:6], namely, the desire to end Malachi on a more positive note (a practice also followed in the case of Isaiah, Lamentations, and Ecclesiastes). Cf. P.A. Verhoef, *The Books of Haggai and Malachi*, 344.

[38] The precise reference of "the law of Moses [תּוֹרַת מֹשֶׁה]" has been a matter of debate. According to A. von Bulmerincq, for example, it refers to the "lawbook" of Ezra, while J. Wellhausen and R. Rendtorff (*The Old Testament. An Introduction*, 242) equate it with Deuteronomy. On the other hand, K. Marti, J.G. Baldwin (*Malachi*, 251), and J.M. O'Brien suggest that it refers to the entire Pentateuch.

[39] For a discussion of the significance of the canonical placement of Malachi at the close of "The Twelve," cf. P.R. House, *The Unity of the Twelve* (1990).

be of even greater import for exegesis than the elusive historical context of Malachi. At almost every point Malachi betrays an intense concern to apply and (re)interpret antecedent scripture — very much in the spirit of Mal. 3:22 [ET 4:4].[40] Such appears to be the case with Malachi's major emphases, especially his exceptional interest in "covenant" (2:4, 5, 8, 10, 14; 3:1).[41] As stressed by R.L. Smith, Malachi's dependence on the work of the Deuteronomists is not simply a matter of shared isolated vocabulary, but also a matter of motifs and perspective (cf., e.g., the theme of election, though the term does not appear in Mal. 1:2-3).[42] Accordingly, R.J. Coggins observes: "Malachi appears to have been attempting to apply the particular emphases of the Deuteronomists in the circumstances of his own day."[43]

In a similar manner, H. Marks notes that, typical of the post-exilic prophets, "the author of Malachi uses intertextual echoes to sharpen his protest against current abuses [of the temple cult]."[44] Marks has in mind the probable "echo" in Mal. 1:6-2:9 mentioned above, which offers an extended allusion to and ironic reversal of the Priestly Blessing in Num. 6:23-27.[45] This is hardly an isolated example; similar "echoes" are evident in texts such as Mal. 1:2f. (Esau and Jacob) and 3:12 ("Then all nations will call you blessed," cf. Gen. 12:3). Compare also A. Tosato's suggestion that Mal. 3:5 may refer to Leviticus 19.[46]

Although B.S. Childs considers 3:23f. [ET 4:5f.] to be secondary, his claim that the appeal to Elijah is informed by typological analogy, if true, suggests a nearly identical hermeneutic with that found elsewhere in Malachi: "Like Malachi, Elijah addressed 'all Israel' (1 Kgs. 18:20). The people of Israel were severely fragmented by indecision of faith (18:21). A curse had

---

[40] Cf. H. Marks, "The Twelve Prophets" (1987) 231f. Cf. also Mal. 3:6.

[41] C.T. Begg sets Malachi alongside Hosea, Jeremiah, Ezekiel, and Deutero/Trito-Isaiah as comprising one of the three great tradition-complexes, namely the prophetic, within which the term בְּרִית figures prominently ("Bᵉrit in Ezekiel" [1986] 79). The other two tradition-complexes are the Deuteronomic/Deuteronomistic (with which Malachi has strong affinities) and the Priestly.

The centrality and sophistication of "covenant" within Malachi has been widely recognized. Cf., e.g., J.G. Baldwin, *Malachi*, 216f.; L.C.H. Fourie, "Die betekenis van die verbond as sleutel vir Maleagi" (1982); S.L. McKenzie and H.N. Wallace, "Covenant Themes in Malachi" (1983); R.L. Smith, "The Shape of Theology in the Book of Malachi" (1987) 24; and P.A. Verhoef, *The Books of Haggai and Malachi*, 179-184.

[42] *Micah – Malachi*, 300. So also R.J. Coggins, *Haggai, Zechariah, Malachi*, 76.

[43] *Haggai, Zechariah, Malachi*, 76.

[44] "The Twelve Prophets," 229.

[45] M. Fishbane, *Biblical Interpretation in Ancient Israel* (1985) 332-334; E.M. Meyers, "Priestly Language," 225; and H. Marks, "The Twelve Prophets" 229f.

Mal. 2:1-9 may also include echoes of Deut. 33:8-11, as noted by R.R. Deutsch, "Calling God's People to Obedience" (1987) 71.

[46] A. Tosato, "Il ripudio: delitto e pena (Mal 2,10-16)" (1978) 553. Tosato similarly compares Lev. 19:17-18 (and also 19:34) to Mal. 2:10 and 16.

C. Stuhlmueller argues for a literary dependence of Malachi on Ezekiel, based on a number of plausible allusions: cf. Mal. 1:7, 12 with Ezek. 44:16; Mal. 1:11 with Ezek. 36:23; Mal. 2:3 with Ezek. 5:10; 6:5; 12:15; 30:36; and Mal. 3:2 with Ezek. 44:27 ("Malachi" [1970] 398f.).

Mal. 1:11 may echo Isa. 45:6; 59:19; and 66:20-1 (cf. also Ps. 50:1; 113:3; Zeph. 3:9-10; Zech. 2:15 [ET 11]).

fallen on the land (18:1 // Mal. 3:24, EVV 4:6). Elijah challenged all Israel to respond to God by forcing a decision between the right and the wrong (// Mal. 3:18). He did it by means of the right offering (// Mal. 3:3) and a fire which fell from heaven (// Mal. 3:3, 19).... The appendix served to equate the hearers of Malachi's prophecy — along with future generations who heard his words in scripture — with the disobedient, vacillating people whose national allegiance to the God of their fathers was in danger of being dissolved."[47]

In summation, we conclude that the book of Malachi derives from a period roughly contemporaneous with the ministries of Ezra and Nehemiah in the mid-fifth century B.C. This dating shifts the burden of proof on to those scholars who deny that Malachi shared the concern of Ezra and Nehemiah with the problem of literal mixed marriage. Furthermore, having been alerted to Malachi's corresponding "canonical context," which allows it to be heir to a substantial body of received scripture including the Pentateuch in particular, the interpreter is prepared for the possibility that Mal. 2:10-16 may presuppose or allude to that antecedent scripture. For example, we shall argue in Chapter 5 below that Mal. 2:15 alludes to Genesis 2, which is central to the argument of Mal. 2:10-16. This allusion may be suggested already in 2:10 by its use of the imagery of creation,[48] and it may be further anticipated in 2:14, if its ideal of marriage parallels Genesis 2.[49] Beyond this indebtedness to Pentateuchal traditions, Mal. 2:10-16 appear also to echo Prov. 2:16f.[50]

On the other hand, this awareness of Malachi's canonical context only heightens the apparent contradiction between the prohibition of divorce in 2:16 and the seemingly lenient attitude toward divorce in a text such as Deut. 24:1-4. This difficulty will be considered in more detail in Chapter 3.

---

[47] *Introduction to the Old Testament as Scripture*, 495f. Cf. also B. Glazier-McDonald, who shares a view regarding 3:22-24 [ET 4:4-6] similar to that of Childs, but accepts this passage as original to Malachi (*Malachi*, 243-270, esp. 257).

Mal. 3:22-24 [ET 4:4-6] may also include echoes of Deut. 34:10-12 and Joel 3:4 [ET 2:31]. Cf. B.S. Childs, *Introduction to the Old Testament as Scripture*, 495; B. Glazier-McDonald, *Malachi*, 253.

[48] This allusion is indirect, however, since the creation immediately in view in 2:10 is not the primeval creation, but the recapitulation of creation in the formation of Israel in the Exodus.

[49] So, e.g., W.C. Kaiser Jr., *Malachi*, 70. Although S. Schreiner does not accept an allusion to Genesis 2 in 2:15a, he does recognize a possible allusion to Gen. 2:23f. in the wider context of Mal. 2:15, citing Tob. 8:6ff. as a parallel ("Mischehen-Ehebruch-Ehescheidung," 226).

[50] This point is argued by A. Robert, "Les attaches litteraires bibliques de Prov. I-IX" (1934/35) especially 44:505-25; and C.V. Camp *Wisdom and the Feminine in the Book of Proverbs*, 235-237 and 269-271. Cf. also Chapter 8, §2.2 below.

3. THE LITERARY STRUCTURE OF MALACHI

Having explored the wider historical and literary context of Malachi, we now turn to examine the literary structure of Malachi as a whole and of Mal. 2:10-16 in particular in the hope that by understanding this immediate context of 2:10-16 we may appreciate its concerns more adequately.

There is a widespread scholarly consensus that the book of Malachi is carefully structured in terms of a heading (1:1), followed by six quite distinct pericopes or "disputations" (1:2-5; 1:6-2:9; 2:10-16; 2:17-3:5 [or 3:6]; 3:6 [or 3:7]-12; 3:13-21 [ET 4:3]), followed by a closing "appendix" (3:22-24 [ET 4:4-6]).[51] Each of these disputational units is relatively coherent in its content and is introduced with an assertion made either by Yahweh or by the prophet: "I have loved you..." (1:2); "A son honours his father, and a servant his master. If then I am a father, where is my honour...?" (1:6f.); "Have we not all one father? Has not one God created us? Why then are we faithless to one another..." (2:10); "You have wearied the Lord with your words" (2:17); "For I the Lord do not change..." (3:6f.); "Your words have been stout against me, says the Lord" (3:13).[52] In each unit also the opening assertion is followed by an anticipated challenge from those being addressed:[53] "But you say [וַאֲמַרְתֶּם], 'How hast thou loved us?'" (1:2); "You say [וַאֲמַרְתֶּם], 'How have we despised thy name?...'" (1:6f.); "You ask [וַאֲמַרְתֶּם], 'Why does he not?'" (2:14); "Yet you say [וַאֲמַרְתֶּם], 'How have we wearied him?'" (2:17); "But you say [וַאֲמַרְתֶּם], 'How shall we return?...'" (3:7f.);[54] "Yet you ask

---

[51] Favouring the above analysis are, *inter alia*, E. Pfeiffer, "Die Disputationsworte im Buche Maleachi" (1959); W. Neil, "Malachi" (1962) 230f.; O. Eissfeldt, *The Old Testament, An Introduction* (1965); J. Ridderbos, *De Kleine Profeten*, 3de druk (1968); R.K. Harrison, *Introduction to the Old Testament* (1969) 958f.; J.A. Fischer, "Notes on the Literary Form and Message of Malachi" (1972); W.J. Dumbrell, "Malachi and the Ezra-Nehemiah Reforms" (1976); A.S. Van der Woude, *Haggai, Maleachi* (1982); R.L. Smith, *Micah – Malachi* (1984) 299f.; R. Rendtorff, *The Old Testament. An Introduction* (1985) 242; and G.V. Smith, "Malachi" (1986) 226f.

P.A. Verhoef agrees with the above analysis but divides the second unit into two: 1:6-14 and 2:1-9 (*Maleachi verklaart* [1972] 35-37 and *The Books of Haggai and Malachi* [1987] 171-179). So does R.R. Deutsch, "Calling God's People to Obedience" (1987) 68. J.G. Baldwin likewise notes a subdivision within 1:6-2:9 between 1:14 and 2:1, although unlike Verhoef Baldwin maintains with the above analysis that there are six principal units (*Haggai, Zechariah, Malachi* [1972]).

Less compelling is the five-fold structure suggested by W.C. Kaiser Jr.: 1:1-5; 1:6-14; 2:1-16; 2:17-3:12; 3:13-24 [ET 4:6] (*Malachi* [1984]).

[52] This selection of verses seems preferable to that offered by W.J. Dumbrell in support of the same outline ("Malachi and the Ezra-Nehemiah Reforms," 43). Dumbrell lists the following six statements by Yahweh (usually in the first person) as providing the theological core for the book: 1:2, 2:14, 2:16, 3:1, 3:6, and 3:17.

[53] At times these are priests (1:6; 2:1, 8; cf. 3:3), but the book does not clearly divide into a speech to priests followed by one to laymen, as G. Wallis has argued ("Wesen und Struktur der Botschaft Maleachis"[1967]).

For a further discussion of the literary problems of Malachi, cf. A. Renker, *Die Tora bei Maleachi* (1979).

[54] *BHS* tentatively suggests that וַאֲמַרְתֶּם בַּמֶּה נָשׁוּב is an addition in 3:7. The lack of any textual support, as well as the literary structure presently being considered, does not favour this suggestion.

[וַאֲמַרְתֶּם], 'What have we said against you?'" (3:13). Each anticipated challenge, in turn, is answered with fuller substantiation by Yahweh or the prophet speaking in Yahweh's behalf. This structure is further reinforced and unified by the repetition of important themes, such as the imagined ignorance or indifference of Yahweh to apathetic worship and evil-doers, especially as this indifference appears to be revealed in the prosperity of the wicked; the problem of deficient offerings and the contemptuous attitude this reveals; the theme of covenant; the "fatherhood" of God; etc.

In addition to this careful linear structuring of Malachi, there may also be an unobtrusive concentric structure to the book as a whole which hitherto has not been recognized, although E. Wendland and others have noted Malachi's fondness for concentric patterning within the individual disputations.[55] The most visible literary indicator of this overall concentric pattern is found in the double introductory assertion ("but you say [וַאֲמַרְתֶּם]") and anticipated response, which are found only in the "B" sections, that is, the 2nd (1:6-2:9) and 5th (3:6-12) disputations.[56] As may be noted, at certain points the concentricity concerns ancillary matters and vocabulary, rather than the main topic of the disputation.

Accordingly, without excluding other possible (even overlapping) outlines, we suggest the following concentric outline:

Heading (1:1) — identifying the source (Yahweh), prophetic intermediary (Malachi), and original recipients (Israel[57]) for this book

A. 1st disputation (1:2-5) — Does God make a distinction between the good and the arrogant wicked? Yahweh's elective love for Jacob vindicated in his judgement against Esau (to be laid waste)

B. 2nd disputation (1:6-2:9) — Israel's begrudging offerings condemned. The profanation of Yahweh through contemptuous priestly service and sacrifice and the corruption of the covenant with Levi judged by Yahweh, who will reverse the priestly blessing into a curse; Yahweh's name to be great among the nations

C. 3rd disputation (2:10-16) — Yahweh is a witness between a man and his wife by covenant. Yahweh is invited to cut off those who intermarry and yet bring an offering; those who

---

[55] "Linear and Concentric Patterns in Malachi" (1985). Cf. also S.D. Snyman, "Chiasmes in Mal. 1:2-5" (1984); *idem*, "Antiteses in die boek Maleagi" (1985); and P.A. Verhoef, *The Books of Haggai and Malachi*, 164-168.

[56] אֲמַרְתֶּם in 3:14 differs not only because it lacks the expected introductory conjunction ו found everywhere else, but also because it does not introduce a second objection. Rather, it merely introduces the answer to the previous question, "How have we spoken against you?" — "You have said [אֲמַרְתֶּם], 'It is vain to serve God.'"

[57] On the significance of applying the name "Israel" to the post-exilic rump state of Judah, identifying Judah as obligated to the covenant and heir to the promises of Yahweh, cf. W.J. Dumbrell, "Malachi and the Ezra-Nehemiah Reforms," 44f.; and R.L. Smith, *Micah – Malachi*, 302f. Cf. also the preponderance of "Israel" over "Judah" in Ezekiel and Ezra.

divorce based on aversion are puzzled over their rejected offerings. Judah is unfaithful to Yahweh through the parallel offences of intermarriage with pagan women and divorce based on aversion

C'. 4th disputation (2:17-3:5 [or 3:6]) — Yahweh is a witness against adultery and other moral offences. The promise is made that the offerings of Judah and Jerusalem will be made pleasing. Yahweh's justice will be vindicated when the "messenger of the covenant" comes to judge the wicked and purify his people

B'. 5th disputation (3:6 [or 3:7]-12) — Israel's begrudging offerings condemned. Repentance demanded in the tithe with a subsequent promise of blessing to be recognized by all nations

A'. 6th disputation (3:13-21 [ET 4:3]) — Does God make a distinction between the good and the arrogant wicked? Yahweh's justice and elective love vindicated in the contrasting fates of the righteous and the evil-doer (the latter to be burned up)

Closing exhortations which summarize the main points of Malachi (3:22-24 [ET 4:4-6]) — Remember the law of Moses (the focus of disputations 1-3) and the promise of Elijah and the coming day of the Lord (the focus of the disputations 4-6)[58]

In addition to this possible concentric outline for the whole of Malachi, as mentioned above E. Wendland and others have argued for the presence of concentricity as a prominent literary feature within each of the individual disputations. With respect to the third disputation, 2:10-16, which is of special interest to the present thesis, Wendland offers the following outline (slightly modified here):

A God who is One [אֶחָד] created [ברא] his people (to be one)
General sin = infidelity [בגד] (10)
B Specific sin = infidelity [בגד] by intermarriage with a pagan (11)
C Verdict: exclusion, rejection of food offering [מִנְחָה] (12)

C' Verdict: rejection of food offering [מִנְחָה] (13)
B' Specific sin = infidelity [בגד] by divorce (14)
A' God who is One [הָאֶחָד] made [עשׂה] husband and wife to be one [אֶחָד]
General sin = infidelity [בגד] (15-16a)
Summary exhortation (particularly of 13-15) not to commit infidelity [בגד] (16b)[59]

---

[58] Cf. also E. Wendland, who interprets 3:23f. [ET 4:5f.] as an appropriate summary of the main points of Malachi's message ("Linear and Concentric Patterns in Malachi," 114).

[59] Note how the mention of "covering [כסה] X with Y" in this verse forms an *inclusio* with verse 13.

To summarize briefly, against those scholars who would excise 2:11f. as secondary, the artful composition and impressive degree of parallelism in 2:10-16 favour the integrity of the whole and suggest a parallelism between the offences of mixed marriage and divorce as instances of infidelity [בגד]. These matters will be treated in more detail in Chapter 4 below. With respect to the concentric literary structure of Malachi as a whole, while many interpretative problems remain, this structure appears to favour a reference to literal marital offences in the 3rd disputation (2:10-16), the first C-section, since this finds a corroborating parallel in the sexual and other ethical offences treated in the second C-section, the 4th disputation (2:17-3:5 [or 3:6]). In the next chapter we shall attempt to build on this suggestive evidence as we examine more closely the interpretation of Mal. 2:14.

CHAPTER TWO

"COVENANT [בְּרִית]" IN MALACHI 2:14:
DOES IT REFER TO MARRIAGE?

Having considered the interpretative framework within which Mal. 2:14 must
be read, we may now sketch the traditional arguments for assuming that the
"covenant" in the expression "your wife by covenant [lit., 'the wife of your
covenant,' וְאֵשֶׁת בְּרִיתֶךָ]" refers to the covenant of marriage and so differs in
its reference from the covenant mentioned in 2:10. As noted earlier it is this
traditional view which many modern scholars have rejected. In the second
half of the chapter we shall examine their objections in detail.

1. THE "TRADITIONAL" VIEW, ACCORDING TO WHICH MALACHI 2:14 IDENTIFIES MARRIAGE AS A COVENANT

Mal. 2:14 reads: "You ask, 'Why does he not [וַאֲמַרְתֶּם עַל־מָה]?' Because the
LORD was witness [עַל כִּי־יְהוָה הֵעִיד] between you and the wife of your youth
[בֵּינְךָ וּבֵין l אֵשֶׁת נְעוּרֶיךָ], against whom you have been faithless [אֲשֶׁר אַתָּה בָּגַדְתָּה
בָּהּ], though she is your companion [וְהִיא חֲבֶרְתְּךָ] and your wife by *covenant*
[וְאֵשֶׁת בְּרִיתֶךָ]."

Although the "traditional" interpretation is more often assumed than
argued, the following arguments may be advanced in its support:[1]

1) Malachi does not use "covenant [בְּרִית]" in a univocal manner.
While the covenant in Mal. 2:10 (and possibly 3:1) may refer to Yahweh's
covenant with Israel, the covenant in 2:4, 5, and 8 ("the covenant of Levi")

---

[1] The most common argument in favour of the "traditional" interpretation is the citation
of Prov. 2:17 and Ezek. 16:8, where "covenant [בְּרִית]" is also used with reference to
marriage. Since the traditional interpretation of these texts is also frequently defended by a
citation of the remaining texts, a degree of circularity results. To avoid this difficulty, these
texts will be treated separately in Chapter 8 after the interpretation of Malachi 2 is
established independently.
   Favouring the "traditional" view of Mal. 2:14 are, among others: Martin Luther,
"Lectures on Malachi"; E.B. Pusey, *The Minor Prophets* (1860) 483; H. Cowles, *The Minor
Prophets* (1867) 392f.; G.A. Smith, *The Books of the Twelve Prophets* (1899); A. von
Bulmerincq, "Die Mischehen im B. Maleachi" (1926); *idem, Der Prophet Maleachi, Band
2: Kommentar zum Buche des Propheten Maleachi* (1932) 289; J.M. Myers, *The World of
the Restoration* (1968); T. Chary, *Aggée — Zacharie — Malachie* (1969) 259; J.G.
Baldwin, *Haggai, Zechariah, Malachi* (1972) 239f.; H.W. Wolff, *Anthropology of the Old
Testament* (1974) 167; S. Schreiner, "Mischehen-Ehebruch-Ehescheidung: Betrachtungen
zu Mal 2 10-16" (1979); W.C. Kaiser Jr., *Malachi* (1984) 69f.; R.L. Smith, *Micah –
Malachi* (1984); R.S. Westcott, "The Concept of *berît* with Regard to Marriage in the Old
Testament" (1985) 73f.; P.A. Verhoef, *Maleachi verklaart* (1972) 181-183; and *idem, The
Books of Haggai and Malachi* (1987) 273-275.

does not. Consequently, there can be no inherent objection to the view that Malachi intends yet another reference by his use of covenant in 2:14.

2) Furthermore, Yahweh is described in 2:14a as a "witness [הֵעִיד] between you and the wife of your youth." The endearing designation "the wife of your youth [אֵשֶׁת נְעוּרֶיךָ]" in 2:14a is in parallel with "the wife of your covenant [וְאֵשֶׁת בְּרִיתֶךָ]" in 2:14b.[2] This implies that the covenant in 2:14b was between the husband and the wife.

Although the precise idiom of בֵּין ... וּבֵין + הֵעִיד ["be a witness between... and..."] is found only here, a close parallel, בֵּין ... וּבֵין + עֵד, is attested in Gen. 31:50, "God is witness between you and me [אֱלֹהִים עֵד בֵּינִי וּבֵינֶךָ]," where the covenant in question exists between the two persons so described, i.e., Jacob and Laban. See also Gen. 31:44 and especially 48f., where the Lord is invited to watch between the covenant parties. Accordingly, this idiomatic usage likewise supports the inference that the covenant in 2:14b was between the husband and the wife.

3) Another reason for holding that the covenant in 2:14 refers to a marriage covenant is the observation that the expression "the wife of your covenant [וְאֵשֶׁת בְּרִיתֶךָ]" is in apposition to "your companion [חֲבֶרְתֶּךָ]." While חָבֵר / חֲבֶרֶת can be a rather general designation for "companion," deriving from its root meaning "to unite, to join together," חבר (verbal or nominal forms) frequently designates persons who have come into association by an agreement or contract.[3] In particular, in some cases חבר is used with reference to covenant partners. According to P. Kalluveettil, for example, covenant associations may be present in Dan. 11:6, 23; 2 Chr. 20:35ff.; and Hos. 4:17.[4] While the evidence is not sufficient to require such a covenantal reference in Mal. 2:14, it does suggest it. Moreover, it is notable that there are no cases where fellow Israelites are designated with the term חבר (verbal or nominal forms) merely on the basis of their mutual involvement in Yahweh's covenant with Israel.[5]

4) The expression ב + בגד, "to act faithlessly against," which appears in Mal. 2:14, is supportive of the recognition of marriage as a covenant between husband and wife: "You ask, 'Why does he not?' Because the LORD was witness between you and the wife of your youth, against whom you have been faithless [אֲשֶׁר אַתָּה בָּגַדְתָּה בָּהּ], though she is your companion and your wife by covenant."

---

[2] Cf. also Prov. 5:18 and Isa. 54:6. Cf. also S. Schreiner, "Mischehen-Ehebruch-Ehescheidung. Betrachtungen zu Mal 2,10-16" (1979) 216, n. 66.

[3] Cf., e.g., H. Cazelles, "חָבַר, chābhar," TDOT 4 (1980) 196, and M. O'Connor, "Northwest Semitic Designations for Elective Social Affinities" (1986) 73-80. Cazelles notes that חבר in Sirach 7:25 may mean "to marry" (op. cit., 197).

[4] P. Kalluveettil, Declaration and Covenant (1982) 51-53. חבר, "become an ally," may also appear with reference to Jonathan and David in 1 Sam. 20:30, if the text is emended with the LXX — so P.K. McCarter Jr., 1 Samuel, 339.

[5] So, e.g., while 2 Chr. 20:35 uses חבר, "become an ally," to describe the Judahite king Jehoshaphat's relation to Ahaziah, the king of Israel, it does so because of a special alliance, not because of their mutual relation to Yahweh.

As noted by S. Erlandsson, בגד is often used of acts of infidelity committed against a covenant partner (cf., e.g., 1 Sam. 14:33, Jeremiah 3:21, Ps. 78:57, etc.).[6] Since ב + בגד can also be used to describe the infidelity of fellow-Israelites bound together under the terms of Yahweh's covenant with his people, however, as it is in Mal. 2:10, the appearance of this idiom in 2:14 is obviously not decisive.

5) Finally, while the semantic parallel between "the wife of your covenant [וְאֵשֶׁת בְּרִיתֶךָ]" in 2:14b and "the wife of your youth [אֵשֶׁת נְעוּרֶיךָ]" in 2:14a has been noted by other scholars, what has been unnoticed elsewhere are the various parallel nominal syntagms of "covenant [בְּרִית]," which offer decisive evidence for the interpretation of the disputed expression "the wife of your covenant [וְאֵשֶׁת בְּרִיתֶךָ]." There are only four such nominal syntagms attested in Biblical Hebrew where the *nomen regens* refers to a person and בְּרִית is suffixed or is in construct.[7] What is noteworthy is the fact that in each case the referenced covenant exists between the person(s) indicated by the *nomen regens* and the person referred to by the pronominal suffix or additional construct, just as is being argued for אֵשֶׁת בְּרִיתֶךָ in Mal. 2:14. The first two nominal syntagms differ somewhat from אֵשֶׁת בְּרִיתֶךָ in that the *nomen regens* is a participle, yielding an objective genitive: לְנֹצְרֵי בְרִיתוֹ, "for those who keep his covenant," found in Ps. 25:10, and לְשֹׁמְרֵי בְרִיתוֹ, "to those who keep his covenant," found in Ps. 103:18. Nevertheless, the referenced covenant exists between the person(s) indicated by the *nomen regens* ("those who keep") and the person referred to by the pronominal suffix (i.e., God).

The third nominal syntagm is בַּעֲלֵי בְרִית־אַבְרָם, "the possessors of Abram's covenant," in Gen. 14:13. As argued by P.J. Naylor, this expression signifies those who were "participants" in a covenant with Abram. The text does not refer to members in covenant with some other, perhaps unnamed, political entity. Rather, a covenant existed between Mamre, Eshcol, and Aner, referred to by בַּעֲלֵי (a term which in this context has no necessary implication of superiority) and Abraham — on an analogy with the covenant which exists between you and your wife in the expression, "the wife of your covenant [אֵשֶׁת בְּרִיתֶךָ]."[8]

The final nominal syntagm is virtually identical to אֵשֶׁת בְּרִיתֶךָ, "the wife of your covenant," differing only in the gender and number of the *nomen regens*: אַנְשֵׁי בְרִיתֶךָ, "the men of your covenant," found in Obad. 7. Although there are some obscurities at both the beginning and the ending of this verse, there is little doubt about its general sense. Edom was betrayed (or will be betrayed) by her allies in a punishment which reflects her own earlier betrayal of Israel: "All your allies [lit., 'the men of your covenant,' אַנְשֵׁי בְרִיתֶךָ] have deceived you, they have driven you to the border; your confederates [lit., 'the men of your peace,' אַנְשֵׁי שְׁלֹמֶךָ] have prevailed against you; your trusted

---

[6] S. Erlandsson, "בָּגַד, *baghadh*," *TDOT* 1 (1974) 471-472. Cf. the fuller discussion of בגד as applied to marriage in Chapter 8 below.

[7] P.J. Naylor, "The Language of Covenant" (1980) 199.

[8] *Ibid.*, 130, 219.

friends have set a trap under you — there is no understanding of it." As indicated in the rendering of the RSV, there is general scholarly agreement that "the men of your covenant [אַנְשֵׁי בְרִיתֶךָ]" does not refer to Edom's co-religionists (as is sometimes argued for "the wife of your covenant [אֵשֶׁת בְּרִיתֶךָ]"), but to "your allies," that is, to those with whom Edom had a covenant.[9] This interpretation is corroborated by the synonymous parallelism between אַנְשֵׁי בְרִיתֶךָ in vs. 7a and אַנְשֵׁי שְׁלֹמֶךָ in v. 7b, an expression which identifies persons with whom Edom shared peace, i.e., "your friends."

With this weight of evidence in mind, especially this last argument concerning the the the nominal syntagms of "the wife of your covenant [אֵשֶׁת בְּרִיתֶךָ]," which have been overlooked by scholars, it is apparent that Malachi employs the expression אֵשֶׁת בְּרִיתֶךָ to refer to a covenant which exists between a husband and his wife. Accordingly, the burden of proof must rest with any interpreters who deny an identification of marriage as a covenant in Mal. 2:14. Objections to this understanding of "the wife of your covenant [אֵשֶׁת בְּרִיתֶךָ]" have often been raised, however, and so we must turn now to a consideration of these.

2. ARGUMENTS AGAINST THE "TRADITIONAL" VIEW OF MALACHI 2:14 ANSWERED

2.1 The uncertain covenant in Malachi 2:14 should be interpreted in the light of the covenant in Malachi 2:10, which refers to Israel's covenant with God

In view of the literary structure of the book of Malachi considered earlier, it is not surprising to find that the covenant mentioned in 2:14, which is located in Malachi's third disputation, bears an altogether different reference from the covenant ("the covenant with Levi") mentioned in 2:4, 5, 8, which is located in the second disputation. On the other hand, it seems reasonable to expect that the covenant in 2:14 may well have the same reference as the covenant in 2:10, since these do occur within the same disputation.[10] Various literary parallels between vss. 10 and 11 on the one hand and vss. 14 and 15 on the other may appear to offer further support for this identification. It may be noted, for example, that within both vs. 10 and vs. 14 Israel is charged with the sin of infidelity [בגד], a charge which is repeated and elaborated in both vs. 11 and the notoriously problematic vs. 15. Further,

---

[9] So, e.g., J.A. Bewer, *Obadiah* (1911) 24f.; G.C. Aalders, *Obadja en Jona* (1958) 27f.; L.C. Allen, *The Books of Joel, Obadiah, Jonah and Micah* (1976) 150f.; H.W. Wolff, *Obadiah and Jonah* (1986) 50f.; D.K. Stuart, *Hosea - Jonah* (1987) 411, 417f.; and D.W. Baker, *Obadiah* (1988) 34f.

[10] A. Isaksson, after urging that marriage could not have been considered a בְּרִית in the period of Malachi, states simply "The covenant mentioned in v. 14 must be the same covenant as in v. 10, viz. the covenant between Yahweh and his chosen people" (*Marriage and Ministry in the New Temple*, 31). Cf. also C.C. Torrey, "The Prophecy of 'Malachi'" (1898) 9.

there is a striking parallel between the double use of "one [אֶחָד]" in vs. 10 and its double appearance in vs. 15. Finally, depending on one's interpretation of vs. 15, there is the possibility of a parallel allusion to creation in these verses, even though the immediate reference in vs. 10 is probably to the formation of Israel, rather than of humanity.[11]

Of course, these observations merely permit the proposed identification of the covenant in vs. 14; they do not require it — especially since, as has already been noted, Malachi uses "covenant" with a very different reference only a couple of verses earlier (vs. 8, cf. vss. 4, 5) in a clause that also closely resembles vs. 10.[12] Indeed, the traditional interpretation of the covenant in vs. 14 takes account of the close relationship between vss. 14 and 10 by suggesting that between these two distinct covenants there is parallelism and close interrelation, not synonymy.[13]

A closer examination of this approach which identifies the covenant in vs. 14 with that in vs. 10 reveals a number of difficulties. In particular, we do not find in vs. 14 an exact repetition of "the covenant of our fathers [בְּרִית אֲבֹתֵינוּ]," the expression which appears in vs. 10, nor do we find simply the term "covenant [בְּרִית]," as if referring back to vs. 10. Rather, what we find is the strikingly dissimilar expression אֵשֶׁת בְּרִיתֶךָ, "the wife of your covenant."

Proceeding on the assumption that the covenant in vs. 14 is the same as that in vs. 10, namely one between Israel and God, some interpreters suggest that the "wife" mentioned is merely a vivid figure for God.[14] Two considerations militate against this view, however. First, everywhere else in Scripture where the marriage figure is applied to Israel's relation to God, it is Israel or Judah who is uniformly depicted as the wife, never God.[15] This practice does not appear to be coincidental in the light of the profound

---

11 The precise parallelism is most explicit in the use of "create [ברא]" in vs. 10, which corresponds to its synonym, "make [עשׂה]," in vs. 15. Both these verbs are notably prominent in Genesis 1-2. Possible, though less clear, allusions to Genesis may be detected in the mention of the "sanctuary of Yahweh" in vs. 11 and the "spirit" in vs. 15. Cf. M.G. Kline, *Images of the Spirit* (1980); and G.J. Wenham, "Sanctuary Symbolism" (1986).
   The following exegetes, among others, support a reference to creation in vs. 15 (although in some cases based on uncertain textual emendations): J. Wellhausen (1892), A. van Hoonacker (1908), E. Sellin (1922), D. Deden (1953), F. Nötscher (1957), A. Deissler (1964), P. Grelot, *Man and Wife in Scripture* (1964) 69, and W. Rudolph (1976).

12 In both vs. 8 and vs. 10 the בְּרִית is in construct with Israel's forebears ("Levi" finds a close parallel in "our fathers"), and in both cases the charge is synonymous ("corrupting [שִׁחֵתֶם]" the covenant in vs. 8 parallels "profaning [חִלֵּל]" the covenant in vs. 10).

13 Cf., e.g., P. Grelot, who offers the following comment on Mal. 2:14-16, "There is, however, no doubt that the fidelity of Jahveh towards Israel, whom he has joined with himself in a *berith*, is implicitly put forward as a model for husband and wife" (*Man and Wife in Scripture*, 69f.).

14 F.F. Hvidberg writes, "'the wife of thy youth', who was a 'companion' and 'the wife of thy covenant'... are similes which denote the cult of Yahweh, the faith in Yahweh. Yahweh is himself very nearly 'the wife of youth', with whom Judah had a covenant" (*Weeping and Laughter in the Old Testament*, 123).

15 This difficulty is acknowledged by A. Isaksson, who defends the identification of Yahweh as a wife here in Malachi as suggested by the image employed in vs. 11, i.e., marriage to "the daughter of a foreign god" (*Marriage and Ministry in the New Temple*, 33). This explanation proceeds only by assuming what needs to be proven, namely that "the daughter of a foreign god" is in fact a reference to a goddess.

similarity between God's self-imposed obligation to provide for Israel and her requisite submission to him as Lord and the corresponding responsibilities of husbands and wives within Israelite society. Second, vs. 14a asserts that Yahweh himself is witness "between you and the wife of your youth." An interpretation that would make Yahweh both the witness and the wife within the same figurative marriage appears contrived.[16]

Taking account of these two objections, an alternative interpretation has been offered by B. Vawter, following C.C. Torrey.[17] These scholars identify the "wife" in vs. 14 as a vivid personification of the "covenant" itself.[18] Although this interpretation succeeds in eliminating the two difficulties mentioned above, it creates difficulties of its own. The metaphor of marriage applied to the relationship between Israel and the covenant is unprecedented elsewhere in the Old Testament. Likewise, it is nowhere to be found in the New Testament or, to the present writer's knowledge, in post-biblical Judaism. Furthermore, the imagery of God's people being "married" to the covenant appears strained precisely because there are so few points of resemblance between a literal marriage and one's relationship to a covenant. Indeed, it is difficult to get beyond the profound dissimilarities which immediately suggest themselves to extract any plausible comparison whatsoever. Not only is a "covenant" impersonal and to that degree dramatically unlike a wife, but also the most prominent obligation of Israelites toward the covenant is obedience, and this would hardly typify an Israelite husband's obligation toward his wife.

In addition, leaving aside for the moment the need to relate the exegesis of vs. 14b to the admittedly problematic vss. 15 and 16,[19] it should be noted that the view of Torrey and Vawter runs into difficulties with both vs. 13 and vs. 14a. In terms of vs. 13, the present view appears to require one to delete שֵׁנִית or וְזֹאת שֵׁנִית תַּעֲשׂוּ or to emend שֵׁנִית in order to avoid its conventional meaning of "second(ly)" or "second time." This is so because if the covenant in vs. 14b is the same as that in vs. 10, and the "marriage" is taken in a figurative sense, then the wrong condemned in vs. 14 is not a "second" failing, but the very same failing as that mentioned in vs. 10. The proposed deletions of שֵׁנִית or וְזֹאת שֵׁנִית תַּעֲשׂוּ, however, are entirely

---

[16] F.F. Hvidberg seems to sense the awkwardness of this (*Weeping and Laughter in the Old Testament*, 123). After noting how Yahweh is both wife and witness and judge, he suggests without support, "It is, however, possible here, too, that the text has been elaborated by later hands, who wanted to reinterpret it in the direction of an attack on faithlessness in marriage."

[17] "The Biblical Theology of Divorce," 621.

[18] C.C. Torrey defines בְּרִית in this expression as "covenant religion" in contrast to בת אל נכר in vs. 11 as "the daughter of a strange god, i.e., a foreign cult" ("The Prophecy of 'Malachi'" [1898] 9f.).

[19] E.g., C.C. Torrey declares them to be "hopelessly corrupt" ("The Prophecy of 'Malachi'," 10, note 20). It is possible, as R.A. Mason notes, that "the very bad state of the text bears its own witness to the probability that it did originally condemn divorce outright. If so, ... it would be small wonder if it suffered from scribal efforts to soften it" (*The Books of Haggai, Zechariah, and Malachi* [1977] 150).

conjectural.[20] On the other hand, the proposed emendation of שְׂנֵיתָ can claim support in the LXX of vs. 13a, καὶ ταῦτα, ἃ ἐμίσουν, ἐποιεῖτε, which interprets שנית as "which I hate" [שְׂנֵאתִי].[21] Nevertheless, it is likely that the LXX reflects a corruption in its *Vorlage* which took place under the influence of שׂנֹא in vs. 16.[22] In addition, the prevalence of the relative particle אֲשֶׁר elsewhere in the MT of Malachi (11x) would lead one to expect its presence here if the reading of the LXX were correct.[23]

Furthermore, in order to relate vs. 14b to 14a, on the view of Torrey and Vawter, it is necessary to interpret the construct in the phrase אֵשֶׁת בְּרִיתֶךָ as appositional: "your wife, that is, the covenant." While such an appositional use of the construct is widely attested, in the present case it requires the reader to ignore the evident parallelism between אֵשֶׁת בְּרִיתֶךָ in vs. 14b and אֵשֶׁת נְעוּרֶיךָ, "the wife of your youth," in vs. 14a, which clearly cannot be understood as appositional. Equally problematic for an appositional interpretation of אֵשֶׁת בְּרִיתֶךָ is the fact that it also requires one to overlook the opposing evidence of אַנְשֵׁי בְרִיתֶךָ, "the men of your covenant," that is, "your allies," found in Obad. 7, as discussed earlier.

A.S. van der Woude avoids some of these objections by accepting a reference to literal marriage in Mal. 2:14. Van der Woude's position needs to be discussed here, however, because of his insistence, shared by a number of other scholars, that the covenant mentioned in vs. 14 refers to Israel's relationship with Yahweh, not to the relationship between a husband and his wife. In effect then, "the wife of your covenant [אֵשֶׁת בְּרִיתֶךָ]" describes the man's wife as a fellow Jew, a partner with her husband in the same national covenant which constituted Israel as the people of God.[24] Trying to account

---

[20] Cf. *BHS*. A.S. van der Woude claims the proposed deletion is "unwarranted (despite LXX) and only based on the false thesis that the prophecy of Malachi originally spoke of divorce only" ("Malachi's Struggle for a Pure Community," 68, n. 19).

[21] One should not minimize this emendation with the term "revocalizing." In Malachi's time Hebrew was written consistently with final *matres lectiones* (the MT must be assumed to involve at least a metathesis of the *yôd*), and in not one of the 112 biblical occurrences of the verb שׂנא does the 'aleph fail to appear. The reading שנית in 4QXII[a] likewise supports the MT. Cf. R. Fuller, "Text-Critical Problems in Malachi 2:10-16," *JBL* 110 (1991) 47-57; and Fuller's forthcoming treatment of 4QXII[a] in DJD.

[22] So, e.g., P.A. Verhoef, *The Books of Haggai and Malachi*, 262.

[23] R. Althann's suggestion that שְׂנֵיתָ should be interpreted as meaning "gnashing of teeth" lacks adequate support ("Malachy 2,13-14 and UT 125, 12-13" [1977] 418-21). Based on a proposal of M. Dahood (*Psalms I*, 42), Althann's other suggestion to interpret וְאֹת as "indignity" has been accepted by A.S. van der Woude, "Malachi's Struggle for a Pure Community," 68, n. 19. While it is claimed that אֹת also appears with the meaning "indignity" in Ps. 7:4; 44:18; 74:18; and Job 17:8, none of these texts require this newly posited sense. Cf., e.g., A.A. Anderson, *Psalms*, 94, 545.

[24] The following scholars likewise equate the בְּרִית in 2:14 with that in 2:10, with the implication that אֵשֶׁת בְּרִיתֶךָ, "the wife of your covenant," is understood as meaning simply "a wife who is a fellow Jew": K. Marti, *Das Dodekapropheton* (1904); W. Nowack, *Das kleinen Propheten* (1922); E. Sellin, *Das Zwölfprophetenbuch* (1929-30); B.M. Vellas, *Israelite Marriage* (1956) 24; W. Rudolph, *Haggai, Sacharja 1-8, Sacharja 9-14, Maleachi* (1976) 274; C. Locher, "Altes und Neues zu Maleachi 2,10-16" (1981) 254f.; and B. Glazier-McDonald, *Malachi*, 101.

for the exact force of the expression בְּרִיתֶךָ, Van der Woude suggests that בְּרִית here bears the special meaning "covenant community." He defends this suggestion by asserting that it is a meaning which is also "*intimated* [italics added] by Mal. 2:10; 3:1c and Ps. 74:20a," as well as Dan. 11:28, 30, 32 and the Dead Sea Scrolls.[25] "Intimated" is not the same as "required," however, and in the work of lexical semantics it is unwise to ignore the principle of parsimony. Accordingly, the evidence is insufficient to posit this new sense for בְּרִית.

In summary, while a parallel clearly exists between the covenant in 2:14 and the covenant in 2:10, it is not one involving an identity of reference. The specific nature of this parallel will be explored more carefully in the next chapter. For the present, it appears that none of the arguments considered thus far are sufficient to overturn the implication of the five arguments considered in §1 above that the covenant mentioned in the expression אֵשֶׁת בְּרִיתֶךָ refers to a covenant between "you," i.e., the husband, and "your wife."

2.2 The expression "the daughter of a foreign god [בַּת־אֵל נֵכָר]" in Malachi 2:11 must refer to a goddess and not to a literal bride, thus requiring a figurative "marriage" throughout Malachi 2:10-16

Another argument which has been advanced in support of a figurative reference for "the wife of your covenant [וְאֵשֶׁת בְּרִיתֶךָ]" in Mal. 2:14 relies on the claim that the expression "the daughter of a foreign god [בַּת־אֵל נֵכָר]" in Mal. 2:11 must refer to a goddess and not to a literal bride, thus requiring a figurative "marriage" throughout Mal. 2:10-16.

1) The first argument for understanding "the daughter of a foreign god" as a reference to a goddess rather than a woman is the simple observation that to be the daughter of a god, if understood literally, is to be a goddess.[26] At least two considerations weigh against this interpretation. First, had it been Malachi's intention to speak of a goddess, it is unclear why he chose to use the circumlocution, "the daughter of a foreign god," rather than simply saying "a goddess" or, better still, explicitly naming the goddess in question.[27] Second, while "the daughter of a foreign god" may be

---

[25] A.S. van der Woude, "Malachi's Struggle for a Pure Community," 69. For other scholars who support a similar interpretation of בְּרִית in Mal. 3:1, cf. P.A. Verhoef, *The Books of Haggai and Malachi*, 289, n. 13.

[26] So F.F. Hvidberg, who writes, "The expression *bat 'ēl nēkār* in verse 11 undoubtedly cannot - as generally maintained - mean 'eine Ausländer,' 'Heiden.' A 'daughter of a god' is a goddess..." (*Weeping and Laughter in the Old Testament*, 121). So also, A. Isaksson, *Marriage and Ministry in the New Temple*, 31, and J.M. O'Brien, *Priest and Levite in Malachi*, 68. Cf. also R. Kraetzschmar, *Die Bundesvorstellung in Alten Testament in ihrer geschichtlichen Entwicklung* (1896) 168, and C.C. Torrey, "The Prophecy of 'Malachi'," 9.
Alternatively, J. Morgenstern has argued that Mal. 2:10-16 refers to a marriage between Menahem (= "Judah") and a Tyrian princess (= בת־אל נכר) ("Jerusalem - 485 B.C." [1957] 15-47). Lacking sufficient evidence for such a specific reference, this view appears fanciful.

[27] E.g., "Ashtoreth," "the Queen of Heaven," etc., mentioned elsewhere in the OT.

understood in a literal manner, such literalism can hardly be insisted upon since, on the present interpretation, this expression is located in the midst of a very striking simile — namely one where human beings are being described as having "married" [בָּעַל] a goddess!

2) A second argument for taking "the daughter of a foreign god" as a reference to a goddess is the observation that this expression would be unparalleled in the Old Testament as a description of a non-Jewish woman.[28] As P.A. Verhoef has argued, however, even if this expression were unprecedented elsewhere as a description of a non-Jewish woman, within Malachi it is entirely fitting.[29] This is so because Malachi intends for it to be understood as antithetical to his description of Yahweh as a father: "Have we not all one Father?" (Mal. 2:10). If Israelites are all the children of Yahweh, their Father, by virtue of their covenant relation to him, then by definition a pagan woman would be the daughter not of Yahweh, but of a "foreign god." Furthermore, the expression "the daughter of a foreign god" is not entirely without parallel in the Old Testament. As pointed out by R.L. Smith, just as Israelites are called "sons and daughters of Yahweh" in Deut. 32:19, Moabites are called "sons and daughters of Chemosh" in Num. 21:29.[30]

3) A third argument for understanding "the daughter of a foreign god" as referring to a goddess is its singular form.[31] This is unpersuasive since in the context Malachi refers to the offending Israelites corporately as "Judah [יְהוּדָה]." This corporate reference leads one to expect a similarly corporate (and so singular) reference for Judah's bride. Clearly, it would have been inappropriate for Malachi to have written: "Judah has profaned the sanctuary of the Lord, which he loves, and has married the daughters of a foreign god" — perhaps yielding an unintended implication of polygyny.[32]

Although unattested elsewhere in Biblical Hebrew, it is plausible that Hebrew did possess such a term, presumably אלה, based on Ugaritic *ilt* and Phoenician אלת (cf. also Akkadian *iltu*). If Biblical Hebrew lacked a specific term for "goddess," however, the expression עשתרת אלהי צדנים in 1 Kgs. 11:5, 33 demonstrates that אֱלֹהִים included "goddess" within its semantic range.

G.W. Ahlström notes that בת־אל נכר, "daughter of a foreign god," finds a reasonably close parallel in the phrase בני אלים, "sons of gods," appearing in Ps. 29:1 and 89:7 [ET 6] (*Joel and the Temple Cult of Jerusalem*, 49). Occurring in such mythopoeic contexts, apparently with reference to angelic beings rather than to pagan deities, the value of this evidence for an interpretation of Mal. 2:11 is greatly diminished.

[28] So A.C. Welch, *Post-Exilic Judaism*, 120, and R.L. Smith, *Micah – Malachi*, 322f. Cf. also G.W. Ahlström, who argues that had it been Malachi's intention to speak of foreign women he would have employed נשים נכריות (1 Kgs. 11:1, 8; Ezra 10:2; Neh. 13:26) (*Joel and the Temple Cult of Jerusalem*, 49).

[29] *The Books of Haggai and Malachi*, 265.

[30] *Micah – Malachi*, 319, n. 11b. So also S.R. Driver, *The Minor Prophets* (1906) 312.

[31] Cf. R. Kraetzschmar, *Die Bundesvorstellung im Alten Testament*, 168, 240; C.C. Torrey, "The Prophecy of 'Malachi'," 9, especially n. 18.; F.F. Hvidberg, *Weeping and Laughter in the Old Testament*, 122.

[32] J.M.P. Smith concedes the awkwardness of the singular, but argues that "it is more natural to interpret the statement as meaning that an alliance has practically been made between Judah and some people that does not worship Yahweh through the common celebration of such [literal] marriages" (*Malachi*, 49).

4) Finally, as noted by C.C. Torrey and A. Isaksson, the LXX and dependent versions interpret Mal. 2:11 as an attack on apostasy to an alien cult.[33] The LXX, in particular, offers καὶ ἐπετήδευσεν εἰς θεοὺς ἀλλοτρίους, "and he [Judah] has gone after other gods," in place of the MT וּבָעַל בַּת־אֵל נֵכָר, "and he has married the daughter of a foreign god." J.M.P. Smith dismisses the LXX reading as paraphrastic and tendentious, an assessment with which P.A. Verhoef agrees.[34] Verhoef explains that mixed marriages had become normal among Hellenistic Jews, and so Malachi's condemnation is avoided. Whether or not this explanation is accepted, the final clause of the MT is widely recognized as preferable on the principle of the *lectio difficilior* and appears to have the support of 4QXII[a].[35]

To sum up, none of the arguments for supposing that the "daughter of a foreign god" refers to a goddess are persuasive. It is more likely that the phrase means a "pagan woman"; hence 2:11, like 2:14, is referring to literal marriage.

2.3 Hostility to literal "mixed" marriages in 2:11, 12 would be antithetical to the "universalist" tenor of the rest of Malachi, thus implying a figurative "marriage" throughout Malachi 2:10-16

Yet a third argument in support of a figurative reference for "the wife of your covenant [וְאֵשֶׁת בְּרִיתֶךָ]" in Mal. 2:14 relies on the outlook of the rest of the book. In particular, it has been argued that if 2:11, 12 is interpreted as a repudiation of literal intermarriage with foreign women, then its perspective would be antithetical to the universalism which is so prominent elsewhere in Malachi (e.g., Mal. 1:5, 11, 14; 2:10). A number of scholars have used this observation to support the identification of 2:11, 12 as a later interpolation, with the conclusion that Mal. 2:10-16 originally opposed only divorce.[36] Since these scholars do not deny a reference to literal marriage in 2:10-16, the point at issue here, we may defer a more detailed consideration of this approach until Chapter 4.

Alternatively, the alleged tension between the perspective of Mal. 2:11, 12 and the sympathetic view of foreigners elsewhere, for example in Mal. 1:11, has been used to argue that 2:11, 12 must not in fact be referring to literal intermarriage. Here is one more important consideration favouring an interpretation of "the daughter of a foreign god" as referring to a goddess and the marriage in these verses as a figure of speech. In response, it may be observed that if "the daughter of a foreign god" is taken as a reference to a

---

[33] C.C. Torrey, "The Prophecy of 'Malachi'," 4, n. 10; and A. Isaksson, *Marriage and Ministry in the New Temple*, 32.

[34] J.M.P. Smith, *Malachi*, 58; and P.A. Verhoef, *The Books of Haggai and Malachi*, 269. In support Verhoef cites, among others, G.J. Botterweck, "Schelt- und Mahnrede gegen Mischehe und Ehescheidung" (1960).

[35] So, according to R. Fuller, "Text-Critical Problems in Malachi 2:10-16," *JBL* 110 (1991) 47-57. See also Fuller's forthcoming treatment of 4QXII[a] in DJD.

[36] So, e.g., K. Marti (1904), E. Sievers (1905), E. Sellin (1922), C. Kuhl (1963), and R.A. Mason (1977).

non-Jewish woman, such an expression may be deemed particularly felicitous because it places the emphasis not on an ethnic or racial disqualification, which would be in tension with Israel's calling to lead the nations into the knowledge of Yahweh, but on a distinctively religious one.[37]

Furthermore, it may be questioned whether scholars have misconstrued the evidence for Malachi's "universalism." Three lines of argument suggest that this is the case.

1) For example, P.A. Verhoef argues that יִגְדַּל יְהוָה מֵעַל לִגְבוּל יִשְׂרָאֵל in Mal. 1:5 should be rendered "Great is the Lord *over* the territory of Israel," rather than the traditional "*beyond* the territory of Israel."[38] Verhoef notes that "over" is by far the more common rendering of מֵעַל לְ elsewhere in Biblical Hebrew, and his interpretation is supported by both the LXX ὑπεράνω and the Vulgate *super*. Even if "*beyond* the territory of Israel" is retained in Mal. 1:5, however, this does not require a kind of "universalism" which would be congenial to interfaith marriage. In the context of 1:2-5, Malachi's point seems to be that Yahweh's coming judgment and wrath against Edom (whether or not "Edom" is understood literally) will elicit Israel's acknowledgment of the reality of Yahweh's election and universal sovereignty. As Israel will see, Yahweh is no mere local deity incapable of expressing his displeasure with offending foreign nations.

2) The verse which has been most featured in the modern scholarly discussion of Malachi's "universalism" is Mal. 1:11: "For from the rising of the sun to its setting my name is great among the nations, and in every place incense is offered to my name, and a pure offering; for my name is great among the nations, says the Lord of hosts."[39] Mal. 1:14b likewise offers a close parallel to vs. 11 and so may be considered together with it for convenience: "for I am a great King, says the Lord of hosts, and my name is feared among the nations."

G.A. Smith's commendation of Mal. 1:11 as "perhaps the most original contribution which the Book of Malachi makes to the development of prophecy" is characteristic of the view of many modern interpreters,[40] but it is precisely the "originality" or, perhaps better, "oddity" of Malachi's alleged acceptance of sincere heathen worship which renders this interpretation so suspect. On Smith's view, Mal. 1:11 does not merely teach that there are

---

[37] Cf. J.G. Baldwin, *Haggai, Zechariah, Malachi* (1972) 238. Cf. also E.M. Yamauchi, "Cultural Aspects of Marriage in the Ancient World" (1978) 250, and *idem*, "Ezra, Nehemiah" (1988) 677.

[38] *The Books of Haggai and Malachi*, 194 and 206.

[39] See the extensive bibliography on this verse in P.A. Verhoef, *The Books of Haggai and Malachi*, 222, n. 64.

[40] *The Book of the Twelve Prophets*, II, 350. Cf., among others, C.C. Torrey, "The Prophecy of 'Malachi'" (1898) 3; K. Marti, *Das Dodekapropheton* (1904); W. Nowack, *Das kleinen Propheten* (1922); E. Cashdan, *The Twelve Prophets* (1948) 336; R.C. Dentan, "The Book of Malachi" (1956) 1120; L.H. Brockington, "Malachi" (1962) 657; and H. Frey, *Das Buch der Kirche in der Weltwende* (1963) 148. Cf. also F. Horst, who refers to the heterodox Jewish worship of Samaria (*Die zwölf kleinen Propheten* [1964] 267).

decent and righteous people in every nation, but that "the very sacrifices of the heathen are pure and acceptable to Him."[41]

We note the following principal objections which have been raised against this view of Smith and others:[42]

a) The claim that Malachi considered pagan sacrifices offered to idols to be acceptable to God ignores the important qualification within 1:11 that the offerings in question are made לִשְׁמִי, "to my name."

b) This view contradicts other indications of uncompromising "particularlism" within Malachi, such as Yahweh's enmity against Edom in Mal. 1:2ff.

c) To suppose that Mal. 1:11 commends pagan sacrifices offered by non-Levitical priests would set this verse completely at odds with Malachi's pervasive concern with the abuses and false teaching of Israel's own priesthood.[43]

d) The claim that Malachi considered "sincere" pagan worship to be acceptable to God sets Malachi at radical variance with the teaching of the Old Testament at almost every other point. The only apparent exceptions are passages such as Isa. 19:18-25 and Zeph. 2:11, which are widely recognized as figurative and having an eschatological reference. Certainly such a view would be difficult to square with Malachi's own exhortation concerning the law of Moses (Mal. 3:22 [ET 4:4]).

e) What makes the proposed interpretation of Mal. 1:11 particularly untenable is the way Malachi presupposes general agreement among his hearers with his assertions about God's relation to the nations.[44] Such a presupposition seems impossible given the unmitigated abhorrence of paganism reflected in the roughly contemporaneous works of Ezra and Nehemiah.[45]

f) Finally, the present interpretation fails to note that the expression "from the rising of the sun to its setting" in Mal. 1:11 appears to echo Isa. 45:6; 59:19; and 66:20-1.[46] If so, this would support an eschatological interpretation of this notorious crux since these antecedent texts are clearly eschatological, referring to a future conversion of the Gentiles.[47] Malachi

---

[41] *The Book of the Twelve Prophets*, II, 351.

[42] To these one may add the claim upheld by some scholars that Mal. 1:11-14 is a later addition to Malachi's prophecy (so F. Horst, *Die zwölf kleinen Propheten*, 265-67; K. Elliger, *Das Buch der zwölf kleinen Propheten*, 194; R. Rendtorff, "Maleachibuch," 628; and A.S. van der Woude, "Malachi's Struggle for a Pure Community," 66).

[43] So J.T. Marshall, "The Theology of Malachi" (1896) 12f.; and G.L. Robinson, *The Twelve Minor Prophets* (1952) 157-169.

[44] So A. von Bulmerincq, *Der Prophet Maleachi*, II (1932) 122; and P.A. Verhoef, *The Books of Haggai and Malachi*, 227. This presupposed agreement assumes a present reference for 1:11. If this verse has a future reference (so NIV), then Malachi's "universalism" is no different from the eschatological hope for the conversion of the nations reflected in Isa. 19:18-25 and Zeph. 2:11.

[45] Cf. J.T. Marshall, "The Theology of Malachi."

[46] Cf. also Ps. 50:1; 113:3; Zeph. 3:9-10; and Zech. 2:15 [ET 11].

[47] Cf. A. van Hoonacker, *Les douze petits prophètes* (1908) 713; J.G. Baldwin, "Malachi 1:11 and the Worship of the Nations in the OT" (1972); E. Achtemeier, *Nahum – Malachi* (1986) 177f.; B. Glazier-McDonald, *Malachi*, 55-61 — less certain is the claim of

may have considered that these promises of Gentile conversion were beginning to be fulfilled in his own day, as evidenced by the worship of contemporary proselytes.[48] The bold language of 1:11, however, in contrast to the modest numbers of proselytes likely to have existed at the time, would seem to favour the view of P.A. Verhoef that Malachi's reference went beyond the worship of contemporary proselytes and diaspora Jews to encompass a still future, more comprehensive fulfilment.[49] The reminder of Yahweh's purpose for the conversion of the nations, a plan entailed in Israel's calling to be a blessing to the nations (cf. Mal. 3:12) and one which features the temple as its focus, would not be out of place in the light of Malachi's prominent interest in eschatology (cf., e.g., Mal. 3:1-5, 17, 19-24 [ET 4:1-6]) and would add force to his condemnation of the apathetic sacrificial cult of his contemporaries.[50]

Possible, but less likely in the light of these antecedent texts, is the view that Mal. 1:11 refers solely to the worship of diaspora Jews[51] or the view that Malachi was speaking in hyperbole — that the ignorant worship of heathen was more acceptable than the slovenly worship of Israelites. If so, Malachi's intention was to condemn Israel, not to approve pagans.[52]

None of these interpretations for 1:11 (and 1:14), except the view of Smith, which seems least likely, raises any difficulty with respect to 2:11; they all allow 2:11 to refer to literal marriage.[53]

3) Mal. 2:10, "Have we not all one Father? Did not one God create us?...," is yet another verse which is alleged to support a "universalism" at variance with the implied bigotry of 2:11, if 2:11 refers to literal mixed marriage. After all, if we acknowledge the common Fatherhood of God, do we not imply the universal brotherhood of mankind? Such an inference may

---

C.V. Camp that Malachi has "literalized" Isaiah's image of the priesthood of the Gentiles into a real expectation (*Wisdom and the Feminine in the Book of Proverbs*, 323 n. 8).

[48] Cf. C. von Orelli, *The Twelve Minor Prophets* (1893) 389, and T.C. Vriezen, "How to Understand Malachi 1:11" (1975).

[49] "Some Notes on Malachi 1:11" (1967).

[50] This "evangelistic" calling of Israel was made clear already in the Abrahamic covenant in Gen. 12:2f. and exemplified in the careers of the Patriarchs, especially Joseph. Cf. H.W. Wolff, "The Kerygma of the Yahwist" (1966). It appears to be reasserted in the career of David and is especially prominent in the following (mainly eschatological) texts: Psalm 47; 87; Isa. 2:1-4; 19:23-25; 41:5; 42:4-6; 45:14; 49:6, 22-23; 60:3; 66; Jer. 4:1-2 (Israel's obedience is the condition of her blessing to the nations); Mic. 4:1-5; Daniel; Jonah; Zech. 2:15 [ET 11]; 8:23; and Esth. 8:17.

[51] Cf., e.g., J.M.P. Smith, *Malachi*; J. Swetnam, who argues that the "sacrifices" in question are metaphorical for prayer and study of the Torah ("Malachi 1,11: An Interpretation" [1969]); and R.R. Deutsch, "Calling God's People to Obedience" (1987) 84-87.

[52] Cf. R.A. Mason, who notes the lack of any blood sacrifice in 1:11 and the fact that Psalm 50, to which the text may allude, rejects animal sacrifice in favour of more spiritual sacrifices of thanksgiving (*The Books of Haggai, Zechariah, and Malachi*, 144f.). So also R.J. Coggins, *Haggai, Zechariah, Malachi*, 78.

[53] Accordingly, if Mal. 1:11 does not contradict the "particularism" elsewhere in Malachi, there is little ground left for viewing this text as secondary (as do, e.g., F. Horst, K. Elliger, R. Rendtorff, and A.S. van der Woude).

seem reasonable to modern man, but it is not at all apparent that this was in
the mind of the prophet. Indeed, Malachi's point of reference for the "we" of
his rhetorical question appears to be his fellow-Israelites, not mankind
indiscriminately.[54] Moreover, the only brotherhood Malachi goes on to
consider is that which derives from the profaned "covenant of our fathers"
(2:10b). Whether this "covenant" is a reference to the Sinaitic covenant or to
the Abrahamic covenant and its subsequent developments which brought
Israel into existence, it is clearly one unique to fellow Israelites.

This parochial perspective for 2:10 may find further support if "one
Father" in 10a is allowed to be defined by the "covenant of our fathers" in
10b, that is, if we follow commentators like J.G. Baldwin in recognizing
"Father" as a reference to Abraham or Jacob.[55] On the other hand, if "one
Father" is defined by synonymous parallelism with "one God" and so refers
to God's "fatherhood," as seems more likely, it has often been observed that
the "fatherhood" of God within the Old Testament defines God's special
relation not to mankind in general, but to Israel in particular: "fatherhood...
not in a natural sense but in the spiritual sense of adoption and on the basis of
his covenant."[56] Passages such as Deut. 32:6, Isa. 63:16, and 64:7 [ET 8],
which describe God as the "creator" and "father" of Israel, offer clear
instances of this usage.

In summary, it appears that the alleged "universalism" in Mal. 1:5, 11,
14 and 2:10 is not such as would prohibit a repudiation of literal
intermarriage with pagan women in 2:11f.

2.4   The treatment of literal marriage in Malachi 2:10-16 is deemed unsuitable to the larger context of Malachi

The fourth argument in support of a figurative reference for "the wife of your
covenant" in Mal. 2:14 similarly relies on the wider context of the book.
Here it is observed that elsewhere in the book the prophet does not especially
concern himself with matters of personal or social ethics. Rather, Malachi
seems absorbed with cultic and priestly matters: condemnation of the priests
(for their complicity) and the people for offering inferior sacrifices (1:6-14);
condemnation of the priests for their violation of the covenant with Levi and
the need for priestly instruction from the law (2:1-9); the promise of the

---

[54] So P.A. Verhoef, *The Books of Haggai and Malachi*, 266.

[55] In support of this interpretation, held earlier by Jerome, Ibn Ezra, David Kimchi, J.
Calvin, and M. Luther, cf., e.g., A. von Bulmerincq, *Der Prophet Maleachi*, II, 243f.; D.R.
Jones, *Haggai, Zechariah, Malachi*, 193f.; and J.G. Baldwin, *Haggai, Zechariah, Malachi*,
237.

A.S. van der Woude, however, notes that some LXX MSS transpose the first two
clauses of vs. 10, probably due to a desire to give God preeminence ("Malachi's Struggle
for a Pure Community," 67). Consequently, the present order may favour an identification
of the "one father" as God.

[56] P.A. Verhoef, *The Books of Haggai and Malachi*, 265. Cf. Mal. 1:6. So also J.G.
Baldwin, *Haggai, Zechariah, Malachi*, 237; A.S. van der Woude, "Malachi's Struggle for a
Pure Community," 67; and most modern commentators.

Lord's coming to his temple to purify the Levites and the securing of pure offerings from Judah and Jerusalem (2:17-3:5); the nation's failure with respect to tithes and offerings (3:6-18); etc. Accordingly, A. Isaksson writes: "This interpretation of Mal. 2.10-16 as an attack on apostasy to an alien cult is in entire agreement with the rest of the contents of the Book of Malachi.... Malachi is a priestly reformer, not a prophetic renovator of the ethics of· marriage."[57]

Three answers may be given in response to this claim of Isaksson:

1) Acknowledging the priority Malachi gives to cultic offences is quite different from saying cultic offences are Malachi's exclusive concern. It is unwarranted for the modern interpreter to reduce everything outside 2:10-16 to cultic matters. For instance, Mal. 1:6, at least incidentally, reinforces the fifth commandment, a concern to which Malachi returns in 3:24 [ET 4:6]. It is also possible that the priestly instruction being neglected or perverted in 2:6ff. may include ethical and legal matters. In any case, in Mal. 3:5 Yahweh quite explicitly threatens His impending judgment against "adulterers," that is, those who violate marriage, as well as his judgment against "sorcerers, ... against those who swear falsely, against those who oppress the hireling in his wages, the widow and the orphan, against those who thrust aside the sojourner...." These cannot all be reduced to merely cultic transgressions. Indeed, highlighting this concern with Yahweh's judgment against "adulterers," etc., in Mal. 3:5 is the overall literary structure of Malachi considered in the previous chapter. There it was suggested that the second C-section, the 4th disputation (2:17-3:5 [or 3:6]), which treats sexual and other ethical offences, offers a corroborating parallel to the literal marital offences treated in the 3rd disputation (2:10-16), the first C-section. Finally, a general concern with the Lord's decrees and laws, rather than an exclusive interest in narrowly cultic matters, seems to be indicated in Mal. 3:7, 14, 18, and 22 [ET 4:4]. In this last verse the laws in question are specified as "the law of my servant Moses, the statutes and ordinances that I commanded him at Horeb for all Israel."

2) Although we may grant a predominant, though not exclusive, interest in cultic matters in the work of Malachi, this need not rule out a concern with mixed marriage and divorce in 2:10-16. As evidence for this, it is widely recognized that the book and ministry of Ezra, and to a lesser degree of Nehemiah, provide a striking and historically relevant parallel to the same blend of interests as we find in Malachi — a predominant concern with cultic matters together with special attention to the problem of mixed marriage.

3) Finally, in keeping with Malachi's cultic orientation elsewhere, it may be noted that the prophet frames much of his objection to Israel's

---

[57] *Marriage and Ministry in the New Temple*, 32. G.W. Ahlström similarly comments, "Malachi is always interested primarily in what he himself considers to be a pure and right Yahweh cult, and the social and moral problems are not his main concern here" (*Joel and the Temple Cult of Jerusalem*, 50).

aberrant marital practice precisely in cultic terms. In 2:11 Malachi condemns
the marrying of "the daughter of a foreign god" as "profaning the sanctuary
of the Lord, which he loves [חִלֵּל יְהוּדָה קֹדֶשׁ יְהוָה אֲשֶׁר אָהֵב]." While "the
sanctuary of the Lord" may plausibly refer to the people of Israel,[58] some
scholars prefer its more customary usage as a reference to the temple.[59] In
either case cultic concepts are being employed as a way of underscoring the
reprehensible character of this sin.[60]

Malachi's imprecation in 2:12 involves a number of difficult
interpretative problems, especially the problematic expression עֵר וְעֹנֶה, "he
who arouses[?] and he who answers[?]," which need not be decided here.[61]
For our purposes it is enough to note that there are two major ways of relating
the expression, "and the one who presents an offering to Yahweh of hosts
[וּמַגִּישׁ מִנְחָה לַיהוָה צְבָאוֹת]" to its context. On the one hand, it may be
coordinate with the expression עֵר וְעֹנֶה and so represents a third group to be
"cut off." On the other hand, perhaps preferably, וּמַגִּישׁ מִנְחָה לַיהוָה צְבָאוֹת may
be coordinate with the expression לָאִישׁ אֲשֶׁר יַעֲשֶׂנָּה, "to the man who does
this," and thus stresses the reprehensible hypocrisy of men who so intermarry
and yet presume to bring offerings to the Lord.[62] On this view, עֵר וְעֹנֶה, "he
who arouses[?] and he who answers[?]," may offer a merism intended to
include everyone between each named extreme, however the terms עֵר and עֹנֶה
are to be rendered. While it is impossible to be sure of this second option
because of the obscurity of עֵר וְעֹנֶה, such an intention for this passage

---

[58] Based largely on context, so C. von Orelli, E. Sellin, and P.A. Verhoef. See also the
arguments of A.S. van der Woude, "Malachi's Struggle for a Pure Community," 67f.

[59] So G.A. Smith, K. Marti, R.C. Dentan. So also G.W. Ahlström, *Joel and the Temple
Cult of Jerusalem*, 49, who cites K. Elliger, *Das Buch der zwölf kleinen Propheten*, 189.
This approach is also preferred by J.G. Baldwin, who notes, "Certainly it is they whom He
loves" (*Haggai, Zechariah, Malachi*, 238f.). A.S. van der Woude considers it more likely
that אָהֵב and בָּעַל have the same subject (hence אֲשֶׁר is not a relative here) ("Malachi's
Struggle for a Pure Community," 67, n. 14).
The view of Schreiner that קֹדֶשׁ יְהוָה refers to the Lord's own "holiness" appears
implausible given the relative clause, "which he loves" (Mischehen-Ehebruch-
Ehescheidung," 210).

[60] C. Stuhlmueller offers the rather improbable view that "'the temple' that 'Judah has
profaned' and 'which the Lord loves' is none other than the divorced wife" ("Malachi"
[1970] 400).

[61] Cf. the intriguing "sexual" interpretation offered by B. Glazier-McDonald, "Malachi
2:12: *'ēr we'ōneh* - Another Look" (1986). This seems more plausible than the "cultic"
understanding of G.W. Ahlström, who writes "The terms עֵר וְעֹנֶה, 'he who arouses himself
and [he who] answers' (or 'sings a lament'), may have something to do with rituals which
the prophet did not accept as Yahwistic" (*Joel and the Temple Cult of Jerusalem*, 49f., n. 8).
Against Glazier-McDonald, however, cf. J.M. O'Brien, *Priest and Levite in Malachi*, 70f.
In support of reading עֵד, "a witness," in place of עֵר, on the evidence of 4QXII[a] (a
suggestion already made by J. Wellhausen, *Skizzen und Vorarbeiten* [1892] 207), cf. R.
Fuller, "Text-Critical Problems in Malachi 2:10-16," *JBL* 110 (1991) 47-57; and also
Fuller's forthcoming treatment of 4QXII[a] in DJD.

[62] P.A. Verhoef renders the verse with this sense: "May the Lord cut off from the tents
of Jacob that man, whoever he may be, even though he brings offerings to the Lord
Almighty" (*The Books of Haggai and Malachi*, 262).

comports with the frequently encountered prophetic indictment of the contradiction between Israel's flagrant sin and her external religiosity.[63]

Furthermore, in 2:13f. Malachi depicts frustrated Israelites grieving at the altar because Yahweh will no longer accept their offerings, and he explains this rejection as due to their marital infidelity. Like the suggested interpretation of 2:12, this verse exemplifies the same prophetic antipathy for a merely external religiosity.

Accordingly, in spite of Malachi's sustained interests in cultic and priestly matters, there is no reason to deem inappropriate a concern with literal marital offences in Mal. 2:10-16, particularly in the light of the example of Ezra, where these same concerns coexist, and given the detrimental effects of these offences on the cult, as stressed by Malachi.

2.5 Alleged ritual weeping in Malachi 2:13 favours the interpretation of 2:11 and 2:14 as referring to idolatry rather than to literal marriage

A final objection to a reference to literal marriage in Mal. 2:14 is based on a supposed allusion to an idolatrous practice in Mal. 2:13. In particular, F.F. Hvidberg has refurbished an older argument that the weeping mentioned in 2:13 is an allusion to syncretistic ritual weeping.[64] Hvidberg's primary argument for this interpretation rests on his identification of "the daughter of a foreign god" in 2:11 as a goddess.[65] Hvidberg explains: "It cannot be doubted that this is a deity of the Anat-Astarte type, and that her lover, for whom the weeping is done, is an 'Adonis' deity." We have already considered the merits of Hvidberg's interpretation of "the daughter of a foreign god." Here we merely need to take up any additional arguments which support a cultic interpretation of the weeping in Mal. 2:13.

At issue is not whether cultic weeping is attested elsewhere in the ancient Near East or elsewhere in Israel's apostasy. For example, it is granted that a similar weeping is recorded in Ezek. 8:14, where Jewish women wept for Tammuz in the temple of the Lord.[66] What is at issue is whether this is what Malachi intends in 2:13, particularly since this weeping is mentioned without an explicit reference to Tammuz or any other alien deity. Hvidberg renders the verse, "And this have ye done again: Covering the altar of Yahweh with tears, with weeping and groaning, insomuch that he

---

[63] P.A. Verhoef offers further support for this interpretation by an attractive, if still uncertain, exegesis of "covering one's garment with violence" in vs. 16.

[64] *Weeping and Laughter in the Old Testament*, 120-123. Cf. also H. Winckler, "Maleachi" (1899) 531-9; H. Ringgren, *Israelite Religion* (1966) 197; and G.W. Ahlström, *Joel and the Temple Cult of Jerusalem*, 49.
  J.M.P. Smith dismissed Winckler's view as "a curiosity of interpretation" (*Malachi*, 52; cf. also p. 57).

[65] Based on this identification, F.F. Hvidberg explains the expression "Judah ... has *married* the daughter of a foreign god" (2:11) as reminiscent of Hosea's depiction of Yahweh as the husband of Israel.

[66] Singled out as supportive of this thesis by A. Isaksson, *Marriage and Ministry in the New Temple*, 33.

regardeth not the offering any more or receiveth gifts with good will at your hand."[67]

Grammatically Hvidberg's argument rests on two points: 1) that in 2:13 שֵׁנִית, rendered by Hvidberg as "again," implies that the weeping is a second *abomination* related to the marriage mentioned in 2:11; and 2) that in 2:13b מֵאֵין bears the meaning "insomuch that ... not," with the implication that Yahweh will not accept Judah's offerings *because of* Judah's reprehensible weeping.[68]

In response to the first of these arguments, while it is appropriate to recall our earlier discussion regarding the uncertainty of שֵׁנִית, both textual and semantic (§2.1 above), we may grant with Hvidberg and others that a rendering such as "again" or "secondly" is plausible.[69] This, however, does not settle the matter at issue. What needs to be proven is that the second abomination is the weeping of Judah, rather than the infidelity mentioned in vs. 15. Strongly favouring this latter interpretation is the interchange recorded by the prophet in vs. 14. Judah wants to know why [עַל־מֶה] Yahweh no longer accepts their offerings. Malachi's explicit answer is that it is because of [עַל כִּי] their infidelity toward "the wife of your youth," not because of their weeping, as we might expect on Hvidberg's view.[70]

In response to the second of Hvidberg's arguments, it is not at all clear that the passage cited by Hvidberg in support of his definition of מֵאֵין, Zeph. 3:6, means what he alleges: "... I have laid waste their streets so that none walks in them; their cities have been made desolate, without a man, without an inhabitant [מֵאֵין יוֹשֵׁב]" (RSV).[71] If this hypothetical resultative use is rejected, one is left with a causal use which yields a sense exactly opposite to that which Hvidberg desires: "You cover the Lord's altar with tears, with weeping and groaning *because* he no longer regards the offering or accepts it with favour at your hand" (RSV). If for the moment the precise force of מֵאֵין is left in abeyance, 2:13f. clearly implies that Judah's weeping and her question "why?" are both due to the fact that Yahweh refuses to accept her offering, not the reverse as Hvidberg supposes.

Entirely consistent with this reading of the evidence, and highly problematic for Hvidberg, is the observation that Judah covers *"Yahweh's* altar [מִזְבַּח יְהוָה] with tears." Indeed, this mention of Yahweh is so

---

[67] *Weeping and Laughter in the Old Testament*, 121.

[68] F.F. Hvidberg, *Weeping and Laughter in the Old Testament*, 121, 122, n. 1. Cf. also A. Isaksson, *Marriage and Ministry in the New Temple*, 29.

[69] So also S.R. Driver, *The Minor Prophets* (1906) 315.

[70] To assert, as Hvidberg does, that this infidelity in vs. 14 "must refer to the same treachery as that mentioned in 11b and 13a" is merely to assume what needs to be proven (*Weeping and Laughter in the Old Testament*, 122).

Cf. also W. Rudolph, who argues that the "tears" are not likely to be cultic, against the view of S. Schreiner, since vs. 13b makes clear that the people's lament is due to Yahweh's refusal to accept their offerings. Moreover, the idea of cultic weeping is rather remote from the context ("Zu Mal 2 10-16," 89).

[71] In support of this rendering, cf., e.g., J.M.P. Smith, *A Critical and Exegetical Commentary on the Book of Zephaniah*, 242, and R.L. Smith, *Micah – Malachi*, 139.

embarrassing for Hvidberg's thesis that he makes the gratuitous suggestion: "It is, however, possible that 'Yahweh's altar' is due to an elaboration by later hands, who reinterpreted the text and would not submit to the mention of the name of a strange god in this passage."[72] Such an *ad hoc* argument lacks conviction.

In his exegesis of Mal. 2:10-16, A. Isaksson reiterates F.F. Hvidberg's conclusions concerning the alleged ritual mourning in 2:13, while adding one further argument of his own (which is repeated by G.W. Ahlström).[73] Isaksson takes issue with interpreters who consider that it is "the divorced wives who, in their sorrow and despair, cover Yahweh's altar with tears."[74] Offering Hvidberg's interpretation as a more satisfying exegesis, Isaksson remarks: "it seems very unlikely that they [the priests] would have admitted divorced women to the altar itself, so that they might weep there in despair."[75]   Whether this is unlikely or not,[76] the vast majority of commentators, convinced that it is the offending men who are weeping at the altar, would agree with Isaksson in rejecting this view concerning divorced wives without feeling the least compelled to embrace the approach of Hvidberg. The argument for cultic weeping is not advanced by the posing of a false dilemma.

A final argument which needs to be considered briefly is one put forth by G.W. Ahlström, building on the views of Hvidberg and Isaksson. Ahlström notes that "the usual mode of designating a rite or phenomenon as non-Yahwistic, i.e. as belonging to ancther deity, is, in the prophetical books,

---

[72] *Weeping and Laughter in the Old Testament*, 122; so also A. Isaksson, *Marriage and Ministry in the New Temple*, 32.

G.W. Ahlström, willing to accept "Yahweh" as original to the text, can only maintain a reference to "cultic weeping" by recourse to special pleading (*Joel and the Temple Cult of Jerusalem*, 28). He writes, "Mal. 2:13 does not quite prove that the rite was Yahwistic from the point of view of the prophet, but it could have been so from the point of view of the priests."

While Israel's syncretism allowed worship of alien gods to take place in the Lord's temple or sanctuary, it appears that it usually involved distinct altars set up to honour the foreign deity — hence repeatedly we read about "the altar of Baal," "the altars for Baalim," "altars for all the host of heaven," etc., in such passages as Judges 6; 1 Kgs. 16:32; 2 Kgs. 11:18; and 2 Chr. 14:3; 33:3ff.

[73] A. Isaksson, *Marriage and Ministry in the New Temple*, 31-32. Cf. also G.W. Ahlström, *Joel and the Temple Cult of Jerusalem*, 49.

[74] This view is based on the Targum and accepted by, *inter alia*, Jerome, "Commentariorum in Malachiam Prophetam"; E. Henderson, *The Twelve Minor Prophets* (1858) 454; H. Cowles, *The Minor Prophets* (1867) 392; and G.H.A. von Ewald, *Commentary on the Prophets of the Old Testament*, 2 (1875) 81.

[75] *Marriage and Ministry in the New Temple*, 29.

[76] Citing J.M.P. Smith, *Malachi*, 51 in support, G.W. Ahlström asserts: "women are not allowed to approach Yahweh's altar" (*Joel and the Temple Cult of Jerusalem*, 49). With Smith, however, clearly the language of "covering the altar with tears" is figurative, and "the legitimacy of the figure does not depend upon the proximity of the women to the altar (cf. Hb. 2:17)." Perhaps more convincing is J.G. Baldwin, who notes that Ahlström's view is untenable since the deserted wives have not yet been mentioned (*Haggai, Zechariah, Malachi*, 239).

to call it תועבה ['an abomination'], as is done here in Malachi [2:11]."[77] For Ahlström to restrict his attention solely to occurrences in the prophetical books, however, is artificial and lacking in justification — particularly given the similarities, if not literary dependence in some cases, between Malachi and Ezra, Nehemiah, Proverbs, and especially Deuteronomy, but also the Pentateuch more generally, as noted earlier.

In any case, while "abomination [תּוֹעֵבָה]" is frequently used in the manner posited by Ahlström, it is not limited to this use.[78] "Abomination" is often used of unspecified wrongs, as well as of sexual offences in particular, in a manner which would support its presence in Mal. 2:11, if Malachi has in mind an offence involving literal intermarriage. Compare, for example, Lev. 18:22-30; 20:13; Deut. 23:19 [ET 18]; 24:4; and perhaps Ezek. 16:22.

Of special interest in the present case, however, are the occurrences of "abomination" in Ezra 9:1, 11, and 14.[79] Here Ezra recalls the reason for the prohibition of intermarriage with pagans — namely their "abominations": "Shall we break thy commandments again and intermarry with the peoples who practice these abominations [הַתֹּעֵבוֹת הָאֵלֶּה]? Wouldst thou not be angry with us till thou wouldst consume us, so that there should be no remnant, nor any to escape?" (Ezra 9:14) Although Ezra does not use "abomination" to refer to the prohibited intermarriage itself, he does use it in the justification of that prohibition making reasonable its presence in Mal. 2:11, where literal intermarriage is also in view. As argued by B. Glazier-McDonald, intermarriage is banned precisely because of the idolatrous practices of the pagan wife, which cause intermarriage to profane the sanctuary of Yahweh.[80]

In summary, against F.F. Hvidberg, G.W. Ahlström, and others, it appears that Mal. 2:13 does not allude to syncretistic ritual weeping and that "abomination" in the same verse does not require a reference to idolatry. Accordingly, Mal. 2:13 does not support a reference to idolatry rather than literal marriage in Mal. 2:11 and 14.

---

[77] *Joel and the Temple Cult of Jerusalem*, 27f. Cf. also p. 50. In support G.W. Ahlström cites numerous authorities, including D.E. Gowan, who asserts תועבה "always seems to refer to cultic irregularities" ("Prophets, Deuteronomy and Syncretistic Cult in Israel" [1968] 107).

[78] Cf. E. Gerstenberger, "תעב *t'b* pi. verabscheuen," *THAT* 2, 1051-1055; and R.F. Youngblood, "תָּעַב abhor, etc.," *TWOT* 2, 976-977.

Cf. also M. Weinfeld, *Deuteronomy and the Deuteronomic School* (1972) 267-9; and R. Westbrook, "The Prohibition on Restoration of Marriage in Deuteronomy 24:1-4" (1986) 405.

[79] Cf. A.S. van der Woude, "Malachi's Struggle for a Pure Community," 67

[80] *Malachi*, 89-91. B. Glazier-McDonald cites Lev. 20:2-5, as well as Ezek. 8:10, 14, and 16, as proof that idolatrous practices, even when conducted outside the temple, defile Yahweh's sanctuary.

3. SUMMARY AND CONCLUSIONS

This chapter began by reviewing the arguments for holding that covenant in Mal. 2:14 refers to marriage. In particular it was argued that although the covenant in vs. 14 bears some relation to the covenant in vs. 10, the claim that it is one of synonymy raises intractable problems. Certainly some attention to the covenant in vs. 10 is appropriate in the attempt to define אֵשֶׁת בְּרִיתֶךָ, "the wife of your covenant," in vs. 14b, but it should not be to the neglect of the parallel expression אֵשֶׁת נְעוּרֶיךָ, "the wife of your youth" in vs. 14a or of the nominal syntagms of אֵשֶׁת בְּרִיתֶךָ, especially אַנְשֵׁי בְרִיתֶךָ, the men of your covenant," in Obad. 7. The implication of these parallels is that the covenant in Mal. 2:14 is one which exists between a husband and his wife (§1-§2.1).

Subsequently, we reviewed the objections which have been raised against interpreting covenant in Mal. 2:14 as a reference to literal marriage. It was concluded that:

The arguments that "the daughter of a foreign god" must refer to a goddess and cannot refer to a non-Jewish woman lack conviction (§2.2).

The so-called "universalism" of Malachi is not such as forbids a reference to literal "interfaith marriage" in 2:11f. and hence a reference to literal marriage throughout 2:10-16 (§2.3).

While Malachi shows a special interest in cultic matters throughout his work, including 2:10-16, as with the work of Ezra, this need not exclude a concern with Judah's literal marital practice (§2.4).

The claim that Mal. 2:13 refers to an idolatrous "cultic weeping" is unconvincing (§2.5).

In short, no objection based on considerations internal to the book of Malachi is sufficient to overturn the weight of evidence of the five arguments considered in §1 that the covenant mentioned in the expression אֵשֶׁת בְּרִיתֶךָ, "the wife of your covenant" or "your covenant wife," refers to a literal marital covenant between "you," i.e., the husband, and "your wife."

CHAPTER THREE

MALACHI 2:16 AND DIVORCE

Traditionally Mal. 2:16 has been understood to be a condemnation of divorce *per se*. This interpretation coheres with the view that the covenant in 2:14 refers to marriage. Many scholars, however, hold that 2:16 does not refer to literal divorce and therefore 2:14 need not refer to literal marriage. This viewpoint will now be evaluated.

"... It must be sincerely doubted whether in Old Testament times even a prophet would have denounced divorce as a crime. Deuteronomy 24 tells against this interpretation." So writes A.S. van der Woude, as he rejects an interpretation of Mal. 2:16 which would construe this verse as a repudiation of literal divorce when based on aversion, an interpretation which on other grounds Van der Woude would be prepared to accept.[1] A. Isaksson echoes this same sentiment when he concludes: "Interpreting the text as a condemnation of divorce means that we are reading into it a view of divorce which was first expounded about 500 years after Malachi...."[2] Accordingly, Isaksson argues that the impossibility of such a reference to literal divorce in Mal. 2:16 offers significant support to the view that Mal. 2:10-16 as a whole is concerned with an attack against apostasy to an alien cult and has nothing to do with literal marriage and divorce.

In support of Van der Woude and Isaksson, there is a wide scholarly consensus that Malachi is heavily indebted to the Deuteronomic perspective.[3] The following points of comparison have been noted:

1) Of all the Old Testament books, only Malachi and Deuteronomy commence with an address to all "Israel."[4]

---

[1] "Malachi's Struggle For a Pure Community" (1986) 71.

[2] *Marriage and Ministry in the New Temple* (1965) 34. At another point Isaksson asserts: "He [Malachi] goes far beyond Dt. 24:1-4, and indeed seems to set himself in downright opposition to what is written there about divorce" (p. 30).

[3] So, e.g., J. Swetnam, "Malachi 1:11 An Interpretation" (1969) 203; W.J. Dumbrell, "Malachi and the Ezra-Nehemiah Reforms," 42; and R.J. Coggins, *Haggai, Zechariah, Malachi*, 75-76.

L.H. Brockington lists five conceptual parallels between Malachi and Deuteronomy: Mal. 1:2 // Deut. 7:8 — God's love for Jacob; Mal. 1:9 // Deut. 10:17 — God does not show favour; Mal. 2:1, 4; 3:3 // Deut. 18:1 — priest and Levite synonymous, Levites may offer sacrifice; Mal. 2:6 // Deut. 33:10 — the law of truth in Levi's mouth; Mal. 3:22 [ET 4:4] // Deut. 4:10 — revelation to Moses on Horeb ("Malachi," 656).

C. Stuhlmueller adds two further examples: Cf. Mal. 1:12 with Deut. 7:8 and Mal. 3:22 with Deut. 4:10 ("Malachi," 399).

[4] So notes W.J. Dumbrell, "Malachi and the Ezra-Nehemiah Reforms," 44. Dumbrell goes on to stress how the post-exilic application of the covenant injunctions in

2) Malachi concludes his work with an emphatically Deuteronomic injunction: "Remember the law of my servant Moses, the statues and ordinances that I commanded him at Horeb for all Israel" (3:22 [ET 4:4]).[5] Horeb is mentioned as the site where Moses and Israel received God's revelation in Deut. 4:10ff.[6]

3) Malachi's special interest in affirming Yahweh's elective love for Israel in spite of her doubt of that love finds a parallel in Deuteronomy's similar affirmation of Yahweh's love over against the anticipated doubts of a "potentially refractory Israel" (Deut. 4:37; 7:6ff.).[7]

4) Malachi's concern for Yahweh's despised "name" (1:6ff.) may presuppose the "Name Theology" of Deuteronomy.[8]

5) Given the relatively infrequent mention of the "fatherhood" of God outside of Deuteronomy (within Deuteronomy cf. Deut. 8:5; 14:1; 32:6), Malachi's appeal to this concept may likewise suggest Deuteronomic influence.

6) Malachi's appeal to the "covenant with Levi" finds a possible source in Deut. 33:8-11.[9] Similarly, it has been argued that Malachi reflects Deuteronomy's usage where, it is claimed, "priest" and "Levite" are employed synonymously (or at least without a rigorous distinction) and "Levites" are permitted to offer sacrifice, as in Deut. 18:1ff.[10]

7) Malachi's concern for the tithe may be related to the provision made in Deut. 26:12ff.[11]   As Dumbrell notes, Malachi's dependence on Deuteronomy regarding the tithe includes not only the stipulation, but also

---

Deuteronomy, such as the call to remember Yahweh's elective love, represents a "bold transference to the rump-state by the post-exilic prophets of the projected ideal."

Whether or not one accepts the reading of אֶל־כָּל־יִשְׂרָאֵל in place of MT אֶל־יִשְׂרָאֵל in Mal. 1:11 (supported by some MSS, for which see *BHS*), this variant suggests a scribal desire to assimilate this verse to Deut. 1:1. Cf. also Mal. 3:22 [ET 4:4].

[5] Accordingly, Dumbrell considers Malachi to be a book "bound together by Deuteronomic inclusions, a fact which tends to underscore the derivative prophetic nature of the work" ("Malachi and the Ezra-Nehemiah Reforms," 44). Cf. A. Renker, *Die Tora bei Maleachi* (1979) 98-101.

[6] So notes L.H. Brockington, "Malachi."

[7] So W.J. Dumbrell, "Malachi and the Ezra-Nehemiah Reforms," 44, and L.H. Brockington, "Malachi," 656.

[8] So U. Kellermann, "Erwägungen zum Esragesetz" (1968) 383, n. 81, and W.J. Dumbrell, "Malachi and the Ezra-Nehemiah Reforms," 45.

[9] So W.J. Dumbrell, "Malachi and the Ezra-Nehemiah Reforms." Against this see S.L. McKenzie and H.N. Wallace, "Covenant Themes in Malachi," 550.

[10] So, e.g., L.H. Brockington, "Malachi," 656.

See J.G. McConville for a careful reappraisal of Wellhausen's reconstruction of the history of the priesthood and, related to this, the supposed synonymy of the terms "priest" and "Levite" in Deuteronomy (*Law and Theology in Deuteronomy* [1984] 124-153). Cf. also J.M. O'Brien, *Priest and Levite in Malachi* (1990).

[11] So W.J. Dumbrell, "Malachi and the Ezra-Nehemiah Reforms," 49. A contrary view is expressed by a number of other scholars who argue that Malachi presupposes the legislation of P rather than D. Cf., e.g., G.A. Smith (*The Book of the Twelve Prophets*, II, 2nd ed. [1929] 328-330), W. Neil ("Malachi," 229), and P.A. Verhoef (*The Books of Haggai and Malachi*, 159).

the blessing sanction of a bounty which will command the respect of the nations (Deut. 26:19).

8) A further possible evidence of Deuteronomic influence is found in Mal. 3:17, where the prophet identifies Israel as God's "special possession [סְגֻלָּה]."[12] Apart from Ps. 135:4, which is regarded as post-exilic and dependent on earlier Deuteronomic texts, this designation for Israel is found elsewhere only in texts which are thought to be Deuteronomic, namely Exod. 19:5, Deut. 7:6, 14:1-2, and 26:18. Moreover, in Deut. 14:1-2 "special possession" is juxtaposed with an assertion of Israel's sonship, much as it is in Mal. 3:17.

9) Finally, perhaps the most notable evidence of Deuteronomic influence within Malachi is the prominence of covenant concepts throughout this brief work.[13] As has been demonstrated by S.L. McKenzie and H.N. Wallace, this importance goes far beyond the six explicit references to "covenant" (Mal. 2:4, 5, 8, 10, 14; 3:1) to include the Deuteronomic vocabulary of covenant (e.g., "love," "hate," "father," "son," "cursed," "great king," etc.), as well as characteristic perspectives and themes.[14]

In view of Malachi's profound debt to the Deuteronomic perspective, a number of scholars have argued that the apparent lenience in Deut. 24:1-4 regarding the practice of divorce should control one's exegesis of Mal. 2:16, thereby disallowing any kind of denunciation of divorce on the part of the prophet.[15] Certainly, if Malachi is so indebted to the Deuteronomic perspective, any interpretation which considers Mal. 2:16 to prohibit divorce will have to give an account for this apparent radical departure from that dependency. Nevertheless, before one seeks to harmonize, compare, or contrast these two texts, it is surely preferable to study each of them in its own right.[16]

---

[12] Or "covenant possession" according to S.L. McKenzie and H.N. Wallace, who cite M. Weinfeld, "The Covenant of Grant in the Old Testament and the Ancient Near East" (1970) 195 ("Covenant Themes in Malachi," 561).

[13] Stressing the centrality and sophistication of "covenant" within Malachi, cf. J.G. Baldwin, *Haggai, Zechariah, Malachi* (1972) 216f.; A. Tosato, "Il ripudio: delitto e pena (Mal 2,10-16)" (1978); L.C.H. Fourie, "Die betekenis van die verbond as sleutel vir Maleagi" (1982); S.L. McKenzie and H.N. Wallace, "Covenant Themes in Malachi" (1983); C.T. Begg, "*Berit* in Ezekiel" (1986) 79; R.L. Smith, "The Shape of Theology in the Book of Malachi" (1987) 24; and P.A. Verhoef, *The Books of Haggai and Malachi*, 179-184.

[14] "Covenant Themes in Malachi." Cf. also R.L. Smith, *Micah – Malachi*, 300, and R.J. Coggins, *Haggai, Zephaniah, Malachi*, 75-76.

[15] See, e.g., A.S. van der Woude, "Malachi's Struggle For a Pure Community," and A. Isaksson, *Marriage and Ministry in the New Temple*, as discussed above.

Cf. also S.L. McKenzie and H.N. Wallace, who leave undecided the question of whether Mal. 2:10-16 has to do with mixed marriage and divorce or apostasy and some other offence, noting: "If Mal 2:13-16 concerns divorce, it is in striking contrast to the law of divorce in Deut 24:1-4" ("Covenant Themes in Malachi," 552f.).

[16] For those who consider that Malachi not only prohibited divorce, but also urged polygyny as a preferable alternative, yet a further tension is introduced between Malachi and Deuteronomy, that is, if the prohibition of polygyny in Deut. 17:17 is taken as implying a general prohibition.

At the close of this chapter we shall turn our attention to Deut. 24:1-4, unquestionably the *locus classicus* for any discussion of divorce in the Old Testament. Before doing so, however, we shall examine Mal. 2:16 by itself. In particular, we shall seek to demonstrate the superiority of the MT of Mal. 2:16 over against the versions or 4QXII[a] (or any conjectural emendations). Furthermore, we shall seek to establish that the text condemns not divorce in general, but specifically what may be called "unjustified divorce," that is, divorce based on aversion. If successful, an important implication of this conclusion for the present thesis will be to eliminate Mal. 2:16 as evidence against a reference to literal marriage in Mal. 2:10-16 and, at the same time, to elucidate a key implication of the identification of marriage as a covenant.

Overlooking minor differences in detail, there are nine major interpretative approaches to Mal. 2:16 which, for convenience, may be divided into four categories: 1) Approaches which deny any reference to divorce in Mal. 2:16; 2) Approaches which interpret Mal. 2:16 as requiring, or permitting divorce; 3) Approaches which interpret Mal. 2:16 as an absolute prohibition of divorce; and 4) Approaches which limit the kind of divorce prohibited in Mal. 2:16.

1. APPROACHES WHICH DENY ANY REFERENCE TO DIVORCE IN MALACHI 2:16

1.1 The text and meaning of Malachi 2:16 is too uncertain to claim that it addresses the subject of divorce

The MT of 2:16a reads: כִּי־שָׂנֵא שַׁלַּח אָמַר יְהוָה אֱלֹהֵי יִשְׂרָאֵל וְכִסָּה חָמָס עַל־לְבוּשׁוֹ אָמַר יְהוָה צְבָאוֹת [lit., "For he hates 'sending,' says Yahweh, the God of Israel, 'and he covers his garment with violence,' says Yahweh of hosts"]. The following is a brief listing of the principle lexical, grammatical, and textual problems associated with this passage: How should the כִּי be understood? The LXX, Vulgate, and Targum take it as a conditional, "*if* a man hates...."[17] Because they do so, the versions (excluding LXX[NABQV]) construe Mal. 2:16 as providing an express permission for divorce. In other words, they consider the apodosis to begin with שַׁלַּח: "If you hate (her), *divorce* (her)...."[18] Alternatively, with LXX[NABQV], it is possible that the apodosis should begin with וְכִסָּה, "*then he covers*...." If one understands כִּי as a causative, "because," or as a more mild conjunction, "for," one must still account for the problematic שָׂנֵא, "he hates." What is the subject of this verb? If the antecedent is Yahweh, the third person is awkward in what purports to be direct discourse. Moreover, the shift in reference from the "he" [= Yahweh]

---

[17] See below for a discussion of these witnesses.

[18] So notes, e.g., A. Isaksson, *Marriage and Ministry in the New Temple*, 32; R.L. Smith, *Micah – Malachi*, 323; and P.A. Verhoef, *The Books of Haggai and Malachi*, 278. Cf. also J.G. Baldwin, *Haggai, Zechariah, Malachi*, 241.

of "he hates" to the "he" [= the divorcing man] of "he covers" appears difficult.

A further difficulty concerns the precise meaning of שַׁלֵּחַ, "sending," a form which lacks an explicit object and which may be parsed as a Piel infinitive construct, or as an alternative form of the Piel infinitive absolute, or as a masculine singular imperative. In spite of the concurrence of both tradition and the vast majority of modern scholars in understanding שׁלח as referring to divorce, it is often noted that the use of this verb with this sense is by no means customary for the Old Testament.

A similar list of problems can be raised for וְכִסָּה חָמָס עַל־לְבוּשׁוֹ, "and he covers his garments with violence." What is the relation of this expression to what precedes? If it is a second thing which is hated, why is וְכִסָּה not an infinitive construct to balance שַׁלֵּחַ (BHS suggests emending it)? Or is this clause an apodosis? Is חָמָס the subject ("*violence* covers...") or is it the object of כִּסָּה ("he covers with *violence*...")?[19] Is לְבוּשׁוֹ, "his garments," to be interpreted as a metaphor referring to the wife, or is there a cultic reference here, etc.?

Despairing in the face of all these problems, C.C. Torrey simply declares Mal. 2:16 (and 2:15) to be "hopelessly corrupt."[20] Similarly, F.F. Hvidberg writes: "nothing definite can be said about Verses 15 and 16, the text being completely unintelligible in these."[21] Repeating the same thought with only a slight elaboration, A. Isaksson writes, "nothing definite can be said as to the content of vv. 15-16 on account of the poor state of the text. When scholars construe from them that Yahweh hates divorces or that the purpose of marriage is to procreate children, they can only do so, as I have already pointed out, by resorting to quite arbitrary emendation of the text."[22]

All interpreters acknowledge the difficulty of the MT of 2:16, as well as the striking disparity in the witness of the versions for this verse. Nevertheless, most scholars are willing to attempt an exegesis of 2:16. The few who demur because the verse is so "hopelessly corrupt" are most often those who also deny any reference to literal marriage in Mal. 2:10-16. May this textual agnosticism be a rather too convenient means of eliminating contrary evidence? Indeed, it is possible, as R. Mason notes, that "the very bad state of the text bears its own witness to the probability that it did originally condemn divorce outright. If so, ... it would be small wonder if it suffered from scribal efforts to soften it."[23] At any rate, it is necessary to see

---

[19] Favouring the identification of חָמָס as the subject are, e.g., LXX, Vulgate, and J.G. Baldwin, *Haggai, Zechariah, Malachi*. Favouring the identification of חָמָס as the object are, e.g., Peshitta, Targum, and P.A. Verhoef, *The Books of Haggai and Malachi*.

[20] "The Prophecy of 'Malachi'," 10, note 20.

[21] *Weeping and Laughter in the Old Testament*, 123. So also A.C. Welch, *Post-Exilic Judaism*, 120.

[22] *Marriage and Ministry in the New Temple* (1965) 34. J.M. O'Brien seems to share this view and, accordingly, offers no interpretation of 2:16a (*Priest and Levite in Malachi*, 72f.).

[23] *The Books of Haggai, Zechariah and Malachi* (1977) 150. Cf. also S. Schreiner, "Mischehen-Ehebruch-Ehescheidung" (1979) 208.

if sense can be made of the verse before giving up and claiming that it is beyond interpretation.

1.2 Malachi 2:16 condemns an idolatrous ritual (I.G. Matthews)

I.G. Matthews offers another approach which denies any reference to literal divorce in Mal. 2:16. Building on the views of C.C. Torrey and H. Winckler, Matthews understands Mal. 2:10-16 as a sustained attack against some variety of Tammuz worship, rather than marital offences.[24] In terms of this context, Matthews renders 2:16, "For I hate stripping off ... and putting a pagan device on one's garment, says Yahweh of hosts. So preserve your good sense and do not apostatise."

In support of this rendering, Matthews proposes to emend the MT שָׂנֵא, "he hates," to read שָׂנֵאתִי, "I hate." As evidence for this emendation Matthews cites the LXX, ἀλλὰ ἐὰν μισήσας ["but if having hated"].[25] The aorist participle in the LXX, however, with its implied second person subject, makes the proposal unlikely.[26] Matthews also deletes אָמַר יְהוָה אֱלֹהֵי יִשְׂרָאֵל, "says Yahweh, the God of Israel," as an expansion. Presumably Matthews shares the opinion of other scholars that the name, "Yahweh, the God of Israel," seems inauthentic, since it occurs only here in Malachi, and that it is also repetitive (a vertical dittography?), given the presence of אָמַר יְהוָה צְבָאוֹת, "says Yahweh of hosts," in the following line. Because the MT has the support of 4QXII[a] and all the versions, however, the proposed deletion appears unwarranted.

In addition, Matthews suggests that שַׁלַּח means "stripping off," a meaning supported by the Targum. Matthews explains that "stripping off ... may have been one of the features in Tammuz worship."[27] There is no evidence, however, for such a cultic practice. Furthermore, the Targum does not require the meaning posited by Matthews.[28] Given the fact that there is no other example where the meaning "strip off" is required for שלח among its 847 biblical occurrences, including 267 instances of the Piel, Matthews' suggestion must be deemed highly improbable.[29]

Finally, Matthews asserts that "no meaning of חמס can be made to fit context."[30] Since the LXX offers καὶ καλύψει ἀσέβεια ἐπὶ τὰ ἐνθυμήματά σου, "and ungodliness will cover your thoughts," Matthews wonders whether its Vorlage may have read חשב, "think." A homograph of

---

[24] I.G. Matthews, "Malachi" (1935) 27.

[25] Ibid., 37.

[26] The LXX aorist participle has an implicit second person subject, based on agreement with the second person aorist subjunctive ἐξαποστείλῃς in LXX[אABQV] or the second person singular aorist imperative ἐξαπόστειλον in LXX[LW].

[27] Ibid., 23.

[28] The Targum reads, אֲרֵי אִם סְנִית לַהּ פַּטְרַהּ, "for if you hate her then divorce her." Jastrow, sub verbo פטר, offers "to free, dismiss, let go; to divorce" for the Pe'al, and "same, esp. to divorce" for the Pa''ēl.

[29] For these statistics see THAT 2, 910f.

[30] Ibid., 37.

חשב means "girdle," an item of dress associated with the high priest's vestments in Exod. 28:27f., etc. Accordingly, Matthews supposes that Malachi's original reference may have been to some pagan equivalent of this garniture. Any such use of חשב is speculative, however, and Matthews' handling of the LXX is unconvincing. While Matthews' suggestion requires ἐνθυμήματα to correspond to חָמָס, it is more likely that it renders לְבוּשׁ, "his garment." With J.M.P. Smith, ἐνθυμήματα, "thoughts," is probably the result of an inner-Greek corruption of ἐνδύματα, "garment," which has the support of LXX^W as well as the daughter versions (Peshiṭta, Arabic, Armenian, Ethiopic, and Georgian).[31]

As a result it is unnecessary to suppose that the *Vorlage* of the LXX differed from the MT in this clause. Therefore we conclude that to find a reference to idolatry in 2:16 and to dismiss its reference to divorce is improbable.

1.3 Malachi 2:16 deals with the secondary status of a former Jewish wife, not with divorce (A.S. van der Woude)

Other scholars, while admitting that 2:16 deals with marriage-related problems, deny that it treats divorce. A.S. van der Woude, for example, argues that the exclusive concern of 2:10-15 is with mixed marriage and that at no point prior to vs. 16 is there any intimation of divorce. In particular, Van der Woude notes that, as with the בגד ["be faithless"] in vs. 10, the בגד in vs. 14 "does not necessarily imply divorce."[32] After reviewing the difficulties mentioned above concerning an overly facile identification of שׁלח ["send out" or "expel"] in 2:16 with divorce, Van der Woude offers his own view, namely that שלח "is an abbreviation of the idiomatic expression *šālaḥ yād* (the same abbreviation can be found in 2 Sam. 6:6 and Obad. 13) that designates a morally detestable hostile act."[33] Accordingly, Van der Woude renders the verse, "For he who neglects (his Jewish wife) puts forth his hand (in hostility), says Yahweh the God of Israel, and covers his garment with violence, says Yahweh Almighty...."[34] Van der Woude explains Malachi's intent in this verse as one of condemning not divorce, but the "subordination and maltreatment of married Jewish women because of foreign heathen wives."

Van der Woude's thesis is appealing for its avoidance of any conjectural emendation of "and covers [וְכִסָּה]," its ability to maintain the

---

[31] *Malachi*, 60. Accordingly, the eclectic text of the Göttingen Septuagint, prepared by J. Ziegler, reads ἐνδύματα in 2:16.

[32] "Malachi's Struggle For a Pure Community," 69. Cf. also p. 67, where he examines vs. 10, adding the observation that Deut. 24:1 demonstrates that "divorce as such could hardly violate the covenant community."

[33] *Ibid.*, 71. In support A.S. van der Woude cites P. Humbert, "Etendre la main" (1962) 383-395.

[34] *Haggai, Maleachi*, POT, 116. Van der Woude cites Gen. 29:31, 33 and Deut. 21:15-17 in support of the rendering "*achterstelt*," that is "discriminates against" or "neglects" for שׂנא (*Haggai, Maleachi*, 124).

same subject for "hate [שָׂנֵא]" and "and covers [וְכִסָּה]," and for the coherency of theme which it supposes for 2:10-16 (mixed marriages). Nevertheless, there are several difficulties which make it doubtful:

1) Van der Woude rejects several alternative views of 2:16 in part because they require conjectural emendation (including revocalization) of the text, but his own view requires revocalizing the MT שַׁלַּח as a Qal perfect, שָׁלַח, a form unsupported by any of the versions.[35]

2) Although Van der Woude's translation obscures the fact, his proposal requires the assumption not only of an ellipsis of the direct object "hand [יָד]," but also of an ellipsis of a prepositional phrase, presumably something like "against her [בָּהּ]" (cf. 1 Sam. 24:7 [ET 6]).[36]

3) More seriously, Van der Woude's entire proposal depends on the identification of שלח as "an abbreviation of the idiomatic expression *šālaḥ yād*." Van der Woude defends this proposal by citing two texts, 2 Sam. 6:6 and Obad. 13, but neither proves the point at issue.

In the case of 2 Sam. 6:6, it appears that ידו את, "his hand," should be restored in this verse (the MT of Samuel is notoriously haplographic), following the multiple witness of 4QSam[a], LXX, Peshiṭta, Targum, and Vulgate.[37] Alternatively, if the MT is retained, an ellipsis of the sort suggested by Van der Woude might be feasible in 2 Sam. 6:6, where the context makes clear what is intended. This is precisely not the case with Malachi. Making this example still less apt for Van der Woude's purpose, the meaning of the expression שלח (את ידו) in 2 Sam. 6:6 is not the same as that proposed by Van der Woude for Malachi! In Samuel it refers to a literal extension of Uzzah's hand, intended to steady the ark, not to an act of hostility.

Turning to Obad. 13b, וְאַל־תִּשְׁלַחְנָה בְחֵילוֹ בְּיוֹם אֵידוֹ, "You should not have looted his goods in the day of his calamity," once again the contention of Van der Woude seems dubious. There appears to be a consensus among modern commentators that the key term for Van der Woude's alleged abbreviation, תִּשְׁלַחְנָה, has suffered some kind of corruption. This conviction is based on the observation that the form of each of the seven other parallel jussives in vss. 12-14 is a third person feminine singular, rather than the third

---

[35] "Malachi's Struggle For a Pure Community," 71, n. 36.

[36] In every one of the fifty-seven examples of שלח יד in the OT (so Even-Shoshan), this expression either 1) refers to a very literal stretching forth of the hand (or an anthropomorphic "stretching forth" in the case of passages having God or an angel as their subject), which in every case is indicated by a complementary infinitive or a coordinate finite verb descriptive of a subsequent action accomplished by the outstretched hand, such as, grasping, seizing, taking, touching, or smiting, or 2) is accompanied by a prepositional phrase (ב is most common, but על and אל are frequent as well). Some, though not all, of the examples in this second category are metaphoric. Based on this evidence, following Van der Woude's interpretation of 2:16, we would expect an appropriate prepositional phrase (perhaps elided, though there are no biblical examples for this), since the metaphoric usages are confined to the second category.

[37] So *BHS*; E.C. Ulrich Jr., *The Qumran Text of Samuel and Josephus*, 56; P.K. McCarter Jr., *II Samuel*, 164 (with some uncertainty); R.P. Gordon, *1 & 2 Samuel*, 356, n. 32; and A.A. Anderson, *2 Samuel* (1989) 98.

person or second person feminine plural as here. The LXX offers further support for an emendation with its expected third person singular, συνεπιθῇ. Not surprisingly, many scholars read יָד וְאַל־תִּשְׁלַח in place of MT וְאַל־תִּשְׁלַחְנָה.[38]

4) A further difficulty with Van der Woude's proposal is that it requires acceptance of his possible, but nevertheless speculative, reconstruction of the social circumstances of Judah's mixed marriages. Van der Woude writes, "By marrying foreign women Judaeans tried to share the privileges of their alien overlords. The common cause they made with them gave rise to severe tensions between a well-to-do class and the poor in one and the same religious community."[39] The problem with this posited class struggle is that there is no hint of it in the text. Nevertheless, since Van der Woude is unwilling to allow an allusion to divorce in vs. 10, he must insist on this reconstruction because only in this way can he explain the faithlessness of Jews toward their brothers mentioned in that verse, as well as the violation of the "covenant community."[40] To be sure, the expression "profaning the covenant of our fathers" (vs. 10) may refer to mixed marriage, as Van der Woude suggests, but it is not enough for Van der Woude to discuss whether divorce may or may not "violate the covenant *community* [italics added]" since Van der Woude has not succeeded in establishing this rather idiosyncratic definition of בְּרִית.[41] Furthermore, even if the question "why are we faithless, a man against his brother" (vs. 10) seems unlikely as a reference to the relationship between a husband and his wife,[42] in the light of a passage

---

[38] So, e.g., C.F. Keil, *The Twelve Minor Prophets*, vol. 1, 364; A.B. Ehrlich, *Randglossen zur hebräischen Bibel*, vol. 5, 261; *BHS*; and J.D.W. Watts, *Obadiah* (1969) 35.

Alternatively, L.C. Allen assumes an ellipse of יָד, "hand," and repoints the MT as a second masculine singular form of the energic imperfect, תִּשְׁלָחֶנָּה (*The Books of Joel, Obadiah, Jonah and Micah* [1976] 157, n. 11).

Yet a third option is favoured by H.W. Wolff, who argues that the MT arose through a corruption of תִּשְׁלַח־נָא (*Obadiah and Jonah* [1986] 37). This suggestion was first made by J.A. Bewer, but Bewer considered it equally possible that the original text read יָד תִּשְׁלַח, or even יָדֶיךָ תִּשְׁלַח (*A Critical and Exegetical Commentary on Obadiah and Joel* [1911] 42).

[39] "Malachi's Struggle For a Pure Community," 66. Van der Woude also states, "Our text envisages the internal controversies in the Judaean community engendered by those who preferred social privileges and economic gains to religious and national loyalty and unity by marrying foreign women" (*ibid.*, 67).

[40] "Malachi's Struggle For a Pure Community," 67.

Of course, if one admits a reference to divorce in Mal. 2:16, it is possible to find ample evidence for the intimation of this problem prior to vs. 16. E.g., cf. P.A. Verhoef, *The Books of Haggai and Malachi*, 262-281, especially 278.

[41] Cf. our discussion of this definition in chapter 2, §2.1. Van der Woude appears to be more tentative in his identification of the בְּרִית in vs. 10, stating it "*may* [italics added] have here already, as in vs. 14, the meaning of covenant community" ("Malachi's Struggle For a Pure Community," 67).

Van der Woude's understanding of the expression "profaning the covenant of our fathers" as a reference to mixed marriage appears plausible. Against Van der Woude, however, it is possible that just as adultery was recognized as a violation of Israel's covenant with Yahweh, in terms of the stipulation of the seventh commandment, frivolous divorce may have been viewed similarly.

[42] So A.S. van der Woude, "Malachi's Struggle For a Pure Community," 67.

such as Gen. 31:50 it is possible that it describes the breach between husbands and fathers-in-law which may have been the result of unjustified divorce.[43]

5) Finally, Van der Woude states but nowhere explains why, on his view, these polygynous mixed marriages *necessarily* resulted in the disdainful treatment of the Jewish wives. If the motive for these second marriages was merely political or economic, as Van der Woude claims, they would appear to be similar to a category of equally utilitarian marriage about which a fair amount is known, namely bigynous marriages contracted for the purpose of procuring offspring. If biblical and ancient Near Eastern parallels are to be trusted, under this kind of circumstance the "wife of one's youth" need not have suffered the disdain of her husband; indeed, it was more commonly the second wife who was relegated to a secondary status.[44]

Thus we conclude that Van der Woude has not proved his case that 2:16 is referring to the abuse of secondary wives. We should therefore leave open the possibility that 2:16 refers to divorce and investigate the thrust of Malachi's remarks.

2. APPROACHES WHICH INTERPRET MALACHI 2:16 AS REQUIRING (OR PERMITTING) DIVORCE

The great majority of commentators from the ancient versions to the modern era agree that Mal. 2:16 refers to divorce, but there is a wide diversity of view as to Malachi's precise attitude toward divorce. At one extreme, some hold that divorce is encouraged, at the other, that divorce is condemned unreservedly. We shall review the main options.

2.1 Malachi urges divorce (4QXII[a], LXX[LW], and Targum)

As noted above, the MT of 2:16 may permit an alternative reading, "*If* he hates, send (her) away...."[45] This interpretation of כִּי as a conditional particle and the related understanding of שַׁלַּח as an imperative are supported by 4QXII[a],[46] as well as by the LXX[LW],[47] Vulgate,[48] Targum,[49] and Talmud.[50]

---

[43] Laban's concern over the future treatment of Leah and Rachel in Genesis 31:50 is instructive as an example of a father-in-law's on-going concern for his married daughters. Viewed from the husband's side, cf. also the corresponding breach of fellowship which was the result of the unjust action of Saul, David's father-in-law, and the Timnahite father-in-law of Samson, when these men attempted to dissolve the inchoate marriages of their daughters.

[44] Cf., e.g., CH §§145f. and the classic biblical examples of Abraham, Sarah, and Hagar; also Elkanah, Hannah, and Peninnah. On the other hand, cf. LI §28, which recognizes the possibility that the second wife may be preferred over the first. Cf. also the case of Jacob's marriage to Leah and Rachel. Cf. further T.E. McComiskey, "The Status of the Secondary Wife: Its Development in Ancient Near Eastern Law" (1965).

[45] See J.G. Baldwin, *Haggai, Zechariah, Malachi*, 241.

[46] According to R. Fuller, 4QXII[a] reads: כִּי אִם שׂנתה שלח [ ] אל ישראל וכסו חמס על [לבנ]שֶׁך ("Does Yahweh Hate Divorce? Malachi 2:16 and Text of Malachi at Qumran" [1988]). R. Fuller notes that שׂנתה represents a second person perfect form (unpublished paper on Malachi 2:10-16 [n.d.]). A quiescent *'aleph*, as in the expected form

Accordingly, this interpretation is accepted by Rashi,[51] David Kimchi,[52] and Maimonides,[53] among others.

In spite of the ancient pedigree of this view, at times called "the traditional Jewish interpretation," the following objections may be noted:

1) LXX[LW] ("But if, *having hated* [or "you hate"], divorce her!") and the other versions to which appeal is made support this view only by eliminating the awkward shift in personal reference in the MT between כִּי־שָׂנֵא, "if *he* hates," and שַׁלַּח, "*you* send away."[54] Accordingly, the MT may be preferable as the *lectio difficilior*.

2) In spite of the apparent support for divorce in LXX[LW], the uniform rendering of the LXX in 16b is καὶ καλύψει ἀσέβεια ἐπὶ τὰ ἐνθυμήματά [LXX[W] ἐνδύματα] σου, "and ungodliness will cover your thoughts [garment]." This rendering is basically supportive of the MT, וְכִסָּה חָמָס עַל־לְבוּשׁ, and only with great difficulty can it be made to support the present interpretation, since it appears implicitly to condemn divorce.[55] Furthermore, it should be noted that LXX[אABQV], understood by J. Ziegler to preserve the Old Greek, differs significantly from LXX[LW] in that it explicitly condemns divorce. LXX[אABQV] reads: ἀλλὰ [LXX[א]: ἀλλ'] ἐὰν μισήσας ἐξαποστείλῃς, λέγει κύριος ὁ θεὸς τοῦ Ισραηλ, καὶ καλύψει ἀσέβεια ἐπὶ τὰ ἐνθυμήματά σου, λέγει κύριος παντοκράτωρ, "But if you divorce, having hated, says the Lord, the God of Israel, then ungodliness will cover your thoughts [or "garment" if LXX[אABQV] are corrected with LXX[W]], says the Lord Almighty."[56]

שנאתה, is often not represented in the orthography at Qumran. Cf. E. Qimron, *The Hebrew of the Dead Sea Scrolls* (1986) §100.61.

Consequently, this text may be rendered: "For if you hate, divorce!... God of Israel, and they cover your garment with violence." Fuller considers that the text of 4QXII[a] in 2:15f. is "so corrupt we must still resort to conjectural emendation" (unpublished paper on Malachi 2:10-16 [n.d.]).

[47] LXX[LW]: ἀλλὰ ἐὰν μισήσας [W: μεισήσας] ἐξαποστείλον..., "But if, having hated (or, "you hate"), divorce!...."

[48] *cum odio habueris, dimitte.*

[49] אֲרֵי אִם סָנֵיתָ לָהּ פַּטְרַהּ, "for if you hate her then divorce her."

[50] See Rabbi Jehuda in *b. Gi̧t.* 90b: "R. Jehuda said, 'If you hate her, you should put her away [...שלח שנאתו[ן] אם]'." For this restoration of the text, cf. C. Locher, "Altes und Neues zu Maleachi 2,10-16," 245.

[51] Rashi (Rabbi Solomon ben Isaac, 1040-1105 A.D.) begins by acknowledging a division of opinion in the Talmud tractate *b. Gi̧ţin* regarding Mal. 2:16: "Some say 'if you hate her send her away with a bill of divorce and marry another [אם שנאת שלח אותה בגט ותנשא לאחר]'." Preferring the alternative imperatival view, Rashi urges that it is kinder to divorce a hated wife than to keep her in a marriage "causing her anger and pain."

[52] So C. Locher, "Altes und Neues zu Maleachi 2,10-16," 245.

[53] *Hil. Geruschin* X, 21, as cited by S. Schreiner, "Mischehen-Ehebruch-Ehescheidung," 228.

[54] Understanding שַׁלַּח as a masculine singular imperative. It should be noted that this view also presupposes an ellipsis of a pronominal direct object for both שָׂנֵא and שַׁלַּח.

[55] See below for a discussion of the view of S. Schreiner, who follows the LXX in this curious shift from the seeming endorsement of divorce in 16aα to an emphatic disapproval of divorce in 16aβ ("Mischehen-Ehebruch-Ehescheidung" [1979]).

[56] For the use of καί to introduce an apodosis, see Blass and Debrunner, §442(7).

3) The reading of the versions with their approval of divorce is considered by many scholars to be tendentious.[57] For example, L. Kruse-Blinkenberg argues that Malachi originally opposed the provision of divorce in Deut. 24:1-4 and that LXX[LW], Targum, and the Peshiṭta of vs. 16 were all corrected in order to bring them into agreement with Deuteronomy. A similar view has been expressed by R. Fuller with respect to the reading of 4QXII[a].[58] In spite of the great antiquity of 4QXII[a], dated to 150-125 B.C. based on its semicursive script, Fuller notes that in more than half of the cases where 4QXII[a] agrees with the LXX over against the MT, it offers a reading which is inferior to the MT.[59]

4) Most seriously, as noted by J. Baldwin, "such a reading undermines all that the prophet is seeking to convey."[60] To be more specific, we may observe with R. Westbrook that this interpretation, which considers that 2:16a commends divorce, is difficult to reconcile with the strenuous disapproval implied at the conclusion of the verse: "So take heed to yourselves and do not be faithless."[61]

2.2 Malachi urges divorce of heathen wives (A. von Bulmerincq)

A significant modification of the previous view has been proposed by A. von Bulmerincq.[62] According to von Bulmerincq, Mal. 2:16 requires the divorce only of heathen wives, a view which comports with von Bulmerincq's identification of Malachi as Ezra's assistant (Ezra being none other than "the messenger of the covenant" in 3:1).

To support this interpretation, however, von Bulmerincq proposes the following five emendations of the MT: 1) transpose שִׁלַּח אָמַר and שָׂנֵא; 2) change אָמַר into אֲשֶׁר; 3) emend the suffix on לְבוּשׁוֹ to לְבוּשֵׁךְ, following the LXX and Targum; 4) insert a לֹא before כִּסָּה, following the Peshiṭta and Targum; and 5) delete וְנִשְׁמַרְתֶּם בְּרוּחֲכֶם וְלֹא תִבְגֹּדוּ in 16b as a superfluous variant of 15b וּבְאֶשֶׁת נְעוּרֶיךָ לֹא תִבְגֹּדוּ, following E. Sellin, J.M.P. Smith, and

---

[57] So L. Kruse-Blinkenberg, "The Pesitta [sic] of the Book of Malachi" (1966) 102-104, 111; J.G. Baldwin, *Haggai, Zechariah, Malachi* (1972) 241; W. Rudolph, *Haggai, Sacharja 1-8, Sacharja 9-14, Maleachi* (1976) 270; C. Locher, "Altes und Neues zu Maleachi 2,10-16," 245; and R.L. Smith, *Micah – Malachi* (1984) 323. R.A. Mason makes a similar point with regard to the seemingly disturbed MT (*The Books of Haggai, Zechariah, and Malachi* [1977] 150).

[58] R. Fuller, unpublished paper on Malachi 2:10-16 (n.d.) 7f.: "The readings preserved in G[WL] and 4QXII[a] and the Targum seem more likely to this writer to preserve an intentional change of the text of v. 16 which is in disagreement with the content of vv. 13-15 and in obvious agreement with Dt 24:1-4."

[59] More precisely, according to Fuller there are seven readings where 4QXII[a] agrees with the LXX against the MT, four of which are inferior. On the other hand, there are four readings where 4QXII[a] agrees with the LXX against the MT, only one of which appears to be inferior. In addition, 4QXII[a] offers one unique reading, the omission of אֲשֶׁר אַתָּה בָּגַדְתָּה בָּהּ in 2:14, which may be superior.

[60] *Haggai, Zechariah, Malachi*, 241.

[61] "The Prohibition on Restoration of Marriage in Deuteronomy 24:1-4," 403, citing Abarbanel in support.

[62] "Die Mischehen im B. Maleachi" (1926) 41-42; and *idem, Der Prophet Maleachi, Band 2* (1932).

others. The following text results for vs. 16: כִּי אִם שַׁלַּח אֲשֶׁר שָׂנֵא יְהוָה אֱלֹהֵי
יִשְׂרָאֵל וְלֹא כִסָּה חָמָס עַל־לְבוּשֶׁךָ אָמַר יְהוָה צְבָאוֹת. We may translate it: "On the
contrary, divorce the one whom Yahweh, the God of Israel, hates, then wrong
will not cover your garment (any more), says Yahweh of hosts."[63]
Consequently, von Bulmerincq views this verse as an encouragement to
divorce a non-Jewish wife, the sort of woman whom Yahweh "hates" because
such a marriage constitutes the most heinous sort of sin and a hindrance to the
advent of Yahweh.

Whatever the merits of von Bulmerincq's third and fourth proposals,
the first two proposals and the last proposal are entirely speculative and
appear to be merely a reflex of von Bulmerincq's attempt to relate Mal. 2:10-
16 to Ezra 10. Such a cavalier treatment of the text renders von Bulmerincq's
approach unconvincing.

*2.3 Malachi recommends divorce in Malachi 2:16 as the lesser of two evils,
i.e., as preferable to polygyny (S. Schreiner)*

S. Schreiner offers a significant modification of the traditional Jewish view,
which understands Mal. 2:16 as urging divorce.[64] Following LXX[LW],
Vulgate, and Targum, Schreiner interprets כִּי as a conditional particle, with
the apodosis beginning with the unemended שַׁלַּח of the MT. Where Schreiner
parts company with the traditional Jewish interpretation is in his contrastive
rendering of the וְ, which introduces the clause, וְכִסָּה חָמָס עַל־לְבוּשׁוֹ, and
especially in his overall interpretation of the text. Schreiner translates the
verse, "If one no longer loves, divorce, says YHWH the God of Israel; but
such a one covers his garment with shame, says YHWH Sebaoth."[65]

Schreiner explains that the husbands in Mal. 2:16 were wanting
children (based on 2:15) and so were taking second wives without regard to
their heathen identity. As a consequence, their conduct entailed a three-fold
violation of the law (perhaps intended by the "covenant" in 2:10).[66] First,
they were committing adultery because they had failed to divorce their first
wife before taking a second (Exod. 20:14; Deut. 5:18; 22:22-29; Lev. 20:10;
19:20). Second, they were marrying pagan women in violation of such texts
as Exod. 34:16 and Deut. 7:3. Finally, they were sinning with respect to their
children (cf. Mal. 3:18-21), since the offspring of these mixed marriages
would be prohibited from the assembly according to Deut. 23:4 [ET 3] (cf.
Neh. 13:1ff.). In response Schreiner argues that Malachi upheld the ideal of

---

[63] A. von Bulmerincq, *Der Prophet Maleachi, Band 2*, 306.

[64] "Mischehen-Ehebruch-Ehescheidung" (1979) 217f.

In certain respects Schreiner's view resembles that of Martin Luther, *Lectures on
Malachi*, 406f., to whom he appeals for support ("Mischehen-Ehebruch-Ehescheidung,"
207), but Luther says nothing about polygyny and interprets Malachi mainly in the light of
Matt. 19:3-10.

[65] "Wenn einer nicht mehr liebt, Ehe scheiden, spricht YHWH, der Gott Israels; aber
derjenige besudelt mit Schande sein Gewand, spricht YHWH Zebaoth" ("Mischehen-
Ehebruch-Ehescheidung," 217f.).

[66] *Ibid.*, 220.

monogamy and urged that men who wanted to marry a second wife must divorce their first wife. Nevertheless, this action is merely the lesser of two evils [*"die Wahl des kleineren Übels"*] because any such divorce constitutes the defiling of one's garments, that is, a personal defilement.[67]

The chief advantage of Schreiner's treatment of Mal. 2:16 is its fidelity to the unemended MT and the support it can claim from the versions. Attractive also is Schreiner's interpretation of שָׂנֵא, "hates," as a reference to the attitude of the divorcing husband, which is consistent with the use of this term when it appears elsewhere in connection with divorce. On Schreiner's view Malachi appeals to Deut. 24:1ff. Following Rashi, Schreiner considers the hatred in 2:16 to be an allusion to "if she does not find favour in his eyes [אִם־לֹא תִמְצָא־חֵן בְּעֵינָיו]" in Deut. 24:1 (cf. also "and he hates her [וּשְׂנֵאָהּ]" in vs. 3). Accordingly, Malachi regarded a second marriage as permissible, but only after a legal divorce, which Malachi tolerates as a lesser evil to the alternative of polygyny.

Nevertheless, there are some serious problems with this otherwise appealing view:

1) As was noted above with respect to the traditional Jewish view, the versions support this view only by eliminating the awkward shift in personal reference in the MT between כִּי־שָׂנֵא, "if *he* hates," and שַׁלַּח, "*you* send away."

2) Although the apodoses of conditionals introduced by כִּי are often unmarked (as in Exod. 21:14, 36, 37 [ET 22:1]; 22:9f. [ET10f.], etc.), hence supporting Schreiner's identification of שַׁלַּח as the apodosis, just as often they are marked, typically employing a converted perfect (as in Gen. 4:24; Exod. 1:10, 12:15, 19; 22:26 [ET 27], etc.). Accordingly, some justification is needed for preferring to begin the apodosis with שַׁלַּח, rather than וְכִסָּה, as is implied by, *inter alia*, LXX^RABQV.

3) The conjunctive position of the ו in its clause וְכִסָּה חָמָס עַל־לְבוּשׁוֹ, that is, its position attached directly to the main verb, may permit but does not favour Schreiner's interpretation of this clause as contrastive: "*but*, such a one covers his garment with shame" (italics added).[68]

4) Related to this grammatical observation, the contradictory change from the seeming approval of divorce in vs. 16aα ("If one no longer loves, divorce") to the disapproval of divorce in 16aβ and 16b ("but such a one

---

[67] *Ibid.*, 226f.

[68] Cf., e.g., T.O. Lambdin, *Introduction to Biblical Hebrew*, §132, and Waltke and O'Connor §39.2.3, who consider one of the main uses of the disjunctive clause, where ו does not attach directly to the verb, to be to express the contrastive idea ("but," "however," etc.).

The apparent clarity of Lambdin's and Waltke and O'Connor's interpretation of interclausal syntax contrasts with the practice of modern English translations, which commonly render examples of conjunctive ו (especially converted imperfects) as "but," etc. Cf., e.g., Gen. 3:9, 6:18, 8:1, etc.

Lacking a full-scale study of the biblical evidence for the contrastive use of ו, a study which would be alert not only to word order, but also to key particles, such as the presumed effect of a prior negative (cf., e.g., F.I. Andersen, *The Sentence in Biblical Hebrew* [1974] 183), etc., the most that can be safely asserted here is that there appears to be a tendency for the contrastive use of ו to manifest itself in disjunctive rather than conjunctive clauses.

covers his garment with shame, says YHWH Sebaoth. Therefore guard your spirit and do not act faithlessly") fails to commend itself as too abrupt and unexpected.[69] Moreover, the language of that disapproval is far too strenuous to allow Schreiner's claim that Malachi considered divorce "the lesser of two evils" — an ethical calculus which seems rather too modern for the fifth century B.C. in any case. Furthermore, Schreiner's assumption that Mal. 2:15-16 alludes to Deuteronomy 24, as opposed to Genesis 1-2, is uncertain and has been challenged by W. Rudolph.[70]

5) Schreiner's conclusion that Mal. 2:16 was an attempt to address the problem of polygyny, which Malachi deemed to constitute adultery is unconvincing. Neither Ezra nor Nehemiah, nor any other ancient source, suggests that polygyny was a problem in the post-exilic community, and the text of Malachi nowhere else mentions this matter.[71]

With such an "astonishing result [erstaunliche Ergebnis]," as his conclusions have been termed by W. Rudolph, Schreiner's interpretation has failed to commend itself among more recent interpreters.[72]

3. APPROACHES WHICH INTERPRET MALACHI 2:16 AS AN ABSOLUTE PROHIBITION OF DIVORCE

Having rejected those interpretations which view Mal. 2:16 as encouraging divorce, we now turn to approaches which interpret Mal. 2:16 as an absolute prohibition of divorce.

"I hate divorce, says the Lord God of Israel, and covering one's garment with violence, says the Lord of hosts." This rendering of the RSV is typical of those who favour a view which has been called "the traditional Christian approach."[73] In reality, however, the interpretation of Mal. 2:16 as a condemnation of divorce is just as well represented among early Jewish commentators as is the "traditional Jewish approach." See, for example, Rabbi Johanan, mentioned in b. Giṭ. 90b, and the medieval commentators, Al-Qumisi, Jephet Ben Eli, and Ibn Ezra (who mentions this as one option), among others.[74]

---

[69] So also C. Locher, "Altes und Neues zu Maleachi 2,10-16," 243.

[70] "Zu Mal 2 10-16" (1981) 85-90. Cf. also Chapter 5.

[71] See W. Plautz, "Monogamie und Polygynie im Alten Testament" (1963) and the discussion of polygyny in Chapter 4, §6 below.

[72] Cf., e.g., C. Locher, "Altes und Neues zu Maleachi 2,10-16" (1981) 242-246; W. Rudolph, "Zu Mal 2 10-16" (1981) 85-90; R.L. Smith, Micah – Malachi (1984) 324; and R. Westbrook, "The Prohibition on Restoration of Marriage in Deuteronomy 24:1-4" (1986) 403.

[73] See R Westbrook for this designation ("The Prohibition on Restoration of Marriage in Deuteronomy 24:1-4," 402).

[74] So, C. Locher, "Altes und Neues zu Maleachi 2,10-16," 245.
See b. Giṭ. 90b: "R. Jehuda said, 'If you hate her, you should put her away' R. Johanan said: 'He that sends his wife away is hated [שׂנוי המשלח].'" The Talmud attempts to reconcile these views by claiming, rather implausibly, that Johanan was speaking only of the second marriage: "They are not differing in opinion, since the one speaks of the first marriage and the other of the second."

P.A. Verhoef's treatment is typical of those who favour this interpretation.[75] He begins by considering the primary interpretative question to be the determination of the subject, or antecedent, of שָׂנֵא. Verhoef apparently considers that there are only two alternatives: either the subject is an impersonal "one," referring to the divorcing man (with this option seeming to necessitate the view of LXX[LW], etc., that the text commends divorce), or the subject is Yahweh. Since the former conclusion is deemed impossible on contextual grounds, a way is found to make Yahweh the subject.

The following suggestions have been offered to accomplish this objective:

a) From an English reader's stand-point Biblical Hebrew tolerates a high degree of variation in personal reference, particularly in prophetic speech.[76] This appears to be the view of T. Laetsch, for example, who explains that "the prophet states a fact, and then claims divine authority for this fact."[77] While this approach has the merit of avoiding textual emendation, it results in what must be deemed an unexpected and awkward change in the subject with "and he covers [וְכִסָּה]."[78]

b) Perhaps the majority of scholars holding this view have suggested an emendation of the text from שָׂנֵא, "he hates," to אֶשְׂנָא[79] or שָׂנֵאתִי,[80] "I hate." The advantage of this approach is that it relieves the grammatical incongruity between the third person verb and the context of direct discourse. The disadvantage is, of course, that these emendations are purely conjectural.

Accordingly, the objection of A. Isaksson must be dismissed as uninformed: "No instance can be quoted of these verses being understood in earlier times as an attack on divorce" (*Marriage and Ministry in the New Temple*, 32).

[75] *The Books of Haggai and Malachi*, 278.

[76] Cf., e.g., E.W. Bullinger, *Figures of Speech Used in the Bible* (1898) 524f., and GKC §144p. Prophetic speech is especially susceptible to this phenomenon because of its self-presentation as both the words of the prophet and simultaneously the word of the Lord.

[77] *The Minor Prophets* (1956) 527. Cf. the AV, which relieves the awkward change in personal reference by assuming the use of indirect discourse, "For the Lord, the God of Israel, saith, that he hateth putting away: for one covereth violence with his garment, saith the Lord of hosts: therefore take heed to your spirit, that ye deal not treacherously."

[78] Laetsch discusses וְכִסָּה, but he does not answer this objection (*The Minor Prophets*, 527). He offers two possible explanations of this clause: Either this is an example of the suppression of the demonstrative pronoun (cites GK §155n and the examples of Isa. 41:24 and Exod. 4:13), "or it may simply add the personal consequence of the sin." On this second approach Laetsch suggests rendering, "and (by doing that) he covers his garment with violence."

[79] So, e.g., J. Wellhausen, *Skizzen und Vorarbeiten* (1892) 199 (who also deletes אָמַר יְהוָה אֱלֹהֵי יִשְׂרָאֵל as secondary and revocalizes וכסה as an infinitive construct, interpreting it as a second object of Yahweh's hatred), perhaps the RSV, and R. Fuller, untitled paper on Malachi 2:10-16 (n.d.).

[80] So, e.g., R.L. Smith, who renders 16a: "Because I hate divorce, says Yahweh God of Israel, and he (who) covers his garment with violence, says Yahweh of hosts" (*Micah – Malachi*, 319f.). Smith offers no support for nominalizing the clause וְכִסָּה חָמָס עַל־לְבוּשׁוֹ or for taking the clause as an object of the emended verb שָׂנֵאתִי.

c) With W. Rudolph and others, שֹׂנֵא may be identified as a verbal adjective, which is being employed as a participle.[81] In addition, Rudolph suggests that שֹׂנֵא has an elided first person singular pronominal subject, an occasional feature of participles (cf. GKC §116s, which expresses reservation concerning this and other alleged examples). Accordingly, שֹׂנֵא may be rendered, "I am hating." This approach has the advantage of avoiding any conjectural emendation of כִּי־שָׂנֵא שַׁלַּח. The supposition of an elided first person singular pronominal subject when there are no other first person pronouns in the context, however, and the fact that a verbal adjective of שׂנא is otherwise unattested fail to commend this approach.[82]

C.F. Keil, P.A. Verhoef, and others prefer a slight revocalization of the text from שָׂנֵא, "he hates," to the Qal participle שֹׂנֵא, "hating," again positing an elided first person singular pronoun.[83] Verhoef explains the significance of this form: "The participle suggests continuity. The Lord continually and habitually hates." While this view has the merit of restoring an attested form, the Qal participle, rather than Rudolph's hypothesized verbal adjective, it does so at the expense of introducing a conjectural emendation of the MT, albeit slight. The appeal to an elided pronoun, which is nowhere explicit in the context, remains problematic.

---

[81] W. Rudolph, *Haggai - Sacharja 1-8 - Sacharja 9-14 - Maleachi* (1976) 270. Cf. also *idem*, "Zu Malachi 2:10-16" (1981) 90, and C. Locher, "Altes und Neues zu Maleachi 2,10-16" (1981) 245-247.
A simpler way of stating this is that for intransitive stative verbs of the form קָטֵל or קְטֹל the participle generally coincides with the third masculine singular perfect. See GKC §50b and Waltke and O'Connor §37.1b.

[82] Probably because שׂנא is transitive, in spite of its stative vowel pattern, it has a well-attested active participle of the form שֹׂנֵא. Even-Shoshan lists eight occurrences. Cf. GKC §50b and Joüon §41c.
A. Tosato appears to accept and to build on Rudolph's approach to 2:16 ("Il ripudio: delitto e pena [Mal 2,10-16]" [1978] 552 — the writer is indebted to Mr. Paul J. Collacott of Cheltenham for his help in translating Tosato). Tosato renders Mal. 2:16, "Since Yahweh the God of Israel has said 'I hate divorce' and Yahweh of hosts has said '(I hate) a man covering his garment with violence,' therefore be careful for your lives and don't act faithlessly."
Although A. Tosato does not discuss this verse at length, he does say that Malachi is persuaded that divorce is sinful because it violates the covenant between Yahweh and Israel (*op. cit.*, 552, esp. note 19). Tosato supports this assessment by noting the fairly extensive terminological parallels between Mal. 2:14-16 and Jer. 3:1-13, where Judea is called בֹּגְדָה (8, 11) and בְּגוֹדָה (10) because of its infidelity toward Yahweh, the friend of its youth (אַלּוּף נְעֻרֶיהָ vs. 4), infidelity which is the cause of its divorce (8). Consequently, Mal. 2:13-16 makes the behaviour of the man who would divorce the wife of his youth equivalent to that of the unfaithful "wife" in Jeremiah with respect to her husband, Yahweh — an equivalence (men are no less obligated to marital fidelity than their wives) found also in the Gospels.
Tosato's view, however, shares the difficulties of the "traditional Christian interpretation" mentioned above. In addition, Tosato's rendering of the third masculine singular perfect וְכִסָּה is problematic (unless Tosato accepts the emended reading כְּכַסֶּה, proposed by E. Sellin and W. Rudolph).

[83] E.g., C.F. Keil, *The Twelve Minor Prophets*, vol. 2, 454; P.A. Verhoef, *Maleachi verklaart* (1972) 190; and *idem*, *The Books of Haggai and Malachi* (1987) 278.
Verhoef cites GK §116s (as does W. Rudolph) in support of the suppressed pronominal subject (*Maleachi verklaart* [1972] 190).

Finally, there are three further problems with this approach to Mal. 2:16 which need to be considered:

1) As Van der Woude has noted, since there is an awkward shift in the subject from שׂנֵא (whether emended or not) to וְכִסָּה, this approach inevitably needs to explain away or to emend וְכִסָּה without textual support.[84] Although Verhoef succeeds in defending the MT of וְכִסָּה, based on the third person suffix on לְבוּשׁוֹ, he fails to support his rendering of this perfect (as if it were a substantive use of the participle): "I hate divorce, says the Lord God of Israel, *even the one who covers* [italics added] his garment with (the marks of) violence, says the Lord Almighty." Some scholars emend וְכִסָּה to an infinitive construct to balance שַׁלַּח,[85] while others prefer an infinitive absolute with a preposition, כְּכַסֵּה.[86] While neither of these suggestions is impossible, they lack textual support.

2) By failing to interpret "hates [שָׂנֵא]" as a reference to the divorcing husband's attitude, this approach overlooks a considerable body of evidence, both biblical and extrabiblical, where hate in the context of divorce is a frequently specified attribute of one of the marriage partners. This evidence will be discussed in detail below.

3) Of the approaches to Mal. 2:16 considered thus far, this is the first which necessarily involves a conflict with the seemingly lenient attitude toward divorce in Deut. 24:1-4. Although we must defer judgment until a more detailed evaluation of that text, it may be useful to note here two alternative responses to this objection which have been made by those wishing to support the "traditional Christian" interpretation of 2:16:

a) W.J. Dumbrell has argued that Malachi's attitude toward divorce need not be considered incongruous with Deuteronomy 24 if, as J. Murray and others have argued, the purpose of Deuteronomy 24 was not "to facilitate divorce (the possibility of which is admittedly presupposed), but rather [to affirm] the indissolubility of the (original) marriage relationship."[87]

b) Alternatively, Malachi's view of divorce may have gone beyond the more lenient provision of Deuteronomy, but in so doing may simply reflect a hermeneutical approach to antecedent scripture which is well-represented during the post-exilic period.[88] For example, P. Grelot observes how

---

[84] "Malachi's Struggle For a Pure Community," 70.

[85] So, e.g., *BHS*.

[86] So E. Sellin, *Das Zwölfprophetenbuch* (1922) 554, and W. Rudolph, *Haggai, Sacharja 1-8, Sacharja 9-14, Maleachi* (1976) 270, n. 16. Cf. A.S. van der Woude, "Malachi's Struggle For a Pure Community," 71, n. 35.

[87] "Malachi and the Ezra-Nehemiah Reforms," 47f. See also J. Murray, *Divorce* (1961).

C.F. Keil offers an alternative explanation, "The thought is not at variance with Deuteronomy xxiv. 1 sqq., where the putting away of a wife is allowed; for this was allowed because of the hardness of their hearts, whereas God desires that a marriage should be kept sacred" (*The Twelve Minor Prophets*, II, 454).

[88] P.A. Verhoef observes, "In the postexilic period stricter demands were made on the marriage bond, apparently in connection with the prohibition of marriages with Canaanites and heathen people in general (Exod. 34:16; Deut. 7:4). The prophecy of Malachi endorses these stricter stipulations..." (*The Books of Haggai and Malachi*, 280f.).

Malachi's view of marriage and divorce goes "far beyond the tolerances of the Torah."[89] To account for this Grelot notes that during this same time the requirements of the Torah were also being made more strict by the reforms of Nehemiah and Ezra. Only Ruth "makes a tactful protest against this severity...."[90] Also of significance is the fact that Malachi appears to base his argument quite explicitly on Genesis 1-2, rather than Deuteronomy 24.[91]

The problem here in reconciling Mal. 2:16 with Deuteronomy is similar to the difficulty of relating Ezra 9-10 to Deuteronomy (in view of Ezra's widely recognized affinity with Deuteronomy). H.G.M. Williamson believes that Ezra did, in fact, go far beyond the stipulations of Deuteronomy both in his identification of the nations of his day with the Canaanites of pre-exilic days and, perhaps also, in his insistence on the dissolution of mixed marriages.[92]

In summary, while the view that Mal. 2:16 prohibits all divorce is easier than the view that it encourages divorce, this absolutist interpretation has enough problems to encourage the search for a better approach.

4. APPROACHES WHICH LIMIT THE KIND OF DIVORCE PROHIBITED IN MALACHI 2:16

4.1 Malachi prohibits divorce only when initiated by the woman (one rabbinic view)

The view of y. Qidd. I 58c, 16 and Gen. Rab. 18, 12c, ascribed to rabbis living in the 4th century A.D., is that the divorce which God "hates" in Mal. 2:16 is "mutual divorce." What is intended by "mutual divorce" is divorce which may be initiated by either the husband or the wife, such as is practiced among pagan couples, not Jewish divorce which may be initiated only by the husband, according to the rabbinic view.[93] An apparent assumption of this interpretation is that it was the offended women who initiated the dissolution of their marriages in Malachi. Perhaps the rabbis based this assumption on the curious order in Malachi's treatment of mixed marriage and divorce. Malachi mentions the problem of mixed marriage before divorce, as if to suggest that the divorces were a response of the offended Jewish wives (forcing their bigamous husbands to divorce them), rather than the preparatory action of husbands anticipating a second marriage (this time to a

---

[89] Man and Wife in Scripture, 69.
[90] Ibid. Against this alleged "tactful protest," cf. A. Phillips, "The Book of Ruth — Deception and Shame" (1986) 2.
[91] Cf. W. Rudolph, Haggai, Sacharja 1-8, Sacharja 9-14, Maleachi, 274f., and R.L. Smith, Micah – Malachi, 325.
[92] Ezra, Nehemiah, 161. For further discussion, cf. M. Fishbane, Biblical Interpretation in Ancient Israel, 114-129.
[93] Cf. M. Barth, Ephesians, 659, n. 311.

pagan).[94] Apart from its interest for the history of interpretation, however, this view has little to commend it.

4.2 Malachi condemns only unjustified divorce, that is, divorce based on aversion

Finally, we turn to consider the interpretative approach which views Mal. 2:16 as condemning divorce when it is based on aversion: "If one hates and divorces, says Yahweh, God of Israel, he covers his garment with violence, says Yahweh of hosts...." We shall seek to establish this approach as that which is most faithful to the text, requiring minimal or no emendation of the MT, and as most congruent with the larger context of Mal. 2:10-16.

4.2.1 How should כִּי be understood?

As has been indicated, there are essentially two options for the interpretation of כִּי: 1) It may be understood in a non-conditional manner, perhaps to be rendered "because" or "for," or possibly to be left untranslated as an emphasizing particle;[95] or 2) it may be intended as a conditional particle, "if one hates...."[96] It is important to clarify these options further. When כִּי functions as a causal subordinating conjunction, the main clause most commonly precedes the כִּי clause.[97] When כִּי functions as a conditional particle introducing a protasis, the apodosis, or independent clause, most often follows the כִּי clause.[98] It should be noted that conditional כִּי may be rendered "if," or it may bear one of its other senses, such as "when," "whenever," etc., especially if the context suggests a higher probability that the condition will actually occur.[99] Given the order of clauses in Mal. 2:16, it is easier to take כִּי as "if."

כִּי is non-conditional (R. Westbrook)

R. Westbrook has recently defended an interpretation of Mal. 2:16 which understands this text as condemning unjustified divorce and, in so doing, favours the non-conditional causal(?) sense of כִּי (against the view preferred above). He renders the verse, "For he has hated, divorced ... and covered his

---

[94] This curious order of treatment is also noted by W.F. Luck, who concludes that the divorce condemned by Malachi is divorce based merely on the desire to be monogamously married to another (*Divorce and Remarriage* [1987] 82).

[95] So NIV. Cf., e.g., T. Muraoka, *Emphatic Words and Structures in Biblical Hebrew* (1985) 158-164, and Waltke and O'Connor §39.3.4.e. A. Aejmelaeus considers that the emphatic use of כִּי is less frequent than is often alleged ("Function and Interpretation of כִּי in Biblical Hebrew" [1986] 208).

[96] The context of Mal. 2:16 appears to exclude the other principal uses of כִּי listed, for example, in Williams, *Syntax*, §§444-452.

[97] In support of this analysis of כִּי clauses, cf. A. Aejmelaeus, "Function and Interpretation of כִּי in Biblical Hebrew" (1986) 193-209, esp. 197-199. Cf. also Waltke and O'Connor §39.3.4.e.

[98] Deut. 4:29; 28:2, 9, offer rare counter-examples.

[99] A. Aejmelaeus, "Function and Interpretation of כִּי in Biblical Hebrew," 197.

garment in injustice."[100] Perhaps the chief advantage of this non-conditional causal(?) interpretation is the way it explicitly relates Mal. 2:16a to 2:15b, "Take heed to yourselves, and let none be faithless to the wife of your youth...," making clear that 2:16a provides the expected underlying reason for this dire injunction.[101] It appears that there must be some such logical connection between 2:16a and this warning in 2:15b since the injunction is essentially repeated in 2:16b, "So take heed to yourselves and do not be faithless," thereby forming an inclusio which frames 2:16a.[102] If this posited logical connection permits the causal כִּי clause in 2:16a to follow the main clause in 2:15b, then this medial position for the כִּי clause conforms to the usual pattern discussed above.

Nevertheless, there are some difficulties connected with Westbrook's view:

a) Although it is only a modest emendation, Westbrook follows J.M.P. Smith, et al., in repointing שִׁלַּח as a Piel perfect, שִׁלַּח, "he divorced," so as to form an asyndetic construction with שָׂנֵא, "he has hated."[103]

b) The ellipsis in Westbrook's translation offers mute testimony to the problematic character of the clause, "says Yahweh, God of Israel [אָמַר יְהוָה אֱלֹהֵי יִשְׂרָאֵל]," for his interpretation. While some scholars have argued that this clause should be deleted as a gloss, this is conjectural and is now opposed by the additional evidence of 4QXIIa.[104] Situated where it is, it appears as an intrusion on Westbrook's interpretation. As such it may favour a view that places a more significant break between what comes before the clause and what comes after, as does the conditional view of כִּי to be considered below.[105]

c) Finally, on Westbrook's view there seems to be an awkward change in pronominal reference from vs. 15b to vs. 16a. To be fair, Westbrook does not discuss this point, and so, apart from any implication which may be drawn from his rendering of the mild causative "for," it is uncertain what exact relation he sees between these verses. In addition to the shift from the second person plural of vs. 15b to the third person singular in 16a (and then back to the second person plural in 16b), one is left to puzzle over the precise

---

[100] "The Prohibition on Restoration of Marriage in Deuteronomy 24:1-4," 403.

[101] Cf. P.A. Verhoef, who, following a different interpretation, argues that 2:16a provides an explanation not merely for 2:15b, but for each of the preceding problems back to 2:13 (*The Books of Haggai and Malachi*, 278).

[102] Although the MT here is supported by the versions, *BHS* and others suggest deleting this.

[103] So also A. van Hoonacker, H. Junker, F. Nötscher, and T. Chary, *inter alios*.

[104] Citing in support J. Wellhausen, W. Nowack, K. Budde, and E. Sievers, J.M.P. Smith favours this proposed deletion (*Malachi*, 55).

[105] Apart from Mal. 2:16, the expression אמר יהוה appears twenty-one times within Malachi and only sixty-eight times elsewhere in the OT (neglecting cases of כה אמר יהוה). In each case within Malachi the clause coincides with a major break in the grammar of the verse: 1:2, 6, 8, 9, 10, 11, 13, 14; 2:2, 4, 8; 3:1, 5, 7, 10, 11, 12, 13, 17, 19 [ET 4:1], 21 [ET 4:3].

antecedent of the "he" in vs. 16a.[106] Furthermore, it is not obvious how the assertion, "for he has hated, divorced...," actually explains the command, "Take heed to yourselves...."[107]

A translation of the whole makes these difficulties readily apparent: "'Take heed to yourselves, and let none be faithless to the wife of your youth. For *he* has hated, divorced,' says Yahweh, God of Israel, 'and covered his garment in injustice.'" Who is the intended referent of this "*he*"? Moreover, as is evident from the capitalization of "For," Westbrook fails to render the כִּי clause in 2:16a in a manner which makes clear its grammatical subordination to 2:15b (although he insists on its logical subordination). If 2:16a is not grammatically subordinate to 2:15b, then the frontal position of the כִּי clause no longer favours the causal interpretation.[108]

כִּי is conditional (the view preferred here)

Given the difficulties of taking כִּי as a causal subordinating conjunction ("because," "for"), an alternative interpretation of כִּי seems preferable, namely that כִּי bears a conditional sense in 2:16: "If one hates and divorces, says Yahweh, God of Israel, he covers his garment with violence, says Yahweh of hosts...."[109] This conditional option has often been rejected to avoid the implication of the versions that Mal. 2:16 endorses divorce, but this implication is not necessary since, as LXX[NABQV] indicates, the apodosis may begin with וְכִסָּה, "he covers," rather than שִׁלֵּחַ, "divorces."[110] If this interpretation is accepted, the objections to the traditional Jewish view listed earlier (§2.1 above) are fully met.

T.V. Moore has raised an additional objection to the conditional interpretation. He notes that while כִּי may at times be rendered "if," this is not its customary sense.[111] To have any force, however, this objection needs to be strengthened by a more nuanced comparison of the syntax of the present verse and the use of כִּי elsewhere in conditional clauses. While it is true that

---

[106] The grammar of third person form יִבְגֹּד in vs. 15b is discussed below. Here we merely note that even if it is left unemended (against the versional evidence), it appears inadequate to account for the wholesale shift to the third person in vs. 16a.

[107] E.g., with such an explanatory clause it would seem more logical for the command to be: "*Expel such a man, for he has hated....*" Alternatively, if the command is to be maintained, it would seem more logical for a rather different explanatory clause: "Take heed to yourselves.... *for I will judge all such faithless husbands.*"

[108] It is possible that special emphasis is intended when a causal כִּי clause precedes the main clause (Joüon §170n). If so, the fact that no particular emphasis is required in 16a does not favour the present causal interpretation of its כִּי clause. Other grammarians, however, fail to confirm this point. Cf., e.g., A. Aejmelaeus, "Function and Interpretation of כִּי in Biblical Hebrew," 196f.

[109] Alternatively, if שֹׂנֵא is identified as a verbal adjective, or participle (cf. GKC §50b and Waltke and O'Connor §37.1b), the MT may be rendered, "if one who hates divorces..., then he covers...."

[110] LXX[NABQV] reads: ἀλλὰ [LXX[NA]: ἀλλ '] ἐὰν μισήσας ἐξαποστείλῃς, λέγει κύριος ὁ θεὸς τοῦ Ἰσραηλ, καὶ καλύψει ἀσέβεια ἐπὶ τὰ ἐνθυμήματά σου, λέγει κύριος παντοκράτωρ, "But if you divorce, having hated, says the Lord, the God of Israel, then ungodliness will cover your thoughts [or "garment" if LXX[NABQV] are corrected with LXX[W]], says the Lord Almighty."

[111] *A Commentary on Haggai and Malachi,* 138.

other uses of כִּי predominate, כִּי is used in a conditional manner in well over fifty verses, as rendered by the RSV.[112] Moreover, in a significant number of cases, the apodosis is marked by a וְ + perfect, as is being suggested for Mal. 2:16 (cf., e.g., Exod. 23:5; Lev. 13:16; 25:25; Num. 27:8; etc.).[113]

4.2.2 Who is the subject of "hates [שָׂנֵא]"?

We have already noted the following difficulties which result from the assumption that the antecedent of "he hates [שָׂנֵא]" is Yahweh: Unless שָׂנֵא is emended or explained, there is a resulting grammatical awkwardness in the presence of a third person verb in what purports to be the direct discourse of Yahweh. Furthermore, there is a puzzling change in subject from Yahweh to the divorcing husband in "and he covers [וְכִסָּה]," or there is a need to emend this latter verb to more adequately parallel שִׁלַּח. Finally, the assumption that Yahweh is the subject of "he hates" ignores a substantial body of evidence that when hate appears in the context of divorce, it typically refers to the disposition of one of the marriage partners.

The alternative approach suggested here is that the subject or antecedent of "he hates" is not Yahweh, but the divorcing man or, more exactly, an impersonal subject: "if *one* hates...." There are several advantages to this interpretation: First, it has the support of the versions, though as we have noted, apart from LXX[NABQV], they interpret the passage as an authorization rather than a condemnation of divorce.[114] Second, this interpretation requires no emendation of "hates [שָׂנֵא]" because it is not in conflict with its context as Yahweh's direct discourse. Third, on this view there is no awkward shift in subject from "hates [שָׂנֵא]" to "covers [וְכִסָּה]" — the subject of both of these third masculine singular perfects is the divorcing man (i.e., the impersonal subject "one"). Finally, it has often been noted how hate [שׂנא] is found elsewhere in the Old Testament in the context of marriage, where it refers to the attitude of husbands toward their wives. So, for example, J.M.P. Smith cites Gen. 29:31 and Deut. 21:15-17.[115] To these we may add Deut. 22:13, 16; 24:3; Judg. 15:2; Prov. 30:23; and Isa. 60:15.

More recently, this association of hate and marriage has received fresh support. On the basis of several Aramaic marriage contracts from Elephantine, where the formula "I hate so and so my husband/wife" is to be pronounced by the divorcing partner, some scholars have argued that "hate" may be a technical synonym for "divorce."[116]

---

[112] Cf., e.g., Gen. 4:24; Exod. 21:14, 37; 22:9f. [ET 10f.], 13 [ET 14], 15 [ET 16]; Lev. 11:38; 13:40; etc.

[113] Cf. also Deut. 18:21f., where a non-converted perfect appears in an unmarked apodosis.

[114] It is also the view of a considerable number of modern scholars, including A. van Hoonacker, H. Junker, F. Nötscher, T. Chary, S. Schreiner, and M. Smith, who render the passage either "if one sends away out of hate" or "if one hates, (let him) send away."

[115] *Malachi*, 56.

[116] The foundational study to make this point was that of J.J. Rabinowitz, "Marriage Contracts in Ancient Egypt in the Light of Jewish Sources" (1953), although the biblical example cited by Rabinowitz, Deut. 21:15, has been rejected by R. Yaron, "On Divorce in

Bringing to bear numerous Akkadian parallels, however, R. Westbrook has recently reviewed this evidence and has concluded that the term "hate" in the context of marriage cannot simply be equated with "divorce."[117] When "hate" occurs alone, it appears to be an encapsulation[118] for the fuller expression, "hate and divorce," and this combination refers to divorce motivated by hatred or, in other words, divorce that is without justification. In support of his contention that "hate" is at most an encapsulation of "hate and divorce" and that "hate" implies something beyond mere divorce, Westbrook notes that while two of the Elephantine contracts employ the term "hate" by itself to express the concept of divorce,[119] a third reads, "if H... says 'I hate my wife W, she shall not be my wife'...."[120] Since "she shall not be my wife" is widely recognized as a divorce formula, there would be an awkward redundancy here if "hate" were simply a synonym for divorce. Similarly, a marriage contract from Alalakh reads, "if W hates H and divorces him...,"[121] implying that these are not identical terms; and another Neo-Assyrian contract has "if W hates (and) divorces, he must pay...," this time lacking the conjunction.[122] Based on references to "hate" in non-marital contexts within various Akkadian legal texts, Westbrook argues that this term stresses the culpable motive of a purely subjective aversion which typically turns an innocent act (like leaving a city in CH §136) into a criminal one.[123]

Turning to Mal. 2:16, Westbrook argues that the MT can be rendered without emendation, "For he has hated, divorced ... and covered his garment in injustice." Since the asyndetic expression, "he has hated, divorced," is

---

Old Testament Times" (1957) 119. Cf. also R. Yaron, *Introduction to the Law of the Aramaic Papyri* (1961).

A.S. van der Woude notes simply that while "hate" bears the sense of "divorce" in Aramaic, it is unattested with this meaning in Biblical Hebrew ("Malachi's Struggle for a Pure Community," 70, n. 32).

[117] "The Prohibition on Restoration of Marriage in Deuteronomy 24:1-4," 398ff.

[118] Westbrook does not use the term "encapsulation." For an examination of the phenomenon of "encapsulation" in lexical semantics, cf. J. Lyons, *Semantics*, I, 262.

[119] Cowley 15 (= PY B2.6) and Kraeling 2 (= PY B3.3).

[120] Kraeling 7 lines 21-22 (= PY B3.8) is obviously intended, correcting the typographical mistake in R. Westbrook, "The Prohibition on Restoration of Marriage in Deuteronomy 24:1-4," 401, n. 51.

[121] D.J. Wiseman, "Supplementary Copies of Alalakh Tablets," *JCS* 8 (1954) 7, No. 94, lines 17-19.

[122] B. Parker, "The Numrud Tablets, 1952 — Business Documents," No. ND 2307, lines 49-50 read *šum-ma ·(m)Mil-ki-ra-mu [itti-ší] e-zi-ra e-zip-pi iddan(an)*. Similarly, R. Westbrook: *šum-ma H e-zi-ra e-zip-pi SUM-an* ("The Prohibition on Restoration of Marriage in Deuteronomy 24:1-4," 400). Westbrook rejects the various alternative interpretations/emendations of this text proposed by *CAD* E (1958) 422; V. Jakobson, "Studies in Neo-Assyrian Law" (1974) 116; and J.N. Postgate, *Fifty Neo-Assyrian Legal Documents* (1976) 105f.

To this evidence, Westbrook adds a legal formula attested in the *ana ittišu* series (VII iv 1-5 = *ana ittišu* A §5): "if a wife hates her husband and says 'You are not my husband'..." (B. Landsberger, *Die Serie ana ittišu*, MSL I, 103).

[123] "The Prohibition on Restoration of Marriage in Deuteronomy 24:1-4," 401. Cf. also LE §30 and CH §§142, 193.

paralleled by the Neo-Assyrian contract mentioned earlier, Westbrook
suggests that it was "taken from a standard legal idiom" and means "divorced
without justification."[124] Nevertheless, it seems better still to take כִּי as "if"
and to translate 2:16, "If one hates and divorces, says Yahweh, God of Israel,
he covers his garment with violence, says Yahweh of hosts...." This proposal
requires us to examine the meaning and form of שַׁלַּח, which is not without its
own problems.

4.2.3 The problematic meaning and form of "divorces [שַׁלַּח]"

In spite of the presence in Biblical Hebrew of other terms for divorce,
including גרשׁ (Lev. 21:7; 22:13; Num. 30:10; Ezek. 44:22) and כְּרִיתוּת (Deut.
24:1, 3; Isa. 50:1; Jer. 3:8), there is adequate evidence to establish the
meaning "divorce" within the semantic range of the Piel of שׁלח, based on
Deut. 22:19, 29; 24:1, 3, 4; and possibly 21:14; Gen. 21:14; Ezra 10:44; Isa.
50:1; and Jer. 3:1, 8.[125] What has made שַׁלַּח in Mal. 2:16 problematic is not
its meaning, but its grammatical form.

Westbrook's claim that the MT of Mal. 2:16 need not be emended on
the basis of a Neo-Assyrian marriage contract may go beyond the evidence.
While it is true that this Akkadian parallel, along with the rest of Westbrook's
evidence, offers impressive support for interpreting "hates [שֹׂנֵא]" as referring
to the husband's attitude (rather than Yahweh's, etc.) and also for permitting
an asyndetic construction, it should be noted that the Akkadian formula
which Westbrook cites has both verbs in the I/1 durative, while the MT of
Mal. 2:16 involves one perfect and one infinitive construct.

---

[124] *Ibid.*, 403f.

[125] On the use of גרשׁ with reference to divorce, see R. Yaron, "On Divorce in Old
Testament Times" (1957) 117-121.

In addition to those terms listed above, H.J. Hendriks mentions עזב (Isa. 54:6, 7; 60:15),
a term which "denotes the position of the divorced, forsaken wife" ("Juridical Aspects,"
57).

W.L. Callison posits a radical contrast between כְּרִיתוּת, which he supposes referred to
legal divorce (requiring a written document and permitting remarriage), and שַׁלַּח, the
informal "putting away" mentioned in Mal. 2:16, which, according to Callison, was little
more than desertion and did not permit remarriage ("Divorce, the Law, and Jesus" [1986]).
Callison, however, commits two linguistic errors. First, he confuses parts of speech when
he compares the distribution of a noun, כְּרִיתוּת, with a verb, שַׁלַּח, and concludes from their
different uses that they are contrastive terms. Second, Callison fails to note that in each of
its four biblical occurrences כְּרִיתוּת appears as a *nomen rectum* for סֵפֶר. This observation
may suggest a restricted usage for this term and so may prove to be crucial when one
considers the matter of lexical choice for terms having to do with divorce.

שַׁלַּח is used to refer to the "sending away" of one's spouse that coincides with and
expresses the termination of marriage. S.L. McKenzie and H.N. Wallace state, "Divorce is
apparently involved, though the use of *šallah* to mean 'divorce' is unusual..." ("Covenant
Themes in Malachi," 552f., n. 14). Cf. also KB, *s.v.* שׁלח. For a fuller discussion of the use
of שַׁלַּח with reference to divorce, cf. D.W. Amram, who includes Gen. 21:14, *The Jewish
Law of Divorce According to Bible and Talmud* (1896) 55ff.; R. Yaron, "On Divorce in Old
Testament Times" (1957); Z.W. Falk, *Hebrew Law in Biblical Times*, 155; H.J. Hendriks,
"Juridical Aspects," 56, 76, n. 288; and J. Scharbert, "Ehe und Eheschliessung in der
Rechtssprache des Pentateuchs und beim Chronisten" (1977) 216, 219f.

It is possible that one should follow the suggestion of J.M.P. Smith and others and repoint שַׁלַּח as a perfect שִׁלַּח.[126] In addition to offering a closer parallel to the Neo-Assyrian marriage contract mentioned above, this modest emendation allows an asyndetic construction which is typical for Biblical Hebrew, with the two perfects to be rendered, "if one hates and repudiates/divorces" (i.e., "if one divorces because of hatred").

A preferable alternative, however, may be to leave שַׁלַּח unemended and interpret this form as a Piel infinitive absolute functioning as a substitute for a finite form, in this case a perfect.[127] Other interpreters may have overlooked this possibility because the Piel infinitive absolute of שׁלח appears twice elsewhere as שַׁלֵּחַ (e.g., Deut. 22:7; 1 Kgs. 11:22). This does not preclude our proposal, however, since in the Piel conjugation the infinitive construct often provides an alternative form for the infinitive absolute.[128]

4.2.4 "he covers his garment with violence [וְכִסָּה חָמָס עַל־לְבוּשׁוֹ]"

Finally, we need to consider how the clause "he covers his garment with violence [וְכִסָּה חָמָס עַל־לְבוּשׁוֹ]" is to be understood on the present interpretation. We have already argued that this clause ought to be construed as an apodosis, against the view of LXX[LW], etc. (see §4.2.1 above). In addition to offering greater congruence with its context, one special advantage of this proposal is that it obviates any need to emend וְכִסָּה.[129]

Even though we may have clarified its grammatical function within its context, because this figure occurs nowhere else in the Old Testament, there remains considerable uncertainty as to its interpretation. In addition, there is further uncertainty regarding the grammar within the clause itself. T.V. Moore rules out the rendering "who covers violence with his garment" on the ground that עַל, when used with כסה, always designates the thing covered.[130] Nevertheless, it may be asked whether "violence [חָמָס]" is the subject of

---

[126] *Malachi, ad loc.* Smith renders the verse, "For one who hates and sends away covers his clothing with violence, says Yahweh of hosts." Cf. also A. van Hoonacker, H. Junker, F. Nötscher, T. Chary, and R. Westbrook.

[127] Joüon §123x and Waltke and O'Connor §35.5.2. Waltke and O'Connor note that all of the narrative examples which they cite occur in direct discourse, a fact which may lend additional support to the recognition of שַׁלַּח in 2:16 as an infinitive absolute. Cf. also W.L. Moran, "The Use of the Canaanite Infinitive Absolute as a Finite Verb in the Amarna Letters from Byblos" (1950) 169-172. Within the immediate context of Malachi, it is possible that כַּסּוֹת in 2:13 offers another, generally undetected, example of an infinitive absolute used as a finite form.

[128] Cf. GKC §52o, which notes that in the Piel the infinitive construct form is "much more frequently" employed for the infinitive absolute than the special infinitive absolute form. Cf. also Joüon §52c.

[129] The most common proposals are to repoint כִּסָּה as an infinitive construct to balance שַׁלַּח (so *BHS*), or to emend it to an infinitive absolute with prefix, כְּכַסֵּה. Cf. discussion of this in A.S. van der Woude, "Malachi's Struggle for a Pure Community," 70 and 71, n. 35.

[130] *Malachi* (1856) 139. So also W.C. Kaiser Jr., *Malachi*, 73. Cf. Deut. 13:8, Hab. 2:14, etc. These parallels, likewise, appear to offer little support for the interpretation of the NIV (assuming that it is not intended to be paraphrastic): "I hate a man's covering himself with violence as well as with his garment."

"covers [כְּסֹה]" (so LXX, Vulgate),[131] or whether it is the object describing that with which "his garment" is covered (so Peshiṭta, Targum).[132] Although the sense of the passage is not greatly affected by the choice, favouring this latter option is the grammatical parallel with "he hates [שָׂנֵא]," to which reference has been made — namely, the desirability of having the same subject, the divorcing man, for both of these perfects.

There are three main alternative interpretations for an identification of "his garments [לְבוּשׁוֹ]."

1) The first view understands "garment" in a literal manner, supposing the reference to be to the worshipper's attire within a cultic setting. There are two variations on this approach. The first assumes a context of idolatrous worship, while the second assumes a context of hypocritical worship. We have already rejected the idolatrous context posited by H. Winckler and I.G. Matthews, which leaves their interpretation of "his garment [לְבוּשׁוֹ]" without foundation (Chapter 2, §2.2 and §2.5; and Chapter 3, §1.2). The second variation on this literal view of "garment" is represented by P.A. Verhoef. Comparing the use of "cover [כסה]" in vs. 13, where the semantic domain is predominantly cultic, Verhoef suggests that "despite the fact that the people were accused of divorcing their wives [unjustly, we might add], they indulged in sacrificial activities."[133] Verhoef suggests that the "violence" may refer to the splashed blood of hypocritically sacrificed animals (cf. Mic. 6:7). In any case, the mention of garments besmirched with violence or injustice would appear to stress their heinous desecration and hypocrisy. While an allusion to 2:13 is plausible, however, the posited connection between "violence [חָמָס]" and "the splashed blood of hypocritically sacrificed animals" is unconvincing.

2) Since the suggestion was first made by E. Pococke, the majority of modern interpreters have understood "his garments [לְבוּשׁוֹ]" as a reference to a wife.[134] Several arguments have been offered in support. Perhaps least convincing is the frequent appeal to the *Qur'ān* 2:187, which is offered as an extrabiblical example where "garment" appears as a poetic reference to one's wife: "... They (your wives) are a covering [*lb's*] to you, and you are a covering [*lb's*] to them." The use of "garment," however, whether as a metaphor (as in the *Qur'ān*) or as a designation, is hardly customary as a

---

[131] The LXX reads, καλύψει ἀσέβεια ἐπὶ τὰ ἐνθυμήματά σου. J.M.P. Smith notes that ἐνθυμήματά is an inner-Greek corruption for ἐνδύματα, based on the daughter versions of LXX, viz., Peshiṭta, Arabic Armenian, Ethiopic, and Georgian (*Malachi*, 60). So also LXX[W].

[132] So, e.g., P.A. Verhoef, *The Books of Haggai and Malachi*, 279.

[133] *Ibid.*, 280.

[134] E. Pococke, *A Commentary on the Prophecy of Malachi* (1740) — so, according to A. von Bulmerincq, *Der Prophet Maleachi, Band 2*, 315. This view is supported by, among others, E. Henderson, *The Twelve Minor Prophets* (1858) 455; J. Wellhausen, *Skizzen und Vorarbeiten* (1892) 199; G.A. Smith, *The Book of the Twelve Prophets* (1899) 365; K. Marti, *Das Dodekapropheton* (1904); 472; R.C. Dentan, "The Book of Malachi" (1956) 1136; and C.M. Carmichael, *Law and Narrative in the Bible* (1985) 198.

reference to a wife, being attested nowhere else in Arabic literature or Biblical Hebrew.[135] A second argument in favour of recognizing "his garments" as a reference to a wife is the intimate proximity of clothes to the wearer, which suggests to some its aptness as a metaphor for a wife in relation to her husband.[136] The final, and perhaps strongest argument for interpreting "his garments" as a reference to a wife is the practice of obtaining a wife by means of covering her with a garment (Deut. 22:30 [ET 23:1], Ruth 3:9, Ezek. 16:8).[137] Based on this association with a marriage rite, "his garments" is used in a transferred sense to refer to the wife.[138]

3) The older view of לְבוּשׁ, which may still be preferable, is that "his garments" is simply another instance of the pervasive biblical image of clothes as the outward expression of the inner state of a man.[139] See, for example, Jer. 2:34, "Also on your skirts is found the lifeblood of guiltless poor"; Ps. 73:6, "Therefore pride is their necklace; violence covers them as a garment [יַעֲטָף־שִׁית חָמָס לָמוֹ]"; and Ps. 109:18, "He clothed himself with cursing as his coat [וַיִּלְבַּשׁ קְלָלָה כְּמַדּוֹ]...!"[140] In addition, the customary use of garments in claiming a woman as a wife, as discussed above, with its implicit pledge of protection and support, may make this metaphor especially apt in the present context.[141]

In any case, against the apparent assumption of Van der Woude, nothing about Malachi's use of this image and its mention of "violence"

---

[135] Cf. E.B. Pusey, *The Minor Prophets* (1883) 484, n. 5, and J.M. P Smith, *Malachi*, 60, against G.H.A. von Ewald, who terms לְבוּשׁ "a genuinely popular phrase... for *his wife*" (*Mal'aki* [1881] 82).

[136] So, e.g., W.E. Barnes, *Malachi* (1917) 125.

[137] So, e.g., J.M.P. Smith, *Malachi*, 55f.; W.C. Kaiser Jr., *Malachi*, 73f.; and E. Achtemeier, *Nahum - Malachi* (1986) 183.

[138] Cf., e.g., A. Phillips, "Uncovering the Father's Skirt" (1980) 38.

[139] Cf. Martin Luther, *Lectures on Malachi*, 406; C.F. Keil, *The Twelve Minor Prophets*, vol. 2 (1868) 454; J. Packard, "The Book of Malachi" (1876) 17; E.B. Pusey, *The Minor Prophets* (1883) 609, n. 13; T.T. Perowne, *Malachi* (1890) 27; C. von Orelli, *The Twelve Minor Prophets* (1893) 397f.; S.R. Driver, *The Minor Prophets* (1906) 317; E. Sellin, *Das Zwölfprophetenbuch* (1922) 554; P.M. Schumpp, *Das Buch der zwölf Propheten* (1950) 396; D.R. Jones, *Haggai, Zechariah, Malachi* (1962) 197; C. Stuhlmueller, "Malachi" (1970) 400; W. Rudolph, *Haggai, Sacharja 1-8, Sacharja 9-14, Maleachi* (1976) 275; and S. Schreiner, "Mischehen-Ehebruch-Ehescheidung. Betrachtungen zu Mal 2,10-16" (1979) 227.

[140] Cf. also Zech. 3:3-5; Ps. 109:29; Prov. 31:25; Isa. 59:17; 61:10; 64:5 [ET 6], etc.

[141] Cf. J.M.P. Smith, *Malachi*, 55f. Smith also cites W.R. Smith, *Kinship and Marriage in Early Arabia*, 1st ed., p. 87, as offering Arabic parallels for the use of garments in claiming a wife. *N.B.*, Smith is careful to distinguish his view from the view which uses these texts to argue an identification of "his garments" with the man's wife (*op. cit.*, 60). Possibly there is also some connection between the garment mentioned in 2:16 and the Akkadian practice of "cutting the hem/veil" as expressive of divorce (perhaps reflected in the expression, סֵפֶר כְּרִיתֻת, bill of divorce [cutting]"). In any case, the expression "the wife of your youth," with its allusion to the time of one's wedding, may offer some indirect support to an association between the garments mentioned in 2:16 and the use of garments in the act of betrothal.

Moreover, it is also possible that an allusion is intended to 2:13, where כסה also appears in what is a distinctly cultic context. Cf. P.A. Verhoef, *The Books of Haggai and Malachi*, 279f. Thus understood, Malachi employs an image which is reminiscent of that found in Zechariah 3 in order to indicate that by his divorce the offerer has been spiritually disqualified from cultic participation.

necessarily implies that he viewed divorce on the ground of aversion to be an illegal act.[142] The concern of the prophet is rather to condemn such divorces as unethical and, as an instance of infidelity [בגד] or covenant breaking (cf. 2:14), liable to divine judgment: "Therefore, take heed to yourselves!"

In summary, we may paraphrase Mal. 2:16, "If one hates and divorces [that is, if one divorces merely on the ground of aversion], says Yahweh, God of Israel, he covers his garment with violence [i.e., such a man visibly defiles himself with violence], says Yahweh of hosts. Therefore, take heed to yourselves and do not be faithless [against your wife]."

5. DEUTERONOMY 24:1-4

We began this chapter noting how A.S. van der Woude rejects an interpretation of Mal. 2:16 which is similar to the one just defended — that Malachi repudiated not divorce in general, but divorce based on aversion.[143] Van der Woude acknowledges that he might be prepared to accept this interpretation on other grounds were it not for the lenient attitude toward divorce attested in Deut. 24:1-4. We turn now to this decisive passage.

It is not possible within the limits of the present study to establish which, if any, of the ten major competing views is to be preferred for the rationale behind the prohibition of palingamy to a former spouse in Deut. 24:4.[144] Nevertheless, in spite of this unresolved debate, there has emerged a

---

[142] "It must be sincerely doubted whether in Old Testament times even a prophet would have denounced divorce as a *crime* [italics added]" ("Malachi's Struggle For a Pure Community," 71).

[143] *Ibid.*

[144] The ten views in question are:

a) To renew such a marriage would be to condone adultery (the adultery is implicit in the second marriage, whether or not a remarriage to the first husband takes place). Cf. Philo, *Special Laws*, 3:30f. Philo's approach is discussed and rejected by R. Yaron, "The Restoration of Marriage" (1966) 6f., and R. Westbrook, "The Prohibition on Restoration of Marriage in Deuteronomy 24:4," 388f.

b) The remarriage of a divorced woman is tantamount to adultery. Cf. C.F. Keil and F. Delitzsch, *The Pentateuch* (1878) 418, and S.R. Driver, *Deuteronomy* (1902) 272. Against this, cf. R. Yaron, "The Restoration of Marriage," 7.

c) Protect the first marriage (a deterrent against rash divorce). Cf. S.R. Driver, *Deuteronomy*, 272. Against this, however, cf. R. Yaron, "The Restoration of Marriage," 5f.; J.A. Thompson, *Deuteronomy* (1974) 244; G.J. Wenham, "The Restoration of Marriage Reconsidered" (1979) 36; and R. Westbrook, *op. cit.*, 389.

d) A consequence of marriage as an unobliterable relationship. Cf. J. Murray, *Divorce* (1961) 14.

e) Codify natural revulsion. Cf. H. Junker, *Das Buch Deuteronomium* (1933) 100; C.M. Carmichael, *The Laws of Deuteronomy* (1974) 203-207; and *idem, Women, Law, and the Genesis Traditions* (1979) 8-21. Against this view, cf. G.J. Wenham, "The Restoration of Marriage Reconsidered," 37, and R. Westbrook, *op. cit.*, 391.

f) Protect the second marriage. Cf. S.R. Driver, *Deuteronomy*, 272, and R. Yaron, "The Restoration of Marriage," 8-11. Against this view, cf. C.M. Carmichael, *The Laws of Deuteronomy*, 204; R. Westbrook, *op. cit.*, 389f.; and G.J. Wenham, "The Restoration of Marriage Reconsidered," 37.

g) Avoid incest. Cf. G.J. Wenham, "The Restoration of Marriage Reconsidered," 37ff., and W.A. Heth and G.J. Wenham, *Jesus and Divorce* (1984) 106-110. Against this view,

scholarly consensus that the intent of this casuistic law is neither to authorize divorce, nor to stipulate its proper grounds, nor to establish its requisite procedure. Rather, its sole concern is to prohibit the restoration of a marriage after an intervening marriage.[145] If so, there is no necessary contradiction between Malachi's prophetic indictment of divorce on the ground of aversion and Deuteronomy 24.[146]

In grammatical terms this consensus reflects the conviction that the only apodosis in Deut. 24:1-4 is the clause which begins לֹא־יוּכַל in vs. 4. Accordingly, as against the AV, for example, the clause beginning וְכָתַב in vs. 1b is not an apodosis, but is rather part of a complex protasis extending from vss. 1 to 3.[147] It may help to illustrate this analysis if we set out the various elements of Deut. 24:1-4 as follows:

---

cf. R. Westbrook, op. cit., 390f., and H.W. Hoehner, "A Response to Divorce and Remarriage [a paper read by W.A. Heth]" (1987) 240-246, at 243.

h) Protect the woman. Cf. W.F. Luck, Divorce and Remarriage (1987) 57. Against this, cf. H.W. Hoehner, "A Response to Divorce and Remarriage [a paper read by W.A. Heth]," 242.

i) Prohibit unjust enrichment (due to estoppel). Cf. R. Westbrook, op. cit., 387-405.

j) Avoid legalized adultery (closing a possible loophole in the prohibition against adultery). Cf. J. Calvin, Commentaries on the Four Last Books of Moses arranged in the form of a Harmony, III, 94: "The reason of the law is, that, by prostituting his wife, he would be, as far as in him lay, acting like a procurer." Cf. also S.F. Bigger, "Hebrew Marriage and Family in the Old Testament Period" (1974) 237, and P.C. Craigie, Deuteronomy (1976) 306f.

It will be noted that these ten main approaches are not necessarily mutually exclusive and that not all scholars confine themselves to just one of these opinions. For example, at various points in his discussion, S.R. Driver supports positions c), which he most favours, but also b) and f). Similarly, C.F. Keil and F. Delitzsch, The Pentateuch, 416ff., appear to hold a combination of b), c), and h); while J.A. Thompson, Deuteronomy, 245, speaks in favour of b), c), and f).

For a further discussion of this issue, see the writer's unpublished paper, "Alternative approaches to Deuteronomy 24:1-4 and a defence of the 'adultery loophole' view" (submitted to G.J. Wenham on 18/8/87).

[145] So, already, J. Calvin, Commentaries on the Four Last Books of Moses, III, 94. Cf. also, e.g., C.F. Keil and F. Delitzsch, The Pentateuch, III, 416f.; S.R. Driver, Deuteronomy (1895) 269; M.G. Kline, Treaty of the Great King (1963) 114f.; A. Phillips, Deuteronomy (1973) 159f.; J.A. Thompson, Deuteronomy (1974) 243.; P.C. Craigie, Deuteronomy (1976) 304; and A.D.H. Mayes, Deuteronomy (1979) 322.

[146] The regulation of a practice does not thereby imply moral approval for that practice. Cf., e.g., Chapter 4, §6.2.1 below.

[147] AV: "When a man taketh a wife, and marrieth her, then it shall be, if she find no favour in his eyes, because he hath found some unseemly thing in her, that he shall write her a bill of divorcement, and give it in her hand, and send her out of his house. And when she is departed out of his house, she may go and be another man's wife. And if the latter husband hate her, and write her a bill of divorcement, and give it in her hand, and send her out of his house; or if the latter husband die, which took her to be his wife; her former husband, which sent her away, may not take her again to be his wife, after that she is defiled; for that is abomination before the LORD: and thou shalt not cause the land to sin, which the LORD thy God giveth thee for an inheritance." (Deut. 24:1-4)

Cf. also the English Revised Version, the American Revised Version, and the ASV of 1901. These translations give the impression that divorce is not merely permitted, it is mandatory under the circumstances described in vs. 1 (so notes J. Murray, Divorce, 4).

Typical of the present scholarly consensus is the view of R.C. Campbell, who writes, "There is scarcely any question that these verses constitute one conditional sentence, the

Complex protasis:

Condition 1: An initial legal marriage

"When a man takes a wife and marries her,..."

24:1 כִּי־יִקַּח אִישׁ אִשָּׁה וּבְעָלָהּ

Condition 2: Because the wife commits some offence

"... if then she finds no favour in his eyes because he has found some indecency in her,..."

וְהָיָה אִם־לֹא תִמְצָא־חֵן בְּעֵינָיו כִּי־מָצָא בָהּ עֶרְוַת דָּבָר

Condition 3abcd: He legally divorces her

a) "... and he writes her a bill of divorce..."

וְכָתַב לָהּ סֵפֶר כְּרִיתֻת

b) "... and puts it in her hand...."

וְנָתַן בְּיָדָהּ

c) "... and sends her out of his house,..."

וְשִׁלְּחָהּ מִבֵּיתוֹ׃

d) "... and she departs out of his house,..."

24:2 וְיָצְאָה מִבֵּיתוֹ[148]

Condition 4: And then she remarries

"... and if she goes and becomes another man's wife,..."

וְהָלְכָה וְהָיְתָה לְאִישׁ־אַחֵר׃

Condition 5: And either the second husband hates her

"... and the latter husband dislikes her..."

24:3 וּשְׂנֵאָהּ הָאִישׁ הָאַחֲרוֹן

Condition 6abc: And legally divorces her

a) "... and writes her a bill of divorce..."

וְכָתַב לָהּ סֵפֶר כְּרִיתֻת

b) "... and puts it in her hand..."

וְנָתַן בְּיָדָהּ

c) "... and sends her out of his house,..."

וְשִׁלְּחָהּ מִבֵּיתוֹ

Alternative to Conditions 5 and 6abc: Or the second husband dies

"... or if the latter husband dies, who took her to be his wife,..."

אוֹ כִי יָמוּת הָאִישׁ הָאַחֲרוֹן אֲשֶׁר־לְקָחָהּ לוֹ לְאִשָּׁה׃

Apodosis: Under such conditions remarriage to the first husband is prohibited

"... then her former husband, who sent her away, may not take her again to be his wife..."

24:4 לֹא־יוּכַל בַּעְלָהּ הָרִאשׁוֹן אֲשֶׁר־שִׁלְּחָהּ לָשׁוּב לְקַחְתָּהּ לִהְיוֹת לוֹ לְאִשָּׁה

Reason part 1: because the woman is defiled

---

protasis of which is to be found in the first three verses and the apodosis of which beings [sic for "begins"] only with v. 4" ("Teachings of the Old Testament Concerning Divorce" [1963] 174f.).

[148] Although the MT of Deut. 24:1-4 is generally reliable, it is possible that one should follow the LXX in omitting מִבֵּיתוֹ וְהָלְכָה, as noted in BHS. In any case, the sense is not greatly affected by the choice.

"... after she has been defiled;..."

אַחֲרֵי אֲשֶׁר הֻטַּמָּאָה

Reason part 2: because it would be an abomination

"... for that is an abomination before the LORD,..."

כִּי־תוֹעֵבָה הִוא לִפְנֵי יְהוָה

Reason part 3: and would bring guilt upon the land

"... and you shall not bring guilt upon the land which the LORD your God gives you for an inheritance."

וְלֹא תַחֲטִיא אֶת־הָאָרֶץ אֲשֶׁר יְהוָה אֱלֹהֶיךָ נֹתֵן לְךָ נַחֲלָה:

Accordingly, since Deut. 24:1-4 is concerned only with the prohibition of palingamy to a former spouse, there is no necessary contradiction with the interpretation being advanced for Mal. 2:16. Moreover, it now appears probable that Deut. 24:1-4 may, in fact, presuppose an outlook similar to Mal. 2:16. This is the case because, as R. Westbrook has argued, this law appears to assume a widely attested legal practice according to which a husband incurs a substantial financial penalty if he divorces his wife merely on the ground of aversion.[149]

Westbrook emphasizes the distinction between the sort of divorce which terminates the first marriage (based on the discovery of "some indecency [עֶרְוַת דָּבָר]" in the wife) and that which terminates the second (based on the husband's "dislike [וּשְׂנֵאָהּ]"). Further, Westbrook notes that there must be some factor, heretofore overlooked, which would account for the remarkable pairing of the second divorce with death. That factor, Westbrook hypothesizes, is the favourable financial consequence for the woman which would result either from the death of her husband or from that particular kind of divorce.

Based on an extensive survey of both ancient Near Eastern and post-biblical Jewish practice, Westbrook concludes that typically when a marriage was dissolved by death or divorce, a woman was entitled to a financial settlement at least consisting of the return of her dowry, but often also including a further payment from her husband's own resources.[150] On the

---

[149] "The Prohibition on Restoration of Marriage in Deuteronomy 24:1-4," 387-405.

[150] Westbrook suggests that if the wife had borne children, LE §59 and CH §137 [Westbrook mistakenly cites CH §147] may indicate that the financial consequences for divorce were still more severe, requiring the husband to forfeit the whole of his property ("The Prohibition on Restoration of Marriage in Deuteronomy 24:1-4," 395, n. 26). This suggestion is not without difficulties. In support, Westbrook cites his *Old Babylonian Marriage Law*, Chapter 4.

Cf. CH §§171b-172; NBL §12; and less explicitly *m. Ketub.* 7:1; 10:1-2. Note that in addition to the returned dowry, the widow in each case is entitled to additional payments (either marital property given to her by her husband or some equitable share of the estate).

For the financial settlement in the case of death, Westbrook notes Rashi's suggestion that the wife contributes to the husband's death, but considers this too farfetched and so remarks that Yaron does not consider it (*op. cit.*, 390, n. 10). While Westbrook is probably correct in rejecting this interpretation for Deuteronomy 24, a law such as CH §153

other hand, in cases where the divorce was justified because of some serious misconduct on the part of the woman (less than adultery, for which the penalty would be death according to Westbrook), the financial consequences were radically different. Under such a circumstance the husband was entitled to keep the dowry and incurred no financial penalty.[151]

Westbrook then argues that the first divorce in Deuteronomy 24 was precisely such as would involve "the kind of misconduct referred to in CH §§141-142 and in *m. Ketub.* 7:6 and therefore justifies the husband in divorcing his wife without a financial settlement."[152] The second divorce, on the other hand, because it specifies a motive of "hate," a term that in numerous other legal contexts expresses "the *mens rea*, the 'guilty mind', which is a necessary constituent of the offence," would entitle the wife to receive the normal financial settlement.[153] We have already considered Westbrook's argument concerning the meaning of "hate [שנא]" in the context of divorce. Here it should be noted that under such a circumstance the second divorce would leave the woman in much the same financial condition as if her husband had died.

Westbrook concludes, "The effect would be that the first husband profits twice: firstly by rejecting his wife and then by accepting her. It is a flagrant case of unjust enrichment which the law intervenes to prevent." In modern law such a prohibition would be grounded in the concept of "estoppel," the principle that a man who has benefited from asserting a

---

demonstrates that the possibility of this kind of murderous intrigue on the part of a wife is anything but farfetched.

For the financial settlement in the case of divorce, cf. LU §§6-7; CH §§138-140; MAL A §§20, 37, 38; and *m. Ketub.* 1:2 (cf. *b. B. Qam.* 82b). CH §138 specifies the general case where the divorced woman is entitled to her returned dowry [*šeriktam*] and a divorce payment equal to her marriage present [*kaspam mala terḥatiša*]. Westbrook argues that MAL A §37 need not be understood as giving the husband total discretion with respect to the divorce settlement (*op. cit.*, 395, n. 27). It may only intend to relieve him of a statutory minimum, such as mentioned in CH §§6-7, 138.

[151] Westbrook cites CH §141, where the wife's misconduct was of a financial nature (according to Westbrook), and the punishment is expulsion "without giving her anything, not her journey-money, nor her divorce-money." Westbrook also notes CH §§142-143, where the wife in an inchoate marriage is to be cast into the water if she was unchaste and involved in some financial misconduct, but if she is innocent of the charge, she may leave with her dowry. Finally, Westbrook cites MAL A §29 (following the interpretation offered by G. Cardascia, *Les lois assyriennes* [1969] 161-163) and *m. Ketub.* 7:6.

Westbrook's assumption of the death penalty for adultery presumably reflects the typical case of a guilty spouse caught *in flagrante delicto*. Cf., e.g., CH §129; LE §28; HL §§195, 197, 198; MAL A §§13, 15, 16, and 23. It is important, however, to stress the condition of being caught *in flagrante delicto* and also to note that some laws suggest the possibility that the death penalty for an adulterous wife, even if caught *in flagrante delicto*, could be waived by her husband as long as equal leniency was shown to the guilty lover. Cf., e.g., CH §129; HL §198; and MAL A §§14, 15, 16, and 23. See the fuller treatment of this topic in Chapter 8 below.

[152] "The Prohibition on Restoration of Marriage in Deuteronomy 24:1-4," 399.

[153] "The Prohibition on Restoration of Marriage in Deuteronomy 24:1-4," 401. Westbrook cites LE §30; CH §§136, 142, 193, as offering examples for this usage of "hate."

particular set of facts may not benefit a second time from conceding that the facts were otherwise.

Whether or not one agrees with Westbrook that estoppel is the underlying rationale for the prohibition in Deut. 24:1-4, his analysis of the distinction between the two divorces and the resulting financial benefit to the first husband, which may have motivated the remarriage, appear plausible. Of course, in the absence of corroborating evidence, some uncertainty about the precise meaning of "some indecency" must remain.[154] Still, there is an inherent plausibility in Westbrook's attempt to distinguish "if then she finds no favour in his eyes because he has found some indecency [עֶרְוַת דָּבָר] in her" in vs. 1 from "and he hates her [וּשְׂנֵאָהּ]" in vs. 3. If these expressions were entirely synonymous, why would the author use the fuller expression when "hate" is sufficiently clear and well attested elsewhere in divorce contexts?[155] Likewise, the evidence from the ancient Near East and post-biblical Judaism presented by Westbrook should predispose the interpreter to discover in the biblical legislation a similar practice of distinguishing various grounds for divorce — in particular, mere aversion (שׂנא) from some more serious failing in one's spouse (presumably עֶרְוַת דָּבָר). Accordingly, as against those scholars who consider Mal. 2:16 to be in tension with Deut. 24:1-4, the implied financial penalty on the second husband who divorces in Deut. 24:3 in reality reflects a disapprobation of divorce when grounded in mere aversion similar to what is attested in Mal. 2:16.[156]

---

[154] Whatever the precise origin and meaning of this *crux interpretum*, it seems warranted to conclude with Westbrook that it refers to a cause serious enough to permit the husband to divorce his wife while avoiding any financial penalty. Cf. also, e.g., M.G. Kline, *Treaty of the Great King*, 115.

Among others, A.D.H. Mayes considers that the entire clause וְהָיָה אִם־לֹא תִמְצָא־חֵן בְּעֵינָיו כִּי־מָצָא בָהּ עֶרְוַת דָּבָר is "probably a later addition" (*Deuteronomy*, 322). Mayes bases this conjecture on the fact that the verse "has a new beginning with the word wᵉhāyāh; see comment on 18:19." Mayes' comment at 18:19 proves to be unilluminating, however, and the argument must be judged unconvincing since וְהָיָה is so widely attested with this same grammatical function in texts of unquestioned integrity (e.g., Mayes himself does not consider 18:19 to be a later interpolation). Indeed, given the repetition in phraseology between the description of the first divorce, where we read וְכָתַב לָהּ סֵפֶר כְּרִיתֻת וְנָתַן בְּיָדָהּ וְשִׁלְּחָהּ מִבֵּיתוֹ וְיָצְאָה מִבֵּיתוֹ, and the second, where we find the only slightly abbreviated וְכָתַב לָהּ סֵפֶר כְּרִיתֻת וְנָתַן בְּיָדָהּ וְשִׁלְּחָהּ מִבֵּיתוֹ, it would be quite surprising to be left, as Mayes would have it, without any expression in the first divorce to parallel (or contrast with) וּשְׂנֵאָהּ in the second.

[155] Here we assume the widely conceded observation that since 24:1 occurs in the protasis of this case law, the legislator was not intending to introduce a novel requirement in the procedure for divorce which would necessitate the unusually full description.

[156] Less convincing is Westbrook's interpretation of הֻטַּמָּאָה, "she has been caused to be unclean," as a reference to the first husband's allegation of defilement: "... the first husband's earlier assertion that she was unclean makes her unclean now for the purposes of marrying her. Having profited from the claim that she was unfit to be his wife, he can not now act as if she were fit to marry him because circumstances have made her a more profitable match" ("The Prohibition on Restoration of Marriage in Deuteronomy 24:1-4," 404f.).

Also problematic is the characterization in 24:4 of any such remarriage as an "abomination [תוֹעֵבָה]" which would bring "guilt upon the land [וְלֹא תַחֲטִיא אֶת־הָאָרֶץ]," statements which appear excessively harsh for the pecuniary wrong he alleges. Although Westbrook cites M. Weinfeld, *Deuteronomy and the Deuteronomic School* (1972) 272-269,

6. SUMMARY AND CONCLUSIONS

We began the present chapter by acknowledging the importance of Mal. 2:16, if it refers to literal divorce, for its support of a reference to literal marriage in Mal. 2:14. Not surprisingly, those scholars who reject a reference to literal marriage in 2:14 either refrain from offering any interpretation of 2:16, claiming that the text is "hopelessly corrupt" (so C.C. Torrey, cf. also F.F. Hvidberg and A. Isaksson), or they resort to unwarranted emendation of the MT of 2:16 and the attribution of otherwise unattested meanings to its vocabulary in order to restore a reference to idolatry (I.G. Matthews).

Following a discussion of these approaches, we considered one other interpretation which also denies a reference to literal divorce in 2:16, namely that of A.S. van der Woude. Van der Woude holds that 2:16 condemns the mistreatment of Jewish wives within polygynous mixed marriages. The principal advantage of this view is that it removes an apparent contradiction between the absolute prohibition of divorce in Mal. 2:16, as it has been traditionally interpreted, and the acceptance of divorce in Deut. 24:1-4. While Van der Woude's interpretation does not exclude a reference to literal marriage in Mal. 2:14,[157] it is unconvincing especially because of its supposition that the key term שלח is an abbreviation for the expression שלח ["put forth"] + יָד ["a hand"] + בָּהּ ["against her"], a usage that lacks any convincing parallel.

Each of the remaining three main alternative interpretations of 2:16 accepts a reference to literal divorce and so coheres with the view of this thesis that the covenant mentioned in Mal. 2:14 refers to literal marriage. The first of these is that Malachi urges divorce, whether of a hated wife (so 4QXII[a], LXX[LW], Targum, and S.), or perhaps of a heathen wife (so A. von Bulmerincq): "If ..., then divorce [שַׁלַּח] [her]!" The versional evidence in support of interpreting שַׁלַּח as an imperative, however, appears to be tendentious, having arisen from a desire to harmonize Malachi with the liberal tolerance of divorce in Deut. 24:1-4. Moreover, this interpretation is opposed by the resulting awkward shift in pronominal reference in 2:16a, a

---

in defence of תּוֹעֵבָה as a reference to "hypocrisy," this definition is uncertain and, even if possible elsewhere, unconvincing for Deut. 24:4 (cf. also S.A. Kaufman, "The Structure of the Deuteronomic Law" [1978-79] 127 and 156, n. 107).

Finally, Jer. 3:1-10 tells against the assumed rationale of estoppel since, on Westbrook's view, the restoration of a marriage after an intervening marriage is entirely permissible if this can be accomplished without estoppel. In other words, the precise terms under which each marriage is ended is of critical importance for determining the propriety of the remarriage. Jer. 3:1, however, repudiates any remarriage without specifying the grounds for the termination of either marriage. Westbrook is aware of the difficulty posed by Jeremiah 3 for his interpretation and so argues against the vast majority of scholars that Jeremiah 3 has no relation to the law in Deuteronomy 24 (*op. cit.*, 405, n. 66.).

[157] Cf. Chapter 2, §2.1 above for a discussion of Van der Woude's understanding of בְּרִית in the expression אֵשֶׁת בְּרִיתֶךָ as a reference to the "covenant community."

shift which can only be eliminated by emending the MT (which should be maintained as the *lectio difficilior*): "if *he* hates [her], then *you* divorce [her] [שַׁלַּח]!" Finally, we noted that this view is difficult to reconcile with the strenuous disapproval implied in 2:16b: "and he covers his garment with violence," and especially the warning, "So take heed to yourselves and do not be faithless."

Alternatively, perhaps the majority of interpreters have held that Mal. 2:16 condemns divorce unconditionally: "I hate divorce, says the Lord God of Israel...." On this view, however, Mal. 2:16 contradicts the lenient attitude toward divorce implied in Deut. 24:1-4. Given Malachi's indebtedness to the Deuteronomic perspective such a contradiction is troubling. In addition, this traditional interpretation of the text finds the form of שָׂנֵא difficult (generally requiring an emendation or the assumption of an ellipsis) and neglects a considerable body of evidence that "hate [שׂנא]," when occurring in the context of divorce, is a frequently specified attribute of one of the marriage partners. Finally, the traditional view struggles with וְכִסָּה and generally emends the form without textual support.

Accordingly, we prefer to maintain the MT and to interpret Mal. 2:16 as condemning only unjustified divorce, that is, divorce based on aversion: "If one hates and divorces, [i.e., if one divorces merely on the ground of aversion] says Yahweh, God of Israel, he covers his garment with violence [i.e., such a man visibly defiles himself with violence], says Yahweh of hosts. Therefore, take heed to yourselves and do not be faithless [against your wife]." This interpretation accepts the evidence of 4QXII[a] and the versions that כִּי is a conditional particle, favoured also by the fronted position of the כִּי-clause. With LXX[NABQV], however, it holds that the apodosis begins with וְכִסָּה, "then he covers...," rather than with שַׁלַּח, "divorces." Unrecognized by other commentators, the present view understands שַׁלַּח as an infinitive absolute functioning as a finite verb — hence, כִּי־שָׂנֵא שַׁלַּח offers an example of asyndeton: "If he hates and divorces...."[158]

Finally, far from contradicting Deut. 24:1-4, on the present view Mal. 2:16 shares the same assessment of divorce based on aversion as seems to be presupposed for the second divorce in Deut. 24:3, with its adverse financial consequences for the offending husband (§5 above). While Malachi says nothing to imply that such divorces were illegal, he condemns divorce based on aversion as ethically reprehensible and as an instance of infidelity [בגד], or covenant breaking (cf. 2:14), susceptible to divine judgment: "Therefore, take heed to yourselves!" Such a perspective offers significant support for the identification of literal marriage as a covenant in 2:14.

---

[158] For this asyndetic construction, cf. Chapter 3, §4.2.2 and §4.2.3 above. Alternatively, if שָׂנֵא is identified as an otherwise unattested verbal adjective, and hence the equivalent of a participle, the MT may be rendered without significant difference in meaning: "if one who hates divorces..., then he covers...." Cf. GKC §50b and Waltke and O'Connor §37.1b.

CHAPTER FOUR

MALACHI 2:10-16 AND THE TOLERATION OF POLYGYNY
ELSEWHERE IN THE OLD TESTAMENT

We turn now to consider the primary argument of C. C. Torrey against the traditional interpretation of Mal. 2:10-16, which finds in this text a condemnation of literal interfaith marriage and divorce. Writes Torrey, "To assume, in the first place, that divorce of Israelitish wives stood in any necessary or even probable connection with the wedding of women from other nations is ridiculous. Jews occasionally married gentiles, not because they were dissatisfied with their own countrywomen, or with their religion, but because they found some of the gentile women attractive."[1] More recently, A. Isaksson has argued in similar terms, "it could not have been necessary for a Jew at this period to divorce his Jewish wife in order to marry a woman belonging to another people and another religion...."[2]

What is at issue in these observations is the apparent implication of Mal. 2:10-16 that polygyny, in spite of its assumed toleration elsewhere in the Old Testament, was no longer an option for Malachi's contemporaries. It is important to realize that this rejection of polygyny, if it is so, was the conviction not only of the prophet, who may have held an idiosyncratic view, but also apparently of the very men Malachi was condemning. The divorce of their Jewish wives was seemingly a necessary prelude to (or a consequence of) the mixed marriages into which these men had entered.

We have already rejected the alternative interpretation which Torrey and Isaksson propose for Mal. 2:10-16, an interpretation which avoids the alleged difficulty by arguing for a figurative reference in the text. It remains for the present chapter to support a reference to literal marriage and divorce by attempting to resolve this apparent contradiction between Mal. 2:10-16 and the assumed toleration of polygyny elsewhere in the Old Testament. Among scholars who support a reference to literal marriage in Malachi, there are five main alternative approaches to resolve this apparent contradiction, each of which we shall consider in turn:

1) Mal. 2:10-16 originally condemned only divorce and therefore carries no implication regarding the practice of polygyny (the majority view among modern critical scholars).

---

[1] "The Prophecy of 'Malachi'," 9.
[2] *Marriage and Ministry in the New Temple*, 30.

2) Mal. 2:10-16 originally condemned only mixed marriage and therefore is not only consistent with the practice of polygyny, but presupposes it (A. S. van der Woude).

3) Mal. 2:10-16 condemns both mixed marriage and divorce in a manner which suggests that these were typically interrelated acts. The divorces in question, however, refer to Ezra's enforced dissolution of mixed marriages in Ezra 9-10, and so the text carries no implication regarding the practice of polygyny (G. H. A. von Ewald, H. H. Spoer, L. Kruse-Blinkenberg, J. J. Collins, and M. Smith).

4) Mal. 2:10-16 condemns both mixed marriage and divorce, but these offences bear no necessary causal relationship to each other. Accordingly, once again, the text carries no particular implication regarding the practice of polygyny (J. Wellhausen and others — perhaps the most convincing view).

5) Mal. 2:10-16 condemns both mixed marriage and divorce in a manner which suggests that these were typically interrelated, with the implication that resort to polygyny under such a circumstance was exceptional, discountenanced, or possibly even illegal in Malachi's day (the traditional view).

Since this traditional view remains possible, it will be necessary to digress in order to examine the widely assumed toleration of polygyny elsewhere in the Old Testament and particularly in the post-exilic period. From this examination it will be concluded that although polygyny was never illegal, monogamy was seen as the marital ideal, particularly in the post-exilic period, and that actual marital practice was monogamous with few exceptions. As a consequence, there is no compelling reason for denying a reference to literal marriage and divorce in Malachi 2 or, more particularly, for denying the identification of literal marriage as a "covenant" in 2:14.

1. MALACHI 2:10-16 ORIGINALLY CONDEMNED ONLY DIVORCE AND THEREFORE CARRIES NO IMPLICATION REGARDING THE PRACTICE OF POLYGYNY (THE MAJORITY CRITICAL VIEW)

Supposing a rejection of polygyny to have been unlikely in post-exilic times, perhaps the majority of modern critical scholars have resolved the seeming rejection of polygyny in Malachi's day by their conclusion that Mal. 2:11f. is unoriginal to the text.[3] In other words, according to this approach, Malachi originally attacked only the practice of divorce, not mixed marriage.

---

[3] So, inter alia, G.A. Smith, The Book of the Twelve Prophets (1899) 340, 363-65; K. Marti, Das Dodekapropheton (1904) 469; E. Sievers, Alttestamentliche Miscellen, 4, Zu Maleachi (1905); W. Nowack, Die kleinen Propheten (1922) 404, 418f.; E. Sellin, Das Zwölfprophetenbuch (1922); K. Elliger, Das Buch der zwölf kleinen Propheten (1950) 189, 193; R. Rendtorff, "Maleachi," RGG[3], IV, col. 629; R.A. Mason, The Books of Haggai, Zechariah, and Malachi (1977) 149; A. Renker, Die Tora bei Maleachi (1979) 90; and R. Vuilleumier, Malachie (1981) 237, 240f.

There are minor differences among scholars as to whether to include vss. 10, 11a, or 13a in the proposed interpolation. So, e.g., R. Vuilleumier considers only 11b-12 to be

Although G. A. Smith maintained the traditional view that foreign marriages in fact had led to the frequent divorces which Malachi condemns, Smith's interpretation prepared for the modern critical consensus by arguing that vss. 11-12 may have been dislocated, or more probably were a later addition.[4] He offers four arguments for considering vss. 11 and 12 to be secondary:

1) Vss. 11 and 12 do not cohere with vs. 10. In vs. 10 the prophet chides his brethren for being faithless to each other, but vss. 11 and 12 "do not give an instance of this: they describe the marriages with the heathen women of the land, which is not a proof of faithlessness between Israelites."[5]

2) If vss. 13-16 are allowed to follow immediately upon vs. 10, they make perfect sense as they offer the expected example of faithlessness between Israelites which is condemned in vs. 10.[6]

3) Vss. 11 and 12 "lack the characteristic mark of all the other oracles of the book: they do not state a general charge against the people, and then introduce the people's question as to the particulars of the charge."[7] In other words, the expected retort of the people, "but you say," occurs not in vs. 11, where it might have been expected, but in vs. 14.[8]

4) One can readily account for how vss. 11 and 12 may have been intruded in the text "when the question of heathen marriages came to the front with Ezra and Nehemiah."[9]

To these arguments of Smith, the following additional arguments have been advanced by others:

5) The criticism of mixed marriage in vs. 11 contradicts the universalism which is characteristic of other portions of Malachi's prophecy (e.g., Mal. 1:11, and perhaps 2:10).[10]

6) The change from the first person in vs. 10 to the third person in these verses is abrupt and so supports the recognition of these verses as secondary.[11]

---

secondary, while K. Elliger prefers 11b-13a. A. van Hoonacker, on the other hand, considers all of vss. 10-12 to be secondary.

[4] *The Book of the Twelve Prophets* (1899) 340, 363-65.

[5] So G.A. Smith, *The Book of the Twelve Prophets* (1899) 340. Cf. also p. 363, where Smith writes, "Certain verses, 11-13a, ... disturb the argument by bringing in the marriages with heathen women...."

This objection is summarized by J.M.P. Smith, "their interest is not in ethics as in v. 10, but in cultus" (*Malachi*, 57).

[6] So also, *inter alia*, R.A. Mason, *The Books of Haggai, Zechariah, and Malachi*, 149.

[7] G.A. Smith, *The Book of the Twelve Prophets* (1899) 340.

[8] So notes R.L. Smith without necessarily agreeing that vss. 11-13b are secondary (*Micah-Malachi*, 320)

[9] G.A. Smith, *The Book of the Twelve Prophets* (1899) 340. Cf. also E. Sellin, *Das Zwölfprophetenbuch*, 551; J. Morgenstern, "Jerusalem - 485 B.C." (1957) 21; and E. Lipiński, "Malachi," *EJ*, 11, col. 814.

[10] So, e.g., E. Sellin, *Das Zwölfprophetenbuch*, 551.

[11] R.A. Mason, *The Books of Haggai, Zechariah, and Malachi*, 149.

7) The descriptive and prosaic character of these verses does not fit Malachi's style elsewhere.[12]

8) Although A. S. van der Woude considers vs. 11 to be original, with respect to vs. 12 he writes, "The metre, the wording and the contents of the verse strongly suggest that it is a gloss."[13] More specifically regarding the contents of the verse, Van der Woude explains, "the curse clashes with the call on the audience of the prophet to heed to their spirit and not to be unfaithful."[14]

9) O. Eissfeldt notes "the removal of these words which condemn the marriage of foreign women, would give a more general character to the reproach made to the people in ii, 10-16, since divorce then would be absolutely condemned here, and not just divorce occasioned by a desire for a foreign wife."[15]

10) Finally, perhaps the most important argument for the secondary character of vss. 11-12 is that the proposed deletion would resolve the problem of an apparent rejection of the option of polygyny.[16]

The following answers may be offered in response to this approach:

1) Contrary to G. A. Smith, vss. 11 and 12 are organically related to vs. 10.[17] First, this unity is evident because they are directed to the same general audience. While 2:1-9 is quite explicitly and narrowly directed against the priests, vs. 10 broadens this perspective to include all Israel: "Have we not all one father? Has not one God created us? Why then are we faithless to one another, profaning the covenant of our fathers?"[18] Vss. 11 and 12 share this same broad perspective, naming Judah as the one who has been faithless, Israel and Jerusalem as the locale of her abomination, and "the tents of Jacob" as the dwelling from which offenders are to be cut off.[19]

---

[12] E. Sellin, *Das Zwölfprophetenbuch*, 551; K. Elliger, *Das Buch der zwölf kleinen Propheten*, 189; G.J. Botterweck, "Schelt- und Mahnrede gegen Mischehe und Ehescheidung. Auslegung von Malachias 2, 10-16" (1960) 181; and A. Renker, *Die Tora bei Maleachi*, 73.

[13] "Malachi's Struggle for a Pure Community," 68.

[14] *Ibid.*, 68, n. 17. In a similar manner, R.A. Mason notes that "the separateness of verses 11-12 is further shown by the finality of the concluding curse in verse 12" (*The Books of Haggai, Zechariah, and Malachi*, 149).

[15] *The Old Testament: An Introduction*, 442.

[16] Cf., e.g., K. Marti, *Das Dodekapropheton*, 469; and A.S. van der Woude, "Malachi's Struggle for a Pure Community," 66. A.S. van der Woude unaccountably cites G.A. Smith and E. Sellin in support of this argument (*op. cit.*, 66, n. 6).

[17] Recognizing this difficulty, A. van Hoonacker has argued that vs. 10 is also secondary, along with vss. 11 and 12 (*Les douze petits prophètes* [1908] 721ff.). Other scholars, however, have not followed Van Hoonacker in this suggestion.

[18] The MT pointing here of a Niphal, בָּגַדְנוּ, a conjugation otherwise unattested for this verb, may have been motivated by a misguided scribal concern to protect Malachi from including himself among the offenders.

[19] G.S. Ogden argues that the priests continue to be the assumed audience of 2:10-16 ("The Use of Figurative Language in Malachi 2:10-16" [1988] 223-230). Ogden, however, fails to take account of the overall literary structure of Malachi, which distinguishes the disputation in 2:10-16 from what precedes. Furthermore, Ogden's assumption that "Judah" in 2:11 is intended as a figurative reference to the priesthood appears unconvincing.

Second, vss. 11 and 12 are further related to vs. 10 in terms of shared vocabulary. In particular, vs. 11 begins with "be faithless [בָּגְדָה]," a verb and concept which not only appears in vs. 10, but also turns out to be a unifying element for the whole of 2:10-16 (forms of בגד are found in Mal. 2:10, 11, 14, 15, 16, but nowhere else in this book). In addition, the verb "profane [חלל]" is employed in both vs. 10 and vs. 11; elsewhere within Malachi it is found only in 1:12. Finally, contrary to Smith, vss. 11 and 12 do "cohere with verse 10" since it is plausible that the prophet would have considered these interfaith marriages to constitute a breach of faith between fellow-Israelites [וּבְנֵד אִישׁ בְּאָחִיו], profaning the covenant of their fathers [לְחַלֵּל בְּרִית אֲבֹתֵינוּ].[20]

Of course, if these interfaith marriages precipitated the divorce of Jewish wives, it would be especially clear that they entailed a breach of faith [בגד] against fellow-Israelites. Even apart from the issue of divorce, Ezra and Nehemiah offer ample testimony to the post-exilic conviction that interfaith marriage put the entire covenant community at risk of the wrath of God; as such this sin necessarily constituted a breach of faith against fellow-Israelites. This notion of a profound corporate responsibility for these prohibited marriages is clear in Ezra's response in 9:3-15, particularly in his use of the first person plural pronoun. Compare also, for example, Ezra 10:10 and Neh. 13:29.

As to whether Malachi would have viewed interfaith marriage as an example of "profaning the covenant of our fathers [לְחַלֵּל בְּרִית אֲבֹתֵינוּ]," it is not certain whether "the covenant of our fathers" refers to the covenant with the patriarchs (as perhaps in Deut. 4:31; 7:12-14; 8:18), or to the covenant at Sinai (as in 2 Kgs. 17:15 and Jer. 4:13), or comprehensively to both.[21] For the present argument it is not necessary to decide the matter since on either interpretation it appears likely that interfaith marriage could be characterized as an instance of covenant profaning or breaking. If a reference to the patriarchs is preferred in 2:10, then intermarriage was implicitly prohibited by the covenant promise of the dispossession of the Canaanites (cf. especially Gen. 24:7) and explicitly opposed in a number of texts associated with the patriarchs (cf. Gen. 24:2-4; 26:34-35; 27:46; 34; and especially 31:50).[22]

---

[20] It should be noted that vs. 10 does not teach that the infidelity and profaning are separate (coordinate) failings. To "profane the covenant" is to break faith with fellow members of the covenant community. ל used with the infinitive construct here is either explanatory, "Why then are we faithless... by profaning the covenant...," or it expresses a result, "Why then are we faithless ... with the result of profaning the covenant...." Cf. Waltke and O'Connor §36.2.3.d and e.

[21] S.L. McKenzie and H.N. Wallace prefer a reference to the patriarchal covenant, based on the references to Jacob (1:2-5), Levi (2:1-9), and perhaps Abraham (2:15) ("Covenant Themes in Malachi," 552). Alternatively, they suggest the reference is intentionally ambiguous because Malachi regarded the Sinaitic covenant and the patriarchal covenants "as standing in continuity with the original covenant of election."

[22] J. Van Seters considers the emphasis on racial purity inherent in the Abrahamic covenant and texts like Gen. 24:7 (which prohibits intermarriage with Canaanites) to reflect exilic and post-exilic concerns (*Abraham in History and Tradition* [1975] 272ff.).

B. Glazier-McDonald, however, challenges Van Seters' emphasis on racial purity to the neglect of the issues of apostasy and syncretism (*Malachi*, 86-88). Glazier-McDonald cites G.W. Ahlström in support of the notion that the threat of apostasy and syncretism remained

Alternatively, as is perhaps more probable in view of Malachi's use of "fathers" in 3:7, if the reference in 2:10 is to the Exodus generation, then interfaith marriage was explicitly prohibited by the stipulations of the Sinaitic covenant (cf. Exod. 34:12-16; Num. 25:1ff.; Deut. 7:3f.).[23]

Further supporting the coherence of 2:11f. with 2:10, it is notable that Ezra specifically relates interfaith marriage to the transgression of God's commandments (e.g., 9:10f., 14) and to breaking faith [מעל] with God (9:2, 4; 10:2, 10). Likewise, Nehemiah explicitly recalls the critical failure of Israel's idolatrous sexual alliance with Moab, when Israel yoked herself with the Baal of Peor (Numbers 25), as well as Solomon's sinful interfaith marriages (13:1ff., 26ff.).[24] Finally, Nehemiah decries interfaith marriage in a manner which closely parallels Mal. 2:10ff., thus supporting its unity: "... they have defiled the priesthood and the covenant of the priesthood and the Levites [עַל גָּאֳלֵי הַכְּהֻנָּה וּבְרִית הַכְּהֻנָּה וְהַלְוִיִּם]" (Neh. 13:29).[25]

2) If a section of text, such as vss. 11-12, can be removed without disrupting the flow of a narrative or argument, this may indicate that the portion is secondary, but it hardly requires this conclusion. As has often been observed, the criterion of excisability is notoriously precarious as a means for determining the originality of a work. This is especially true with biblical and ancient Near Eastern texts, which are fond of such literary techniques as repetition, digression, layering, etc. As a matter of fact, removal of vss. 11 and 12 does not leave a coherent result without radical philological emendation or outright deletion of vs. 13a, "and this again you do [וְזֹאת שֵׁנִית תַּעֲשׂוּ]." The suggested philological emendation of R. Althann, who renders vs. 13a, "Even indignity, gnashing of teeth you perform," does not commend itself.[26] The alternative expedient of deletion, although widely accepted, offends the principle of parsimony and is not favoured by 4QXII[a] or the versional evidence.[27]

---

issues in the exilic and post-exilic periods (G.W. Ahlström, *Joel and the Temple Cult of Jerusalem*, 27).

[23] Further supporting a reference to the Exodus generation, it has been argued that the designation of God in 2:10 as our "father" (cf. Mal. 1:6) and as the one who "created us" probably alludes to the formation of Israel as a people at Sinai (cf. Deut. 32:6; Isa. 43:1, 15; 44:7; 63:16; 64:8; etc.). So, e.g., E. Sellin, *Das Zwölfprophetenbuch*, 551; A.S. van der Woude, "Malachi's Struggle for a Pure Community," 67; and P.A. Verhoef, *The Books of Haggai and Malachi*, 265f.; as against, *inter alia*, J. Wellhausen, *Skizzen und Vorarbeiten* (1892) 198; and W. Nowack, *Die kleinen Propheten* (1922) 417f.

[24] Cf. discussion of Ezra 9:10f. in H.G.M. Williamson, *Ezra, Nehemiah*, 137.

[25] H.G.M. Williamson would prefer to relate Nehemiah's statement to Mal. 2:4-8, where the covenant of Levi is explicitly mentioned (*Ezra, Nehemiah*, 401). To be sure, the perspective of this passage does offer some parallel to that found in Nehemiah. Nevertheless, it is only in Mal. 2:10ff. that the problem of interfaith marriage is treated.

[26] "Malachy 2, 13-14 and UT 125, 12-13" (1977) 418-19.

[27] In support of deleting 13a, cf., *inter alia*, G.A. Smith, *The Book of the Twelve Prophets* (1899) 340; K. Marti, *Das Dodekapropheton* (1904) 470; and W. Nowack, *Die kleinen Propheten* (1922) 419.

Against the proposal to delete שֵׁנִית in Mal. 2:13 on the basis of the LXX, cf. A.S. van der Woude, "Malachi's Struggle for a Pure Community," 68, n. 19. The LXX, ἃ ἐμίσουν,

3) G. A. Smith's observation that vss. 11 and 12 do not include the expected prophetic charge and the anticipated retort of the people at first seems plausible. Each of the other disputations of Malachi (1:2-5; 1:6-2:9; 2:17-3:5; 3:6-12; 3:13-21 [ET 4:3]) is introduced by an assertion made by Yahweh or by the prophet. In each case this assertion is closely followed by the anticipated retort of the people, "but you say [וַאֲמַרְתֶּם]...."

Smith's observation fails for two reasons, however. First, if Smith is correct about the uniform structure of each of Malachi's disputations, then the logic of his objection ought to require him to delete not only vss. 11 and 12, but also vs. 10. This is so because the assertion, "... he no longer regards the offering or accepts it with favour at your hand," and the retort, "But you say, 'Why does he not?'," found in vss. 13 and 14 have no direct relation to the opening rhetorical questions in vs. 10. Nevertheless, neither Smith nor the majority of modern scholars has favoured this proposal because of the evident authenticity of that verse (supported in terms of vocabulary, style, and viewpoint).[28]

Second, the literary structure of Malachi is not so rigid as would prohibit an elaboration of the charge before the retort, as is found in the canonical text of 2:10-16. This variety in the structure of the various pericopes of Malachi is most evident simply in terms of length. While the length of each of the other disputations ranges between four verses and nine verses, the second disputation, 1:6-2:9, includes eighteen verses, twice the length of any other pericope, yet the originality of the whole of this disputation has never been seriously challenged.[29] Another evidence for variety in the literary structure of the disputations is the observation that in three of these, 1:6-2:9, 3:6-12, and 3:13-21 [ET 4:3], there are actually two distinct retorts, each introduced by the key word אֲמַרְתֶּם(ו), "(but) you say." In general, critical scholarship has accepted each of these as original.[30] Finally, it should be noted that two of the disputations, 1:6-2:9 and 3:6-12, closely resemble the structure of 2:10-16 without the proposed deletion of vss. 11 and 12. This is so because in each of these sections the retort of the people is not made in response to the *initial* assertion of Yahweh or his prophet. Rather, there is a significant development in the opening assertion (in the case of 2:10-16, extending over four verses), and in each case the retort is directed only against the *last* point in the discourse.

4) While the concern of Ezra and Nehemiah with mixed marriage might account for some later editorial insertion of a reference to this problem in the present text of Malachi, it hardly requires this conclusion. This

---

supports the consonantal text of the MT although it apparently read שָׂנֵתִי, "which I hate" (perhaps under the influence of 2:16), rather than שֵׁנִית, "second."

[28] On the other hand, cf. A. van Hoonacker, who argues against the originality of vs. 10 (*Les douze petits prophètes* [1908] 721ff.).

[29] 1:2-5 has but four verses; 1:6-2:9 has eighteen verses; 2:10-16 has seven verses; 2:17-3:5 has six verses; 3:6-12 has seven verses; 3:13-21[ET 4:3] has nine verses.

[30] Cf. *BHS* on 3:7, however.

supposition of a later interpolation would be greatly helped, of course, if it could be shown that Malachi was written long before Ezra and Nehemiah (as was argued, e.g., by A. C. Welch, who considered Malachi to be a contemporary of Haggai and Zechariah, cir. 520 B.C.[31]). Such an early date for Malachi appears unlikely and has been all but abandoned among modern scholars. Curiously, G. A. Smith himself argues for a period contemporaneous with Ezra and Nehemiah, offering as evidence the mention of mixed marriages in Malachi![32] If Malachi can be dated on other grounds to a period nearly contemporaneous with Ezra and Nehemiah, as it appears it can, it would be quite surprising if there were no reference to this problem, given the overlap of Malachi's concerns with those of Ezra and Nehemiah (e.g., tithes, sacrifice, priesthood, the law of Moses) and especially given his intention to treat the subject of marriage.[33]

5) The alleged contradiction between the universalism of 1:11-14 and the parochialism of 2:12f. need not require the conclusion that 2:12f. is secondary. Indeed, A. S. van der Woude draws the very opposite conclusion; he argues that Mal. 1:11-14 is the later addition,[34] but this too is unnecessary. As was argued in Chapter 2 above, Malachi's "universalism" has been grossly distorted if it is imagined by modern scholars to have been in any way congenial to idolatry.[35] Further, as was discussed earlier, the "parochialism" of 2:12, 13 has nothing to do with racism or nationalism. Rather, the concern here is emphatically religious as is suggested by the unusual reference to "daughter of a foreign god."[36] R. A. Mason explains, "They are foreigners who, unlike Ruth the Moabitess, refused to become worshippers of Yahweh."[37]

6) The observation concerning the change in person from vs. 10 (first person plural) to vss. 11 and 12 (third masculine singular) may make too much of what appears as a natural transition. The first person plural is entirely appropriate in the rhetorical questions of vs. 10, but would seem less fitting in the specific charge levelled in vss. 11 and 12, unless Malachi himself had been guilty of an interfaith marriage. It should be noted that while the grammatical reference of the verbs does change from vs. 10 to vss. 11 and 12, there is a consistency of reference between these verses in the way they represent the prophet's direct discourse: God or Yahweh is maintained in

---

[31] *Post-Exilic Judaism* (1935) 113-25. Cf. the discussion of Welch's views in R.L. Smith, *Micah - Malachi*, 298f.

[32] *The Book of the Twelve Prophets*, 334f.

[33] On the dating of Malachi, cf. our discussion in Chapter 1, §1.

[34] "Malachi's Struggle for a Pure Community," 66, citing in support K. Elliger, F. Horst, and R. Rendtorff, "Maleachibuch," as well as his own commentary, *Haggai, Maleachi*.

[35] Cf. also P.A. Verhoef, "Some Notes on Malachi 1:11" (1967); J.G. Baldwin, "Malachi 1:11 and the worship of the nations in the Old Testament" (1972) 117-24; and T.C. Vriezen, "How to Understand Malachi 1:11" (1975) 128-136.

[36] Cf., e.g., C.F. Keil, *The Twelve Minor Prophets*, 449; and R.A. Mason, *The Books of Haggai, Zechariah, and Malachi*, 150.

[37] Cf. the similar assessment of 2:11, 12 offered by, e.g., J.G. Baldwin, *Haggai, Zechariah, Malachi*, 238; and W.C. Kaiser Jr., *Malachi*, 68.

the third person. In any case, Hebrew is well-known to tolerate fluctuations in personal reference to a degree which would be unacceptable for English, and Malachi elsewhere offers numerous examples of this phenomenon.[38] Compare, for example, Mal. 1:7, 9; 2:3, 10, 15;[39] 3:1, 5, 18, and 23 [ET 4:5]. It is doubtful that all of these examples are secondary or stand in need of emendation, and the prevalence of this practice should caution one against a too hasty rejection of vss. 11 and 12. Furthermore, the proposed deletion of vss. 11 and 12 would not, in fact, eliminate the "problem" of altered personal reference from the first person plural forms of vs. 10, since vs. 13 switches to the second person masculine plural.

7) The suggestion that the descriptive and prosaic character of vss. 11 and 12 does not fit Malachi's style elsewhere is amply refuted by a passage such as Mal. 3:16 (of undoubted authenticity), as A. S. van der Woude has argued.[40]

8) Van der Woude's objection that the curse in vs. 12 does not fit the "metre" of Malachi can be dismissed partly based on the fact that too little is known regarding metre, particularly in late Biblical Hebrew, and also based on the likelihood that, while Malachi is characterized by elevated prose exhibiting a number of poetic features, it is not poetry.[41]

As for the supposed discrepant "wording" of this curse, there should be no particular difficulty with the expression, "and brings an offering to the LORD of hosts [וּמַגִּישׁ מִנְחָה לַיהוָה צְבָאוֹת]," based on the close parallel found in Mal. 1:11. Nor should there be any objection to Malachi's use of the proper nouns "Jacob [יַעֲקֹב]" or "Yahweh [יהוה]," well attested elsewhere in Malachi, nor to any of the elements of the expression, "to the man who does this [לָאִישׁ אֲשֶׁר יַעֲשֶׂנָּה]."[42] All that is left of vs. 12 is the initial יַכְרֵת, "May [Yahweh] cut off," and the admitted crux עֵר וְעֹנֶה מֵאָהֳלֵי, "the one who arouses[?] and the

---

[38] Cf., e.g., GKC §144p and the examples of heterosis of person and number offered by E.W. Bullinger, *Figures of Speech Used in the Bible*, 524f. R. Yaron makes a similar observation with respect to Akkadian; he notes that abrupt changes of person in the LE may offend our *Sprachgefühl*, but, apparently, did not so affect the ancient speaker (*The Laws of Eshnunna*, 2nd ed. [1988] 284).

[39] The clause, "Let none be faithless to the wife of *your* youth," is a parade example of the fluidity of personal reference permissible in Hebrew even within a sentence. Cf. also S. Schreiner, "Mischehen-Ehebruch-Ehescheidung," 213; and A.S. van der Woude, "Malachi's Struggle for a Pure Community," 70, n. 30. Van der Woude finds similar examples in Isa. 1:29 and Ps. 49:20.

[40] "Malachi's Struggle for a Pure Community," 66. On the lack of scholarly agreement concerning the prosody of Malachi, see below.

[41] Cf. J.M.P. Smith, *Malachi*, 4f.; and P.A. Verhoef, *The Books of Haggai and Malachi*, 166. So also the RSV, NEB, and most English commentators and translations. A contrary opinion is expressed by a number of German scholars, including K. Marti, E. Sievers, W. Nowack, and W. Rudolph, who have been joined in their opinion most recently by R.L. Smith, *Micah-Malachi*, 301.

[42] The other examples of יַעֲקֹב are found in Mal. 1:2 and 3:6. Apart from the two in 2:12, there are thirty-nine other examples of the tetragrammaton יהוה (Mal. 1:1, 2 [*bis*], 4 [*bis*], 5, 6, 7, etc.) Excluding 2:12, the verb עשה appears seven times (Mal. 2:13, 15, 17; 3:15, 17, 19 [ET 4:1], 21 [ET 4:3]); the noun אִישׁ three times (Mal. 2:10; 3:16, 17); and the relative particle אֲשֶׁר ten times (Mal. 1:4; 2:9, 11, 14; 3:1 [*bis*], 17, 18, 19 [ET 4:1], 21 [ET 4:3]).

one who answers[?] from the tents of."[43] Given the observation that every
other word in this verse is entirely at home within Malachi, it would appear
unwarranted to judge the wording of this curse unlikely for Malachi. This is
so not only because of the uncertainty of the meaning of עֵר וְעֹנֶה מֵאָהֳלֵי, but
also because of the extremely limited corpus of Malachi's undisputed
writings by which one is to judge his customary manner of expressing
curses.[44]

Finally, Van der Woude's explanation that "the curse clashes with the
call on the audience of the prophet to heed to their spirit and not to be
unfaithful" lacks cogency. Not only is the Bible replete with examples of
curses used as dire warnings, but also the prophets provide a number of apt
parallels where imprecation based on past sin is followed by an urgent appeal
to repentance (cf., e.g. Jer. 17:5-21; 11:3ff.).[45] Indeed, a particularly striking
parallel for this exact phenomenon can be found elsewhere in Malachi itself,
namely in 1:14ff. In this text Malachi prays a curse against those who offer
blemished sacrifices, but then Yahweh proceeds to warn the priests that they
will indeed be cursed, if they will not "take it to heart" to give glory to his
name.

9) In response to O. Eissfeldt, who wants to remove vss. 11 and 12 so
that "divorce then would be absolutely condemned here [in 2:16], and not just
divorce occasioned by a desire for a foreign wife," just such a limitation
makes sense of 2:16, as we have argued above in Chapter 3, §4. The
unconditional prohibition of divorce, which Eissfeldt would wish for 2:16,
would place that verse in intolerable and unnecessary tension with the
testimony of the rest of the Old Testament concerning the practice of divorce
(including Deut. 24:1-4).[46]

10) Finally, it is notable that the interests and perspective, if not
vocabulary, of Mal. 2:10-16 find significant parallels in Neh. 13:23-29, a fact
which tells against the proposed deletion of vss. 11-12. Nehemiah's
emphasis on the unholy children born of interfaith marriage in 13:24 recalls
by contrast the "godly seed [זֶרַע אֱלֹהִים]" of Mal. 2:15, however the rest of
this problematic verse is to be rendered. Nehemiah's use of cursing in 13:25,
29 and his remedy of excommunication in 13:28 invite a comparison with
Mal. 2:12, where Malachi's curse implies excommunication. Lastly, as

---

[43] For yet another, not entirely convincing, attempt to interpret this expression, cf. B.
Glazier-McDonald, "Malachi 2:12: 'ēr we'ōneh - Another Look" (1986) 295-298. R. Fuller
notes that 4QXII[a] reads וענה עד, "witness and respondent [perhaps one who speaks in
defence of the accused]," which would support J. Wellhausen's proposed emendation of the
MT (R. Fuller, "Text-Critical Problems in Malachi 2:10-16," *JBL* 110 [1991] 47-57).

[44] Without implying agreement with their methodology, it may be noted that Y.T.
Radday and M.A. Pollatschek consider Malachi 1 and 2 to exhibit a coherency of
vocabulary throughout ("Vocabulary Richness in Post-Exilic Prophetic Books" [1980] 333-
46).

[45] For curses used as dire warnings, cf. Gen. 17:14; Exod. 12:15; etc.

[46] J.M.P. Smith makes the further suggestion that had divorce alone been in view in
2:10-16, rather than the additional offence of mixed marriage, one might expect some term
designating the wronged women in vs. 10 in place of the mentioned "brothers" (*Malachi*,
48).

mentioned above, Nehemiah's description of the dire consequences of "the
Jews who had married women of Ashdod, Ammon, and Moab" seems to echo
the indictment of Mal. 2:10-11. Nehemiah asserts: "... they have defiled the
priesthood and the covenant of the priesthood and the Levites [עַל גָּאֳלֵי הַכְּהֻנָּה
וּבְרִית הַכְּהֻנָּה וְהַלְוִיִּם]" (Neh. 13:29).

We conclude, then, that there are no compelling literary-critical
arguments for regarding Mal. 2:11 and 12 as secondary; indeed, the evidence
supports their originality. The only remaining reason for considering these
verses to be secondary is their supposed conflict with the alleged tolerance of
polygyny elsewhere in the Old Testament. This prompts us to examine other
exegetical options to determine if Mal. 2:10-16 really does disparage or reject
polygyny and then to examine the remainder of the Old Testament to
determine if it does, by contrast, approve polygyny.

2. MALACHI 2:10-16 ORIGINALLY CONDEMNED ONLY MIXED MARRIAGE AND THEREFORE IS NOT ONLY CONSISTENT WITH THE PRACTICE OF POLYGYNY, BUT PRESUPPOSES IT (A. S. VAN DER WOUDE)

Agreeing with scholars who claim "that in a community that permitted
polygamy, contracting a new marriage with a foreign woman has in principle
nothing to do with divorce," A. S. van der Woude has argued that Mal. 2:10-
16 makes no reference to divorce.[47] Rather, according to Van der Woude, the
concern of 2:16 is to attack "the subordination and maltreatment of married
Jewish women because of [polygamous marriages with] foreign heathen
wives."[48]

Although this approach succeeds in eliminating the assumed failure of
Malachi to reckon with polygyny and, accordingly, allows a reference to
literal marriage throughout 2:10-16, Van der Woude's translation of 2:16 is
unconvincing: "For he who neglects (his Jewish wife) puts forth his hand (in
hostility), says Yahweh the God of Israel, and covers his garment with
violence, says Yahweh Almighty...."[49] See our criticism of Van der Woude's
view in the previous chapter (Chapter 3, §1.3). Here we simply add that our
objections to Van der Woude's treatment of vs. 16 are made even more
compelling by the evidence provided by R. Westbrook and others regarding
the widespread use of "hate" [whether Hebrew or Aramaic שׂנא or Akkadian
zērum] in connection with divorce.[50] Furthermore, as will be discussed in §6

---

[47] A.S. van der Woude, "Malachi's Struggle for a Pure Community" (1986) 66.
[48] *Ibid.*, 71.
[49] *Haggai, Maleachi*, 116: "Immers, wie (zijn vrouw) achterstelt, strekt zijn hand uit
(ten onheil), spreekt YHWH, de God van Israël, en bedekt zijn gewaad met onrecht, spreekt
YHWH almachtig...."
[50] "The Prohibition on Restoration of Marriage in Deuteronomy 24:1-4," 399-402. Cf.
also D. Daube, "Terms for Divorce," (1973) 366. This evidence was discussed in detail in
Chapter 3 above.

below, it is far from evident that polygyny was as prevalent among post-exilic Jews as Van der Woude supposes.

3. MALACHI 2:10-16 CONDEMNS EZRA'S ENFORCED DISSOLUTION OF MIXED MARRIAGES IN EZRA 9-10 AND SO CARRIES NO IMPLICATION REGARDING THE PRACTICE OF POLYGYNY (G. H. A. VON EWALD, H. H. SPOER, L. KRUSE-BLINKENBERG, J. J. COLLINS, AND M. SMITH)

In contrast to those who argue that Mal. 2:10-16 originally opposed only divorce, but also in contrast to Van der Woude who argues that Mal. 2:10-16 opposes only mixed marriage, each of the three views remaining for our consideration concedes that Malachi opposed both mixed marriage and divorce. The first of these is represented by L. Kruse-Blinkenberg, who in his influential study of the Peshitta of Malachi renewed a suggestion made earlier by G. H. A. von Ewald and H. H. Spoer that the "I hate divorce" of Mal. 2:16 may have been intended to oppose the dissolution of marriages recorded in Ezra 9-10.[51]

Offering more argumentation, J. J. Collins similarly observes, "Many scholars have assumed that Malachi supported Ezra's reform, but that view is difficult to reconcile with Mal. 2:13-16, which unequivocally rejects divorce as itself a breach of covenant."[52] In support, Collins notes: "There is nothing to suggest that Malachi opposes only the divorce of Jewish wives, nor is there any reason to believe that the Jews who married foreign women had divorced the wives of their youth. Malachi's objection is to divorce as such."[53] In addition, Collins considers that the unqualified rejection of divorce in Mal. 2:16 amply refutes those scholars who speculate that Malachi may have helped prepare for Ezra's reform. The weeping at the altar suggests that an attempted reform had already taken place, presumably the one which was led by Ezra. In other words, it is possible that those who had complied with Ezra's mandate and had divorced their wives were now perplexed as to why Yahweh still did not accept their offerings. If this evidence is accepted, then not only did Malachi fail to pave the way for Ezra's work, it must be assumed that he condemned it. Finally, as argued by Collins, if certain of these intermarriages led to idolatry, this would constitute an abomination, but it is not a necessary consequence of intermarriage as such. Malachi's starting point, that we all have one Father, demonstrates his fundamental openness to

---

[51] "The Pesitta [sic] of the Book of Malachi" (1966) 95-119, cf. esp. 103-104. Although not cited by Kruse-Blinkenberg, the same suggestion was made earlier by G.H.A. von Ewald, *Commentary on the Prophets of the Old Testament, Vol. 5* (1881) 79f., and by H.H. Spoer, "Some New Considerations towards the Dating of the Book of Malachi" (1908) 179f. — the latter as part of his argument for a second century date for Malachi.

Cf. also M. Smith, who considers Malachi to be the work of a "segregationist" prophesying before Ezra, but 2:16 to be a later interpolation into the text by an "assimilationist" who repudiated Ezra's program of enforced divorce ("Jewish religious life in the Persian period" [1984] 273).

[52] "The Message of Malachi" (1984) 212.

[53] *Ibid.*, 212.

intermarriage with Gentiles. This openness, which is diametrically opposed to the view of Ezra, is similar to that expressed in Isa. 56:1-8.

The following four considerations weigh against this proposal. First, it is plausible that the expression "the wife of your covenant" in vs. 14 may not require that this wife was Jewish.[54]   Nevertheless, Mal. 2:10-16 does not readily give the impression that the mixed marriages, which Malachi so vehemently condemns in vss. 11 and 12, are the self-same marriages which he so adamantly defends in vss. 14-16.

Second, Collins correctly observes that Malachi does not explicitly relate the offence of divorce to that of mixed marriage. Contrary to Collins, however, we have already argued in the previous chapter that Malachi's condemnation is directed only against divorce based on aversion [שׂנא] and not against divorce as such.

Third, it is unclear that there is any necessary relation between the weeping at the altar mentioned in vs. 13 and the reforming work of Ezra. Nevertheless, even if this verse does reflect that reforming work, it hardly requires the view that Malachi intended to repudiate Ezra's program of the enforced dissolution of interfaith marriages. Vs. 11 explicitly condemns interfaith marriages as an "abomination [תּוֹעֵבָה]" and a profanation of the sanctuary of the Lord [חִלֵּל יְהוּדָה קֹדֶשׁ יְהוָה].   Similarly, however the crux עֵר וְעֹנֶה מֵאָהֳלֵי יַעֲקֹב in vs. 12 is to be rendered, Malachi's curse leaves little doubt that it is interfaith marriage, and not merely divorce, which renders Israel's offerings repulsive to Yahweh: "May the LORD cut off to the man who does this ... and brings an offering to the LORD of hosts!" (cf. 1:10). It is hard to imagine how Malachi could use stronger language to condemn these marriages; accordingly, there appears little difference between his attitude and that of Ezra.

As for Malachi's repudiation of divorce, the chief difficulty for Collins' suggestion is whether what Ezra 10 describes can legitimately be termed "divorce." W.A. Heth and G.J. Wenham, for example, argue that what took place in Ezra 10 was not divorce, but the dissolution of invalid unions (perhaps similar to the presumed dissolution of Michal's marriage to Paltiel).[55]   Support for this contention may be found first in the unusual vocabulary employed by Ezra to describe both the original unions (Hiphil forms of ישׁב are used in 10:2, 10, rather than the expected לקח, etc.) and the subsequent dissolution of those unions (לְהוֹצִיא in 10:3 and וְהִבָּדְלוּ in 10:11, rather than שׁלח, גרשׁ, or even שׂנא).   In particular, it should be noted that Malachi's terms in 2:16 are not those employed by Ezra.

Perhaps no less striking are the remarkable circumstances which prompted these dissolutions. Specifically, unlike divorce these dissolutions

---

[54] Contrary, e.g., to W.C. Kaiser Jr., *Malachi*, 70.
[55] *Jesus and Divorce*, 162-164. This interpretation has also been argued by, *inter alia*, G. Rawlinson, *Ezra and Nehemiah* (1890); H.M. Wolf, *Malachi*, 95; and W.F. Luck, *Divorce and Remarriage*, 282, n. 27.

were initiated neither by the husband, nor by the wife, but by a corporate action imposed on the guilty husbands. As such, in this respect particularly, they resemble the dissolution of Michal's invalid "marriage" to Paltiel at the instigation of Ishbosheth (2 Sam. 3:15).[56] In any case, by contrast to Ezra, the divorces which Malachi condemns in 2:16 are explicitly divorces which are the result of a husband's unjustified aversion (שׂנא) and not the result of a corporate action. This last point merits particular emphasis since both Kruse-Blinkenberg and Collins, based on their rendering "I hate divorce," assume that Malachi condemns divorce in an unqualified manner. As argued above in Chapter 3, this rendering and interpretation are unsatisfactory.

Fourth, Collins' appeal to Mal. 2:10 is unconvincing; as we have already argued, the reference to our "one Father" may not intend anything beyond God's paternal/covenantal relationship to Israel by which all members of the covenant community (but not those outside it) are constituted brothers. Nevertheless, it is possible, though uncertain, that Malachi might have accepted intermarriage with a converted Gentile (as in Boaz's marriage to Ruth).[57] Certainly the phrase "daughter of a foreign god" appears to stress the threat of idolatry, rather than racial miscegenation, as the basis for Malachi's rebuke. On the other hand, at least a superficial concern with biological descent does appear prominent in Ezra. In part, this emphasis may be a reflex of the need for priestly genealogical purity, which may also have been extended to all the people as a "kingdom of priests."[58] On closer inspection, Ezra implies that the primary motive for the prohibition against intermarriage was the danger of religious syncretism (cf., e.g., Ezra 9:2, 11, 14).[59] Such a perspective is entirely congenial with Malachi and, accordingly, does not favour Collins' hypothesis.

In conclusion, while the view that Malachi condemned Ezra's enforced divorces does succeed in eliminating the alleged contradiction between Mal. 2:10-16 and the assumed toleration of polygyny elsewhere and, as such,

---

[56] Cf. G.P. Hugenberger, "Michal" (1986).

[57] Cf. Ruth 1:16. For a similarly open attitude toward intermarriage with presumably converted Gentiles and the inclusion of converted Gentiles in Israel, cf. Gen. 41:45; Exod. 12:38; Num. 12:1ff.; 32:12; Deut. 20:14; 21:10-14; Josh. 6:25; 2 Sam. 23:39; Esth. 8:17; Ps. 87; Isa. 56:3, 5ff.; 60:7, 10; 61:5-6; 66:18ff.; Zech. 2:11; etc.

Cf. further Jdt. 14:10; Tobit; and examples of intermarriage at the Jewish colony in Elephantine (Cowley 14, 25, 28). Cf. also S.J.D. Cohen, "Conversion to Judaism in Historical Perspective: From Biblical Israel to Post-Biblical Judaism" (1983).

[58] Cf. Lev. 21:14. Cf. also D. Bossman, "Ezra's Marriage Reform: Israel Redefined" (1979) 32-38, and M. Fishbane, *Biblical Interpretation in Ancient Israel*, 121-123.

[59] For a discussion of Ezra's prohibition of intermarriage understood as an exegetical extension of the law in Deut. 7:1-3, 6 and Deut. 23:4-9 [ET 3-8], and perhaps Leviticus 18, cf. S.J.D. Cohen, "From the Bible to the Talmud: The Prohibition of Intermarriage" (1984) and especially M. Fishbane, *Biblical Interpretation in Ancient Israel* (1985) 114-129.

The Pentateuchal texts to which Ezra alludes leave little doubt that the Canaanites, and hence by analogy Ezra's non-Israelite contemporaries, were disqualified for intermarriage because of their idolatry and abominable religious practices. Cf. Exod. 34:16. Cf. also J. Blenkinsopp, *Ezra - Nehemiah*, 176f.

permits Mal. 2:14 to identify literal marriage as a "covenant," the difficulties listed above leave this interpretation in serious doubt.

4. THERE IS NO NECESSARY INTERRELATION BETWEEN MIXED MARRIAGE AND DIVORCE IN MALACHI 2:10-16, APART FROM A SIMILARITY OF THEME. ACCORDINGLY, THE TEXT CARRIES NO IMPLICATION REGARDING POLYGYNY (THE VIEW PREFERRED HERE)[60]

A number of scholars who acknowledge an original reference both to literal mixed marriage and to literal divorce in Mal. 2:10-16 consider these two offences to have been causally independent of each other. C. von Orelli, for example, notes that the text nowhere requires the view that each of these mixed marriages was preceded by the divorce of a Jewish wife, though some, or even many, may have been.[61] In any case, the laws against mixed marriage in Exod. 34:16 and Deut. 7:3f. are sufficiently general to apply whether or not there has been a previous divorce.[62] Furthermore, given that the text does not explicitly relate the divorces in 2:14-16 to the mixed marriages in 2:11-12, there is little reason to deny that at least some mixed marriages may have been formed without a previous divorce, just as some divorces need not have been followed by remarriage to a Gentile.[63]

This is not to suggest that Malachi intended no relation whatsoever between the offence of mixed marriage in vss. 11-12 and that of divorce in vss. 13-16. T. Chary, for example, distinguishes three sermons in 2:10-16, namely 2:10, 2:11-12, and 2:13-16, which are linked by the shared theme and vocabulary of infidelity [בגד].[64] J.G. Baldwin shares this view and suggests that these three sermons may be related in terms of their concern with "covenant loyalty" or, alternatively, in terms of a family concept: "... for the prophet begins (vs. 10) with a question that bears on the nation as one family.

---

[60] J. Wellhausen, *Skizzen und Vorarbeiten* (1892) 198f.   So also, *inter alia*, E. Henderson, *The Twelve Minor Prophets* (1858) 453-455; C. von Orelli, *The Twelve Minor Prophets* (1893) 397; T. Chary, *Aggée - Zacharie - Malachie* (1969) 255-263; and J.G. Baldwin, *Haggai, Zechariah, Malachi* (1972) 237.

[61] *The Twelve Minor Prophets* (1893) 397.

[62] As with Ezra and Nehemiah, Malachi extended the application of this law to include the non-Israelite women living in Palestine in his day. Von Orelli considers this extension to have been warranted based on the original reasons for the prohibitions as stated in Exod. 34:16 and Deut. 7:4, namely the concern to avoid the idolatrous influence of a heathen wife (*The Twelve Minor Prophets*, 398).

For a more recent discussion of this matter, cf. D. Bossman, "Ezra's Marriage Reform: Israel Redefined" (1979) 32-38; S.J.D. Cohen, "From the Bible to the Talmud: The Prohibition of Intermarriage" (1984); and especially M. Fishbane, *Biblical Interpretation in Ancient Israel* (1985) 114-129.

[63] Less convincing is J. Wellhausen's observation that since the text characterizes the divorced wife as "the wife of your youth" (vs. 14), it implies that these divorces may have been motivated not by any plans to enter into a mixed marriage, but simply by the fact that these Jewish wives were no longer youthful and attractive (*Skizzen und Vorarbeiten* [1892] 199).

[64] T. Chary, *Aggée - Zacharie - Malachie* (1969) 255-263.

He continues (vss. 11, 12) to see the nation as a spiritual family, and in the last four verses turns to individual family life within the nation."[65]

Perhaps clearest is the view of J. Wellhausen, who observes that mixed marriage with Gentiles (vss. 11-12) and the divorce of Jewish wives (vss. 13-16) are simply two different examples of the more general offence prohibited in vs. 10.[66]

Arguing against Wellhausen's interpretation, C.C. Torrey insists that "it is not possible thus to separate vs. 13-16 from vs. 10-12."[67] Torrey's objection, however, fails to do justice to Wellhausen's concern to stress the unifying role of vs. 10. Further neutralizing Torrey's objection, it is not difficult to detect literary and thematic parallels between vs. 10, as the controlling rubric, and vss. 11-12 and vss. 13-16, which suggest that mixed marriage and divorce are merely parallel offences without any necessary causal connection between them. C.V. Camp notes, for example, the significant repetition of several catchwords: "'one' (*'eḥad*, vv. 10 [*bis*], 15 [*bis*]); 'faithlessness' (*bgd*, vv. 10, 11, 14, 15, 16); 'covenant,' (*berît*, vv. 10, 14); 'offering' (*minḥâ*, vv. 12, 13); 'do' (*'śh*, vv. 11, 12 [*bis*], 15)."[68]

As has already been discussed, had it been the intention of the text to suggest that these divorces were the necessary prerequisite for the subsequent mixed marriages, one might have expected Malachi to treat these two offences in the reverse order of what is found. In any case, the present order appears to have been dictated largely by a literary purpose, rather than by any attempt to reproduce the chronology of offences. In particular, as was argued above in the first chapter, the present arrangement yields an artful envelope structure for Mal. 2:10-16:

A God who is One [אֶחָד] created [ברא] his people (to be one)
    General sin = infidelity [בגד] (10)
  B Specific sin = infidelity [בגד] by intermarriage with a pagan (11)
    C Verdict: exclusion, rejection of food offering [מִנְחָה] (12)

    C' Verdict: rejection of food offering [מִנְחָה] (13)
  B' Specific sin = infidelity [בגד] by divorce (14)
A' God who is One [הָאֶחָד] made [עשׂה] husband and wife to be one [אֶחָד]
    General sin = infidelity [בגד] (15-16a)
    Summary exhortation (particularly of 13-15) not to commit infidelity [בגד] (16b)[69]

---

[65] *Haggai, Zechariah, Malachi*, 237. Cf. also W.C. Kaiser Jr., *Malachi*, 65.
[66] *Skizzen und Vorarbeiten* (1892) 199.
[67] "The Prophecy of 'Malachi'," 9.
[68] *Wisdom and the Feminine in the Book of Proverbs* (1985) 323, n. 12. To Camp's list one might add "profane" (חלל, vss. 10, 11) and "cover" (כסה, vss. 13, 16), among other terms.
[69] Note that the mention of "covering [כסה] X with Y" in this verse forms an *inclusio* with vs. 13.
This suggested outline of 2:10-16 is based on the study of E. Wendland, "Linear and Concentric Patterns in Malachi" (1985) 108-21.

In addition to general subject matter (i.e., marital offences), shared vocabulary, and parallel literary structure, there may be yet other indications of an intended parallelism between vss. 11-12 and vss. 13-16, the two parade examples of the more general offence set forth in vs. 10. It is possible, for instance, that both vss. 11-12 and vss. 13-16 intend to stress the unacceptability and particularly the hypocrisy of offerings made by worshippers who have so flagrantly sinned by committing infidelity [בגד] (cf. the rejected offering in vs. 12 and the reference to garments covered in violence in vs. 16, if "garment" is to be taken as a reference to literal cultic attire).[70]

Noteworthy is the manner in which "one [אחד]" in vs. 10 is picked up again in vs. 15. To appreciate fully the import of this stress on "oneness" and its possible indirect support for monogamy, it will be necessary to turn our attention in the next chapter to a closer study of vs. 15. Nevertheless, in the words of C.V. Camp, the unmistakeable effect of all this parallelism "is to equate the faithlessness to the Lord involved in marrying foreign women to the faithlessness to one's wife involved in divorce."[71]

Finally, if 2:15 asserts that Yahweh's purpose for marriage is that it should produce a "seed of God/godly seed [זֶרַע אֱלֹהִים],"[72] then in Malachi's view divorce may have frustrated this purpose in a manner analogous to mixed marriage. Compare Neh. 13:23ff., where Nehemiah stresses the adverse impact of mixed marriage on the children of these unions. Compare also Ezra 10:3, 44. Certainly it appears that the expression "seed of God" reflects the imagery established in 2:10 (and 1:6) of God as the "one father to all of us," that is, to his people in virtue of his redemptive acts and covenant, and offers an intentional contrast to the phrase, "the daughter of a foreign god," in Mal. 2:11.

To sum up, if Malachi's intention in juxtaposing the offences of mixed marriage and divorce was to stress their similarity as instances of infidelity [בגד], rather than to imply that they were causally interrelated, then Mal. 2:10-16 carries no implication regarding polygyny and so is in no conflict with the alleged toleration of polygyny elsewhere in the Old Testament.[73] Accordingly, this view supports the identification of literal marriage as a "covenant" in 2:14.

---

[70] Cf. P.A. Verhoef for this possible interpretation, which reflects an important subtheme of Malachi (cf. 1:10) (*The Books of Haggai and Malachi*, 279f.). Cf. also our discussion in Chapter 3, §4.2.4.

[71] C.V. Camp, *Wisdom and the Feminine in the Book of Proverbs* (1985) 323, n. 12. Camp adds that "a similar sort of implicit equation is also made by the use of the zarâ-figure in Proverbs. The editors of both books seemed to have had such an equation in mind."

[72] Cf. Chapter 5, §8.1.5 below.

[73] Cf. W. Rudolph, "Zu Malachi 2:10-16" (1981) 86.

While the present interpretation seems preferable, the traditional interpretation of Mal. 2:10-16 (that the offences of mixed marriage and the divorce of Jewish wives were typically interrelated) remains a possibility which cannot easily be excluded. We turn now to examine this approach and its implications.

5. MALACHI 2:10-16 CONDEMNS BOTH MIXED MARRIAGE AND DIVORCE IN A MANNER WHICH SUGGESTS THAT THESE WERE TYPICALLY INTERRELATED, WITH THE IMPLICATION THAT POLYGYNY WAS EXCEPTIONAL, DISCOUNTENANCED, OR POSSIBLY EVEN ILLEGAL IN MALACHI'S DAY (THE TRADITIONAL VIEW)

As C.C. Torrey noted, the traditional interpretation of Mal. 2:10-16, which has been popular since the time of Jerome, considers that the problems of mixed marriage and divorce were interrelated.[74] In O. Eissfeldt's words, "Jewish men have divorced their Jewish wives in order to marry foreign women in their place."[75] Although this causal connection is more often assumed than argued, the following considerations may be advanced in support:

1) The fact that Mal. 2:10-16 juxtaposes its condemnation of mixed marriage and its condemnation of divorce suggests a possible causal linkage between these two marital offences. It is important to realize that this approach does not require that every mixed marriage was preceded by a divorce, nor that every divorce was necessarily followed by a mixed marriage. It only requires that these two offences were typically related. This recognition of the presence of possible exceptions may help to explain why Mal. 2:10-16 does not relate these two offences in a more explicit fashion. Furthermore, the traditional view does not exclude the various literary and conceptual parallels which may exist between these offences, as illumined by the previous approach.

2) Only by positing a typical connection between these divorces and subsequent mixed marriages, which presumably would have been materially advantageous, can a reasonable explanation be offered for the apparent prevalence of the problem of divorce based on aversion in Malachi's day.[76]

3) It is significant that the divorces condemned in Mal. 2:16 are specifically those which are based on mere aversion [שׂנא]. Such a description

---

[74] "The Prophecy of 'Malachi'," 4.

[75] *Introduction*, 442. Cf. also, e.g., C.F. Keil, *The Twelve Minor Prophets* (1878) 447f.; S.R. Driver, *The Minor Prophets* (1906) 312; J.M.P. Smith, *Malachi* (1912) 47, 52; G.L. Robinson, *The Twelve Minor Prophets* (1955) 164; J. Kodell, *Lamentations, Haggai, Zechariah, Malachi, Obadiah, Joel, Second Zechariah, Baruch* (1982)102; P.C. Craigie, *Twelve Prophets*, II (1985) 236; E. Achtemeier, *Nahum - Malachi* (1986) 181; and J.A. Soggin, *Introduction to the Old Testament* (1989) 344.

[76] P.A. Verhoef, *The Books of Haggai and Malachi*, 275.

is eminently suitable for divorce motivated by the desire to enter into another marriage.[77]

4) It appears likely that most divorces in Malachi's day would have been followed by a remarriage. In the context of life in post-exilic Palestine, where the population of available Jewish women would have been at a minimum, many of these remarriages would have been mixed.[78]

5) More specifically, it is often supposed that the appellation "the wife of your youth" in Mal. 2:14 suggests that the aging of one's wife, and by implication the presence of younger, more attractive (Gentile) women, was the primary motive for the divorces and subsequent mixed marriages.[79]

6) Attempting to account for the lack of opposition when the mixed marriages of Ezra 9-10 were forcibly dissolved, H.G.M. Williamson has suggested that "knowledge of this fact [that the guilty men had previously divorced their Jewish wives in order to enter into these mixed marriages] may have reduced the sympathy of the majority of the families concerned."[80]

7) It is possible that Malachi's stress in 2:15 on "godly offspring" as Yahweh's intention for marriage is best explained as due to Malachi's assumption that such divorces would be followed inevitably by a mixed marriage and that mixed marriage poses a clear threat to this purpose (cf. Neh. 13:23ff.; Ezra 10:3, 44).[81]

While these considerations have merit, perhaps especially the last, the following objections may be mentioned:

1) The fact remains that Mal. 2:10-16 nowhere explicitly interrelates the offences of intermarriage and divorce. As noted earlier, it is possible, for example, that the two offences are juxtaposed not to suggest a causal connection, but simply to emphasize how each of them is a prime example of the more general infidelity [בגד] condemned in 2:10.

2) It is uncertain whether divorce based on aversion was especially prevalent in Malachi's day, particularly given the fact that neither Ezra nor Nehemiah mentions the problem. Nevertheless, if the divorce rate was particularly high among Malachi's contemporaries, alternative explanations are possible. For example, the upsurge of religious relativism (Mal. 1:13; 2:17; 3:14f.; etc.), the disregard of vows (Mal. 1:14), and the disintegration of family and moral values (Mal. 3:5, 24 [ET 4:6]) may all have contributed to

---

[77] As M.T. Roth has observed with respect to Neo-Babylonian marriage documents, it appears that the clauses anticipating such unjustified divorces are all predicated on the assumption that the offending man will divorce in order to marry another woman ("She will die by the iron dagger," 188, n. 8).

[78] Cf. A.C. Welch, *Post-Exilic Judaism*, 251. If the first marriages (with Jewish wives) were formed while still in exile, and then the divorces and subsequent mixed marriages took place back in Judah, one might compare the concern and remedy of Laban with respect to Jacob's marriage to his daughters in Gen. 31:50.

[79] Such was the view of Rabbi Johanan (cf. Yamauchi, "Ezra," 677). Cf. also W. Neil, "Malachi," 231; and R.L. Alden, "Malachi," 717.

[80] *Ezra, Nehemiah*, 160.

[81] In a private communication dated 17/4/91, A.C.J. Phillips suggests this argument.

increased marital breakdown. In any case, Malachi offers no hint as to the particular motivation for divorce based on aversion in 2:16, perhaps because he intends to make his condemnation of unjustified divorce as general as possible.

3) While it is likely that divorce for the sake of marrying another would constitute a case of "aversion," it is uncertain that every or even most subsequent remarriages were necessarily mixed or that every or even most mixed marriages were necessarily preceded by a divorce. Nothing about Malachi's condemnation permits one to conclude that he would have approved mixed marriage in cases where it was not preceded by a divorce or that he would have approved unjustified divorce as long as it was not followed by a mixed marriage.

4) It is uncertain that there was such a disparity in the relative number of marriageable Jewish women versus men in the mid-fifth century B.C. province of Judah (Yehud).[82] Moreover, had there been such a disparity, presumably this would have affected the majority of first marriages as well, since it is likely in this later period that most of these would have been contracted in Judah.

5) There is no evidence that the expression "the wife of your youth [אֵשֶׁת נְעוּרֶיךָ]" was in any way intended to allude to the fact that these Jewish wives had now become aged and unappealing! Of course, even if they had, this fact cannot explain why the problem of divorce had become acute in the post-exilic community since wives, along with their husbands, inevitably aged in every period of Israel's history.[83] In any case, when one compares the use of "the wife of your youth" elsewhere in the Old Testament (e.g., Prov. 2:17; 5:18; Isa. 54:6; cf. also Joel 1:8), it appears that, far from having any pejorative connotation, it was an expression of endearment and may have been employed by Malachi to offer the strongest possible incentive for revivified love.[84]

Furthermore, as opposed to the hypothesized motive of romance, it is more likely that most of the mixed marriages in Malachi's day were *mariages de convenance*. In a world where property frequently was inalienable and where wealth and status were primarily in non-Israelite hands, the temptation for the returned exiles to secure these through intermarriage must have been

---

[82] A.C. Welch bases his argument in favour of this disparity on the doubtful assumption that Malachi should be dated nearly a century earlier than is argued by most scholars, namely about 520 B.C. (*Post-Exilic Judaism*, 251).

[83] Given the modern flavour of the suggestions of some scholars about how pretty young Canaanite women might have seemed (cf., e.g., W. Neil, "Malachi," 231), as an *ad hominem* argument it may be noted that in modern times divorce is most common among younger couples, not those who have matured together.

[84] There may be a nostalgic allusion in this expression to the first blush of marital love. Cf. Deut. 24:5; Cant. 8:5; and Rev. 2:4, 5. T.T. Perowne speaks about "the tender recollection of 'the kindness of youth and the love of espousals' (Jerem. ii. 2), and the binding force of years since spent together in intimate companionship..." (*Malachi* [1910] 26).

significant.[85]   Consistent with this, Neh. 6:17-19 and 13:4, 28 enumerate instances of intermarriage between members of the Jewish aristocracy and the powerful families of Sanballat the Horonite, later governor of Samaria, and of Tobiah the Ammonite, perhaps a governor of the sub-province of Ammon or deputy to Sanballat.[86]   Similarly, J.M. Myers notes the disproportionate prominence of members of the upper classes in the list of offenders in Ezra 10.[87]

6) H.G.M. Williamson's explanation for the lack of opposition to the forcible dissolution of the mixed marriages of Ezra 9-10 appears unconvincing.[88]   Neither Ezra nor Nehemiah makes any mention of the problem of divorce, perhaps suggesting that many individuals had entered their mixed marriages without a previous divorce. Furthermore, what is surprising is not the lack of opposition from some imagined third parties who may have been injured (i.e., the previously divorced wives and their families), but the lack of opposition from the offending husbands themselves or from their present Gentile wives and in-laws. Of course, there may have been plenty of opposition which was simply unrecorded.[89]

7) Malachi's order of treatment of mixed marriage followed by divorce is unexpected on the traditional view. H. Cowles, among others, explains this order by suggesting that a man who was already married to a Jewish wife practiced polygyny by taking a second wife who was a Gentile. Subsequently, the slighted Jewish wife would find the situation intolerable and be put away.[90]   In other words, Malachi's order of treatment reflects the proper chronological order: the divorce of one's Jewish wife typically followed a second marriage to a Gentile wife.

This explanation, however, is unconvincing for several reasons. First, while there is evidence to support the practice of a wife-initiated divorce intended as a response to an unwanted polygynous marriage, Cowles' view reads too much into a text which nowhere hints that these divorces were

---

[85] G.A. Smith argues "such alliances were the surest way both to wealth and to political influence" (*The Book of the Twelve Prophets*, 344). Cf. also W.J. Dumbrell, "Malachi and the Ezra-Nehemiah Reforms," 47; and A.S. van der Woude, "Malachi's Struggle for a Pure Community," 66.

[86] Cf. J. Blenkinsopp, who also cites an account of the marriage between Manasseh, the brother of the high priest Jaddua, and a daughter of Sanballat, recorded in Josephus, *Antiquities* 11.302-312 (*Ezra - Nehemiah*, 365).

[87] *The World of the Restoration* (1968) 88f., 98, 122.

[88] *Ezra, Nehemiah*, 160. Ezra 10:15 is ambiguous in its implication.

[89] It is possible, for example, that Joiada refused to divorce his wife and so was ostracised in Neh. 13:28 (as suggested by J.M. Myers, *Ezra, Nehemiah*, 218).

[90] H. Cowles, *The Minor Prophets* (1867) 391-393. Cf. also C.F. Keil, *The Twelve Minor Prophets*, 447; L.H. Brockington, "Malachi," 657; and W.J. Dumbrell, "Malachi and the Ezra-Nehemiah Reforms," 48.

Rashi's interpretation may be mentioned here, although his understanding of vs. 16 is unconvincing (see previous chapter). On his view, Malachi rebukes his contemporaries for two offences: first for interfaith marriage, which would be reprehensible under any circumstances, and second for the injury to one's Jewish wife which is the result of bringing the rival Gentile wife into the home. Consequently, Malachi urges such men to divorce their Jewish wives, rather than to treat them with such cruelty.

instigated by, or were a response to, the Jewish wives' discontent.[91] Second, in most cases of polygyny in the ancient Near East, the pre-eminent status of the first wife was protected.[92] Indeed, if Jewish men contracted their mixed marriages for economic or social reasons, as is widely argued, it is questionable whether the Gentile aristocracy would have permitted their daughters to enter such polygynous marriages, where they would be relegated to a secondary status. Finally, Cowles' view assumes that an unrestricted polygyny was practiced in Malachi's day and that Malachi would have preferred polygyny to divorce. Against these assumptions, there is little evidence for unrestricted polygyny anywhere in the ancient Near East and considerable doubt whether even a restricted polygyny would have been prevalent in post-exilic Israel. There is a wide scholarly consensus that not only was monogamy seen as the marital ideal in this period (post-exilic Israel), but also it was actually practiced with few, if any, exceptions.[93]

Alternatively, G.A. Smith, among others, considers that Malachi's order of treatment of mixed marriage and divorce is logical, rather than chronological. Smith suggests that "the relatives of their half-heathen brides made it a condition of the marriages that they should first put away their old wives...."[94] While this view succeeds in recognizing the normal pre-eminence accorded a first wife and the likely concern of Gentile families to safeguard the status interests of their daughters, it must still be acknowledged that the text offers no hint that Gentile families in fact made such demands.

8) It is possible that Malachi viewed the purpose of marriage (to produce "godly offspring") to be directly threatened only by mixed marriage, but that he mentions this matter in the context of divorce in 2:15 because he assumes that mixed marriage would inevitably follow divorce. It is also possible, however, that Malachi recognized that both mixed marriage (with the "daughter of a foreign god") and divorce equally endanger this purpose. As such, this implied consequence for divorce may offer an additional parallel between the offences of mixed marriage and divorce (see §4 above).

In summary, the weight of evidence appears to favour the view that the offences of mixed marriage and divorce are juxtaposed not because they were causally interrelated, but because they are parallel instances of the more general infidelity [בגד] condemned in 2:10. Nevertheless, since the traditional view remains possible, the identification of marriage as a covenant in 2:14 needs to be secured against the claim that a literal reference would be contradicted by the toleration of polygyny in Malachi's day. To accomplish

---

[91] For example, cf. Nuzi marriage tablets Nos. 1 and 2 discussed above. Cf. also E. Lipiński, "The Wife's Right to Divorce in the Light of an Ancient Near Eastern Tradition" (1981).

[92] Cf., e.g., T.E. McComiskey, "The Status of the Secondary Wife: Its Development in Ancient Near Eastern Law" (1965) 1 and *passim*.

[93] For evidence, cf. the fuller discussion below in §6.

[94] *The Book of the Twelve Prophets*, 344. Cf. J.M.P. Smith, *Malachi*, 52; P.A. Verhoef, *The Books of Haggai and Malachi*, 275.

this it is necessary to examine the practice of polygyny elsewhere in the Old Testament and particularly in the post-exilic period.

6. EXCURSUS ON THE PRACTICE OF POLYGYNY IN ANCIENT ISRAEL

No one denies that polygyny was practiced within Israel throughout much of the Old Testament period. Unfortunately, a similar scholarly consensus for virtually every other important question surrounding this practice is lacking. In particular, it would be helpful to know the prevalence and class distribution of polygyny during each period.[95] Furthermore, there is

---

[95] A useful summary of the evidence for polygyny in the OT is provided by W. Plautz, "Monogamie und Polygynie im Alten Testament" (1963) 3-27.

It should be noted, however, that it is often difficult or impossible to ascertain whether a particular example is one of polygyny, rather than of successive monogamous marriages (cf., e.g., the doubtful example of polygyny in 1 Chr. 8:8-11 based on multiple descent lines). Cf. also J.M. Breneman, who acknowledges the same problem with respect to evidence from Nuzi, "It is clear that in some cases a man has two wives; however, sometimes when another wife and her sons are mentioned (as in texts 6 and 13) we can not be sure if it refers to a former wife, either deceased or divorced, or to another living wife. In text 4 the other sons are definitely from a divorced wife" (*Nuzi Marriage Tablets*, 291). Breneman goes on to note the same problem in treating the evidence of wills.

In an attempt to gain more reliable evidence for the possible prevalence of polygyny in ancient Israel, a number of scholars have sought to extrapolate from the practice attested in comparative Semitic cultures. One of the most influential sources for this comparison has been the meticulous work of H. Granqvist. Granqvist notes that of the 112 men residing in the modern village of Artas near Bethlehem, eleven had two wives, and one had three. Granqvist was rightly sceptical, however, about attempts to draw parallels between twentieth century Palestinian Arabs and ancient Israelites. Regrettably, biblical scholars have not always been so judicious (*Marriage Conditions in a Palestinian Village* [1935] II, 205).

While much of the biblical and epigraphic evidence for the relative prevalence of polygyny is ambiguous or inconclusive, one apparent exception is provided by A. van Selms' analysis of UT 119 (*Marriage and Family Life in Ugaritic Literature* [1954] 20). Where the text can be read or reasonably restored, there appears to be a list of twenty households, among which four are listed as having two wives and one as having three wives. This would imply a 25% rate of polygyny.

This evidence is problematic, however, in that there is considerable uncertainty as to the nature of the list. While C.H. Gordon lists this as "census of households in the town of Alašiya," A. Alt has expressed an alternative view that this is a list of captives from Cyprus (C.H. Gordon, *UT*, 262; A. Alt, "Ein phönikisches Staatswesen des frühen Altertums," 207-209). Certainly the closing notice given for each family, that they are "in the house of" [*b.bt*] some other individual, makes this list rather peculiar. Also striking is the unparalleled identification of some of the wives as "a mighty wife" [*aṭṭ adrt* in 119:4, 7, 9, 16, 18], interpreted by Gordon as an "upper-class wife" (*op. cit.*, 352). Regardless of the outcome of this debate, given the damaged nature of the text and the limited sample it represents, it would seem precarious to draw conclusions for Ugaritic society as a whole, much less for ancient Israel. Van Selms appends his own qualifying judgment: "A percentage of 25 for polygamic marriages may certainly be regarded as high" (*op. cit.*, 20). Moreover, since the time of Van Selms' study a number of additional Ugaritic texts, which C. Gordon classifies as "household statistics or census records," have come to light to dramatically change this ratio: UT 1080, 1142, 2044, and 2068.

UT 1080 is a list (with relatively few lacunae) of eight households, which mentions wives, children, and animals. Based on Gordon's transliteration and occasional reconstruction of the text, in each case we read of only one wife. UT 1142 is too fragmentary to be of use. UT 2044 is also rather fragmentary, but yields clear information about three households, one of which may possibly mention "two wives." The critical *ṯt*, "two," in line 11 is reconstructed by Gordon within a lacuna, but Gordon indicates his own

considerable uncertainty regarding the legal status of concubines and the precise distinctions, if any, between a concubine [פִּילֶגֶשׁ], a slave-wife [whether אָמָה or שִׁפְחָה], and a captive-wife [as in Deut. 20:14; 21:10-14; etc.].[96] Finally, assuming that polygyny was a legally valid form of marriage

---

serious reservations about the reconstruction (*UT*, Supplement, 14). Text 2068 lists ten households and in each case mentions only one wife (*w . aṯṯh*, "and his wife").

Finally, to these texts we may add one more particularly significant text, UT 1077, classified by Gordon under the heading "Lists of personal and/or geographical names" (*UT*, 291). After a broken beginning, the text lists four men each simply identified as a *b'l aṯṯ*, "the husband of a wife." Following this are listed six men each identified as a *b'l ššlmt*, "the husband of a concubine(?)." No individual is recorded as having more than one wife. (This text may offer corroboration for an interpretation of Abraham as monogamously married to his concubine Keturah and the Levite of Judges 19 as monogamously married to his concubine).

There is no point in summing up these totals to offer a new measure for the relative prevalence of polygyny in Ugaritic society. An undetected special purpose behind any or all of these lists would radically skew the results of any such computation. We need merely observe that even this modest amount of new data leaves one with a very different impression of typical marital practice from what Van Selms was able to offer on the basis of UT 119 alone.

[96] Without denying that there are important distinctions in the usage of these terms, such as the fact that פִּילֶגֶשׁ is only used of a married woman, it is notable that a number of OT texts employ them in an overlapping manner. For example, Bilhah is variously identified as Rachel's אָמָה (Gen. 30:3), Rachel's שִׁפְחָה (Gen. 29:29; 30:4, 7; 35:25), Jacob's שִׁפְחָה (Gen. 32:23 [ET 22]; and possibly 30:43; 32:6 [ET 5]), Jacob's פִּילֶגֶשׁ (Gen. 35:22), as well as Jacob's wife, אִשָּׁה (Gen. 30:4). Reflecting their views of Mesopotamian practice, however, many scholars have sought to distinguish "concubines" from slave-wives, though with decidedly dissimilar results. For example, while E. Neufeld insists that the legal status of the פִּילֶגֶשׁ, אָמָה, and שִׁפְחָה vis-à-vis their husband was probably identical, nevertheless he considers it likely that the פִּילֶגֶשׁ was originally a prostitute and so had a distinctly lower social status than the אָמָה and שִׁפְחָה, who were originally slaves (*Ancient Hebrew Marriage Laws* [1944] 121-123). On the other hand, L.M. Epstein and S.F. Bigger take the opposite view, placing the פִּילֶגֶשׁ both legally (as a free woman) and socially over the אָמָה and שִׁפְחָה (L.M. Epstein, *Marriage Laws in Bible and Talmud* [1942] 35, 50; and S.F. Bigger, "Hebrew Marriage and Family in the Old Testament Period" [1974] 105f.). With uncertain success, other scholars attempt to distinguish further an אָמָה from a שִׁפְחָה. Cf., e.g., A. Jepsen, "*Amah* und *Schiphchah*" (1958); Ch. Cohen, "Studies in Extra-Biblical Hebrew Inscriptions I. The Semantic Range and Usage of the terms אָמָה and שִׁפְחָה," *Shnaton* 5-6 (1978-79) xxv-liii; and P. Trible, *Texts of Terror* (1984) 30, n. 9.

Perhaps most problematic, however, is the view of some scholars who simply disqualify all biblical examples of "concubines" by insisting that they do not offer instances of marriage. Cf., e.g., E. Neufeld, who writes, "The concubine was not married by her master, and her status differed very slightly from that of a slave" (*op. cit.*, 124). So also C.J.H. Wright, *An Eye for an Eye* (1983) 176; and P. Trible, *op. cit.*, 66.

Such an assessment of the meaning and status of the פִּילֶגֶשׁ, however, rests largely on conjecture, on an uncritical acceptance of S.I. Feigin's classic study of concubinage in Mesopotamia, and on assumed parallels with occidental practice, in part fostered by the misleading traditional rendering "concubine" (S.I. Feigin, "The Captives in Cuneiform Inscription" [1934]). Unfortunately, Feigin's results are in urgent need of re-examination in view of his consistent identification of *šugîtum* as a "concubine." Given that CH §184, for example, appears in the midst of legislation concerned with the dowries of priestesses, and given the frequent association elsewhere (as in CH §§137, 144, 145 and 183) between the *šugîtum* and the *nadîtum* (a high priestess who was prohibited from bearing children), it appears that the older view of B. Landsberger and W. Eilers that the *šugîtum* was some kind of "lay priestess" is still to be preferred. It is true that in occidental practice a concubine was, in general, a mere sexual consort and was not considered to be a member of her

in every period, what legal restrictions were placed on this practice, if any, and what was its ethical status. Was it required (for example, in the case of levirate marriage), recommended, approved, merely tolerated, or condemned? Obviously, it is impossible to treat these matters in detail within the scope of the present study. Nevertheless, it is hoped that the evidence to be presented will be adequate to challenge the overly facile assumption that in post-exilic Israel polygyny was a viable alternative to the divorces indicated in Mal. 2:16.

6.1 The prevalence of polygyny in the Old Testament

With respect to the prevalence and class distribution of polygyny, it is well-known that although the Old Testament offers numerous examples of tribal leaders and kings who practiced polygyny, the only clear instance of a non-monogamous marriage for any "commoner" is Elkanah in 1 Samuel 1.[97] Based on this slender evidence, E. Neufeld, for example, claims that "among the middle classes, of which Elkanah of the Book of Samuel may be taken as representative, it was probably the normal practice to have two wives."[98] Of course, if this were so, then this would greatly help those scholars who reject the traditional interpretation of Mal. 2:10-16, including C.C. Torrey and A. Isaksson mentioned above.

Against Neufeld, however, it appears necessary to qualify drastically the example of Elkanah by giving more adequate attention to the likely special motive for this bigyny, namely Hannah's infertility.[99] It is a remarkable fact that perhaps the majority of legal texts and marriage documents from Mesopotamia which bear on the question of polygyny authorize it precisely in the exceptional circumstance that one's wife proves to be infertile (cf., e.g., CH §145 and LE §59; the only other specific case where polygyny was expressly permitted was when one's wife was gravely ill, cf. CH §148).[100] This is not to claim that polygyny was never practiced

---

partner's household. Because her relationship was not one of marriage, it was protected neither by the laws of adultery, nor by the requirement of some sort of formal divorce for its dissolution. Such an understanding, however, fails to do justice to the complex phenomena of concubinage both in the Bible and elsewhere in the ancient Near East (cf., e.g., the following texts which identify concubines as wives: Gen. 16:3; 25:1, 6; 1 Chr. 1:32; 2 Sam. 16:22; and Judg. 19:1-5).

[97] To this one example we could possibly add 1 Chr. 7:4f., if the commonly proposed emendation to restore a comparative ב at the beginning of vs. 5 is accepted. This would yield "...because they had more wives and sons *than* their brothers" (cf. E.L. Curtis and A.A. Madsen, *A Critical and Exegetical Commentary on the Books of Chronicles*; and W. Rudolph, *Chronikbücher*).

Based on the armies they could muster, etc., it appears that J. Bright has correctly identified the patriarchs as "chieftains of semi-nomadic clans" and not "commoners" (*A History of Israel*, 3rd. ed. [1981] 92f.).

[98] *Ancient Hebrew Marriage Laws* (1944) 118.

[99] So the Talmud, *b. Yebam.* 64b, and most modern commentators. Cf. also L.M. Epstein, *Marriage Laws in Bible and Talmud* (1942) 20.

[100] Cf. R. Westbrook, "Old Babylonian Marriage Law" (1982) I, 56f.

While CH §145 pertains to the special case of marriage to a *nadîtum*-priestess (who was prohibited from bearing children), the presence of other laws, such as LE §59, and similar stipulations within extant marriage tablets supports the inference that this law was applied more generally. For a discussion of LE §59, cf. R. Yaron, *The Laws of Eshnunna* (1988) 79, 211-222.

Demonstrating that these laws reflect actual practice, the following Nuzi marriage contracts contain an explicit prohibition against bigyny unless the first wife proves to be infertile: Nuzi marriage contracts 1, 2, 4, 5, 6, 8, and 101 (cf. also 104), as edited by J.M. Breneman, "Nuzi Marriage Tablets" (1971). Cf. also C.H. Gordon, "Nuzi Tablets Relating to Women" (1935) 163-84.

For a similar provision at Alalaḫ, cf. texts 91:24-31 and 92 (D.J. Wiseman, *The Alalakh Tablets* [1953]). Cf. I. Mendelsohn, "On Marriage in Alalakh," 355-357. Mendelsohn concludes that the prohibition of a second wife was "probably inserted in all marriage contracts of well-to-do brides where the girl's father was in a position to impose such a pledge on his future son-in-law" (*ibid.*, 355).

Cf. also similar clauses in three Old Assyrian marriage contracts, I 490, ICK 3, and TC 67, discussed by J. Lewy, "On some Institutions of the Old Assyrian Empire," 6-10; A.J. Skaist, "Studies in Ancient Mesopotamian Family Law" (1963) 71; and T.L. Thompson, *The Historicity of the Patriarchal Narratives*, 262.

For the Neo-Babylonian period, cf. No. 3 in M.T. Roth, *Babylonian Marriage Agreements: 7th - 3rd Centuries B.C.* This contract is for a concurrent second marriage for a man whose first wife was infertile (lines 10f.). Otherwise fifteen of the forty-five agreements preserve a clause anticipating what will happen if the husband divorces his wife because he wants to marry another woman (Nos. 1, 2, 4, 5, 6, 8, 15, 16, 17, 19, 20, 25, 26, 30, and 34). No contract anticipates the possibility of an additional marriage without a preceding divorce.

Alternatively, other laws permit a wife to pre-empt the action of her husband by providing him with a concubine of her own choosing (so CH §§144-47) or, going one step further, require a barren wife to provide her husband a second wife or concubine — so Nuzi *HSS* 5 (1929) No. 67, as treated by E.A. Speiser in "New Kirkuk Documents Relating to Family Laws" (1930) 31ff.; "Ethnic Movements in the Near East in the Second Millennium" (1933) 44; and *Genesis* (1964) 120f. Cf. also R. de Vaux, *Ancient Israel*, I, 24. Cautioning against certain aspects of Speiser's application of these texts to Genesis, cf. J. Van Seters, "The Problem of Childlessness in Near Eastern Law and the Patriarchs of Israel" (1968); and T.L. Thompson, *op. cit.*, 252-280.

LI §28 may appear to offer an exception. It is more likely, however, that since this law mandates the support of the first wife, it merely parallels CH §148. Unfortunately a lacuna occurs at the decisive point where the original text may have mentioned the first wife's illness.

Laws which treat the inheritance rights of the children of different wives may not contradict the assumption that bigyny was typically limited to cases of infertility or illness (e.g., CH §§146, 147, 170, 171; LI §§24, 25; SL §§12, 13, 14; Deut. 21:15-17). These laws may have been intended to address the case of the offspring of successive monogamous marriages or cases such as that of Abraham and Sarah and Elkanah and Hannah, where the barren wife had her children later after a second marriage had already been concluded (this seems probable in the case of CH §§146, 147). In any case, even if these laws envision the consequences of a more general polygyny, they may not approve polygyny any more than the laws regarding premarital intercourse (Exod. 22:15f. [ET 16f.] and Deut. 22:20f.) necessarily authorize or approve that practice. They merely provide a remedy to mitigate some adverse consequences of these perhaps disapproved practices.

It is unclear whether CH §141 authorizes bigyny as a penalty against a wayward wife or whether, as seems more likely, the first wife is stripped of her wifely status and reduced quite literally to the status of a slave as a *lex talionis*. Cf., perhaps, 2 Sam. 6:23 and Hosea 3.

For other examples of bigyny motivated by infertility, cf. Abraham's simultaneous marriage to Sarah and Hagar (Genesis 16), motivated by Sarah's infertility. Although Jacob already had three sons by his wife Leah, it seems likely that Jacob's marriage to Rachel's maid Bilhah (Gen. 30:4) should be considered as an example of this motive. As such, this example is particularly instructive in that the biblical text stresses the role of Rachel and her

apart from infertility or sickness. Indeed, the opposite is implied by the very presence of these laws and marriage contracts, some of which stipulate stiff financial penalties and authorize the offended wife to leave, should her husband acquire a second wife after she has borne children. Nevertheless, the legal texts leave little doubt that unjustified polygyny, that is, polygyny unmotivated by infertility or illness, was officially and widely discountenanced. Accordingly, the majority of cuneiform texts which allude to marriage, whether in the legal corpora or wisdom literature, etc., presuppose monogamy as the normal, if not also the ideal, form of marriage in Mesopotamia.[101]

Thus, the case of Elkanah, far from suggesting widespread polygyny, indicates that actual Israelite practice closely resembles that of Mesopotamia and of ancient Egypt. In the latter case, excluding the royal family, polygyny is attested only twice throughout the whole of Egyptian antiquity — a fact which is all the more remarkable because, as S. Allam has noted, "we are relatively well informed about Egyptian marriage, due to numerous documents beginning in the Late Period (11th - 4th centuries B.C.)."[102]

---

desire for children ("Give me children, or I shall die!" Gen. 30:1) as the cause of polygyny, not Jacob's desire. Cf. also Gen. 30:9, where Leah gives her maid Zilpah to Jacob because she "saw that she had ceased bearing children."

On the other hand, it should be noted that the acute need posed by barrenness did not always lead to bigyny (cf. Isaac and Rebekah in Gen. 25:21, Manoah and his wife in Judges 13, and, presumably, Seled and his wife in 1 Chr. 2:30). Further, the modern reader should not suppose that the ancients were unaware of male infertility as a contributing factor to childlessness. Cf. Abraham's incredulous response to the divine promise: "Shall a child be born to a man who is a hundred years old?" (Gen. 17:17). Similarly other passages readily acknowledge that a moral deficiency in a man, just as in a woman, can be the precipitating cause of infertility as a divine judgment: E.g., Gen. 20:17f. and possibly Lev. 20:20f. Cf. also K. van der Toorn, *Sin and Sanction in Israel and Mesopotamia*, 85-87.

[101] Accordingly, I. Mendelsohn, J. Klíma, and others summarize the evidence by stating that Babylonian marriage was with few exceptions essentially monogamous. Cf. I. Mendelsohn, *Slavery in the Ancient Near East* (1949) 50; *idem*, "On Marriage in Alalakh" (1959) 351-57; J. Klíma, "Marriage and Family in Ancient Mesopotamia" (1966) 100, 102; R. Yaron, *The Laws of Eshnunna* (1988) 79, 211-222; and R. Westbrook, "Old Babylonian Marriage Law" (1982) I, 56f.

Cf., e.g., MAL A §55, which is of special interest in that it explicitly presupposes monogamy. Resembling Deut. 22:23-27, this law specifies that if a married man ravishes an unbetrothed virgin, his wife will be ravished in a talionic punishment and taken from him; then he must marry the ravished virgin at the discretion of her father. If the ravisher is unmarried, he must pay an inflated marriage present (perhaps to be understood as threefold the customary amount as a penalty [*šalšāte kaspa šīm batūlte*], vs. *ANET*); once again, he must marry the ravished virgin at the discretion of her father.

[102] So S. Allam, *Everyday Life in Ancient Egypt* (1985) 27. Cf. also p. 35; *idem*, "Ehe" (1975) 1162-81; and P.W. Pestman, *Marriage and Matrimonial Property in Ancient Egypt* (1961) *passim*.

W.A. Ward confirms that monogamy was the exclusive form of marriage for non-royalty throughout Egypt's history and denies any evidence for the existence of harems or concubinage even among royalty during the Old and Middle Kingdoms. Only with the new internationalism of the Empire did royal polygyny (not concubinage) for the purpose of diplomacy become a necessity ("Reflections on some Egyptian terms presumed to mean 'harem, harem-woman, concubine'" [1983] 67f., 74).

6.2 The ethical stance of the Old Testament with respect to polygyny

Concerning the ethical status of polygyny in the Old Testament, nowhere do we find an express biblical permission for polygyny comparable to what obtains in the Code of Hammurabi, for example, much less the *Qur'ān* or Talmud.[103] Nevertheless, it has often been argued that the Old Testament does not merely recognize polygyny as a legal form of marriage, but that it also approves it. This conclusion does not rest on any particular Old Testament examples of polygyny since most of these are reported without any indication of moral approbation.[104] Rather, it seeks its support in eight specific texts: Exod. 21:10f.; Lev. 18:17f.; Deut. 21:15-17; Deut. 25:5-10; 2 Sam. 12:7f.; Jer. 3:6-13; Ezekiel 23; and, of particular interest to our study, Mal. 2:10-16. On closer examination, however, it is not so clear that any of these texts require the conclusion that polygyny was ethically approved.

6.2.1 Texts which are alleged to approve polygyny

Jeremiah 3:6-13 and Ezekiel 23
Jer. 3:6-13 and Ezekiel 23 depict Yahweh as a bigynist in his relationship to Israel and Judah. Accordingly, R. Holst and B. Vawter, among others, consider these texts to reflect the prophets' ethical approval of polygyny.[105] Because these texts are allegorical, however, it is precarious to press their details in an attempt to derive from them legal or ethical norms. This is

---

[103] Cf. CH §§144-148 and *Qur'ān* 4:3. Cf. W.M. Watt, who argues that *Qur'ān* 4:3 does not merely limit polygyny to four wives, as it is generally understood, since it would condemn Muhammed himself, who is said to have taken thirteen wives, but it encourages men who had only one or two wives to marry as many as four (*Muhammad, Prophet and Statesman* [1964] 151-159).
  Although contradictory opinions are expressed, Mishnaic and Talmudic interpretation sees polygyny not as a tolerated deviation, but as a legal right (cf., e.g., *b. Yebam.* 65a). Furthermore, according to the positive view, polygyny is obligatory in the case of infertility (*b. Yebam.* 61b; *b. Soa* 24a) and the levirate (cf., e.g., *b. Yebam.* 44a). Cf. also *m. Yebam.* 4:11; *m. Ketub.* 10:1-6; *m. Git.* 2:7; 3:1; *m. Qidd.* 2:6-7; *m. Soa* 6:2; and *m. Ber.* 8:4.
  Nevertheless, the Talmud shows a general tendency to favour monogamy and specifically commends monogamy for priests (cf. E. Neufeld, *Ancient Hebrew Marriage Laws* [1944] 119, n. 4; and L.M. Epstein, *Marriage Laws in Bible and Talmud* [1942] 10). In fact, it seems likely that the discussion concerning the right of polygyny was largely theoretical. For this reason neither a single rabbi among the more than two thousand sages in the entire Talmud nor a single plaintiff is mentioned as actually having more than one wife — so, according to G.F. Moore, *Judaism in the First Centuries of the Christian Era,* II (1927) 122; D.M. Feldman, *Marital Relations, Birth Control, and Abortion in Jewish Law* (1968) 37; and R. Biale, *Women and Jewish Law* (1984) 49. Contrarily, L.M. Epstein challenges this observation (*Marriage Laws in Bible and Talmud* [1942] 17).
[104] Indeed, moral disapprobation is suggested by some of these examples: e.g., Lamech, Abraham, David, Solomon, and possibly Jacob and "the sons of the gods" in Genesis 6. For one possible interpretation of this last, obviously problematic text, which finds in it a reference to royal polygyny, cf. M.G. Kline, "Divine Kingship and Genesis 6:1-4" (1961/62). Supporting Kline's interpretation over against the more common view may be the recognition that nowhere in Ugaritic literature do the gods have sexual relations with men (so A. van Selms, *Marriage and Family Life in Ugaritic Literature* [1954] 19).
[105] R. Holst, "Polygamy and the Bible" (1967) 205-213; and B. Vawter, "The Biblical Theology of Divorce" (1967) 226f.

especially so given the historical exigencies which these texts seek to symbolize; the two kingdoms with their separate destinies could not easily be made to fit the pattern of monogamy except in the eschaton (cf. Ezek. 16:53-63).[106]

As evidence of the need for caution, both Jeremiah 3 and Ezekiel 23 depict Yahweh's "wives" as "sisters" (Jer. 3:7f. and especially Ezek. 23:2ff., which further specifies that they were uterine sisters). This detail admirably suits the religio-historical relationship between Israel and Judah and their ostensibly common faith in Yahweh, but Lev. 18:18, if it is not to be interpreted as a prohibition against polygyny in general, is emphatic in explicitly prohibiting this form of polygyny in particular. A similar problem obtains in the treatment of parables and allegories in the New Testament. For example, although most scholars concede that Paul would have rejected polygyny, nevertheless he was quite willing to use Abraham's bigynous marriage to Hagar and Sarah as an allegory for the old and new covenants in Galatians 4.[107]

2 Samuel 12:7f.

Although Nathan's words to David in 2 Sam. 12:7f. appear to endorse royal polygyny by implicating the deity in the acquisition of David's wives ("I gave you your master's house, and your master's wives into your bosom"), unfortunately moral approbation cannot be inferred so easily from Yahweh's acts.[108] 2 Sam. 12:11, for example, appears to offer a deliberate parallel to 12:8. Here Yahweh threatens David with a talionic punishment, that he will "take your wives before your eyes, and give them to your neighbour, and he shall lie with your wives in the sight of this sun." Nevertheless, even though this text asserts that Yahweh will "give" David's concubines to another, 2 Samuel leaves little doubt that the fulfillment of this threat in what Absalom did on the palace roof "in the sight of all Israel" (2 Sam. 16:22) constituted a flagrant act of adultery deserving the death penalty.[109]

---

[106] Cf. also Isa. 54; 61:1-6. The warning against the over-interpretation of allegory cuts both ways, however. It cautions equally against the emphasis P. Grelot wishes to place on the fact that in the eschatological wedding feast of Ezek. 16:53-63, and hence in the ideal state, Jerusalem is Yahweh's only bride, with the other cities identified as her daughters ("The Institution of Marriage: Its Evolution in the Old Testament" [1970] 46). Similarly, not too much should be made of the other prophetic texts which metaphorically depict Yahweh in a monogamous marriage with Israel (e.g., cf. Isa. 1:1; Jer. 2:2; Ezek. 16:8; and Hos. 2:18 [ET 16]). Against such arguments, S.F. Bigger correctly insists that the pre-eminent concern in these texts is with fidelity to the marital bond, not with the number of one's wives ("Hebrew Marriage and Family in the Old Testament Period" [1974] 97).

[107] Cf. also the parable in Matthew 25 of the wise and foolish virgins awaiting the bridegroom.

[108] Since they do not affect the point at issue, we leave aside a number of text critical problems in 2 Sam. 12:7f. Cf., e.g., P.K. McCarter Jr., *II Samuel*, 292, 295.

[109] For an alternative approach to 2 Sam. 12:7f. which denies any reference to polygyny, cf. C.J. Goslinga, *Het Tweede Boek Samuël* (1962) 215; and W.C. Kaiser Jr., *Toward Old Testament Ethics* (1983) 187.

Exodus 21:10f. and Deuteronomy 21:15-17

Exod. 21:10f. and Deut. 21:15-17 may regulate polygyny and, as such, support the view that polygyny was considered to be a legally valid form of marriage (unlike homosexual unions, for example, or marriage to a woman who was already another man's wife[110]). This is not enough, however, to support the inference that these texts tacitly *approve* polygyny.[111] Such a phenomenon, where a law regulates an existing practice without thereby according it approval, is a recognized feature in both ancient and modern jurisprudence.

For instance, one would be reluctant to conclude that Deut. 21:15-17 endorses or approves the practice of a husband "hating" one of his wives, although this law seeks to mitigate the potential injury from such hatred. Additional examples are easily multiplied. Does the prohibition against bringing the hire of a harlot or "dog" into the temple in Deut. 23:19 [ET 18] approve these practices as long as the earnings are not brought into the temple? Or is this law strictly regulatory, intended to prohibit the compounding of these offences by the additional sacrilege of forbidden offerings? In modern jurisprudence one may compare various regulatory statutes, such as the stipulation of the U.S. Revenue Code which requires all tax-payers to report income derived from embezzlement, theft, etc. Such a provision, which regulates one's earnings from embezzlement, theft, etc., should not be misconstrued as if it accorded these acts official approval.

Furthermore, depending especially on the interpretation of "designate [יעד]" in Exod. 21:8f., it is possible that Exod. 21:10f. does not treat polygyny at all, but considers instead the case of a broken engagement (betrothal).[112]

In support of a reference to polygyny in 2 Sam. 12:7f., cf. M. Tsevat, "Marriage and Monarchical Legitimacy in Ugarit and Israel" (1958) 237-43; and J.D. Levenson and B. Halpern, "The Political Import of David's Marriage" (1980) 507-518.

[110] Cf., e.g., the case of Paltiel's "marriage" to Michal, the wife of David (1 Sam. 25:44; 2 Sam. 3:14f.). Presumably the fact that David never divorced Michal (nor did he willingly flee his city — cf. MAL A §36) rendered Paltiel's marriage invalid. Accordingly, it could be dissolved and their own marriage be restored, apparently without violation of Deut. 24:1-4. Cf. J.D. Martin, "The Forensic Background to Jeremiah III 1" (1969) 82-92; Z. Ben-Barak, "The legal background to the restoration of Michal to David" (1979) 15-29; and G.P. Hugenberger, "Michal" (1986) 348.

[111] As against, e.g., W. Plautz, "Monogamie und Polygynie im Alten Testament" (1963) 8.

[112] Cf. the detailed treatment of this text in §3.4 below.

Similarly, L.M. Epstein has questioned whether Deut. 21:15-17 treats a case of polygyny. Noting the usage of שׂנא elsewhere in connection with divorce, including at Elephantine, Epstein argues that שׂנואה, "hated," implies that the wife in question had been divorced (*Marriage Laws in Bible and Talmud* [1942] 4).

The complete expression, הָאַחַת אֲהוּבָה וְהָאַחַת שְׂנוּאָה, however, does not appear to favour Epstein's suggestion since אֲהוּבָה, "loved," is offered as a contrastive term. Cf. also S.F. Bigger, "Hebrew Marriage and Family in the Old Testament Period," 95, n. 1.

Deuteronomy 25:5-10

The law of levirate marriage in Deut. 25:5-10 provides a starting point for the Talmudic discussion of polygyny, and it remains a key evidence for modern scholars who consider that the Old Testament approved, rather than merely tolerated, polygyny.[113]   According to the school of Shammai, since Deuteronomy makes no provision for exempting a married brother from his levirate duty, it thereby implicitly requires, and hence approves, polygyny under such a circumstance. Closer examination, however, reveals that this law does not bear on the issue.

To begin with, it is important to recognize that Deut. 25:5-10 makes no pretence at an exhaustive coverage of the situations to which it might apply.[114] So, for example, there is no attempt to treat the possibility that there is no living brother or that a living brother might be disqualified by his immaturity from entering a levirate marriage.[115] Given this incompleteness, it is entirely possible that if a brother were already married, this too may have disqualified him from assuming the levirate obligation. The evidence of Genesis 38 suggests this possibility since the direction of levirate responsibility seems to have been downward to increasingly younger, and hence normally unmarried, brothers.

Deut. 22:23-27, the law requiring a ravisher to marry his victim, may offer an instructive analogy in that this law does not consider the case of a ravisher who is already married. One might be tempted to argue from this omission that under such a circumstance this law also would require and thus approve polygyny. The comparative evidence of MAL A §55, however, challenges such an inference. MAL A §55 provides a close parallel to Deut. 22:23-27, but it is more complete in several of its specifications, including its treatment of the exceptional case of the ravisher who is already married (in this case the law requires both a talionic ravishing of the ravisher's wife and the prior dissolution of that marriage before any marriage to the victim).

---

[113] Cf. *b. Yebam.* 44a (and *m. Yebam.* 4:11). Cf. also B. Vawter, "The Theology of Divorce," 226, n. 8; and W.F. Luck, *Divorce and Remarriage*, 230ff.

[114] On the typical incompleteness of biblical and ancient Near Eastern law, cf. R. Westbrook, "Biblical and Cuneiform Law Codes" (1985) 247-264. It was the incompleteness of Deut. 25:5-10, of course, which stimulated so much of the Talmudic speculation in *Yebamot.*

[115] That such exceptional cases were not unknown is clear from their presence within the biblical record. Cf., e.g., the situation of the widowed Ruth, left without any living brother-in-law, in Ruth 1:11f. The "kinsman-redeemer" (גֹּאֵל) appears to function in a manner which is analogous to the brother-in-law (יָבָם), and yet Ruth 1:11f. implies that the levirate responsibility was, strictly speaking, considered to be limited to the immediate family (in the wording of Deut. 25:5, "If brothers dwell together..."). Evidently, such was also the view of the Sadducees in Matt. 22:23-33. Cf. the fuller treatment of these complex issues in D.A. Leggett, *The Levirate and Goel Institutions in the Old Testament* (1974); E. Levine, "On Intra-familial Institutions of the Bible" (1976); A.A. Anderson, "The Marriage of Ruth" (1978); and W.C. Kaiser Jr., *Toward Old Testament Ethics* (1983) 190ff.

On the other hand, immaturity was the ostensible reason for postponing Shelah's levirate marriage to Tamar in Genesis 38. Cf. MAL A §43; and J. Morgenstern, "The Book of the Covenant, Part II," (1930) 164.

More explicit support for the view that levirate marriage may not have required polygyny appears in the Targum for Ruth 4:6: "I cannot marry her, because I am already married; I have no right to take an additional wife, lest it lead to strife in my home." While offering an inferior text for the passage, the Targum nevertheless reveals what must have been the common understanding in its day, namely that an existing marriage would exempt one from performing the duty of the levirate.[116]

Leviticus 18:17, 18

According to the traditional interpretation, Lev. 18:17, 18 prohibits a man from simultaneously marrying a woman and her daughter, or a woman and her sister. Such a prohibition, it is argued, implies a more general permission for (or approval of) polygynous marriage to women unrelated to each other. This implication is possible, but it is by no means necessary. For example, the fact that Lev. 19:29 forbids a man from turning his daughter into a harlot does not necessarily imply permission for him to turn other women into harlots, etc.

More problematic for these verses, however, is the likelihood that the traditional interpretation of Lev. 18:18 is wrong and that this text, in fact, offers a general (ethical) prohibition of polygyny.[117] The following seven arguments may be advanced in support of this alternative interpretation.

1) The operative expression אִשָּׁה אֶל־אֲחֹתָהּ (lit., "a woman to her sister") is used everywhere else in the Old Testament in the distributive sense of "one to another" and nowhere else refers to literal sisters.[118] Likewise, the masculine equivalent, אִישׁ אֶל־אָחִיו (lit., "a man to his brother") invariably has an analogous distributive sense, "one (man) to another," and does not refer, except by coincidence, to literal brothers.[119] Indeed, had it been the intention of Lev. 18:18 to prohibit a man from marrying two women who were literal sisters, it could have done so with considerably less ambiguity by the use of the conjunction "and [ו]," rather than the preposition "to [אֶל]," that is, "a

---

[116] Cf. J.H. Hertz, "Foreword" to *The Babylonian Talmud*, Seder Nashim, I, xvii. Cf. also the notice of the death of Judah's wife in Gen. 38:12, which appears to be recorded in order to establish the transference of the levirate responsibility now to Judah. Cf. HL §193. On this view, the text implies that Judah was not responsible to perform the levirate duty while his wife was still alive.

[117] So, according to, *inter alia*, M. Poole, *Annotations upon the Holy Bible* (1803) *ad loc.*; S.E. Dwight, *The Hebrew Wife* (1836) 105-27; anon., "Art. IV - The General Assembly of 1842" (1842) 518-520; J. Murray, *Principles of Conduct* (1957) 250-256, esp.p. 253; and A. Tosato, "The Law of Leviticus 18:18: A Reexamination" (1984). Against this view, cf. G. Bush, *Notes, Critical and Practical, on the Book of Leviticus* (1842) 192-98, cited with approval by W.C. Kaiser Jr., *Toward Old Testament Ethics*, 114-16. At other points, however, Kaiser interprets Lev. 18:18 as a prohibition of polygyny (*op. cit.*, 93-94, 186, 189).

[118] This is so whether or not persons are in view: Exod. 26:3(*bis*), 5, 6, 17; Ezek. 1:9, possibly 11 (cf. *BHS*), 23; 3:13. Cf. J. Murray, *Principles of Conduct* (1957) 253. This summary of actual usage is not intended to imply that the expression could not refer to literal sisters.

[119] I.e., Gen. 42:21, 28; Exod. 16:15; 25:20; 37:9; Num. 14:4; Isa. 9:18 [ET 19]; Jer. 13:14; 23:35; 25:26; and Ezek. 24:23.

woman *and* her sister [אָשָׁה וַאֲחֹתָהּ]." The grammar of this expression would then be precisely analogous to that of "a woman *and* her daughter [אָשָׁה וּבִתָּהּ]," the phrase employed by the author in the immediately preceding verse, where he forbids sexual relations with a woman and her daughter (cf. also Lev. 20:14). It appears likely that it was the awareness of this usage which already led the Zadokites and the Qumran community in the first century B.C., as well as the much later Karaites, to interpret Lev. 18:18 as an explicit prohibition against polygyny.[120]

2) Even apart from any consideration of the expression אָשָׁה אֶל־אֲחֹתָהּ, the possibility of a non-literal sense for "sister [אָחֹות]" (or "brother [אָח]") is widely recognized.[121] In the past such a meaning in Lev. 18:18 has often been overlooked because of the assumption that vs. 18 must be interpreted in the light of the long series of incestuous unions which are prohibited in vss. 7-17, where אָחֹות consistently refers to a literal sister.[122] A. Tosato has noted, however, "Elsewhere in Leviticus 18 we find *'aḥôt*, and not as in v. 18 *'iššâ... 'aḥōtāh*. A simple equation between these two philologically different expressions seems to be false."[123]

3) Moreover, according to Tosato, the overall literary structure of Leviticus 18 suggests that there is a major break between vss. 17 and 18. As Tosato outlines the chapter, there is a parenetic framework consisting of vss. 1-5 and 24-30. Vs. 6 then introduces two series of laws: the first series prohibits incestuous unions; the second series prohibits a variety of non-incestuous sexual unions. Up to this point virtually all scholars are in agreement; the problem comes in determining the dividing point between the two series. While some interpreters favour a division between vs. 18 and vs. 19, others, including Tosato, divide the two series between vs. 17 and vs. 18. Supporting this second analysis, whereby vs. 18 is placed with other non-incestuous sexual unions, Tosato notes that the eleven prohibitions in vss. 7-17 have the same formal structure: each begins with "the nakedness of

---

[120] For the Zadokite interpretation of Lev. 18:18, cf. "Fragments of a Zadokite Sect," 7:1, in R.H. Charles, ed., *The Apocrypha and Pseudepigrapha of the Old Testament in English*, II (1913) 810. Cf. also R. Holst, who summarizes the whole of 7:1-4 in the Fragments, noting that the Zadokites prohibited polygyny based not only on Lev. 18:18, but also on Gen. 1:27 and Deut. 17:17 ("Polygamy and the Bible" [1967] 210). Cf. G.F. Moore, *Judaism in the First Centuries of the Christian Era*, I, 202; and L.M. Epstein, *Marriage Laws in Bible and Talmud*, 13.

For the Qumran interpretation of Lev. 18:18, cf. CD 4:20-21, which reads "and you shall not take a woman as a rival wife to another...." This interpretation is further confirmed in 11QTemple 57:17-19, "And he (=the king) shall not take in addition to her another wife, for she alone shall be with him all days of her life; but if she dies, then he can take to himself another...." Cf. A. Tosato, "The Law of Leviticus 18:18" (1984) 199-201.

For the Karaite interpretation of Lev. 18:18, cf. L.M. Epstein, *Marriage Laws in Bible and Talmud* (1942) 22f.

[121] Cf., e.g., A. Tosato, "The Law of Leviticus 18:18," 201f., n. 8 and n. 9.

[122] So, e.g., G.J. Wenham, *Leviticus*, 258, n. 27, arguing against J. Murray.

[123] "The Law of Leviticus 18:18," 202, n. 8.

Tosato is not denying that other pronominally suffixed forms of אָחֹות appear in 18:6-17. Rather, presumably, his point is that the precise syntagm, אָשָׁה אֶל־אֲחֹתָהּ, must be interpreted on its own.

[עֶרְוַת]" and culminates in "you shall not uncover [לֹא תְגַלֵּה]." On the other hand, none of the second series of prohibitions, including the disputed vs. 18, begins with "the nakedness of [עֶרְוַת]," and none culminates in "you shall not uncover [לֹא תְגַלֵּה]." Rather, each of the six prohibitions in vss. 18-23 begins with the conjunction "and [ו]," and the main verb, which is preceded by the negative לֹא, is some second person imperfect other than "uncover [תְגַלֵּה]."

4) Further supporting Tosato's analysis is the observation that all but one of the anti-incest laws conclude with a justification based on the identity of the forbidden individual.[124] In form each justification appears as a verbless clause with a pronominal subject: "she is your mother [אִמְּךָ הִוא]" (v 7); "it is your father's nakedness [עֶרְוַת אָבִיךָ הִוא]" (v 8); "for they are your own nakedness [כִּי עֶרְוָתְךָ הֵנָּה]" (v 10); "she is your sister [אֲחוֹתְךָ הִוא]" (v 11); "she is your father's near kinswoman [שְׁאֵר אָבִיךָ הִוא]" (v 12); "she is your mother's near kinswoman [כִּי־שְׁאֵר אִמְּךָ הִוא]" (v 13); "she is your aunt [דֹדָתְךָ הִוא]" (v 14); "she is your son's wife [אֵשֶׁת בִּנְךָ הִוא]" (v 15); "she is your brother's nakedness [עֶרְוַת אָחִיךָ הִוא]" (v 16); "they are your near kinswomen [שַׁאֲרָה הֵנָּה]" (v 17). As is readily apparent, however, the prohibition in vs. 18 lacks a similar explanatory clause; one would be expected if the writer had intended it to be classified with the first series of laws, rather than the second.[125]

5) What is perhaps even more striking, the justification offered in vs. 18, "to be a rival to her [לִצְרֹר ... עָלֶיהָ]," far from emphasizing the intrinsic perversity of this wrong, is quite general and applicable to any bigynous marriage. As Tosato remarks, "the harm which the law wants avoided is such (rivalry, enmity) that any woman (and not necessarily a sister of the first wife) is capable of causing...."[126] Indeed, the same root, צרר, "to be a rival" or "to be hostile," is used in 1 Sam. 1:6 to describe the discordant relationship between Peninnah and Hannah, who need not have been literal sisters.[127] Accordingly, if the motive for this prohibition was to avoid vexation to one's wife, there is little reason for limiting its prohibition to a literal sister; both the Bible and anthropology provide ample testimony to the unpleasant reality of contention among co-wives, whether sisters or not.[128]

6) Further, if Lev. 18:18 had been concerned to avoid the incestuous implication of marriage to a woman and her literal sister, it would be difficult

---

[124] Vs. 9 is the only exception.

[125] As Tosato notes, had the writer intended Lev. 18:18 to prohibit the simultaneous marriage of sisters and thus to have this law complete the first series of prohibitions, it should have read something like, עֶרְוַת אִשָּׁה וַאֲחֹתָהּ לֹא תְגַלֵּה שְׁאֵרָה הִוא ("The Law of Leviticus 18:18," 206, n. 19).

[126] *Ibid.*, 206f.

[127] Some scholars consider צָרָר, "adversary," in 1 Sam. 1:6 to be a technical term for a co-wife (cf. Akkadian ṣerritum). This is possible, but unnecessary, given the actual hostility between Peninnah and Hannah described in the text.

[128] Cf. also the example of contention between Sarah and Hagar in Genesis 16 and 21; Sir. 26:6; 37:11.

Indeed, in G.P. Murdock's classic survey of 250 cultures, the majority of those cultures which permit polygyny actually prefer polygyny involving natural sisters, apparently to help minimize conflict (*Social Structure* [1949] 284ff.)!

to account for the explicit time limit on the application of the present law, "while she is alive [בְּחַיֶּיהָ]," found nowhere else in the anti-incest laws.

7) Finally, such a prohibition against polygyny ought not be dismissed as out of character for the Holiness Code because of its impossible idealism. Rather, it compares favourably with a number of other equally idealistic provisions, such as the prohibition against hatred in Lev. 19:17f.! The fact that Lev. 18:18 and many other "idealistic" stipulations lack criminal sanctions suggests that these may have been intentionally ethical, rather than legal norms. Putting this somewhat differently, Lev. 18:18 can be categorized as a *lex imperfecta*, a law which prohibits something without thereby rendering it invalid (reflecting a society which would have lacked the requisite means of enforcement in any case).[129]

6.2.2 Texts which presuppose or may encourage monogamy as the ideal form of marriage

Having concluded that Lev. 18:18 may plausibly be interpreted as it was at Qumran, namely as an ethical prohibition of polygyny, we need to consider whether other texts within the Old Testament similarly discourage or disapprove polygyny, even if polygyny remained a legally valid form of marriage. Certainly a number of texts appear to presuppose monogamy and perhaps even to advocate monogamy as desirable, if not normative. As R. de Vaux, B. Vawter, W. Plautz, and other scholars have noted, this preference for monogamy seems to be the case especially in the wisdom literature and the J account of creation (i.e., the paradigmatic monogamous marriage of Adam and Eve in Genesis 2, to be discussed more fully in Chapter 5 below, and the decidedly unflattering account of the origin of polygyny in the reprobate line of Cain in Gen. 4:19ff.).[130] As argued by W. Plautz, however, many of the texts which initially appear to favour monogamy may do so only because they reflect monogamy as the prevalent and typical practice at the time. They need not require the conclusion that monogamy was the exclusive or even the ideal form of marriage.[131]

---

[129] For other examples and a more general discussion of *leges imperfectae*, cf. S.E. Loewenstamm, "The Laws of Adultery and Murder in Biblical and Mesopotamian Law" (1980) 153, n. 9; and R. Yaron, *The Laws of Eshnunna* (1988) 212.

[130] R. de Vaux, *Ancient Israel*, II, 25f.; B. Vawter, *Genesis*, 76; *idem*, "The Biblical Theology of Divorce," 223f.; and W. Plautz, "Monogamie und Polygynie im Alten Testament" (1963) 3-6.

Cf. Ps. 128:3 (discussed by W. Plautz, *op. cit.*, 4); Prov. 5:15-21; 12:4; 18:22; 19:14; 31:10-31; Eccl. 9:9; and Canticles (according to "the Shepherd Hypothesis"). Other "non-Wisdom" passages could also be added, such as Deut. 28:54, 56; Jer. 5:8; 6:11; Mal. 2:14 — cf. discussion of these verses in W.C. Kaiser Jr., *Toward Old Testament Ethics*, 189f.

By contrast, texts which attest to the inexpedience of polygyny (factiousness and jealousy of wives, favouritism toward children, etc.) abound. Cf. Genesis 16; 21; 29-31; 1 Samuel 1 (including the use in vs. 6 of the term צָרָר, "adversary," for a co-wife); 2 Chr. 11:21; Deut. 21:15; Sir. 26:6; and 37:11.

[131] "Monogamie und Polygynie im Alten Testament," 5. Cf. also S.F. Bigger, "Hebrew Marriage and Family in the Old Testament Period" (1974) 86ff. As will be argued in Chapter 5, however, this objection appears to be unjustified in the case of Genesis 2.

6.2.3 Texts which undermine or prohibit the motive for polygyny
Nevertheless, it is a striking fact that the Old Testament excludes both of the most clearly approved, if not the only approved motives for polygyny among Israel's neighbours (omitting the case of grave illness), namely infertility and, in the case of royalty, the need to secure diplomatic alliances. The promise of fertility for covenant fidelity, taught both by example, as in the case of Abraham (recourse to Hagar because of Sarah's infertility only demonstrated Abraham's lack of faith), and by precept, as in Exod. 23:26, Deut. 7:14, and 28:4, should have obviated the most common need for polygyny.[132] Similarly, foreign alliances were forbidden to Israel (cf., e.g., Deut. 17:16; Isa. 7; 30:1f.; 31:1), and royal polygyny, the means by which such alliances were secured, was condemned both by example (cf. Solomon in 1 Kgs. 11:1-10) and by precept in Deut. 17:17.[133]

Admittedly, the prohibition in this last text, "he [the king] shall not increase wives for himself [וְלֹא יַרְבֶּה־לֹּוֹ נָשִׁים]," seems less than precise — "increase" over what maximum number, one might ask. It appears, however, that the expression, "he [the king] shall not increase wives for himself," was chosen not to facilitate some more modest level of polygyny, but to achieve an artful parallelism between the three characteristic sins of Canaanite (and Israelite) kingship:

סוּסִים לֹא־יַרְבֶּה־לּוֹ רַק, "only *he must not increase* horses *for himself...*"

נָשִׁים וְלֹא יַרְבֶּה־לּוֹ, "and *he must not increase* wives *for himself...*"

וְכֶסֶף וְזָהָב לֹא יַרְבֶּה־לּוֹ מְאֹד, "and *he must not increase* greatly silver and gold *for himself...*"

What makes these sins particularly dangerous for any would-be king of Israel, the evident reason for conjoining them here, is that each of them constitutes an acute temptation for the king to vaunt himself over his brethren and, especially, to apostatise. As A.D.H. Mayes notes, horses and wealth are the very things which would later lead the king "to pride, to a loss of awareness of the need to trust in Yahweh, and so to unfaithfulness and apostasy" (cf. Isa. 2:7-9 and Mic. 5:10ff.; and for the related problem of an

---

[132] Cf. also W. Berg, who argues that narrative analogy may offer a key to condemning the patriarch's practice of polygyny: Abraham is presented as a second Adam figure, who falls when he heeds the advice of Sarah, his Eve ("Der Sündenfall Abrahams und Saras nach Gen 16,1-6" [1982] 7-14).

Less clear, but nevertheless possible, is the example of Hannah's temporary infertility, which may have motivated Elkanah to take Peninnah as a second wife, but which the text explains was an evidence of Yahweh's judgment (cf., e.g., 1 Sam. 1:5f., 11, perhaps reflected also in Hannah's unwillingness, or inability, to partake of the peace offerings in Shiloh until after Eli's priestly benediction).

[133] Cf. also 1 Kgs. 3:1 and Neh. 13:26.

I. Mendelsohn notes that the anti-monarchical polemic of 1 Samuel 8 and Deuteronomy 17, including its prohibition of royal polygyny, was very likely an early direct repudiation of the excesses of Canaanite kingship, rather than a late reflection of Israel's own bitter experience from Solomon *et al.* ("Samuel's Denunciation of Kingship in the Light of the Akkadian Documents from Ugarit" [1956] 17-22).

alliance with Egypt, cf. Isa. 30:1-7; 31:1-3).[134] Similarly, the prohibition against "increasing" wives is not so much concerned with the legality of polygyny in the abstract, but with the inevitable result of *royal* polygyny in apostasy and accommodation to the gods of one's wives: as the text explicitly states, "lest his heart turn away" (cf. 1 Kgs. 11:1ff.; 16:31-33).[135] Since this danger can attend diplomatic polygyny practiced to any degree and since the text insists that the king should neither allow his heart to be "lifted above his brethren" nor to think himself above the law (vss. 18-20), it appears that the seemingly vague expression, "he [the king] shall not increase wives for himself," was intended precisely to prohibit the king from having any more wives than other men were permitted, just as the parallel lines prohibit him from having any more horses or wealth.[136] In other words, the Zadokites and the community at Qumran were not misguided in their interpretation of Deut. 17:17 as requiring monogamous marriage for the king.[137]

6.3 Malachi 2:10-16 and conclusions

Based on our brief survey above, we offer the following conclusions regarding the practice of polygyny in the Old Testament:

1) Although polygyny appears to have been practiced within Israel throughout most, if not all, of the pre-exilic period, it was largely confined to Israel's chieftains and royalty and only rarely attested outside this circle.

2) Although polygyny was implicitly recognized as a legally valid form of marriage throughout the Old Testament, and one or two texts even regulate this practice (Deut. 21:15-17 and, perhaps, Exod. 21:10-11), nevertheless no text requires it or commends it as ethically approved.

3) On the other hand, a number of texts appear to advocate monogamy as the assumed, if not also the normative and ideal form of marriage (e.g., Genesis 2; Proverbs; etc.).

---

[134] *Deuteronomy* (1979) 272f.

[135] By its very nature royal polygyny typically involves foreign, and hence heathen, wives. Cf. especially 1 Kgs. 11:1-8, where all or most of Solomon's wives appear to be of foreign extraction. Cf. also 2 Sam. 3:3; 1 Kgs. 3:1; 14:21, 31; and 16:31.

[136] It is this implicit comparison with other men which rescues these prohibitions from meaningless imprecision.

In terms of this sustained concern to promote humility, if status display was ever a motive for Israelite polygyny, such a motive would also be forbidden for the king.

[137] Cf. 11QTemple 57:17-19, "And he (=the king) shall not take in addition to her another wife, for she alone shall be with him all days of her life; but if she dies, then he can take to himself another...."

For the Zadokite interpretation of Deut. 17:17, cf. "Fragments of a Zadokite Sect," 7:4, in R.H. Charles, ed., *The Apocrypha and Pseudepigrapha of the Old Testament in English*, II (1913) 810. Cf. also G.F. Moore, *Judaism in the First Centuries of the Christian Era*, I, 202; and R. Holst "Polygamy and the Bible" (1967) 210.

As an aside, one may object that this prohibition would have been clearer had it simply stated "the king shall not take a second wife" or "shall not have more than one wife," etc. Given the undeniable right to remarry following divorce or the death of a spouse, however, the expression as it exists in 17:17 may be deemed adequate.

4) Consistent with this ideal, other texts demonstrate the inexpedience of polygyny; a few suggest that it was ethically disapproved, and perhaps even prohibited (e.g., Gen. 4:19ff.; Lev. 18:18; and Deut. 17:17).

5) The two motives for polygyny which were most generally approved elsewhere in the ancient Near East, namely the securing of diplomatic alliances for leaders and a remedy for infertility, were obviated or excluded within the Old Testament.[138] Of course, even apart from this idealistic exclusion, if Mal. 2:15 implies that the Jewish wives of Malachi's day had borne children, then recourse to polygyny under such a circumstance would be unexpected and disapproved even by non-Israelite norms.

With respect to the post-exilic period, although Mal. 2:10-16 has been supposed by some scholars to assume (A.S. van der Woude) or even to commend polygyny (e.g., H. Cowles and W.F. Luck), it is far more likely that monogamy was seen as the marital ideal in this period and that actual marital practice was monogamous with few, if any, exceptions.[139] Such an assumption may find some support in the rejection of polygyny among the Jews in 5th century B.C. Elephantine, as well as in later sectarian Judaism.[140] In any case, at least in terms of the biblical record, there is not a single example of polygyny among the Israelites during the post-exilic period (excluding Esther). Even apart from any consideration of the relevant biblical and epigraphic evidence, however, the rarity of polygyny in Malachi's day should be readily apparent from the sociological observation that polygyny is

---

[138] This is not to deny the existence of many other possible motives for polygyny in the OT, as well as elsewhere in the ancient Near East, including love (Gen. 29:26-30); guilt (2 Sam. 11:27); the desire to please parents (Gen. 27:46; 28:8f.); and perhaps display status (Esther 1, 2), among others. No law or marriage document appears to accord any of these its approval, however, while many would penalize the husband who takes a second wife on these grounds (apart from the infertility or grave illness of the first wife).

[139] Cf. W. Nowack, *Die kleinen Propheten* (1922) 417; E. Sellin, *Das Zwölfprophetenbuch* (1930) 550ff.; R. Yaron, *Introduction to the Law of the Aramaic Papyri* (1961) 61; B. Vawter, "The Biblical Theology of Divorce" (1967) 223-43; S. Schreiner, "Mischehen-Ehebruch-Ehescheidung" (1979) 226; A. Tosato, "The Law of Leviticus 18:18" (1984) 199-214; E. Achtemeier, *Nahum - Malachi* (1986) 181; and B. Glazier-McDonald, *Malachi* (1987) 114.

As argued by these scholars, Gen. 2:18-25 appears to support monogamy as an ideal, and many of the Pentateuchal laws and statements in the wisdom literature seem to presuppose it as the normal or ideal marriage form. Cf., e.g., Exod. 20:7; 21:5; Lev. 18:8, 16, 18; 20:10; 21:13; Num. 5:12; Deut. 5:21; 22:22; Prov. 5:18-20; 12:4; 18:22; 19:13; 31:10-31; Eccl. 9:9; Sir. 26:1-4; Tob. 7:12; 8:6-8; and the Damascus Document.

[140] Cf., e.g., R. Yaron, *Introduction to the Law of the Aramaic Papyri*, 60.

This growing tendency to reject polygyny in a more explicit manner may reflect a later inclination to apply earlier priestly standards to the covenant people as a whole. Cf., e.g., D. Bossman, "Ezra's Marriage Reform: Israel Redefined," 37f.; and M. Fishbane, *Biblical Interpretation in Ancient Israel*, 114ff.

In support, it may be noted that there is no clear example of polygyny among the priesthood throughout Israel's history. (In favour of Moses as a monogamist, cf. W. Plautz, "Monogamie und Polygynie im Alten Testament," 4; and F.M. Cross, *Canaanite Myth and Hebrew Epic*, 204). Cf. also the New Testament requirement for church leaders to be the "husband of but one wife," an uncertain expression which may have a more general application, perhaps intending to prohibit remarriage, but which appears to exclude polygyny as well (1 Tim. 3:2, 12 and Titus 1:6; cf. also 1 Tim. 5:9).

most commonly associated with men who enjoy considerable wealth and status, characteristics which hardly typified Malachi's beleaguered contemporaries living in the rump state of Judah.[141]

7. SUMMARY

The present chapter has been concerned to answer an objection of C.C. Torrey, A. Isaksson, and others to a reference to literal marriage in Mal. 2:10-16, and hence to the identification of literal marriage as a "covenant" in 2:14. Their objection is based on a contradiction between the traditional interpretation of these verses and the scholarly assumption that polygyny was freely tolerated by Malachi and his contemporaries. More particularly, on the traditional view Malachi condemns both mixed marriage and divorce in 2:10-16 because Israelite men were committing both of these offences when they divorced their Jewish wives in order to marry Gentile women. If polygyny was freely tolerated, there would have been no reason for these divorces; hence, as argued by these scholars, Malachi must not refer to literal marriage and divorce.[142]

In response we noted that the traditional interpretation of the relationship between the offences of mixed marriage and divorce in Mal. 2:10-16 represents only one of five alternative views, each of which supports a reference to literal marriage. In considering these views, it appeared that the fourth was the most probable interpretation, namely the view of J. Wellhausen and others that the offences of mixed marriage and divorce were merely parallel examples of the infidelity [בגד] which Malachi condemns in 2:10 and that there was no necessary causal connection between them. As a result, on this view Mal. 2:10-16 carries no implication for the practice of polygyny.

Nevertheless, since the traditional view remains possible, it was necessary to examine the practice of polygyny elsewhere in the Old Testament. In the course of this study it was concluded that, although polygyny was never illegal, monogamy is seen as the marital ideal in a number of texts and that actual marital practice was monogamous with few, if any, exceptions, particularly in the post-exilic period.

Consequently, there is no contradiction between Mal. 2:10-16, when understood as referring to literal marriage and divorce, and the probable attitudes toward and practice of polygyny in Malachi's day; hence there is no

---

[141] So also B. Glazier-McDonald, *Malachi: The Divine Messenger*, 114.

[142] As we noted in the course of the chapter, this same argument regarding the apparent contradiction between Mal. 2:10-16, if it refers to mixed marriage and divorce, and the assumed toleration of polygyny elsewhere is advanced by critical scholars to eliminate any reference in Mal. 2:10-16 to the offence of mixed marriage and, alternatively, by A.S. van der Woude to eliminate any reference to the offence of divorce. Neither expedient is required, however, if there is no causal relationship between these offences, as is argued, for example, by J. Wellhausen, *et al.* See §4 above.

compelling reason for denying a reference to literal marriage as a "covenant" in 2:14.

CHAPTER FIVE

MALACHI 2:15: MALACHI'S APPEAL TO ADAM AND EVE FOR HIS UNDERSTANDING OF MARRIAGE AS A "COVENANT [ברית]"

"Interpreting the text [of Mal. 2:10-16] as a condemnation of divorce means that we are reading into it a view of divorce which was first expounded about 500 years after Malachi and a view of the wife's status in marriage which did not begin to be put into practice in this part of the world until about 2500 years after the prophet Malachi worked there."[1] So writes A. Isaksson, who adds at another point in his discussion, "A really quite decisive argument against interpreting these verses as dealing with marriage and divorce is that the O.T. concept ברית ["covenant"] is quite incompatible with what marriage meant at this period. Marriage was not a compact entered into by man and wife with Yahweh as witness but a matter of commercial negotiation between two men."[2]

While recognizing the intimate connection between intermarriage and the threat of idolatry which underlies Malachi's condemnation of intermarriage, we have already rejected the view held by Isaksson and others that Malachi was employing the image of marriage just as a metaphor for idolatry.[3] Moreover, although "covenant" in 2:10 refers to Israel's covenant with God, which was being desecrated by intermarriage, we have rejected the view that "covenant" in vs. 14 refers to Israel's covenant in which the husband and the wife (or, according to some, the wife's family) are considered to be fellow partners, rather than to the marital relation itself.[4]

We still need to consider this more fundamental and intriguing criticism of Isaksson's, namely his assertion that Malachi could not have considered literal marriage and divorce in terms of covenant concepts since such a view of marriage would be unprecedented and anachronistic within the post-exilic period. Of course, if Malachi did indeed consider marriage and divorce in terms of covenant concepts, as we have argued, one cannot rule out *a priori* the possibility that Malachi was a religio-ethical genius and that he articulated a theory of marriage which was in many respects unprecedented. Nevertheless, as Isaksson seems to have appreciated, such an hypothesis of originality is ruled out in the present case because of the manner in which

---

[1] A. Isaksson, *Marriage and Ministry in the New Temple* (1965) 34.
[2] *Ibid.*, 31. In support Isaksson cites R. Kraetzschmar, *Die Bundesvorstellung im Alten Testament*, 168, 240; and C.C. Torrey, "The Prophecy of 'Malachi'," 9.
[3] For the danger of idolatry resulting from mixed marriage, cf., e.g., Exod. 34:11-16; Deut. 7:1-4; 1 Kgs. 11:1-11; Ezra 9:1ff.; and Neh. 13:23-31.
[4] See Chapter 2, §2.1 above.

Malachi conducts his argument. Nowhere else is Malachi averse to anticipating objections and misunderstandings on the part of the people, but in 2:10-16 there is not the least hint that his contemporaries might object to his identification of their wives as "your companion and your wife by covenant [חֲבֶרְתְּךָ וְאֵשֶׁת בְּרִיתֶךָ]." In other words, in this section as throughout his work, Malachi's argument proceeds not by way of bold new insights and novelties, but by way of reminder and appeal to the ancient standards and common convictions (cf. Mal. 3:22 [ET 4:4]).[5] No doubt some were prepared to justify their divorces and to insist that they had not committed infidelity [בגד] against their wives. Perhaps many even assumed that Yahweh would be indifferent to such acts (cf. 2:17; 3:15, 18) and that he would never act as a "witness" against them and so reject their offerings (2:14, cf. 3:5).[6] Malachi's condemnation of his contemporaries would lose all its force, however, if the underlying understanding of marriage as a covenant could not command their assent or be substantiated from the ancient texts.

In Chapter 8 we shall attempt to place Malachi's conception of marriage in its proper context in terms of other biblical texts which appear to view marriage as a covenant (or which presuppose such a view). Our immediate concern, however, is to establish the plausibility of that interpretation of Mal. 2:15a according to which Malachi grounds his view of marriage in the "law of my servant Moses" and specifically in the paradigmatic marriage of Adam and Eve.[7] After this we shall seek to establish that the character of Adam and Eve's marriage lent itself to being identified by Malachi as a covenant (2:14) and, as such, provided a plausible justification for Malachi's understanding of marriage.

To facilitate our discussion it will help to have before us the following citation of the MT, a proposed translation, and the LXX, with each segment labelled according to a scheme of reference commonly employed among commentators:

2:15a αα וְלֹא־אֶחָד עָשָׂה   aβ וּשְׁאָר רוּחַ לוֹ   aγ וּמָה הָאֶחָד מְבַקֵּשׁ זֶרַע אֱלֹהִים
2:15b bα וְנִשְׁמַרְתֶּם בְּרוּחֲכֶם   bβ וּבְאֵשֶׁת נְעוּרֶיךָ אַל־יִבְגֹּד:

---

[5] For example, Mal. 2:10 begins with the rhetorical question, "Have we not all one Father?" — a question which presupposes a body of theological common knowledge. Of course, Judah may have been ignoring this fact of its "sonship" and mutual "brotherhood," and certainly many offenders were prepared to conveniently overlook the idolatrous paternity of their foreign wives (hence Malachi's pointed reminder that such a wife was a בַּת־אֵל נֵכָר). Malachi's argument and condemnation, however, presuppose an essential agreement on the part of his contemporaries with his own rather nuanced understanding of Israel's existence as a people in covenant with Yahweh.

[6] According to certain interpretations, vs. 15a offers this kind of self-justification either by appeal to the example of Abraham (cf., e.g., E. Cashdan, "Malachi" [1948] 347) or by reference to the mandate to have children, which may have motivated the taking of a new wife.

[7] Cf. Chapter 1, §§2-3 above for a defence of the authenticity of 3:22 [ET 4:4] within Malachi and an interpretation of ... תּוֹרַת מֹשֶׁה which takes this as a plausible instance of synecdoche intended by Malachi to encompass the Pentateuch as a whole.

2:15 ᵃᵃ"Did He not make [you/them] one, ᵃᵝwith a remnant of the spirit belonging to it? ᵃᵞAnd what was the One seeking? A godly seed! ᵇᵃTherefore watch out for your lives ᵇᵝand do not act faithlessly against the wife of your youth."

2:15a ᵃᵃκαὶ οὐκ ἄλλος⁸ ἐποίησε⁹, ᵃᵝκαὶ ὑπόλειμμα πνεύματος αὐτοῦ. ᵃᵞκαὶ εἴπατε Τί ἄλλο ἀλλ' ἢ σπέρμα ζητεῖ ὁ θεός; 2:15b ᵇᵃκαὶ φυλάξασθε ἐν τῷ πνεύματι ὑμῶν, ᵇᵝκαὶ γυναῖκα νεότητός σου μὴ ἐγκαταλίπῃς·

The LXX may be rendered: ᵃᵃ"And another has not done [so] [or "And did not another do (it)?"], ᵃᵝand [there was] a remnant of his spirit. ᵃᵞBut you say, 'What else does God seek but a seed?' ᵇᵃBut guard your spirit, ᵇᵝand do not forsake the wife of your youth."

"This is unquestionably the most difficult v. in Mal."[10] So noted J.M.P. Smith, who at another point commented, "The beginning of this verse as found in 𝔐 [= the Masoretic Text] is hopelessly obscure."[11] After surveying a variety of interpretative approaches, including a conjecture of his own, Smith was forced to conclude, "No satisfactory solution of the problem of this verse has yet been found."[12] Taking account of the proliferation of contradictory attempts to elucidate this verse in the seventy years since Smith, A.S. van der Woude recently observed: "Mal. 2:15 is one of the most difficult passages of the whole Old Testament. It would be a hopeless task to record all the attempts that have been made to explain this verse."[13] It is hard to imagine a greater disincentive to new scholarship than such an assessment coming from a scholar of Van der Woude's stature. Nevertheless, the very proliferation of those failed attempts offers its own witness to the conviction of the majority of modern scholars that the text and sense of Mal. 2:15 may not be so irrecoverable after all. In any case, although the evidence is such as will require any conclusions to be tentative, the apparent centrality of Mal. 2:15 in Malachi's argument and its potential importance for insight into

---

8 So LXXᵂᶜᵒⁿˢᵗⁱᵗ· ᶜʰʳ·ᴵᴵᴵ²²¹ (and AQΓ). LXXᴮ⁻ℵ*⁻⁶⁸ read οὐ καλὸν ἐποίησε; ("Did he not do a good thing?").

9 So J. Ziegler's edition (Duodecim Prophetae). A. Rahlfs reads ἐποίησεν.

10 A Critical and Exegetical Commentary on Haggai, Zechariah, Malachi and Jonah, 59. Cf. also, e.g., E. Sellin, Das Zwölfprophetenbuch (1922) 553; and W. Rudolph, Haggai, Sacharja 1-8, Sacharja 9-14, Maleachi, 270.

11 Malachi, 54.

12 Ibid., 55. J.G. Baldwin suggests, "Here the text becomes difficult, having suffered perhaps at the hand of scribes who took exception to its teaching" (Haggai, Zechariah, Malachi, 240). Cf. A. Tosato, "Il ripudio: delitto e pena [Mal 2,10-16]," 553.

13 "Malachi's Struggle for a Pure Community," 69. Cf. also the comment of W. Rudolph, "V. 15a ist die große crux des Maleachibuchs, und es wäre uferlos, alle vorgetragenen Deutungen Revue passieren zu lassen" (Haggai, Sacharja 1-8, Sacharja 9-14, Maleachi, 270, n. 15).
Other scholars who share W. Rudolph's and A.S. van der Woude's assessment regarding the difficulty of Mal. 2:15 include J.C. de Moor, De profeet Maleachi (1903) ad loc.; R.C. Dentan, "Malachi," IB, 6 (1956) 1136; H. Frey, Das Buch der Kirche in der Weltwende (1957) 159; and P.A. Verhoef, Maleachi (1972) 183.

Malachi's theory of marriage, not to mention its possible bearing on the teaching of Jesus, make imperative the present attempt at understanding.

As forewarned by Van der Woude, it is not possible within the limits of the present study to review in detail the host of previous interpretations of Mal. 2:15a.[14] It is apparent, however, that the primary interpretative issues posed by this verse concern: a) the grammar and reference of אֶחָד, "one," in 2:15aα (whether it is the subject or object of its clause; whether it is pronominal; its relationship to הָאֶחָד, "the one," in 2:15aγ and אֶחָד, "one" in 2:10), b) the decision whether וְלֹא־אֶחָד עָשָׂה is to be understood as a declarative ("he did not make one" or "no one made") or an interrogative clause ("and did he not make one?"), and c) the possibility that the MT should be emended (the three most common proposals are to emend אֶחָד, "one," and/or הָאֶחָד, "the one" to אַחֵר, "other," as implied by the LXX; to emend וְלֹא, "and not," to הֲלֹא, "did not?", following Targum Jonathan, the Peshiṭta, and the Vulgate; and to revocalize *ad sensum* וּשְׁאָר, "and a remnant of," to וּשְׁאֵר, "and flesh"[15]).

Although there have been numerous conflicting attempts to resolve these interpretative issues, two alternative approaches have succeeded in commanding the greatest degree of assent among modern scholars.[16] The first of these understands "one [אֶחָד]" in 15aα in a pronominal sense, while the second approach, which is favoured here, understands "one [אֶחָד]" as the object of its clause and, more particularly, considers that this verse offers an allusion to Gen. 2:24. We shall consider each of these approaches in turn.

---

[14] Without claiming to be exhaustive, the present author surveys the most important interpretations of Mal. 2:15a on pages 127-172 of his dissertation, "Marriage as a Covenant" (1991). Eight major approaches are distinguished based on whether they consider אֶחָד to be the subject of עָשָׂה (the direct object of which may be variously "it," referring to the offence described in vs. 14, or, requiring some emendation, "her" or "them") and if so, whether (I.) אֶחָד in 15aα or הָאֶחָד in 15aγ or both refer to Abraham, or whether (II.) אֶחָד refers to God, or whether (III.) אֶחָד is employed in a pronominal sense (i.e., לֹא־אֶחָד means "no one" or "nobody"), or whether (IV.) אַחֵר is read in place of the MT אֶחָד, following the LXX. Alternatively, some views understand אֶחָד as an attributive adjective, or delete it altogether, in that (V.) they follow the Peshiṭta and read אֵשׁ in place of עָשָׂה. Finally, there are views which consider אֶחָד as the direct object of עָשָׂה, with "Yahweh" as its assumed subject. These may be distinguished based on whether (VI.) אֶחָד has some reference other than Genesis 1 and 2, or whether (VII.) אֶחָד refers to Adam or to Eve, or whether (VIII.) אֶחָד refers to the "one flesh" marital unity of Adam and Eve in Gen. 2:24.

Other useful surveys are offered by J.C. de Moor, *De Propheet Maleachi* (1903); A. von Bulmerincq, *Der Prophet Maleachi*, 2 vols. (1926-1932); P.A. Verhoef, *Maleachi* (1972); and B. Glazier-McDonald, *Malachi: The Divine Messenger* (1987).

[15] This proposal was first advanced by A. van Hoonacker, *Les douze petits prophètes* (1908) 726, 728. Among those who have accepted this proposal are E. Sellin, *Das Zwölfprophetenbuch übersetzt und erklärt* (1922); D. Deden, *De Kleine Profeten* (1953); T. Chary, *Aggée - Zacharie - Malachie* (1969); W. Rudolph, *Haggai, Sacharja 1-8, Sacharja 9-14, Maleachi* (1976); NAB; and JB.

[16] For a discussion of the strengths and weaknesses of six other major approaches to Mal. 2:15a, cf. G.P. Hugenberger, "Marriage as a Covenant" (1991) pp. 127-137 and 141-153.

1. VIEWS WHICH CONSIDER "ONE [אֶחָד]" TO BE EMPLOYED IN A
PRONOMINAL SENSE (I.E., לֹא־אֶחָד IS TAKEN TO MEAN "NOT ONE," "NO
ONE," OR "NOBODY") WITH "ONE [אֶחָד]" UNDERSTOOD AS THE
SUBJECT OF ITS CLAUSE

Currently the interpretation of Mal. 2:15 perhaps most popular among
scholars is that "one [אֶחָד]" in 15aα is to be understood in a pronominal
sense, that is, לֹא־אֶחָד is taken to mean "not one," "no one," or "nobody."[17]
So, for example, S. Schreiner renders Mal. 2:15, "And no one does (any such
thing), so long as he has an ounce of sense; for what does such a one seek
(who does any such thing): Children! So guard (for yourselves) your sense,
and let no one treat the wife of his youth faithlessly."[18]

In support of this approach, it is often noted that "not [לֹא]" + "one
[אֶחָד]" elsewhere bears a similar pronominal meaning in a number of
passages, including Exod. 8:27 [ET 31]; 9:6; Job 14:4; etc. Although
virtually everyone who follows this approach considers וְלֹא־אֶחָד עָשָׂה to be a
declarative clause ("and no one does"), nevertheless, there are considerable
differences over the precise interpretation of the text, particularly 15aγ, and
the possible need for textual emendation (although it is a notable strength of
this view that a number of scholars support the unemended MT in 15a: A.B.
Ehrlich, P.M. Schumpp, S. Schreiner, A. Tosato, C. Locher, P.A. Verhoef,
and B. Glazier-McDonald, *inter alios*).

While one may wonder about the justification for Schreiner's
parenthetical addition, "any such thing," found nowhere in the text, and doubt
Schreiner's interpretation of רוּחַ as "sense" or "understanding [*Verstand*],"
unsupported by BDB, KB, or *THAT*, the most serious difficulty with
Schreiner's exegesis of vs. 15 is the resulting logic of vss. 14-16, as Schreiner
construes these verses. As noted by W. Rudolph, it would be very strange for
Malachi to insist that divorce is perfidy in 14b, 15b, and 16b and that it is a

---

[17] The present view is held by the following: B. Duhm, *Die zwölf Propheten in den
Versmassen der Urschrift übersetzt* (1910); A.B. Ehrlich, *Randglossen zur hebräischen
Bibel*, V (1912) 360; A. von Bulmerincq, "Die Mischehen im B. Maleachi" (1926); *idem,
Der Prophet Maleachi*, II (1932) 290ff.; F. Horst, *Nahum bis Maleachi* (1964) 268; I.G.
Matthews, "Haggai, Malachi" (1935) 23f.; K. Elliger, *Das Buch der zwölf kleinen
Propheten*, II (1950) 189; D.R. Jones, *Haggai, Zechariah, Malachi* (1962); A. Tosato, "Il
ripudio: delitto e pena [Mal 2,10-16]" (1978) 552; S. Schreiner, "Mischehen – Ehebruch –
Ehescheidung. Betrachtungen zu Mal 2 10-16" (1979) 217; P.M. Schumpp, *Das Buch der
zwölf Propheten* (1950) 393; P.A. Verhoef, *Maleachi* (1972); *idem, The Books of Haggai
and Malachi* (1987) 277; and B. Glazier-McDonald, *Malachi: The Divine Messenger*
(1987).

K. Budde's view is similar, but he interprets Mal. 2:15aα as an interrogative (*Zum Text
der drei letzten kleinen Propheten* [1906]).

[18] "Mischehen – Ehebruch – Ehescheidung. Betrachtungen zu Mal 2 10-16" (1979) 217:
"Und niemand tut (so etwas), sofern er einen Rest von Verstand besitzt; denn was sucht
derjenige (der so etwas tut): Kinder! Doch bewahrt (euch) euren Verstand, und die Frau
seiner Jugend behandele niemand treulos."

moral and religious offence of such gravity that it causes Yahweh to reject Israel's sacrifices, while in vs. 15a he brands it as mere stupidity![19]

In addition to these, several more fundamental objections have been raised against this approach, which considers "one [אֶחָד]" to be employed in a pronominal sense:

1) Various scholars note the inherent difficulty which this view seems to entail for "the one [הָאֶחָד]" in 15aγ. J.M.P. Smith, for example, objects that the "sudden shift of stand-point in the word 'one' is most remarkable and unnatural."[20] Putting this same objection somewhat differently, Van der Woude simply asserts, "it is unlikely that the author of the verse could refer to 'no one' by 'that one' (*ha'ehād*)."[21]

2) J. Packard, among others, notes that the present view assumes an ellipsis of the direct object of "does [עָשָׂה]" in the first clause and typically also an ellipsis of a predicate for "the one [הָאֶחָד]" in the second clause.[22]

3) Packard further objects to the present view by noting that an interrogative sense appears to be indicated for 15aα both by the position of וְלֹא־אֶחָד, preceding the verb in its clause, and by the explicit question introduced by "and what [וּמָה]" in the second clause (conjoined to the first clause by "and [וְ]").[23]

4) Finally, Packard and others observe that the pronominal rendering "no one" for לֹא־אֶחָד lacks lexical support.[24] Packard asserts, "Had the prophet meant to say that no one ever did so, he would have used אֵין אִישׁ, as Gen. xxxix. 11, or simply אַיִן." Although Packard is cited approvingly by W.C. Kaiser Jr., this assertion somewhat oversimplifies the evidence.[25] While it is true that the Old Testament does commonly use אַיִן or אֵין אִישׁ to mean "no one," this is by no means its exclusive practice;[26] in fact, אַיִן and

---

[19] "Zu Malachi 2:10-16" (1981) 85-90.

[20] *Malachi*, 55.

[21] "Malachi's Struggle for a Pure Community," 69. Cf. J. Packard, who notes that the presence of an article on the second "one," הָאֶחָד, favours a reference back to the first "one," אֶחָד ("The Book of Malachi" [1876] 17).

K. Budde appears to appreciate this difficulty when he suggests that the MT הָאֶחָד represents a corruption from an original הָא. Indeed, had Malachi intended what the present interpretation alleges, one might have expected the text to read הוּא. This emendation is purely conjectural, however, lacking any versional support.

[22] "The Book of Malachi" (1876) 17. Similarly, J.M.P. Smith objects to the RVmargin, "And not one hath done so who had a residue of the spirit...," because "so" is missing from the MT (*Malachi*, 54).

[23] Cf. also J. Owen's comment: "The position of the words shows that it is a question, for there is no interrogative particle. So it is in our language, 'Has he not made one?' And that it is a question, is evident from what follows, 'and why one?'" (John Owen, translator, in John Calvin, *Zechariah and Malachi*, 555, n. 1). J.M.P. Smith notes, "it is in an unusual position for the subject of a verbal sentence, unless it is intended to be emphatic; and it is just as abnormal a position for the object" (*Malachi*, 59). This argument favouring an interrogative sense for 15aα will be developed more fully at the end of the present chapter.

[24] W. Nowack, for example, objects without elaboration that neither לֹא־אֶחָד nor רוּחַ bear the meanings alleged by this view (*Die kleinen Propheten übersezt und erklärt* [1922] 420).

[25] W.C. Kaiser Jr., *Malachi* (1984) 72.

[26] The NIV, for example, offers the rendering "no one" 291 times in the Hebrew OT; 139 of these employ neither אִישׁ + אַיִן nor אַיִן.

אֵין אִישׁ are nowhere employed with a perfect, as would be required in the present case.

Nevertheless, the essence of Packard's objection stands. In the vast majority of instances when an Old Testament author intends to say "no one" with some verb in the perfect, this is accomplished by employing לֹא + אִישׁ + a perfect (as in Gen. 41:44), or more simply לֹא + a perfect (as in Gen. 41:21), or even לֹא + a third person plural perfect (as in Gen. 26:22 and 35:5). On the other hand, no example of אֶחָד + לֹא offers clear support for the pronominal rendering posited for Mal. 2:15. Although "one [אֶחָד]" in its various forms occurs some six hundred and ninety-nine times in the Old Testament,[27] there are only nineteen occurrences in seventeen verses where "not [לֹא]" and "one [אֶחָד]" appear together within the same clause;[28] of these, there are only three verses where the precise phrase לֹא אֶחָד is attested: the *Kethib* of Ps. 139:16, Job 14:4, and Mal. 2:15.[29]

In none of the sixteen occurrences where "not [לֹא]" and "one [אֶחָד]" occur together, but not in the phrase לֹא אֶחָד, does "one" bear an indefinite pronominal sense. Instead, in each case the numerical sense of "one" is clearly prominent. Seven examples employ אֶחָד as an attributive adjective describing "one" item or individual singled out from, or contrasted with, a larger number mentioned in the context (i.e., Num. 11:19; 35:30; Deut. 19:15; Josh. 17:17; 23:14 [*bis*]; and 1 Kgs. 8:56). In eight other examples אֶחָד appears as a substantive, but again it refers to "one" item or individual singled out from, or contrasted with, a larger number mentioned in the context (i.e., Exod. 8:27 [ET 31]; 10:19) and is often accompanied by either מִן, hence "one *out of*" (Exod. 9:6; Num. 16:15 [*bis*]; 2 Sam. 13:30; and Ps. 106:11), or בְּ, "one *among*" (2 Sam. 17:12).

The single remaining example of "not [לֹא]" and "one [אֶחָד]" occurring together, but not in the phrase לֹא אֶחָד, is Job 31:15: הֲלֹא־בַבֶּטֶן עֹשֵׂנִי עָשָׂהוּ וַיְכֻנֶנּוּ בְּרֶחֶם אֶחָד, "Did not he who made me in the womb make him? And did not *one* fashion us in the womb?" (RSV). Two difficulties with this example require special comment. First, on almost any interpretation, it is necessary to assume that "not [לֹא]" has been elided in the second clause. Second, it is uncertain whether אֶחָד should be understood as a reference to God ("And did not *one* [or *the same God*] fashion us in the womb?") or as an attributive adjective modifying רֶחֶם ("And did he not fashion us in *one* [or, *the same*] womb?"). Although this latter interpretation of Job 31:15 may be preferable, on either interpretation אֶחָד appears to have been chosen in order to

---

[27] So Even-Shoshan, *s.v.*

[28] I.e., Exod. 8:27 [ET 31]; 9:6; 10:19; Num. 11:19; 16:15; 35:30; Deut. 19:15; Josh. 17:17; 23:14; 2 Sam. 13:30; 17:12; 1 Kgs. 8:56; Mal. 2:15; Pss. 106:11; 139:16 (*Kethib*); Job 14:4; and 31:15.

[29] אֵין + אֶחָד is equally rare, occurring only in Ps. 14:3, its parallel, Ps. 53:4 [ET 3], and Dan. 10:21.

emphasize the fact that Job and his slave had *one* rather than *two* distinct origins.[30]

Finally, turning to the two examples (apart from Mal. 2:15) where the phrase לֹא אֶחָד occurs, we shall first consider Ps. 139:16, וְעַל־סִפְרְךָ כֻּלָם יִכָּתֵבוּ יָמִים יֻצָּרוּ וְלֹא [וְלוֹ] אֶחָד בָּהֶם, "All the days ordained for me were written in your book when as yet there was not *one* of them." Unfortunately, this difficult verse requires the resolution of several lexical and text-critical uncertainties, not the least of which is the need to decide whether to follow the *Qere* reading of לוֹ, "to him," in place of לֹא, "not," which would eliminate this as an example altogether. If one accepts the *Kethib*, however, once again "one" is employed as a cardinal and not as an indefinite pronoun; its numerical sense is emphasized both by contrast to "all of them [the days]," mentioned earlier in the verse, and by the subsequent modifying prepositional phrase, "among them [בָּהֶם]" (or "of them [מֵהֶם]," as in some MSS).[31]

Regrettably, both the text and sense of לֹא אֶחָד in Job 14:4 are also disputed. After the question, "Who can bring what is pure out from the impure?", the answer, "not one," would seem unexpected in view of Job's insistence on the omnipotence of God. As a result, a number of scholars suggest following the sense of the Vulgate (which offers, *nonne tu qui solus est* ["is it not you alone?"]) and the Targum (which adds, "except God") and emend the MT, for example, by repointing לֹא as לֵא, "the Mighty One."[32] F.I. Andersen, who notes that Hebrew normally expresses the idea "not one" by employing the negative existential predicator אֵין, offers the alternative suggestion that אֶחָד should be understood as a reference to God, "The One."[33] On this approach Job 14:4 would presumably be interpreted with the Vulgate as an unmarked rhetorical interrogative: "Is it not 'The One'?" Whatever the proper solution to Job 14:4 might be, M.H. Pope has argued that from a metrical point of view the MT לֹא אֶחָד appears to be "entirely too short."[34] Thus, with so many uncertainties surrounding Job 14:4, it would appear unwise to allow this single example to overturn the impression gained from the widely established patterns of Hebrew usage, which render implausible the proposal to interpret וְלֹא־אֶחָד in Mal. 2:15 in a pronominal sense.

---

[30] In support of taking אֶחָד as an attributive adjective modifying רֶחַם, cf. J.H. Kroeze, *Het Boek Job* (1961) 346f. Cf. also G.P. Hugenberger, "Marriage as a Covenant" (1991) §5.2.1.

[31] A.A. Anderson, *Psalms*, II, 910, considers the MT of 139:16b (לֹא אֶחָד בָּהֶם) to be "obscure," as does L.C. Allen, *Psalms 101-150*, 252, n. 16d.; and M. Dahood, *Psalms III*, 295 (who attempts to resolve this "baffling" phrase by repointing אֶחָד as a Niphal).

In support of the MT we have already considered a number of examples where אֶחָד is modified by a prepositional phrase introduced by בְּ or מִן (i.e., Exod. 9:6; Num. 16:15 [*bis*]; Josh. 23:14 [*bis*]; 2 Sam. 13:30; 17:12; 1 Kgs. 8:56; and Ps. 106:11).

[32] Cf. M. Dahood, *Psalms I*, 46, 144; *idem, Psalms II*, 212-213; and *idem*, "Hebrew-Ugaritic Lexicography IV (1966) 408. Cf. *RSP* III, I, 118f, h; A.C.M. Blommerde, *Northwest Semitic Grammar and Job* (1969) 118; L. Sabottka, *Zephanja* (1972) 17f.; F.I. Andersen, *Job* (1976) 171; and E.B. Smick, "Job" (1988) 926.

[33] *Job* (1976) 171.

[34] *Job* (1973) 106f.

2. VIEWS WHICH CONSIDER "ONE [אֶחָד]" TO OFFER AN ALLUSION TO
THE "ONE FLESH" MARITAL UNITY OF ADAM AND EVE IN GENESIS
2:24. ON THIS APPROACH "ONE [אֶחָד]" IS THE DIRECT OBJECT OF
"MAKE [עָשָׂה]" AND "YAHWEH" IS THE ASSUMED SUBJECT OF "MAKE
[עָשָׂה]"

Perhaps the most widely held alternative approach to Mal. 2:15 considers
Yahweh to be the implied subject of "make [עָשָׂה]" based on vs. 14 and
favours an interrogative interpretation of וְלֹא־אֶחָד עָשָׂה, "and did he not make
one?"[35] The major textual issue for this approach is the decision whether to
maintain the MT of וּשְׁאָר, "and a remnant of," or to accept A. van
Hoonacker's proposal to revocalize the MT to read וּשְׁאֵר, "and flesh."[36] The

---

[35] D.A. Bruno is the only exception since he emends לֹא־אֶחָד to לְאֶחָד (*Das Buch der
Zwölf. Eine rhythmische und textkritische Untersuchung* [1957] 181, 233).
    For an analysis of six other approaches to Mal. 2:15 that are less commonly supported
by current scholars, cf. G.P. Hugenberger, "Marriage as a Covenant" (1991) pp. 127-137
and 141-153.

[36] A. van Hoonacker renders Mal. 2:15, "Did he not make 'them' to be a single [being],
which has its flesh [and] its life? And what does this unique [being] seek? A posterity for
God! Therefore take care of your life, - and 'do not be' faithless to the wife of your youth"
[= "Ne 'les' a-t-il point faits pour n'être qu'un seul [*être*], qui a sa chair [et] sa vie? Et cet
[*être*] unique à quoi tend-il? A une postérité pour Dieu! Ayez donc soin de votre vie, — et
ne 'sois' point perfide envers l'épouse de ta jeunesse"] (*Les douze petits prophètes* [1908]
726, 728).
    Those scholars who hold views similar to Van Hoonacker's include D. Deden, *De
Kleine Profeten* (1953) 393; T. Chary, *Aggée - Zacharie - Malachie* (1969) 258, 260; NAB;
JB; and perhaps J.G. Baldwin, *Haggai, Zechariah, Malachi* (1972) 240f.; and the NIV.
    Likewise, E. Sellin revocalizes וּשְׁאָר, "and a remnant of," as וּשְׁאֵר, "and flesh" (*Das
Zwölfprophetenbuch übersetzt und erklärt* [1922] 550ff.). Accepting several other
proposed emendations, Sellin also follows the LXX in reading אַחֵר (ἄλλος, ἄλλο) in place
of the MT אֶחָד in 15aγ. As a result, Sellin renders Mal. 2:15, "Did he not make into one,
flesh and life for you (sing.)? But you (pl.) say: What does God require other than
progeny? Indeed, take heed for your (pl.) life! And do not be faithless against the wife of
your (pl.) youth!" [= "Hat er nicht zu Einem gemacht / <Fleisch> und Leben <dir>? / <Aber
ihr sprecht: Was anderes> / <Als> Nachkommenschaft verlangt Gott? / Doch hütet euch für
euer Leben! / Und gegen das Weib <eurer> Jugend <seid> nicht treulos!"].
    Offering views similar to that of Sellin are N. Nowack, *Die kleinen Propheten übersezt
und erklärt* (1922) 420f.; J.E. McFadyen, "Malachi" (1929) 835; A. Deissler in A. Deissler
and M. Delcor, *Les petits prophètes, II, Michée-Mal* (1964); A. Deissler, *Zwölf Propheten,
Die Neue Echter Bibel, 4* (Stuttgart: Echter, 1981); and A. Renker, *Die Tora bei Maleachi.
Ein Beitrag zur Bedeutungsgeschichte von tôra im Alten Testament* (1979) 73.
    Among those scholars who support the present approach while maintaining the MT of
וּשְׁאָר are Rashi (against the implication of E. Cashdan, "Malachi," 347); John Calvin,
Zechariah and Malachi, 554; E. Pococke, "A Commentary on the prophecy of Malachi"
(1740); T. Scott, *The Holy Bible with Explanatory Notes, Practical Observations, and
Copious Marginal References* (1788-1792); W. Newcome, *Minor Prophets* (1836); E.
Henderson, *The Book of the Twelve Minor Prophets* (1858); J. Packard, "The Book of
Malachi" (1876) 16; E.B. Pusey, *The Minor Prophets*, vol. 2 (1883); T.T. Perowne,
Malachi (1890); W.H. Lowe, "Malachi" (no date); H. Frey, *Das Buch der Kirche in der
Weltwende. Die kleinen nachexilichen Propheten* (1957) 157-160; T.J. Delaughter,
Malachi, Messenger of Divine Love (1976) 101; W.C. Kaiser Jr., *Malachi* (1984) 71f.; and
R.L. Smith, *Micah-Malachi* (1984) 319; as well as the RV, ASV, and the RSVmargin.
    Kaiser's view is typical of many of these scholars who maintain the MT. He translates,
"Did not he [God] make them one? — even though he had the residue of the spirit [i.e.,
'enough creative power in reserve'] [presumably to 'supply many partners']. So why only
one [partner]? Because he was seeking godly offspring" (*Malachi* [1984] 139). "The

major interpretative issue, which understandably relates to this textual decision, is whether or not to understand the clause וּשְׁאָר רוּחַ לוֹ in a concessive sense: "*though* he [i.e., Yahweh] had a remnant (or abundance) of the spirit [with which God might have made more than one wife for Adam, had he so desired]." This concessive interpretation is held to imply that Malachi intended to oppose polygyny by an appeal to the primordial monogamous marriage of Adam and Eve. Rather than assuming that Mal. 2:15 opposes polygyny, however, it seems more probable from the context that Malachi appeals to the "one flesh" unity of the paradigmatic marriage of Adam and Eve in order to oppose divorce. Accordingly, we suggest rendering Mal. 2:15 as follows: "Did He not make [you/them] one, with a remnant of the spirit belonging to it? And what was the One seeking? A godly seed! Therefore watch out for your lives and do not act faithlessly against the wife of your youth."

In particular, "one [אֶחָד]" is to be understood as an allusion to the "one flesh" character of the primeval marriage described in Gen. 2:24. Nevertheless, while "one" derives from and alludes to that text, Malachi's rhetorical question has as its immediate referent the contemporary marriage described in the preceding verse, Mal. 2:14. Just as God had made Adam and Eve to be "one" in their marriage, the husband and wife of Malachi's day must also recognize that God made them to be "one."

To better appreciate this dual referencing, it may help to note that in vs. 10 Malachi employs a similar melding of a paradigmatic historical event with a contemporaneous application. In that verse Malachi asks, "Have we not all one father? Did not one God create us?" Yet, as argued in a previous chapter, this fatherhood of God, this creative work primarily alludes to the redemptive events surrounding Sinai which, in terms of the biblical representation, formed the nation of Israel nearly a millennium before Malachi's own day. While those redemptive events involved Israelites who lived centuries earlier (hence Malachi speaks of the "the covenant of our fathers"), nevertheless Malachi interprets them as applying equally to his own contemporaries (hence, "Have *we* not all one father? Did not one God create *us*?").

2.1 Special features of the present view

Before attempting to answer the various objections which have been raised against this view, it will help to consider in some detail five major features which distinguish this present view from those which share its basic

---

thought would then run like this: Why did God make Adam and Eve only one flesh, when he might have given Adam many wives, for God certainly had more than enough of the Spirit, or his creative power, in reserve to furnish many partners? However, our God was seeking a godly offspring, and such plurality would not have been conducive to this result" (*op. cit.*, 71f.).

perspective, namely that "one [אֶחָד]" is to be understood as an allusion to the "one flesh" character of the primeval marriage described in Gen. 2:24.

2.1.1 The antecedent of לוֹ, "to him/it," in the expression וּשְׁאָר רוּחַ לוֹ, "though a remnant of the spirit belonged to him/it," is "one [אֶחָד]," not Yahweh

As already mentioned, many interpreters who share the present approach consider the antecedent of לוֹ, "to him/it," in the expression וּשְׁאָר רוּחַ לוֹ, "though a remnant of the spirit belonged to him/it," to be Yahweh and so interpret this clause as polemic against polygyny. Allegedly, Malachi is recalling how God had plenty of spirit left after creating Eve; so the divine choice not to create more than a single wife for Adam implies a repudiation of polygyny.[37]

This interpretation fails on at least three different grounds. First, such an interpretation of "though a remnant of the spirit belonged to him" virtually demands that "one [אֶחָד]" be understood primarily as a reference to Eve, not to marriage: "Did he not make just *one* [wife for Adam], even though he had a remnant of the Spirit?" Yet such an interpretation would expect the feminine form אַחַת, "one," or even אִשָּׁה אַחַת, "one woman," not the masculine form אֶחָד, "one," as in the MT. Second, it seems strange that there would have been any need in the post-exilic context for Malachi to insist that Yahweh's creative potential, that is, his "spirit [רוּחַ]," was not exhausted after the creation of the first two souls. Surely, not even the most ardent polygynist would have thought otherwise. Finally, a repudiation of polygyny in vs. 15 would appear unexpected in its context. Nowhere else in 2:10-16 is polygyny mentioned, nor is there any allusion to this as a problem elsewhere in the post-exilic biblical corpus.[38] Moreover, at least according to some interpreters, Malachi's condemnation of exogamous marriage in 2:10-12 and of divorce in 2:13-16, if anything, presupposes monogamy among Malachi's contemporaries. In other words, if polygyny had been a common practice, there would have been little reason for a man who wished to marry a pagan woman to divorce "the [Jewish] wife of his youth." In addition, there is a clear linkage between vss. 14, 15, and 16 (with the latter two sharing the parallel conclusion, וְנִשְׁמַרְתֶּם בְּרוּחֲכֶם, "Therefore watch out for your lives," and all three verses linked by the term בגד, "be unfaithful"), and in vs. 16 the practice condemned is explicitly identified as divorce, not polygyny.

H. Frey and others offer an alternative interpretation. They argue that the antecedent of "to him/it [לוֹ]" in the expression וּשְׁאָר רוּחַ לוֹ is "one [אֶחָד]" rather than Yahweh: "with a remnant of the spirit belonging to *it*?" Admittedly, this interpretation has its own difficulties — although it is salutary to recognize that the expression is problematic on virtually every interpretation. Other texts support the notion that an individual may possess

---

[37] So, e.g., J. Calvin, *Malachi*, 556. Cf. P.A. Verhoef, *The Books of Haggai and Malachi*, 277.
[38] Cf. the discussion of polygyny in Chapter 4, §6 above.

the spirit, but nowhere else does the Bible suggest that a married couple as such might similarly possess the spirit. Nevertheless, there are a number of texts which teach that the *community* of Israel corporately possesses the spirit, who is present as a witness to the covenant, and this may provide an appropriate analogy for the present passage.[39]

2.1.2 In spite of its admitted difficulty the MT רֹוּחַ וּשְׁאָר, *"and a remnant of the spirit," in 15aβ should be maintained*

As mentioned above, the expression "and a remnant of the spirit belongs to him/it [לֹו רֹוּחַ וּשְׁאָר]" is problematic on virtually any view of 2:15. J.M.P. Smith, for example, has noted, "'remnant of the Spirit' is scarcely a Hebrew point of view, and it lacks all analogy."[40] Smith's observation has often been thought to favour an alternative interpretation of רֹוּחַ וּשְׁאָר, for example, "a remnant of *sense*," which would not support the present approach to vs. 15a.[41] While this interpretation may be suggestive of various modern idioms, such as "an ounce of sense," it finds little lexical support in the ancient texts. Moreover, it appears to be opposed by the use of רוּחַ in vs. 15b, since "guard your sense" is not particularly convincing for בְּרוּחֲכֶם וְנִשְׁמַרְתֶּם. Accordingly, many scholars have accepted A. van Hoonacker's attractive proposal to emend *ad sensum* the MT רֹוּחַ וּשְׁאָר, "and a remnant of spirit," to שְׁאָר וְרוּחַ(וֹ), "flesh and spirit." The result of this emendation comports with the present interpretative approach to 2:15 because it makes more explicit the assumed allusion to Gen. 2:24 — the emended text recalls how God "made one (both) flesh and spirit." The fact that Gen. 2:24 employs בָּשָׂר, rather than שְׁאָר, for "flesh" need not detract from this view since these two terms function as synonyms elsewhere.

While we recognize the plausibility of Van Hoonacker's proposal, nevertheless, our interpretation assumes the integrity of the MT לֹו רֹוּחַ וּשְׁאָר. There are a number of reasons for this choice.

1) Although the discussion of the proposed emendation normally focuses on the merits of an admittedly modest repointing of שְׁאָר, "remnant of," as שְׁאָר, "flesh," in fact the emendation requires at least one and very often two additional changes in the text: the introduction of the conjunction וְ before רוּחַ (hence, "*and* spirit") and often the deletion of the initial וְ, "and," prefixed to וּשְׁאָר. These changes are not trivial and require a more adequate defence according to the canons of textual criticism.

2) The MT vocalization for וּשְׁאָר, "remnant," is uniformly supported by the versions (LXX: ὑπόλειμμα; Peshiṭta: ܣܪܟܐ; Vulgate: *residuum*) in spite of the marked divergence from the MT of those same versions elsewhere in vs. 15. Given the acknowledged difficulty of the expression

---

[39] E.g., cf. Hag. 2:5 and the interpretation of this verse offered in M.G. Kline, *The Structure of Biblical Authority* (1972) 201f. Cf. also, M.M. Kline, "The Holy Spirit as Covenant Witness" (1972) *passim*.
Cf. H. Frey, *Das Buch der Kirche in der Weltwende* (1957) *ad loc.*
[40] *Malachi*, 54.
[41] Cf., e.g., P.A. Verhoef, *The Books of Haggai and Malachi*, 276.

"and a remnant of the spirit belongs to him/it [וּשְׁאָר רוּחַ לוֹ]," this uniform witness of the versions is remarkable and would be hard to explain on any other basis than the assumption of the originality of the MT.

3) Related to the comment just made, even apart from the supportive witness of the versions, it is hard to imagine how a supposed original text which was understood as שְׁאֵר, "flesh," could have been uniformly corrupted by the versions into שְׁאָר, "remnant," precisely because this resulting reading is so difficult (principle of *lectio difficilior*).[42]

4) Further, as noted by A. Tosato, there is at least a slight grammatical confirmation for the suitability of וּשְׁאָר, "and a remnant *of*," in the expression וּשְׁאָר רוּחַ, since שְׁאָר is commonly found elsewhere in the Old Testament in the construct state, just as it appears in the present verse.[43]

5) Finally, the claim of J.M.P. Smith and others, namely that "remnant of the spirit" lacks analogy elsewhere in the Old Testament, is true only for the usual view, which holds that "to him/it [לוֹ]" has Yahweh for its referent.[44] As mentioned earlier, however, our interpretation holds that the antecedent of "to it" is "one."

With A. von Bulmerincq and others, "spirit [רוּחַ]" in both 15aβ and 15bα is to be understood as in Ps. 104:29f.; Job 32:8; Dan. 5:12; and 6:4, namely as a reference to the spirit of God which resides in man. If "spirit" is considered as a reference to the divine spirit, then a possible analogy for our text may be found in Num. 11:25, where the Lord "took some of the spirit that was upon him [i.e., Moses] and put it upon the seventy elders."[45]

Nevertheless, since the presence of the spirit which comes from God and a creature's life are coterminous (cf. Ps. 104:29f.[46]), "spirit" may be at one and the same time a reference both to the spirit of God and to the breath of life (cf. נִשְׁמַת חַיִּים in Gen. 2:7).[47] If "spirit" is understood as a reference to one's life breath, then the present clause may find an analogous text in Dan.

---

[42] Accordingly, L. Kruse-Blinkenberg argues that it is impossible to reconstruct or improve the MT in 2:15 by the help of LXX, Peshṭta, or Targum ("The Pesitta [*sic*] of the Book of Malachi," 113).

[43] E.g., Isa. 10:19f.; 11:11, 16; 28:5; Neh. 11:20; 1 Chr. 11:8; and 2 Chr. 24:14, according to A. Tosato, "Il ripudio: delitto e pena (Mal 2,10-16)," 551, n. 15.

Tosato adds to this the observation that there is a certain linguistic congruence between לֹא־אֶחָד and שְׁאָר as is apparent from a number of examples, including Exod. 8:27 [ET 31]; 10:19; and 14:28. This observation, however, lacks conviction because in the cases cited שְׁאָר appears in the Niphal verbal form, not as a (G-stem) noun.

[44] T. Chary shares the objection that the unemended expression וּשְׁאָר רוּחַ לוֹ makes no sense; he notes that this applies particularly if Yahweh is the antecedent (*Aggée - Zacharie - Malachie* [1969] 261).

[45] This parallel is acknowledged by P.A. Verhoef, *The Books of Haggai and Malachi*, 276.

It is less common, but not exceptional, for an unqualified and anarthrous רוּחַ to refer to the Spirit of God. Cf., e.g., Isa. 32:15; Ezek. 3:12; 11:1, 24; 43:5.

[46] RSV: "When thou hidest thy face, they are dismayed; when thou takest away their breath [רוּחָם], they die and return to their dust. When thou sendest thy Spirit [רוּחֲךָ], they are created; and thou renewest the face of the ground."

[47] T.T. Perowne compares Gen. 7:22, "in whose nostrils was the breath of the spirit of life [נִשְׁמַת־רוּחַ חַיִּים בְּאַפָּיו]" (*Malachi* [1890] 27).

10:17, where the Niphal of שׁאר is used to describe the near depletion of one's life-breath [נְשָׁמָה]: "How can my lord's servant talk with my lord? For now no strength remains in me, and no breath is left in me [וּנְשָׁמָה לֹא נִשְׁאֲרָה־בִי]." Tosato recognizes an advantage of this interpretation, namely that it maintains the same sense for "spirit [רוּחַ]" in the present expression in 15aβ as it bears later in vss. 15b and 16c.[48] Tosato notes that the warning to guard one's life-spirit in those two later passages corroborates his interpretation here of an implied threat of being completely deprived of "life-spirit [רוּחַ]."

Finally, in support of the present interpretation of 2:15aβ, H. Frey makes the interesting proposal that Malachi, having already drawn attention to creation and the marriage of Adam and Eve, now also obliquely alludes to Genesis 6, where God determined that his holy life-giving spirit would not continue to strive with mankind (Gen. 6:3) as a result of the marital infractions described in that context. So here, men who have similarly transgressed have only a residue of his spirit [וּשְׁאָר רוּחַ], which now they must guard [וְנִשְׁמַרְתֶּם בְּרוּחֲכֶם].[49]

2.1.3 The MT of 15aγ should be maintained in spite of the evidence of the LXX and 4QXII[a]

While the general quality of the MT in Malachi should be recognized, nevertheless, with E. Sellin, A. Deissler, and others, the evidence of the LXX, "and you say [καὶ εἴπατε]," cannot easily be disregarded as an expansion.[50] It is true that most scholars who support the restoration of "and you say [וַאֲמַרְתֶּם]" also urge emending the remainder of 15aγ in accord with the LXX, but this more radical emendation of the MT is unnecessary, and, as we have argued above, the reading of the LXX is not convincing.[51] Furthermore, as noted by R. Fuller, while the text of Mal. 2:15 in 4QXII[a] is off the leather, considerations of line length favour the assumption that this verse was slightly longer in 4QXII[a] than it is in the MT and hence support the inference that it included וַאֲמַרְתֶּם.[52]

The following observations, however, weigh against the originality of "and you say [וַאֲמַרְתֶּם]" in 15aγ. First, the presence of the conjunction ו on

---

[48] In support, A. Tosato cites D. Lys, "Rûach" (1962) 336, who presents evidence that this is the prevalent sense which רוּח bears in all the post-exilic texts where it is found ("Il ripudio: delitto e pena [Mal 2,10-16]," 551, n. 16)

[49] H. Frey, Das Buch der Kirche in der Weltwende, 160.

[50] It is true that the unemended MT in 15aγ is not particularly difficult and, as such, may not seem to demand the presence of וַאֲמַרְתֶּם or correction by recourse to the LXX. Yet one may question the consistency of a text-critical methodology which resorts to the versions only when the MT is considered difficult or corrupt. Cf., e.g., R.W. Klein's warning, "A common mistake in Old Testament textual studies is to resort to LXX only when the MT, for one reason or another, seems difficult or corrupt" (Textual Criticism of the Old Testament From the Septuagint to Qumran [1974] 62).

[51] For scholars who emend the remainder of 15aγ in accord with the LXX, cf. E. Sellin, W. Nowack[3rd ed.], A. Deissler, A. Renker, and R. Fuller (in "Does Yahweh Hate Divorce? Malachi 2:16 and the Text of Malachi at Qumran").

[52] R. Fuller, "Does Yahweh Hate Divorce? Malachi 2:16 and the Text of Malachi at Qumran." Cf. also R. Fuller's forthcoming edition of 4QXII[a] in the DJD series.

וּמָה, "*and* what," which immediately follows the proposed restoration of "and you say" does not favour the restoration. Furthermore, if "and you say" is restored in 15aγ, the question "And what does He desire?" is no longer a rhetorical question on Malachi's lips, but a question which Malachi anticipates or actually hears from his audience. Unlike every other example of "and you say [וַאֲמַרְתֶּם]" in Malachi (1:2, 6, 13; 2:14, 17; 3:7, 8, 13), however, there is nothing about the context of this question which would allow one to understand how it would ever have arisen in the mind of Malachi's audience. In every other case, Malachi makes an assertion to which his audience directly objects using synonyms, if not identical vocabulary. Here there is nothing of the kind; the supposed direct discourse does not even appear to be an objection. Finally, it should be noted that elsewhere the LXX, and presumably its *Vorlage*, frequently expands texts by the interpretative insertion of some form of "to say [λέγειν / εἰπεῖν / ἐρεῖν]" to introduce what was believed to be direct discourse. Compare, for example, Gen. 31:32 [LXX^A], 44 [LXX^A], 46; Num. 9:2; Josh. 22:34; 1 Sam. 1:20; etc. While it is significant that 4QXII^a probably read ואמרתם in 15aγ and hence supports the LXX at this point, the textual quality of this witness should not be exaggerated. R. Fuller observes that in Malachi 4QXII^a holds a middle position between the MT and the LXX. Specifically, 4QXII^a agrees with the LXX against the MT seven times (four of these readings are inferior to the MT); it agrees with the MT against the LXX four times (one of which appears to be an inferior reading); and once it offers a unique reading (which may be superior to both the LXX and the MT).[53]

In any case, on the present interpretation of Mal. 2:15, the presence or absence of "and you say" in 15aγ does not greatly affect the sense of the text. Any decision to "restore" "and you say" to 2:15aγ, however, would call into question the concentricity of the overall literary structure of Malachi as discussed in Chapter 1 and is, therefore, to be resisted in the absence of more compelling evidence.

2.1.4 *"One [אֶחָד]" alludes to Genesis 2:24 while "the one [הָאֶחָד]" refers to God*

Unlike most interpretations, the present view considers it likely that "one [אֶחָד]" and "the one [הָאֶחָד]" in Mal. 2:15 do not share an identical reference. Even if this conviction were proved false, however, once again our conclusions concerning the overall interpretation of Mal. 2:15 would not be greatly affected.

Certainly it is possible to render 15aγ, "But you say, 'Why one [וּמָה הָאֶחָד]?' He was seeking a godly seed [מְבַקֵּשׁ זֶרַע אֱלֹהִים]." This rendering does have the advantage of allowing "one [אֶחָד]" and "the one [הָאֶחָד]" to bear an identical reference, but three difficulties weigh against this alternative. First, while an unaccompanied מָה may on occasion mean "why," this is

---

[53] "Does Yahweh Hate Divorce? Malachi 2:16 and the Text of Malachi at Qumran."

hardly its most common sense since it is found in only seventeen or so of its 554 occurrences in the OT.[54] It may also be significant that in none of these examples does מָה bear the meaning "why" in a verbless clause, such as would be required in 15aγ. Second, the rendering "why one?" appears to ignore the article on הָאֶחָד without justification. Finally, it is extremely rare in Hebrew to elide the pronominal subject of a participle, such as is posited by the rendering: "*he* was seeking a godly seed."[55] The single other example in Malachi, namely 2:9, differs significantly from the present case. In that verse there is an obvious parallelism between אֵינְכֶם שֹׁמְרִים אֶת־דְּרָכַי, "you have not been keeping my ways," and the following coordinate clause, וְנֹשְׂאִים פָּנִים בַּתּוֹרָה, "and [you] have been showing partiality in your instruction." This parallelism between two coordinate participial clauses makes the elided subject for the second participle readily apparent, but it is precisely this sort of parallelism that is lacking in Mal. 2:15.

An alternative interpretation which would construe "God [אֱלֹהִים]" as the subject of "was seeking [מְבַקֵּשׁ]" (cf. the LXX) requires an unusual word order for the clause (participle-object-subject) and appears to be excluded by the resulting sense: "And why one? Because God was seeking a seed!"[56] Since the Bible recognizes that progeny can result equally from exogamous, adulterous, as well as other illicit unions, there is no obvious logical relation between God's desire for mankind to reproduce and the question posed concerning this marital "oneness."[57] Further, even if some connection were posited, this line of discussion would be at best tangential to Malachi's concern to oppose divorce and exogamous marriage (indeed, it could be argued that this interpretation of the clause would actually justify the divorce of an infertile wife).

---

[54] Cf. Even-Shoshan. BDB, *s.v.*, 553, offers the following examples of מָה with the meaning "why": Exod. 14:15; 17:2; 2 Kgs. 6:33; 7:3; Ps. 42:6; Job 15:12; and Cant. 8:4. While KB, *s.v.*, offers additional examples, each of these actually reads מַה־זֶּה, and, in any case, may not require the rendering "why": Gen. 3:13; 12:18; 26:10; Judg. 18:24; 1 Kgs. 21:5; and 2 Kgs. 1:5.

Eliminating cases of מָה לְךָ, מַה־לָּמָּה, . . . כִּי מַה־זֹּאת, מַה־זֶּה, תַּחַת מֶה, יַעַן מֶה, מָה־לְךָ, and מֶה־הַדָּבָר הַזֶּה, none of which could support a rendering "why" in Mal. 2:15, the following 17 examples of מָה (excluding Mal. 2:15) are rendered "why" in either the NIV or RSV: Exod. 14:15; 17:2; Josh. 7:25; 2 Kgs. 6:33; 7:3; Jer. 2:36; 30:15; 49:4; Pss. 42:6; 42:12; 43:5; 52:3 [ET 1]; Job 7:21; 15:12; Cant. 7:1 [ET 6:13]; Eccl. 7:10; and Lam. 3:39.

[55] It is acknowledged that the decision to separate הָאֶחָד from what follows, rather than taking it as the subject of מְבַקֵּשׁ, has the support of the Masoretic cantillation marks (as indicated by the *zāqēp qᵉtannāh*).

[56] F.I. Andersen notes that there are only five examples (out of 355) in the Pentateuch where a participial predicate introduces an independent verbless clause (*The Hebrew Verbless Clause in the Pentateuch*, 48).

[57] E.g., cf. Lot and his daughters in Genesis 19, Esau and his Canaanite wives in Genesis 36, or David and Bathsheba in 2 Samuel 11.

2.1.5 זֶרַע אֱלֹהִים, *"seed of God" or "godly seed," includes, but need not be confined to, literal children in their minority*

It is granted that from the biblical perspective all children are viewed as having come from God (cf. Ps. 127:3).[58] Nevertheless, it appears unlikely that the phrase זֶרַע אֱלֹהִים, lit. "seed of God," was intended as a tautology or poetic elaboration meaning merely "children," such as is supposed by S. Schreiner. Indeed, given our interpretation that "seed of God" answers the question "What was the One [i.e., Yahweh] seeking?" it is doubtful that Malachi intends the construct to express merely the origin of this seed, that is, "seed from God."[59] Rather, in the context of Mal. 2:10-16, "seed of God" seems to reflect the imagery established in 2:10 (and 1:6) of God as the "one father to all of us [אָב אֶחָד לְכֻלָּנוּ]," that is, to his people in virtue of his redemptive acts and covenant, and seems to offer an intentional contrast to the phrase "the daughter of a foreign god [בַּת־אֵל נֵכָר]" in Mal. 2:11.[60]

Since God's paternity in 2:10 is not restricted to youngsters and "the daughter of a foreign god" is similarly not confined to girls in their minority, this context has been used by J. Ridderbos to suggest that "seed of God" is intended as a reference to Israel herself, rather than the actual dependent children of some human couple. This interpretation may find further support in Ezra 9:2, where זֶרַע הַקֹּדֶשׁ, "seed of holiness" or "holy race," appears to refer to Israel as a whole. Compare also זֶרַע יִשְׂרָאֵל, "seed of Israel," in Neh. 9:2. This broader reference in Mal. 2:15 appears plausible, but it would seem unwarranted to exclude a reference to literal children as well, particularly in the light of the parallel concern in Ezra and Nehemiah regarding the spiritual disqualification and erosion of faith and Hebrew culture in the literal children born to mixed marriages (cf. Ezra 10:3, 44; and Neh. 13:24f.), as well as the threat to faith entailed in the sin of giving and taking literal daughters in mixed marriage (Ezra 9:2, 12; and Neh. 13:25ff.).[61]

Combining these perspectives, H. Frey notes that "the One" who is the Father of Israel desires not merely indiscriminate procreation, but the proliferation of covenant children — seed born not just of the will of man but of God (cf. 1 John 5:1, 4; John 3:3ff.). In other words, the seed mentioned in 2:15aγ should be understood as having the same kind of dual interdependent paternity as does Israel in Mal. 2:10: "Have we not all one *father* ... why then are we faithless to one another, profaning the covenant of our *fathers*?" Given the allusion to Gen. 2:24 in Mal. 2:15aα (and allusions to the Genesis narrative elsewhere in Malachi — cf., e.g. Mal. 1:2), significant support for

---

[58] As noted by J. Wellhausen, *Die kleinen Propheten* (1898) 240.

[59] Cf. S. Schreiner, "Mischehen – Ehebruch – Ehescheidung," 217, n. 71.

[60] *Ibid.* Cf. also P.A. Verhoef, *The Books of Haggai and Malachi,* 265.

[61] If it is objected that Ezra and Nehemiah are concerned primarily with mixed marriage and not divorce (as in Mal. 2:15), divorce would not have been any less perilous to the goal of securing a "godly seed." Ezra and Nehemiah offer supportive evidence that children went with their divorced mothers and as such were disinherited and spiritually disqualified from involvement in the Israelite cultus (cf. Ezra 10:3, 44). Cf. the similar fate of Ishmael in the expulsion of Hagar. Cf. also Isa. 50:1; Jer. 3:14; and Hos. 1:2; 2:6 [ET 4].

the present understanding of "seed of God" appears to be offered by the ensuing parallel and sustained concern within Genesis with the bifurcation between the "seed" of the woman and the "seed" of the serpent beginning with Gen. 3:15.[62]

Finally, Malachi returns to this concern with godly children in the closing promise concerning the ministry of Elijah, who will "turn the hearts of the fathers to their children and the hearts of children to their fathers" (Mal. 3:24 [ET 4:6]). Once again there may be an intentional twofold reference in this promise. On the one hand, and most simply, the "fathers" and "children" are to be understood as literal members of the same families. In this respect Malachi's promise finds support not only in the biblical picture of family discord as an evidence of divine curse (cf. Mic. 6:6), but also in ancient Near Eastern eschatology, which similarly promises a period of restored social harmony.[63] On the other hand, it is likely that a more spiritual (or covenantal) family is also in view in 3:24 [ET 4:6], based on the references to Israel's forebears described as "fathers" elsewhere in Malachi: Levi (Mal. 3:3), Jacob (Mal. 3:6), and the exodus generation (Mal. 2:10), etc. The "children" represent the present, much later generation of Israel. This possibility finds further support in the immediate context, in 3:22 [ET 4:4], where family solidarity is presupposed between post-exilic Israel and the exodus generation. In Malachi's view "all Israel" including Malachi's contemporaries were obligated by the covenant at Horeb. On this interpretation, when the "hearts of the children are turned to their fathers" Israel will recapture the faith and loyalty of Levi, etc.[64] Alternatively, since Abraham, Levi, etc., have long since died, the promise that "he will turn the hearts of the fathers to their children" would then have to be understood figuratively, perhaps in a manner which would resemble Isa. 63:16.[65]

---

[62] Already in Genesis 4 and 5 there is a sharp differentiation between the Cainites and the Sethites. Only the latter share a family likeness to God: God "made him [Adam] in the likeness of God" (Gen. 5:1), and subsequently Adam "became the father of a son [Seth] in his own likeness, after his image" (Gen. 5:3), etc., down to Noah, who "found favour in the eyes of the Lord." (Gen. 6:8).

Later, in a manner which parallels the experience of Malachi's contemporaries, Abraham moved from Ur *of the Chaldeans* to live in the occupied land of promise, where Sarah gave birth to a son, Isaac, the godly child of the promise (cf. Gen. 21:12). Yet this was only after the birth of Ishmael, the fruit of merely human plans and a mixed marriage, which threatened the marriage of Abraham and Sarah, the wife of his youth. (Cf. H. Frey, *Das Buch der Kirche in der Weltwende*, 160.) To safeguard the covenant line, later Abraham's servant is prohibited from procuring a wife for Isaac from among the Canaanites and is commanded to find a wife from among Abraham's own relatives instead (Gen. 24:3f.). Still later while Esau weds some local Hittite women, Rebekah pleads with Isaac to instruct Jacob to find a wife from among their kinsmen and so to beget children who would be heirs of the Abrahamic blessing in Genesis (cf. Gen. 27:46ff.).

[63] Cf. P.A. Verhoef, *The Books of Haggai and Malachi*, 342, citing A. Jeremias, *The Old Testament in the Light of the Ancient East*, vol. 2 (1911) 312.

[64] This more spiritual reference may also be favoured by Mal. 1:6, where Malachi takes it for granted that sons generally honour their fathers (an assumption which Micah, for example, might not have found so gratuitous).

[65] Cf. P.A. Verhoef, *The Books of Haggai and Malachi*, 342.

*2.2 Objections to the present approach which considers "one [אֶחָד]" to offer
an allusion to the "one flesh" marital unity of Adam and Eve in Genesis 2:24*

Having considered certain distinctive features of the interpretation of Mal.
2:15 which is favoured here, we now need to examine a variety of objections
which have been raised against the present approach.

2.2.1 The problem of conjectural textual emendations

A. Tosato and A.S. van der Woude, among others, have objected that
interpretations of Mal. 2:15 which consider "one [אֶחָד]" to allude to the "one
flesh" marital unity of Adam and Eve frequently require a number of purely
conjectural textual emendations in the latter part of vs. 15a.[66] Obviously, an
uncertain theory is not rendered more convincing by the accumulation of
additional uncertainties. The present view, however, neither requires nor
favours any emendation of the MT.[67]

We have already discussed our reasons for rejecting the common
proposal to emend וּשְׁאָר רוּחַ, "remnant of the spirit," in 15aβ and for rejecting
the proposed restoration of וַאֲמַרְתֶּם, "and you say," in 15aγ, although this
latter emendation would not greatly affect the sense of the text. We also
noted that while הֲלֹא or וַהֲלֹא, "(and) did not...?", has often been suggested as
an emendation of the MT וְלֹא, "and did not...?", in 15aα (based on Targum
Jonathan, the Peshiṭta, and the Vulgate), this emendation too is unnecessary.[68]

Finally, two proposals have been advanced to temper or eliminate the
odd shifts of personal reference in the MT of 15b (from second masculine
plural, to second masculine singular, to third masculine singular): וְנִשְׁמַרְתֶּם
בְּרוּחֲכֶם וּבְאֵשֶׁת נְעוּרֶיךָ אַל־יִבְגֹּד., lit. "Therefore watch out for your lives and let
one not act faithlessly against the wife of your youth." Some scholars follow
the Peshiṭta and read a third masculine singular suffix, נְעוּרָיו, "*his* youth,"
while others follow the LXX, Targum Jonathan, Vulgate, and a few MSS of
the MT read a second masculine singular form, תִּבְגֹּד, "do (not) act
faithlessly," in place of the third masculine singular jussive verb, יִבְגֹּד, "let
one (not) act faithlessly."[69] Neither of these proposals is required. It is
widely recognized (cf., e.g., E.W. Bullinger, *Figures of Speech*, 524f.; GKC
§144p) that Hebrew tolerates heterosis (= change) of person and number to a

---

[66] Cf. A. Tosato, "Il ripudio: delitto e pena (Mal 2,10-16)," 548-553; and A.S. van der
Woude, "Malachi's Struggle for a Pure Community," 69.

[67] It is entirely possible with A. Tosato that the confusion of the ancient versions
concerning 2:15 may be less the result of variations in their *Vorlagen* or misunderstandings
of the meaning of the text than studied attempts to avoid that meaning ("Il ripudio: delitto e
pena [Mal 2,10-16]," 553).

[68] See our more detailed discussion of unmarked rhetorical interrogatives below.
Favouring הֲלֹא are, among others, J. Wellhausen, *Die kleinen Propheten* (1898); W.
Nowack, *Die kleinen Propheten übersezt und erklärt* (1903); A. van Hoonacker, *Les douze
petits prophètes* (1908); and O. Isopescul, *Der Prophet Malachias* (1908); E. Sellin, *Das
Zwölfprophetenbuch* (1922); D. Deden, *De kleine profeten* (1953); F. Nötscher,
Zwölfprophetenbuch (1957); and A. Deissler in A. Deissler and M. Delcor, *Les petits
prophètes, II, Michée-Mal* (1964).

[69] נְעוּרָיו is favoured by, *inter alios*, W. Nowack, K. Marti, B. Duhm, and J.M.P. Smith.
On the other hand, תִּבְגֹּד is favoured by J. Wellhausen, W. Nowack, S.R. Driver, C. von
Orelli, E. Sievers, and A. van Hoonacker.

much greater degree than English.   As such, the Hebrew Bible includes numerous examples of exactly the kind of mixing of personal reference as is found in our text.   Not all of these can be dismissed as the result of textual corruption; some of them may even reflect an intentional stylistic choice.[70] Moreover, in the light of the contradictory versional evidence for Mal. 2:15b, emendation to remove the heterosis of person in the MT appears to be misguided.   This is so because it is only on the assumption of the originality of the MT, which has both second and third person references in tension, that a reasonable account can be given for the simpler uniform third person reference of the Peshiṭta as well as the simpler uniform second person reference of the LXX, Targum Jonathan, and Vulgate.   In other words, the MT should be maintained on the principle of *lectio difficilior*.

2.2.2 The problem of the supposed need for an interrogative ה in 15aα

It has often been argued that had it been Malachi's intention to express a rhetorical interrogative in 15aα, which is required by the present approach, Malachi would have done so by utilizing an interrogative ה as he does in vs. 10.   This is not to deny the possibility that at times Hebrew may omit the interrogative ה in rhetorical questions.   As argued by A. Tosato, however, who cites Joüon §161a in support, the cases where Hebrew omits the interrogative ה significantly differ from the present instance.[71]   Opposing those who would emend וְלֹא to הֲלֹא (J. Wellhausen, et al.) or וְהֲלֹא (H. Graetz) in order to bring vs. 15 into conformity with Malachi's practice in vs. 10, A. von Bulmerincq notes that the corrected LXX opposes an interrogative sense for 15aα and so supports the MT in opposition to the suggestion to emend.[72]

In response to these arguments against an interrogative interpretation for this verse, Mal. 1:8 appears to offer two more examples within Malachi of the use of an unmarked rhetorical interrogative.   Furthermore, the appeal to vs. 10 proves only that Malachi was capable of using the interrogative ה to express a rhetorical question; it does not prove that Malachi was incapable of expressing a rhetorical question without the use of an interrogative ה.

It is commonly recognized that in Hebrew a clause may be interrogative without being explicitly marked by an interrogative pronoun, an interrogative adverb, or the interrogative ה.   GKC, for example, notes that "frequently the natural emphasis upon the words is of itself sufficient to indicate an interrogative."[73]   In particular, GKC notes the relative frequency

---

[70] So S. Schreiner, "Mischehen – Ehebruch – Ehescheidung," 213, who appeals to E. König, *Stilistik, Rhetorik, Poetik* (1900) 238ff. Cf. also J. Sperber, "Der Personenwechsel" (1918/19) 23-33. Cf. further the discussion of this same point in C. Locher, "Altes und Neues zu Maleachi 2,10-16," 256; and A.S. van der Woude, "Malachi's Struggle for a Pure Community," 70, n. 30. Cf. also M. Fishbane, who discusses shifts of personal reference in Deuteronomy 1-6, denying that they have any implication for the isolation of variant sources in that context (*Biblical Interpretation in Ancient Israel* [1985] 321f.).

[71] "Il ripudio: delitto e pena (Mal 2,10-16)," 550.

[72] *Der Prophet Maleachi*, II, 294f.

[73] GKC §150a. Cf. C. Brockelmann, *Grundriss der vergleichenden Grammatik der semitischen Sprachen* (1908-1913) II §113a. Cf. also the comments on 15aα offered by L.

of cases where the unmarked interrogative clause is introduced with וֹ (cf. Jonah 4:11, among numerous other examples) or (וֹ)לֹא (cf. Exod. 8:22 [ET 26]; 2 Kgs. 5:26; and Lam. 3:38).[74] Although it is not mentioned by GKC in this connection, inverted word order has also been identified as a common indicator of the kind of "emphasis" which GKC considers to be a frequent characteristic of unmarked interrogative clauses.[75] As such, inverted word order is mentioned by P. Joüon and R. Meyer, among others, as a prominent, though not invariable, feature of otherwise unmarked interrogative clauses.[76] Tosato's citation of Joüon §161a against an interrogative interpretation of 2:15aα is misleading because Tosato fails to give adequate attention to Joüon's insight concerning inverted word order.

Reinke, G.H.A. von Ewald, C. von Orelli[3rd ed.], J.C. de Moor, E. Sellin, and W. Nowack[3rd ed.], each of whom maintains an interrogative sense for the unemended MT וְלֹא־אֶחָד.

The definitive study of this phenomenon is still that of H.G. Mitchell, "The Omission of the Interrogative Particle," in *Old Testament and Semitic Studies in memory of William Rainey Harper*, I (Chicago, 1908) 115-129.

Mitchell, *op. cit.*, p. 117, objects to GKC's characterization of unmarked interrogatives as occurring "frequently" given that he is able to discover only 27 clear examples of this phenomenon within the OT (e.g., Gen. 3:1; 18:12; Judg. 11:9; 1 Sam. 21:16 [ET 15]; 22:7, 15; 2 Sam. 16:17; 19:23 [ET 22]; 1 Kgs. 1:24; 21:7; Isa. 14:10; Hos. 10:9; Hab. 2:19; Zech. 8:6; Prov. 22:29; 26:12; 29:20; Job 2:9f.; 11:3; 14:3; 37:18; 38:18; 40:30 [ET 41:6]; Cant. 3:3; and Lam. 3:36, 38). He considers 12 other cases to be the likely result of textual corruption (e.g., Gen. 27:24; 1 Sam. 16:4; 30:8; 2 Sam. 18:29; 2 Kgs. 5:26; 9:19; Ezek. 11:3, 13; 17:9; Prov. 5:16; 30:24; and Job 40:25 [ET 41:1]).

[74] For a further discussion of the interrogative/affirmative use of לֹא, cf. G.R. Driver, "'I was [am] no prophet, neither was [am] I a prophet's son.' (RV)" (1955-56) 91-92.

[75] Though cf. GKC §141n, where inversion of word order is observed in interrogative verbless clauses. The example which GKC cites, namely 1 Sam. 16:4, is problematic, however, both because it may be textually corrupt and also because, at least according to the analysis of F.I. Andersen, its word order (P-S) may be construed as entirely normal for such a clause where P is indefinite (*The Hebrew Verbless Clause in the Pentateuch* [1970] 106).

While recognizing the remaining uncertainties regarding word order in Biblical Hebrew, for our present purpose we accept as valid the main conclusions of F.I. Andersen concerning the typical core sequence of P-S in independent verbless clauses of classification (i.e., clauses where P is indefinite), of S-P in clauses of identification (i.e., clauses where P is definite), of S-P in a circumstantial clause of classification, and of S-P in participial clauses. In so doing, we do not necessarily accept each of Andersen's explanations of the exceptions to these sequences, and particularly, we do not need to accept his exclusion of "emphasis" as an appropriate, even if subjective, explanatory category (*op. cit.*, 18, 24). Cf. also Williams, *Syntax* §§577-582.

Andersen's aversion to the notion of "emphasis" has been challenged both by J. Hoftijzer, "The Nominal Clause Reconsidered" (1973) 475 (whose analysis stresses the notion of "contrastiveness") and by T. Muraoka, *Emphatic Words and Structures in Biblical Hebrew* (1985) 1-46, at p. 6.

With respect to the word order of verbal clauses, we accept the consensus summary offered by Williams, *Syntax* §§571-576, and T. Muraoka, *Emphatic Words and Structures in Biblical Hebrew*, 28-46, both of whom begin by acknowledging verb-subject(-object-prepositional phrase/adverb) as the normal sequence of independent verbal clauses. To be noted also is the often overlooked, but helpful distinction between conjunctive and disjunctive verbal clauses (not just circumstantial clauses, as in Muraoka), which is offered in Lambdin §§133, 197.

[76] Joüon §161a, 495 and R. Meyer, *Hebräische Grammatik*, III (1972) §111, 1.

Specifically, we may note that of the thirty-two examples of unmarked interrogative clauses cited by GKC §150a, a list which is by no means exhaustive,[77] inverted word order occurs in twenty-two cases: Gen. 18:12; Exod. 33:14;[78] Judg. 11:23; 14:16; 1 Sam. 11:12;[79] 20:9; 22:7; 2 Sam. 11:11; 15:20; 1 Kgs. 1:24;[80] 2 Kgs. 5:26;[81] Job 2:10;[82] 10:9; Isa. 37:11; 44:19b; Jer. 25:29; 45:5; 49:12; Lam. 3:38; Ezek. 20:31; Zech. 8:6; and Jonah 4:11. Concerning the remaining ten examples where word order is not inverted, five of these appear to be in need of textual emendation (i.e., Gen. 27:24;[83] Exod. 8:22 [ET 26];[84] 1 Sam. 16:4;[85] 2 Sam. 18:29;[86] Prov. 5:16[87]), and three appear more likely to be declarative clauses (i.e., 2 Sam. 16:17;[88] Isa. 28:28;[89]

---

[77] Cf., e.g., H.G. Mitchell, "The Omission of the Interrogative Particle," 117; and C.L. Meyers and E.M. Meyers, *Haggai, Zechariah 1-8,* 417.

[78] Alternatively, this may be a declarative clause, as in the NIV. Cf. also H.G. Mitchell, "The Omission of the Interrogative Particle," 118.

[79] Unless the MT should be emended with the LXX to include a negative: "Who was it who said, 'Saul shall *not* reign over us!'?" (so also H.P. Smith, *A Critical and Exegetical Commentary on the Books of Samuel,* 81; H.G. Mitchell, "The Omission of the Interrogative Particle," 118; P.K. McCarter Jr., *1 Samuel*; contra S.R. Driver, *Notes on the Hebrew Text and the Topography of the Books of Samuel,* 87; and R.W. Klein, *1 Samuel,* 103).

[80] It will be noted below with Mitchell that questions which are expressed by an unmarked interrogative clause are invariably rhetorical. 1 Kgs. 1:24 may not *require* this conclusion because it is possible that Nathan wished to appear uncertain of the answer to his question. Since to presuppose David's complicity with Adonijah's revolt would be to accuse David of disobedience, however, it appears more likely that Nathan asked his question in a rhetorical fashion.

[81] H.G. Mitchell considers the MT to be corrupt, but this appears unnecessary ("The Omission of the Interrogative Particle," 115f.). Cf., e.g., M. Cogan and H. Tadmor in support of the MT (*II Kings* [1988] 66). Alternatively, with G.H. Jones, this may be a declarative clause (*1 and 2 Kings,* II, 420).

[82] Frequently rendered, "shall we accept good... and not evil?," but with É. Dhorme, perhaps better is a conditional rendering: "if we accept good, shall we not accept evil?" (*Job,* 20).

[83] Correct with the Samaritan Pentateuch to include the interrogative ה.

[84] Delete ולא with LXX, Syriac, and Vulgate, resulting in a declarative clause: "they will stone us!"

[85] The elliptical inquiry here concerning one's well-being may be idiomatic, cf. 2 Sam. 18:29, or the text may need to be emended to include an interrogative ה following the LXX and Sebir — so H.G. Mitchell, "The Omission of the Interrogative Particle"; P.K. McCarter Jr., *1 Samuel,* 274; and R.W. Klein, *I Samuel,* 157.

[86] The elliptical inquiry here concerning one's well-being may be idiomatic, cf. 1 Sam. 16:4, or the text may need to be emended to include an interrogative ה, as in 18:32, with some MSS, Sebir, Targum [codex Reuchlinianus], Vulgate — so Mitchell, "The Omission of the Interrogative Particle"; and BHS; contra S.R. Driver, *Notes on the Hebrew Text,* 332.

[87] The text may need to be emended with LXX$^{B-\aleph^*-68}$, which prefix μή. This reading may imply an initial פֶּן. Cf. BHS.

[88] Most interpreters understand Absalom's first question to Hushai as rhetorical and sarcastic, "Is this your loyalty to your friend?!" Cf., e.g., P.K. McCarter Jr., *2 Samuel,* 378, 388; H.W. Hertzberg, *I and II Samuel,* 348f.; and J.P. Fokkelman, *Narrative Art and Poetry in the Books of Samuel, Vol. 1: King David (II Sam. 9-120 & I Kings 1-2)* (1981) 207.

It is not at all obvious, however, why Absalom would have been so sarcastic on this occasion. What could Absalom hope to gain by offending Hushai if he had, in fact, transferred his loyalty, as had been the case, presumably, with many of Absalom's supports (cf., e.g. Ahithophel)? On the other hand, it would not be at all unexpected for Absalom to doubt and wish to test Hushai's supposed transfer in loyalty. For this reason it seems preferable to understand this clause in a declarative sense, expressing an accusation: "This is [only] an act of loyalty to your friend! Why did you not go with your friend?" Absalom

and Hos. 4:16[90]). This leaves only two examples (1 Sam. 24:20 [ET 19];[91] 25:11), of which both happen to be apodoses and one gains its interrogative sense from an initial explicit interrogative pronoun (1 Sam. 25:10f.[92]).

We may summarize the data to this point by saying that where the text of the MT is sound and an interrogative sense is clear, the word order of unmarked interrogative verbal clauses is frequently inverted (having other core elements fronted before the verb).[93] We may also note that in every case there is a passionate rhetorical character to the unmarked interrogative with the expected answer never in doubt.[94] As such, the evidence clearly supports H.G. Mitchell's contention that the purposeful omission of the interrogative ה lends to the clause an element of incredulity, sarcasm, or irony.[95] While the inverted word order of Mal. 2:15 can be explained differently, it appears plausible that it is best explained as an indicator of an otherwise unmarked interrogative.[96]

Confirmation for an interrogative interpretation of 15aα at times has be sought in the possible co-ordination of 15aα with 15aγ, which is explicitly

---

suspected that Hushai had remained behind in order to serve David in some way. Now he demanded to know what Hushai was up to, what he hoped to accomplish by not accompanying David.

[89] This may be a declarative clause, so NIV; O. Kaiser, *Isaiah 13-39* (1974) 258; H. Wildberger, *Jesaja 28-39* (1982) 1083f.; J.D.W. Watts, *Isaiah 1-33* (1985) 374; and J.N. Oswalt, *The Book of Isaiah: Chapters 1-39* (1986) 523.

[90] Based on the usual precative function of the introductory עַתָּה, it seems preferable to take Hos. 4:16 as a declarative clause Cf. F.I. Andersen and D.N. Freedman, *Hosea* (1980) 334, 377.

[91] "And if a man finds his enemy *will he send him on his way in peace?*" Rather than intending a rhetorical appeal to common sense, it is possible that Saul was quoting a proverbial expression which summarizes the legal requirement to love one's enemies (cf., e.g., Exod. 23:4), on the grounds of which David's obedience would merit God's blessing — "And if a man finds his enemy, he should send him on his way in peace."

[92] "*Who* is David... that I should take my bread...."

[93] By "core elements" is meant either a subject or an object, not simply a conjunction, negative particle, or adverb, all of which commonly precede verbs in verbal clauses.

[94] Omitting only the textually dubious Gen. 27:24.

In cases where there might be some doubt as to the appropriate answer, such as 2 Sam. 11:11, where David puzzles over Uriah's unwillingness to go home, considerable effort is expended to introduce the unmarked interrogative so that no doubt could remain concerning its answer. Uriah rehearses for David how the ark and Israel's army are all in tents — recalling in an ironic manner David's own sentiment in 2 Sam. 7:2. Obviously, under such a circumstance it would be unthinkable for him to return home. Cf. also Judg. 11:23; 14:16; Isa. 37:11; and Jonah 4:11.

An exception to this observation may be offered by the special case of inquiries concerning another's well-being, which were asked, presumably, without knowledge of the answer (i.e., 1 Sam. 16:4 and 2 Sam. 18:29). Both of these examples involve some textual uncertainty, but if the MT is to be maintained, manners may have dictated the appearance of a presumption of well-being for the inquirer ("He is well, isn't he?").

[95] "The Omission of the Interrogative Particle," 209.

[96] This conclusion obtains whether one interprets אֶחָד as a negated subject or a negated direct object fronted before the finite verb. If the former is so, Mal. 2:15 finds a precise parallel in 2 Kgs. 5:26; if the latter, a precise parallel exists in 1 Sam. 20:9.

Referring to the fronting of אֶחָד in 15aα, J.M.P. Smith remarks, "It is an unusual position for the subject of a verbal sentence, unless it is intended to be emphatic; and it is just as abnormal a position for the object" (*Malachi*, 59).

interrogative. In any case, our conclusion in favour of an interrogative sense in 2:15aα enjoys the support of the major versions. In particular, the reading of LXX[B-ℵ*-68], καὶ οὐ καλὸν ἐποίησε ["And did he not do a good thing?"], supports, if not requires, an interrogative interpretation of Mal. 2:15aα.[97] Less clearly interrogative, but still likely, is the reading of LXX[WConstit. Chr.III221] (and AQΓ), καὶ οὐκ ἄλλος ἐποίησε(ν) ["And did not another do (it)?"], favoured by A. Rahlfs and J. Ziegler.[98] While some uncertainty regarding the LXX may remain, unambiguous corroborative support for an interrogative interpretation of 15aα is found in the Peshitta (ܪܠܐ ܘܠܐ), Targum (הלא), and Vulgate (*nonne*).

2.2.3 The problem of the use of "create [ברא]" in vs. 10 to refer to God's creative act which appears to oppose the use of "make [עָשָׂה]" in vs. 15 as an allusion to creation

Contrary to the present view, which interprets "he made [עָשָׂה]" in 2:15 as an allusion to the creation narrative, A. Tosato objects that in vs. 10 God's creative act is referred to by "create [ברא]," not "made [עשה]," even if vs. 10 probably refers to the creation of Israel as the people of God, rather than to the original creation of Genesis 1-2. In answer to Tosato, however, the use of ברא in vs. 10 does not exclude a similar use for עָשָׂה in vs. 15 since Genesis 1 exhibits this same diversity of usage and, in particular, uses "made [עשה]" for the creation of man in 1:26.[99] Compare also Gen. 2:4, where both ברא and עשה appear. Furthermore, while Tosato draws attention to Malachi's use of עָשָׂה elsewhere with reference to the misconduct of his compatriots (i.e., 2:11, 12, 13), this need not control our interpretation of 2:15.[100] It is hardly to be expected that Malachi would use such a common verb as עָשָׂה in some univocal sense (cf. 3:17 and 3:21 [ET 4:3], where Malachi employs עָשָׂה to describe Yahweh's eschatological redemptive intervention!).[101]

2.2.4 The problem of Yahweh as the assumed antecedent of "made [עָשָׂה]"

A. von Bulmerincq has objected to the present view that it appears forced because it requires "Yahweh" to be the implied subject of "made [עָשָׂה]" in vs. 15aα, while the closest explicit reference to "Yahweh" is found in vs. 14a,

---

[97] So, e.g., both E. Sellin (*Das Zwölfprophetenbuch* [1922] 553) and W. Nowack (*Die kleinen Propheten übersezt und erklärt* [1922] 420) cite the LXX as supporting their conjecture that one should read הלא in place of the MT ולא.

[98] A. Rahlfs, *Septuaginta* (1935) and J. Ziegler, ed., *Septuaginta. Vetus Testamentum Graecum Auctoritate Academiae Scientiarum Gottingensis editum* (1984).
   A. von Bulmerincq asserts that the LXX (οὐκ ἄλλος/ν) favours a declarative sense in vs. 15a (*Der Prophet Maleachi*, II, 294f.). In support of recognizing οὐ at the head of its clause as a marker of a rhetorical question expecting an affirmative answer, however, cf. Blass and Debruner §§427, 433, 440; and R.W. Funk, *A Beginning-Intermediate Grammar of Hellenistic Greek* (1973) §617.7.

[99] Cf. also W. Rudolph, "Zu Mal 210-16," 90, esp. note 12.

[100] Cf. also 3:19 [ET 4:1].

[101] On the present view, of course, עָשָׂה in Mal. 2:15 refers not to creation in general, but to the special creative activity of God (related in Gen. 2:18-24) by which he made Adam and Eve to become one flesh in Gen. 2:24.

seemingly too distant to allow it to be the required antecedent.[102] Against this objection, however, T. Chary has observed that although the explicit mention of "Yahweh" does occur at some remove from 15aα, he can still be the subject of 15aα because, in fact, he dominates the logic of the entire preceding verse.[103]

2.2.5 The problem of a lack of parsimony in requiring "one [אֶחָד]" and "the one [הָאֶחָד]" to bear a different reference

A final argument against the present view, which understands "one [אֶחָד]" and "the one [הָאֶחָד]" to bear a different reference, is that such an interpretation lacks parsimony. We have already considered, however, numerous arguments which appear to demand the conclusion that, in fact, "one [אֶחָד]" and "the one [הָאֶחָד]" do bear a different reference. Here we need only add the observation that the dual referencing of "one" in 2:15 finds adequate preparation in the logic of Mal. 2:10. As R.L. Smith has noted, the whole burden of 2:10 is to impress upon Malachi's hearers that because Yahweh is "one" so should they be "one."[104] By analogy with 2:10 Malachi may imply in 2:15 that the One God who made Adam and Eve likewise made them to be "one" and hence, on penalty of their lives (2:15bα, cf. Gen. 2:23), requires that they should act as "one" (cf. Gen. 1:27 and 2:24).

2.3 Further support for an allusion to Genesis 2:24 in Malachi 2:15

In addition to what has already been observed regarding the language of Yahweh "making one" [וְלֹא־אֶחָד עָשָׂה] and Yahweh's purpose for marriage in securing "a godly seed [זֶרַע אֱלֹהִים]," there are five further arguments in support of an allusion to Gen. 2:24 in Mal. 2:15.

First, in terms of the wider context of Malachi, an allusion to Genesis 2 in Mal. 2:15 can come as no surprise in a book which is so conscious of its subservience to the law of Moses (cf. Mal. 3:22 [ET 4:4]) and so fraught with allusions to Pentateuchal texts, especially Genesis.[105]

Second, focusing more narrowly on Mal. 2:10-16, it has been observed that Mal. 2:10 in particular prepares for an allusion to Genesis by its use of the imagery of creation, although this allusion is indirect since the creation immediately in view is not the primeval creation, but a recreation in the formation of Israel (also accomplished by way of a judicial separation of the waters and subsequent habitation of a paradise land, etc.). This creational imagery in 2:10 has significance for the interpretation of 2:15 because of the substantial verbal and conceptual linkage between these two verses.[106]

---

[102] A. von Bulmerincq, *Der Prophet Maleachi*, II, 294.

[103] *Aggée - Zacharie - Malachie*, 261.

[104] *Micah-Malachi*, 321.

[105] For a discussion of תּוֹרַת מֹשֶׁה and examples of Malachi's dependence on Pentateuchal texts, see our discussion in Chapter 1, §§1-2 above.

[106] E.g., cf. אחד and בגד in both 2:10 and 2:15 and the correspondence between ברא in 2:10 and עשׂה in 2:15. Cf. also the relationship between God as the "one father to all of us [אָב אֶחָד לְכֻלָּנוּ]" in 2:10 and "seed of God [זֶרַע אֱלֹהִים]" in 2:15. This linkage is such that an

Third, as W.C. Kaiser Jr. has noted, already in Mal. 2:14 there appears to be a conceptual framework for marriage which parallels Genesis 2, if it is not directly indebted to it, in its radical view of the position of the wife.[107] In Genesis not only is the wife called "a helper, suitable for him," but also the highest natural loyalty owed by a man to his parents is now to be superseded by an even higher loyalty to his wife — as a husband, he "leaves his father and mother and cleaves [a term employed elsewhere in covenantal contexts] to his wife." Consequently, Kaiser writes, "Perhaps there is an echo of the 'one flesh' of Gen. 2:24 in the word 'companion [חֲבֶרְתֶּךְ],' which means 'united, or joined together.'" Similarly, although S. Schreiner does not accept the present interpretation of 2:15a, he recognizes a possible allusion to Gen. 2:23f. in the wider context of Mal. 2:15 and cites Tob. 8:6ff. in support.[108]

Fourth, perhaps the most striking point of similarity between Genesis 2 and Malachi 2 is the fact that the primary obligation of marriage as stressed in both of these texts is not that of the wife toward her husband, as might be expected from their ancient contexts, but that of the husband toward his wife. We will leave to the end of this chapter a closer examination of Adam's obligation to nurture and to love his wife. This obligation is already-implied in the mode of Eve's creation, but it is explicit in Adam's recognition of Eve as "bone of my bones and flesh of my flesh," as well as in the narrator's conclusion in Gen. 2:24. In a similar manner, throughout Mal. 2:14-16 the prophet repeatedly stresses the fidelity which is required not of the wife, but of the husband, whose disloyalty against his wife constitutes a threat against his own life. Apart from Genesis 2 (and much later texts, such as Eph. 5:21-33, which are dependent on it), such a perspective is almost unparalleled.

Finally, in the past scholars have been understandably impatient with interpreters who read a fully developed New Testament theology back into associated Old Testament texts. In recent years, however, there has been a fresh appreciation for the Jewish background of the teachings of Jesus of Nazareth and his radical dependence on the Old Testament in keeping with his own disavowal of originality (Matt. 5:17-20).[109] Having established the likelihood of the present interpretation of Mal. 2:15, whereby Malachi grounds his prohibition of divorce in the conjugal unity effected by God in marriage, as taught in Genesis 2, we join many scholars (such as A. van

---

allusion in Mal. 2:15 to Genesis is widely accepted even among interpreters who reject the present exegesis of Mal. 2:15a. Cf. G.P. Hugenberger, "Marriage as a Covenant" (1991) pp. 127-137 and 141-153.

[107] *Malachi*, 70

[108] "Mischehen – Ehebruch – Ehescheidung," 226. According to Schreiner, this possibility was also favoured by J. Saurin, *Kurtzer Entwurff der Christlichen Theologie und Sitten-Lehre* (= abregé de theologie et morale chretienne, dt.) (1723) 473.

[109] Cf., e.g., C.H. Dodd, *According to the Scriptures: The Substructure of New Testament Theology* (1952); R.T. France, *Jesus and the Old Testament* (1971); and D.A. Carson and H.G.M. Williamson, eds., *It is Written: Scripture Citing Scripture* (1988). Cf. also J.H. Charlesworth, *Jesus Within Judaism. New Light from Exciting Archaeological Discoveries* (1988).

Hoonacker, E. Sellin, and H. Frey), who appropriately cite Matt. 19:4-9 as evidence that Jesus was dependent on Mal. 2:15 or, at least, that he understood the implication of Gen. 2:24 in a manner which parallels and corroborates the present interpretation of Mal. 2:15. It is a remarkable fact that the Adam and Eve narrative similarly influenced the understanding of marriage in at least two works dating from the 2nd century B.C., Tob. 8:5-6 and Sir. 25:24-26, besides several well-known New Testament texts in addition to Matt. 19:4-9 (// Mark 10:6-9), namely, Eph. 5:21-33; 1 Cor. 6:16; 11:8, 9; and 1 Tim. 2:13.[110]

2.4 Concluding remarks on the view that "one [אֶחָד]" offers an allusion to the "one flesh" marital unity of Adam and Eve in Genesis 2:24

We began this chapter (§1) by reviewing the major alternative interpretative approach to Mal. 2:15, which takes "one [אֶחָד]" in 15aα as the subject of its clause and understands it in a pronominal sense (i.e., לֹא־אֶחָד is taken to mean "not one," "no one," or "nobody"). Deeming the evidence for that approach to be unconvincing, in the present section (§2) we examined the view that "one [אֶחָד]" is the direct object of "he made [עָשָׂה]." This recognition brings with it two further implications, namely that "Yahweh" (from 2:14) is the implied antecedent of "he made" and that וְלֹא־אֶחָד עָשָׂה is to be understood as an unmarked rhetorical interrogative. Accordingly, we suggest rendering Mal. 2:15: "Did He not make [you/them] one, with a remnant of the spirit belonging to it? And what was the One seeking? A godly seed! Therefore watch out for your lives and do not act faithlessly against the wife of your youth."

In support, it was noted that the present view requires no emendation of the MT. Furthermore, it was argued that an unmarked rhetorical interrogative in 15aα is paralleled elsewhere in Malachi (1:8) and is favoured by the inverted word order of its clause (§2.2.2 above), by the co-ordination of 15aα with 15aγ, which is explicitly interrogative, and by the versional evidence for 15aα (LXX[B-א*-68], Peshiṭta, Targum, Vulgate, and probably LXX[WConstit. Chr.III221] (and AQΓ)).

An advantage of the present view, as noted by A. van Hoonacker, E. Sellin and others, which helps to confirm it, is its ability to account for the dire warnings in 15b and 16b ("Therefore watch out for your lives"). These warnings carry the radical implication that for an unfaithful spouse divorce is an offence against one's own life. In other words, concern for one's life and fidelity to one's legitimate spouse are considered virtually synonymous (cf. Eph. 5:28). It follows that in 15a Malachi must have intended to articulate a

---

[110] P.W. Skehan and A.A. Di Lella render Sir. 25:24-26, "In a woman was sin's beginning: on her account we all die. Allow water no outlet, and be not indulgent to an erring wife; If she walks not by your side, cut her away from your flesh with a bill of divorce" (*The Wisdom of Ben Sira*, [1987] 343f., cf. also 348f.).
    Cf. N. Lohfink and J. Bergman, "אֶחָד *'echadh*," *TDOT*, I, 198, who cite Sirach 25:24-26 and Mal. 2:15.

principle which would establish this equivalence. As elucidated by the present approach, that principle is the profound communion of life which God effects between a man and a woman within marriage, as established in Gen. 2:24: "Did He not make [you/them] one...?" Thus interpreted, as noted above, there is a remarkable similarity between the logic of Mal. 2:15 and the teaching of Jesus in Matt. 19:5ff.

We conclude the present section by noting that from Malachi's own perspective his view of marriage was not unprecedented, but was consciously derived from, or at least supported by, the paradigmatic marriage of Adam and Eve (Gen. 2:24) — a fact which is entirely at home in a book replete with allusions to Pentateuchal texts.

3. THE LIKELIHOOD THAT MALACHI JUSTIFIED, OR PERHAPS EVEN DERIVED, HIS VIEW OF MARRIAGE AS A COVENANT (2:14) FROM GENESIS 2-3

In this concluding section we shall consider the evidence of Genesis 2 more directly, not so much to determine the grammatico-historical "correctness" of Malachi's implied exegesis, but to determine whether the character of Adam and Eve's marriage would have lent itself to being identified as a covenant by Malachi (2:14).[111]

3.1 Adam and Eve as a paradigm for marriage

Obvious to any reader of Genesis 2-3 is the fact that the account of Adam and Eve is characterized by a luxuriance of meaning and intention. One need not exclude any of the various aetiological concerns which have been posited for the narrative (particularly the need to explain the origin and character of the human race), or any literary concerns (such as to provide an introduction to Genesis, or to the entire J document, etc.), however, in order to recognise the prominence, at least in the canonical form of the text, of a didactic concern to provide in the account of Adam and Eve a normative paradigm for marriage.[112]

---

[111] In support, cf. G.J. Wenham, *Genesis 1-15* (1987) 71; and V.P. Hamilton, *The Book of Genesis, Chapters 1-17* (1990) 181, both of whom identify Adam's marriage to Eve as covenantal.

[112] Besides the need to explain the origin and character of the human race, various other aetiological purposes have been suggested for Genesis 2-3 including the following: the need to explain the lack of ribs about the abdomen; the presence of the navel; embarrassed consciousness of sexuality in 3:7; the use of clothes in 3:7, 21; the origin of (or perhaps new postlapsarian significance for) the leglessness of snakes in 3:14 ; woman's fear of snakes (3:15); pain in childbearing (3:16); futility of labour (3:17ff.); the existence of death (3:19); man's need to till the ground to gain a living and why he is buried in the ground when he dies (based on a pun between אָדָם and אֲדָמָה in 2:7 and 3:19) — cf. H. Gunkel, *Genesis übersetzt und erklärt, ad loc.*; P. Humbert, "Études sur le récit du Paradis et de la chute dans la Genèse," 57f.; N. Lohfink, "Gen 2-3 as 'historical etiology';" G. von Rad, *Genesis, ad loc.*; J. Rogerson, *The Supernatural in the Old Testament*, 27; M. Oduyoye, *The Sons of the Gods and the Daughters of Men*; C. Westermann, *Genesis 1-11, ad loc.*

Admittedly, certain strands of critical scholarship have tended to obscure this purpose by minimizing the function of Gen. 2:24, the *locus classicus* of marriage: "Therefore a man leaves his father and his mother and cleaves to his wife, and they become one flesh [עַל־כֵּן יַעֲזָב־אִישׁ אֶת־אָבִיו וְאֶת־אִמּוֹ וְדָבַק בְּאִשְׁתּוֹ וְהָיוּ לְבָשָׂר אֶחָד]." In the existing text this verse unquestionably offers a climactic summary for the whole of Gen. 2:18-24.[113] Instead of this

---

Recent OT scholarship has been increasingly alert to the literary function of the Adam and Eve narrative within the framework of Genesis in particular, but also within the larger literary work of the Pentateuch. For example, A.J. Hauser has explored the literary parallels between Genesis 2-3 and the story of Cain and Abel in Genesis 4 ("Linguistic and Thematic Links between Genesis 4:1-16 and Genesis 2-3" [1980]).

Likewise, I.M. Kikawada stresses ways in which the Adam and Eve narrative anticipates and prepares for the account of the deluge, which in turn offers a kind of judicial decreation followed by a redemptive recreation ("Literary Convention of the Primaeval History" [1975]). Cf. also the similar observations in D.J.A. Clines, "The Theology of the Flood Narrative" (1972-73); and *idem, The Theme of the Pentateuch* (1978) 73ff.; M.G. Kline, *Kingdom Prologue* (1981-85); I.M. Kikawada and A. Quinn, *Before Abraham Was. The Unity of Genesis 1-11* (1985); and W.A. Gage, *The Gospel of Genesis. Studies in Protology and Eschatology* (1984). The possible identification of the mysterious אֵד of Gen. 2:6 as a "flood," fructifying in the case of Eden, but nevertheless a major water source in view of the mentioned four rivers in Gen. 2:10ff., may provide further support (D. Kidner, "Genesis 2:5,6: wet or dry?").

Similarly, D.J.A. Clines emphasizes the parallels between Adam and Abraham (*The Theme of the Pentateuch* [1978]; cf. also W. Berg, "Der Sündenfall Abrahams und Saras nach Gen 16,1-6" [1982]). On the other hand, B.T. Dahlberg notes how Genesis 2-3 and the Primeval History more generally are paralleled by the Joseph Narrative (Genesis 37-50), thereby forming an inclusio for the book ("On recognizing the unity of Genesis;" cf. also D.J.A. Clines, *The Theme of the Pentateuch*, 84-85).

Looking beyond Genesis, I.M. Kikawada and A. Quinn demonstrate how the Primeval History offers a close literary parallel to Exodus 1-2 (*Before Abraham Was*). They also briefly suggest a much broader comparison of the whole of Exodus with Creation by identifying Genesis as a "foretelling of the Exodus," much as Deuteronomy offers a "retelling."

Further afield, and for this reason less secure, is a purpose first articulated by W. Brueggemann, who argues for an intentional extended parallel between Adam and Eve, on the one hand, and David and Bathsheba, on the other ("David and His Theologian" [1968]). As summarized by G.W. Coats, Gen. 2:4-3:24 "derives from circles (wisdom?) who stand over against the king to admonish, instruct, and correct him, or finally to impeach him.... At earlier stages, the tradition may have served as a critical judgment on the power of the king. It reflects the efforts to limit and thus to instruct the king in his administration of state affairs. It calls on mythological tradition which, by annual repetition in the ritual of the royal cult, secured the stability of the king's world" (*Genesis with an Introduction to Narrative Literature* [1983] 39, 59f.). Cf. the similar views of W.M. Clark, "The Flood and the Structure of the Pre-patriarchal History" (1971); J.W. Rosenberg, "The Garden Story Forward and Backward: The Non-Narrative Dimension of Gen. 2-3" (1981) 1-27; and *idem, King and Kin: Political Allegory in the Hebrew Bible* (1986); J.M. Kennedy, "Peasants in Revolt: Political Allegory in Genesis 2-3" (1990) 3-14. Against this approach, however, cf. D.J.A. Clines, *The Theme of the Pentateuch*, 73f.; and W. Richter, "Urgeschichte und Hoftheologie."

[113] Vs. 25 then functions as a transitional verse, connected to 3:1ff. perhaps by the verbal linkage of a pun between "naked [עֲרוּמִּים]" in 2:25 and "subtle [עָרוּם]" in 3:1, but especially by the relation of this verse to the mentioned shame and remedy for their nakedness in 3:7ff. Qualifying the recognition of a deliberate pun, in a language like Hebrew with only twenty five consonantal phonemes (if one accepts the view of J. Blau, *On Polyphony in Biblical Hebrew*, regarding bivalent ח, ע, and שׂ) and largely triconsonantal roots, one should not be surprised by frequent assonance, which may be purely accidental.

canonically explicit purpose, scholars at times have preferred to highlight other purposes within the text, some of which would be evident only in hypothesized pre-canonical sources.

So, for example, C. Westermann asserts that Gen. 2:24 is a later addition which bears an aetiological motif to explain "the basic drive of the sexes to each other" (citing von Rad) and that its purpose is extraneous to that of the larger narrative unit, which is concerned with the "creation of the humankind which reaches its goal in the complementary society of man and woman."[114] Thus viewing 2:24 as secondary, not surprisingly Westermann explicitly rejects the claim of von Rad (with which we would agree) that "in this statement [2:24] the entire narrative so far arrives at the primary purpose toward which it was oriented from the beginning."[115] Consistent with this devaluation of 2:24, Westermann also strenuously rejects the claim of F. Delitzsch, A. Dillmann, and others that "the narrative is the foundation of monogamy" since "it is not concerned with the foundation of any sort of institution, but with primeval event."[116]

It appears that Westermann may have allowed his form/source critical presuppositions to obscure a vital and even determinative purpose within the present narrative — a purpose which would not have been missed in Malachi's day by those who read the text with pre-critical eyes. For such readers, the explicit introductory "therefore [עַל־כֵּן]," the generalized language of "man [אִישׁ]," rather than "Adam [(הָ)אָדָם]," and especially the mention of leaving one's father and mother, a qualification which could not have applied literally to Adam, all make plain the narrator's intention: this summary is to be interpreted as a general norm substantiated by the preceding narrative. As G.W. Coats concludes, Gen. 2:24 is the aetiological goal of the entire narrative unit (Gen. 2:18-25).[117]

There are yet other indications that the Adam and Eve narrative was intended, at least in part, to offer a normative paradigm for marriage, as Malachi appears to have understood the text. For example, supportive of this conclusion is the generic naming in Gen. 2:23 of "wife/woman [אִשָּׁה]" because she was taken out of "husband/man [כִּי מֵאִישׁ לֻקֳחָה־זֹּאת]." Also clear is the more universal reference of the punishment articulated in Gen. 3:14-19 and especially vs. 16. As noted by N.M. Sarna, the curse of multiplied pain in childbirth in 3:16, as also the curse in 3:15, presupposes the blessing and universal mandate of Gen. 1:28: "And God blessed them, and God said to them, 'Be fruitful and multiply, and fill the earth and subdue it; and have

---

[114] *Genesis 1-11*, 232f. The only proof offered by Westermann for his assessment of 2:24 is the criterion of excisability: "It is clear then that v. 24 is but an addition to the narrative which is complete without it, ending with v. 23."

[115] *Ibid.*, 233. G. von Rad, *Genesis*, 84. Later, however, C. Westermann somewhat inconsistently states that "the narrative 2:4b-8, 18-24 is brought to a conclusion in v. 24" (*Genesis 1-11*, 234).

[116] *Genesis 1-11*, 232. Of course F. Delitzsch and A. Dillmann were "misled" in their assessment by the fact that 2:24 clearly does, in fact, have the institution of marriage in view.

[117] *Genesis with an Introduction to Narrative Literature*, 53.

dominion over the fish of the sea and over the birds of the air and over every living thing that moves upon the earth.'"[118] Just as this blessing was not restricted to or exhausted by the original pair (cf. Gen. 9:1), the correlative curse appears similarly to go beyond Adam and Eve to encompass every one of their descendants in its baleful grip.[119]

Finally, in view of the literary parallels between Genesis 1-11 and various ancient Near Eastern creation accounts and other myths (e.g., the Sumerian King List, the Sumerian Flood Story or its reconstructed form as the Eridu Genesis, the Memphis creation documents, the Atra-ḥasīs Epic, Enūma Eliš, the Gilgameš Epic, the Adapa Myth, etc.), the inclusion of an intentionally paradigmatic marriage in Genesis 2-3 should not be surprising.[120] In fact, such an account may even serve to foster the pervasive anti-pagan polemical intent underlying the biblical account, as detected by many scholars.[121] While many specific facets of this polemic have been identified, none is more foundational than the implied repudiation in Genesis

---

[118] *Genesis* (1989) 27.

[119] This universal reference is apparent even though 2 f.s. and 3 m.s. forms occur throughout the Hebrew text. Apart from such an extended application, the seemingly intentional parallelism of a universal scope in the other two cursings (of the serpent in 3:14f. and of the ground/Adam in 3:17-19) would inexplicably break down in this middle member (3:16). For this reason there is virtual unanimity among exegetes that such a wider application is intended, whether or not one accepts the Augustinian theory of "original sin." Cf. S.E. Porter, "The Pauline Concept of Original Sin, in Light of Rabbinic Background" (1990) 3-30.

[120] The secondary literature on these myths and their comparison with Genesis is vast. Cf., e.g., T. Jacobsen, *The Sumerian King List* (1939); A. Heidel, *The Gilgamesh Epic and Old Testament Parallels*, 2nd ed. (1949); *idem*, *The Babylonian Genesis. The Story of Creation*, 2nd ed. (1951); W.G. Lambert, "A New Look at the Babylonian Background of Genesis" (1965); A.R. Millard, "A New Babylonian 'Genesis' Story" (1967); W.G. Lambert and A.R. Millard, *Atra-ḥasīs: The Babylonian Story of the Flood with the Sumerian Flood Story by Miguel Civil* (1969); W.M. Clark, "The Flood and the Structure of the Pre-Patriarchal History" (1971); I.M. Kikawada, "Literary Convention of the Primaeval History" (1975); T. Frymer-Kensky, "The Atrahasis Epic and its Significance for our Understanding of Genesis 1-9" (1977); W.H. Shea, "Adam in Ancient Mesopotamian Traditions" (1977); T. Jacobsen, "The Eridu Genesis" (1981); N.E. Andreasen, "Adam and Adapa: Two Anthropological Characters" (1981); W.H. Shea, "A Comparison of Narrative Elements in Ancient Mesopotamian Creation-Flood Stories with Genesis 1-9" (1984); J.D. Bing, "Adapa and Immortality" (1984); I.M. Kikawada and A. Quinn, *Before Abraham Was. The Unity of Genesis 1-11* (1985); G.J. Wenham, *Genesis 1-15* (1987) xxxvii-xlii, xlvii-l, 52f.; W.G. Lambert, "Old Testament Mythology in its Ancient Near Eastern Context" (1988); and J.H. Walton, *Ancient Israelite Literature in its Cultural Context* (1989) 19-47.

Of course, this is not to say that scholars have established any direct awareness of, say, Enūma Eliš on the part of the biblical author. Indeed, such is unlikely to have been the case. The point is rather that many of the religious concepts instanced in the various pagan creation myths appear to have had wide currency in the ancient Near East. It is these concepts which Genesis appears to be refuting using, appropriately, a genre which finds a close parallel in Enūma Eliš, and especially the Eridu Genesis and the Atra-ḥasīs Epic. Hence this constitutes a genre where the ancient reader expected such questions to be addressed.

[121] Cf., e.g., A. Heidel, *The Gilgamesh Epic and Old Testament Parallels*, 225f.; *idem*, *The Babylonian Genesis*, 89-96, 120-126; A.C.J. Phillips, *Lower than the Angels*, 24; and I.M. Kikawada and A. Quinn, *Before Abraham Was*, 51, 57.

of the polytheism and related theomachy, the begetting of subordinate deities, etc., of its ancient Near Eastern antecedents.[122]

Germane to our thesis and of special interest in a number of recent studies is the extent to which the ancient Near Eastern myths may explicitly address the relation between the sexes. This theme in the myths may suggest an additional corresponding polemical interest within Genesis. H. Ringgren notes how Enkidu in the Gilgameš epic "attains civilization through sexual intercourse with a temple prostitute... [who] then addresses him, 'You are wise, you have become like a god.'"[123] A degree of similarity between this tale and the Genesis narrative has often been noted.[124] Based on that similarity, Ringgren suggests "it might be possible to find in the Israelite narrative a tacit polemic against the role of women in the Canaanite fertility cult." In his more extensive study of these same parallels, J.A. Bailey concludes:

> "the Gilgameš parallel is of significance not because it indicates the path which J followed, but rather the path which he knew but from which he departed. Within the context of Mesopotamian fertility religion it is understandable that sexual experience would be considered the means of initiation into civilization. But in the context of the religion of Israel, which does not see fertility as the ground of all being human and divine, there was not place for such an initiation. J therefore altered the tradition he knew at this point."[125]

S.F. Bigger offers further support for this perspective with the observation that the ancient Near Eastern myths typically feature divine prototypes for marriage.[126] It is widely supposed that these prototypes may have been acted out in the cultus in terms of sacred prostitution or a representative divine marriage of the king.[127] In the Sumerian mythology he

---

[122] Cf. A. Heidel, *The Babylonian Genesis*, 96-114. Genesis also distances itself from the mythical by its quasi-precise location of Eden near the Tigris and Euphrates rivers, its insistence that Adam and Eve are the progenitors of the entire human race, etc. These features demand that the biblical creation and subsequent history be understood as real events at the head of the continuum of real time and space. Cf., e.g., W. Brueggemann, *Genesis*, 96f., 102-115; and H. Blocher, *In The Beginning*, 154-170.

[123] *Israelite Religion*, 111. n. 24.

[124] Cf., e.g., E.A. Speiser, *Genesis*, 26f.; and S.G.F. Brandon, *Creation Legends of the Ancient Near East*, 131f., both cited by Ringgren.

[125] "Initiation and the Primal Woman in Gilgamesh and Genesis 2-3," 147.

[126] "Hebrew Marriage and Family in the Old Testament Period," xviiff.
This is not to claim that there are no parallels for a concern with the human institution of marriage. The Atra-ḫasīs Epic, I, lns. 255ff., records the creation of an original seven human couples and considers the topic of human marriage in ln. 301. The first of these observations qualifies the claim of J.A. Bailey that Genesis 2 provides the only account of the creation of a woman to be found in all the extant ancient Near Eastern literature ("Initiation," p. 143).

[127] In support of these suggestions concerning the cultus and royal marriages, Bigger cites S.H. Hooke, ed., *Myth and Ritual* (1935); *idem, Myth, Ritual and Kingship* (1958); E.D. James, *Myths and Rites in the Ancient Near East* (1958); and P. Grelot, *Man and Wife in Scripture*, 22f.
Bigger may be on less secure ground, however, as he proceeds to affirm the commonly repeated notion that the purpose of such cultic re-enactments was to secure "fertility to

points especially to the two divine couples, Inanna and Dumuzi and Enki and Ninhursaga. In the Babylonian mythology Ishtar and her numerous divine marriages (affairs?) are mentioned; at Ugarit El and his consort *Aṯrt*, as well as other wives, and the marriage between *Nkl* and *Yrḫ* are offered as important examples.[128] When Bigger turns to Israel's "mythology," he notes by contrast: "Yahweh had no consort, so the Old Testament presents no divine prototype for marriage....[129] However, a human prototype for marriage was postulated. Marriage was instituted, according to Hebrew mythology, with the first couple, Adam and Eve...."[130]

For all these reasons and especially because of Gen. 2:24, it appears that Malachi, as well as certain intertestamental and New Testament authors, was justified in his understanding of the Adam and Eve narrative as providing a normative paradigm for marriage.[131]

3.2 The paradigmatic marriage of Adam and Eve as a "covenant"

If Genesis 2-3 was correctly perceived by Malachi as a normative account of Hebrew marriage, does it support his description of marriage as a covenant? If it could be established that Genesis 2-3 views marriage as covenantal, A. Isaksson's claim that Malachi's views, if taken as a reference to literal marriage, were an unprecedented novelty would be refuted.[132]

---

families, flocks and fields." Cf. the recent cautions of W.G. Lambert about "the modern term 'fertility', beloved of historians of religion but not so easily found in the ancient texts" ("Trees, snakes and gods in ancient Syria and Anatolia," 436).

[128] A. van Selms appears to share Bigger's understanding of these divine marriages as prototypical of human marriage or at any rate as so highly reflective of human marriage that one may freely draw upon the epic texts for a study of the dynamics of purely human marriage at Ugarit (*Marriage and Family Life in Ugaritic Literature*, 10-12.)

[129] Later Bigger offers two modest qualifications of this statement. First, he notes the common prophetic image of Yahweh's marriage to his people ("Hebrew Marriage and Family in the Old Testament Period," xix-xx), and second, he accepts the interpretation of Gen. 6:1-4 which understands this text as the residue of an earlier myth of divine-human marriages (*ibid.*, xx).

The assumed lack of a consort for Yahweh has been challenged recently on archaeological grounds. Cf., e.g., W.G. Dever, "Asherah, Consort of Yahweh? New Evidence from Kuntillet 'Ajrûd" (1984) 21-37. The absence of any such consort in Genesis, however, is hardly debatable. In any case, against Dever's interpretation of the 'Ajrûd inscriptions which refer to "Yahweh and his Asherah," cf., e.g., J.A. Emerton, who objects that Hebrew does not affix pronominal suffixes to proper nouns as Dever supposes ("New Light on Israelite Religion: the Implications of the Inscriptions from Kuntillet 'Ajrud" [1982] 3-9, 14-15). Cf. also J.H. Tigay, "Israelite Religion: The Onomastic and Epigraphic Evidence" (1987) 157-194, esp. 173f.

[130] *Ibid.*, xviii-xx.

[131] For allusions to Adam and Eve's marriage, cf. Job 18:12 (uncertain); Tob. 8:5f.; Sir. 25:24-26; Matt. 19:4-9; Eph. 5:21-33; etc. Cf. G.P. Hugenberger, "Women in Church Office: Hermeneutics or Exegesis? A Survey of Approaches to 1 Timothy 2:8-15," *JETS* 35 (1992) 341-360; and especially P. Grelot, "The Institution of Marriage: Its Evolution in the Old Testament" (1970) 39-50.

[132] *Marriage and Ministry in the New Temple* (1965) 34.

Admittedly, the precise term "covenant [בְּרִית]" is not employed in Genesis 2-3. By itself, however, this observation does not prohibit the recognition of Adam and Eve's marriage as a covenant since Malachi apparently was unencumbered by what modern linguists term the "word-thing fallacy."[133] For example, Malachi recognizes another otherwise unrecorded "covenant [בְּרִית]," namely one with Levi in Mal. 2:4, 5, and 8. This covenant seemingly refers to the special privileges accorded the Levites as a reward for their self-ordaining zeal in executing their idolatrous brethren in Exod. 32:26-29 (cf. Deut. 33:8-11). The later recognition of such a covenant may have been inferred by analogy from the explicitly identified "covenant of peace [בְּרִיתִי שָׁלוֹם]" and "covenant of a perpetual priesthood [בְּרִית כְּהֻנַּת עוֹלָם]" with Phinehas and his descendants, which was grounded in a similar act of zeal recorded in Num. 25:11-13 (cf. also Jer. 33:20-21).

In any case, although Genesis 2-3 lacks the term "covenant [בְּרִית]," for anyone with Malachi's penchant for covenant concepts, there is sufficient evidence in Genesis 2-3 to suggest the appropriateness of this designation for the relationship between Adam and Eve.[134] Without anticipating the results of the next chapter, where we shall attempt to establish the definition of "covenant [בְּרִית]," it is enough to note here that if the Old Testament can identify David's relationship with Jonathan as a "covenant," for example, which it does in 1 Sam. 18:3; 20:8; and 23:18, then clearly "covenant" can be used for a relationship between private individuals and is not restricted to "divine-human" relationships, on the one hand, or international "treaty" relationships, on the other. More particularly, although the "covenant" commitment cannot be reduced to "love," since Jonathan's love for David preceded their covenant and, in fact, provided its explicit motive (1 Sam. 18:1, 3), nevertheless it is remarkable that Jonathan fulfils his covenant obligation to David by showing David greater loyalty than he shows to his own father (1 Sam. 19:2ff.; 20:9, 13, 30).[135] In an analogous manner, Gen. 2:24 summarizes the husband's obligation to his wife as one of "leaving [יַעֲזָב]" his father and mother and "cleaving [דָבַק]" to his wife.

---

[133] A scholarly consensus that warns against the frequent error of denying the presence of a בְּרִית merely because of the absence of the term has emerged. Cf., e.g., W. Eichrodt, *Theology of the Old Testament*, I (1961) 17f.; G. von Rad, *Old Testament Theology*, I (1962) 133; J. Barr, "Some Semantic Notes on the Covenant" (1977); P.J. Naylor, "The Language of Covenant" (1980); and P. Kalluveettil, *Declaration and Covenant* (1982) 3; 91, n. 356.

[134] On the importance and sophistication of covenant concepts in Malachi, cf. J.G. Baldwin, *Haggai, Zechariah, Malachi* (1972) 216; P.J. Naylor, "The Language of Covenant" (1980) 422; L.C.H. Fourie, "Die betekenis van die verbond as sleutel vir Maleagi" (1982); P.A. Verhoef, *Malachi*, 180, n. 2; S.L. McKenzie and H.N. Wallace, "Covenant Themes in Malachi" (1983); and R.L. Smith, "The Shape of Theology in the Book of Malachi" (1987) 24.

[135] Cf. the classic study of W.L. Moran, "The Ancient Near Eastern Background of the Love of God in Deuteronomy" (1963).

3.2.1 "Therefore a man shall leave his father and his mother and cleave to his wife..." (Genesis 2:24a)

The implication of this command in Gen. 2:24 has been much contested among biblical scholars. Beginning with W.R. Smith, a number of scholars have argued that Gen. 2:24 reflects a hypothesized primitive matriarchy.[136] While this view offers a plausible parallelism between "leaving" and "cleaving," in that the authority of the wife over her husband replaces the former authority of the husband's parents, in fact most of those who hold this view do not consider the implied matriarchy to operate in this fashion. As R. de Vaux notes, such a thorough-going matriarchy is rare within "primitive" societies and, in any case, is contradicted by the quite emphatic patriarchal order upheld elsewhere in Genesis and stated explicitly in Gen. 3:16.[137] The kind of matriarchy most commonly defended is not one where the wife exercises authority over her husband, but a more limited type where a child is considered to belong to the mother's family and social group (i.e., matrilineal descent). This theory, however, is unconvincing in the few biblical examples it offers as proof, for which reason it has been largely discredited among recent scholars; in any case, it fails to support the proposed exegesis for Gen. 2:24.[138]

Alternatively, C.H. Gordon, among others, has argued that Gen. 2:24 is a "survival" from a primitive form of marriage termed an *erēbu* marriage.[139] It is argued that in this kind of marriage the husband enters his father-in-law's house in effect to be adopted as the son of the father-in-law in

---

[136] W.R. Smith, *Kinship and Marriage in Early Arabia*, 2nd ed. (1903) 82-87; J. Morgenstern, "Beena Marriage (Matriarchat) in Ancient Israel and its Historical Implications" (1929); and *idem*, "Additional Notes on Beena Marriage (Matriarchat) in Ancient Israel" (1931).

[137] *Ancient Israel, Social Institutions*, 19.

The discussion of an original Semitic matriarchy often has been flawed by a tendency to apply conclusions drawn from modern "primitive" societies to the far less accessible ancient societies, which were frequently anything but primitive.

Some scholars prefer to assign Gen. 2:24 and 3:16 to different recensions (e.g. H. Gressmann, "Mythische Reste in der Paradieserzählung," *Archiv für Religionswissenschaft*, 10 [1907] 345-367). Even so, since Gen. 2:24 is "an editorial comment," one would expect on the critical methodology that it would represent one of the latest elements in our text and hence would come from a time in Israelite history when such a marital arrangement would be least imaginable.

[138] For a more fundamental critique of the assumption of an original matriarchy, cf. T.C. Vriezen, *Onderzoek naar de paradijsvoorstelling bij de oude semietische volken* (1937) 170f.; D.R. Mace, *Hebrew Marriage* (1953) 35-43, 76-94; and R. de Vaux, *Ancient Israel, Social Institutions*, 19f.

Against matrilineal descent, cf. R.W. Wilson, "Sociology of the Old Testament" (1985) 970-971. For a recent attempt to rehabilitate the notion of an early "non-patriarchal" social system in ancient Israel, including matrilineal descent, cf. S.J. Teubal, *Sarah the Priestess* (1984). Teubal, however, does not discuss Gen. 2:24.

[139] C.H. Gordon, "*Erēbu* Marriage" (1981) 159. Previous advocates of the view that an *erēbu* marriage was a recognized marriage form in the ancient Near East, rather than an exceptional condition arising out of individual circumstances, include H. Gunkel (*Genesis übersetzt und erklärt* [1910]); M. Burrows ("The Complaint of Laban's Daughters" [1937] 259-276); C.H. Gordon ("The Story of Jacob and Laban in the Light of the Nuzi Tablets" [1937] 25-27); and E. Neufeld (*Ancient Hebrew Marriage Laws* [1944] 56-67).

the absence of any true sons. The evidence frequently cited for this hypothesized form of marriage, however, appears doubtful.[140] Nevertheless, even if some examples of an *erēbu* type of marriage remain after closer scrutiny, this is far from establishing the widespread practice which would be required for this interpretation of Gen. 2:24.

Moreover, it is not at all clear that "leave" ought to be understood in such a literalistic manner, as if this term could refer only to a change in domicile (although, cf. Ruth 2:11).[141] Rather, it is far more likely that the terms "leave" and "cleave" are intended to define each other. Since it is unlikely that the author of Gen. 2:24 intended to require a literal or physical "cleaving" or "fastening" to one's wife, it is doubtful that in this context a literal "leaving" of one's parents was intended. As C. Westermann notes wryly, the text says "leaves his parents," not his "parents' house"![142]

Accordingly, the language of "leave" and "cleave" appears intended to stress the necessity of a radical change, not of domicile, but of one's pre-eminent loyalty — a husband is to transfer to his wife the primary familial

---

[140] *Erēbu* is the Akkadian word "to enter" and is utilized to describe this hypothesized form of marriage based on its appearance in MAL A §27, where it is found in the I/3 ("frequentive") stem: "If a woman is living in her father's house (and) her husband has been frequently entering [*ētanarrab*], any marriage-gift [*nudunnā*, perhaps better rendered, "widow's settlement"], which her husband gave her, he may take back as his own, (but) he may not touch what belongs to her father's house." It is possible, however, that the husband in MAL A §27 is authorized to take back the *nudunnū* because his father-in-law has thwarted the consummation of the marriage by refusing permission for his daughter to leave home (the husband's intent is made clear by his repeated "entering"). On such a view, the existing marriage is an "inchoate" marriage, not an *erēbu* marriage as often supposed.

Alleged examples of *erēbu* marriage in the Bible include Jacob, Moses, and Samson. Since Jacob and Moses were both fugitives when they entered marriage, however, and since they later relocate their domicile outside the home of their in-laws, their value as evidence for this theory is greatly diminished. Had Jacob's marriage been of the *erēbu* type, T.L. Thompson argues that he should not have paid a marriage present consisting of his labour, the equivalent of a *terḫatu* (*The Historicity of the Patriarchal Narratives*, 279f.). Least convincing is the case of Samson since his Timnahite father-in-law was emphatically unaware of the *erēbu* theory and, as a result, interpreted Samson's temporary absence as a repudiation of the marriage!

For a detailed refutation of the example of Jacob and challenge to the alleged parallel between Jacob's marriages and the Nuzi marriage contract Gadd 51, which is frequently cited in support of *erēbu* marriage, cf. J. Van Seters, "Jacob's Marriages and Ancient Near East Customs: a re-examination" (1969) 377-95; T.L. Thompson, *The Historicity of the Patriarchal Narratives* (1974) 269-280; M.J. Selman, "Published and Unpublished Fifteenth Century B.C. Cuneiform Documents and Their Bearing on the Patriarchal Narratives of the OT" (1975) 29, 251-259; and J. Van Seters, *Abraham in History and Tradition* (1975) 72-82.

Against the theory of *erēbu* marriage, cf. also G.R. Driver and J.C. Miles, *The Assyrian Laws*, 134ff.; and S.F. Bigger, "Hebrew Marriage and Family in the Old Testament Period" (1974) 163-174.

[141] Cf. also the reading of Targum Onkelos for Gen. 2:24, "Therefore a man leaves the sleeping-abode [בֵּית מִשְׁכְּבֵי] of his father and mother." It is likely that this interpretative reading arose to avoid the impression that Gen. 2:24 might require a man to leave his parents' house, rather than just their bedroom, since in Talmudic times it was customary for the new bride to come to live in her father-in-law's house. Cf. M. Aberbach and B. Grossfeld, *Targum Onkelos to Genesis* (1982) 33.

[142] *Genesis 1-11*, 233.

loyalty which he once owed to his parents.[143]   A modern generation of readers who at times may be all too willing to "forsake father and mother" can hardly appreciate the impact such a stipulation would have had in its ancient societal context.[144]

In support, it may be noted that "leave [עָזַב]" is often used elsewhere in a figurative manner, offering many examples where it expresses the relinquishment of one's commitment to another (cf., e.g., Gen. 24:27; Deut. 28:20; 29:24 [ET 25]; 31:8, 16, 17; Josh. 1:5; etc.).   In particular, "leave [עָזַב]" is frequently used in covenantal contexts, as when Israel is warned not to forsake [עזב] the covenant (Deut. 29:24 [ET 25]) or is condemned for forsaking [עזב] Yahweh and so breaking the covenant (Deut. 31:16), while the promise is affirmed that Yahweh will not forsake [עזב] Israel (Deut. 31:8; Josh. 1:5).[145]   Similarly, "cleave [דָּבַק]" is used elsewhere in a figurative manner, offering a number of examples where it refers to the assumption of an ardent covenant loyalty.[146]   These covenantal associations seem especially clear in such passages as Deut. 4:4; 10:20; 11:22; 13:5 [ET 4]; 30:20; Josh. 22:5; and 23:8; where דָּבַק is juxtaposed with terms like עָבַד, "to serve"; יָרֵא, "to fear"; שָׁמַר, "to keep (his commandments)"; and אָהַב, "to love"; among others.

3.2.2 "... and they will become one flesh" (Genesis 2:24b)
Another key feature of Gen. 2:24 which also suggests the presence of a covenant is its mention of "they will become one flesh [וְהָיוּ לְבָשָׂר אֶחָד]." Understandably, this enigmatic clause has occasioned a great deal of scholarly discussion.

---

[143] A psychological reference, as is suggested by M.M. Bravmann, seems unlikely ("Concerning the Phrase 'and shall cleave to his wife'" [1972]; *idem*, "The Original Meaning of 'A Man Leaves His Father and Mother' (Gen 2.24)" [1975]; and *idem*, *Studies in Semitic Philology* [1977] 593-95).   Bravmann considers that the text reflects the typical case where a husband experiences an easier emotional detachment from his family than does a wife. Against this, cf. V.P. Hamilton, *Genesis 1-17*, 180f.

[144] Cf. W. Neuer, *Man and Woman in Christian Perspective*, 68. For a discussion of the loyalty normally due one's parents, see A. Mawhinney, "God as Father: Two Popular Theories Reconsidered" (1988) 181-189. Cf. also P.A.H. De Boer, *Fatherhood and Motherhood in Israelite and Judean Piety* (1974); and K. van der Toorn, *Sin and Sanction in Israel and Mesopotamia* (1985) 13-15.

[145] V.P. Hamilton notes that "the verb *forsake* frequently describes Israel's rejection of her covenant relationship with Yahweh (Jer. 1:16; 2:13, 17, 19; 5:7; 16:11; 17:13; 19:4; 22:9; many other examples from the OT could be cited)" (*Genesis 1-17*, 181).

[146] Cf. G. Wallis, "דָּבַק, *dābhaq*," *TDOT*, III, 80-84; W. Brueggemann "Of the Same Flesh and Bone (Gn 2,23a)," 540; U. Cassuto, *Genesis, Part I*, 137; and V.P. Hamilton, *Genesis 1-17*, 181.
Others have taken "cleave" to refer to sexual union. So, apparently, D. Kidner, who writes "Note the order: 'leaving' before 'cleaving'; marriage, nothing less before intercourse" (*Genesis*, 66. n. 1). Such a sexual sense for "cleave" fails to offer the expected parallelism with "leave" and, in any case, is elsewhere unattested (1 Kgs. 11:2 is doubtful). Against this, cf. also G. Wallis, "דָּבַק, *dābhaq*," 81.
In other texts the ardour implied in דָּבַק is especially prominent, as in Shechem's love (דָּבַק) for Dinah in Gen. 34:3. Yet the concept of loyalty seems almost always to be stressed, as in Prov. 18:24, where again דָּבַק offers a synonym for love (אָהַב) in its parallel member. Cf. also Ruth 1:14.

The view of Rashi, repeated by G. von Rad and others, that we have here an allusion to offspring, seems least likely.[147] This is so not only because on this view the expression seems to equate parents with their own children ("they will become..."), but also because it requires a sense for בָּשָׂר, "flesh," which is unattested elsewhere in biblical Hebrew.

A second view which is possible, but on closer examination unlikely, is that of J. Skinner and others, who equate "become one flesh" with sexual union.[148] This interpretation rests mainly on an inference from the chronological sequence of what might be expected to follow "leaving" and "cleaving" and also on contextual clues which suggest a reference to sexual intimacy. It is self-evident that the sexual associations of "flesh [בָּשָׂר]" elsewhere, as in Lev. 15:2-3, 7, and 19, where "flesh [בָּשָׂר]" appears as a euphemism for male and female genitals, cannot be applied to the present case.[149] Certainly we are prepared for an interpretation of 2:24 which stresses a physical union of man and woman because of their derivation from a very literal "one flesh" in the preceding verses.[150] What appears decisive for this interpretation, however, is the implication of sexual intimacy in the immediately following verse, Gen. 2:25, where we read "and the man and his wife were both naked, and were not ashamed."[151]

Nevertheless, had it been the author's intention to refer just to the act of sexual union, it is unclear why he employed such an unusual expression as "become one flesh," rather than, for example, "... and he will know her [וְיִדְעָהּ]." Furthermore, in the present sequence of "he will leave [יַעֲזָב]" and "he will cleave [וְדָבַק]," especially given the semantic implication of "cleaving" as expressive of on-going adherence and loyalty, rather than a punctiliar act, one expects the third member of the sequence likewise to refer to an enduring state, rather than a single act of intercourse, or even a series of such acts. In other words, it is doubtful that the reader is to imagine that following the consummation of the marriage in sexual union or following each successive act of intercourse, the couple reverts to their former state of being two separate fleshes!

---

[147] For Rashi's views, cf. A.M. Silbermann and M. Rosenbaum, *Chumash with Targum Onkelos, Haphtaroth and Rashi's Commentary: Bereshith* (1934) 12. Cf. also O. Procksch, *Die Genesis, ad loc.*; and G. von Rad, *Genesis*, 85.

Although J. Skinner considers that the interpretative addition of משניהם in the Samaritan Pentateuch suggests that it may have understood the text in this manner (the full Samaritan text reads והיה משניהם לבשר אחד), it seems forced in the present context and may require an assumption of the death of the parents, which is nowhere suggested in the text (*Genesis*, 70). Cf. also H.W. Wolff against this view (*Anthropology of the Old Testament*, 93).

[148] J. Skinner, *Genesis* (1930) 70; and N.M. Sarna, *Genesis* (1989) 23.

[149] For more examples, cf. N.P. Bratsiotis, "בָּשָׂר, *bāśār*," *TDOT*, II, 319, par.f.

[150] A.J. Hauser says that the mention of בָּשָׂר in Gen. 2:21, where God closes Adam's wound with flesh, prepares the reader for the one flesh union in verse 24 ("Genesis 2-3: The Theme of Intimacy and Alienation" [1982] 23). Cf. also G. von Rad, *Genesis*, 85.

[151] G. von Rad, *Genesis*, 85. C. Westermann acknowledges verse 25 as "a bridge" between what precedes and what follows; he agrees with H. Gunkel, however, against G. von Rad, in stressing the latter rather than the former (*Genesis 1-11*, 234).

Moreover, this objection and its underlying assumption find support in each of the several ancient texts which allude to this passage. The advice in Sir. 25:26 with respect to a wayward wife is to "cut her off from your flesh with a bill of divorce." The implication here is that being one flesh expresses the on-going state of matrimony, while separation from the one flesh reality constitutes divorce (not merely a period of sexual abstinence). Similarly, 1 Cor. 6:16 makes emphatic that becoming "one flesh" is a result of sexual union, rather than to be equated with it: "Do you not know that he who joins himself to a prostitute becomes one body with her? For, as it is written, 'The two shall become one flesh.'" The same implication of an enduring state obtains in Matt. 19:5, 6: "'For this reason a man shall leave his father and mother and be joined to his wife, and the two shall become one flesh'? So they are no longer two but one flesh. What therefore God has joined together, let not man put asunder."[152]

Possibly the most common view of what it means to "become one flesh" considers the expression to refer not to sexual union itself, but to the bondedness which results from and is expressed by sexual union.[153] As H.W. Wolff writes, "It means the physical union of man and woman, whose utter solidarity is expressed in this way."[154] Appealing to the context of 2:24, as well as to the support of Sir. 25, 1 Cor. 6, etc., considered above, M. Gilbert concludes that the "one flesh" reality is not simply carnal union, but a bond which is founded on a love commitment which exceeds even filiation.[155] Such an interpretation enjoys the strengths of the previous view (in its attempt to relate "one flesh" to physical intimacy) while avoiding some of its difficulties (by referring to a resultant state, rather than a punctiliar act). Nevertheless, the view lacks lexical support for its interpretation of בָּשָׂר.[156]

Perhaps more attractive is a melding of this view (that "become one flesh" refers to the bondedness which results from and is expressed by sexual union) with the suggestion that becoming "one flesh" refers to the

---

[152] Cf. Mark 10:6-9.

[153] Cf. especially M. Gilbert, "'Une seule chair' (Gn 2,24)" (1978) 66-89. Cf. also J. de Fraine, *Genesis uit de grondtekst vertaald en uitgelegd* (1963) 52; A. van Selms, *Genesis deel I*, 4e druk (1984) 60f.; N. Lohfink, *s.v.* "אָחַד," *TDOT*, I, 198; N.P. Bratsiotis, "בָּשָׂר," *TDOT*, II, 328; and W. Neuer, *Man and Woman in Christian Perspective*, 63.

Others share a similar view, considering "they shall become one flesh" to be expressive of a profound emotional, if not also spiritual union, but without indicating any possible relation between this union and the sexual act. Cf., e.g., S.R. Driver, *The Book of Genesis with Introduction and Notes*, 3rd. ed. (1904) 43. W.H. Gispen argues against the similar view of H. Junker, who considers "they shall become one flesh" to be merely a poetic way of saying "two people have become one heart and soul." Gispen notes that this approach fails to do justice to the context (*Genesis vertaald en verklaard*, 131).

[154] *Anthropology of the Old Testament*, 93.

[155] "'Une seule chair' (Gn 2,24)."

[156] While acknowledging that "becoming one flesh" in part refers to the physical side of marriage, B. Vawter cites Ps. 84:3 to demonstrate that "flesh" can also refer to one's "very being itself, his identity, his heart and soul" (*On Genesis*, 75f.). While the principle of *pars pro toto* is unobjectionable, Vawter's conclusion that "becoming one flesh" means, accordingly, "a union of persons who together make up a new person" is unconvincing, if not unimaginable.

establishment of a new family unit — in other words, the "bondedness" expressed by "flesh [בָּשָׂר]" is more precisely a *familial* bondedness.[157]   A special benefit of this interpretation is the manner in which it achieves a balance in Gen. 2:24 between the parents, namely, the family which is "left," and the result of "cleaving" to one's wife, namely the establishment of a new family: "they become one [or "the same"] flesh."

The principal support for this view, however, is the use of בָּשָׂר in Gen. 29:14; 37:27; Lev. 18:6; 25:49; 2 Sam. 5:1; and Isa. 58:7, where the term refers to the members of one's family (or kin).[158]   While the case of Lev. 25:49 is indecisive, in the five other texts it seems plausible that the designation of another person as one's "flesh" not only identifies him as a member of one's family, but also implies a requirement of caring and loyalty. This is transparently so in the case of Gen. 29:14; 37:27; and 2 Sam. 5:1, to which we shall return later.   Likewise, in Lev. 18:6 the wording of the general prohibition against sexual relations with "any of the flesh of his flesh [כָּל־שְׁאֵר בְּשָׂרוֹ]" seems intended to underscore how reprehensible such an illicit act with one of these individuals would be, an emphasis which is continued throughout the incest prohibitions in vss. 6-17 with their analogous appended motive clauses: "because she is your nakedness!" etc.[159]   This emotive connotation is perhaps even clearer in Isa. 58:7: "Is it not to share your bread with the hungry, and bring the homeless poor into your house; when you see the naked, to cover him, and not to hide yourself from your own flesh [וּמִבְּשָׂרְךָ]?"[160]   The implied logic here recalls the one "body" or one "flesh" imagery employed by Paul in 1 Corinthians 12 and Ephesians 4, with respect to the love obligation of Christians toward their fellow believers, and in Ephesians 5, with respect to marriage.

In summary, it appears likely that "they become one flesh" refers to the familial bondedness of marriage which finds its quintessential expression in sexual union.   Given the widely recognized purpose of covenant to create unity and, especially, given the tendency to employ familial terminology to articulate that unity (covenant partners are frequently designated "father" and "son" or "brothers"), the implication of "they become one flesh," as understood above, entirely comports with the assumption that Adam and Eve's marriage was viewed as a covenant.[161]

---

[157] J. Skinner considers this view possible, though he prefers a reference to the *"connubium"* (*Genesis*, 70). U. Cassuto also appears to favour this view, though he offers no argumentation (*Genesis, Part One*, 137). Cf. especially G.J. Wenham, "The Restoration of Marriage Reconsidered" (1979) 36-40; *idem, Leviticus* (1979) 253-61; A.F.L. Beeston, "One Flesh" (1986) 115-117; and G.J. Wenham, *Genesis 1-15* (1987) 71.

[158] For kinship terminology utilizing בָּשָׂר, cf. S. Rattray, "Marriage Rules, Kinship Terms and Family Structure in the Bible" (1987) 537-544.

[159] Cf. G.J. Wenham, *Leviticus*, 254f.

[160] Cf. also Neh. 5:5.

[161] Cf., e.g., P. Kalluveettil who summarizes, "Covenant is relational, in one way or other it creates unity, community" (*Declaration and Covenant*, 51 — cf. also pp. 51-57; 102f.). Similarly, D.J. McCarthy concludes that the basic idea of a covenant was "a union based on an oath" (*Treaty and Covenant* [1963] 96). At another point he notes that

3.2.3 The Bundesformel*: "This at last is bone of my bones and flesh of my flesh..." (Genesis 2:23)*

While some features of Genesis 2-3 suggest the possibility that the marriage of Adam and Eve was viewed as a covenant and other features may be illuminated by such an interpretative assumption (e.g., Adam's naming of Eve), the relational formula in Gen. 2:23 virtually requires this conclusion.[162]

It is commonplace in recent discussion to consider Gen. 2:23 as Adam's "jubilant welcome" of Eve.[163] The context and phraseology chosen for Adam's declaration, however, appear to carry a further important implication. There is an unmistakeable formulaic quality about the expression, "this ... is bone of my bones and flesh of my flesh," which finds remarkably close parallels in Gen. 29:14; 2 Sam. 5:1; 19:13f. [ET 12f.]; and 1 Chr. 11:1 (cf. also Judg. 9:2).

While we shall leave to the next chapters a closer examination of these texts and their implication for Gen. 2:24, here we may briefly anticipate some of our conclusions. First, each of these texts employs "the relationship formula" to affirm familial propinquity, thereby suggesting that Adam's intention goes beyond the mere acknowledgement of Eve's origin (including

---

covenant was "the means the ancient world took to extend relationships beyond the natural unity by blood" (*ibid.*, 175).

For the use of the terms "father" and "son" and "brothers" to refer to covenant partners, cf., e.g., P. Kalluveettil, *Declaration and Covenant*, 98-101, and *passim*.

[162] It seems likely that Adam's naming of Eve bears some relation to God's own naming of his creation (cf. Gen. 1:5, 8, 10; 5:2) as well as Adam's previous naming of the animals (Gen. 2:19). One possible background for such naming activity may be discerned elsewhere in the biblical record and the ancient Near East in the example of kings, who name animals and plants, perhaps as an expression of their royal dominion, but especially to exhibit their great wisdom and discriminating judgment (cf., e.g., 1 Kgs. 4:33).

How such parallels should be applied to the case of the naming of Eve is less clear. Cf., e.g., O. Eissfeldt, "Renaming in the Old Testament," 69-79; P. Trible, *God and the Rhetoric of Sexuality*, 133f.; G.F. Hawthorne, "Name," 480-483; P. Kalluveettil, *Declaration and Covenant*, 76; and D.J.A. Clines, *What Does Eve Do to Help?* (1990) 38f.

If this naming activity is understood in terms of covenant concepts, there is an especially intriguing parallel for consideration. H. Blocher observes that ancient suzerains often (re)named their covenant partners when entering into a covenant. For instance, Nebuchadnezzar renamed Eliakim as Jehoiakim (2 Kgs. 23:34) and Mattaniah as Zedekiah (2 Kgs. 24:17), etc. (*In The Beginning*, 91). It would be easy to multiply examples (cf., e.g., Dan. 1:7). This practice may provide a more adequate explanation for God's practice of naming his creation than simply the expression of his wisdom (for the idea of a covenant with creation, cf., e.g., Gen. 9:16) and for renaming his human vassals, such as when Abram became Abraham or Jacob became Israel, than the frequent claim to find here an evidence of conversion.

In terms of this background, Adam names Eve "woman" or better "wife [אִשָּׁה]" at the moment when they enter into a covenant (of marriage), as indicated by the *Bundesformel*, "This is bone of my bones...." Adam's renaming of his wife as "Eve" in Gen. 3:20 coincides with the renewal of their marriage following its acute breakdown in the alienation expressed in Gen. 3:7, 12.

[163] So J.G. Herder, as quoted by C. Westermann, *Genesis 1-11*, 231. Similarly, cf. J.A. Bailey, "Initiation and the Primal Woman in Gilgamesh and Genesis 2-3," 142f.; A.J. Hauser, "Genesis 2-3: The Theme of Intimacy and Alienation," 24; and W. Neuer, *Man and Woman in Christian Perspective*, 67.

any "jubilant welcome" or descriptive praise) to an acknowledgement of Eve as a family member, that is, as his wife.

Second, as argued by W. Brueggemann and others, in several of these texts it is clear that the "relationship formula" is not merely an assertion of an existing blood tie, "but is rather a covenant oath which affirms and establishes a pattern of solidarity."[164] This appears to be the case, for instance, when Israel gathered at Hebron to make David their king declaring, "Behold, we are your bone and flesh" (2 Sam. 5:1) — compare 2 Sam. 5:3, where the resulting commitment is explicitly identified as a covenant. In other words, under certain circumstances, which we shall seek to identify in Chapter 7, "the relationship formula" may constitute a solemn "Declaration Formula," which will be seen to be functionally indistinguishable from a covenant-ratifying oath.[165]

In favour of this interpretation of the "relationship formula" in Gen. 2:23, Adam does not address his "jubilant welcome" to Eve ("*you* are now bone of my bones..."), as one would expect for a mere welcome, but to God as witness ("*this* is now bone of my bones [זֹאת הַפַּעַם עֶצֶם מֵעֲצָמַי וּבָשָׂר מִבְּשָׂרִי] ...").[166] Surely Adam recognized that God did not need to be informed concerning Eve's origins. Rather, these words appear to have been intended as a solemn affirmation of his marital commitment, an elliptical way of saying something like, "I hereby invite you, God, to hold me accountable to treat this woman as part of my own body." As will be demonstrated in the next chapter, the concise statement in 2:23 is entirely in keeping with the elliptical character of ancient oath formulae.

4. SUMMARY

We began this chapter by noting what is perhaps A. Isaksson's most fundamental objection to the identification of literal marriage as a "covenant [בְּרִית]" in Mal. 2:14, namely, the claim that such a view would be unprecedented and anachronistic in the post-exilic period. While we shall defer to Chapter 8 the evidence of other biblical texts which view marriage as

---

[164] W. Brueggemann, "Of The Same Flesh and Bone," 535ff.

Although it goes beyond the scope of the present study, the text implies reciprocal obligations for both Adam and Eve based on the mode of Eve's creation from the rib of Adam (not just obligations on the part of Adam, as stressed by earlier commentators such as Calvin). For a fuller discussion, cf. G.P. Hugenberger, "Rib" (1988) 183-185.

[165] Cf. N.P. Bratsiotis, "בָּשָׂר, *bāśār*," *TDOT*, II, 319, where this is called the "relationship formula." The following partial examples are also offered: Neh. 5:5; Lev. 18:6; 25:49; Gen. 37:27.

[166] Cf. Mal. 2:14. In support, cf. also W. Reiser, "Die Verwandtschaftsformel in Gen. 2,23" (1960) 1-4.

It does not detract from the present view that the relationship formula is pronounced by Adam, rather than Eve. P. Kalluveettil notes that the superior party typically utters the *Bundesformel (Declaration and Covenant*, 213).

For an alternative explanation for the use of the third person in Gen. 2:23, which views this as an evidence of "descriptive praise," cf. C. Westermann, *Genesis 1-11*, 231. Westermann, however, does not consider this interpretation to exclude the recognition of 2:23 as a relationship formula.

a covenant (or presuppose such a view), it has been our concern in the present chapter to argue that from Malachi's own perspective his view of marriage was not unprecedented, but was consciously derived from, or at least supported by, the paradigmatic marriage of Adam and Eve (Gen. 2:24), to which he makes allusion in Mal. 2:15.

After rejecting the principal alternative interpretative approach, we determined that Mal. 2:15 is best rendered, "Did He not make [you/them] one, with a remnant of the spirit belonging to it? And what was the One seeking? A godly seed! Therefore watch out for your lives and do not act faithlessly against the wife of your youth."[167]

Although we stressed the grammatical and textual support for this interpretation, which has the advantage of requiring no emendation of the MT, it was noted that important confirmation for this view comes from the concluding admonition in 2:15b (cf. also 2:16b). This warning carries the radical implication that for an unfaithful spouse divorce is an offence against one's own life. Only when 2:15a is rendered as suggested above ("Did He not make [you/them] one...?") is this equivalence between concern for one's life and fidelity to one's spouse explained; it is the result of the profound communion of life which God effects between a man and his wife, as established in Gen. 2:24. In a book replete with allusions to Pentateuchal texts, the present allusion to the "one flesh" marital unity of Adam and Eve in Gen. 2:24 is hardly out of place — particularly given the preparation for this allusion in the imagery of creation in Mal. 2:10 and given the widely recognized verbal and conceptual links which exist between 2:10 and 2:15. Further confirming Malachi's indebtedness to Gen. 2:23f. is the remarkable stress throughout Mal. 2:14-16 on the primacy of a husband's obligation of fidelity toward his wife, a viewpoint which is almost unparalleled apart from these two texts.[168]

As throughout his work, the prophet's argument in Mal. 2:10-16 proceeds by way of reminder and appeal to the ancient standards and common convictions (cf. Mal. 3:22 [ET 4:4]), rather than by way of innovatory insights. Indeed, Malachi's condemnation of his contemporaries would have lost all its force if the underlying understanding of marriage as a covenant could not command their assent or be substantiated from the received texts — particularly since he tosses off the expression "though she is your companion and your wife by covenant [וְהִיא חֲבֶרְתְּךָ וְאֵשֶׁת בְּרִיתֶךָ]" as though this would be readily understood.

We concluded the chapter by arguing that the character of Adam and Eve's marriage would have lent itself to being identified by Malachi as a "covenant [בְּרִית]" (2:14) in spite of the absence of this term in Genesis 2-3. This identification is suggested by the original purpose of marriage, which

---

[167] For other interpretative approaches to Mal. 2:15a, cf. G.P. Hugenberger, "Marriage as a Covenant" (1991) pp. 127-137 and 141-153.

[168] Cf. §2.3 for a survey of arguments in support of an allusion to Genesis 2 in Mal. 2:15.

parallels that of covenant, namely, to create a unity between unrelated persons. It is further suggested by the vocabulary and content of the husband's obligation to "leave [יַעֲזָב]" his father and mother and to "cleave [דָּבַק]" to his wife — terms frequently associated with covenant contexts. Especially clear, however, is Adam's use of the relationship formula, "This at last is bone of my bones and flesh of my flesh" (Gen. 2:23). This expression finds a close parallel in texts such as 2 Sam. 5:1 and 1 Chr. 11:1, where it is employed as a covenant-ratifying declaration formula.

While we still need to clarify the definition of "covenant [בְּרִית]" and to examine more carefully the nature of covenant-ratifying oaths (including declaration formulae), to which we shall turn our attention in the following chapter, we may conclude provisionally that Malachi was justified in grounding his view of marriage as a "covenant" in the paradigmatic marriage of Adam and Eve.

CHAPTER SIX

"COVENANT [ברית]" AND "OATH" DEFINED

Having established that Malachi and Genesis 2-3 probably regard marriage as a covenant, we need to address a fundamental objection to this view raised by J. Milgrom and M. Greenberg. It is claimed that a ratifying oath is indispensable for the existence of a covenant [בְּרִית].[1] Lacking evidence for any such oath in marriage, Milgrom and Greenberg have questioned the identification of marriage in the Old Testament as a covenant.[2] To deal with this objection, we must look at what constitutes a covenant in the Old Testament, as well as elsewhere in the ancient Near East, to determine whether marriage fits this understanding. Accordingly, the present chapter endeavours first to establish the definition of "covenant [בְּרִית]." In particular, we shall examine the claim that a ratifying oath is indispensable for a "covenant" in its normal sense. Leaving aside the question whether such an oath exists in marriage, we will then consider the appropriateness of the use of the term "covenant" in reference to marriage. In the second half of the chapter, we will suggest that the search for the requisite covenant-ratifying oath in marriage has been hampered by two factors: first, by the tendency to expect evidence in the wrong place; second, by the tendency to reduce "oath" to verbal self-malediction. In contrast, it will be demonstrated that biblical oaths in general and hence covenant-ratifying oaths in particular may be gestural or enacted (= "oath-signs") and that they need not always be overtly self-maledictory. The following chapter will apply these arguments to the search for the requisite covenant-ratifying oath or oath-sign for marriage in the Old Testament.

1. THE DEFINITION OF "COVENANT [בְּרִית]"

1.1 A field-oriented approach

In the Introduction we observed that in the past too often the recognition of marriage as a "covenant [בְּרִית]" in the Old Testament proceeded from the now-discredited notion that "covenant [בְּרִית]" is essentially a synonym for "relationship." While such a definition for בְּרִית appropriately stresses a prominent aspect of covenants and reflects the wide range of application for

---

[1] Cf., e.g., M. Weinfeld, "בְּרִית berîth," TDOT, II, 256.
[2] J. Milgrom, Cult and Conscience (1976) 134; and M. Greenberg, Ezekiel 1-20 (1983) 278.

this term in biblical texts, its inadequacy is apparent in a text such as Mal. 2:14. Here the prophet appeals to the identity of the wife as וְאֵשֶׁת בְּרִיתֶךָ, "your wife by covenant," in order to underscore the heinous character of the infidelity [בגד] of these guilty husbands. If "covenant" conveyed nothing more than "relationship," Malachi's comment would seem strangely vacuous and add little to what is already more forcefully implied in the designation אֵשֶׁת . . . ךָ, "your wife."

To generalize the evidence of this single example, among its 283 occurrences in 263 verses some sense of obligation typically attends the presence of a covenant.[3] For this reason covenants are said to be kept (שׁמר - 15x; נצר - 2x), commanded (צוה - 7x), remembered (זכר - 14x), or confirmed (העמיד - 3x), and one is to be faithful in a covenant (נאמן - 1x) or to hold fast in a covenant (החזיק - 1x). Alternatively, covenants are said to be broken (הפר - 20x), transgressed (עבר - 9x), forgotten (שׁכח - 4x), forsaken (עזב - 5x), profaned (חלל - 3x), despised (נאר - 1x), acted falsely against (שׁקר - 1x), or violated (שׁחת - 1x).[4]

Also problematic for an interpretation of "covenant [בְּרִית]" which would reduce it to a "relationship" are a number of examples, such as Ezra 10:3; 2 Kgs. 11:4; 2 Chron. 23:1; and Jer. 34:8-10, where a covenant does not appear to effect a relationship at all, but merely secures a stipulated course of action. In other texts, far from creating a relationship *de novo*, the making of a covenant seems to presuppose an existing relationship, to which explicit appeal is made during the negotiations to make the covenant. This seems to be the case, for example, in the covenant between Abraham and Abimelech in Gen. 21:22ff.[5]

For reasons such as these, E. Kutsch has argued that בְּרִית never establishes a relationship.[6] Instead, virtually everywhere it consists of an obligation, whether self-imposed, as in a promise or the undertaking of a commitment, or imposed on another, as in a law.[7] While many texts support

---

[3] Statistics are from Even-Shoshan, *s.v.* E. Kutsch offers 287, presumably including in that count the textually uncertain Ezek. 20:37 ("בְּרִית *berît* Verpflichtung," *THAT*, I, 341).

For a careful examination of all extra-biblical examples of *br(y)t*, having the meaning "agreement, compact, or covenant," cf. K.A. Kitchen, "Egypt, Ugarit, Qatna and Covenant" (1979) 453-464.

[4] For a more exhaustive treatment of these and other syntagms of בְּרִית, cf. P.J. Naylor, "The Language of Covenant. A Structural Analysis of the Semantic Field of ברית in Biblical Hebrew, with Particular Reference to the Book of Genesis" (1980).

[5] D.J. McCarthy summarizes the pattern of some 13 older accounts of "secular" covenant making within the Bible: Gen. 21:22-34 (J and E); 26:23-33; 31:25-32:5 (at least 2 narratives); Josh. 9:1-10:1; 1 Sam. 11:1-3; 18:1-4 + 20:5-8; 20:11-17 + 23:16-18; 2 Sam. 3:17-21 + 5:1-3; 3:12-21; 1 Kgs. 15:19; 20:31-34; 2 Kings 11 (∥ 2 Chronicles 23) (*Treaty and Covenant* [1981] 19f.). McCarthy concludes, "the negotiations ... begin regularly with an affirmation that a real though general relationship already exists between the parties." Cf. *ibid.*, 297.

[6] E. Kutsch, *Verheissung und Gesetz* (1973); and *idem*, "Gesetz und Gnade. Probleme des alttestamentlichen Bundesbegriff" (1967) 18-35. Cf. also L. Perlitt, *Bundestheologie im Alten Testament* (1969); and E.W. Nicholson, *God and His People. Covenant and Theology in the Old Testament* (1986).

[7] For self-imposed examples, cf., e.g., Gen. 14:13; Exod. 23:32; 34:12, 15; Deut. 7:2; Judg. 2:2; 2 Sam. 5:3; 1 Kgs. 15:19; Isa. 33:8; Jer. 34:10; Mal. 2:14; Obad. 7; Ps. 55:21[ET

this emphasis on the obligations implied in covenants, Kutsch has gone too far in denying that בְּרִית ever creates a relationship. J. Barr argues against Kutsch's conclusions noting the logical dependence of Kutsch's view on the very uncertain etymology which he proposes — deriving בְּרִית from the rare and uncertain root ברה II, supposed to mean "to look for, to choose" (related to the Akkadian *barûm*, "to look"), hence "determining," and finally "obligation [*Verpflichtung*]."[8] Barr further suggests that in spite of Kutsch's appropriate concern with the context in each of the appearances of בְּרִית, nevertheless Kutsch's argument appears to confuse the words spoken when a בְּרִית is made and the effects which are promised or which actually follow the making of a בְּרִית with the semantic content of the term בְּרִית.[9] Finally, Barr wonders whether Kutsch was unduly influenced by a theological agenda since "the whole discussion seems dominated by a strong sense of the opposition between grace and law, promise and law, which makes the reader uncomfortable."[10]

20]; Job 31:1; 40:28 [ET 41:4]; 1 Chron. 11:3; and 2 Chron. 16:3. For examples where a בְּרִית is imposed on another, cf., e.g., Josh. 24:25; 2 Chron. 23:1, 3; Jer. 34:8; Ezek. 17:13-16:18; and Job 5:23. Covenants with mutually assumed obligations appear in 1 Kgs. 15:19; Amos 1:9; Ps. 83:6; and 2 Chron. 16:33.

[8] E. Kutsch, "Sehen und Bestimmen. Die Etymologie von ברית" (1970) 165-178; *idem, Verheissung und Gesetz* (1973). Kutsch proposes the following etymological development for ברה II to ברית: sehen – ersehen – auswählen – bestimmen – Bestimmung – Verpflichtung (*Verheissung und Gesetz*, 39).

Cf. J. Barr, "Some Semantic Notes on the Covenant" (1977) 24, 25 and 36. Barr notes that as a matter of procedure Kutsch is careful not to begin with this etymological argument: "But *logically* his proposal depends rather more on etymology than this would suggest. The total effect of his reasoning depends very considerably on the proposal...." Later Barr observes that an analogy based on the older English term "beholden" (which appears to suggest a development from "to see" to "to be obligated"), which is offered by Kutsch in support, is inapplicable. This is so because "beholden," in the sense of "to be obligated," comes from a term meaning "to hold, retain," and not from "to behold" in the sense of "to see," as Kutsch supposes.

Not surprisingly, Kutsch's proposal has found little support. Cf. M.L. Newman, "Review of *Verheissung und Gesetz*" (1975); M. Weinfeld, "בְּרִית *berîth*," *TDOT*, II, 255. It should be acknowledged, however, that none of the proposed etymologies for בְּרִית has received notable support. Perhaps most widely favoured is the proposal of E. Meyer, followed by L. Köhler and others, that בְּרִית derived from the root ברה I, which means "to eat," alluding to the meal which frequently accompanies the covenant-making ceremony (E. Meyer, *Die Israeliten und ihre Nachbarstämme* [1906]; L. Köhler, "Problems in the Study of the Language of the Old Testament" [1956] 3-24).

Others, however, prefer to relate בְּרִית to the Akkadian term *birtu / birîtu* meaning "a fetter" (so M. Weinfeld, "בְּרִית *berîth*," *TDOT*, II, 255; and K.A. Kitchen, "Egypt, Ugarit, Qatna and Covenant" [1979] 461), or to go further back and relate בְּרִית to the Akkadian preposition *birît* meaning "between," from which *birtu* possibly derives (so, O. Loretz, "Berît — Band, Bund" [1966] 239-41; M. Noth, "Old Testament Covenant Making in the Light of a Text from Mari" [1967] 108-117).

A more recent suggestion is that of E.B. Smick, who relates בְּרִית to the Akkadian term *burru* (D) meaning "to establish a legal situation by testimony with an oath" ("בְּרִית" (*bᵉrît*) covenant," *TWOT*, I, 128; cf. *CAD*, B, 125ff.).

[9] J. Barr, "Some Semantic Notes on the Covenant" (1977) 37.

[10] *Ibid.*, 37. Barr's reservations about Kutsch have been cited with approval by D.J. McCarthy, *Treaty and Covenant* [1981]16, n. 26. McCarthy likewise suggests that "there is more than merely scientific interest at work [behind the concern to demonstrate that בְּרִית

As noted in the Introduction, any attempt to reduce the numerous occurrences of "covenant [בְּרִית]" to some univocal sense, basic meaning, or original meaning, whether one chooses "relationship," "obligation," "oath," or "solemn promise," is unwarranted.[11] Although a predisposition against this sort of reductionism or oversystemization is now a common feature of modern linguistics, this point has been made with particular force by P.J. Naylor with reference to the study of בְּרִית.[12] Naylor's primary concern is to develop a "field-oriented" approach to the various senses of בְּרִית, elucidating their paradigmatic and syntagmatic relationships. In so doing, Naylor offers a salutary reminder that, at least in principle, one must be prepared to identify any possible features of linguistic differentiation for בְּרִית, such as diachrony, dialect, idiolect, style, and other incidental features, rather than lumping every occurrence together indifferently as R.B. Girdlestone, P. Buis, and other scholars appear to have done.[13] If this differentiation is recognized, it turns out that stylistic variation (whether בְּרִית occurs in a narrative, legal, prophetic, or poetic context) is by far the most dominant.

1.2 A concept-oriented approach to the distinct senses of "covenant [בְּרִית]"

While Naylor's "field-oriented" approach is to be appreciated, it does not exclude a more "concept-oriented" approach to the various senses of בְּרִית, which may be of greater use in the present study.[14] In terms of this alternative approach to lexical semantics, we may delineate the following senses of בְּרִית:

1) The predominant sense of בְּרִית in Biblical Hebrew is an elected, as opposed to natural, relationship of obligation established under divine sanction.[15] It is this sense in particular which we intend by the English term

---

means *Verpflichtung*, 'obligation']. There are theological positions, probably subconscious but still very real, in the background. There is the fear of seeming to tie God to a contract and creating a *quid pro quo* pharisaism..." (*op. cit.*, 17).

For further critical discussion of Kutsch's views, cf. M. Weinfeld, "*Bᵉrît* — Covenant vs. Obligation" (1975) 120-128, esp. 124f.; D.J. McCarthy's substantial review article of L. Perlitt, *Bundestheologie im Alten Testament*, entitled "*bᵉrît* in Old Testament History and Theology" (1972) 110-121; and P.J. Naylor, "The Language of Covenant," 34ff., 42. Cf. also M.J. Buss, "Review: L. Perlitt, *Bundestheologie im Alten Testament (WMANT 36)*" (1971).

[11] Appropriately, *BDB* suggests the richness of this term by offering the following translational equivalents: "pact," "compact," "covenant," "treaty," "alliance," "league," "constitution," "ordinance," "agreement," and "pledge."

[12] P.J. Naylor, "The Language of Covenant" (1980). Cf. also D.J. McCarthy, *Old Testament Covenant* (1972) 4; and P Kalluveettil, *Declaration and Covenant* (1982) 15f.

[13] Cf. P.J. Naylor, "The Language of Covenant," 70-72.

[14] For a discussion of the distinction between "field-oriented" and "concept-oriented" approaches to lexical semantics, cf. P. Cotterell and M. Turner, *Linguistics and Biblical Interpretation* (1989) 145-181.

[15] Cf. M.G. Kline, who defines בְּרִית as a "sanction-sealed commitment to maintain a particular relationship or follow a stipulated course of action. In general, then a covenant may be defined as a relationship under sanctions" (*By Oath Consigned*, 16). The definition

"covenant."[16] Not only does בְּרִית occur most frequently with this sense in the biblical corpus, it does so most often while referring to covenants between Yahweh and his people, as in Exod. 19:5, etc. (appearing in what Naylor terms the 3rd dimension of its semantic field, after the first two dimensions of literal and figurative uses). בְּרִית also bears this sense while referring to secular relationships, as in Gen. 14:13, 1 Sam. 18:3, etc. (Naylor's 1st dimension). An important special case of this usage occurs when the relationship in question is of an international political nature, where a more specific English rendering for בְּרִית would be "treaty" (e.g., cf. 1 Sam. 11:1 and 1 Kgs. 5:26 [ET 12]).

As is well-known, a great deal of scholarly attention has been devoted to the apparent analogy between the ancient Near Eastern treaty texts and various portions of the Bible which refer to a covenant between Yahweh and Israel since this comparison was first suggested, apparently independently, by D.J. Wiseman, E. Bickerman, G.E. Mendenhall, and K. Baltzer.[17] Without entering further into this vast area of scholarly discussion, it is sufficient to emphasize here that not all covenants are treaties. Thus it should not be expected that wherever a covenant is mentioned it will necessarily exhibit any or all of the features of some single "covenant form" derived from a detailed comparison of international treaty texts.[18] In particular, it is the concern of the present thesis to argue that a number of Old Testament texts, and Malachi in particular, conceive of marriage as a בְּרִית — not as a "treaty," and thus not necessarily in a manner which exhibits each of the well-rehearsed features of

---

offered by G.E. Mendenhall is similar: "A solemn promise made binding by an oath, which may be either a verbal formula or a symbolic oath" ("Covenant," 714). Cf. W. Dyrness, *Themes in Old Testament Theology* (1979) 113. Cf. also M.L. Newman, who defines covenant as a "formal relationship of obligation between two parties, normally resulting from some prior common experience and sealed by a solemn oath or cultic rite" ("Review of *Verheissung und Gesetz*" [1975] 120).

[16] Although this translational choice is rather arbitrary, it reflects a common convention established by the translational practice of the AV (which so renders בְּרִית 260 times). As a translation, "covenant" has been faulted because of the many inappropriate senses which attach to this term in contemporary English (e.g., a mutual agreement, especially regarding the use of land; a financial or church membership pledge; etc.). As J. Barr observes, however, the objections raised by, e.g., E. Kutsch against the traditional German rendering "Bund" (since בְּרִית does not mean "alliance" or "agreement") do not apply to the English term "covenant" ("Some Semantic Notes on the Covenant," 36). In any case, the utility of "covenant" as a translation choice can be defended based on the fact that for most English speakers this term is largely an "empty word," deriving any meaning it may have from biblical usage (J. Barr, *op. cit.*, 36).

[17] D.J. Wiseman, in a paper read to the Society of Old Testament Studies in January 1948, according to M.G. Kline, *The Structure of Biblical Authority*, 114, n. 2; E. Bickerman, "Couper une alliance" (1950-51), according to E.W. Nicholson, *God and His People* (1986) 57; G.E. Mendenhall, "Law and Covenant in Israel and the Ancient Near East" (1954); and K. Baltzer, *Das Bundesformular* (1960). These scholars base their work on V. Korošec's foundational study of the structure of the Hittite treaties, *Hethitische Staatsverträge: Ein Beitrag zur ihrer juristischen Wertung* (1931).

[18] Cf. D.J. McCarthy, *Old Testament Covenant*, 4.

ancient Near Eastern treaty relationships, but in the presently understood sense of its hypernym, "covenant."[19]

Because this first sense of בְּרִית is the primary concern of the present research, we shall consider it in fuller detail after briefly surveying, for the sake of completeness, the remaining attested senses of בְּרִית.[20]

2) A less frequent sense of בְּרִית is that of a shared commitment to a stipulated course of action, established under divine sanction. A common English rendering for בְּרִית when it bears this sense is "pact." Understood in this manner, a "pact" differs from a "covenant" primarily in the more limited nature of the commitment undertaken. An example of בְּרִית with this sense is found in Ezra 10:3: "Therefore let us make a *covenant* with our God to put away all these wives and their children, according to the counsel of my lord and of those who tremble at the commandment of our God; and let it be done according to the law."[21]

3) Occasionally בְּרִית bears the sense of the documentary witness (book/tables) of the covenant. This appears to be related by encapsulation to either of the common expressions, "the book of the covenant [סֵפֶר (הַ)בְּרִית]" (Exod. 24:7; 2 Kgs. 23:2, 21; 2 Chron. 34:30) or "the tables of the covenant [לוּחֹת הַבְּרִית]" (cf. Deut. 9:9).[22] An example of בְּרִית with this third sense is found in 1 Kgs. 8:21, "And there I have provided a place for the ark, in which is the *covenant* of the LORD [בְּרִית יְהוָה אֲשֶׁר־שָׁם]...".[23] Clearly the ark did not contain the covenant relationship itself, but only the documentary witness to the covenant.[24] Based on this example, it is plausible that the forty-two biblical occurrences of the expression אֲרוֹן בְּרִית, "ark of the covenant," including its various congeners, should all be considered additional examples of בְּרִית bearing this third sense.

4) A further case of encapsulation may be noted in instances where בְּרִית bears the sense, "the sign of the covenant" — where בְּרִית encapsulates the expression אוֹת (הַ)בְּרִית (Gen. 9:12, 13, 17; 17:11). An example of this

---

[19] The texts which are most explicit in their identification of marriage as a בְּרִית are Mal. 2:14; Prov. 2:17; and Ezek. 16:8.

As noted by D. L Magnetti, there is a considerable conceptual and terminological overlap between the treaties and the interpersonal covenants of the ancient Near East ("The Oath in the Old Testament in the Light of Related Terms and in the Legal and Covenantal Context of the Ancient Near East" [1969] 94).

[20] There are some examples where בְּרִית is used with this first sense, but in a figurative manner. The fact that these examples are confined to poetic and highly rhetorical contexts and the fact that one of the covenant partners is typically an impersonal entity, but personified for the purpose of the figure, confirm the recognition of these uses as figurative. Cf., e.g., Isa. 28:15, 18.

[21] It is not always possible to be certain which of the first two senses of בְּרִית is intended (e.g., cf. Isa. 33:8; Hos. 10:4). The following instances appear to be fairly clear examples of בְּרִית bearing its second sense: Ezra 10:3; 2 Kgs. 11:4 (∥ 2 Chron. 23:1); Jer. 34:8, 10, 15, 18 (*bis*); and Ps. 83:6 [ET 5].

[22] "Encapsulation" is a term coined and defined by J. Lyons as the "lexicalization of ... [a] syntagmatic modifying component" (*Semantics*, I, 262). Cf. also P.J. Naylor, "The Language of Covenant," 93.

[23] Cf. also the parallel in 2 Chron. 6:11.

[24] Apart from the expression אֲרוֹן בְּרִית, "Ark of the Covenant," the only other clear example is 2 Chron. 6:11, the parallel text to 1 Kgs. 8:21.

sense is offered in Gen. 17:13. Already in vs. 11 circumcision is explicitly identified as "a sign of the covenant," but in vs. 13 we read with respect to the rite of circumcision, בְרִיתִי בִּבְשַׂרְכֶם, "so shall my *covenant* be in your flesh." In this clause בְּרִית does not refer to the covenant relationship itself, but to the sign of the covenant.[25]

5) While in the first two senses considered above בְּרִית refers to the covenant or pact as a whole, by synecdoche בְּרִית may at times signify a specific obligation undertaken within the covenant. An example of this sense may be found in Lev. 24:8: "Every sabbath day Aaron shall set it in order before the LORD continually on behalf of the people of Israel as a perpetual *covenant* (stipulation) [בְּרִית עוֹלָם, lit. "a covenant (stipulation) of eternity"]." Compare the parallel expression חָקַּת עוֹלָם, "a statute of eternity" or "a perpetual statute" in 24:3 (and חָק־עוֹלָם in 24:9).[26]

6) There are also two idiomatic expressions involving בְּרִית to be noted. The first is the characteristic, though not exclusive, expression for making (remaking) a covenant/pact, כָּרַת בְּרִית, "to cut a covenant." Several alternative etymologies have been proposed to account for this remarkable idiom.[27] With G.E. Mendenhall, however, "it seems most likely that the original meaning was lost in antiquity before the time of Moses, and had simply become a technical term [for making/remaking a covenant]."[28]

The second idiomatic expression is נָתַן + object + לִבְרִית, found in Isa. 42:6 and 49:8, where the servant of the Lord is "given as a covenant" to the people [וְאֶתֶּנְךָ לִבְרִית עָם]. Based on the remarkable semantic proximity of אָלָה, "curse," to בְּרִית, "covenant," P.J. Naylor argues that נתן לברית, "to give/present as a covenant," should be understood as an example of emphatic metonymy, as is the case with the parallel syntagm נתן לאלה, "to give/present as a curse," in Num. 5:21; Jer. 29:18; 42:18; and 44:12.[29] Accordingly, as the cursed woman in Num. 5:21 was an embodiment of that curse, so the servant of Yahweh in Isaiah, "constitutes the embodiment, and personal existentialisation, of all that the covenant entailed."[30]

It will be helpful to return now to a more detailed discussion of the first and primary sense of בְּרִית, namely that of "an elected, as opposed to natural, relationship of obligation established under divine sanction."

---

[25] Cf. also, possibly, Lev. 24:8.

[26] Cf. also, possibly, Exod. 31:16.

[27] Cf., e.g., M.G. Kline, *By Oath Consigned* (1968) 42, n. 8; D.L. Magnetti, "The Oath in the Old Testament" (1969) 70; E. Kutsch, *Verheissung und Gesetz* (1973) 40-49, *idem*, "בְּרִית *berīt* Verpflichtung," *THAT*, I (1984) 339-352; M. Weinfeld, "בְּרִית *berîth*," *TDOT*, II (1977) 253-279; D.J. McCarthy, *Treaty and Covenant* (1981) 16ff., 92f.; K.A. Kitchen, "Egypt, Ugarit, Qatna and Covenant" (1979) 460f.; and P Kalluveettil, *Declaration and Covenant* (1982) 92f., n. 25.

[28] G.E. Mendenhall, "Covenant," 716.

[29] "The Language of Covenant," 380-395.

[30] *Ibid.*, 394.

Other possible idiomatic expressions or examples of further distinct senses of בְּרִית include עָמַד בַּבְּרִית, found in 2 Kgs. 23:2 ("all the people joined in the covenant") and שׁלח + בַּבְּרִית, found in 1 Kgs. 20:34 ("I will let you go on these terms").

A chief difficulty which vexes any discussion of the term בְּרִית is the broad semantic range of בְּרִית, but the curious lack of contrastive terms occupying the same semantic field.[31] This fact alone renders implausible, for example, the overly precise analysis of A. Jepsen, who argues that בְּרִית always refers to the constitutive act which produces a relationship, rather than to the relationship itself.[32] Certainly some texts employ בְּרִית to refer to the constitutive act (e.g., Exod. 24:8). Other texts, however, seem equally clear in their reference to the relationship more generally. For instance, the expression, "an everlasting covenant [בְּרִית עוֹלָם]," which occurs sixteen times, would seem rather odd if only the constitutive act were in view.[33]

A second problem that needs to be discussed is the apparent complexity of the definition which has been offered: "an elected, as opposed to natural, relationship of obligation established under divine sanction." This is especially true because it will be argued that this definition is operative for בְּרִית in Mal. 2:14.

Reflecting a fundamental assumption of modern linguistics, J. Barr has warned biblical scholars against what he has termed "illegitimate totality transfer." This error is committed when "the 'meaning' of a word (understood as the total series of relations in which it is used in the literature) is read into a particular case as its sense and implication there."[34] Stating this principle more positively, E.A. Nida urges that "the correct meaning of any term is that which contributes least to the total context."[35]

While this principle offers an important corrective for certain past interpretative excesses, it appears to overstate the case and has recently been criticized and replaced by a more nuanced approach offered by A. Wierzbicka and P. Cotterell and M. Turner.[36] Offering the English word "bicycle" as an example, Cotterell and Turner note that any English speaker would recognize as semantically anomalous the sentence: "It's a bicycle, but you steer it with

---

[31] Cf. J. Barr, "Some Semantic Notes on the Covenant" (1977) 31-33; and M. Weinfeld, "בְּרִית berîth," TDOT, II, 256-262.

[32] A. Jepsen, "Berith. Ein Beitrag zur Theologie der Exilszeit" (1961) 161-179.

[33] Gen. 9:16; 17:7, 13, 19; Exod. 31:16; Lev. 24:8; 2 Sam. 23:5; Isa. 24:5; 55:3; 61:8; Jer. 32:40; 50:5; Ezek. 16:60; 37:26; Ps. 105:10; and 1 Chron. 16:17. By contrast, no text speaks of an "everlasting oath" (עוֹלָם + אלה/(נ)שבע) or an "everlasting meal / banquet" (עוֹלָם + מִשְׁתֶּה / אָכְלָה), etc. For a discussion of the meaning of עוֹלָם in covenant contexts, cf. M. Tsevat, "Studies in the Book of Samuel," 75-77. Cf. also J. Barr, "Some Semantic Notes on the Covenant," 33.

Other attributes of בְּרִית may also favour a reference to the relationship itself, rather than to its constitutive act. For example, בְּרִית שָׁלוֹם ("covenant of peace") in Num. 25:12; Isa. 54:10; Ezek. 34:25. Cf. M. Noth, "Old Testament Covenant Making in the Light of a Text from Mari" (1967) 108-117.

Finally, although Dan. 9:27 teems with interpretative difficulties, the fact that it can be said of the anointed, וְהִגְבִּיר בְּרִית לָרַבִּים שָׁבוּעַ אֶחָד ["he will make a strong covenant with many for one week (of years)"], implies that בְּרִית does not refer to the constitutive act.

[34] J. Barr, The Semantics of Biblical Language, 218.

[35] E.A. Nida, "The Implications of Contemporary Linguistics for Biblical Scholarship" (1972) 86. Cf. also A.C. Thiselton, "Semantics and New Testament Interpretation" (1977) 84.

[36] A. Wierzbicka, Lexicography and Conceptual Analysis (1985); P. Cotterell and M. Turner, Linguistics and Biblical Interpretation, 122-123.

handlebars." This is so because the possession of handlebars is properly part of the sense or lexical concept of the term "bicycle," even if handlebars are not normally a contextually focused element for "bicycle."[37] Not only is the sense or lexical concept of a term frequently more detailed than might first be imagined, but, as Cotterell and Turner observe, the context of a term often further enriches its meaning (its "discourse concept") so that the resulting sense goes considerably beyond "that which contributes least to the total context."[38]

In the case of Mal. 2:14, from the context of the whole book it is clear that Malachi employs בְּרִית and its related terms with a degree of sophistication (cf. P.J. Naylor, who concludes his dissertation with an extended abstract from Malachi, stressing its "abundant evidence of language oriented to covenant"[39]). Even apart from a consideration of that relatively sophisticated use of terminology, however, we have already noted the inadequacy of any attempt to reduce בְּרִית in Mal. 2:14 merely to "relationship."

1.3 Four diagnostic sentences to help test the first sense posited for "covenant [בְּרִית]"

It remains for us to attempt to justify each of the elements in our definition of the first sense of בְּרִית and to consider these elements as they relate to marriage. Ideally, it would be desirable to construct a series of diagnostic sentences in order to discover which, if any, of these appear anomalous to a native speaker of Biblical Hebrew. While we shall begin each section of our discussion with a proposed diagnostic question, obviously, in the absence of native speakers and with the limited body of evidence at our disposal, our conclusions will necessarily be far more tentative.

1.3.1 "He made a covenant, but it was with another person."

While בְּרִית cannot be reduced to "relationship," nevertheless supporting the centrality of relationship in the vast majority of biblical examples is the observation that virtually everywhere בְּרִית implies the existence of two parties between whom the בְּרִית exists.[40] In particular, the majority of the occurrences of בְּרִית in the Old Testament refer to covenants where God is one of the partners, as for example the covenants between: Yahweh and Noah (Gen. 6:18; 9:9-17), Yahweh and Abraham (Gen. 15:8-18; 17:1-4; etc.), Yahweh and Abraham together with his descendants (Gen. 17:7; etc.),

---

[37] *Linguistics and Biblical Interpretation*, 148f. Cotterell and Turner draw this example from Wierzbicka's work.

[38] *Ibid.*, 152.

[39] "The Language of Covenant," 422f.

[40] Among those scholars who reject "relationship" [*Verhältnis*] as central to בְּרִית are E. Kutsch (*Verheissung und Gesetz*); and, following Kutsch, L. Perlitt (*Bundestheologie im Alten Testament*) and E.W. Nicholson (*God and His People*). Cf. also M.J. Buss, "Review: L. Perlitt, *Bundestheologie im Alten Testament (WMANT 36)*"; and D.J. McCarthy, "*berît* in Old Testament History and Theology" (1972).

Yahweh and Isaac (Gen. 17:21; etc.), Yahweh and the Patriarchs (Exod. 6:4), Yahweh and Israel (Exod. 19:5; etc.), Yahweh and Phinehas (Num. 25:12f.), Yahweh and David (2 Chron. 7:18; etc.), Yahweh and Levi (Mal. 2:4ff.), Yahweh and the eschatological Israel (Jer. 31:31; Isa. 42:6; 49:6-8; 55:3; etc.), and so on.

Besides these theological covenants, there are numerous examples of secular covenants, that is, covenants between persons other than God, although God remains their guarantor. Apart from possible instances involving marriage, the biblical text mentions covenants which exist between: individuals (Gen. 21:22f.; 26:23ff.; 31:44ff.; 47:29; 1 Sam. 18:3; 20:8; 22:8; 23:18; 2 Sam. 3:12f.; 1 Kgs. 2:42-46; etc.), leaders often acting as representatives of their peoples (Gen. 14:13; 1 Kgs. 5:26 [ET 12]; 15:19; 20:34; perhaps 2 Sam. 3:13, 21; etc.), people groups (Josh. 9:6, 11, 15f.), leaders and their subjects (2 Sam. 5:3 // 1 Chron. 11:3; 2 Kgs. 11:17 // 2 Chron. 23:16, 3; perhaps Hos. 6:7-11a; 10:3-4), an individual and the representatives of a people (Joshua 2), and a priest and military leaders (2 Kgs. 11:4 // 2 Chron. 23:1).

In only a few cases do we read about covenants involving impersonal entities, such as a covenant between: men and animals (Job 5:23; 40:28 [ET 41:4]; and perhaps Hos. 2:20 [ET 18], where Yahweh is mediator), a man and the stones of the field (Job 5:23), Israel's apostate leaders and death (Isa. 28:15-18), Job and his eyes (Job 31:1), and Yahweh and day and night (Jer. 33:20, 25). These examples, however, all appear in poetic contexts, often involving hyperbole, personification, or other rhetorical features which suggest that בְּרִית is being employed only in a figurative manner.[41] It is notable that even in these cases there are no examples of a בְּרִית which involves only a single party. In this respect a בְּרִית differs markedly from, for instance, a vow (cf., e.g., the Nazirite vow in Num. 6:2ff.).[42]

Also supportive of the centrality of relationship in covenant is the frequency with which familial or social relationships appear to provide a model for the obligations of a covenant and, consequently, for the terminology by which reference is made to the partners of a covenant. For example, scholars have noted that "brother" may be employed as a designation of a partner in a covenant. This is clearly the case in certain extra-biblical texts.[43] It may also be the case in Judg. 9:3; 1 Kgs. 9:13; 20:32;

---

[41] So M. Weinfeld, "בְּרִית berîth," *TDOT*, II, 264; and J.A. Thompson, "Covenant (OT)" *ISBE Revised*, I, 791, who lists these (and, curiously, Zech. 11:10) as "metaphorical covenants."

[42] Apart from the Nazirite vow, most vows also differ from covenants in being conditional (cf., e.g., Gen. 28:20; 1 Sam. 1:11). On the other hand, like covenants vows include an oath and hence involve God as a witness or guarantor.
D.L. Magnetti defines a "vow [נדר]" as "a solemn promise made to God to do or to perform a certain act in the context of the cult" ("The Oath in the Old Testament," 199).

[43] D.J. McCarthy, *Treaty and Covenant* (1981) 106ff. Cf. P Kalluveettil, *Declaration and Covenant*, 99-101.

2 Sam. 1:26; and perhaps Num. 20:14.[44] Possibly the clearest example is the expression בְּרִית אַחִים, "a covenant of brothers," used in Amos 1:9 of the treaty between Tyre and Israel.[45] Similarly, the terms for "father" and "son" appear in extra-biblical texts as designations of covenant partners; they may so appear within biblical texts in 1 Sam. 25:8; 2 Sam. 7:14; 2 Kgs. 16:7; Isa. 63:16 (bis); 64:7 [ET 8]; Jer. 31:9; Ps. 2:7; 89:27f. [ET 26f.]; and 116:16.[46]

Furthermore, of special interest to the present study, the husband-wife analogy, although unattested outside the Bible, is used extensively to depict the deity's relationship to Israel in Hosea, Isaiah, Jeremiah, and Ezekiel and is perhaps already implied in the language of "jealousy [קָנָא]" and "whoring [זָנָה]" elsewhere.[47] Whether or not some of these texts demand an interpretation of marriage as a covenant, as will be argued later, they certainly support an emphasis on the relational aspect of בְּרִית (perhaps even including an emotional component).[48]

Turning to the social sphere, the terms "lord" and "servant" are well attested as designations of covenant partners in extra-biblical covenants.[49] Within the Bible there are numerous plausible examples of "lord" and "servant" used in this manner in both theological and secular covenants. For instance, compare Gen. 50:18; Josh. 9:8; 1 Sam. 25:8; 27:12; 2 Kgs. 10:5-6; 16:7; 24:1; and Ps. 116:16.[50] Further, the language of "friend" or "companion" is similarly used of covenant partners in the extra-biblical texts and possibly within the Bible.[51] Compare אָהֵב, "be a friend," used of Hiram's

---

[44] So P. Kalluveettil, *Declaration and Covenant*, 198-210 (Chapter 6: "The Formula 'Brother'").

One needs to be careful not to fall into "pan-covenantalism," however, since "brother" may often be simply a polite designation or even a term of endearment. In this respect one may compare examples where a wife is called "sister." Apart from the problematic case of the Patriarchal narratives (Gen. 12:13, 19; 21:2ff.; 26:7ff.), each of the remaining examples occurs in a highly poetic context, and none appears to have any necessary covenantal implication (i.e., Prov. 7:4; Cant. 4:9f., 12; 5:1f.).

[45] Cf. J.F. Priest, "The Covenant of Brothers" (1965) 400-406; and F.C. Fensham, "The Treaty between the Israelites and Tyrians" (1969) 80.

[46] For a discussion of "father" and "son" terminology in extra-biblical texts, cf. P. Kalluveettil, *Declaration and Covenant*, 98f.; 129f. For the biblical use of these terms with reference to covenant partners, cf. F.C. Fensham, "Father and Son Terminology for Treaty and Covenant" (1971); D.J. McCarthy, "Notes on the Love of God in Dt. and the Father-Son Relationship between Yahweh and Israel" (1965) 144-147; J.W. McKay, "Man's Love for God and the Father/Teacher – Son/Pupil Relationship" (1972) 426-435; and M. Weinfeld, "Covenant, Davidic" (1976) 190f. Cf. also the developed father-son analogy in Hosea 11.

[47] Cf., e.g., Hosea 1, 3; Isaiah 43, 49, 51, 62, 63; Jeremiah 2, 3, 30; Ezekiel 16, and 23.

For the absence of this analogy in extra-biblical texts, cf. M. Weinfeld, *Deuteronomy and the Deuteronomic School*, 81f., n. 6. Qualifying Weinfeld's claim, however, cf. Chapter 7, §1.1.5 below.

[48] So M. Weinfeld, *Deuteronomy*, 81f., n. 6; and *idem*, "בְּרִית *berîth*," *TDOT*, II, 278. Cf. G. Wallis, "אָהַב, *'āhabh*," *TDOT*, I, 113f.

[49] Cf. D.J. McCarthy, *Treaty and Covenant* (1981) 79, n. 80; and P. Kalluveettil, *Declaration and Covenant*, 93-99.

[50] For Josh. 9:8, cf. F.C. Fensham, "The Treaty Between Israel and the Gibeonites" (1964) 96-100.

[51] Cf., e.g., W.L. Moran, "The Ancient Near Eastern Background of Love of God in Deuteronomy" (1963); F.C. Fensham, "The Treaty between the Israelites and Tyrians"

relationship to David in 1 Kgs. 5:15 [ET 5:1], or אהב, "love," used of
Jonathan's relationship to David in 1 Sam. 18:1, 3; compare also the uses of
חבר, "companion" or "partner," in Mal. 2:14; Ps. 94:20; Dan. 11:6, 23; 2
Chron. 20:35, 37; and Hos. 4:17.

Related to these familial and social models for covenant is the
pre-eminent covenantal obligation of "love [אהב]" (cf. Deut. 6:5; 7:8, 13;
23:6 [ET 5]; 30:6, 15, 16, 20), or "brotherhood [אחוה]" (Zech. 11:14), or
"peace [שָׁלוֹם]" (Num. 25:12; Isa. 54:10; Ezek. 34:25; 37:26).[52] Recognizing
this, P. Kalluveettil writes, "even these texts where 'obligation' outshines
other aspects of covenant, do not deny the idea of relation, from which
obligation originates."[53] Putting this somewhat speculatively, Kalluveettil
states, "For Semitic peoples, obligation, for instance, was not an isolated
concept."[54]

Summarizing these observations, D.J. McCarthy writes: "Covenant is
not contract, as we have had occasion to repeat more than once. It is personal
union pledged by symbol and/or oath. The relationship comes first."[55]
Similarly, P. Kalluveettil asserts, "Covenant is relational, in one way or other
it creates unity, community."[56] At another point he states:

> "The idea, 'I am yours, you are mine' underlies every covenant
> declaration. This implies a quasi-familial bond which makes sons
> and brothers. The act of accepting the other as one's own reflects
> the basic idea of covenant: an attempt to extend the bond of blood
> beyond the kinship sphere, or, in other words, to make partner
> one's own flesh and blood. The study of the DF [declaration
> formulae] has shown that covenant is relational."[57]

(1969) 71-87; P. Kalluveettil, *Declaration and Covenant*, 51-53, 99f., 101-102; and E.W.
Nicholson, *God and His People* (1986) 61f.
[52] Cf. W.L. Moran, "The Ancient Near Eastern Background of Love of God in
Deuteronomy" (1963); D.J. McCarthy, *Treaty and Covenant* (1981) 160f., n. 6; P.J. Naylor,
"The Language of Covenant," 27; and P. Kalluveettil, *Declaration and Covenant*, 84.
  This "love" should not be reduced to mere loyalty, as if it were entirely dispassionate.
Cf. Jer. 2:2 and M. Weinfeld, *Deuteronomy and the Deuteronomic School*, 81f.
  Cf. also D.J. Wiseman, "Is it Peace? – Covenant and Diplomacy" (1982) 311-326.
[53] *Declaration and Covenant*, 91, n. 354.
[54] *Ibid.*, 18, n. 9.
[55] D.J. McCarthy, *Treaty and Covenant* (1981) 297. At another point McCarthy notes,
"rites and cultic acts are what bring the covenant relationship into being. They are
'sacrifices of union' (*šᵉlāmîm*) which establish a certain community between God and
Israel. The treaties aim at the same effect designated by the cognate term, 'peaceful union,'
(*šalîmu*) but the means is not rite but the agreement based on a pledge which they
represent (*ibid.*, 295).
[56] *Declaration and Covenant,*, 51. Cf. also Kalluveettil's comment on p. 91: "Secular
covenant actually means, 'relation and obligation, commitment and action'; one cannot
separate the idea of relationship from it."
[57] *Ibid.*, 212. Cf. also McCarthy's summary, "there is no doubt that covenants, even
treaties, were thought of as establishing a kind of quasi-familial unity" (*Old Testament
Covenant*, 33).
  Cf. M.L. Newman, who writes with respect to E. Kutsch's one-sided emphasis on
obligation in covenant, "Although obligation is invariably one element in the meaning of
bᵉrît, it does not exhaust that meaning. *Relationship* is also an essential feature. *Bᵉrît*

In terms of this relational aspect of covenant and the primacy of the obligation of love, it should hardly be surprising if a text such as Mal. 2:14 did, in fact, identify marriage as a covenant. Indeed, so impressive are the parallels between marriage and other kinds of covenant within the Old Testament, some scholars have argued that marriage, along with adoption, provides the underlying model and subsequently formulae for the theological covenants of the Old Testament.[58] Alternatively, if this conclusion is not accepted, J. Ziegler's view that the covenant between Yahweh and Israel suggested the marriage metaphor of the prophets precisely because marriage was also understood as a covenant seems plausible.[59]

1.3.2 "He made a covenant, but it was with a non-relative."
Supportive of the emphasis in our definition on an elected, as opposed to natural, relationship, D.J. McCarthy remarks that covenants were "the means the ancient world took to extend relationships beyond the natural unity by blood."[60] The same point was made a generation earlier by W.R. Smith, who noted, "a covenant means an artificial brotherhood."[61] Appropriately בְּרִית is nowhere employed of naturally occurring relationships and the ordinary obligations which attend them, such as those which exist between parents and a child or between blood brothers (cf. Gen. 4:9). On the other hand, stressing their special and volitional character (even if volitional only on the part of the suzerain), covenants are frequently said to be cut or (re)made (כרת - 63x), confirmed or established (הקים - 12x), given (נתן - 3x), entered (בוא - 3x; הביא - 1x; עבר - 1x), issued (שׂים - 1x), etc.[62]

---

always involves two parties and a specific *relation* between them" ("Review of *Verheissung und Gesetz*," 120).

[58] R. Smend and N. Lohfink, among others, have argued that marriage and adoption were the ultimate models for covenant and hence the "Bundesformel," the declaration "I will be your God and you will be my people," may itself derive from the legal formulae for marriage and adoption. Cf. R. Smend, *Die Bundesformel* (1963); *idem, Die Mitte des Alten Testaments* (1970) 49-54; and N. Lohfink, "Dt 26,17-19 und die Bundesformel" (1969) 517-53.

Cf. also M. Weinfeld, who asserts that the "Bundesformel" is "a legal formula taken from the sphere of marriage, as attested in various legal documents from the ancient Near East (cf. Hos. 2:4 [2])" ("בְּרִית *berîth*," *TDOT*, II, 278). Less convinced is P. Kalluveettil, *Declaration and Covenant*, 213.

L. Perlitt has argued against the assumed covenant setting for the "Bundesformel" (*Bundestheologie im Alten Testament* [1969] 105-115). His objections, however, are refuted by D.J. McCarthy, *Treaty and Covenant* (1981) 182-185.

[59] J. Ziegler, "Die Liebe Gottes bei den Propheten" (1930) 73-77. Cf. also T.C. Vriezen, *An Outline of Old Testament Theology* (1958) 146; and M.H. Woudstra, "The Everlasting Covenant in Ezekiel 16:59-63" (1971) 25.

[60] *Treaty and Covenant*, 1st ed. (1963) 175. This section was eliminated from the second edition, but its essential point is reiterated and nowhere disavowed. Cf., e.g., *idem, Treaty and Covenant*, 2nd ed. (1981) 295. Cf. also McCarthy's assertion, "there is no doubt that covenants, even treaties, were thought of as establishing a kind of quasi-familial unity" (*Old Testament Covenant* [1972] 33).

[61] W.R. Smith, *Lectures on the Religion of the Semites* (1927) 318.

[62] Cf. P.J. Naylor, "The Language of Covenant," 126-127.

In terms of this aspect of the character of covenants, marriage in general, and the marriage of Adam and Eve in particular, is eminently qualified as a plausible example of a covenant. Texts such as Leviticus 18 and 20 suggest that marriage quite literally extends family relationships so that incest with an affine is no less heinous than incest with a consanguine.[63] Additionally, Gen. 2:24 describes the obligation of a husband toward his wife precisely in terms of a familial loyalty which is comparable to that owed to one's parents: "Therefore a man leaves his father and his mother and cleaves to his wife, and they become one flesh."

1.3.3 "He made a covenant, but it was one with obligations."

E. Kutsch defends the centrality of "obligation" in covenant, although, as previously noted, has gone too far in insisting that בְּרִית should always be rendered "duty" or "command" [*Verpflichtung*].[64] In a more balanced presentation of the evidence, M. Weinfeld begins with the notion of "obligation," citing certain passages wherein a covenant is "commanded" (Ps. 111:9 and Judg. 2:20), while noting that in other passages the terms "covenant" and "commandment" function synonymously (e.g. Deut. 4:13; 33:9; Isa. 24:5; Ps. 50:16; and 103:18).[65]

Not surprisingly, there seems to be a scholarly consensus that "covenant" entails obligation.[66] Yet there has been considerable debate whether the obligations of a covenant are necessarily mutual, particularly in connection with certain covenants between Yahweh and his people, or whether covenants of promise (where Yahweh is considered to assume all necessary obligations) may be distinguished rather sharply from law covenants (where the obligations are more clearly mutual).[67] Favouring the assumption that there is invariably a degree of mutual obligation, D.J. McCarthy states that "all covenants ... have their conditions," and he goes on to observe that these conditions or obligations may often be assumed as matters of cultural convention.[68]

What is intended by "an *elected* as opposed to natural relationship of obligation" could also be expressed as a "*formal* [italics added] relationship of obligation," as does M.L. Newman, "Review of *Verheissung und Gesetz*" (1975) 120.

[63] Cf. G.J. Wenham, "The Restoration of Marriage Reconsidered," 36-40.

[64] E. Kutsch, *Verheissung und Gesetz* (1973) 28-39. Cf., *idem*, "בְּרִית *berīt* Verpflichtung," *THAT*, I, 339-352. For a critique of Kutsch, cf. D.J. McCarthy, *Treaty and Covenant* (1981) 16-22; M. Weinfeld, "*Bᵉrît* — Covenant vs. Obligation" (1975) 120-128; and M.L. Newman, "Review of *Verheissung und Gesetz*" (1975) 117-120.

[65] M. Weinfeld, "בְּרִית *berîth*," *TDOT*, II, 255.

[66] For a discussion of the metonymic synonyms for covenant based on the stipulations of the covenant, cf. P. Kalluveettil, *Declaration and Covenant*, 30ff.

[67] What we are terming a "covenant of promise" is called by G.E. Mendenhall a "patron" covenant ("Covenant," 717). Mendenhall uses the term "promissory covenant" to describe the kind of covenant found in Ezra 10:3 where no new relationship is established, but where the covenant serves to guarantee a stipulated course of action.

[68] *Old Testament Covenant*, 3. In support of the "inseparability of covenant and commandment," D.J. McCarthy cites E. Gerstenberger, *Wesen und Herkunft des*

Whether McCarthy's analysis is correct or not, in terms of this aspect of (mutual) obligation marriage is very plausibly identified as a covenant. With respect to the paradigmatic marriage of Adam and Eve, we noted in the previous chapter the obligations (without any denigration) of a wife toward her husband. In part, as we have argued elsewhere, these obligations are already implied in the mode of the creation of Eve, having been made from the rib of the man,[69] but they are also made more explicit in her identification as a עֵזֶר כְּנֶגְדּוֹ, "a helper corresponding to him." A similar implication may be detected in Mal. 2:14 in the identification of the wife as חֲבֶרְתֶּךָ, "your partner."[70]

What is especially striking, as was noted in the previous chapter, is the fact that the primary obligation of marriage as stressed in both Genesis 2 and Malachi 2 is not that of the wife toward her husband, as might be expected from their ancient context, but that of the husband toward his wife. An obligation of nurture and love on Adam's part is already implied in the mode of Eve's creation as well as in Adam's recognition of Eve as "bone of my bones and flesh of my flesh." Removing any doubt concerning this pre-eminent obligation, however, the narrator concludes in Gen. 2:24 that a man should "leave his father and his mother" and "cleave to his wife, and they will become one flesh." The greatest and most enduring natural love and loyalty which a man once owed to his parents is now to be superseded by an even greater love and loyalty to his wife. Similarly, in Mal. 2:14-16 the prophet stresses the fidelity which is required, not of the wife, but of the husband. Indeed, in both vss. 15 and 16 Malachi makes it clear that a man threatens his own life if he is guilty of disloyalty toward the wife of his youth.

1.3.4 *"He made a covenant, but it was one with an oath."*

While one need not accept N. Lohfink's definition of בְּרִית as "oath," the relative indispensability of an oath for ratifying a covenant commands a widespread scholarly consensus.[71] Accordingly, G.M. Tucker states: "the

---

Apodiktischen Rechts, 145-6 (*op. cit.*, 3, n. 4). M.G. Kline similarly favours the mutuality of obligations in a covenant (*The Structure of Biblical Authority*, 125f., 145f.).

[69] Cf. G.P. Hugenberger, "Rib," *ISBE Revised*, 4 (1988) 183-185.

[70] On the covenantal associations of חבר, cf. P. Kalluveettil, *Declaration and Covenant*, 51-53.

Kalluveettil notes that while the stipulations of a covenant are generally indicated, at times these may be left unspecified apart from the general obligation of behaviour befitting friends (as in the Abimelech-Abraham pact) (*op. cit.*, 91). Kalluveettil cites approvingly the comment of W.R. Smith, *Religion of the Semites*, 315f.: "Primarily the covenant is not a special engagement to this or that particular effect, but a bond of troth and life-fellowship to all the effects for which kinsmen are permanently bound together."

[71] N. Lohfink, *Die Landverheissung als Eid* (1967) 101-13. For a brief critique of Lohfink, cf. D.J. McCarthy, who, nevertheless, acknowledges that both originally and subsequently in "many" OT texts בְּרִית may mean "oath" (*Treaty and Covenant* [1981] 22).

Conversely, it is interesting that although the Akkadian phrase *riksu* [/ *rikiltu*] *u māmītu* ("bond and oath") is the standard expression for "treaty," the term *māmītu*, "oath," by itself can refer to a treaty by metonymy.

covenant formula was based on the oath pattern and the contract was not."[72] M. Weinfeld similarly concludes: *"berith* as a commitment has to be confirmed by an oath...: Gen. 21:22ff.; 26:26ff.; Dt. 29:9ff. (10ff.); Josh. 9:15-20; 2 K. 11:4; Ezk. 16:8; 17:13ff.... The oath gives the obligation its binding validity...."[73]

Offering compelling support for this conclusion, P.J. Naylor has established the remarkable semantic proximity of אלה, "curse," to ברית in terms of collocation, idiomatic overlap, functional commutativity, and especially syntagmatic intersection.[74] Reflecting this proximity, instead of "cutting a covenant" [בְּרִית + כָּרַת], at one point we read "his oath which Yahweh your God cut [= made] with you" [וּבְאָלָתוֹ אֲשֶׁר יְהוָה אֱלֹהֶיךָ כֹּרֵת עִמָּךְ] (Deut. 29:11 [ET 12]). Alternatively, just as one can swear an oath, several texts speak about the "swearing of a covenant" [בְּרִית + נשׁבע]: Deut. 4:31; 7:12; and 8:18. Similarly, rather than entering a covenant, two passages

---

[72] "Covenant Forms and Contract Forms," 500. If oaths were optional in the contract form, as Tucker argues, this need not imply that they are infrequently attested. Indeed, as D.L. Magnetti argues, it seems that "the swearing of an oath was part of the normal procedure" for contracts in Egypt, Mesopotamia, and Syria-Palestine ("The Oath in the Old Testament," 47, cf. also pp. 49, 65-85).

[73] M. Weinfeld, "בְּרִית *berîth*," *TDOT*, II, 256.
Likewise, D.J. McCarthy concludes that the basic idea of a treaty is "a union based on an oath" (*Treaty and Covenant* [1981] 141). Cf. the similar insistence on oaths as an indispensable feature of covenants in G.E. Mendenhall, "Covenant" (1962) 716; H.C. Brichto, *The Problem of 'Curse' in the Hebrew Bible* (1963) 70; G.M. Tucker, "Covenant Forms and Contract Forms" (1965) 488-490; D.L. Magnetti, "The Oath in the Old Testament" (1969) 72-4, 113, 123 and *passim*; K.A. Kitchen, *The Bible in Its World* (1977) 80f.; J. Barr, "Some Semantic Notes on the Covenant" (1977) 23-38, esp. p. 32.; J. Scharbert, "אָלָה *'ālāh*," *TDOT*, I (1978) 264; and E.W. Nicholson, *God and His People* (1986) 103.

[74] "The Language of Covenant," 380-395.
In support of the semantic proximity of אלה to ברית in terms of collocation, אלה appears with ברית: in Hos. 10:4; in an hendiadys in Deut. 29:11, 13 [ET 12, 14]; in synonymous parallelism in Ezek. 16:59; 17:16, 18, 19; and in functional parallelism in Gen. 26:28.
Idiomatic overlap is apparent in the hendiadys mentioned above, which is comparable to the Akkadian phrase *riksu u māmîtu*. Of interest also is a Phoenician incantation text involving a covenant granted by the god Ashur, along with other deities, to the people (Z. Zevit, "A Phoenician Inscription and Biblical Covenant Theology" [1977] 110-118). The text reads עלם . אלה [cognate of Hebrew אלה] . לן , כרת, which offers a striking parallel for Jer. 32:40, וְכָרַתִּי לָהֶם בְּרִית עוֹלָם.
Functional commutativity is illustrated in a text such as Gen. 24:1-67. Here it appears that אלה and שבועה may be used interchangeably (cf. vss. 3, 9, and 37 with vss. 8 and 41). Elsewhere it is apparent that כרת ברית and נשׁבע שבעה commute. Hence, it may be suggested that אלה (נשׁבע) may be parallel to, though not necessarily interchangeable with, כרת ברית.
Finally, the following are shared syntagms, demonstrating syntagmatic intersection:
זאת/היתה ברית // זאת/היתה אלה
בוא/הביא בברית // בוא/הביא באלה
נשבע ברית // נשבע אלה
נתן ברית // נתן אלה
נתן לברית // נתן לאלה
כתב ברית // כתב אלה
הגיד ברית // הגיד אלה
שמע את דברי הברית // שמע את דברי האלה

speak of entering [בא / עבר] an oath: Deut. 29:11 [ET 12] and Neh. 10:30 [ET 29]. Finally, also of interest are a number of texts which closely associate בְּרִית, "covenant," or בְּרִית + כָּרַת, "make a covenant," with either אָלָה, "oath" (Gen. 26:28; Deut. 29:11, 13, 20 [ET 12, 14, 21]; Ezek. 16:59f.; 17:13, 16, 18, 19; Hos. 10:4; Neh. 10:31 [ET 30]), or שְׁבוּעָה, "oath" (Deut. 7:8f.; Jer. 11:3-5; Ps. 105:9; Neh. 10:30 [ET 29]; 2 Chron. 15:12-15), or נשבע, "swear" (Gen. 21:31-32; 26:28-31; 31:44 compared with 31:53; Deut. 7:8f.; 31:20; Josh. 9:15f.; Judg. 2:1; 1 Sam. 20:8 compared with 20:17; 2 Kgs. 11:4; Isa. 54:9f.; Jer. 11:3-5; Ezek. 16:8; Ps. 89:4 [ET 3]; 132:11f.; Ezra 10:3-5; and 2 Chron. 15:12-15).

Having established four essential ingredients in the Old Testament understanding of בְּרִית, viz., that it is used of 1) a relationship 2) with a non-relative 3) which involves obligations and 4) is established through an oath, the first three of which are clearly present in marriage, we must now examine the evidence for this fourth element of a ratifying oath in marriage. From the evidence considered above, it appears that such a ratifying oath may well be the *sine qua non* of covenant precisely because it invokes the deity to act against any subsequent breach of the covenant. If this is so, the lack of an oath in marriage, as J. Milgrom has argued, indeed would appear to prohibit marriage from being considered a covenant. Milgrom observes, "though countless marriage contracts and laws from [the] ancient Near East are known, not a single one to my knowledge stipulates an oath."[75]

Milgrom proceeds to counter specific arguments which might imply that an oath did accompany marriage whether elsewhere in the ancient Near East or in Israel. He argues, perhaps not altogether convincingly, that the fact that the cuneiform laws so frequently allow an injured husband to mitigate or waive the death penalty against an adulterer implies that adultery did not entail the breach of an oath.[76] He notes that the oath mentioned in Gen. 31:50ff. has to do with prohibiting future marriages to Jacob, not with the contraction of his already existing marriages to Rachel and Leah.[77] Referring to Ezek. 16:8, Milgrom observes that the oath "is taken by God whereas it should have been expected of the bride, Israel, for it is the bride, not the husband, who is subject to the laws of adultery." Milgrom adds that there is a similar anomaly with respect to the charge of infidelity in Mal. 2:14.

Milgrom goes on to counter the assumption of an oath connected with marriage as a means of accounting for the remarkable use of the term מַעַל, "trespass," in Num. 5:11ff. He argues that this term is used of an oath violation in Num. 5:6-8 and is everywhere else used exclusively of sins

---

[75] *Cult and Conscience* (1976) 134.
[76] *Ibid.*, 134, where he cites CH §129; MAL A §§14-16; and HL §§192f.
[77] While Milgrom discusses this example at some length, with the implication that it is erroneously used to buttress the theory of covenantal marriage, he does not cite any scholar who has made the mistake he alleges. Concern about prohibiting other marriages is a common feature of ancient Near Eastern marriage contracts (e.g. from Nuzi).

against God. Nevertheless, Milgrom considers that its usage in Num. 5:11ff. is best understood as a "literary metaphor."

Finally, the actual reason for his digression into the subject of marriage as a covenant, Milgrom denies that the penalty prescribed for the violation of a betrothed slave-girl in Lev. 19:20-22, namely an אָשָׁם, a "guilt/reparation offering," is not to be explained on the supposition that adultery violates an individual oath made at the time of her betrothal (after all, the paramour is punished although he had not taken an oath!).[78] Rather, according to Milgrom, the "guilt/reparation offering" is required because adultery violates the prohibition made within the Decalogue and hence violates Israel's collective oath of commitment to Yahweh by which they bound themselves to the Sinaitic covenant.[79]

We need now to consider the possibility that there may yet be an "oath" associated with marriage, both a verbal oath and, more importantly, an "oath-sign," which hitherto has generally been overlooked.

2. TOWARD A SOLUTION REGARDING THE APPARENT LACK OF AN OATH IN MARRIAGE

2.1 The lack of any explicit reference to an oath within marriage in the ancient Near Eastern law collections or extant marriage contracts is not unexpected

Although Milgrom observes that none of the extant marriage contracts or laws from the ancient Near East stipulates an oath for marriage, three considerations may help to put this objection into perspective.[80]

1) First, it should be recalled that ancient Near Eastern law in general, just as biblical law in particular, is predominantly concerned with the unusual and difficult, not with what could be assumed.[81] For example, limiting our

---

[78] According to J. Milgrom, the אָשָׁם offering was the appointed means for expiating crimes against God when committed under mitigating circumstances (*Cult and Conscience* [1976] 133). These crimes divide between "sancta trespass" (the subject of Chapter 2) and "oath violation" (the subject of Chapter 3).

[79] *Ibid.*, 135f. We may add here that Milgrom qualifies his own objections by acknowledging that "the betrothal/marriage rite might be conceived as a covenant if there were a mutual exchange of verba solemnia even though an oath formula was not used" (*ibid.*, 135, n. 487). Milgrom goes on to cite some evidence for the likelihood of such a verbal exchange, including Hos. 2:4 [ET: 2]. On the crucial oath-like function of such solemn declarations, see our discussion below in Chapter 6, §2.3.3.

[80] *Ibid.*, 134.

[81] On the problematic nature of the so-called "law codes," their purpose, incompleteness, and emphasis on exceptional cases, etc., cf., e.g., G.E. Mendenhall, "Ancient Oriental and Biblical Law" (1954) 26-46; J.J. Finkelstein, "Ammisaduqa's Edict and the Babylonian Law Codes" (1961) 103-104; D.J. Wiseman, "The Laws of Hammurabi Again" (1962) 161-72; S. Greengus, "Law in the OT," *IDBSup.* (1976) 533; R. Westbrook, "Biblical and Cuneiform Law Codes" (1985) 247-264; and M. Fishbane, *Biblical Interpretation in Ancient Israel* (1985) 91-97. In fact, according to Fishbane, the frequent lacunae and ambiguities in biblical law impelled subsequent innerbiblical and extrabiblical interpretation, apart from which the law would have been inoperative.

attention to sexual issues within the Old Testament legislation, many
surprising gaps have often been observed, such as the lack of an explicit
prohibition against father-daughter incest, rape of a married woman, self-
induced abortion, or lesbianism.[82]   In terms of positive stipulations, the
unexpected omission within the Old Testament of an explicit requirement for
a "marriage present [מֹהַר]" or, for that matter, for the drafting of a marriage
contract [כְּתֻבָּה or כְּתוּבָה in post-biblical Hebrew] has frequently been noted.[83]
As a result of this well-documented tendency toward lacunae in both biblical
and ancient Near Eastern law, it should not be surprising that an oath
connected with marriage is nowhere stipulated even if such an oath were
customary or mandatory.

2) In spite of the widespread scholarly recognition of the
indispensability of an oath, whether verbal or symbolic, as the requisite
means for ratifying covenants, K.A. Kitchen has noted that in the fifty-seven
extant extra-biblical treaty documents a ratifying oath is only rarely
stipulated.[84]   G. Mendenhall makes a similar observation: "The oath itself is
lacking in both the Israelite and the Hittite covenants, though there is no

---

[82] Contrast CH §154; HL §195; and MAL A §53. Of course, a prohibition against
father-daughter incest, for example, might be inferred from Lev. 18:6, 10, 17, or Gen.
19:30ff. Similarly, it is possible that a prohibition against the rape of a married woman
could be inferred from the more difficult case of the rape of a betrothed woman in Deut.
22:25-27. Also cf. the anti-rape theme of Judges 5 treated by M.Z. Levin, "A Protest
Against Rape in the Story of Deborah" (in Hebrew) [reviewed in *OTA* 4:1 (1981) #142].
For a discussion of the legal status of abortion on the basis of Exod. 21:22-25, cf., e.g., B.S.
Jackson, "The Problem of Ex. xxi 22-25 (*Ius Talionis*)" (1973) 273-304; S.E.
Loewenstamm, "Exodus xxi 22-25" (1977) 352-60; M.G. Kline, "*Lex Talionis* and the
Human Fetus" (1977) 193-201; R. Westbrook, "Lex talionis and Exodus 21:22-25" (1986)
52-69; and M. Fishbane, *Biblical Interpretation in Ancient Israel*, 92-94.

[83] Exod. 22:16 and Deut. 22:29 treat exceptional cases of the "marriage present" [מֹהַר].
     Marriage contracts are attested for Jews in the post-exilic period. For the earliest such
evidence, cf. the seven Aramaic marriage contracts (termed סֵפֶר אִנְתּוּ, "a document of
wifehood," in Cowley 14:4, etc.), which have survived from the fifth century B.C. Jewish
community at Elephantine. The seven contracts may be found in Cowley, Kraeling, and
recently re-edited in Porten-Yardeni. Cf. also the fragmentary betrothal contract, Cowley
48. For the use of contracts among Jews in the second century B.C., cf. Tob. 7:13, 14.
     For the later practice of the early second century A.D. Jews, cf. three fragmentary
Aramaic Jewish marriage contracts, two of which were published in *DJD*, II, as no. 20 (pp.
109ff.) and no. 21 (pp. 114ff.). For the third, cf. *DJD*, II, 253, n. 5. In addition two more
Jewish marriage contracts written in Greek were found at Murabba'at and published in
DJD, as no. 115 (243ff.) and no. 116 (254ff.). Cf. M.A. Friedman, *Jewish Marriage in
Palestine: A Cairo Geniza Study* (1980-81) I, 7-9.
     For Talmudic practice, cf. *b.* Qidd. 2b. For the much later Gaonic period (10th and 11th
centuries A.D.), cf. M.A. Friedman, *op. cit.*
     It is less clear whether the Jews utilized marriage contracts in the pre-exilic period. In
favour of this assumption, cf. R. de Vaux, *Ancient Israel*, I, 33. More cautious is R. Yaron,
Introduction to the Law of the Aramaic Papyri, 49; and *idem*, "Aramaic Marriage Contracts
from Elephantine," 36f.

[84] K.A. Kitchen, *The Bible in Its World* (1977) 79-85, esp. 80f.; *idem*, "Law, Treaty,
Covenant and Deuteronomy" (1988). So also D.J. McCarthy, *Treaty and Covenant* (1981)
182; and J.H. Walton, *Ancient Israelite Literature in its Cultural Context* (1989) 95.
     Kitchen's summary of the evidence contradicts E. Gerstenberger, who mistakenly
equates the common documentary curse, "If anyone changes the words of this tablet...,"
with the ratifying oath, or treaty curse ("Covenant and Commandment" [1965] 38-51). Cf.
F.B. Knutson, "Literary Genres in *PRU* IV," *RSP*, II, 157f.

doubt that this was the formality which made the covenant valid."[85] One evidence in support of this assumption of a ratifying oath in biblical covenants is seen in later texts which frequently refer to such an oath, even though it was unrecorded in the original instance.[86] Hence, by analogy with the practice of the treaty documents, it appears unwarranted to assume from the omission of a similar stipulation in marriage documents that a ratifying oath was necessarily lacking in actual practice.[87]

3) Contrary to Milgrom's assertion that none of the extant marriage contracts stipulates an oath, in point of fact, a considerable number of marriage contracts do include an oath. For instance, eight of the forty-five neo- and late-Babylonian marriage contracts assembled by M.T. Roth invoke a curse against anyone who would violate the terms of the agreement (Nos. 2, 5, 8, 14, 18, 19, 26, and 30).[88] In one case (No. 6), and possibly a second (No. 16), the contract specifies a mutual oath by which both bride and groom are bound to the terms of the contract.

Roth offers the following translation for No. 6:

(1-4) Nabû-aḫ-iddin, son of Aplā, spoke to Daḫli-eššu, son of Arba'ilā, as follows: (4-6): "Please give me ꝭBanât-Esagil, your daughter, the lass. Let her be my wife."

---

[85] G.E. Mendenhall, "Covenant" in *IDB*, I, 720. Cf. also D.L. Magnetti, "The Oath in the Old Testament," 72ff.

Analogous to the situation with covenants and their assumed attending verbal oaths or oath-signs, M. Malul notes that the ancient Near Eastern law compendia in general, "except for one or two cases in MAL, do not make reference to symbolic acts...," although there can be little doubt that a rich variety of symbolic acts were customary and even mandatory (*Studies in Mesopotamian Legal Symbolism*, 12f.). Cf. also *ibid.*, 449-452.

[86] Cf., e.g., the reference in 2 Sam. 3:9 to Yahweh's oath to David to establish his throne, nowhere suggested in the earlier narrative. Cf. similar examples in Isa. 54:9, which mentions Yahweh's oath not to allow another deluge after Noah, and Ezek. 16:8 and 20:5-6, which mention Yahweh's otherwise unrecorded oath with respect to the Mosaic covenant. Finally, although Gen. 22:16 does record an explicit oath taken by Yahweh to bless Abraham and his progeny, it nowhere mentions Yahweh's intention to give Israel the promised land (as in Gen. 15:18-20 and 17:8). Nevertheless, in more than forty OT texts, reference is made to Yahweh's oath guaranteeing possession of the promised land (e.g., cf. Gen. 24:7; 26:3; Exod. 32:11-13; Deut. 8:18; Judg. 2:1; Jer. 11:3-5; and 2 Chron. 15:15). Cf. also D.L. Magnetti, who discusses these texts and notes that while it is unusual, an oath sworn by the sovereign is attested in extra-biblical treaties ("The Oath in the Old Testament," 70f., 113ff., 125, cf. *AT* nos. 3 and 456).

[87] While this argument assumes some similarity between the treaties as international covenants and marriage as an interpersonal covenant (cf., e.g., D.L. Magnetti, "The Oath in the Old Testament," 94), it does not presuppose a particularly close analogy between treaty documents and betrothal/marriage documents. As will be stressed below, marriage documents, in fact, are not closely related to treaties since they are typically contract documents (following a contract form and primarily concerned to list human witnesses, though at times they may include curses, etc.) and not covenant documents (which have an altogether distinct form including the mention or assumption of a divine witness).

[88] M.T. Roth, *Babylonian Marriage Agreements: 7th - 3rd Centuries B.C.* (1989), 19.

Cf. also the MB Ḫana marriage document, discussed by A.J. Skaist, wherein the couple "swore an oath by the god and the king before Pagirum" ("Studies in Ancient Mesopotamian Family Law Pertaining to Marriage and Divorce," 89-93), and a 17th century B.C. marriage contract from Sippar discussed by J. Klíma, wherein the bride (a priestess) and groom "both swore in the names of God Shamash, God Marduk and the town of Sippar" ("Marriage and Family in Ancient Mesopotamia" [1966] 100).

(7-9) Dalīli-eššu consented to his (proposal), and gave ᶠBanât-Esagil, his daughter, the lass, to him in marriage.

(10-13) Should Nabû-aḫ-iddin release ᶠBanât-Esagil and marry another, he will give her six minas of silver and she may go where she wishes.

(14-16) Should ᶠBanât-Esagil <be found> with another man, she will die by the iron dagger.

(17-19) They swore[89] by Nabû and Marduk their gods, and by Nebuchadnezzar, the king, their lord, not to contravene (this agreement).

(20) At the sealing of this document (21-27) before: Šulā, son of Šamaš-iddin, descendant of Rab-bāni; Šamaš-mukīn-apli, son of Nūrea, descendant of Zērija; Marduk-nādin-aḫi, son of Zababa-iddin, descendant of Rab-bāni; Mār-šarri-ilūa, son of Arba'ilā; Nabû-uṣuršu, son of Abī-ul-idi; and Nabû-aḫḫē-iddin the scribe, son of Šulâ, descendant of Egibi.

(28-29) Opis, month II, day 13, year 41, of Nebuchadnezzar, king of Babylon.

While the discovery of the oath in lines 17-19 might seem attractive for the present thesis, on closer examination it appears unlikely that this oath effected the marriage (covenant) itself. If it had, one would expect it to be mentioned immediately after the "historical" sketch of the marriage in lines 1-9, rather than following the stipulations of lines 10-16. Located where it is, it seems more likely that this oath is to be viewed solely in terms of the precise stipulations of this contract. That is, the couple agreed in advance to the sanctions to be applied in the event that Nabû-aḫ-iddin were to choose a second wife, or that ᶠBanât-Esagil were to commit adultery (and be caught *in flagrante delicto*); for reasons that elude us, they decided to make this a matter of a contract sealed in the presence of witnesses and confirmed by means of a mutual oath.[90]

Supporting this interpretation, a comparison with the remaining marriage agreements suggests that this oath is the functional equivalent of the curses mentioned in the eight other contracts indicated above; those curses are similarly placed after the stipulations and immediately before the list of human witnesses. Although there is significant variety in detail, the curse in No. 5 is typical (lines 26-29): "May Marduk and Zarpānītu decree the destruction of whoever contravenes this matter, and may Nabû, the scribe of

---

[89] *iz-ku-ru*, is a I/1 Preterite, expressive of simple past action. As such, this text does not stipulate an oath for marriage, but merely records as a matter of fact that the couple (the antecedent is clearly Nabû-aḫ-iddin and ᶠBanât-Esagil, not Nabû-aḫ-iddin and Dalīli-eššu) swore their agreement. For the typical use of historical narrative in the first millennium "subjective" contractual form, cf. M.T. Roth, *Babylonian Marriage Agreements*, 1f. Cf. also T.G. Pinches, "Babylonian Contract-Tablets with Historical References" (1890).

[90] I.e., this marriage agreement indicates that the couple were oath bound to the terms of the marriage contract, but not necessarily that they were oath bound to the marriage itself. Cf. also M.T. Roth, "'She will die by the iron dagger': Adultery and Neo-Babylonian Marriage" (1988) 186-206.

Esagila, cut short his long days. May Nebuchadnezzar, king of Babylon, decree his destruction." What makes this functional equivalence of mutual oath and curse significant is the observation that in marriage agreement No. 8, at least, a third party besides the husband and wife is bound by the curse. This is so because No. 8 is a betrothal agreement. Although the mother of the bride has promised her daughter in marriage (lines 1-5), the marriage has not been consummated and a later stipulation in the contract (lines 8-11) anticipates the possibility that the mother may renege on her promise: "Should ᶠQudāšu [the mother of the bride] not give ᶠImmertu [her daughter] (in marriage) to Nabû-balāssu-iqbi [the groom], ᶠQudāšu will pay five minas of silver from her own dowry to Nabû-balāssu-iqbi." Since ᶠQudāšu is a party to this agreement and has an obligation which is included within its stipulations, presumably she, along with the bride and groom, is also an object of the curse (lines 20-24): "May Marduk and Zarpānītu decree the destruction of whoever contravenes this matter; may Nabû, the scribe of Esagil, cut short his long days; may Nergal, the almighty, the overpowering among the gods, not save his life from plague and massacre." Being bound by this curse, alternatively the mother could have been made the subject of a mutual oath, at least in principle, but clearly such an oath bears little resemblance to the exclusive oath between a husband and wife which ought to be expected of marriage if indeed it was a covenant.

Considering the presence of oaths and curses in contracts which already have human guarantors, D.L. Magnetti notes that while "contracts were made in a sphere in which men could take care of the situation... the fact remains that evidence indicates that oaths were sworn as part of contract procedure in at least some ancient Near Eastern civilizations. Perhaps this was due to influence by the procedure in the law court [where oaths of clearance or oaths for witnesses were required at times] or to a desire for the additional sanction of the supernatural."[91]

On the other hand, contrary to Milgrom's expectation, it is unlikely that any betrothal or marriage contract would necessarily stipulate a marriage-ratifying oath precisely because of the special commercial and ancillary focus of these contracts. With respect to the extant marriage contracts, Milgrom himself notes, "it seems that in Babylonian betrothal / marriage, contracts were not even written, except when additional stipulations had to be made."[92]

---

[91] D.L. Magnetti, "The Oath in the Old Testament," 49f.

[92] J. Milgrom, *Cult and Conscience*, 134, n. 484.

Supplementing what was said in the previous note with respect to Jewish marriage contracts, it may help to enumerate here, at least in an approximate manner, the quantity and provenance of the extant non-Jewish marriage contracts:

• a number of Sumerian marriage contracts (cf. A. Falkenstein, *Neusumerische Gerichtsurkunden*, I, 107f.)

• 4 from the Old Assyrian period (so J.M. Breneman, *Nuzi Marriage Tablets*, 13; cf. *ANET*, 543; A.J. Skaist, *Studies in Ancient Mesopotamian Family Law*, 70-84)

• the Middle Babylonian Ḫana text (A.T. Clay, *Babylonian Records in the Library of J. Pierpont Morgan*, Part IV (1923) 4, no. 52, 50-52; cf. also A.J. Skaist, *op. cit.*, 89-93; and M. Malul, *Studies in Mesopotamian Legal Symbolism*, 130f.)

What Milgrom correctly acknowledges for Babylonian betrothal and marriage contracts, based on the landmark studies of S. Greengus, has since been confirmed by R. Westbrook and others and has also been convincingly demonstrated for Late Babylonian and Neo-Babylonian marriage contracts as well as the Jewish Aramaic marriage contracts from Elephantine.[93] In other

---

• 1 Middle Assyrian text (A.J. Skaist, *op. cit.*, 85-89)
• Approximately 29 tablets from the Old Babylonian period (so J.M. Breneman, *op. cit.*, 13; A.J. Skaist, *op. cit.*, 43-68; cf., e.g., G.R. Driver and J. . Miles, *The Babylonian Laws*, I, 253-9; S. Greengus, "The Old Babylonian Marriage Contract"; R. Harris, "The Case of Three Babylonian Marriage Contracts" [1974] 363-365; and especially R. Westbrook, "Old Babylonian Marriage Law," I [1982] 60-325. Of the large number of private legal documents related to marriage which Westbrook presents, he considers only 19 to be straightforward marriage contracts [*op. cit.*, II, 109])
• Over 100 tablets relating to marriage from Nuzi, many of which appear to be marriage contracts (cf. J.M. Breneman, *op. cit.*, A.J. Skaist, *op. cit.*, 93-107)
• some marriage tablets from Kultepe (so J.M. Breneman, *op. cit.*)
• some marriage tablets from Ashur (so J.M. Breneman, *op. cit.*)
• 4 from Alalaḫ (cf. D.J. Wiseman, *The Alalakh Tablets*, texts 91-94, 54ff. Cf. also I. Mendelsohn, "Marriage in Alalakh," 352f.; A.J. Skaist, *op. cit.*, 108-115; and the translation and discussion of *AT* 92 in M. Malul, *op. cit.*, 111f.)
• 9 (a couple of which are fragmentary) Neo-Assyrian marriage documents (V.A. Jakobson, "Studies in Neo-Assyrian Law" [1974] 115-121; and J.N. Postgate, *Fifty Neo-Assyrian Legal Documents* [1976] 101-107)
• 45 Neo- and Late Babylonian marriage contracts (M.T. Roth, *Babylonian Marriage Agreements: 7th - 3rd Centuries B.C.* [1989])
• a number of marriage contracts from Egypt (cf. J.J. Rabinowitz, "Marriage Contracts in Ancient Egypt in the Light of Jewish Sources" [1953]; E. Lüddeckens, *Ägyptische Eheverträge* [1960]; P.W. Pestman, *Marriage and Matrimonial Property in Ancient Egypt* [1961]).
[93] S. Greengus, "Old Babylonian Marriage Ceremonies and Rites" (1966) 55-72; *idem*, "The Old Babylonian Marriage Contract" (1969) 505-532; R. Westbrook, "Old Babylonian Marriage Law," II, 52ff.; J.J. Finkelstein, "Cutting the *sissiktu* in Divorce Proceedings," 236; and M. Malul, *Studies in Mesopotamian Legal Symbolism*, p. 160; H.J. Hendriks, *Juridical Aspects*, 20 (noting the surprising absence of any mention of a marriage contract in MAL A §41), 51; M.T. Roth, *Babylonian Marriage Agreements: 7th - 3rd Centuries B.C.* (1989) 24-28; and B. Porten, *Archives from Elephantine* (1968) 208.
The Mesopotamian legal tradition reflected in the LE §§27-28 and CH §128, which stipulates the use of a marriage contract (*riksatu*) is not unambiguous in its implication. An earlier view considered it possible that marriages in general did not require a *riksatu*, but that apart from this written document a woman who lived with a man would not be accorded the legal status of *aššatu* (so G.R. Driver and J.C. Miles, *The Babylonian Laws*, I, 245-249; and H.J. Hendriks, *Juridical Aspects of the Marriage Metaphor in Hosea and Jeremiah*, 20). Cf. also CH §§150, 151, 165; MAL A §§34, 36; and NBL §8.
S. Greengus, however, argues that while *riksātu* meant a "written contract" in Neo-Babylonian times, in the Old Babylonian period it meant a "contract" whether or not this was written ("The Old Babylonian Marriage Contract"). In part, Greengus bases his interpretation of *riksātu* on the root *rakāsum*, meaning "to bind" or "to tie." There appears to be nothing in the terms *riksātu* or *rakāsum* which indicates a written document. On the contrary, when, for example, CH intends to prescribe a written document, "it does so unambiguously and employs for unmistakable clarity terms like *tuppum, kanikum*, and *kunukkum*" (*op. cit.*, 507).
Greengus explains that cases where a marriage contract was committed to writing invariably reflect a special need to address certain abnormal family circumstances. He concludes, "In our judgment, therefore, the primary purpose of the so-called marriage documents was not to record marriage, but to record important transactions which could affect the status and rights of husbands or wives" (*op. cit.*, 512). Supporting such a conclusion for OB as well as later practice are the significant number of contracts which

words, documentary attestation for marriages appears to have been largely concerned to specify extraordinary requirements, not to belabour what was typical and could be assumed. Hence, the lack of an explicit stipulation of a ratifying oath in marriage need occasion no surprise. Agreeably, P. Kalluveettil writes, "since the main concern of marriage contracts were economic, the marriage ratifying rites as such were not described in them."[94]

It seems, therefore, that the stipulation of an oath within extant betrothal and marriage contracts should not generally be expected precisely because these were *contracts*; they were documents intended to attest to various ancillary agreements related to marriage (often between the husband and his father-in-law, though other arrangements are not uncommon), but they were not intended to attest to the marriage covenant itself. Indeed, not infrequently, as in the arrangement between Laban and Jacob in Genesis 31, these documents were not drafted until long after the marriage was contracted.[95] As forcibly argued by R. Westbrook in his recent study of Old

---

indicate the presence of children (requiring the clarification of property rights in the event of the dissolution of the marriage). In support of Greengus' view, cf., e.g., B. Porten, *op. cit.*, 208; and P.W. Pestman, *Marriage and Matrimonial Property in Ancient Egypt*, 28-30.

R. Yaron, however, has some reservations regarding Greengus's view (*The Laws of Eshnunna* [1988] 200-205). Unfortunately, the Nuzi marriage tablets, studied in detail by J.M. Breneman, neither support nor refute the claim made by Greengus concerning *riksatu* (*Nuzi Marriage Tablets*, 257-261). They do suggest, however, that at times marriage contracts may have been intended only to provide legal protection for the wife and not to address any unusual family circumstance or property concern.

M.T. Roth, however, concludes that it is unlikely that a written agreement always accompanied marriage in the Neo-Babylonian period (*Babylonian Marriage Agreements*, 26). As an impressive example she offers the case of the 6th-5th century family of Itti-Marduk-balāṭu concerning whom "hundreds of documents pertaining to the family's economic and legal activities have survived, including documents revealing the dowry transfers of nine women (five daughters who married out, four brides who married into the family) over three generations." In spite of this impressive documentation, no marriage contracts have survived from this family almost certainly because none were written.

[94] P. Kalluveettil, *Declaration and Covenant*, 110. In general, Kalluveettil's conclusion seems well founded (and especially convincing in the case of Elephantine — cf. B. Porten, *Archives from Elephantine*, 208). "Main concern," however, should not be misunderstood as "only concern." For example, there are a number of Nuzi marriage tablets which say nothing about inheritance or personal property (i.e., texts 1, 3, 9, 11, 12, 14, 15, as well as all the slave marriage texts, 16-22), and some texts are silent about the bride-price as well (i.e., texts 14 and 21). As a consequence, J.M. Breneman concludes that at times marriage tablets may have been drafted merely for the legal protection of the wife (*Nuzi Marriage Tablets*, 258-260).

Similarly, M.T. Roth emphasizes economics as the most frequent consideration in the Neo- and Late Babylonian marriage contracts, but also acknowledges that the purpose or purposes behind many other texts is entirely elusive (*Babylonian Marriage Agreements*, 28). One evidence of this ancillary focus in the marriage contracts is the fact that only a tiny fraction of the extant marriage contracts, namely ten, all from the Neo-Babylonian period, consider the subject of adultery. Cf. M.T. Roth, "'She will die by the iron dagger': Adultery and Neo-Babylonian Marriage" (1988) 186, n. 1.

[95] Cf., e.g., P.W. Pestman, *Marriage and Matrimonial Property in Ancient Egypt*, 28.

Babylonian marriage law, "marriage is a legal status and must be distinguished from the marriage contract which is incidental thereto."[96]

In terms of G.M. Tucker's analysis of covenant forms and contract forms, the marriage documents are characterized by features which are typical of contracts rather than covenants: that is, they usually include a date, the names of the parties, a description of the transaction and its conditions, and they conclude with the names of human witnesses.[97] It is this last feature particularly which demonstrates that the principal guarantors of these agreements were the courts and community, rather than God or the gods.[98] Hence, these arrangements represent private legal and commercial agreements, that is, contracts, rather than covenants (which, ratified by oath, do not require witnesses or the apparatus of the court to be enforced). This acknowledgement that the extant marriage documents are contracts does not affect the hypothesis that marriage itself is a covenant. Tucker recognizes other examples of a similar mixture of contract and covenant, for instance, the commercial arrangement between Solomon and Hiram in 1 Kgs. 5:15ff. [ET 5:1ff.] (called a בְּרִית in the text, but undoubtedly included aspects of conveyance as well).[99]

---

[96] R. Westbrook, "Old Babylonian Marriage Law," I, ii. Westbrook considers this observation to be the central thesis of his study. Cf., especially, R. Westbrook, *op. cit.*, II, 149-157.

This understanding contrasts radically with the view of I. Mendelsohn, for example, who defines marriage in the ancient Near East as "a civil affair based on a written contract" ("On Marriage in Alalakh," 351). Other scholars similarly confuse the covenant of marriage with the marriage contract. Cf., e.g., R. de Vaux, *Ancient Israel, Vol. 1, Social Institutions* (1961) 33; A. Isaksson, *Marriage and Ministry*, 31; and R.S. Westcott, "The Concept of *berît* with Regard to Marriage in the Old Testament" (1985) 43.

[97] G.M. Tucker, "Covenant Forms and Contract Forms" (1965) 487-503; cf. J.B. Torrance, "Covenant or Contract?" (1970) 51-76.

Evidence for the contract form within the OT can be detected in Gen. 23:9-18; Ruth 4:9-11; 2 Sam. 24:18-25 (∥ 1 Chron. 21:18-27); and Jer. 32:10-12. Cf. discussion of these texts in G.M. Tucker, *op. cit.*, 499-500.

[98] Tucker appears to have overstated the evidence slightly in that some contracts do, in fact, include oaths. Cf. the discussion earlier in the present section (§2.1) concerning the oath in Roth No. 6. Cf. also M.T. Roth, *Babylonian Marriage Agreements*, 19; and D.L. Magnetti, "The Oath in the Old Testament," 49f.

[99] Cf. G.M. Tucker, "Covenant Forms and Contract Forms," 502; and F.C. Fensham, "The Treaty between Solomon and Hiram and the Alalakh Tablets" (1960) 59-60.

In a similar fashion, R. Westbrook sharply distinguishes marriage as a status, analogous to adoption, from the betrothal and/or marriage contracts which at times attended it ("Old Babylonian Marriage Law," II, 56f., 149-152).

An additional example of the sometimes complimentary function of contracts and covenants may be found in Nehemiah 8-10. According to D.J. McCarthy the people enter into a written contract to observe the already obligatory covenant law of Yahweh — a contract which stresses, notably, their economic obligations ("*berît* in Old Testament History and Theology," 119). Though בְּרִית is not used of this arrangement (cf. Neh. 10:1 [ET 9:38]), cf. Ezra 10:3, where a similar commitment is termed a בְּרִית. Cf. F.B. Knutson, who argues against Baltzer that neither Nehemiah nor Ezra depicts a covenant renewal ("Literary Genres in *PRU* IV," *RSP*, II, 177-180). Rather, in Nehemiah "we have not a covenant, but a promise, a pledge, to keep the covenant already in effect." On the other hand, in Ezra we have a covenant intended for a special purpose, namely, the putting away of foreign wives.

2.2 Oaths may often be accompanied by, or even consist of, symbolic acts ("oath-signs")

In attempting to discern the presence or absence of an oath in marriage, it is vital to be clear about what exactly constitutes an oath.[100] We understand by "oath" any solemn declaration or enactment which invokes the deity to act against the one who would be false to an attendant commitment or affirmation.[101]

Although oaths are referred to in a wide variety of ways in the Old Testament, שְׁבוּעָה and אָלָה are the specific terms in Hebrew for "oath" (including both the act of swearing and the content of what is sworn as distinct senses).[102] The fact that אָלָה (originally meaning "curse," cf. Gen.

---

[100] M. Malul has lamented the fact that prior to his own work no comprehensive study had been made of the complex subject of the legal symbolism of Mesopotamia (*Studies in Mesopotamian Legal Symbolism*, v). Because a similar deficiency exists with respect to biblical practice, with a few notable exceptions such as P. Kalluveettil, *Declaration and Covenant*, the reader's indulgence is asked as we build on these works and undertake a methodical consideration of the specialized topic of biblical oath-signs (cf. M. Malul, *op. cit.*, 36).

Although it appeared too late to be of benefit to the present work, see now the welcome study of A. Viberg, *Symbols of Law. A Contextual Analysis of Legal Symbolic Acts in the Old Testament* (1992).

[101] While this definition covers the great majority of cases and, in particular, all examples involving covenant making, to take full account of the evidence it is necessary to acknowledge that some less solemn oaths could be sworn by the life of another individual, generally the king (what Fensham terms "profane" as opposed to "sacred" oaths; cf. Gen. 42:15f.; 1 Sam. 17:55; 2 Sam. 11:11). This implies that the king or other individual, rather than God (or in addition to God, as in 1 Sam. 20:3; 25:26; 2 Kgs. 2:2, 4, 6; 4:30; 15:21), is invoked to examine and act against any perjury. For ancient Near Eastern parallels to oath-taking by the life of the overlord, cf. the examples cited by P. Kalluveettil, *Declaration and Covenant*, 87, n. 329 (although note that some biblical oaths are sworn by the life of an equal, as in 2 Kgs. 2:2, 4, 6).

For a more adequate treatment of oaths, see the full-scale study of D.L. Magnetti, "The Oath in the Old Testament in the Light of Related Terms and in the Legal and Covenantal Context of the Ancient Near East" (1969). Cf. also S.H. Blank, "The Curse, Blasphemy, the Spell, and the Oath" (1950-51) 73-95; H.C. Brichto, *The Problem of "Curse" in the Hebrew Bible* (1963); A.D. Crown, "Aposiopesis in the Old Testament and the Hebrew Conditional Oath" (1963-64) 96-111; F.C. Fensham, "The Treaty Between Israel and the Gibeonites" (1964) 96-100; F.C. Fensham, "Oath," *ISBE Revised*, III (1986) 572-574; M. Greenberg, "The Hebrew Oath Particle, *hay / hê*" (1957) 34-39; F. Horst, "Der Eid im AT" (1957) 366-384; C.A. Keller, "אָלָה *'ālā* Verfluchung," *THAT* I (1984) 149-152; *idem*, "שבע *šb'* ni. schwören," *THAT*, II (1984) 855-863; M.G. Kline, *By Oath Consigned* (1968); M.R. Lehmann, "Biblical Oaths" (1969) 74-92; J. Pedersen, *Der Eid bei den Semiten* (1914); M.H. Pope, "Oaths," *IBD*, III, 575-577; J.M. Price, "The Oath in Court Procedure in Early Babylonia and the Old Testament" (1929) 22-29; H. Ringgren, "חָיָה, *chāyāh*," *TDOT*, IV, 339-340; J. Scharbert, "'Fluchen' und 'Segnen' im Alten Testament" (1958) 1-26; *idem*, "אָלָה *'ālāh*," *TDOT*, I, 261-266; M. Tsevat, "Neo-Assyrian and Neo-Babylonian Vassal Oaths and the Prophet Ezekiel" (1959) 199-204; M. Weinfeld, "The Loyalty Oath in the Ancient Near East" (1976) 379-414; H.C. White, "The Divine Oath in Genesis" (1973) 165-179; and J.A. Wilson, "The Oath in Ancient Egypt" (1948) 129-156.

[102] For example, apart from explicit references employing the verb שבע or the nouns שְׁבוּעָה or אָל, oaths may be referred to by the mention of an accompanying rite (such as the dividing of animals in Jer. 34:18ff.), or an accompanying gesture (such as the raising of the hand in Exod. 6:8), or by the presence of a formula (with חי, e.g., Judg. 8:19; or חלילה, e.g., Gen. 44:7; or וכה יוסיף ... , e.g., 1 Sam. 3:17; 14:44; 20:13; 25:22; 2 Sam. 3:9, 35; 19:14 [ET 13]; 1 Kgs. 2:23; 19:2; 20:10 [a pagan oath]; 2 Kgs. 6:31; Ruth 1:17), or by the

24:41; Deut. 29:19 [ET 20]; 30:7; Isa. 24:6; Jer. 23:10; Ps. 10:7; 59:13) is used in this manner serves to emphasize the hypothetical self-curse which underlies biblical oaths — that is, if the oath should be broken, a curse will come into effect.[103]

As implied in our definition, one important misunderstanding to be avoided is the tendency to equate oaths exclusively with verbal acts. As elsewhere in the ancient Near East, oaths in the Old Testament are not infrequently symbolic rather than verbal, or at least not just verbal. In particular, such symbolic oaths, or "oath-signs" as they have been termed, were frequently employed in the ratification of covenants.[104] So, for example, G.E. Mendenhall defines a covenant as "a solemn promise made binding by an oath, which may be either a verbal formula or a symbolic action."[105]

As an especially vivid illustration of the use of such an oath rite, M.G. Kline cites the eighth-century treaty of Ashurnirari V and Mati'ilu, the King of Arpad.[106] According to the treaty a ram was to be removed from its herd, and "If Mati'ilu [sins] against the treaty sworn by the gods, just as this ram is broug[ht here] from his herd and to his herd will not return [and stand] at its head, so may Mati'ilu with his sons, [his nobles,] the people of his land [be brought] far from his land and to his land not return [to stand] at the head of his land."[107] Not content with this malediction of exile, the treaty goes on to specify that the ram was to be decapitated: "This head is not the head of a ram; it is the head of Mati'ilu, the head of his sons, his nobles, the people of his land. If those named [sin] against this treaty, as the head of this ram is c[ut off,] his leg put in his mouth [...] so may the head of those named be cut off." Finally, the shoulder of the ram is torn off, and once again the treaty

---

use of certain grammatical constructions involving אם, particularly if stated before God (Ps. 137:5f.; 7:4ff.; Job 31:5ff.; etc.), or by the content of the oath itself spoken before God (e.g., Exod. 24:3; 2 Sam. 5:1). Cf. D.L. Magnetti, who employs such criteria to discover 127 oaths employed in non-legal and non-covenantal contexts within the OT ("The Oath in the Old Testament," 147-193).

[103] Cf. 1 Kgs. 8:31; Ezek. 16:59; 17:16, 18f.; Zech. 5:3; Job 31:30; Prov. 29:24; 2 Chron. 6:22.

As D.L. Magnetti notes, "every oath contains at least an implicit self-curse" ("The Oath in the Old Testament," 40). J. Scharbert similarly notes, "In translating the different forms [of אלה], one should always begin with the meaning, 'to pronounce a conditional curse'" ("אלה 'ālāh," TDOT, I 261).

[104] E.g., cf. M.G. Kline, By Oath Consigned, passim.

[105] G.E. Mendenhall, "Covenant," IDB, I, 714.

[106] M.G. Kline, By Oath Consigned, 41.

Cf. also the vivid oath rites enumerated in the Sefire Treaty, I A 35-42, as pointed out to the author by A. Lemaire (A. Lemaire and J. M. Durand, Les inscriptions araméennes de Sfiré et l'Assyrie de Shamshi-Ilu (1984) 114ff.

[107] This translation, followed by Kline, is offered by D.J. McCarthy, Treaty and Covenant, 1st edition (1963) 195. For a more recent translation, cf. S. Parpola and K. Watanabe, eds. Neo-Assyrian Treaties and Loyalty Oaths (1988) 8ff.

threatens that the shoulder of Mati'ilu, and his sons, etc., would similarly be torn out if Mati'ilu sins against the treaty.

In view of this and many other similar examples, it is possible, with D.J. McCarthy and others, that the prominence of such cutting oath-signs in the ratification ceremony for covenants gave rise to the widespread terminology of "cutting" a covenant as well as "cutting" a curse (Deut. 29:13 [ET 14]), etc., attested in Hebrew, Aramaic, and Phoenician texts, and the cuneiform texts from Qatna.[108] This example from the treaty of Ashurnirari V and Mati'ilu is especially instructive in that it offers a clear instance of a self-maledictory oath-sign which does not involve cutting, namely the separation of the ram from its herd.

Likewise, the Old Testament provides numerous examples of both cutting and non-cutting rites employed in connection with the swearing of oaths and, more particularly, in the ratification of covenants. Unlike the treaty of Ashurnirari V and Mati'ilu, however, the Bible is not always so helpful in making explicit the precise symbolism of these acts. For this reason, there is often room for doubt whether any individual covenant rite, for example, the animal cutting ceremony recorded in Genesis 15, is necessarily intended to depict such an oath.[109]

---

[108] D.J. McCarthy, *Treaty and Covenant*, 2nd ed. (1981) 91ff.; *idem, Old Testament Covenant*, 42. Cf. also W.F. Albright, "The Hebrew Expression for 'Making a Covenant' in Pre-Israelite Documents" (1951), 21-22; D.R. Hillers, *Treaty-Curses and the Old Testament Prophets* (1964) 20, n. 27; M.G. Kline, *By Oath Consigned* (1968) 42; and K.A. Kitchen, "Egypt, Ugarit, Qatna and Covenant" (1979) 453-464.
   The Akkadian expression *ḫaram qatālum berît X u Y*, "to kill an ass," which was idiomatic at Mari for covenant making, offers additional conceptual support for the prominence of a ratificatory oath-sign in covenant making. Cf. D.J. McCarthy, *Treaty and Covenant* (1981) 91.

[109] Cf. Jer. 34:18ff. In support of this widely held interpretation, cf., e.g., M.G. Kline, *By Oath Consigned*, 16f., 42; E. Kutsch, "כָּרַת *krt*," *THAT*, I, 857-860; E. Speiser, *Genesis*, 112; E.B. Smick, "כָּרַת *(kārat)*," *TWOT*, I, 456-457; and L. Perlitt, *Bundestheologie im Alten Testament* (1969) (who uses a comparison between Gen. 15:18ff. and Jeremiah 34, as well as an 8th century treaty between Ashurnirari V and Mati'ilu, the King of Arpad, as evidence for a late dating for Gen. 15:18ff. — cf. the counter-argument by D.J. McCarthy, *"berît* in Old Testament History and Theology," 115). Cf. also J. Ha, *Genesis 15: A Theological Compendium of Pentateuchal History* (1989).
   In further support, cf. Gen. 24:7, where Abraham himself refers to an otherwise unrecorded oath on Yahweh's part, unless he intended a reference to the rite in Genesis 15.
   G.F. Hasel ("The Meaning of the Animal Rite in Genesis 15" [1981] 61-78) and G.J. Wenham ("The Symbolism of the Animal Rite in Genesis 15: A Response to G.F. Hasel, *JSOT* 19 (1981) 61-78" [1982] 134-137; *idem, Genesis 1-15* [1987] 332-333), among others, however, reject a comparison with Jeremiah 34 and *ANESTP*, 532. While these scholars also reject an identification of the theophanic procession between divided animals as a hypothetical self-malediction, this conclusion may not be necessary. Cf., e.g., D.J. McCarthy, who rejects the traditional comparison of Genesis 15 with Jeremiah 34, but nevertheless accepts an interpretation of Genesis 15 as a self-maledictory rite (*Old Testament Covenant* [1972] 60f.). Cf. also D.J. McCarthy, *Treaty and Covenant* (1981) 91-96, 255, and *idem, "berît* in Old Testament History and Theology" (1985) 115f.
   A. Viberg, on the other hand, accepts a comparison of Genesis 15 with Jeremiah 34, and he allows that self-imprecation may have played a part in the formation of this act. He denies, however, that this act symbolizes a (self-)malediction in these texts (*Symbols of Law* [1992] 52-69).

In any case, circumcision appears to be one obvious example of an Old Testament cutting rite which was intended as a covenant-ratifying oath-sign.[110] As noted by M.G. Kline, the explicit curse mentioned in Gen. 17:14, that one who breaks God's covenant of circumcision would be "cut off [כָּרַת]" from among his people, suggests that it was this dreadful curse which was meant to be dramatized in the cutting rite of circumcision.[111] Offering further corroboration for identifying circumcision as an oath-sign, Kline points out that the manner in which Genesis 17 identifies the covenant with circumcision (vss. 9, 10, 13) exactly parallels the identification of a covenant with its oath elsewhere in the Old Testament as well as in the extra-biblical treaties.

This is not to say that the symbolism of circumcision is exhausted in its self-maledictory aspect. On the contrary, Kline argues that since the oath symbolized by circumcision was an oath of allegiance, circumcision incorporates simultaneously a more positive symbolism, namely that of "consecration."[112] This is the meaning of circumcision, for example, which is reflected in Jeremiah's call to repentance: "Circumcise yourselves to the Lord, remove the foreskin of your hearts" (Jer. 4:4a).[113]

2.3   Oaths and oath-signs may invoke the deity to witness an attendant declaration or promise without employing an explicit self-malediction. At times they may only implicitly invoke the deity by a solemn *declaration or depiction of a commitment being undertaken*

The obscurity and variety of the various gestures and acts attested in the Old Testament in connection with oaths or covenant making, including the lifting of the hand, placing hands under another's thigh, the exchange of gifts, the exchange of clothes, shaking hands, eating common meals, the use of salt, oil, etc., have led D.J. McCarthy and others to suggest that at times the ratification of a covenant was accomplished by a rite rather than by an oath.[114] In this manner, for example, McCarthy attempts to distinguish the covenant ratification in Exod. 24, accomplished by the rites of a common

---

[110] For a fuller treatment of circumcision, cf. M.G. Kline, *By Oath Consigned*, 39-49, 86-89. Cf. also E. Isaac, "Circumcision as Covenant Rite" (1964) 444-456. For an alternative interpretation, cf. W.H. Propp, "The Origins of Infant Circumcision in Israel" (1987) 355-370.

[111] M.G. Kline, *By Oath Consigned*, 43: "In the cutting off of the foreskin the judgment of excision from the covenant relationship was symbolized." Noting that circumcision was performed on the organ of generation, Kline later supplements this interpretation of its symbolism stating, "we may now add that the specific malediction expressed by the symbolic action of circumcising the foreskin was the cutting off of the vassal's descendants so as to leave him without heir or name in the kingdom" (*op. cit.*, 87).

[112] *Ibid.*, 43ff.

[113] Cf. also the figurative use of עָרֵל in Lev. 19:23-25. Cf. also the use of "circumcision / uncircumcision" as descriptive of one's heart in Lev. 26:41; Deut. 10:16; 30:6; and Jer. 6:10; 9:24, 25 [ET 25, 26].

[114] So D.J. McCarthy, *Treaty and Covenant* (1981) 254ff., 294, n. 39; *idem*, "Three Covenants in Genesis," 179-89; *idem*, *Old Testament Covenant*, 41; and E.W. Nicholson, *God and His People*, 69, 171.

meal, the sacrifice of peace offerings [זְבָחִים שְׁלָמִים], and the manipulation of blood, from the ratifying practice of oath swearing attested in the suzerainty treaties.[115]

Similarly, P. Kalluveettil has argued at length that while "covenant generally implies oath"[116] and "the oath is the most important factor"[117] for covenant making, it is also the case that "a covenant can be ratified by pledged word or by rites,"[118] which in many cases may not have an oath function.[119]   Kalluveettil is especially interested in demonstrating that a "Declaration Formula," such as the solemn assertion of Israel to David at Hebron that "we are your bone and flesh," by itself can effect a covenant between parties. In support he notes that 2 Sam. 5:1-3 (∥ 1 Chron. 11:1-3) offers no mention of an accompanying oath.[120] Hence, on McCarthy's and Kalluveettil's view, an oath may not always be the *sine qua non* constitutive element of covenant; on the contrary, other acts may well serve to ratify a covenant.[121]

2.3.1 Not all rites connected with covenant making are oath-signs

It must be acknowledged that not all rites connected with oath taking or covenant making are necessarily intended as oath-signs. For example, the placing of one's hand "under the thigh [תַּחַת יְרֵכִי]" of another (i.e., on or near the genitals) during an oath, as recorded in Gen. 24:2, 9 and 47:29, may well be intended as an act of acknowledgement on the part of the subordinate concerning his continuing obligation of fidelity to the progeny of his superior, whose genitals are being touched.[122]

---

115 *Treaty and Covenant* (1981) 256.
116 P. Kalluveettil, *Declaration and Covenant*, 5.
117 *Ibid.*, 91.
118 *Ibid.*, 9.
119 *Ibid.*, 9, n. 14 and p. 15.
120 *Ibid.*, 13. Kalluveettil also cites 1 Kgs. 20:31-34 as a second possible example.
121 *Ibid.*, 9, 20. P. Kalluveettil distinguishes certain rites connected with covenant making from the ratifying oath by means of their differing purposes (*op. cit.*, 10). Discussing the E account of the Abimelech-Abraham covenant in Gen. 21:22-24; 27:31, Kalluveettil writes, "Although the swearing makes *bᵉrît* binding and gives it a sacred and inviolable character, it does not directly constitute the covenant *relationship*, i.e., union. The other covenant ceremony, that of accepting sheep and oxen, does that function, the gift is directed at forming the fellowship between Abraham and Abimelech."
   While a conceptual distinction between making a בְּרִית binding and constituting a covenant relationship is perhaps useful in the modern analysis of covenant-making narratives, it is not so easy to derive this distinction from the texts themselves.
122 Cf. Z.W. Falk, "Gestures Expressing Affirmation" (1959) 269; M. Malul, "More on *paḥad yiṣḥāq* (Genesis xxiv 42,53) and the oath by the thigh" (1985) 192-200; and *idem*, "Touching the Sexual Organs as an Oath Ceremony in an Akkadian Letter" (1987) 491-2.
   The OB letter from Kisurra, to which Malul refers, seems to impose an oath on the envoy, which is accompanied by a more explicit reference to the gesture posited here for Gen. 24:2, 9 and 47:29: "Let your envoy grasp my testicles and my penis, and then I will give (it) to you" (Malul, "Touching the Sexual Organs," 491).
   Other interpretations of this gesture are possible. Cf., e.g., E. A. Speiser, "'I Know Not the Day of My Death' [Gen 27:2]" (1955) 252-256; *idem, Genesis*, 178; M.H. Pope, "Oaths" (1962) 576; T.C. Vriezen, "Eid" *Biblische-historisches Handwörterbuch*, I (1962) 374-76; D.L. Magnetti, "The Oath in the Old Testament," 209; O Böcher, "Der Judeneid"

Likewise, the erection of stones in Gen. 31:45ff., Josh. 24:26f., and Isa. 19:19-20 appears not to be intended as a symbolized oath, but to recognize these as a figurative enduring witness to the covenant-making procedure.[123] Of course, neither of these examples supports Kalluveettil's thesis since elsewhere in the context of each an accompanying oath is explicitly mentioned.

Similarly, in covenant contexts the exchange of gifts and less commonly the giving of clothes at times may be intended only to foster amity.[124] Depending upon the context, however, these same acts may carry various legal implications, of which perhaps the most prominent is to serve as a legal witness to the existence of a covenant.[125] In spite of the frequent association between gift giving and covenant, contrary to P. Kalluveettil there is no compelling evidence that gift giving or the exchange of clothes ever effected a covenant in the absence of an oath.[126]

For example, modern scholars generally disassociate the covenant-ratifying oath mentioned in Gen. 21:23, 31b from the gift of the seven ewe lambs in 21:27-31a. Regardless of how one resolves the difficult source-critical issues posed by Genesis 21, nowhere does the text suggest that apart from any oath "the gift served to establish the covenant relationship," as suggested by Kalluveettil.[127] Instead, Abraham explicitly identifies his gift and Abimelech's acceptance of the same as "a witness [עֵדָה]" to Abraham's contested ownership of the well at Beersheba.[128]

Similarly, Kalluveettil's attempt to identify Jonathan's act of clothing David in 1 Samuel 18 as a symbol of "the gift of himself" which effected a covenant seems less likely than the widely held interpretation that the gift of these particular clothes (e.g., the מְעִיל, cf. 1 Sam. 24:5 [ET 4]) represented a willing abdication to David of Jonathan's rights as crown prince.[129] At least

---

(1970) 671-681; R.D. Freedman, "'Put Your Hand Under My Thigh' - The Patriarchal Oath" (1976) 3-4; D.G. Burke, "Gesture," *ISBE Revised*, II (1986) 451f.; Å. Viberg, *Symbols of Law* (1992) 45-51.

[123] Cf. Deut. 27:2ff. Cf. also Exod. 24:4; Josh. 4:20f.; 24:26f.; 1 Kgs. 18:31; Isa. 19:19f.

[124] Such a purpose is unsurprising based on non-covenantal contexts. Cf., e.g., Prov. 19:6.

[125] Cf., e.g., E. Neufeld, *Ancient Hebrew Marriage Laws*, 115-117; D.G. Burke, "Gift," *ISBE Revised*, II, 465-467; and G.A. Anderson, *Sacrifices and Offerings in Ancient Israel* (1987) 57-75 (for a discussion of Ehud's gift of tribute to Eglon in Judges 3).

[126] P. Kalluveettil, *Declaration and Covenant*, 10-12, 29. P. Kalluveettil cites J. Pedersen (*Der Eid*, 25, 49, 52; *idem*, *Israel*, 1-2, 296ff.) for evidence that "gift created *relationship* and effected covenant among the ancient Semites and Hebrews" (*op. cit.*, 10, n. 16.).

[127] *Declaration and Covenant*, 10.

[128] "It [i.e., Abimelech's reception of the lambs] will be a witness for me [תִּהְיֶה־לִּי לְעֵדָה]" is preferable to the RSV, "you will be a witness for me." Cf., e.g., C. Westermann, *Genesis 12-36*, 349.

[129] This royal outfitting appears to be ironically prefigured in Saul's clothing of David in 1 Sam. 17:38f. Cf. J. Morgenstern, "David and Jonathan" (1959) 322; T.N.D. Mettinger, *King and Messiah* (1976) 39; D.K. Jobling, *The Sense of Biblical Narrative* (1978) 12; P.K. McCarter Jr., *I Samuel*, 305; R.W. Klein, *1 Samuel* (1983) 182; and R.P. Gordon, *I & 2*

this appears to have been Saul's view of the substance of this covenant (cf. 1 Sam. 20:30ff.; 22:8). Accordingly, the purpose of such a gift would be, once again, not to effect the covenant, but rather to constitute a public and enduring evidence, a "witness" to Jonathan's commitment. In the nature of the case, for such an abdication to be effective it was necessary for David to have the sort of tangible evidence which the possession of these clothes and weapons offered.[130]

2.3.2 In spite of their opacity to modern readers some rites may prove to be self-maledictory oath-signs after all

With respect to covenant-making narratives which fail to mention a ratifying oath or oath-sign, in most cases it is doubtful whether one may exclude the possibility that the covenants in question were ratified by other unrecorded acts (oaths or oath-signs) or that the rites which are mentioned may be better understood as oath-signs after all, in spite of their opacity to the modern reader.[131] As two examples of this latter option, one may consider the frequently overlooked, but possible self-maledictory symbolism of salt (as in Num. 18:19, Lev. 2:13, and 2 Chron. 13:5) and of oil (as in Hos. 12:2 [ET 12:1]) when these appear in covenant contexts.[132]

Samuel (1986) 159. Cf. also the use of royal garments in *RS 17.159:22-31* — cf. F.B. Knutson, "Political and Foreign Affairs," *RSP*, II, 120-122.

[130] Other texts likewise suggest an association between the donning of clothes and the acquisition of throne rights (or inheritance rights) or, alternatively, between the removal of clothes and the loss of throne rights (or inheritance rights). Cf. *RSP*, II, 122-215, where 1 Kgs. 11:30-31; Genesis 37 (the special garment of Joseph); Isa. 22:21; Num. 20:24-28; and 1 Kgs. 19:19-21 are discussed. Cf. also the fuller discussion below and in Chapter 7 on the use of garments. Cf. also M. Malul, who discusses cuneiform texts which require the removal/leaving of one's garment as an expression of disinherison (*Studies in Mesopotamian Legal Symbolism*, 93ff.).

[131] Frequently preferring to build his case on negative evidence P. Kalluveettil seems to overlook the option that there may have been a ratifying oath or oath-sign which the narrator did not bother to record. For example, at times Kalluveettil attaches special significance to the observation that an oath is not mentioned in a particular account. Cf., e.g., "the fact that oath does not appear in 2 Kg 10,15f. and Lam 5,6 deserves special attention" (*Declaration and Covenant*, 26). Cf. also p. 91, n. 357. At other points, Kalluveettil's observation that a particular covenant lacks a ratifying oath applies only to one source-critical strand of the account. E.g., P. Kalluveettil notes that according to the J account there was no oath in the Abimelech-Abraham covenant, although an oath is mentioned three times in verses frequently assigned to E, i.e., Gen. 21:23, 24, 31 (*op. cit.*, 10). Cf. *ibid.*, 29.

·   E. Gerstenberger appears to have a similar objection in mind when he suggests that McCarthy fails to take into consideration that in the OT we do not have "*drafts* of treaties, but, at best, *narratives* and *sermons* about covenants.... [McCarthy's] distinction of 'ritual' and 'verbal' treaty form (162f., 176) may be a direct result from this oversight" ("Review of *Treaty and Covenant*" [1964] 199).

[132] In support of the possible self-maledictory symbolism of salt, cf. F.C. Fensham, "Salt as Curse in the Old Testament and the Ancient Near East" (1962) 48-50; and D.J. McCarthy, *Old Testament Covenant*, 42. Cf. also J.F. Ross, "Salt," *IDB*, IV, 167; P.J. Naylor, "The Language of Covenant," 200; and D. Stuart, *Old Testament Exegesis* (1984) 63f., who also cites H.C. Trumbull, *The Covenant of Salt* (1899).

2.3.3 Other covenant-making rites may be oath-signs, but they need not be overtly self-maledictory
Perhaps the most telling objection against McCarthy's and Kalluveettil's understanding of oaths is their implied assumption that oaths and oath-signs must be overtly self-maledictory.[133] To be sure, oaths are at times explicitly self-maledictory; as we have seen, oath-signs frequently share this same characteristic, but not all do so.[134]

Verbal oaths are frequently not explicitly self-maledictory
Many verbal oaths include only a highly abbreviated or incomplete self-malediction. For example, in 2 Sam. 3:35 David explicitly invokes God in a statement which is identified in the text as an oath, but the precise self-malediction is left stereotypically undefined: "but David swore saying, 'God do so to me and more also, if I taste bread or anything else till the sun goes down!'" [וַיִּשָּׁבַע דָּוִד לֵאמֹר כֹּה יַעֲשֶׂה־לִּי אֱלֹהִים וְכֹה יֹסִיף כִּי אִם־לִפְנֵי בוֹא־הַשֶּׁמֶשׁ אֶטְעַם־לֶחֶם אוֹ כָל־מְאוּמָה].[135]

Alternatively, oaths frequently consist of a protasis alone with the apodosis (the assumed details of the self-malediction) unmentioned. Compare, for example, 1 Kgs. 2:8, "... I swore to him by the LORD, saying, 'If I put you to death with the sword...!' [וָאֶשָּׁבַע לוֹ בַיהוָה לֵאמֹר אִם־אֲמִיתְךָ בֶּחָרֶב]." Presumably the ellipsis was meant to imply something like, "then

---

For alternative views of the symbolism of salt, cf. P.J. Budd, *Numbers*, 206; G.J. Wenham, *Numbers*, 144; M. Malul, *Studies in Mesopotamian Legal Symbolism*, 378; and especially J.E. Latham, *The Religious Symbolism of Salt* (1982).

In support of the self-maledictory symbolism of oil, cf. D.J. McCarthy, "Hosea XII 2: Covenant by Oil" (1964) 215-21; K. Deller, "*šmn bll* (Hosea 12, 2). Additional Evidence" (1965) 349-52; K.R. Veenhof, review of E. Kutsch, *Salbung als Rechtsakt im Alten Testament und im alten Orient* (1966) 308-13; D.J. McCarthy, *Old Testament Covenant*, 41f., n. 2; *idem, Treaty and Covenant* (1981) 119, n. 46; P. Kalluveettil, *Declaration and Covenant*, 14, n. 34; and D. Stuart, *Hosea —Jonah* (1987) 189f. Cf. also lines 622ff. of the Vassal-Treaty of Esarhaddon with Ramataya in *ANET*, 540; and Ps. 109:18.

An alternative view (perhaps involving an altogether different use of oil) is posited by M. Malul, *Studies in Mesopotamian Legal Symbolism*, 161, 176.

[133] This assumption may have been influenced by the use of אָלָה (literally "curse") for "oath." As J. Scharbert notes, "In translating the different forms [of אָלָה], one should always begin with the meaning, 'to pronounce a conditional curse'" ("אָלָה *'ālāh*," *TDOT*, I, 261).

Further strengthening this identification, one may note the uses of curse [אָלָה] and oath [שְׁבוּעָה] in close proximity in Num. 5:21; Neh. 10:29 [ET 28]; and Dan. 9:11.

[134] The full unexpurgated oath with an elaboration of curses is found in Num. 5:19-28; Ps. 7:4-5; 137:5-6; Job 31:5, 7-8; 31:9-10; 31:16-17, 19-22. Cf. Deut. 21:1-9.

[135] For further examples, cf. 1 Sam. 3:17; 14:44; 20:13; 25:22 (cf. S.R. Driver, *Notes on the Hebrew Text of Samuel*, 199, for proposed emendation); 2 Sam. 3:9, 35; 19:14 [ET 13]; 1 Kgs. 2:23; 2 Kgs. 6:31; Ruth 1:17; and Jer. 42:5. Compare 1 Kgs. 19:2 and 20:10, where the same formula in the plural is used by Jezebel and Ben-hadad with reference to their pagan deities: "So may the gods do to me, and more also...." Cf. D.L. Magnetti, "The Oath in the Old Testament," 200f.; and G.M. Tucker, "Covenant Forms and Contract Forms," 491.

may I also be put to death" or "may I be cursed."[136]   To avoid the awkwardness of an incomplete sentence in English, typically such a formation is rendered as a negative oath, as in the RSV: "I swore ..., 'I will not put you to death with the sword!'"   But such renderings should not be allowed to obscure the underlying implied self-malediction or, as a consequence, the implied invocation of the deity to act against the one who is false to his commitment or affirmation.[137]

Other oaths merely acknowledge God as a witness to the statement or promise of the swearer. Although these examples may not include even an abbreviated self-malediction, the acknowledgement of God as witness brings with it the clear implication that God will take action against any perjury or infidelity. This is the case, for example, in Gen. 31:50: "If you ill-treat my daughters, or if you take wives besides my daughters, although no man is with us, remember, God is witness between you and me [אִם־תְּעַנֶּה אֶת־בְּנֹתַי וְאִם־תִּקַּח נָשִׁים עַל־בְּנֹתַי אֵין אִישׁ עִמָּנוּ רְאֵה אֱלֹהִים עֵד בֵּינִי וּבֵינֶךָ]."[138]   Similarly, a very common oath formula entails the invocation of God simply by a solemn confession of the deity's existence: "as the Lord/God lives [... חַי]," but again this carries the implication that the deity will now hold the swearer responsible for what he states or promises.[139]

Finally, yet other oaths consist merely of the solemn declaration of one's commitment, with God's presence either assumed from the context or invoked only by implication. These *verba solemnia* or "declaration formulae," as they are termed by Kalluveettil, are not solemn simply because they are made with deliberation. Rather, they are solemn because they are uttered before the deity.[140]   Accordingly, a number of texts underscore the

---

[136] Cf. M.R. Lehmann, "Biblical Oaths," 88.

[137] Note that just as an incomplete conditional introduced with אִם results in a negative oath, one introduced by אִם לֹא will result in a positive oath. Cf., e.g., Josh. 14:9, "And Moses swore on that day, saying, 'If the land ... shall not be an inheritance for you..,'" becomes, "Surely the land ... shall be an inheritance for you...." (RSV). On the grammatical usage of אִם and אִם לֹא, cf. GKC §149; and J. Pedersen, *Eid*, 117f. Cf. M.R. Lehmann for a more thorough discussion of these incomplete conditionals, not all of which are introduced with אִם ("Biblical Oaths," 86-92).

[138] Cf. Judg. 11:10; 1 Sam. 12:5; 20:12; Jer. 42:5; Mic. 1:2; Mal. 2:14; and 3:5. Cf. also Gen. 31:53.

[139] Cf., e.g., G.M. Tucker, "Covenant Forms and Contract Forms," 491.
The emphasis suggested here on the implicit curse in all oaths contrasts with the conclusions of M.R. Lehmann regarding oaths employing the חַי formula ("Biblical Oaths" [1969] 74-92). Lehmann's hypothesis of an original blessing-oath signalled by חַי, of which Deut. 32:40 is the lone surviving example, appears unconvincing.
In support of the interpretation of the חַי-oath formula as a solemn acknowledgement of the existence of the guarantor of an oath, cf. F.C. Fensham, "Oath," *ISBE Revised*, III, 573; H.-J. Kraus, "Der lebendige Gott" (1967) 169-200; and H. Ringgren, "חָיָה *chāyāh*," *TDOT*, IV, 339-340. Cf. also D.L. Magnetti, "The Oath in the Old Testament," 202ff. After discussing this oath form in detail, Magnetti cites approvingly the interpretation of Moshe Segal, "Yahweh is a witness who lives forever" (*op. cit.*, 215, n. 38).
Cf. also M. Greenberg, "The Hebrew Oath Particle, *hay* / *hê*" (1957) 34-39.

[140] By contrast, P. Kalluveettil distinguishes rather sharply the purpose of the declaration formulae [DF] from that of oaths (*Declaration and Covenant*, 212). According to Kalluveettil, "The DF contained in a nutshell all the duties and privileges of an ally.... The oral declarations [*sic*] of relationship is not a substitute for oath. Both of them are

importance of words when uttered in God's presence: Judg. 11:11, "... and Jephthah spoke all his words before the LORD at Mizpah."[141] Compare also 1 Kgs. 8:31f.; 2 Chron. 6:22f.; Jer. 34:15; and Hos. 4:15.[142] Of course, the point of this stress in the biblical record on how particular oaths were made in various sanctuaries is just a reflection of the more pervasive concern to have God be a witness to one's oath.[143]

For example, as we noted in the previous chapter, the third person reference in Gen. 2:23, with God's presence asserted in the immediate context, implies that Adam was addressing his affirmation not to Eve, nor, presumably to himself but to God as witness when he said, "This at last is bone of my bones and flesh of my flesh... [זֹאת הַפַּעַם עֶצֶם מֵעֲצָמַי וּבָשָׂר מִבְּשָׂרִי]." Indeed, as in Gen. 2:23, *verba solemnia* are frequently though not exclusively couched in the third person with the apparent implication that they are being stated before God as witness.[144] Compare also the affirmation of the men of Shechem concerning Abimelech, "he is our brother" (Judg. 9:3).[145]

Alternatively, an example of *verba solemnia* couched in the second person is offered in 2 Sam. 5:2f., where the context makes plain their function as part of a covenantal commitment made "before the LORD": "Then all the tribes of Israel came to David at Hebron, and said, 'Behold, we are your bone and flesh....' So all the elders of Israel came to the king at Hebron; and King

---

important covenant elements, but destined to fulfil different functions. Oath has stipulations as its object, one swears to the observance of the covenant terms.... The DF is concerned with the covenant union; it serves to affirm and effect the relationship."

This distinction, however, may be more a product of modern scholarship than ancient reality since, as Kalluveettil acknowledges, often the declaration formulae constitute the content of the oath (*op. cit.*, 212, n. 9; cf. also 93f.).

[141] Cf. R.G. Boling, *Judges*, 199; and P. Kalluveettil, *Declaration and Covenant*, 33f.

[142] The sanctuaries at Gilgal and Beth-aven were places where oaths were administered — cf. M.H. Pope, "Oaths," 576.

[143] The emphasis on God as a divine witness to oaths and covenants is manifest in Gen. 31:50; Josh. 24:22, 27; 1 Sam. 12:5; 20:23 [if MT עֵד is to be emended to עֵר]; Jer. 42:5; Gen. 31:49 (where God is to watch); and Gen. 31:53 (where God is to judge). Cf. 1 Sam. 20:42; and Judg. 11:10. Cf. also Ezekiel 17, where God determines to punish Zedekiah for breaking "my covenant" and "despising" "my oath," although in fact it was a covenant imposed on Zedekiah by the Babylonian overlord,

[144] In the case of Gen. 2:23, the absence of any human witnesses to these *verba solemnia*, such as the elders of the city, other family members, etc., helps to clarify God's role as witness.

In terms of ancient Near Eastern parallels, cf. the use of the third person in the formulae: "this is our king" (cf. P. Kalluveettil, *Declaration and Covenant*, 94, n. 5; p. 107); "he is the king" (*op. cit.*, 107); "this is my brother" (*op. cit.*, 105); and especially "she is my wife" [*assiti sit*] in MAL A §41 (also cf. *op. cit.*, 111).

Note that in a NB letter, *ABL* 280, r. 3, Belibni reports to king Ashurbanipal how the leaders of two cities surrendered to Mushezi-Marduk: "They took the oath of loyalty to Mushezib-Marduk declaring: we are vassals of the king of Assyria" (P. Kalluveettil, *Declaration and Covenant*, 93). This is a clear example of a declaration formula, identified as the content of their oath (even though it lacks any self-malediction).

For second person formulae, cf. Gen. 29:14; 2 Sam. 5:2f.; and "our life is yours" (P. Kalluveettil, *Declaration and Covenant*, 87).

[145] Cf. P. Kalluveettil, *Declaration and Covenant*, 209ff. Cf. also 1 Kgs. 20:32.

David made a covenant with them at Hebron before the LORD, and they anointed David king over Israel."

D.J. McCarthy and P. Kalluveettil both agree that solemn declarations are "solemn" precisely because they implicitly invoke the deity; both go to considerable lengths to stress how "oath-like" are certain examples of such *verba solemnia*. For example, McCarthy concedes with respect to his interpretation of Exod. 24:3 ("All the words which the LORD has spoken we will do") that any such "public commitment to follow Yahweh who has just presented Himself in all his power is *the equivalent of an oath* [italics added]."[146] Similarly, Kalluveettil writes with respect to Israel's affirmation in Exod. 19:8 ["All that the LORD has spoken we will do"]: "From this pledging of the people to obedience (*it amounts almost to the oath of a vassal treaty* [italics added]) results the lord-servant relationship among the parties, and this fellowship paved the way for the proclamation of covenant laws and for the formal realization of pact as described in ch. 24."[147] In the same manner, Kalluveettil comments with respect to the people's acclamation of Saul in 1 Sam. 10:24 ["Long live the king!"], made in the presence of the prophet Samuel and immediately after the Lord had revealed his choice of Saul: "they bind themselves to him [i.e., Saul]; the act *amounted to an oath* [italics added]."[148]

If solemn declarations result in sanction-sealed commitments to which God is witness, then there appears to be little justification for McCarthy's and Kalluveettil's reluctance to identify them as "oaths," rather than "the equivalent of an oath," etc. To refuse to recognize such *verba solemnia* as oaths merely because they are not explicitly self-maledictory is to introduce a distinction where there is no difference.

An uplifted hand, though not overtly self-maledictory, may function as an oath-sign since it expresses an appeal to the deity to act as a witness
What is true of solemn declarations appears to be equally true of solemn enactments, i.e., oath-signs. While, as we have seen, some oath-signs consist

---

[146] D.J. McCarthy, *Treaty and Covenant* (1981) 253. So also D.L. Magnetti, "The Oath in the Old Testament," 128. While McCarthy makes this concession, his analysis of the Sinai covenant as a ritual covenant, rather than a verbal covenant in the tradition of the ancient Near Eastern treaties, requires him to reassert a fundamental difference between what is "the equivalent of an oath" and what is actually an oath. "The ritual is a familial thing and not the terrorizing acted out oaths of some treaty rituals" (*op. cit.*, 276). This difference, however, is not altogether convincing in the face of McCarthy's acknowledgment that the oath-bound treaties similarly effected a familial union between the covenant partners. Cf. the similar point made by M.G. Kline, *The Structure of Biblical Authority*, 2nd ed., 116.

[147] P. Kalluveettil, *Declaration and Covenant*, 157.

[148] P. Kalluveettil, *Declaration and Covenant*, 61. Though the text does not identify this as a covenant, Kalluveettil is convinced that the reality was there.

Cf. also Kalluveettil's earlier discussion where he calls Laban's words in the E version of his covenant with Jacob (Gen. 31:45, 49, 50, 53b, 54) "analogous to an oath formula, vv. 49 and 50b" (*op. cit.*, 11).

of a *drohritus*, that is, an acted-out conditional curse, not all oath-signs are so explicitly self-maledictory. For example, perhaps the most common symbolic action in connection with swearing is that of raising the hand (נשא + יד; הרים + יד; הרים + ימינו [+ שמאלו]). Specifically, when used of oaths נשא + יד, "lift a hand," refers exclusively to oaths taken by God: Exod. 6:8; Num. 14:30; Deut. 32:40; Ezek. 20:5 (*bis*), 6, 15, 23, 28, 42; 36:7; 44:12; 47:14; Neh. 9:15; and Ps. 106:26. On the contrary, the related expression הרים + יד, "raise a hand," appears as an oath-accompanying gesture on the part of Abraham in Gen. 14:22, while the expression שמאלו + ימינו + הרים, "raise his right hand and his left hand," appears as a gesture of swearing on the part of an angel in Dan. 12:7.[149]

Although there is little doubt that the upraised hand is intended as a symbol of swearing in the texts which have been mentioned, as with many symbolic acts, the same gesture may bear a different significance when found in a different context (cf., e.g., Exod. 17:11). Furthermore, it is possible that this gesture assumed different meanings over time or that it was so stereotypically associated with oaths that its precise meaning was lost sight of.[150] Nevertheless, without excluding other possibilities, it seems most probable that in oath contexts the upraised hand represents an appeal to the deity to act as a witness against any perjury or infidelity.[151] Supporting this interpretation, it may be noted that in certain non-oath contexts the raising of the hand(s) also seems to symbolize an appeal to the deity, functioning as a gesture of supplication (e.g., cf. נשא + ידים, "lift hands," in Ps. 28:2; 134:2; and Hab. 3:10; נשא + כף, "lift a palm," in Ps. 63:5 [ET 4]; 119:48; and Lam. 2:19; and הרים + יד, "raise a hand," in Exod. 17:11).[152] If this is the proper interpretation of "raising the hand," then this gesture is only implicitly self-maledictory and, as such, appears to be a symbolic equivalent of the widely-attested oath formula, "as the Lord lives."[153]

---

[149] Cf. also Isa. 62:8. For a plausible explanation for the interesting distribution of these three closely related idioms, cf. Å. Viberg, *Symbols of Law* (1992) 19-31. For a more extensive discussion of the various expressions for upraised hands and their Akkadian equivalents, cf. M.I. Gruber, *Aspects of Nonverbal Communication in the Ancient East* (1980) 22-89.

[150] M. Malul warns about a further possibility with respect to Mesopotamian legal symbolic acts: what may seem like a performable gesture is in fact merely a graphic figure of speech, much like the English expression "to pull one's leg" (*Studies in Mesopotamian Legal Symbolism*, 19, 23-27). In the present case this seems unlikely because of the use of varied phraseology (an important indicator according to Malul, *op. cit.*, 25) and especially because of the abundant iconographic evidence of actual performance to be adduced below. Naturally, when applied to the deity, this gesture is being attributed as a vivid anthropomorphism.

[151] So, e.g., S.R. Driver, *Deuteronomy*, 379; and J.A. Thompson, *Deuteronomy*, 303.

[152] It is possible that this gesture of supplication in turn derived from the use of raising hands as a hailing or greeting gesture. Cf. the use of נשא + יד in Isa. 49:22. Cf. also Keel #414 and Keel's discussion on p. 311.

[153] Alternatively, even if the oath-sign of the upraised hand symbolizes an incomplete self-malediction (cf. the frequent use of upraised hands in non-oath contexts as a sign of surrender as in Keel ##15, 25, 39, 40, 63, etc.), implying the hypothetical surrender of oneself to the deity to do with the swearer as he pleases if there is any perjury or infidelity, nevertheless, it does not constitute a *drohritus*.

Certain other oath-signs likewise do not appear to be overtly or exclusively self-maledictory. In contrast to "raising the hand," which represents a direct appeal to the deity to act as witness, these oath-signs function by offering a solemn depiction of the covenant commitment being undertaken and thereby only implicitly invoke God as witness. As such, these oath-signs operate in a manner which is comparable to the *verba solemnia* discussed earlier. We shall focus on two examples of this kind of oath-sign, namely eating together and shaking hands, not only because of their intrinsic importance, but also because of manifest similarities which exist between these well-recognized oath-signs and the oath-sign to be posited for marriage in the next chapter, namely sexual union. In proceeding to discuss these two examples, however, it is again necessary to keep in mind that the symbolism involved in these acts need not be univocal (as was seen above in the case of circumcision) and that their function may change according to context; the same act may not be an oath-sign when it appears in a different setting.

At times eating together may function as an oath-sign by solemnly depicting the covenant commitment (and possibly its sanction)
One need not agree with scholars like E. Meyer and L. Köhler, who suppose that the idea of "covenant" originally derived from the practice of a shared meal (reflected in an assumed etymology of בְּרִית from ברה I, "to eat"), to be impressed with how frequently such meals are associated with covenant ratification within the Old Testament and elsewhere in the ancient Near East.[154] Given certain widely acknowledged cultural attitudes regarding shared meals evident throughout the Old Testament, such an association with covenants seems entirely appropriate. This is not to suggest that every instance of a common meal within the Old Testament is fraught with significance. Even seemingly incidental references to such meals, however, often betray important cultural presuppositions of expected behaviour and attitudes to which the reader should be alert.[155]

---

[154] Cf., e.g., Gen. 26:30; 31:46-54; Josh. 9:14; Exod. 18:12; Ps. 23:5; 41:10 [ET 9]; 69:23 [22]; 1 Kgs. 1:9, 25; 1 Chron. 12:39f.; 29:22; and 2 Chron. 18:2. For extra-biblical examples, cf., e.g., *EA* 162, 22f. (= *AL*, p. 249); and D.J. McCarthy, *Treaty and Covenant* (1981) 254, n. 19.
Cf. also E. Meyer, *Die Israeliten und ihre Nachbarstämme* (1906) 558 n. 1; L. Köhler, "Problems in the Study of the Language of the Old Testament" (1956) 4-7; and Å. Viberg, *Symbols of Law* (1992) 70-76.
[155] Cf. P. Farb, *Consuming Passions: The Anthropology of Eating* (1980), cited approvingly by M. Malul (*Studies in Mesopotamian Legal Symbolism*, 377f.) in support of the general importance of shared meals throughout history as a means of securing comity.
Focusing on biblical and ancient Near Eastern practice, cf., e.g., W.T. McCree, "The Covenant Meal in the Old Testament" (1926) 120-128; J.F. Ross, "Meal," *IDB*, 3, 315-318; D.J. McCarthy, *Treaty and Covenant* (1981) 254, n. 19; P. Kalluveettil, *Declaration and Covenant*, 11, 12f., 118; and M. Malul, *op. cit.*, 176, 346, 353, 356, 376-378.

1) For instance, just as fasting can be expressive of grief, feasting together in a common meal can be expressive of well-being and rejoicing.[156] Given how often covenants were intended to end a period of alienation, hostility, need or deprivation, or to introduce a period of peace and prosperity, it is not surprising to find plausible examples of this celebratory use of common meals in covenant-making or renewing contexts, where the meals in question do not function as oath-signs. See, for instance, 1 Kgs. 3:15.[157] See also Deut. 12:7; 14:26; 27:7; and perhaps 1 Chron. 29:22, all of which stress how Israel was to eat together rejoicing before the Lord.[158]

2) A second widely-attested cultural assumption concerning shared meals was the expectation that mutual amity and loyalty would attend and be secured by the sharing of a meal. Accordingly, at times common meals functioned analogously to the giving of a gift, as discussed above.[159] This expectation of amity appears to be presupposed in the prophetic image for the last days when, "The wolf and the lamb shall feed together..." (Isa. 65:25).[160] For this reason also, not only is the lack of love at shared banquets seen to be a contradiction (cf. Prov. 15:17), but any subsequent acts of disloyalty are judged particularly reprehensible when they are committed by those who have eaten together (without any necessary implication that the common meal had effected a covenant). Compare, for example, Ps. 41:10 [ET 9], "Even my bosom friend in whom I trusted, who ate of my bread, has lifted his heel against me."

---

[156] Thus the biblical record mentions common meals which were held to celebrate, *inter alia*, a birthday (Gen. 40:20), the day when a child is weaned (Gen. 21:8), the conclusion of sheep shearing (1 Sam. 25:4-13; 2 Sam. 13:23f.), the conclusion of the grape harvest (Judg. 9:27), the conclusion of a temple building project (2 Chron. 7:8; 30:23), and, with special significance for the present thesis, the conclusion of marriage negotiations (Gen. 24:33, 54) and a wedding (Gen. 29:22; Judg. 14:10). Cf. also Gen. 31:27f. For Jewish practice beyond the OT, cf. Tob. 8:19f.; 10:7ff.; 2 Esdr. 9:47; Matt. 22:2; John 2; and *m. Šeb.* 7:4.

Related to this sense of conviviality and gratitude for one's well-being, a number of texts imply an expectation that such festive meals would be shared often with neighbours and persons who were less fortunate. Cf., e.g., Exod. 12:4; Deut. 12:12, 18; 1 Sam. 30:24; 2 Kgs. 7:9; Esth. 1:3, 5, 9; and Job 31:16f.

[157] Cf. S.J. DeVries, *I Kings* (1985) 53. The fact that this feast was not one which was shared between the covenanting parties (the covenant was between Yahweh and Solomon, not Solomon and his servants) makes clear that this feast functioned in a celebratory manner, rather than as an oath-sign.

[158] Cf. also Isa. 55:2f. Alternatively, the meal in 1 Chron. 29:22 may be part of a covenant-ratifying ceremony presided over by David and designed to establish Solomon as king.

[159] Cf., for example, the protest of the Judahites against the men of Israel, "Because the king is near of kin to us. Why then are you angry over this matter? Have we eaten at all at the king's expense? Or has he given us any gift?" (2 Sam. 19:43 [ET 42])

[160] Cf. Isa. 11:7. Cf. also Ps. 23:5. While the traditional view that Ps. 23:5 alludes to food on a common table (perhaps from a sacrifice in view of the implied temple setting in vs. 6) remains probable, it is possible that one should read this text in the light of *ANEP*, #608 (= Keel # 122, 96, cf. discussion on 95f.), which also appears to have a temple setting. If so, there were covenant documents on the table, rather than food.

Related to this expectation of amity, the invitation to join in a common meal was an expression of good will and favour, as in Ruth 2:14.[161] Correspondingly, the willingness to avail oneself of the hospitality of another implies a willingness for amity, while the refusal to share another's food implies condemnation, alienation, or hostility. Compare, for example, 1 Sam. 20:5; 1 Kgs. 13:8; and Ps. 141:4. With such associations, it is not surprising that there is abundant evidence of the use of common meals in the context of covenant, perhaps often intended as an expression of the family-like amity (since families typically eat together) which is secured or formalized in covenant.[162] Compare, for example, Gen. 26:30.

On the other hand, where it is stated or implied that a common meal was eaten in the presence of the Lord, the reader has warrant to suppose that the meal may have functioned as a covenant-ratifying oath-sign. In such a case the solemn depiction of friendship and mutual loyalty would function analogously to the *verba solemnia* considered earlier.[163] The possibility that some covenants were sworn by a common meal seems to be required by the comparative ancient Near Eastern evidence, such as the mention of the oath "by the laden table and by drinking from the cup" in lines 154-156 of the Vassal-Treaty of Esarhaddon with Ramataya.[164] A plausible example of a common meal employed as a covenant-ratifying oath-sign appears in Gen. 31:46 (where the common meal is consumed in the presence of the heap and perhaps also the pillar, if it is not a secondary expansion, which function as symbols of the deity) and possibly Gen. 31:54.[165] An interesting special case

---

[161] Perhaps similar in its romantic associations is the mention of how Tamar prepared and then fed Amnon "heart-shaped cakes" [לבבות] in 2 Sam. 13:6, 8, 10.

The obligation to extend hospitality to strangers may be compared here, although some texts make clear that in such contexts it was not always necessary to eat together. Cf. Gen. 18:5, 8 (where the men ate while Abraham stood by) and Judg. 13:15ff. (this is an important text since the substitution of a burnt offering in this theophanic context implies an equivalence between burnt offerings shared with God and common meals shared with mortals). Cf. also Gen. 19:3; 43:32; Judg. 19:4, 8, 19, 21.

For examples where the king shows his munificence and personal favour by invitations to share in a common meal, cf. 2 Sam. 9:7-13; 19:29, 43 [ET 28, 42]; 1 Kgs. 2:7; 18:19; and Esth. 5:12. Cf. also Judg. 1:7; and 2 Kgs. 25:27-30.

[162] This point is made by D.J. McCarthy (*Treaty and Covenant* [1981] 253ff., 266, 276) and P. Kalluveettil (*Declaration and Covenant*, 11: "Indeed they become kinsmen, since only kinsmen eat together"), *inter alios*.

[163] In some contexts, particularly where sacrifices are included with their symbolism of the deity figuratively sharing in the table fellowship (cf. Judg. 13:15ff.), such meals express simultaneously a renewed commitment to the deity. Cf. S.R. Driver, *Genesis*, 289.

[164] Cf. *ANET*, 536, as noted by M.G. Kline, *The Structure of Biblical Authority* (1975) 117, n. 8. Cf. also D.J. Wiseman, *The Vassal Treaties of Esarhaddon* (1958) 84; R. Borger, "Zu den Asarhaddon Verträgen aus Nimrud" (1961) 173-196; and S. Parpola and K. Watanabe, *Neo-Assyrian Treaties and Loyalty Oaths* (1988) 35.

For another example, cf. *EA* 162 (= *AL*, p. 249).

[165] On the complex source-critical issues raised by Gen. 31:43-54, cf., e.g., D.J. McCarthy, "Three Covenants in Genesis" (1964) 179-189; and, offering a different analysis, C. Westermann, *Genesis 12-36*, 490, 498ff.

It appears that the heap (and perhaps the pillar) was intended as a symbol of the deity, who is identified as a witness to the covenant, אֱלֹהִים עֵד בֵּינִי וּבֵינֶךָ (Gen. 31:50), by Laban, employing the same terms as he uses of the heap in vs. 48: הַגַּל הַזֶּה עֵד בֵּינִי וּבֵינְךָ הַיּוֹם. It is this context and symbolism which make particularly significant the fact that "they ate there

is found in instances where a common meal serves in the recognition of a new king. Compare, for example, 1 Kgs. 1:9, 25, 41; 4:20; 1 Chron. 12:39f.; 29:22; 2 Chron. 18:2; and especially 2 Sam. 3:12-21.[166] Finally, mention should be made of two important, though controversial, examples of common meals functioning as oath-signs: Exod. 18:12 and Josh. 9:14.[167] The efficacy of the Gibeonite covenant in Joshua 9, in spite of the Gibeonite's deception, finds an intriguing nineteenth-century parallel, cited by D.J. McCarthy: "Doughty frequently snatched bread and salt in the tent of an Arab whom he feared. Even such a forced eating with the other was enough to assure protection, in effect, a covenant."[168]

3) There is a third possible symbolism for common meals within the Old Testament, namely that of a self-maledictory rite. In particular, the hypothetical implication of such a meal consumed in the presence of the deity might be to invite the deity to act as a witness against any perjury or infidelity by abandoning the offender to a similar fate as that experienced by the devoured animals.[169] Putting it this way makes clear that, as opposed to the previously considered symbolism, the proposed meaning is not concerned with the *communal* nature of such meals, i.e., that they would be eaten together. Rather, any self-maledictory symbolism applies only to the antecedent death of animals in preparation for the meal and perhaps also to the physical act of consumption, whether of food or drink.[170]

Reflecting this difference in the symbolism, it should be possible, at least in principle, for the same occasion of eating and drinking to function as

---

by the heap" (Gen. 31:46). The arrangement of pillar and heap, if original to the text, may recall an earlier dual representation of the deity in the "smoking fire pot and a flaming torch" in Genesis 15 and may have been intended to replicate the twofold pillar of God's presence in oath posture (Exod. 13:21, etc.; cf. 1 Kgs. 7:21). Cf. M.M. Kline, "The Holy Spirit as Covenant Witness" (1972).

[166] Cf. P. Kalluveettil, *Declaration and Covenant,* 12f., who also cites D.J. McCarthy, "*Bᵉrît* and Covenant in the Deuteronomistic History," 80f.; W.T. McCree, "The Covenant Meal in the Old Testament," 126f.; A. Malamat, "Organs of Statecraft in the Israelite Monarchy," *BAR III,* 164f.; and T.C. Vriezen, "The Exegesis of Exodus 24:9-11," 112 (*op. cit.,* 13, n. 26). R. Smend, however, denies a covenant implication for this meal ("Essen und Trinken – ein Stück Weltlichkeit des AT," 456).

[167] For Exod. 18:12, cf. A. Cody, "Jethro Accepts a Covenant with the Israelites" (1968) 153-166. For Josh. 9:14, cf. F.C. Fensham, "The Treaty Between Israel and the Gibeonites" (1964) 96-100; J.M. Grintz, "The Treaty of Joshua with the Gibeonites" (1966) 113-126; D.J. McCarthy, *Old Testament Covenant,* 43; and P. Kalluveettil, *Declaration and Covenant,* 116f.

[168] D.J. McCarthy, *Treaty and Covenant* (1981) 254, n. 19, referring to events recorded in C.M. Doughty, *Travels in Arabia Deserta* (1888).

[169] In terms of modern sensibilities, by which we prefer to dissociate the slaughter of animals from our subsequent dining by the services of a butcher, any such symbolism may appear far-fetched. In antiquity, however, the connection between slaughter / sacrifice and eating was patently closer and in covenant-making contexts, as we have seen, frequently explicit. Cf. W.W. Hallo, "The Origins of the Sacrificial Cult: New Evidence from Mesopotamia and Israel" (1987) 3-13.

[170] Some scholars would prefer to stress how the sacrificial blood is a symbol of life rather than threat of death. Cf. D.J. McCarthy, *Treaty and Covenant* (1981) 255, 294f. It is not obvious that these alternatives are mutually exclusive.

an oath-sign by offering simultaneously both a positive symbol of the covenant commitment and a negative symbol of the covenant sanction. For this kind of symbolic multivalence, one may recall the example of circumcision considered earlier with both its self-maledictory symbolism and its more positive consecratory symbolism, neither of which excludes the other.[171]

In support of this proposed maledictory symbolism for shared meals, numerous texts within the Old Testament and elsewhere in the ancient Near East depict God's judgment with the imagery of having one's flesh devoured or one's blood drunk, etc.[172] Compare, for example, Ezek. 39:17-20; Jer. 12:9; 19:7; and 34:20.[173] More explicit evidence that these stereotypical curses may have been enacted in a self-maledictory rite is found in the proliferation of curses which conclude the Vassal-Treaty of Esarhaddon with Ramataya:

> "Just as (these) yearlings and spring lambs, male and female, are cut open and their entrails are rolled around their feet, so may the entrails of your sons and daughters be rolled around your feet.... Just as [this?] bread and wine enter the intestines, so may they (the gods) let this oath enter your intestines and the intestines of your sons and daughters.... Just as [this?] honey is sweet, so may the blood of your women, your sons and daughters taste sweet in your mouths.... Just as (this) gall is bitter, so may you, your women, your sons and daughters be bitter to each other."[174]

Within the Old Testament, the jealousy-ordeal in Num. 5:11-31 (however one interprets the outcome for the woman) and the "anti-

---

[171] Perhaps an even closer parallel is afforded by the New Testament Eucharist, referred to by Pliny the Younger in his letter to Trajan: "[Christians] come together to bind themselves by an oath." Paul's threat that whoever eats and drinks unworthily will "eat and drink judgment upon himself" (1 Cor. 11:27ff.) supports a self-maledictory symbolism underlying the Lord's Supper (our infidelity deserves the same dreadful curse which overtook Christ, whose death is symbolized in the elements). At the same time, Paul affirms a more positive symbolism entailed in the *communal* nature of this meal: "Because there is one bread, we who are many are one body, for we all partake of the one bread" (1 Cor. 10:17). In the following verse Paul invites a comparison between the symbolism of the Lord's Supper and OT sacrifices similar to that being presently suggested: "Consider the people of Israel; are not those who eat the sacrifices partners in the altar?" (1 Cor. 10:18)
Cf., e.g., G.E. Mendenhall, who relates the cup of the New Covenant to OT concepts of oath and curse ("Covenant," 722). Cf. also C. F.D. Moule, "The Judgment Theme in the Sacraments," 464-481; A.R. Millard, "Covenant and Communion in First Corinthians," 242-248; and M.G. Kline, *By Oath Consigned*, 80f. For a similar approach to Passover, cf. K. van der Toorn, "Ordeal Procedures in the Psalms and the Passover Meal" (1988) 427-445.
[172] Cf. The Vassal Treaty of Esarhaddon with Ramataya, *ANET*, 538, lines 425ff., where the curse is that Ninurta would "give your flesh to eagles and vultures to feed upon," and lines 440ff., where Adad is asked to bring such famine that you would eat your own children, and, rather than grinding barley, "they [your enemies?] grind your bones" and the bones of "your sons and daughters."
[173] Cf. also Num. 26:10; Deut. 11:6; Ps. 69:16 [ET 15]; Isa. 5:14; 9:12; 34:6-7; Jer. 46:10, 20-21; 50:6f.; Ezek. 34:28; Dan. 7:5; and Amos 3:12.
[174] *ANET*, 539f., lines 551ff.

communion service" in Jer. 25:15 offer clear examples of explicit self-
maledictory eating or drinking.[175]   Alternatively, perhaps the most
controversial example of a covenant-ratifying meal is that found in Exod.
24:11, "And he did not lay his hand on the chief men of the people of Israel;
they beheld God, and ate and drank." M.G. Kline summarizes the ancient
Near Eastern comparative evidence for eating and drinking as a self-
maledictory oath-sign and asserts, "Israel's eating and drinking in the persons
of her representatives on the mount of God (Exod. 24:11) was a recognized
symbolic method by which people swore treaties."[176]   Other scholars,
however, are less certain.

For example, D.J. McCarthy's central thesis in *Treaty and Covenant* is
his claim that the Sinai pericope (Exodus 19-24), whether in whole or in any
of its parts, does not exhibit the treaty pattern known from ancient Near
Eastern parallels. According to McCarthy, the Sinai pericope in its original
form lacks curses, oath taking, and an historical prologue, all expected from
the treaty tradition. As a consequence in Exodus 19-24 we find a "ritual," as
opposed to "verbal," covenant building on Yahweh's theophany, which is
terrible enough (without historical appeals or sanctions) to arouse obedience
to the divine will. According to McCarthy, then, in terms of that theophany
the purpose of the covenant-ratifying meal in Exodus 24 was not an oath-
pledge of obedience on the part of the people (as would be expected from the
treaty pattern), but a gesture of comity to reassure a terrified people of the
benevolence of the deity and to symbolize their acceptance into the family of
God. Likewise, the sacrifices of communion effect a union between God and
people; the blood sprinkled on the altar and people expresses the reality that
Yahweh and his people share the same blood and are members of one
family.[177]

Without attempting to resolve the problematic source analysis of
Exodus 24 or to address the related controversy regarding the history of the

---

[175] Cf. M. Fishbane, "Accusations of Adultery, A Study of Law and Scribal Practice in
Numbers 5:11-31" (1974) 24-45; H.C. Brichto, "The Case of the *Sōṭā* and a
Reconsideration of Biblical 'Law'" (1975) 55-70; G.J. Wenham, *Numbers* (1981) 79-85;
P.J. Budd, *Numbers* (1984) 60-67; and T. Frymer-Kensky, "The Strange Case of the
Suspected Sotah (Numbers v 11-31)" (1984) 11-26.
    Cf. also Isa. 51:17, 22; Zech. 12:2; and Hab. 2:15.
[176] M.G. Kline, *The Structure of Biblical Authority* (1975) 116f.
[177] Alternatively, noting that "eating and drinking in the presence of God cannot be
understood as *ipso facto* the making of a covenant with God," E. Nicholson has urged that
the meal in Exod. 24:11 need not be covenant making in any sense (*God and His People*
[1986] 126). Cf. also *idem.*, "The Origin of the Tradition in Exodus XXIV 9-11" (1976)
148-160; and *idem., God and His People*, 121-133, 164-178.
    Nicholson prefers to view this meal as an expression of their enjoyment of life or the
simple fact that they continued to live after their *visio dei.* In support of this interpretation
of "eat and drink," Nicholson cites 1 Kgs. 4:20, Jer. 22:15, and Eccl. 5:16. Unlike the case
of Exodus 24, however, none of these texts implies that the eating and drinking in question
was of a shared meal nor that the meal was consumed in the presence of God. Furthermore,
Nicholson's claim that Exod. 24:11 offers an instance of *parallelismus membrorum*, where
"they saw God" is balanced with "they ate and drank," is unconvincing (*God and His
People*, 131).

covenant concept in Israel's religion, we may note that in the present form of the text, the common meal in vs. 11 appears to presuppose the earlier sacrifices of vs. 5. Further, the text is explicit that this meal was eaten by Israel's representatives (Moses, Aaron, and the elders of Israel) in the presence of their God. As has been widely recognized, the confluence of these details closely parallels the common meal before God in Exod. 18:12 and, as such, may support their coherence in the present context.[178] Following Israel's solemn affirmation, "all that the Lord has spoken we will do, and we will be obedient," the meal in Exod. 24:11 appears to serve in the ratification of Yahweh's covenant with Israel. Whether it is preferable to view the underlying symbolism of this oath-sign exclusively in terms of its positive depiction of communion between Israel and Yahweh, as does D.J. McCarthy, or whether there may also be a self-maledictory aspect for this meal and its antecedent sacrifices is less clear.[179]

The giving of a hand may function as an oath-sign by solemnly depicting the covenant commitment
The gesture of giving one's hand in a handshake, נתן + יד, appears with plausible covenant-making implication in 2 Kgs. 10:15; Jer. 50:15; Ezek. 17:18; Lam. 5:6; Ezra 10:19; 1 Chron. 29:24; and 2 Chron. 30:8.[180]   In addition, Ps. 144:8, 11, "whose right hand [ימינם] is a right hand [ימין] of falsehood," may allude not to the oath gesture of an upraised hand, as is often assumed, but to the gesture of "giving the right hand," that is, "shaking hands."[181]   Finally, there are a number of references to handshakes in extra-

---

[178] Further support may be offered by the frequent association elsewhere of a common meal shared in a covenant-making context accompanied by antecedent sacrifices (e.g., cf. Gen. 31:54, where the parties tarry on the mountain in a manner which resembles Exodus 24; 1 Kgs. 1:9, 25; 1 Chron. 29:22; 2 Chron. 18:2).

[179] D.J. McCarthy, *Treaty and Covenant* (1981) 294, n. 34. Alternatively, cf., e.g., M.G. Kline, *By Oath Consigned*, 18; *idem, Treaty of the Great King*, 15f.
It is possible that McCarthy's analysis of Exodus 24 was influenced by the view of earlier scholars who hypothesized an evolution from covenant ratification through symbolic ritual, supposed to be a characteristic feature of second millennium treaties, to ratification by verbal oaths, supposed to be a characteristic feature of first millennium treaties (cf. I.J. Gelb, "Review of D.J. Wiseman, *The Vassal-Treaties of Esarhaddon*," 161-162; M. Weinfeld, "Deuteronomy — The Present State of Inquiry," 225, n. 34). This supposed evolution has been rejected by more recent scholars. Cf., e.g., D.L. Magnetti, who argues that oath and ritual are, in fact, integrally connected in the earlier treaties, while rituals, even if less elaborate ones, continue to accompany oaths in the later treaties ("The Oath in the Old Testament," 106, n. 59).

[180] In support of the covenant-making associations of this gesture in these texts, cf., e.g., J.W. Wevers, *Ezekiel* (1969) 106; D. Hillers, *Lamentations* (1972) 98; J.M. Myers, *2 Chronicles* (1979) 175 (who cites in support, R. Kraetzschmar, *Die Bundesvorstellung im Alten Testament*, 47; and J. Wellhausen, *Reste arabischen Heidentums*, 186); F.C. Fensham, *The Books of Ezra and Nehemiah* (1982) 143; R.L. Braun, *1 Chronicles* (1986) 285; and M. Cogan and H. Tadmor, *II Kings* (1988) 115. Cf. also Å. Viberg, *Symbols of Law* (1992) 33-44.

[181] So Keel, p. 96. The ancient Near Eastern iconographic evidence supports the assumption here that it was the right hand which was used for shaking hands (cf., e.g., Keel #123, 96.).

biblical texts and in ancient Near Eastern iconography which support the biblical evidence for the use of this gesture as a pact or covenant-making rite.[182]

The biblical text perhaps clearest in its association between the gesture of giving the hand and covenant making, is Ezek. 17:18: "Because he despised the oath and broke the covenant [וּבָזָה אָלָה לְהָפֵר בְּרִית], because he gave his hand and yet did all these things [וְהִנֵּה נָתַן יָדוֹ וְכָל־אֵלֶּה עָשָׂה], he shall not escape [לֹא יִמָּלֵט]" (Ezek. 17:18 RSV). Kalluveettil writes with respect to this example, "There are two covenant-making acts in Ez 17,11-21: an oath (v. 13 wayyābē’ ’ōtô be‘ālâ) sworn in the name of God (2 Chr 36,13) and the rite of nātan yād (v. 18) which was not merely a gesture of assent to the covenant terms, but a sign which effected the covenant relationship."[183] Kalluveettil offers the plausible suggestion that "the hand stands for the person"; as such, giving one's hand to another symbolizes the giving of oneself.[184]

As mentioned earlier, however, Kalluveettil wishes to distinguish between rites or actions which "effect" or "constitute the covenant relationship, i.e., union" and any oath which merely makes the covenant binding and "gives it a sacred and inviolable character."[185] In the present case, as elsewhere, this distinction is not entirely convincing because there is no suggestion in vs. 18 that Yahweh considers the commitment symbolized in

---

Some scholars suggest that the gesture of "giving a hand" is the same as "striking hands" (כפים + תקע / ø / יד?), particularly as found in Prov. 6:1; 11:15; 17:18; 22:26; and Job 17:3. This is the view, for example, of Keel, p. 96; and C.H. Toy, *Proverbs*, 120. Against this, however, cf. Ps. 47:2 [ET 1] and Nah. 3:19, which suggest that "striking hands" consisted of clapping one's own hands (less probably of slapping the other person's hands), but not of a handshake [= כפים + הכה, cf., e.g., 2 Kgs. 11:12].

[182] The Akkadian expressions leqûm + qātātim ("take hands"), nasāḫum + qātātim ("remove hands"), and ṣabātum + qātātim ("seize hands") all have to do with the assumption or repeal of suretyship and do not appear to be related to the handshake being considered here (cf. M. Malul, *Studies in Mesopotamian Legal Symbolism*, 219-231).

On the contrary, the less well attested nadānu + qātu ("give the hand"), discussed by Kalluveettil, does appear to describe a similar gesture, possibly with similar significance, as does its Hebrew cognate, נתן + יד (*Declaration and Covenant*, 21f.).

Kalluveettil also mentions a related Egyptian idiom, which appears in the Instruction of the Pharaoh Amenem-Het, "It was the eater of my food that made insurrection, I gave to him my two hands (rai’.n.i’ n.f ‘wy.i’) and he produced terror" (op. cit., 22, n. 25). Kalluveettil suggests that the giving of hands "seems to be used here metonymically for the covenant-making itself." Cf. F.L. Griffith, "The Millingen Papyrus" (1896) 35-51. Cf. also Keel #123, 96.

[183] P. Kalluveettil, *Declaration and Covenant*, 14.

[184] *Ibid.*, 21, based on the gesture of "striking the hand," as in Prov. 6:1; 11:15; 17:18; Job 17:3 (cf. Prov. 22:26).

M. Malul prefers to interpret the hand as emblematic of a person's power (*Studies in Mesopotamian Legal Symbolism*, 221, 225, and *passim*). This interpretation is reasonable in the contexts of concern to Malul, for example, in the expression ana qātāti(m) nadānu(m), "to give into the hands" (op. cit., 220), but in other contexts the hand appears to represent the person as a whole on the principle of *pars pro toto*. For example, compare the symbolism of washing one's hands to represent the cleansing of the whole person in Lev. 5:11 and Job 9:30 (cf. 2 Sam. 22:21; Deut. 21:6-7; Ps. 73:13).

[185] *Ibid.*, 10, with reference to the Abimelech - Abraham covenant.

the offer of Zedekiah's hand to Nebuchadnezzar to be any less inviolable than the oath which Zedekiah despised. Indeed, contrary to Kalluveettil, vs. 18 seems to imply that the oath which Zedekiah despised, resulting in the breach of the covenant, was one and the same as the gesture of giving his hand!

This interpretation becomes even more plausible if the protasis of vs. 18 begins with וְהִנֵּה, as it would more typically in Biblical Hebrew and as it does in vs. 10, rather than with the unmarked וּבָזָה, as the RSV implies (leaving uncertain the purpose of the subsequent וְהִנֵּה).[186] Consequently we may render the verse: "He despised the oath by breaking the covenant [cf. the identical expression in 16:59]. If he gave his hand and (yet) did all these things, he shall not escape."[187] The inexorable judgment which will overtake Zedekiah will come because he "gave his hand," a gesture for which Yahweh intends to act as guarantor, and yet in violation of this he sought an alliance with Egypt.[188] Given this context, not surprisingly M. Greenberg identifies the giving of the hand as "a gesture of promise and compact."[189]

---

[186] Cf. D.J. McCarthy, "The Uses of *wᵉhinnēh* in Biblical Hebrew," 336f.

[187] This seems preferable to the rendering of M. Greenberg, who takes the וְהִנֵּה clause as concessive and parenthetical (*Ezekiel 1-20*, 308). Greenberg translates: "He flouted the curse-oath to violate the covenant – although he gave his hand to it yet he did all these things! – he shall not escape!"

[188] Further confirmation for this suggestion may be offered if vs. 18 is read in the light of the literary structure of its context. As analyzed by M. Greenberg, Ezekiel 17 reveals a chiastic structure, A-B-B'-A', with each end member consisting of an extended allegory (*Ezekiel 1-20*, 317-324). The first allegory (vss. 1-10) begins by describing an eagle who lops off the top of a cedar and later plants it, but the planting turns to another great eagle who transplants it. In this figure Ezekiel considers the activities of Nebuchadnezzar and Pharaoh Psammetichus II, the two eagles, with respect to Nebuchadnezzar's rebellious vassal, Zedekiah. The closing allegory (22-24) opens similarly, but rather than speaking of an eagle (representing a merely human agent), it speaks directly of Yahweh, who personally lops off the top of the cedar and later himself plants and cultivates it. In this manner the prophet represents the promised restoration of his people. The change in focus from human agents to Yahweh evident in the allegories is likewise reflected in the two central interpretative sections. While the first B section (vss. 11-18) considers the role of Nebuchadnezzar and Psammetichus II, the second B section (vss. 9-21) attributes the impending judgment of Judah exclusively to Yahweh.

In terms of this structure, coming at the end of its section, vs. 18 summarizes Zedekiah's crime (12-15) and threatened punishment (16-17) and repeats key terms which appear in the rhetorical question of vs. 15 and its answer in vs. 16:

וּבָזָה אֶת־אָלָה (vs. 18a)// בָּזָה אֶת־אָלָתוֹ (vs. 16; cf. וַיָּבֶא אֹתוֹ בְּאָלָה in vs. 13)

לְהָפֵר בְּרִית (vs. 18b)// וְהֵפֵר בְּרִיתוֹ (vs. 15) הֵפֵר אֶת־בְּרִיתִי (vs. 16; cf. וַיִּכְרֹת אִתּוֹ בְּרִית in vs. 13)

וְכָל־אָלֶּה עָשָׂה (vs. 18c)// הֶעָשֹׂה אֵלֶּה (vs. 15)

לֹא יִמָּלֵט (vs. 18d)// הֲיִמָּלֵט ... וְנִמְלָט (vs. 15)

As a summary verse, so closely related to what precedes (particularly vss. 15-16), one should expect to find an appropriate antecedent for the gesture of "giving his hand" mentioned in vs. 18b which makes Zedekiah's perfidy so reprehensible and the judgment against him consequently inescapable. On the present interpretation that gesture was understood as the oath(-sign) by which Zedekiah became Nebuchadnezzar's vassal.

[189] *Ezekiel 1-20*, 315.

Other examples of symbolic acts which may function as oath-signs by solemnly depicting the covenant commitment

There are other symbolic acts, less frequently attested in the Old Testament, which may function as oath-signs by their solemn depiction of the covenant commitment. Included among these are the water libation mentioned in 1 Sam. 7:6 (cf. 2 Sam. 14:14; Isa. 30:1; Lam. 2:19)[190] and especially the act of "taking hold of [the hem of] a garment," as in Zech. 8:23.[191] This latter gesture and its converse, "letting go of the hem of a garment" or "cutting [the hem of] a garment," are well-attested in cuneiform sources. While not limited to covenant contexts, both these gestures appear with transparent significance in one of the stipulations of the treaty between Abba-AN of Yamkhad and Yarimlim of Alalakh: "If he lets go of the hem of Abba-AN's robe and takes hold of another king's robe, he [shall forfe]it his cities and territories."[192] Such a covenantal implication in Zech. 8:23 would comport with the more explicit perspective of Zech. 2:15 [ET 11], "And many nations shall join themselves to the LORD in that day [וְנִלְווּ גוֹיִם רַבִּים אֶל־יְהוָה בַּיּוֹם הַהוּא], and shall be my people [וְהָיוּ לִי לְעָם]...."[193] Compare also the ironic use of this gesture in Saul's inadvertent tearing of Samuel's garment in 1 Sam. 15:27. The unintended implication of this gesture seems to be that Saul had now expressed and sealed his rebellion against Samuel and consequently against Yahweh, whom Samuel represented. As Yarimlim of Alalakh would forfeit his kingdom as a vassal monarch should he "let go of the hem of Abba-AN's robe," so now Saul would forfeit his right to rule as Yahweh's vassal over the kingdom of Israel.[194]

3. SUMMARY

We began this chapter by acknowledging a fundamental objection raised by J. Milgrom and M. Greenberg against the identification of literal marriage as a "covenant [בְּרִית]." Milgrom and Greenberg argue that because literal marriage lacks a ratifying oath, which is considered to be indispensable for any בְּרִית, marriage cannot be identified as a "covenant [בְּרִית]." Having

---

190 Cf. P. Kalluveettil, *Declaration and Covenant,* 28.

191 Cf. R.A. Brauner, "'To Grasp the Hem' and 1 Samuel 15:27" (1974) 35-38; E.L. Greenstein, "'To Grasp the Hem' in Ugaritic Literature" (1982) 217-218; H. Tadmor, "Treaty and Oath in the Ancient Near East: An Historian's Approach" (1982) 134; M. Malul, *Studies in Mesopotamian Legal Symbolism* (1988) 422-431; and W.G. Lambert, "Devotion: The Language of Religion and Love" (1987) 36.

192 As translated in D.J. McCarthy, *Treaty and Covenant* (1981) 307.

Cf. also an Aramaic (Zenjirli) example of "grasp the hem" in Panammu 11 (J.C.L. Gibson, *Textbook of Syrian Semitic Inscriptions,* II [1975] 80-81, 84), as pointed out to the author by A. Lemaire.

193 For the theme of the eschatological ingrafting of the nations, cf., *inter alia,* Isaiah 66 and Psalm 87. For its partial realization in the post-exilic period, cf. Esth. 8:17; and 9:27.

P. Kalluveettil adds as further support the observation that Abimelech likewise was motivated to conclude his covenant with Abraham and Isaac because of his conviction that "God/Yahweh is with you" (Gen. 21:22; 26:28). Cf. also Josh. 2:9-11; 9:9-11.

194 Cf. also 1 Sam. 24:5, 6, 12 [ET 4, 5, 11].

argued in previous chapters, especially Chapter 2, that Mal. 2:14 does, in fact, identify literal marriage as a "covenant [בְּרִית]," in the present chapter we intended to respond to this important objection of Milgrom and Greenberg first by establishing the definition of the term בְּרִית in order to confirm the posited indispensability of a ratifying oath, and then by examining more carefully the characteristics of covenant-ratifying oaths.

From our lexical study it was determined that the predominant sense of בְּרִית in Biblical Hebrew is that of "an elected, as opposed to natural, relationship of obligation established under divine sanction." With the help of four "diagnostic" sentences, it was argued that there are four essential ingredients in the Old Testament understanding of בְּרִית, namely 1) a relationship 2) with a non-relative 3) which involves obligations and 4) is established through an oath. Since the first three of these ingredients were seen to be clearly present in marriage, Milgrom and Greenberg have correctly focused scholarly attention on the fourth element.

Unfortunately, however, the attempt to determine whether marriage possesses a ratifying oath has been hindered by two problems. First, there has been a tendency to seek evidence where it is unlikely to be found, as in the marriage contracts, which address various economic and other matters ancillary to the marriage itself and so should not be confused with the marriage covenant.[195] Second, there has been a tendency to reduce "oath" to verbal self-malediction. In response to this second, more serious defect, we have argued that an "oath" can be any solemn declaration or enactment (an "oath-sign") which invokes the deity to act against the one who would be false to an attendant commitment or affirmation. In particular, it was noted that oaths are often not self-maledictory and may consist simply of a solemn positive declaration (i.e., *verba solemnia*) or a solemn depiction of the commitment being undertaken (i.e., oath-signs such as sharing in a meal or the giving of a hand).[196]

Having thus established the indispensability of a ratifying oath for בְּרִית in its normal sense, in agreement with Milgrom and Greenberg, and having elucidated the character of such oaths as often positive in their solemn articulation or depiction of the covenant commitment, in the following chapter we shall complete our answer to Milgrom's and Greenberg's objection as we attempt to discover if such an oath and/or oath-sign was employed in the case of biblical marriage.

---

[195] Cf. §2.1 above.

[196] Particular attention was given to these last two oath-signs, not only because of their intrinsic importance as examples of positively oriented oath-signs, but also because of manifest similarities which exist between these well-recognized oath-signs and the oath-sign to be posited for marriage in the next chapter.

CHAPTER SEVEN

VERBA SOLEMNIA AND SEXUAL UNION: THE REQUISITE COVENANT-RATIFYING OATH AND OATH-SIGN FOR MARRIAGE

In the previous chapter it was argued that for marriage to constitute a "covenant [בְּרִית]" in its normal sense it must be accompanied by a ratifying oath and/or oath-sign. In the course of investigating the precise characteristics of such oaths and oath-signs, it was noted that while some are explicitly self-maledictory (though the self-malediction is frequently truncated), many others are only implicitly so in that they function by invoking the deity merely by a solemn declaration or depiction of the commitment being undertaken.

The present chapter will seek first to demonstrate that during the Old Testament period *verba solemnia* were typically employed as the requisite covenant-ratifying oath for marriage. Second, evidence will be offered that sexual union likewise functioned as a mandatory covenant-ratifying oath-sign for marriage. It will be recalled how ancient covenants were frequently ratified by an accumulation of oath(s) and oath-sign(s). In the present case, because of the necessarily private, though no less binding, nature of sexual union as an oath-sign, the complementary *verba solemnia* were especially appropriate as they offer essential public evidence of the solemnization of a marriage.

1. EVIDENCE FOR THE USE OF A VERBAL OATH (*VERBA SOLEMNIA*) IN MARRIAGE

Given that no Old Testament text expressly stipulates the use of declaration formulae in marriage, it is, of course, impossible to be certain that any such formulae accompanied or were expected to accompany Israelite marriages. Nevertheless, there are a number of arguments which in their cumulative weight render it highly probable that *verba solemnia* were in fact normally employed in Israelite marriage. We shall consider each of these arguments in turn, beginning with the extra-biblical comparative evidence first from ancient Near Eastern texts preceding or contemporary with the Old Testament and then from Jewish texts later than the Old Testament. Finally, we shall consider evidence within the Old Testament itself.

1.1 Ancient Near Eastern parallels

Although the cuneiform legal corpora of the Old Babylonian period nowhere stipulate the use of *verba solemnia* for marriage in the OB period, nevertheless in his classic essay, "The Old Babylonian Marriage Contract," S. Greengus argued that *verba solemnia* were so employed.[1] Greengus based his argument mainly on the following: 1) a document recording a litigation, 2) scattered references in various OB literary sources, 3) the implication of the better attested corresponding divorce formulae, 4) evidence from later periods (especially MAL A §41), and finally 5) an OB magical text.[2] Given the wide scholarly acceptance of Greengus' view on this matter, it would be enough just to cite his classic defence were it not for the fact that recently it has received a detailed critique by R. Westbrook in his comprehensive study of Old Babylonian marriage law.[3] As a result, it is necessary to reevaluate Greengus' evidence in the light of Westbrook's criticisms.

1.1.1 An Old Babylonian legal document from Ishchali

One OB legal document from Ishchali includes the positive formula, "You are my husband [*muti atta*]."[4] With Greengus, however, it is clear that this text does not record the actual *verba solemnia* of a marriage. This is the case because the text refers to the results of a litigation which stipulated the dissolution of a marriage, or perhaps an engagement, between Abu-ṭabum and Sin-nada, that is, a *kallūtum*-relationship (so Westbrook). The result of the court's decision is that a fine is imposed on Sin-nada (which was paid to the father, or perhaps owner, of Abu-ṭabum) and "the hem of Sin-nada is cut [*sí-sí-iq-ti ᵖᵈEN.ZU-na-da ba-at-qá-at*]."[5] Further, it is stipulated that Abu-ṭabum cannot "raise claims against Sin-nada in respect to her being a wife.

---

[1] S. Greengus, "The Old Babylonian Marriage Contract" (1969) 514ff.

For earlier scholars holding a similar view, cf., *inter alia*, G.R. Driver and J.C. Miles, *The Babylonian Laws*, I (1952) 402, n. 2; and A.J. Skaist, "Studies in Ancient Mesopotamian Family Law Pertaining to Marriage and Divorce" (1963) 124.

[2] For convenience, the order of this evidence differs slightly from that found in Greengus. To these Mesopotamian examples could be added further evidence from Egypt. In Egyptian marriage contracts there is ample documentation for the use of the following marriage declaration formulae (*Eheschliessungsklausel*): "The woman has said to the man: 'You have made me your wife.' The man has said to the woman, 'I have made you my wife.'" Cf. P.W. Pestman, *Marriage and Matrimonial Property in Ancient Egypt* (1961) diagram A par. 12-15; diagram B par 11-12.

[3] R. Westbrook, "Old Babylonian Marriage Law" (1982) 120-125.

[4] S. Greengus, *Old Babylonian Tablets from Ishchali and Vicinity* (1979) 25. S. Greengus refers to this text as A 7757 prior to its publication ("The Old Babylonian Marriage Contract," 517, n. 57).

Cf. the more recent edition of this text in R. Westbrook, "Old Babylonian Marriage Law," I, 193-195, with relevant discussion in II, 121f.

[5] Or "the hem of Sin-nada has been cut." For such a rendering of the I/1 Stative *batqat*, cf. J. Huehnergard, *An Introduction to Old Babylonian Akkadian*, §18.2.

For a recent study of this well-attested symbolic act employed in Old Babylonian and Nuzi documents to effect a divorce, cf. M. Malul, *Studies in Mesopotamian Legal Symbolism*, 197-208. Cf. also the discussion of other examples of this action used outside the context of divorce in *ibid.*, 153-159, 196-198. Cf. also S. Greengus, "The Old Babylonian Marriage Contract," 515, n. 44.

Sin-nada shall not say to Abu-ṭabum, 'you are my husband [*muti atta*]'" (lns. 19-24).

If "you are my husband" were understood as referring to the *verba solemnia* of marriage, this text would prevent Sin-nada from marrying Abu-ṭabum against his will and in spite of the dissolution of their previous relationship.[6] Any such concern seems doubtful. Accordingly, the prohibited declaration, "you are my husband," must be understood as some kind of formal legal claim on the part of the woman that her marriage (or perhaps her inchoate marriage) still exists. Nevertheless, Greengus suggests that the wife's prohibited words "could be patterned after the marriage formulas: *lū mutī attā* or *attā lū mutīma*."[7]

Objecting to Greengus' suggestion, R. Westbrook notes that the present formula bears an "entirely different" function from that required for the *verba solemnia* of marriage and therefore denies any necessary resemblance between this declaration and that which is posited for marriage.[8] In response to Westbrook, however, perhaps an *"entirely* [italics added] different" function overstates the case. The primary legal function of the posited *verba solemnia* is, to be sure, the *formation* of a marriage. Nevertheless, a declaration such as "you are my husband," which formally asserts the *existence* of a relationship, is not so far from the solemn acknowledgement of a relationship, that is, a *"Bundesformel,"* which carries with it implications of consent and commitment. With Westbrook, however, it appears likely that the hypothesized formulae, *lū mutī attā* or *attā lū mutīma,* "surely you are my husband,"[9] fail to take sufficient account of the differing contexts of these legal declarations. If, however, the posited reflex for the wife's formal claim, "you are my husband," is the husband's prior *verba solemnia,* "I am your husband[10] [*lū anāku mutka*]," then Westbrook's objection is answered.

1.1.2 Old Babylonian literary texts

Other texts cited by Greengus for the OB period include a few lines of the Assyrian version of the Gilgameš Epic, where Ištar proposes to Gilgameš, "Come Gilgameš, be thou my (var. *an)* espouser (var. *groom);* give me thy charms for a gift; be thou my husband, I will be thy wife" (vi 7-9), and a similar text in the myth of Nergal and Ereshkigal, where the queen of the underworld proposes to Nergal, "You be my husband, I will be thy wife.... Be thou master, I will be mistress" (*EA* 375, lns. 82-85).[11] As R. Westbrook notes, however, since each of these texts records a *proposal* for marriage,

---

[6] So R. Westbrook, "Old Babylonian Marriage Law," II, 121f.
[7] "The Old Babylonian Marriage Contract," 517, n. 57.
[8] "Old Babylonian Marriage Law," II, 181, n. 8.
[9] Or "may you be my husband."
[10] Or "may I be your husband." In this case, greater semantic congruence is to be preferred over the greater lexical similarity afforded by Greengus' proposal.
[11] "The Old Babylonian Marriage Contract," 516f. (cf. especially n. 55 and n. 56 for additional examples). (*EA* 375 is not included in *AL.*)

rather than discourse from the marriage itself, their value as evidence for the posited *verba solemnia* of marriage is greatly diminished.[12]

1.1.3   Declaration formulae in marriage may be inferred from the widely attested use of corresponding divorce formulae
An additional evidence favouring of the assumption of the use of *verba solemnia* in the formation of marriage is noted by S. Greengus in the well-attested counterpart *verba solemnia* of divorce or the disavowal of marriage: "you are not my wife"[13] and "you are not my husband,"[14] attested in the OB period; and "she / ᶠPN is not my wife,"[15] "he is not my husband,"[16] and "I will not be your wife,"[17] attested for later periods. If such solemn declarations were required to dissolve marriage, it seems a reasonable inference that corresponding positive statements may have been used for the formation of marriage.

This inference of a close reciprocal relationship between formulae for marriage and divorce is further strengthened by the analogous counterpart formulae for adoption, or the legitimating of children, and the repudiation of the adoptive relationship, or disinherison. As in the case of marriage, the positive formulae are poorly attested, though still probable.[18] Compare, for

---

[12] "Old Babylonian Marriage Law," II, 122.

[13] Cf. *ana ittišu* A §6, "If a husband says to his wife, 'You are not my wife' [*ul aššati atta*], he shall pay 1/2 mina of silver by weight" (G.R. Driver and J.C. Miles, *The Babylonian Laws*, II, 310f.).
As just one example, cf. the use of this formula in the OB marriage document *CT* 48:50, "You are not my wife [*ul aššati attī*]." For other examples, cf., e.g., M. Schorr, *Urkunden des Altbabylonischen Zivil- und Prozessrechts* (1913) p. 7, no. 2; and *passim*; A.T. Clay, *Babylonian Records in the Library of J. Pierpont Morgan*, Part IV (1923) 50-52, text 52; R. Harris, "The Case of Three Babylonian Marriage Contracts" (1974) 363-365; and R. Westbrook, "Old Babylonian Marriage Law," II, 192f. For Sumerian parallels, cf. A. Poebel, *Babylonian Legal and Business Documents* (1909) 35-38.

[14] Cf. *ana ittišu* A §5, "If a wife has hated her husband and says, 'You are not my husband' [*ul muti atta*], they shall throw her into the river" (G.R. Driver and J.C. Miles, *The Babylonian Laws*, II, 310f.). For example, cf. the use of this formula in the OB marriage document *CT* 48:50, "You are not my husband [*ul mutī attā*]." For other examples, cf. the sources cited in the previous note.

[15] Cf. document No. 5 in M.T. Roth, *Babylonian Marriage Agreements: 7th - 3rd Centuries B.C.*, 44-47, discussed below. Roth considers the use of the third person divorce formula, "W is not my wife," to be "the most obvious difference between the OB formulation and that found in No. 5" (*op. cit.*, 13).
Similarly, Kraeling 7 (= Porten-Yardeni, B3.8) lines 21-22, "Tomorrow or (the) next day, should Ananiah stand up in an assembly and say: 'I hated my wife Jehoishma; she shall not be my wife [לא חוה לי אנתתן]," ...."

[16] Cf. also S. Greengus, "A Textbook case of Adultery in Ancient Mesopotamia" (1969-70) 40ff.; and *idem*, "The Old Babylonian Marriage Contract" (1969) 516ff. Cf. the MB marriage contract from Ḥana in A.T. Clay, *Babylonian Records in the Library of J. Pierpont Morgan*, Part IV (1923) 4, no. 52, 50-52; and a MA marriage document, *TIM* IV, 45.

[17] Kraeling 7 (= Porten-Yardeni, B3.8) lines 24-25, "And if Jehoishm[a] hate [*sic*] her husband Ananiah and say to him: 'I hated you; I will not be your wife [לא אהוה לך אנתתן]' ...."

[18] Cf. also Ps. 2:7, a text which is generally thought to include *verba solemnia* for adoption: "I will tell of the decree of Yahweh: He said to me, 'You are my son, today I have

example, the declaration formula, "my children [*mārū'a*]!," mentioned in CH §§170-171, by which a man legitimates his natural children born by a slave. The corresponding repudiation formulae, however, appear frequently.[19] Compare, for example, "you are not my father [*ul abi atta*]" and "you are not my mother [*ul ummi atti*]," found in CH §192.[20] See also the declaration, "you are not my son [*ul māri atta*]," mentioned in tablets of adoption cited by G.R. Driver and J.C. Miles.[21] Compare further the disinherison formulae used with natural children: "you are not our son" and "[PN] is not my son."[22]

Finally, it should be observed that the rarity of positive *verba solemnia*, whether for marriage or for adoption, relative to the frequency of their negative counterparts, is only to be expected considering the nature of the extant sources. The majority of marriage documents were drafted upon completion of the marriage and often, as noted in the previous chapter, even after the birth of children. Their interest is typically with economic and other issues ancillary to the marriage itself. As a result, they reveal little about any words, *verba solemnia* or otherwise, or any other ceremony, for that matter, which may have been formative of the marriage, though some such words or rite or both are likely to have existed.

In the same manner, the silence of the legal corpora concerning the hypothesized *verba solemnia* for marriage is quite expected. As also argued

---

begotten you.'" Cf. also the corresponding acknowledgement by David in Ps. 89:27 [ET 26], "You are my Father."

Cf. H.-J. Boecker, "Anmerkungen zur Adoption im AT" (1974) 86-89; S.M. Paul, "Adoption Formulae" (1978) 31-36; *idem*, "Adoption Formulae: A Study of Cuneiform and Biblical Legal Clauses" (1979-1980) 173-85; H.J. Hendriks, "Juridical Aspects of the Marriage Metaphor in Hosea and Jeremiah," 61; and M. Malul, "Adoption of Foundlings in the Bible and Mesopotamian Documents" (1990) 99, 111f.

Rejecting this interpretation is H. Donner, "Adoption oder Legitimation?" (1969) 87-119. Against Donner, however, cf. H.J. Hendriks, "Juridical Aspects of the Marriage Metaphor in Hosea and Jeremiah," 61f.

[19] Cf. the many examples cited by Greengus, "The Old Babylonian Marriage Contract," 518, n. 60.

[20] Cf. also *ana ittišu* A §1, which appears to refer to a natural son, "If a son says to his father, 'You are not my father,' [*ul abi atta*] he may/will shave him, he may/will put a slave-mark on him [and] sell him" (G.R. Driver and J.C. Miles, *The Babylonian Laws*, II, 308f.). Cf. also *ana ittišu* A §2 and SL §4 (in *ANET*, 526).

ARN 36, ln. 3 and *BE* 6/1 59 offer important evidence that these examples of *verba solemnia* were actually recited in a public (court-room) setting. Cf. S. Greengus, "The Old Babylonian Marriage Contract," 518.

[21] *The Babylonian Laws*, I, 402f.

Cf. *ana ittišu* A §3, which appears to refer to a natural son, "If a father says to his son, 'You are not my son [*ul māri atta*],' he forfeits house and wall" (G.R. Driver and J.C. Miles, *The Babylonian Laws*, II, 308f.). Cf. also, *ana ittišu* A §4, "If a mother says to her son, 'You are not my son,' she forfeits house and furniture" (G.R. Driver and J.C. Miles, *The Babylonian Laws*, II, 310f.).

Cf. also SL §§5-6, which has the father and mother saying, "You are not our son" (*ANET*, 526).

[22] Cf. *BE* 6/2, p. 31, text 57; and HSS 19, 27, discussed by M. Malul, *Studies in Mesopotamian Legal Symbolism*, 85. Underscoring the possible primacy of symbolic actions over declaration formulae, the document goes on to specify that "from [this] day I have broken his clod [...PN] is no more my s[on!]" Cf. also *ibid.*, 88.

in the previous chapter, the legal corpora are typically concerned with the exceptional and the difficult, such as issues surrounding adultery, desertion, the dissolution of marriage, or inheritance under special circumstances, etc., not with what was normal or could be assumed, such as would be the case with *verba solemnia*, if these were employed in the manner argued by Greengus.

Although R. Westbrook argues for a profound similarity between marriage and adoption, he questions whether Greengus' critical example of the positive use of *verba solemnia* recorded in CH §§170-171 is applicable beyond the very limited circumstances envisaged in this law.[23] If Westbrook is correct that *verba solemnia* may not have been employed in adoption more generally, then the assumed reciprocal relationship between "my children!" and the repudiation formulae, "you are not my son," etc., evaporates. Westbrook agrees that CH §§170-171 demonstrates that *verba solemnia* could be constitutive of a legal relationship in OB law and, therefore, that it is possible that they were used in the formation of marriage as. well. Nevertheless, Westbrook insists that a stricter analogy with CH §§170-171 at most allows the inference that *verba solemnia* may have been employed only when a woman who was already *de facto* wife, i.e. a concubine, was elevated to the legal status of "wife."[24]

In response to Westbrook, however, it is doubtful that the use of the *verba solemnia*, "my children," found in CH §§170-171, was as restricted as he suggests. Indeed, if these *verba solemnia* were not more generally employed to effect adoptions elsewhere, one would be left to wonder about their origin within this law. Why use *verba solemnia* at all, rather than some other rite invented solely for the purpose? Without the assumption of the more normal usage, would contemporaries have understood a father's intention under these particular circumstances?

It should be recalled that the purpose of CH §§170-171 is not to introduce a novel procedure for legitimation, but merely to establish the rights of inheritance by the legitimated sons born to a concubine (or to deny the same if the natural sons by the concubine were not so legitimated). Further, as noted by M. David and G.R. Driver and J.C. Miles, this more general use of *verba solemnia* appears to be implied by a legal text in which a mother surrenders her son for adoption saying, "Take the lad away; surely (he is) thy son [*tabli ṣuḥāram lû mâruki*]."[25]

---

[23] R. Westbrook, "Old Babylonian Marriage Law," II, 123f.

In the "Abstract" for his dissertation, R. Westbrook writes, "The central thesis of the dissertation is that marriage is a legal status and must be distinguished from the marriage contract which is incidental thereto. Marriage should therefore be compared to other forms of status such as adoption rather than to forms of contract" ("Old Babylonian Marriage Law"). Cf. also R. Westbrook, *op. cit.*, II, 56f., 149-152.

[24] Of course, this is precisely the case envisaged in MAL A §41.

[25] M. Schorr, *Urkunden des altbabylonischen Zivil- und Prozessrechts* Vorderasiatische Bibliothek, 5, 78:10-11. Similar is *VAT* 8946:6-7, "PN$_1$ is her father and PN$_2$ is his daughter." Cf. P. Kalluveettil, *Declaration and Covenant*, 109.

Finally, M.T. Roth discusses a very impressive example, found in a Neo-Babylonian marriage document (No. 5), of the reciprocal relationship between the *verba solemnia* of marriage and divorce.[26] In lns. 9-10 the positive declaration is made: "ᶠBazītu is the wife of Qul-dibbīja-ile'i-Nusku [*ᶠba-zī-tum al-ti ᴵqul-dib-bi-ia-DA-ᵈNusku ši-i*]." Subsequently, a third person declaration of divorce, "she is not my wife," appears in lns. 12-16: "Should Qul-dibbīja-ile'i-Nusku declare: 'ᶠBazītu is not a wife [*ᶠba-zī-tum ul áš-ša-tum ši-i*],' Sîn-aḫḫē-iddin will give to ᶠBazītu six minas of silver as her divorce settlement, and send her back to her (father's) house." Roth observes, "The renunciation of marriage in No. 5 [*W ul aššatu šî*] is a direct negation of the statement made earlier in the document in connection with the formation of the marriage: *W alti H šî*, W is the wife of H.'"[27]

1.1.4 Middle Assyrian *verba solemnia*

Certainly the clearest evidence for the mandatory use of marriage-forming *verba solemnia* in Mesopotamia is found in MAL A §41. This law concerns itself with a man who has a captive wife, an *esirtu*.[28] If such a man wishes to confer on his *esirtu* the higher status of a "wife [*aššat a'īli*]" or "veiled wife [*aššatu paṣṣuntu*]," thereby conferring full rights of inheritance on any children of their union, he must "assemble five or six of his neighbours and he shall veil her [cf. MAL A §40] in their presence and say, 'she is my wife.' Then she will be his wife [*ḫamšat šeššat tappā'ēšu ušeššab ana pânīšunu upaṣṣanši ma aššiti šît iqabbi aššassu šît*]."[29] The specification of witnesses helps underscore the solemn and binding character of this pronouncement.

According to Greengus, several Neo-Babylonian sources exhibit similar formulae, such as Strassmaier *Liverpool* 8:6, "may she be my wife [*lu-ú aš-šá-ti ši-i*]," and VS 6 6:3f., "may she be my wife [*lu-ú DAM-a ši-i*]."[30] The apparent one-sidedness of these declaration formulae may be

---

Accordingly, M. David has argued in favour of the assumption of the use of *verba solemnia* for adoption under normal circumstances (*Die Adoption im altbabylonischen Recht* [1927] 79-81). Cf. G.R. Driver and J.C. Miles, *Babylonian Laws*, I, 401f.

[26] *Babylonian Marriage Agreements: 7th-3rd Centuries B.C.*, 13, 44-47.

[27] *Ibid.*, 13.

[28] Although "concubine" is commonly offered for *esirtu* (*CAD*, E, 336), because of the inappropriate connotations of the English term "concubine," perhaps the rendering "slave-wife" or "captive-wife" would be more felicitous.

[29] Cf. G.R. Driver and J.C. Miles, *The Assyrian Laws*, 186-189.

P. Kalluveettil notes that in most cases the superior party utters the "Bundesformel" (*Declaration and Covenant*, 213). It is possible, however, that the androcentricity of this law is exceptional or merely conventional and that in actual practice brides also pronounced corresponding *verba solemnia*. After noting the declaration formula of the bride Ereskigal in *EA* 357:84f. (not included in *AL*), "Be thou master, I will be mistress," S. Greengus concludes, "We see therefore that the patriarchal character of Babylonian family structure, even with possible legal subordination of its women, need not preclude brides from participating in the formation of the marriage contract via recitation of *verba solemnia*" ("The Old Babylonian Marriage Contract," 521).

[30] "The Old Babylonian Marriage Contract," 516, n. 48.

merely conventional. S. Greengus notes, for example, the remarkable mutuality exhibited in *TIM* IV 45:1-9:[31]

> *PN ū ᶠPN ina migratîšunu mutūtu ū aššutūta idbubū PN mussa ū ᶠPN aššassu ina eqli ū libbi ā[lim] palāḫa aḫu a[ḫa] ippušū*
> "PN and ᶠPN of their own accord agreed to marriage; PN is her husband; ᶠPN is his wife. They shall show respect to one another at· home and abroad."

R. Westbrook argues, however, that the formation of marriage by *verba solemnia* attested in MAL A §41 cannot be extended beyond the very narrow circumstance envisaged in this law, namely the elevation to the status of "wife" of an *esirtu* who is already *de facto* wife.[32] Westbrook argues that since the woman in question was already living in her husband's house, neither *in domum deductio* nor *copula carnalis* could serve the desired purpose of granting her the full legal status of "wife." Accordingly, "the pronouncement of *verba solemnia* before witnesses would certainly be among the most appropriate modes."[33] Thus rejecting a broader application for MAL A §41, R. Westbrook summarizes his critique: "Accordingly, while we must reject for lack of evidence Greengus' theory of *verba solemnia* for the formation of marriage in general, it seems to us an acceptable hypothesis in the very narrow case of the subsequent marriage of one's own concubine."[34]

Like the use of *verba solemnia* in adoption, however, it appears doubtful that MAL A §41 intends to introduce an entirely novel mode for the formation of marriage. On the contrary, the fact that this law specifies the procedure for elevating an *esirtu*-wife, rather than for taking a wife under more normal circumstances, in many respects only increases its value as evidence for the general use of the declaration formula, "she is my wife [*aššiti šīt*]." Had the law treated marriage under entirely unremarkable circumstances, the stipulation of a declaration formula would raise the question whether it represented a (perhaps unsuccessful) legal innovation.[35]

1.1.5 Old Babylonian magical texts

Of the OB texts the first and clearest example cited by S. Greengus is "the *eṭlu* tablet," a much discussed bilingual magical text, originally published by T.G. Pinches, but re-edited by S. Lackenbacher.[36] In this text betrothal is

---

[31] *Ibid.*, 521, n. 75. The normalization is from Greengus.

[32] *Old Babylonian Marriage Law*, II, 125.

[33] Based on an analogy drawn from CH §170, Westbrook is prepared to allow the provision of MAL A §41 to apply to the OB period.

[34] *Old Babylonian Marriage Law*, II, 125.

[35] As we discussed in Chapter 5, §2.1 above, cuneiform law is predominantly concerned with the unusual and difficult, not with what could be assumed.
The special circumstances of this law may help to account for the absence of any specification of a marriage contract (cf. MAL A §§34, 36) or marriage present, etc.

[36] T.G. Pinches, "Notes" (1892-93); S. Lackenbacher, "Note sur l'*ardat-lilî*" (1971) 124ff.

used as a metaphor for demon possession, which metaphor is well-attested elsewhere.[37] In the course of the "marriage" the following apparent *verba solemnia* are spoken by the demon to the young man [the *eṭlu*], who assumes the role of bride-victim:[38]

11. dumu-nun-na gá-e-me-en ba-ni-in-du$_{11}$ // *ma-ri ru-bi-e a-na-ku iq-bi-iš*

12. guškin kù-babbar úr-zu ba-ni-in-si // *KÙ.BABBAR GUŠKIN su-un-ka ú-ma-lu*

13. dam-mu ḫé-me-en // *at-ta*[39] *lu-ú aš-ša-tú*

14. gá-e dam-zu ḫé-a // *ana-ku lu-ú mu-ut-ka*

15. mu-un-na-ab-bé // *iq-bi-ši*

"'I am of princely descent' he said to her; 'thy lap I will fill with silver and gold; you be my (!) wife, I will be thy husband' - he said to her."[40]

Supporting this interpretation of the text, the reverse of the *eṭlu* tablet, col. I, lns. 1ff., refers to a ritual for delivering the *eṭlu* from his demonic possession and so curing him of a demonically induced illness. The text prescribes a symbolic "marriage" between a piglet and a sickness-figurine in which the god Šamaš acts as witness.[41] Deliverance from the demon is accomplished, apparently, by tricking the demon to leave its victim in order to marry the figurine instead. Although *verba solemnia* are not explicitly mentioned in this second marriage, their presence may be inferred from the intended parallel between this "marriage" and the earlier one, a parallel which is reinforced by the shared mention of the well-attested marriage rite of tying

---

For the history of interpretation of this text, cf. S. Greengus, "The Old Babylonian Marriage Contract," 516, n. 53. For a more recent discussion, cf. M. Malul, *Studies in Mesopotamian Legal Symbolism*, 127, 171f., 173, n. 55 and 182ff.

[37] Cf. *CAD* Ḫ, s.v. *ḫâru*. Cf. also S. Greengus, "The Old Babylonian Marriage Contract," 516.

[38] Lackenbacher (*RA* 65, 126) Text No. 1, col II, lns. 11-15.

[39] S. Greengus is troubled by the unexpected masculine *attā* in place of the feminine *attī* and similarly the masculine *-ka* in place of the expected feminine *-ki* ("The Old Babylonian Marriage Contract," 516, n. 51). He suggests that this may reflect Aramaic influence where the final vowels of some forms became indistinguishable. Cf. *GAG*, §13 b-c.
This difficulty disappears if, with M. Malul, the *eṭlu* is the victim who is espoused by the unnamed demon (*Studies in Mesopotamian Legal Symbolism*, 171f., n. 49). This interpretation seems preferable to Lackenbacher's view that the *eṭlu* has been transformed into a demon on an analogy with the *ardat lilî* described in text no. 2 (the *ardat lilî* tablet). This is so especially since, as Malul notes, the reverse of the *eṭlu* tablet, col. II, lns 18-20, refers to the *eṭlu* as the one to be cured and delivered.

[40] As rendered by S. Greengus, "The Old Babylonian Marriage Contract," 516. M. Malul prefers, "I am filling" for the II/1 durative, *ú-ma-lu* (*Studies in Mesopotamian Legal Symbolism*, 183).

[41] Cf. W.G. Kunstmann, *Die babylonische Gebetsbeschwörung*, Leipziger semitische Studien, NF 2, 106, n. 9, as cited by M. Malul, *Studies in Mesopotamian Legal Symbolism*, 173, n. 55.

a purse of gold and silver into the hem of the bride.[42] The fact that the god Šamaš acts as witness to this procedure, and hence to its accompanying solemn declarations, supports the interpretation of the recitation of such words as *verba solemnia*.

A second bilingual magical text, the *ardat lilî* tablet, unavailable to Greengus, appears to offer a close parallel to the *eṭlu* tablet including the mention of the indicated *verba solemnia*. As reconstructed by Lackenbacher, the text of rev. col. II, lns 1-6 reads:

1. [	// *lu-u mu-ut-ka a]na-ku*
2. [	// *lu-u áš-šatu a]t-ta-mi*
3. [	// *an-nu-ú? q]î?-bi-šu*
4. [	// *xx(x) KÙ.B]ABBAR ù GUŠKIN*
5. [	// *i-na qa-]an-ni-ša*
6. [	// *ir-t]a-kas*

"I [be your husband, be y]ou [(my) wife, these are] his [wo]rds(?), ... [si]lver and gold [he t]ied [in] her [h]em."[43]

In his critique of Greengus, Westbrook unaccountably overlooks these magical texts, which comprise perhaps the most compelling evidence in support of Greengus' theory for the use of *verba solemnia* in the OB period.[44]

1.2 Extrabiblical evidence for the use of verba solemnia *among Israelites and Jews*

1.2.1 Elephantine[45]

The marriage formula, "she is my wife and I am her husband from this day and forever [הי אנתתי ואנה בעלה מן יומא זנה עד עלם]," appears with virtually the same wording in four marriage documents from Elephantine: Cowley

---

[42] For this practice, cf. M. Malul, *Studies in Mesopotamian Legal Symbolism*, 171f.; 173, n. 55; 183ff.

[43] Text no. 2 in S. Lackenbacher, "Note sur l'*ardat-lilî*," 138 (cf. 142f., n. 20). Cf. M. Malul, *Studies in Mesopotamian Legal Symbolism*, 183, and 184, n. 98.

[44] The *eṭlu* tablet was also the key example used by G.R. Driver and J.C. Miles, before Greengus, for their argument in favour of the supposition of *verba solemnia* in marriage (*Babylonian Laws*, I, 402).

It should be noted with M. David and others that the magical nature of this text in no way diminishes its value as evidence for the normal marriage rite. Indeed, it is precisely in such an unusual context that one is prepared to find a more complete account of the normal marital practice, including details which would be abbreviated or omitted in other less remarkable texts because they were so widely assumed. Cf. M. David, *Die Adoption im altbabylonischen Recht* (1927) 80, n. 46. Cf. also S. Greengus, "The Old Babylonian Marriage Contract," 516, n. 53; and M. Malul, *Studies in Mesopotamian Legal Symbolism*, 127, 171f., 173, n. 55 and 182ff.

[45] Cf. B. Porten, *Archives from Elephantine* (1968) 206, esp.n. 23; J.A. Fitzmyer, "A Re-Study of an Elephantine Aramaic Marriage Contract (AP 15)" (1971) 137-68; M.J. Geller, "The Elephantine Papyri and Hosea 2, 3: Evidence for the Form of the Early Jewish Divorce Writ" (1977) 139-148; and, for further bibliography, Porten-Yardeni, 30, 60, 82, 132.

15:4;[46] Kraeling 2:3f.;[47] 7:4;[48] and 14:3f.[49]   As noted by R. Yaron, nothing similar occurs in Egyptian marriage contracts, an observation which increases the value of this evidence as indicative of an indigenous Hebrew practice.[50] In each case this formula appears at the conclusion of a brief introductory narrative in which the husband reviews, in a stereotypical manner, how he secured consent for the marriage from his wife's guardian (father, mother, brother, or master), the other party in the marriage contract with the husband. For example, Cowley 15:1-4 reads: "On the 26th [of] Tishri ... Eshor ... said to Mah[seiah ...]..., 'I [c]ame to your house (and asked you) to give me your daughter Mipta(h)iah for wifehood. She is my wife and I am her husband from this day and forever.'"[51]

With respect to the double form of the marriage formula, R. Yaron considers that "she is my wife" is the principal affirmation because, according to Yaron, the documents mainly stress wifehood.[52] Compare, for example, "I [c]ame to your house (and asked you) to give me your daughter Mipta(h)iah for *wifehood* ";[53] "I hated my wife Jehoishma; she shall not be my *wife*";[54] "I hated you; I will not be your *wife*."[55] Yaron acknowledges that the addition "'and I am her husband' does indicate an element of mutuality, but exactly what legal consequences are attached to it is doubtful."[56] Here, however, it may be that Yaron is being overly cautious. The contracts elsewhere do not hesitate to threaten the husband with penalties or to impose on him various restrictions, such as the prohibition against acknowledging any other wife or

---

[46] = Porten-Yardeni, B2.6, 4: ... הי אנתתי ואנה בעלה מן יומא זנה ועד עלם.

[47] = Porten-Yardeni, B3.3, 3f.: ... הי אנתתי ואנה בעלה מן יומא זנה ועד עלם.

[48] = Porten-Yardeni, B3.8, 4: ... הי אנתתי ואנה בעל[ה] מן יומא זנה עד עלם.

[49] = Porten-Yardeni, B6.1, 3f.: [... הי אנתתי] ואנה בעלה מן יומא זנה עד על[ם].

Fragments from three more marriage documents exist, Cowley 36 (= Porten-Yardeni, B6.2), Cowley 46 (= Porten-Yardeni, B6.3), and Cowley 18 (= Porten-Yardeni, B6.4), but they do not include the introductory section in which the marriage formula would be expected.

[50] "Aramaic Marriage Contracts from Elephantine," 30. In support of the Israelite origin the legal procedures of the Elephantine texts, particulary in matters of family law, cf. J.C. Greenfield, "Aramaic Studies and the Bible" (1981) 121.

This is not to imply, however, that Egyptian marriage contracts were altogether lacking in a documentary formula for marriage. E.M. Yamauchi observes that Egyptian contracts typically began with the phrase, "I have made you my wife" ("Cultural Aspects of Marriage in the Ancient World," 245).

[51] = Porten-Yardeni, B2.6:1-4. As indicated by the use of ellipses, the translation is abbreviated here for greater clarity.

[52] *Introduction to the Law of the Aramaic Papyri*, 47.

[53] Cowley 15:3 (= Porten-Yardeni, B2.6:3).

[54] Kraeling 7:21f. (= Porten-Yardeni, B3.8:21f.).

Here and eslewhere a present tense "hate" for the stative perfect שניה may be preferable to the past tense "hated" offered by Porten and Yardeni. Alternatively, these may be instances of the present perfect usage for certain first person perfect verbs in Aramaic documents (= "I hereby hate"), as also in Biblical Hebrew and other Semitic languages, discussed by Y. Muffs, *Studies in the Aramaic Legal Documents from Elephantine*, 2nd ed. (1973) 32, n. 2. Cf. also M.A. Friedman, "The Minimum *Mohar* Payment as Reflected in the Geniza Documents: Marriage Gift or Endowment Pledge?" (1976) 42, n. 56.

[55] Kraeling 7:25 (= Porten-Yardeni, B3.8:25).

[56] *Introduction to the Law of the Aramaic Papyri*, 47.

heir or the prohibition against removing property from a wife, each with specified penalties for its contravention.[57]

Furthermore, although the contracting parties in each of these documents are the husband and his wife's guardian, rather than the husband and his wife, there are so many indications of mutuality that there is little reason to doubt that similar "legal consequences" as attached to "she is my wife" did, in fact, attach to "I am her husband." It is notable, for example, that the contracts stipulate a similar right for both husband and wife to inherit the estate of a spouse who dies without issue. Even more striking, the contracts recognize that the wife enjoys a right to initiate divorce like that of her husband — and both face considerable financial penalties if they exercise this right unjustifiably or merely because of "hatred."[58]

Furthermore, two contracts, Kraeling 7 and Cowley 18, prohibit both the wife and the husband from palingamy by using much the same language.[59] See, for example, Kraeling 7:33f., 36f.: "But Jeho[ishma] does not have the right [to] acquire another husband be[sides] Anani. And if she do thus, it is hatred; they shall do to her [the law of ha]tred;"[60] "Moreover, [Ananiah shall] n[ot be able to] take anoth[er] woman [besides Jehoishma] for himself for wifehood. If he do [thus, it is hatred. H]e [shall do] to her [the la]w of [ha]tred."[61] Although the precise interpretation of this

---

[57] Cf., e.g., Cowley 15:32ff. (= Porten-Yardeni, B2.6:32ff.) and Cowley 15:35f. (= Porten-Yardeni, B2.6:35f.).

[58] Cf. Chapter 3, §4.2.2, where it was argued with R. Westbrook, against R. Yaron, that while שנא, "hatred," is often associated with divorce, it is not to be equated with it. Rather, this term implies an unjustified divorce, that is, a divorce based merely on aversion. Cf. also M.A. Friedman, *Jewish Marriage in Palestine*, I, 314f., n. 10.

R. Yaron considers that the recognition of a wife's capacity to initiate divorce is in contrast to the practice of the entire ancient East, as well as Talmudic law, and must, therefore, derive from Egyptian influence (*Introduction to the Law of the Aramaic Papyri*, 53).

Favouring Semitic rather than Egyptian influence for the right of the wife to initiate divorce, cf. A.J. Skaist, "Studies in Ancient Mesopotamian Family Law Pertaining to Marriage and Divorce," 154-160; and E. Lipiński, "The Wife's Right to Divorce in the light of an Ancient Near Eastern Tradition" (1981) 22f. Cf. also R. Westbrook, "Old Babylonian Marriage Law," II, 223-238, who rejects Driver and Miles' view that the wife had no right at all to initiate divorce in OB law, as well as the earlier view of A. van Praag, that the wife's rights were nearly identical to that of her husband. Cf. further I. Mendelsohn, "On Marriage in Alalakh" (1959) 352-353.

Note that *Mur* 20 (DJD II, 109ff.) recognizes the wife's right to divorce in the 2nd century A.D., a view that was continued in the Palestinian tradition of Judaism represented in the Cairo Geniza. Cf. M.A. Friedman, *Jewish Marriage in Palestine*, I, 312-346. Based on this evidence, B. Porten considers it hazardous to assume that women did not have the right to divorce in the OT (*Archives from Elephantine* [1968] 261f.). Cf. also J.C. Greenfield, "Aramaic Studies and the Bible" (1981) 123-124.

[59] Kraeling 7 = Porten-Yardeni, B3.8; Cowley 18 = Porten-Yardeni, B6.4. Because the beginning of Cowley 18 is missing, only the prohibition against the husband taking another wife is preserved.

[60] Kraeling 7:33f. (= Porten-Yardeni, B3.8:33f.). This rendering, taken from Porten-Yardeni, 82, is somewhat lacking in the felicity of its English (e.g., "do," rather than "does"; "thus" rather than "so"; "the law of hatred" rather than "according to 'the law of hatred'").

[61] Kraeling 7:36f. (= Porten-Yardeni, B3.8:36f.).

prohibition has been disputed (whether it prohibits palingamy or, less likely, polygamy or adultery), a degree of mutuality appears self-evident and is supported by the heretofore undetected parallel literary structure of the protective clauses (lines 21b-40a) as a whole.[62]

Offering a refinement of the traditional interpretation of the marriage formula at Elephantine, M.A. Friedman argues that "she is my wife and I am her husband from this day and forever" is perhaps better identified as a documentary formula, rather than as an exact reproduction of the *verba solemnia* of marriage.[63] In introducing this distinction, Friedman is concerned to argue that the original oral formulae would have been mutual, perhaps with the husband declaring, "you are my wife," and the wife responding, "you are my husband." In any case, Friedman insists that the *verba solemnia* were accurately summarized in the documentary formula.[64]

Alternatively, as appears from Porten-Yardeni, Fold-out No. 19, ln 37b may be restored as יע[ב]דין [ל]הן די[ן]][ש]נ[אה, which yields, "The]y [shall d]o to him [the la]w of [ha]tred." The implication of this restored text is that a husband must relinquish the wealth of his first wife (presumably to her family) if he married another woman following the death of his first wife who died without issue. This consequence resembles the case where a man divorces his wife merely on the ground of aversion.

[62] Favouring a reference to palingamy is E. Volterra, "Review of *The Brookline Museum Aramaic Papyri*," *Iura* 6 (1955) 359, as noted by B. Porten, *Archives From Elephantine*, 224. For an alternative view, cf. R. Yaron, *Introduction to the Law of the Aramaic Papyri*, 60f., 73f.; *idem*, "Aramaic Marriage Contracts from Elephantine," 24ff.
   Confirming a reference to palingamy, or at least some mutually prohibited act, is the linguistic parallelism and balanced literary structure of the protective clauses as a whole:
   A. Divorce by husband who declares his hatred for his wife and the consequence thereof (she receives back her dowry and is free to go where she pleases) — lns. 21b-24a
   A'. Divorce by wife who declares her hatred for her husband and the consequence thereof (she forfeits her dowry and returns to her father's house) — lns. 24b-28a.
   B. Predecease of husband without issue, wife inherits everything; penalty for anyone who attempts to thwart this provision
      Prohibition against the wife acquiring another husband and the consequence of any contravention thereof — lns. 28b-34a
   B'. Predecease of wife without issue, husband inherits everything;
      Prohibition against the husband taking another wife and the consequence of any contravention thereof — lns. 34b-37a.
   C. Prohibition against the husband not doing to his wife "the law of one or two" [= conjugal rights?] and the consequence of any contravention thereof — lns. 37b-39a.
   C'. Prohibition against the wife not doing to her husband "the law of one or two" and the consequence of any contravention thereof — lns 39b-40a.
[63] "Israel's Response in Hosea 2:17b: 'You are my Husband'" (1980) 203. For the traditional view that the marriage formula do reproduce the *verba solemnia* of marriage, cf. B. Porten, *Archives from Elephantine*, 206.
[64] To Friedman's arguments we may add the observation that similar documentary formulae are attested elsewhere among the marriage documents which have survived from the ancient Near East. Cf., e.g., "Kikkinu is her husband; Bitti-Dagan is his wife" (lns. 4f. of the MB marriage document from Ḥana in A.T. Clay, *Babylonian Records in the Library of J. Pierpont Morgan*, Part IV, text 52, 50-52).
   The mutual negative *verba solemnia* of divorce which immediately follow this documentary formula, "thou art not my wife" (ln. 8) and "thou art not my husband" (ln. 13),

1.2.2 Five second century A.D. marriage documents from Wadi Murabba'at
Among the important discoveries found at the Wadi Murabba'at were five
fragmentary Jewish marriage contracts written during the early second
century A.D. prior to the Bar Kokhba revolt. Three of these are written in
Aramaic (*Mur* 20, 21, Babata's marriage contract); the remaining two are in
Greek (*Mur* 115, 116).[65]

Mur 20 is dated by its editors about 117 A.D.[66] Like the other
marriage contracts from Murabba'at (as far as can be determined from their
poor state of preservation) *Mur* 20 appears to exhibit the following
established pattern: 1) date, 2) contracting parties, 3) report of the marriage
formula and any general promises, 4) record of financial matters, 5)
protective clauses for the wife and children in the case of death or divorce,
and 6) concluding list of witnesses. Specifically, *Mur* 20, lns. 1-3, read:
"[On] the seventh of Adar, in year e[leven of ..., the son] of Manasseh from
the sons of Eliashib [...,] that you[67] shall become mine in wifehood according
to the law of M[oses] [[משה]] כדין לאנתה תהוא לי [ד]ין[68]." The end of this line
is missing, but it may proceed to detail various promises from the groom to
care for his wife from this day "and forever [ולעלם]]" (the start of line 5),
such as are found in the later Geniza marriage contracts.

The marriage formulae attested in *Mur* 21 and Babata's marriage
contract are similar, though the texts are fragmentary. Unfortunately, due to
its poor state of preservation *Mur* 116 lacks the marriage formula. On the
other hand, *Mur* 115, dated 124 A.D., offers a significant variation in the
wording of its marriage formula in line 4: "the same Elaios Simon now
agrees[69] to live with her in love," σ[υ]νβιώσεος χάριν νυνεὶ ὁμολογεῖ ὁ
αὐτὸς Ἐλαῖος Σίμω[νος]. While there is a tendency to repeat stereotypical
formulae in the extant Jewish marriage documents, especially those from the

---

support the suggestion that the documentary formula may reflect the earlier unrecorded
mutual marriage *verba solemnia*, "you are my wife" and "you are my husband."

[65] P. Benoit, J.T. Milik, and R. de Vaux, *Les Grottes de Murabba'ât*, DJD II (1961)
109ff., 114ff., 243ff., 254ff. Cf. also the reprint of these texts in E. Koffmahn, *Die
Doppelurkunden aus der Wüste Juda* (1968) 114ff.
The full text of "Babata's marriage contract" is apparently still unpublished. It is
mentioned in *Mur*, p. 253, n. 5, however, and portions have been published by Y. Yadin,
"Expedition D - The Cave of the Letters" (1962) 244-245.

[66] Confusingly, *Mur* 20 has been variously referred to as the "Bar Menasheh marriage
deed" as well as the "Kephar Bebhayu marriage deed." Cf. S.A. Birnbaum, "The Kephar
Bebhayu Marriage Deed" (1958) 12-18; *idem, The Bar Menasheh Marriage Deed* (1962) 7;
and S. Greengus, "Old Babylonian Marriage Contract," 522, n. 83.

[67] In support of an interpretation of תהוא as a second feminine singular, cf. M.A.
Friedman, *Jewish Marriage in Palestine*, I, 158, n. 31.

[68] J.T. Milik proposes [אן]י for the start of line 3, which he understands as the
(intensive) second person feminine singular pronoun. M.A. Friedman has challenged this
by arguing that the expected second person form would be אנת, as in no. 21, line 12 (*Jewish
Marriage in Palestine*, I, 158). As a result he proposes to restore the relative [ד]י.

[69] Though uncertain, S. Bigger's rendering "swears" for ὁμολογεῖ is an intriguing
possibility ("Hebrew Marriage and Family in the Old Testament Period," 75).

later quite rigid Gaonic Babylonian tradition, the evidence of *Mur* 115 provides a salutary reminder that creative variation was permitted among Jews operating within other traditions.[70]

1.2.3 Talmudic evidence

No complete formulary of the marriage contract (*k*e*tubbâ*) is preserved in the Talmud. Almost all extant marriage contracts and references in the Tannaitic literature, however, support the following proposal for the groom: "Be to me a wife according to the law of Moses and Israel [הוֹאי לי לאנתו כדת משה וישראל]."[71]

Of special interest is an Alexandrian marriage document, which was studied by Hillel (about 30 B.C.) and is cited in the Tosefta and both Talmuds.[72] This *k*e*tubbâ* exhibits a form which is similar to that of the contracts from Murabba'at and the Palestinian-type contracts from the Cairo Geniza (10th and 11th century A.D.).[73] The marriage formula is "When you enter my house/the wedding chamber, you will be mine in wifehood [לכשתיכנסי לביתי / לחופה תהויין לי לאנתו]."

From the evidence thus far considered it appears that *verba solemnia* were a regular feature in the contraction of marriage throughout the ancient Near East and into post-biblical times. This fact predisposes us to find allusions to marital *verba solemnia* in the Old Testament. We turn now to an examination of the relevant biblical texts.

1.3 Biblical texts

1.3.1 Genesis 2:23

Already in Chapter 5, §3.2.3 above we observed that the paradigmatic marriage of Adam and Eve was accompanied by *verba solemnia*, spoken by Adam before God: "This at last is bone of my bones and flesh of my flesh; she shall be called Woman, because she was taken out of Man." As we argued, the fact that the "bone of my bones" formula is well-attested elsewhere within the Old Testament helps to identify these words as covenant-forming *verba solemnia*, rather than merely an ejaculatory comment of delight. With variations this formula is found in Gen. 29:14; Judg. 9:2-3; 2 Sam. 5:2 (and the parallel in 1 Chron. 11:1); and 2 Sam. 19:13f. [ET 12f.]. Although in each case some notion of kinship is in view, the formula produces an effect well beyond the bare recognition of a familial relationship to include a commitment of loyalty and an appeal for reciprocal allegiance

---

[70] L.M. Epstein fails to take adequate account of this potential for variation, both here and in the 66 Palestinian-style marriage contracts found among the Cairo Geniza (*The Jewish Marriage Contract* [1927] 57). On the latter, cf. M.A. Friedman, *Jewish Marriage in Palestine*, 2 vols. (1980)

[71] Cf. L.M. Epstein, *The Jewish Marriage Contract* (1927) 57; and M.A. Friedman, *Jewish Marriage in Palestine*, I, 147.

[72] Cf. *t. Ketub.* 4:9; *y. Ketub.* 4:8, 29a; *y. Yebam.* 15:3, 14d; and *b. B. Meṣ.* 104a.

[73] Cf. M.A. Friedman, *Jewish Marriage in Palestine*, I, 156-8.

(i.e., as expected for *verba solemnia*, it effects a covenant commitment).[74] As D. Daube has observed, in the ancient world the solemn acknowledgement of a relationship was frequently the very means of creating it.[75] These parallels as well as Adam's words spoken in the presence of the deity in Gen. 2:23 appear to offer unmistakable examples.

1.3.2 Hosea 2:4 [ET 2]

Given the use of similar formulae for divorce, or the disavowal of marriage, elsewhere in the ancient Near East (i.e., "you are not my wife," "you are not my husband," "she is not my wife," "he is not my husband," "I will not be your wife"), the expression, "she is not my wife, and I am not her husband [הִיא לֹא אִשְׁתִּי וְאָנֹכִי לֹא אִישָׁהּ]," in Hos. 2:4 [ET 2] has long been recognized as a possible example of such *verba solemnia*.[76] During the Middle Ages, for example, the Karaites used this formula, presumably in dependence on this biblical text.[77] Since the Elephantine marriage documents attest to the corresponding marriage formula "she is my wife and I am her husband from this day and forever [הי אנתתי ואנה בעלה מן יומא זנה עד עלם]," whether this is to be understood as the marriage-forming *verba solemnia* or, with Friedman, as their reflex in a documentary formula, it seems likely, with S. Greengus, that Hosea's words were "apparently modelled upon a marriage formula similar to the one used in the papyri."[78] If so, Hosea's words offer indirect

---

[74] On this formula, cf. W. Reiser, "Der Verwandschaftformel in Gen 2,23" (1960); and W. Brueggemann, "Of the Same Flesh and Bone (Gen 2,23a)" (1970). Cf. also D. Daube and R. Yaron, "Jacob's Reception by Laban" (1956); F.I. Andersen, "Israelite Kinship Terminology and Social Structure" (1969); R.G. Boling, *Judges* (1975) 171; and P. Kalluveettil, *Declaration and Covenant*, 209f.

[75] D. Daube, *Studies in Biblical Law* (1947) 7f.

[76] Cf., e.g., C.H. Gordon, "Hosea 2:4-5 in the Light of New Semitic Inscriptions" (1936); R. Yaron, "On Divorce in Old Testament Times" (1957); *idem*, "Aramaic Marriage Contracts from Elephantine" (1958) 30-31; R. de Vaux, *Ancient Israel*, I (1961) 35; S. Greengus, "Old Babylonian Marriage Contract" (1966) 522, n. 82; U. Cassuto, "Second Chapter of the Book of Hosea" (1973) 120-122; H.W. Wolff, *Hosea* (1974) 33f.; and M. Fishbane, "Accusations of Adultery. A Study of Law and Scribal Practice in Numbers 5,11-31" (1974) 40.

M.A. Friedman suggests that Hosea actually introduced two modifications to the original formula ("Israel's Response in Hosea 2:17b: 'You are my Husband'" [1980] 199). First, Friedman considers it likely that the original formula was expressed in the second person, "You are not my wife, and I am not your husband." Though possible, this suggestion may not be required since third person disavowal formulae (presumably stated before witnesses) are attested elsewhere. Cf., e.g., M.T. Roth, *Babylonian Marriage Agreements: 7th - 3rd Centuries B.C.*, No. 5, 13.

Second, Friedman supposes that the original formula employed the expression בעל for "husband," as attested in the Elephantine papyri. Hosea eschewed this term, however, because of its association with the Baal cult. Cf. Hos. 2:18f. [ET 16f.].

M.J. Geller has offered an alternative explanation for Hos. 2:18f. [ET 16f.], suggesting that in this text בעל bears the meaning "lover," as he supposes it does in Kraeling 7:33 (= Porten-Yardeni, B3.8:33) ("The Elephantine Papyri and Hosea 2,3: Evidence for the form of the Early Jewish Divorce Writ," 146, n. 21). Against this view, cf. M.A. Friedman, "Israel's Response in Hosea 2:17b," 201, n. 9.

[77] Cf. M.A. Friedman, "Israel's Response in Hosea 2:17b," 198, n. 1.

[78] S. Greengus, "Old Babylonian Marriage Contract," 522, n. 82. Cf. also J.C. Greenfield, "Aramaic Studies and the Bible," 122.

testimony to the use of the positive *verba solemnia* in eighth-century B.C. Israelite practice.

This recognition of Hos. 2:4a [ET 2a] as containing a formula for divorce or the disavowal of marriage, however, raises questions for the precise function of such a formula within the larger context of Hos. 2:4-25 [ET 2-23]. It goes beyond the limits of the present study to attempt to resolve this issue. Nevertheless, it is apparent from the larger context that the expression, "she is not my wife, and I am not her husband," in Hos. 2:4 does not immediately effect a divorce or dissolution of the relationship between Yahweh and Israel. On the contrary, as noted by F.I. Andersen and D.N. Freedman, among others, the verses which follow at least to vs. 15 [ET 13] presuppose the continuance of the marriage between Yahweh and his people, for which reason Israel continues to be accused of "adultery," not just "promiscuity."[79]

As a consequence, it is possible, with Andersen and Freedman, that Hos. 2:4a [ET 2a] should be viewed as Yahweh's private acknowledgment that his wife's adultery and desertion have rendered his marriage dissolved *de facto*, but since these words have no legal effect (because of their nonjuridical/informal setting and purpose), the marriage remains in force *de jure*.[80] This interpretation does not require, however, Andersen and Freedman's denial that Hos. 2:4a [ET 2a] includes the divorce formula.[81] It merely recognizes the potential effect of context on an expression which elsewhere constitutes performative discourse.

Alternatively, it may be preferable to understand Hos. 2:4a [ET 2a] as entailing an imminent and well-deserved *threat* of divorce by its invocation of the divorce formula — a threat which is realized by the end of vs. 15 [ET 13].[82] In this manner, the interpretation of Hos. 2:4a [ET 2a] better parallels that of Hos. 1:9, which similarly threatens the imminent dissolution of

---

Cf. Cowley 15:4 (= Porten-Yardeni, B2.6); Kraeling 2:3f. (= Porten-Yardeni, B3.3); 7:4 (= Porten-Yardeni, B3.8); and 14:3f. (= Porten-Yardeni, B6.1).

[79] F.I. Andersen and D.N. Freedman, *Hosea*, 219-224.

[80] Against this view, J.L. Mays posits a juridical setting for Hosea 2, but rejects 2:4a [ET 2a] as a divorce formula (*Hosea*, 35ff.). Alternatively, A. Phillips recognizes 2:4a [ET 2a] as a divorce formula, but insists that as a matter of family law, neither a juridical setting, nor even necessarily a public setting, was required for divorce ("Some Aspects of Family Law in Pre-Exilic Israel," 352).

[81] F.I. Andersen and D.N. Freedman explicitly reject the proposed identification of Hos. 2:4a [ET 2a] as a divorce formula (*Hosea*, 200f.). This conclusion is demanded only if it is assumed that the divorce formula necessarily terminates a marriage then and there.

Other scholars have disputed the identification of a divorce formula in Hos. 2:4a [ET 2a], including R. Gordis, "Hosea's Marriage and Message: A New Approach" (1954) 9-35, esp. 20f.; H.H. Rowley, "The Marriage of Hosea" (1963) 92; W. Rudolph, *Hosea* (1966) 65; J.A. Fitzmyer, "A Re-Study of an Elephantine Marriage Contract (AP 15)," 150; and J.L. Mays, *Hosea* (1969) 37f.

Cf., however, H.J. Hendriks' response to Gordis ("Juridical Aspects of the Marriage Metaphor in Hosea and Jeremiah," 57ff.).

[82] In support of Hos. 2:4a [ET 2a] as a threat of divorce based on its nonjuridical setting and the conditional threat of vs. 3, cf. H. McKeating, *Amos, Hosea, Micah*, 83.

Yahweh's covenant with Israel by its use of the parallel covenant dissolution formula, "for you are not my people and I am not your God [כִּי אַתֶּם לֹא עַמִּי וְאָנֹכִי לֹא־אֶהְיֶה לָכֶם]," which appears in the context of the oracular names of Hosea's children.[83] Although positing a complex redactional history for Hosea, G.A. Yee considers that the author of Hos. 2:4 avoids using the customary divorce formula in order to highlight this reversal of the covenant reflected in Hos. 1:9.[84]

Accordingly, just as the threatened covenant dissolution in Hosea 1 is followed by an unexpected promise of covenant renewal in Hos. 2:1-3 [ET 1:10-2:1], so also the threatened divorce in Hos. 2:4ff. [ET 2ff.] is followed by an unexpected promise of a new marriage in Hos. 2:16ff. [ET 14ff.]. Moreover, in each case the promised restoration is expressed in terms of the use of positive declaration formulae which correspond to and reverse the preceding negative dissolution formulae.[85] This structural parallelism is clearly intentional since Hosea identifies the effects of the restored marriage at the end of chapter 2 with the effects of the earlier promised restored covenant:

> And in that day, says Yahweh, I will answer the heavens and they shall answer the earth; and the earth shall answer the grain, the wine, and the oil, and they shall answer Jezreel [cf. 1:4f., 11]; and I will sow him for myself in the land. And I will have pity on Not pitied [cf. 1:6f.; 2:3 [ET 2:1]], and I will say to Not my people [cf. 1:9f.; 2:3 [ET 2:1]], "You are my people"; and he shall say "Thou art my God." (Hos. 2:23-25 [ET 21-23])

In addition to these structural considerations which underscore the parallel between Hos. 2:4 [ET 2:2] and 1:9 and in addition to the ancient Near Eastern parallels to Hos. 2:4 [ET 2:2] already mentioned, H.J. Hendriks offers a number of arguments in support of interpreting Hos. 2:4a [ET 2a] as a

---

[83] F.I. Andersen and D.N. Freedman are inconsistent in their interpretation of these parallel verses (*Hosea*, 197f., 223f.). As mentioned, they consider Hos. 2:4a [ET 2a] to be a private complaint or perhaps even an affirmation if לֹא is asseverative, but on either view Yahweh has no intention to dissolve the marriage. By contrast, noting the positive covenant-making formulae in Lev. 26:12 and 2 Sam. 7:14, they consider that with the corresponding negative formulae in Hos. 1:9, "All this is now undone; a relationship hundreds of years old *has been dissolved* [italics added]."
Cf. also Exod. 6:5-7; Jer. 7:21-23; 11:4; Ezek. 11:20; 14:11; 37:26-27, for other examples of the corresponding positive covenant formula.
[84] G.A. Yee, *Composition and Tradition in the Book of Hosea: A Redaction Critical Investigation* (1987) 105-108.
Yee posits a four-stage redactional history for Hosea, yielding some interpretative novelties, such as his view that the original adulterous mother of chapter 2 is Rachel, the favourite wife of Jacob, not Gomer, and that her children are the northern tribes, the House of Israel (*op. cit.*, 305).
[85] Cf. "Children of the Living God [בְּנֵי אֵל־חָי]" in 2:1 [1:10], perhaps by contrast to "I am not Ehyeh to you [וְאָנֹכִי לֹא־אֶהְיֶה לָכֶם]" in 1:9; "My People [עַמִּי]" in 2:3 [ET 2:1], by contrast to "not my people [לֹא עַמִּי]" in 1:9; 2:1 [ET 1:10]; and "Shown Compassion [רֻחָמָה]" in 2:3 [ET 2:1], by contrast to "not pitied [לֹא רֻחָמָה]" in 1:6, 8. Cf. the use of "my children" as the formula for legitimation in CH §§170-171, discussed earlier.
For Hos. 2:16-25 [ET 14-23], cf. the discussion below.

divorce formula which threatens the dissolution of Yahweh's "marriage" to Israel.[86]   Only three will be briefly repeated here.   First, the remarriage promised in Hos. 2:16-25 [ET 14-23] appears to presuppose the dissolution of a previous marriage in 2:4-2:15 [ET 2:2-13].[87]   Second, the threat of stripping in vs. 5 [ET 3] is a well-attested symbolic action for dissolving relationships and, specifically, effecting divorce; it is thus congruent with the initial threat of divorce posited for 2:4 [ET 2:2].[88]   Finally, Jeremiah, a book which is widely recognized as having been influenced by Hosea's message and his use of the marriage metaphor in particular, interprets in 3:8 Israel's broken relationship with Yahweh as a divorce.[89]

1.3.3 Hosea 2:17-19 [ET 15-17]

17וְנָתַ֨תִּי לָ֜הּ אֶת־כְּרָמֶ֣יהָ מִשָּׁ֗ם וְאֶת־עֵ֤מֶק עָכוֹר֙ לְפֶ֣תַח תִּקְוָ֔ה
וְעָ֤נְתָה שָּׁ֨מָּה֙ כִּימֵ֣י נְעוּרֶ֔יהָ וּכְי֖וֹם עֲלֹתָ֥הּ מֵאֶֽרֶץ־מִצְרָֽיִם׃ ס
18וְהָיָ֤ה בַיּוֹם־הַהוּא֙ נְאֻם־יְהוָ֔ה תִּקְרְאִ֖י אִישִׁ֑י וְלֹא־תִקְרְאִי־לִ֥י ע֖וֹד בַּעְלִֽי׃
19וַהֲסִרֹתִ֛י אֶת־שְׁמ֥וֹת הַבְּעָלִ֖ים מִפִּ֑יהָ וְלֹֽא־יִזָּכְר֥וּ ע֖וֹד בִּשְׁמָֽם׃

15And there I will give her her vineyards, and make the Valley of Achor a door of hope.   And there she shall answer as in the days of her youth, as at the time when she came out of the land of Egypt. 16And in that day, says Yahweh, you will call me, 'My husband,' and no longer will you call me, 'My Baal.'   17For I will remove the names of the Baals from her mouth, and they shall be mentioned by name no more.

As noted in the preceding discussion, Hos. 2:17-19 [ET 15-17] appears within an oracle (Hos. 2:16-25 [ET 14-23]), which promises a new marriage between Yahweh and his people "in that day."[90]   It has already been

---

[86] Cf., e.g., H.J. Hendriks, "Juridical Aspects of the Marriage Metaphor in Hosea and Jeremiah," 58.

[87] In support, Hendriks appeals to his overall treatment of Hosea 2-3, which cannot be reproduced here.

[88] *Ibid.*, 47f.

[89] It is possible that the reference to Yahweh as "my first husband" in Hos. 2:9 [ET 2:7] implies the prior dissolution of the marriage.   If it is objected that the promised renewed marriage between Yahweh and Israel would contravene the express prohibition of Deut. 24:1ff., it may be responded that Jer. 3:1 raises the very same objection.   Perhaps Hosea employs this imagery to threaten Israel's irreparable ruin if she continues in her religious harlotry.   Alternatively, if Hosea depicts Israel's state as already irremissible, then this poses an insuperable legal obstacle which, in the end, only the relentless love of God can overcome.   P. Grelot observes with respect to Yahweh's promised remarriage of his bride, "according to the law and customs of those days no husband would have acted like this" ("The Institution of Marriage: Its Evolution in the Old Testament," 46)

On the relationship between Hosea and Jeremiah, cf., e.g., J. Skinner, *Prophecy and Religion. Studies in the Life of Jeremiah* (1922) 21; H.J. Hendriks, "Juridical Aspects of the Marriage Metaphor in Hosea and Jeremiah," 182-186; and J.A. Thompson, *The Book of Jeremiah* (1980) 81-87.   Thompson cites the full-scale study of this subject provided by K. Goss, "Die literarische Verwandschaft Jeremias mit Hosea" (1930); and *idem*, "Hoseas Einfluss auf Jeremias Anschauungen" (1931).

[90] Unfortunately, there is some dispute about the precise beginning of the oracle of restoration.   E.g., J.L. Mays, H.W. Wolff, and D.K. Stuart favour starting with the

mentioned that the parallel promise of covenant renewal in Hos. 2:1-3 [ET 1:10-2:1] employs positive declaration formulae which correspond to and reverse the preceding negative dissolution formulae. It seems that, in the very same manner, Hos. 2:17-19 [ET 15-17] uses "my husband [אִישִׁי]" as an example of the wife's *verba solemnia*, establishing this new marriage and so reversing the preceding divorce formula, "she is not my wife, and I am not her husband [וְהִיא לֹא אִשְׁתִּי וְאָנֹכִי לֹא אִישָׁהּ]," in Hos. 2:4 [ET 2].

In a careful study of this text, M.A. Friedman concludes that 2:18 [ET 16] alludes to the content of the wife's "response [וְעָנְתָה]" mentioned in 2:17 [ET 15].[91] That is, in 2:16 [ET 14] Hosea alludes to God's proposal of (re)marriage, which is made explicit in Hos. 2:21f. [ET 19f.].[92] Naturally, Hosea assumes his audience knows what must have been the customary marriage formula of the time, perhaps one in which the husband declares, "You are my wife [אִשְׁתִּי אַתְּ]," and the wife responds, "You are my husband [בַּעְלִי אַתָּה]." In contrast to the Elephantine use of בַּעַל, 'husband" or "lord," in its marriage formulae, however, vs. 18 [ET 16] instructs the bride that her response can no longer be "my Baal (= "husband" or "lord") [בַּעְלִי]," but rather "my husband [אִישִׁי]."[93]

Most commentators consider that this change in vocabulary signals a total repudiation of Baal worship (cf. 2:19 [ET 18]). It may also be the case, with C.V. Camp and others, that the wife's response of אִישִׁי, "my husband," implies a heightened character of intimacy in this renewed marriage.[94] As Camp tentatively suggests, "'In that day' this relationship will be transformed. No longer will Israel call the deity 'my *ba'al*,' my master, but

---

eschatological "In that day [וְהָיָה בַיּוֹם־הַהוּא]" of 2:18 [ET 2:16], while J. Lindblom (*Prophecy in Ancient Israel* [1962] 243); H.J. Hendriks, and F.I. Andersen and D.N. Freedman, prefer starting with "therefore [לָכֵן]" in 2:16 [ET 2:14]. Besides allowing the preceding section to end with the structural indicator, נְאֻם־יְהוָה, the principal advantages of this second approach are not only that it better reflects the change in tone from judgment to promise, which occurs at 2:16 [ET 2:14], but also that it preserves the coherence between 2:17 [ET 2:15] and 2:18 [ET 2:16]. On this last point, cf. M.A. Friedman, "Israel's Response in Hosea 2:17b." Accordingly, the entire oracle is the unexpected (because of its positive tone) third member in a series of לָכֵן passages (cf. 2:8 [ET 6] and 2:11 [ET 9]) which follow Yahweh's complaint against his adulterous wife in 2:4-7 [ET 2-5]. Cf. also H.J. Hendriks, "Juridical Aspects of the Marriage Metaphor in Hosea and Jeremiah," 157-160.

[91] M.A. Friedman, "Israel's Response in Hosea 2:17b: 'You are my Husband'" (1980) 199-204.

[92] Friedman cites Judg. 19:3, especially, as well as 2 Sam. 19:8 [ET 7]; Isa. 40:2; 2 Chron. 30:22; and 32:6 in support of this implication for the expression, וְדִבַּרְתִּי עַל־לִבָּהּ.

[93] M.A. Friedman, "Israel's Response in Hosea 2:17b: 'You are my Husband'," 200. Friedman rejects M.J. Geller's proposal that בַּעְלִי means "my lover" in favour of the traditional view that Hosea's opposition to the term בַּעְלִי stems from a repudiation of Baal worship (*op. cit.*, 201, n. 8).

[94] C.V. Camp, *Wisdom and the Feminine in the Book of Proverbs* (1985) 106f. Elsewhere, however, Camp acknowledges that בַּעַל need not always have domineering connotations, as in its repeated appearance in Prov. 31:11, 23, and 28 (*op. cit.*, 91f.). Cf. also L.M. Muntingh, "Married Life in Israel according to the Book of Hosea" (1964-65) 80; C. van Leeuwen, *Hosea* (1968) 72; J.L. Mays, *Hosea*, 48; and H.J. Hendriks, "Juridical Aspects of the Marriage Metaphor in Hosea and Jeremiah," 145.

rather 'my *'îš*,' my husband, my man." In support, she cites studies by W. Brueggemann and P. Trible which argue for an implied mutuality in the terms אִישׁ, "husband," and אִשָּׁה, "wife," as used in Gen. 2:23, in contrast to the term בַּעַל with its stress on the husband's legal rights over his wife as her "lord" or "possessor."[95]

In any case, the marriage-forming declaration, "my husband [אִישִׁי]," and its assumed counterpart declaration, "you are my wife [אַתְּ אִשְׁתִּי]," prepare for and clearly parallel the later declaration formulae in vs. 25 [ET 23]. In that verse Yahweh declares of Israel, who had been repudiated as "Not my people [לֹא־עַמִּי]," "You are my people [עַמִּי־אַתָּה]"; to this Israel will respond simply, "my God [אֱלֹהָי]."

1.3.4 Proverbs 7:4f.

Although its use is metaphoric, Z.W. Falk suggests that there is a plausible allusion to a marriage-forming *verba solemnia* in Prov. 7:4f.: "Say to wisdom, 'You are my sister,' and call insight your intimate friend [אֱמֹר לַחָכְמָה אֲחֹתִי אָתְּ וּמֹדָע לַבִּינָה תִקְרָא]; to preserve you from the loose woman, from the adventuress with her smooth words."[96]

With respect to the wording of the posited *verba solemnia*, it appears that "You are my sister [אֲחֹתִי אָתְּ]" and "intimate friend [וּמֹדָע]" are intended as approximate synonyms because of the chiastic arrangement of 7:4f. Unfortunately, however, there is considerable dispute regarding the meaning of מֹדָע. The only other appearance of מֹדָע is in the *q°rē* of Ruth 2:1, if מוֹדָע is the same term. Terms which appear to be closely related to מֹדָע include מוֹדַעַת, found in Ruth 3:1, and מְיֻדָּע, the Pual masculine singular participle of ידע, found in the *k°tîb* of Ruth 2:1 and also in 2 Kgs. 10:11; Ps. 31:12 [ET 11]; 55:14 [ET 13]; 88:9, 19 [ET 8, 18]; and Job 19:14.

While "acquaintance," "friend," and "relative" have been suggested for each of these מ-noun formations from ידע, none of these definitions is without difficulty. Alternatively, E.F. Campbell has argued that these nouns may include the same covenantal associations as does the cognate verb analyzed in the studies of H.B. Huffmon and S. Parker.[97] Accordingly, Campbell renders מְיֻדָּע as "covenant-brother" and מֹדַעְתָּנוּ as "our covenant circle." In a similar manner, J. Gray explains the sense of מידע in Ruth 2:1: "The term means one known to another, probably with the more pregnant

---

[95] W. Brueggemann, "Of the Same Flesh and Bone (Gn 2,23a)," 538f.; and P. Trible, *God and the Rhetoric of Sexuality* (1978) 100-102.

[96] Z.W. Falk, *Hebrew Law in Biblical Times. An Introduction* (1964) 134f. So also M.A. Friedman, "Israel's Response in Hosea 2:17b: 'You are my Husband'," 203, n. 18.

[97] Cf. E.F. Campbell Jr., *Ruth* (1975) 88-90, 117; H.B. Huffmon, "The Treaty Background of Hebrew *yāda'*" (1966) 31-37; and H.B. Huffmon and S.B. Parker, "A Further Note on the Treaty Background of Hebrew *yāda'*" (1966) 36-38.
Against Campbell cf., e.g., J.M. Sasson, *Ruth* (1979) 39. Sasson's inconsistent renderings of מְיֻדָּע in Ruth 2:1 as "acquaintance" (doubtful in view of the subsequent identification of Boaz as "of the family of Elimelech [מִמִּשְׁפַּחַת אֱלִימֶלֶךְ]" in the same verse) and of מֹדַעְתָּנוּ in Ruth 3:2 as "our relative," however, are unconvincing.

sense of mutual *acknowledgement* of social obligations as between kinsmen, as indicated in 2:20...."[98]

Whatever the precise meaning of וּמֹדָע in Prov. 7:4f., the acknowledgement of wisdom as "my sister [אֲחֹתִי]" seems clear in its implications of intimate friendship and commitment. It is helpful to recognize not only that "sister" and "brother" are favourite epithets for lovers, for example in Egyptian love poetry, but also that the term "sister" is often specifically marital, as when it is paired with "bride [כַּלָּה]" in Canticles (e.g. 4:9, 10, 12; 5:1).[99] Perhaps also the use of "brother" as an established term for the recognition of covenant partners should be compared here.[100] In any case, if one's bride is wisdom, the greater implications of mutuality implicit in the term "sister" seem eminently appropriate.[101]

1.3.5 Tobit 7:12

The book of Tobit, which probably was composed in Hebrew or Aramaic during the second century B.C., offers the modern scholar one of the most detailed narratives regarding the contraction of a marriage available from the ancient world.[102] In the course of the narrative in chapters 7 and 8, Raguel gives his daughter Sarah to be married to Tobias and says, "Here she is; take her according to the law of Moses."[103] Just prior to doing so, Raguel addresses Tobias, "From henceforth you are her brother, and she is your sister [ἀπὸ τοῦ νῦν σὺ ἀδελφὸς εἶ αὐτῆς καὶ αὐτὴ ἀδελφή σου].[104] She has been given to you from today and forever."

While it is the case that "brother" and "sister" are used within Tobit of mother (5:20), relatives (3:14; 5:13), and liberally of fellow Jews (1:3, 10, 16; 2:2; 4:12, 13; 5:6, 11; etc.), they are also used of husbands and wives (cf. Tob. 7:16; 8:4, 7), as in the case of Prov. 7:4 and Canticles. Accordingly,

---

[98] *Joshua, Judges, Ruth* (1986) 390.

[99] On the use of "sister" in Egyptian marriage contracts from the sixth century B.C., cf. E. Lüddeckens, *Ägyptische Eheverträge* (1960) nos. 3, 4, 13-15. Cf. also J.B. White, *A Study of the Language of Love in the Song of Songs and Ancient Egyptian Poetry* (1978) 95.

[100] Cf. J. Priest, "The Covenant of Brothers" (1965) 400-406; D.J. McCarthy, *Treaty and Covenant* (1981) 98, 104, 106; P. Kalluveettil, *Declaration and Covenant*, 99-101; and H. Tadmor, "Treaty and Oath in the Ancient Near East: An Historian's Approach" (1982) 131.

[101] Cf. also the words of 'Anat, who is trying to win Aqht's confidence: "You are my brother and I am [your sister] [*at ah wan [ahtk]*]" (III Aqht rev. 24 = Aqht B i 24 in *ANET*, 152). Although the following lines are too fragmentary to secure the interpretation of this line, A. van Selms compares this affirmation to the formulae used in adoption and marriage in Mesopotamia and Israel (*Marriage and Family Life in Ugaritic Literature* [1954] 120).

[102] On marriage in Tobit, cf. P. Grelot, "The Institution of Marriage: Its Evolution in the Old Testament" (1970) 39-50.

[103] The reference to the "law of Moses" may be compared to the same formula attested in the *Mur* 20 and the Babata marriage contract from Muraba'at, marriage contracts from the Cairo Geniza, and the "traditional" Jewish marriage contract. Cf. M.A. Friedman, *Jewish Marriage in Palestine*, I, 163.

[104] So, according to LXXᴬ. LXXᴮ reads, "you are her brother and she is yours [σὺ δὲ ἀδελφὸς εἶ αὐτῆς, καὶ αὐτή σού ἐστιν]."

M.A. Friedman has plausibly identified this declaration in 7:12 as the *verba solemnia* of the marriage.[105]

Although it is surprising, based on the examples thus far considered, for the father-in-law to pronounce the *verba solemnia*, nevertheless, it is clear that these words do, in fact, effect the requisite change in the status of Tobias and Sarah.[106] Furthermore, they provide the content of the binding agreement requested by Tobias in 7:12 [ET 11]: "until you agree and swear to me [ἕως ἄν στήσητε καὶ σταθῆτε πρός με]."[107] Appropriately, after Raguel's declaration and following the drafting of a marriage contract and a meal (7:14), the couple sleep together, and Tobias addresses Sarah, his wife, as "sister" (8:4, 7).

1.4 Further biblical texts, or expressions, which may allude to the marriage formula

Although some scholars have suggested that the idiomatic expressions היה + ל + לאיש, "to become a husband to...," and לאשה + ל + היה, "to become a wife to...," may derive from marriage formulae, the evidence for this hypothesis is not compelling.[108] More likely is a possible allusion to the marriage *verba solemnia* in an expression found in Canticles, repeated with variations: "My beloved is mine and I am his [דּוֹדִי לִי וַאֲנִי לוֹ]" (2:16); "I am my beloved's and my beloved is mine [אֲנִי לְדוֹדִי וְדוֹדִי לִי]" (6:3); and "I am my beloved's [אֲנִי לְדוֹדִי]" (7:11 [ET 10]). While these texts are comparable to other examples of relationship formulae, none of them occurs within the context of marriage formation.[109] Accordingly, their evidence for the use of *verba solemnia* in marriage is, at best, indirect. Nevertheless, these texts may help to underscore the mutual belonging of (marital?) love and, as such, may support the assumption of reciprocal marriage formulae during the biblical period.

1.5 Conclusions

In his rejection of the identification of marriage as a covenant, J. Milgrom concedes that "The betrothal/marriage rite might be conceived as a covenant if there were a mutual exchange of *verba solemnia* even though an oath formula was not used."[110] While not every example considered above proved

---

[105] M.A. Friedman, "Israel's Response in Hosea 2:17b: 'You are My Husband," 203.

[106] Z.W. Falk explains this as due to the fact that Sarah was a potential heiress, requiring marriage to a relative, and the related fact that there had been no marriage present (*Introduction to Jewish Law of the Second Commonwealth*, vol. 2 [1978] 281).

[107] So LXX^BA. LXX^ℵ reads, "until you settle my affairs [ἕως ἄν διαστήσῃς τὰ πρὸς ἐμέ]."

[108] Gen. 20:12; 24:67; Lev. 21:3; etc. Cf., e.g., L.M. Epstein, *The Jewish Marriage Contract* (1927) 1-52, esp. 55; Z.W. Falk, *Hebrew Law in Biblical Times* (1964) 142; H.L. Ginsberg, "Studies in Hosea 1-3," 53; and H.J. Hendriks, "Juridical Aspects of the Marriage Metaphor in Hosea and Jeremiah," 60.

[109] Cf.. Deut. 26:17f.; 29:12 [ET 13]; Hos. 2:25 [ET 23]; Jer. 7:23; 11:4; 24:7; 31:33; Ezek. 34:30f.; 36:28; 37:23; and perhaps Ps. 95:7; 100:3 — so M.H. Pope, *Song of Songs*, 405.

[110] *Cult and Conscience*, 135, n. 487.

equally convincing, from a broad range of biblical and extrabiblical evidence there can be little doubt that marriage in biblical times was, in fact, typically formed with the use of *verba solemnia*. Furthermore, from the many different examples discussed, it is apparent that a wide variety of formulae were permissible; hence a case such as Gen. 2:23 cannot be rejected merely because it fails to reproduce the standard formula of the much later (Gaonic) Babylonian *keṯubbâ*. In addition, while *verba solemnia* were nearly always declared by the groom (Tob. 7:12 is the only exception), it is notable that at times a reciprocal formula was pronounced by the bride as well.[111]

Finally, in many cases the *verba solemnia* may have been articulated before human witnesses, as often they were repeated in documentary form (i.e., in the marriage contracts) before human witnesses. If so, presumably this served the practical purpose of providing necessary public evidence for the new marital status of the individuals involved.[112] Most examples, however, fail to mention the presence of human witnesses,[113] perhaps allowing the implication that the primary witness was the deity.[114] In any case, a few examples, in particular "the *eṭlu* tablet," perhaps Tobit 7-8, and especially Gen. 2:23, are explicit in their recognition that the deity was witness to the marriage-forming *verba solemnia*.[115] Furthermore, the marriage analogy in Hosea 1-2, which utilizes the *verba solemnia* of marriage to represent divine covenant-forming *verba solemnia* (2:17-19 [ET 15-17]), tends to a similar conclusion. In Chapter 8 supportive evidence will be sought for this implication, namely that in the minds of at least some Old Testament authors, the deity was understood to be a witness to the marital *verba solemnia* (and/or oath-sign) and, accordingly, would judge marital offences even in cases which might not be humanly judiciable. Compare Mal. 2:14 and perhaps Gen. 31:50.

---

[111] The clearest evidence for mutual formulae is from the OB legal document from Ishchali and from Hos. 2:17-19 [ET 15-17]. Mutual formulae may also be implied, however, by the corresponding mutual formulae for the disavowal of marriage or divorce, which are attested for most periods. Finally, it is possible that the mutual character of documentary formulae such as "she is my wife and I am her husband," attested at Elephantine, for example, may imply that the corresponding original oral formulae were pronounced by both husband and wife (although the similar oral formula known from the OB *eṭlu* tablet and the *ardat lilî* tablet demonstrate that this is not a necessary conclusion).

[112] Cf. MAL A §41. Cf. also R. Westbrook, "Old Babylonian Marriage Law," II, 125.

[113] Cf. the analogous situation of the legitimating formula in CH §§170-171.

[114] Cf. the treatment of the oath-like character of *verba solemnia* in the previous chapter.

[115] The context of the *verba solemnia* in Tobit is thoroughly religious; Raguel pronounces a blessing on the couple immediately following his declaration. Cf. also Raguel's command to Tobias, "take her [Sarah] according to the law of Moses" in Tob. 7:12, with its apparent implication that his marital responsibilities were defined in the Scripture, which, if so, would imply their sanctioning by the deity. Cf. the similar mention of "the law of Moses" in the *verba solemnia* attested in the Babata marriage contract, marriage contracts from the Cairo Geniza, and the "traditional" Jewish marriage contract.

2. EVIDENCE SUGGESTING THAT SEXUAL UNION MAY BE THE REQUISITE COVENANT-RATIFYING (AND RENEWING) OATH-SIGN FOR MARRIAGE

Having established that *verba solemnia* were customary for marriage in the Old Testament, we shall now investigate the significance of gifts and especially sexual union in the contraction of marriage. In general, *verba solemnia* do not take the place of symbolic acts in effecting changes in legal status, contracts, or covenants, but instead typically supplement them.[116] In fact, contrary to our modern prejudice in favour of consensual contract with its almost exclusive emphasis on the written word, or at least the spoken word, it appears that the ancients often considered a symbolic act to be the constitutive instrument for effecting a desired legal outcome.[117] As a consequence, there is a *prima facie* likelihood that if marriage was a covenant there may have been a covenant-ratifying oath-sign or even a variety of such oath-signs associated with the formation of marriage.

A considerable number of ceremonies and symbolic rites are known to have been associated with the formation of marriage elsewhere in the ancient Near East (e.g., cf. a prenuptial bath, perhaps for both bride and groom; pouring oil on the bride's head; clothing of the bride [or perhaps tying clothes together between bride and groom]; sewing the dowry into the bride's garment; and a processional celebration for the removal of the bride from her father's home to that of her husband).[118] Some of these rites were even mandatory (e.g., cf. the need to settle a marriage contract [*riksātu*] in LE §§27-28 and CH §128; the required *kirrum* in LE §§27-28, generally understood as some kind of formality involving beer; or the veiling of the bride in MAL A §§40-41). Nevertheless, the biblical evidence for these or any other wedding ceremonies is regrettably scant.[119] Some texts are so terse

---

[116] So M. Malul, *Studies in Mesopotamian Legal Symbolism*, 2-3, 51, 85, and *passim*.

[117] *Ibid.*, 2ff., 88, and *passim*.

[118] Cf. MAL A §§42-43. Cf. also S. Greengus, "Old Babylonian Marriage Ceremonies and Rites" (1966) 55-72; R. Yaron, *The Laws of Eshnunna*, 2nd. ed. (1988) 59, 200-205; R. Westbrook, "Old Babylonian Marriage Law," I, 52; II, 155; and M. Malul, *Studies in Mesopotamian Legal Symbolism*, 152, 161-197, 345.

M. Malul, for example, notes how the garments of the bride and groom could be tied together to symbolize marriage (*op. cit.*, 200 n. 197, 345). By contrast, there is some evidence that when a couple divorced their clothes would again be tied together, only this time it would be in order to immediately cut them apart (*op. cit.*, 206f.).

[119] Cf., e.g., O.J. Baab, "Marriage" *IDB* 3 (1962); S.B. Parker, "The Marriage Blessing in Israelite and Ugaritic Literature" (1976); E.M. Yamauchi, "Cultural Aspects of Marriage in the Ancient World" (1978) 241-252; P.A. Kruger, "The Hem of the Garment in Marriage" (1984); and M. Malul, *Studies in Mesopotamian Legal Symbolism*, 196 n. 125, 336f.

Prior to the formation of marriage, there are examples of circumcision (Gen. 34:22ff., Exod. 4:24-26 is doubtful); a gift of clothes or covering of the bride (Ezek. 16:10-12, and perhaps Ruth 3:9); and anointing the bride (Ezek. 16:9, though it is more likely that this anointing, as well as washing and clothing, is merely illustrative of Yahweh's exemplary care, by contrast to Ezek. 16:4-5).

Actions which are expressive of the joy of a wedding include music, songs, and group celebrations, which need not imply any particular formalities (Ps. 78:63; Jer. 7:34; 16:9;

the impression is left that marriage, at least at times, could have been contracted almost entirely without ceremony. Compare, for example, Gen. 24:67, "Then Isaac brought her into the tent, and took Rebekah, and she became his wife; and he loved her."[120] Even where ceremonies are mentioned, or alluded to, it would seem unwarranted to assume that any given rite was necessarily universally practiced. Furthermore, because of the limitations of our evidence, the symbolism and legal consequences, if any, of any individual ceremony are often very much in doubt.

In any case, besides the *verba solemnia* discussed earlier, two actions especially have dominated scholarly discussion of the *formation* of marriage and are thought to be indispensable for its validity. These are the payment of a betrothal present (*terḥatum* / מֹהַר)[121] and sexual intercourse (*copula carnalis*).

25:10; cf. also Isa. 62:4-5), as well as the donning of special wedding attire (Isa. 61:10; perhaps Cant. 3:11; Ps. 45:13-14; Jer. 2:32; a veil is mentioned in Gen. 24:65 and may be implied in implied in Gen. 29:23, 25 — cf. MAL A §§40-41), though not royal attire (cf. M. Pope, *Song of Songs*, 141-144), a procession of bride and groom (1 Macc. 9:37-39), and a common meal (Gen. 24:54; 29:22).

While Gen. 24:54 indicates that the common meal lasted only a single evening (though the family may have wished for ten days, cf. Gen. 29:55), from Gen. 29:27 it appears that the wedding feast and celebration were intended to last an entire week. Judg. 14:12, likewise, mentions a week long marriage feast, but from the context it is clear that either this practice was confined to Philistia, or at least it was no longer being observed in Israel in the period of the author/editor of the text: "And his father went down to the woman, and Samson made a feast there; for so the young men used to do" (Judg. 14:10). On the other hand, by the time of Tob. 8:19; 10:7, the wedding banquet lasted two weeks (preceded by a meal between the father-in-law and groom in 7:14 and 8:1). Cf. also Judg. 19:4-9.

Other briefly mentioned ceremonies and rites include the giving of a dowry [שִׁלּוּחִים] to the bride from her family (1 Kgs. 9:16; Mic. 1:14; Tob. 8:21; and perhaps 1 Sam. 25:42), bridal gifts given by the husband to his bride at the time of the wedding (termed בְּרָכָה, "blessing," in Josh. 15:19 and Judg. 1:15, but appearing without the term in Hos. 2:17 [ET 15]), and a possible allusion to the *kirrum* ceremony in Gen. 49:6 (as pointed out to the writer by G.J. Wenham; cf. D.W. Young, "A Ghost Word in the Testament of Jacob [Gen 49:5]?" [1981] 335-342).

Other actions may be intended primarily as expressions of the consent of the bride's family. These include the presentation of the bride to the groom by her father (Tob. 7:13; cf. also Gen. 2:22; 29:23); the writing of a marriage contract, or a contract for cohabitation (if, with S. Zeitlin, Raguel's contract was not the marriage contract, the כְּתוּבָה of Tannaic literature, obligatorily written by the groom, but was instead the שְׁטַר קִידּוּשִׁין, written by the father of the bride ["The Origin of the Kethubah: A Study in the Institution of Marriage"]); and a blessing on the couple by the family and other guests (Gen. 24:60; Ruth 4:11; and Tob. 10:12).

[120] Even this text mentions Rebekah's self-veiling in vs. 66, perhaps reflective of the ancient Near Eastern practice cited above. In any case, naturally this marriage takes place under exceptional circumstances, since most of the attested celebrations appear to have taken place at the wife's home, while Rebekah's marriage takes place hundreds of miles from her father's house. Cf. also Gen. 38:2.

[121] The terminology and significance of marriage prestations in cuneiform law and practice are complex and at many point uncertain. For a recent discussion of this topic, cf. G. Cardascia, *Les lois assyriennes* (1969); R. Westbrook, "Old Babylonian Marriage Law," II, *passim*; M.T. Roth, "Marriage and Matrimonial Prestations in First Millennium B.C. Babylonia" (1989) 245-255; and R. Westbrook, *et al.*, "Responses to Prof. Roth's Paper" (1989) 256-260.

The following chart may be useful for the present discussion.

Label = Definition	OB laws	OB dcmts	MAL	NB	NA
Dowry = property provided by the bride's family (a daughter's share of her father's estate). The meaning of *širku*, appearing only in MAL A §9, is uncertain according to G. Cardascia and R. Borger, *Babylonisch-Assyrische Lesestücke*, II, 275. Dowry is termed *mulūgu* in Amarna and Nuzi texts.	*širiktum*	*nudunnūm*	*širku*(?)	*nudunnū*	*nudunnū*
Alternative term for dowry, when restricted to slaves				*mulūgu*	
Alternative term for dowry, when restricted to cash — perhaps more accessible to the wife, with the husband's access correspondingly more limited.				*quppu*	
Bridewealth or marriage present = property given by the husband, or his family, to the bride's family (this use of *biblu(m)* is mentioned only in CH §§159-161, MAL A §30, and M.T. Roth, *Babylonian Marriage Agreements*, Nos. 34, 35).	*biblum*		*biblu*	*biblu*	
Alternative term for bridewealth or marriage present	*terḫatum*	*terḫatum*	*terḫutu*		*terḫutu*
Alternative term for bridewealth or marriage present	*zubullûm*		*zubullû*		
Widow's settlement = property given by the husband to the wife in anticipation of her maintenance needs as a widow.	*nudunnūm*	*širiktum*	*nudunnū*	*širiktu*	
"Dower" or the *nungurtu*-settlement = property given by the father of the groom to the groom.				*nungurtu*	

R. Westbrook differs with M.T. Roth over the *nudunnūm* / *širiktum*, "widow's settlement" ("Responses to Prof. Roth's Paper" [1989] 256f.). Westbrook considers this

2.1 The מֹהַר / terḥatum *as a "betrothal present" (purchase marriage and the* מֹהַר / terḥatum *as a "bride price" refuted)*

According to the majority view of an earlier generation of scholars, especially following P. Koschaker and E. Neufeld (who applied Koschaker's theory to Israelite practice), marriage throughout the ancient Near East (or at least in OB, Nuzian, and MA practice) conforms to the pattern of "marriage by purchase."[122] In other words, it was argued that the husband legally purchased his bride from her guardian, usually her father, by paying a "bride

---

term in the OB period (and CH) to describe the totality of the property of the wife, or what is assigned to the dowry as well as any other special gifts to the bride from the groom. Confusingly, these special gifts may also be called *nudunnûm*, hence the *nudunnûm* in its broad sense includes the *nudunnûm* in its narrow sense. In other words, while *nudunnûm* elsewhere includes the *širiktum*, in CH §§171-172 these terms are used contrastively because in this case *nudunnûm* refers merely to the special gifts from the husband (for which reason these laws are careful to qualify the term with "which her husband gave to her [*ša mussa iddinūšim*]" or "her husband did not give to her [*mussa ... la iddinūšim*]").

Unfortunately, there are no examples in either CH or MAL where *nudunnū(m)* bears the comprehensive meaning posited by Westbrook. Besides CH §§171-172, the term appears also in MAL A §27. According to the restored text of G.R. Driver and J.C. Miles, *nudunnū* also appears in MAL A §32, but this is almost certainly wrong since *nudunnū* is not feminine, as would be required by the following *tadnat* (a third person, feminine singular I/1 Stative of *tadānu*).

According to W. Lambert (private communication) the *biblu(m)* mentioned in CH §§159-161 as well as MAL A §30 may have been a douceur. The key to this interpretation is the recognition that there are two engagements in MAL A §30; the initial one (where *sinniltu* is used) has not progressed as far as the second one (where *aššatu* is used). The *biblu(m)* only expresses interest in a marriage; it is not a "bride price" or "marriage present." Lambert suspects that this is a gift given to the future father-in-law when the man initiates his own marriage, rather than having his parents arrange it. The *biblu(m)* would offer tangible proof that the young man was at one point quite eager for the marriage. For other evidence for this older view that the *biblu(m)* was an engagement gift, by contrast to the *terḥatum*, the bridal gift, cf. P. Koschaker, *Rechtsvergleichende Studien zur Gesetzgebung Hammurapis* (1917) 133f.; F. Mezger, "Promised but not engaged" (1944) 28-31; and G.R. Driver and J.C. Miles, *The Babylonian Laws*, I (1952) 249-265.

Against this view, cf. J. Renger, "Who are all those People?" (1973) 259-273; and R. Westbrook, "Old Babylonian Marriage Law," II, 303-306. Westbrook concludes that the *biblu(m)* "is a gift of various items other than money made on the occasion of 'marriage' celebrations by members of the groom's family to members of the bride's family" (*op. cit.*, 305).

[122] P. Koschaker expressed his views regarding OB purchase marriage in "Zum Eherecht," Chapter 2 in his *Rechtsvergleichende Studien zur Gesetzgebung Hammurapis* (1917) 111-235, and *idem*, "Eheschliessung und Kauf nach altem Recht, mit besonderer Berücksichtigung der älteren Keilschriftrechte" (1950) 210-296. Koschaker's views for MA practice are expressed in his "Quellenkritische Untersuchungen zu den altassyrischen Gesetzen" (1921), and his views regarding Nuzi practice are in "Neue keilschriftliche Rechtsurkunden aus der El-Amarna Zeit" (1928).

Koschaker later argued that all marriages in which a *terḥatum* is mentioned are purchase-marriages ("Fratriarchat, Hausgemeinschaft und Mutterrecht in Keilschriftrechten" [1933] 24).

Cf. also E. Neufeld, *Ancient Hebrew Marriage Laws* (1944) 94-117.

price," the *terḥatum* / מֹהַר.[123] As in all sales transactions, the sale would be completed not by the use of the object purchased (in the case of marriage this would be the *copula carnalis*), but simply by its transfer, the *traditio* (which in the case of marriage would imply a consummation of the marriage by the *in domum deductio*).[124]

Repeatedly criticized from its inception, especially by G.R. Driver and J.C. Miles, Koschaker's theory of "marriage by purchase" and his corresponding identification of the *terḥatum* / מֹהַר as a "bride price" have been all but abandoned among recent Assyriologists.[125] In addition to several studies which have challenged its applicability to Hittite, Egyptian, Nuzian, and Israelite practice, most recently the theory has been rejected decisively by R. Westbrook for the OB period, the very period for which the evidence had been considered the strongest.[126]

---

[123] P. Koschaker, *Rechtsvergleichende Studien zur Gesetzgebung Hammurapis*, 130, 137, 197; and *idem*, "Eheschliessung und Kauf nach altem Recht, mit besonderer Berücksichtigung der älteren Keilschriftrechte," 212.

[124] P. Koschaker, *Rechtsvergleichende Studien zur Gesetzgebung Hammurapis*, 115, 141 (where Koschaker denies that Babylonian law ever regards *copula carnalis* as decisive); *idem*, "Eheschliessung und Kauf nach altem Recht, mit besonderer Berücksichtigung der älteren Keilschriftrechte," 287.

The *in domum deductio* may not be strictly necessary for there to be the requisite removal of the bride from the physical control of her parents. Cf. R. Westbrook, "Old Babylonian Marriage Law," II, 126.

[125] G.R. Driver and J.C. Miles, *The Assyrian Laws* (1935) 142-173; and *idem*, *The Babylonian Laws*, I (1952) 259-265. Cf. also M. Burrows, *The Basis of Israelite Marriage* (1938) *passim*; A. van Praag, *Droit matrimonial assyro-babylonien* (1945) 139-143; A.J. Skaist, "Studies in Ancient Mesopotamian Family Law Pertaining to Marriage and Divorce" (1963); and R. Yaron, *The Laws of Eshnunna* (1988) 174-179.

[126] R. Westbrook, "Old Babylonian Marriage Law," II, 137-149.

Against the identification of Hittite *kušata* (HL §§29-30, 34) as a "bride price" and the applicability of the theory of marriage by purchase to Hittite practice, cf. F. Mezger, "Promised but not engaged" (1944) 28-31.

Against the application of the theory of purchase marriage to Egyptian practice (or the identification of the *šp* as a "bride price"), cf. E. Lüddeckens, *Ägyptische Eheverträge*, I (1960) 3; P.W. Pestman, *Marriage and Matrimonial Property in Ancient Egypt* (1961) 49f., 182-184; and H.J. Hendricks, "Juridical Aspects of the Marriage Metaphor in Hosea and Jeremiah," 27-28.

With respect to Nuzi practice, cf., e.g., K. Grosz, "Some Aspects of the Position of Women in Nuzi" (1989) 171.

Naturally, if the theory of marriage by purchase is untenable for cuneiform practice, this removes a principal argument for its application in Israel. Nevertheless, for arguments against this theory based on the biblical evidence, cf., *inter alia*, M. Burrows, *The Basis of Israelite Marriage*, *passim*; H. Weiss, "The Use of *QNH* in Connection with Marriage" (1964) 246; and W. Plautz, "Die Form der Eheschliessung im Alten Testament" (1964) 298-318.

Ironically, Gen. 31:14-16, a text which frequently is cited in support of the theory of purchase marriage in the OT (cf., e.g., E. Neufeld, *Ancient Hebrew Marriage Laws*, 98, n. 2), proves on closer examination to offer significant evidence against this view. Had Rachel and Leah held that marriage consisted of a woman being *sold* to her husband, they could have raised no complaint at what Laban had done. On the contrary, however, the very force of their complaint stems from the irregularity of Laban's demeaning treatment of them — "Are we not regarded by him as foreigners?" they ask, the implication being that one might sell a foreigner, but surely never a daughter! As a result, they insist that Laban had defrauded them of what was rightfully theirs, namely "the money given for us." Whatever מֹהַר had accrued from Jacob's years of labour, Laban was using up when it

Since none of the alternative views of מֹהַר excludes the possibility that marriage may have been consummated in sexual union, as does Koschaker's view, or that marriage itself may have been a covenant between husband and wife, we do not need to examine these views any further in the present context. Here we simply record our agreement with the main substance of M. Burrows' view regarding the מֹהַר, stated with more precision by R. Westbrook with respect to the *terḥatum*.

In contrast to Koschaker's attempt to compare the law of marriage to that of sale, and hence to identify the *terḥatum* as the price, Westbrook argues persuasively that the comparison ought rather to be between marriage and adoption and that this analogy was one which was recognized by ancient jurisprudence.[127] Like adoption, marriage is a status with rules peculiar to itself.[128] Just as there are two modes of adoption, there are also two modes of marriage. In the primary mode, where no third party is involved, a man adopts a foundling, an orphaned baby he finds in the market place.[129] Under such a circumstance, by the unilateral act of adoption without any contract the law simply accords the relationship the status of "sonship [*mârūtum*]."

The second mode of adoption differs from the first by the fact that the adoptee has natural parents. In this case, before the adoptive relationship can be created, the legal relationship of the adoptee to his natural parents must first be extinguished. This dual transaction in which the natural parents first relinquish their rights of control over the child to allow the adoptive parent to perform his act of adoption is typically recorded in an adoption document (the form and content of which are remarkably parallel to those of the marriage documents[130]). The contract, however, is ancillary to the adoption itself.

---

should have been returned in their dowry, or inheritance, as was customary throughout the ancient Near East. Rightfully, it belonged to them. In other words, Leah and Rachel themselves reject Laban's self-serving theory of marriage by purchase! Cf., e.g., C. Westermann, *Genesis 12-36*, 492.

For the practice of returning the *terḥatum* / מֹהַר with the dowry, a practice which undermines the theory of marriage by purchase, cf., e.g., CH §§163f. Cf. also A. van Praag, *Droit matrimonial assyro-babylonien* (1945) 152ff.; M. Burrows, *op. cit.*, 44; G.R. Driver and J.C. Miles, *The Babylonian Laws*, I, 253ff.; I. Mendelsohn, "On Marriage in Alalakh" (1959) 352ff.; R. de Vaux, *Ancient Israel*, I, 26-29; R. Yaron, *Introduction to the Law of the Aramaic Papyri* (1961) 47ff.; S. Dalley, "Old Babylonian Dowries" (1980) 53-74, at 57f.; K. Grosz, "Dowry and Brideprice in Nuzi" (1981) 161-182, esp. 170; R. Westbrook, "Old Babylonian Marriage Law," II, 300-303; and M.T. Roth, *Babylonian Marriage Agreements: 7th - 3rd Centuries B.C.*, 11f.

[127] "Old Babylonian Marriage Law," II, 150.

[128] Westbrook defines a "status," which he distinguishes from "contract," as a "set of rights and obligations between persons the extent and character of which is determined by the general rules of law.... But it is its own rules, not the agreement of the parties, which give the status its substance" ("Old Babylonian Marriage Law," II, 151f.). Cf. also the distinction between status and contract discussed by M.T. Roth, "'She will die by the iron dagger': Adultery and Neo-Babylonian Marriage," 187, 189, 190.

[129] Westbrook notes that this is the situation, for example, recorded in *UET* 5 260 ("Old Babylonian Marriage Law," II, 186, n. 74).

[130] Westbrook considers this parallelism of form and content between the marriage contracts and adoption contracts to be supportive of the analogy between marriage and adoption ("Old Babylonian Marriage Law," II, 150f.).

While the adoption documents offer no direct analogy for the *terḥatum*, Westbrook argues that the *terḥatum* was the price paid not for ownership of the bride, as Koschaker argued, nor even for the right of cohabitation, since at times someone other than the groom paid the *terḥatum*, but for the right to exercise control over the bride for a specified purpose.[131] "In the marriage documents the marriage formula expresses the transfer of control over the bride from her parents to the groom for the purpose of marriage; in the *kallūtum* documents the formula expresses transfer of control from parents to parents-in-law for the purpose of daughter-in-lawship."[132] In each case the parents are not ceding all of their rights as parents, but only this one aspect which is necessary for the parents-in-law to perform their duty or for the groom to perform the act of marriage.

2.1.1 מֹהַר *formative not of marriage, but of betrothal*

Is the payment of the *terḥatum* or מֹהַר formative of marriage? Whether or not these payments were obligatory to gain the required consent of in-laws, there is no evidence that the payment or receipt of the *terḥatum* or מֹהַר was constitutive of the marriage itself. As summarized by M. Burrows, "what *mohar* effected was not marriage but betrothal."[133] Compare, for example, 2 Sam. 3:14, in which David is quite explicit about the legal import of the מֹהַר as effecting his betrothal [ארשׂ]: "Give me my wife Michal, whom I betrothed at the price of a hundred foreskins of the Philistines [תְּנָה אֶת־אִשְׁתִּי אֶת־מִיכַל אֲשֶׁר אֵרַשְׂתִּי לִי בְּמֵאָה עָרְלוֹת פְּלִשְׁתִּים]."

Certainly, when the *terḥatum* is paid, a woman gains the title of "wife" [*aššatum* according to CH §161];[134] but, with Westbrook, it appears that this does not imply the full legal status of wife. This intermediate status, termed "inchoate marriage" by Driver and Miles, has implications only for third persons.[135] In Westbrook's words, the *terḥatum* "is effective to change betrothal into inchoate marriage, with a sharp rise in the protection of the groom's interest and drastic consequences upon the conduct of third parties [LE §26]."[136] With respect to the couple themselves, however, it is still

---

131 *Ibid.*, II, 155.

132 *Ibid.*, II, 156. In both cases *aḥāzum* expresses the transfer of control.

133 *The Basis of Israelite Marriage*, 20.

134 Cf. V. Korošec, "Ehe," in *RLA*, II, 282.

   H.J. Hendriks cites CH §160 as evidence that "a marriage is legally effected" with the bringing and acceptance of a *terḥatum* ("Juridical Aspects of the Marriage Metaphor in Hosea and Jeremiah," 19). CH §160, however, does not support this view. It proves only that acceptance of the *terḥatum* (and/or *biblum*) obligates a father-in-law to give his daughter in marriage and that, should he fail to do so, he will incur a financial penalty.

135 Cf. R. Westbrook, "Old Babylonian Marriage Law," II, 50. Cf. LE §26. Cf. also Deut. 20:7; 22:23-29; Exod. 22:15, 16 [ET 16, 17]; 1 Sam. 18:25; and 2 Sam. 3:13.

   Following common practice, the present study employs the terms "betrothal" and "inchoate marriage" interchangeably to refer to the married status of couples prior to their cohabitation. R. Westbrook, however, prefers to distinguish these terms and employs "betrothal" to refer only to the preliminary stage in the marriage negotiations preceding the giving of the *terḥatum* (*op. cit.*, 51).

136 *Ibid.*, II, 153.

legally possible to prevent the marriage from taking place; hence the *terḥatum* did not itself effect a marriage.[137]

As A. Skaist observes more generally, one must be careful to distinguish two distinct relationships involved in the formation of marriage in ancient Near Eastern practice.[138] The first is attested in the documents (i.e., the *riksātum*) and consists of a contract between a husband (or his guardian) and his father-in-law (or other guardian of the bride).[139] In this relationship in which the *terḥatum* plays a vital role, the wife appears as an object with the husband invariably marrying the wife, acquiring her from her father or other guardian (he "takes" her, she is "given" to him, etc.). The second relationship is the marriage proper, a relationship which exists between a husband and his wife.

If one considers only the first of these aspects of marriage, for example, if one supposes that the husband and the father-in-law create the marriage, it should be expected that only the husband and the father-in-law would have the authority to dissolve the marriage. Conversely, just as a piece of land cannot alter an agreement between a buyer and a seller, so it might be supposed that the wife would have no right to dissolve the marriage. In reality, however, there is no evidence that the bride's father can dissolve a marriage once it is formed; in fact, there is no evidence that he plays any continuing role in the marriage. Furthermore, contrary to expectation, for most of the ancient Near East there is substantial evidence that the wife did have a legal right to dissolve the marriage.[140]

Accordingly, it is the conclusion of the present study that the *terḥatum* / מֹהַר was not a "bride price," but was instead a "betrothal present," that is, a gift or payment which effected not marriage but betrothal, as noted already by M. Burrows.[141] Furthermore, although other ceremonies may have accompanied a wedding, no rite other than *copula carnalis* may be deemed constitutive of the marriage itself such as would permit it to be identified as an oath-sign.

---

[137] *Ibid.*, II, 50.

[138] A.J. Skaist, "Studies in Ancient Mesopotamian Family Law Pertaining to Marriage and Divorce" (1963) 7f.

[139] This understanding of the *riksātum* is preferable to that of S. Greengus, who assumes that the contract mentioned in LE §§ 27-28 and CH §128 is a contract between the bride and groom. Against S. Greengus on this point, cf. R. Westbrook, "Old Babylonian Marriage Law," II, 56-58.

[140] Cf. CH §142. For examples among OB marriage documents, cf. A. Poebel, *Babylonian legal and business documents from the time of the 1. Dynasty of Babylon*, vol. 6:2 (1906) nos. 40, 59. Cf. also A.J. Skaist, "Studies in Ancient Mesopotamian Family Law," 154-160; E. Lipiński, "The Wife's Right to Divorce in the light of an Ancient Near Eastern Tradition" (1981) 22f.; and Y. Zakovitch, "The Woman's Rights in the Biblical Law of Divorce" (1981) 28-46. Cf. also R. Westbrook, "Old Babylonian Marriage Law," II, 223-238. See also footnote 58 above.

[141] *The Basis of Israelite Marriage*, 20.

2.2 Sexual Union

It is the burden of the present section to demonstrate that sexual union (*copula carnalis*), when engaged in with consent (i.e., both parental, in the case of dependent daughters, and mutual), was understood as a marriage-constituting act and, correspondingly, was considered a requisite covenant-ratifying (and renewing) oath-sign for marriage, at least in the view of certain biblical authors.   Before turning to this posited covenant-ratifying implication, however, we must first consider the evidence that sexual union did, in fact, consummate marriage (contrary to the implication of the theory of purchase-marriage).

2.2.1 Ancient Near Eastern evidence for the role of sexual union in the consummation of marriage

G.R. Driver and J.C. Miles argue that in both OB and MA practice "inchoate marriage" was effected by the giving and receiving of the *terḫatu(m)*, while marriage itself was completed by sexual union, for which the *riksu* offered confirmatory evidence.[142]   This understanding of sexual union as consummating marriage is perhaps most evident in CH §§155f. If a man is caught having relations with a daughter-in-law whom he chose for his son [*ana mârīšu kallatam iḫīrma*], it is a capital offence if it takes place after his son has "known her [*ilmassi*]." If, however, his son has "not yet known her [*la ilmassīma*]," a financial penalty is imposed on the father-in-law, and the girl is permitted to leave and be married to another man.   Other laws demonstrate that betrothal already confers on a woman the protective status of "wife [*aššatum*]" with respect to outside parties, rendering any extramarital

---

[142] *The Assyrian Laws*, 172. Cf. also M. Burrows, *The Basis of Israelite Marriage*, 19.

Similarly, A. van Praag argues that *copula carnalis* consummates marriage, while the *terḫatu(m)* was originally intended to provide evidence for the legitimacy of the marriage, i.e., that it was not merely "concubinage" (*Droit matrimonial assyro-babylonien* [1945] 87f.). According to Van Praag, although the *terḫatu(m)* continued to be paid in later periods, its evidentiary value was rendered redundant with the advent of written marriage contracts.

R. Westbrook criticizes Van Praag, however, for identifying *aḫāzum* in CH §§128, 142, 159-61, etc., as a reference to sexual relations (*Old Babylonian Marriage Law*, II, 182, n. 22). Westbrook argues that in legal contexts related to marriage *aḫāzum* is not euphemistic for sexual intercourse, but is used to express "the acquisition of control over a woman by a man, sometimes expressly by way of transfer from her parent or guardian, and specifically for the purpose of placing both in the status of marriage" (*op. cit.*, 4; cf. also pp. 1-19).

While this understanding of *aḫāzum* is convincing for expressions like *ana aššūtim aḫāzum*, "to take for wifeship," which find a counterpart in the parents' promise *ana aššūtim nadānum*, "to give for wifeship," it is not so clear in other contexts, such as CH §142 or *CT* 8 37d. Westbrook's otherwise careful treatment appears to assume a false disjunction: either *aḫāzum* in marital-legal contexts must always refer to sexual union (which he demonstrates is certainly not the case), or it may never do so (here his treatment is less convincing).   In fact, it appears that OB *aḫāzum* may at times have a sexual reference, as it does in MB — a usage conceded by Westbrook (*op. cit.*, 19). Cf. the fuller discussion of *aḫāzum* below.

Accepting *aḫāzu(m)* as a reference to intercourse in the relevant texts, M. Burrows argues that sexual union regularly consummates marriage in Mesopotamian practice (*op. cit.*, 19, n. 13).

sexual intercourse to be treated as adultery.[143]   It is readily apparent, however, from a comparison of the present two cases that when a woman is betrothed or promised, sexual union with her promised husband decisively changes her status with respect to this man and any other persons having control over her (e.g., her father-in-law).

2.2.2 Biblical evidence for the formation of marriage by sexual union

Deuteronomy 21:10-14
R. Westbrook's analogy between marriage and the two modes of adoption is helpful for understanding the mode of marriage in Deut. 21:10-14, which is analogous to the primary mode of adoption, that is, a case in which a third party (the adoptee's natural parent) is not involved:

> When you go forth to war against your enemies... and see among the captives a beautiful woman, and you have desire for her and would take her for yourself as wife, then you shall bring her home to your house, and she shall shave her head and pare her nails. And she shall put off her captive's garb, and shall remain in your house and bewail her father and her mother a full month;[144] after that you may go in to her, and be her husband, and she shall be your wife [וְאַחַר כֵּן תָּבוֹא אֵלֶיהָ וּבְעַלְתָּהּ וְהָיְתָה לְךָ לְאִשָּׁה]. Then, if you have no delight in her, you shall let her go where she will; but you shall not sell her for money, you shall not treat her as a slave,[145] since you have had your way with her.

Because this woman was taken captive, there is no need to secure her parents' consent or to transfer control over her from them to the groom; accordingly, there is no mention of any marriage negotiations, marriage present, etc. Instead, in vs. 13 the would-be husband merely "goes into her [תָּבוֹא אֵלֶיהָ]," that is, has sexual relations with her, and the result of this single act is that he becomes her husband, and she becomes his wife. In other words, vs. 13 does not describe three separate actions in temporal sequence, as if the husband first "goes into her [תָּבוֹא אֵלֶיהָ]," and then sometime later "he becomes her husband [וּבְעַלְתָּהּ]," and still later "she becomes his wife [וְהָיְתָה לְךָ לְאִשָּׁה]." Rather, the last two clauses are epexegetical and, as such, are simultaneous reciprocal consequences of the first clause.[146]

Deuteronomy 25:5
A second example of Westbrook's "primary mode of marriage" is found in Deut. 25:5, the case of levirate marriage, where because of her widowed status a bride can once again enter marriage without a transfer of control from

---

[143] So G.R. Driver and J.C. Miles, *The Babylonian Laws*, I, 318f. Cf. also *idem, The Assyrian Laws*, 162-164.

[144] It may have been of more than incidental benefit that the month of mourning would also serve to assure the captor of his paternity of any children born to the union.

[145] Or "merchandise." Cf., e.g., P.C. Craigie, *Deuteronomy*, 282.

[146] For the converted perfect used to express epexegesis, cf. Waltke and O'Connor §§32.1e, 32.2.3e, 39.2.4.

her father (or other guardian): "If brothers dwell together, and one of them dies and has no son, the wife of the dead shall not be married outside the family to a stranger [לֹא־תִהְיֶה אֵשֶׁת־הַמֵּת הַחוּצָה לְאִישׁ זָר]; her husband's brother shall go in to her [יְבָמָהּ יָבֹא עָלֶיהָ], and take her as his wife [וּלְקָחָהּ לוֹ לְאִשָּׁה], and perform the duty of a husband's brother to her [וְיִבְּמָהּ]."

Without attempting to resolve here the many complexities of the institution of the levirate, this text identifies the brother's act of sexual union with marriage. The clause, "her husband's brother shall go in to her," is explained in the two subsequent clauses, each of which is introduced by a converted perfect: "he shall take her [וּלְקָחָהּ] as his wife" and "he will perform the duty of a husband's brother to her [וְיִבְּמָהּ]." This sequence is hardly chronological, since the normal idiom would be first to "take" a wife and then to "go in to her."[147]

Genesis 38:8, 18

An illustration of Deut. 25:5 is offered in Gen. 38:8: "Then Judah said to Onan, 'Go in to your brother's wife, and perform the duty of a brother-in-law to her, and raise up offspring for your brother.'" In this situation of widowhood, where marriage negotiations, etc., are neither present nor expected, the whole duty and formation of a levirate marriage is identified with sexual union. Accordingly, Judah's own unwitting sexual intercourse in vs. 18 appears to have sufficed to form a legal marriage, from which issued Perez and Zerah as legitimate offspring, and to have fulfilled Judah's shirked obligation for levirate marriage (for which reason Judah rescinds his condemnation of Tamar for her supposed adultery).[148] Whatever the precise explanation for Gen. 38:26, "... And he did not lie with her again," this statement appears to presuppose the existence of a marriage between Judah and Tamar, in which such relations would have been expected.[149]

Genesis 29:21-28

Perhaps the clearest example of sexual union consummating a marriage is provided by Gen. 29:21-28. Having met his contractual obligation to work for Laban seven years in exchange for Rachel, "Then Jacob said to Laban, 'Give me my wife that I may go in to her, for my time is completed'" (Gen.

---

[147] Cf. the previous note. As is also the case with Deut. 21:10-14, this abbreviated account does not exclude the possibility that there may have been various unrecorded ceremonies or rites which attended the marriage. It merely implies that these were without the decisive legal import which is accorded to sexual intercourse.

[148] Cf. Ruth 4:12.

[149] C. Westermann, for example, suggests that apart from the initial sexual union intended to father a child for the deceased husband, any subsequent relations may have been deemed incestuous (*Genesis 37-50*, 55). However, given the acceptance elsewhere in Genesis of endogamous marriage (cf., e.g., Abraham and his half-sister, Sarah, etc.), this suggestion appears unconvincing.

29:21).[150] From this verse it is apparent that *copula carnalis* is not just a characteristic feature of marriage, it is the decisive expression of the end of mere betrothal and, as such, consummates the marriage.

From the modern point of view where contracts are routinely nullified for an *error in essentialibus*, the following verses, Gen. 29:23-28, offer a surprising example of the irrevocable consequences of sexual union following the appropriate preliminaries of betrothal (payment of the marriage present, here in the form of seven years' labour, as well as the expressed desire for consummation on the part of the groom, and the consent of the guardian of the bride). On Jacob's wedding night Laban tricked Jacob into having sexual intercourse with Leah, rather than Rachel (perhaps helped by an unmentioned customary use of veiling[151]). In the morning Jacob discovers his error and complains bitterly about Laban's deceit.[152] At no point, however, is any question raised about the validity of the marriage which was thus formed by sexual union. The legal consequences of this action for the creation of a valid marriage appear to have been deemed irreversible.[153]

The legal implications of "premarital" sex
Consistent with a predisposition to view sexual union as a marriage-forming act, Exod. 22:15, 16 [ET 16, 17]; Deut. 22:28f.; as well as the seductions of Dinah in Genesis 34 and Tamar in 2 Samuel 13, all encourage or insist on the formalizing of marriage following an act of "premarital" sex. This formalization consists simply of paying the marriage present, which, if accepted, constitutes an *ex post facto* approval of the union by the girl's parents and extinction of their parental authority over her.

Exodus 22:15, 16 [ET 16, 17]
Exod. 22:15, 16 [ET 16, 17] stipulates, "If a man seduces a virgin/girl of marriageable age who is not betrothed, and lies with her, he shall give the marriage present for her, making her his wife. If her father utterly refuses to give her to him, he shall pay money equivalent to the marriage present for virgins/girls of marriageable age."

15 וְכִי־יְפַתֶּה אִישׁ בְּתוּלָה אֲשֶׁר לֹא־אֹרָשָׂה וְשָׁכַב עִמָּהּ מָהֹר יִמְהָרֶנָּה לּוֹ לְאִשָּׁה׃

16 אִם־מָאֵן יְמָאֵן אָבִיהָ לְתִתָּהּ לוֹ כֶּסֶף יִשְׁקֹל כְּמֹהַר הַבְּתוּלֹת׃

As recognized by most interpreters, the present law considers the case of the seduction of an unbetrothed nubile woman. The first condition,

---

[150] Ezek. 16:32 differs because its subject is a woman rather than a man, but also because it refers to adulterous unions as well as the rejected marital sexual union: "Adulterous wife, who takes strangers instead of her husband!"

[151] So, e.g., D. Daube, *Studies in Biblical Law*, 191f.

[152] Cf. Z. Jagendorf, "'In the morning, behold, it was Leah': Genesis and the Reversal of Sexual Knowledge" (1984) 187-192.

[153] Deut. 22:13-21 is less clear in the implication it attaches to sexual union because the husband's act may be mentioned not for its legal consequence, but for its practical consequence in accounting for the ensuing pregnancy.

namely that the man seduces [פתה] the girl, is important not only because it emphasizes the man's primary responsibility for this illicit act — he seduces her, not the reverse (cf., e.g., MAL A §56 or SL §8[154]) — but especially because it distinguishes the present case from that of rape, which is not explicitly considered in the Covenant Code.[155] Such a concern with the presumption of consent, or lack thereof, on the part of a woman is recognized as of critical importance in determining culpability in cases of extramarital sex (i.e., whether such acts are to be prosecuted as adultery or rape)[156] and would be a necessary consequence of the recognized need for volition in the contraction of covenants and the resulting nullity of covenants made under duress.[157]

The further qualification that the woman in question is "not betrothed" serves to distinguish the present case from that of adultery (cf. Deut. 22:23-29).[158] It is not immediately clear, however, why the girl is identified as a

---

[154] MAL A §56: "If the virgin has given herself to the seignior, the seignior shall (so) swear and they shall not touch his wife; the seducer shall give the (extra) third in silver as the value of a virgin (and) the father shall treat his daughter as he wishes" (*ANET*, 185).

SL §8: "If (a man) deflowered the daughter of a free citizen in the street, her father and her mother having known (that she was in the street) but the man who deflowered her denied that he knew (her to be of the free-citizen class), and, standing at the temple gate, swore an oath (to this effect, he shall be freed)" (*ANET*, 526).

With respect to the woman in SL §8, J.J. Finkelstein notes that her presence "in the street" implies loitering in a manner that causes the man to mistake her for a prostitute, to which misimpression he swears ("Sex Offences in Sumerian Laws" [1966] 357ff.).

Cf. further the legal recognition of the possibility of a (married) woman seducing a man in LU §4, "If a wife of a man, by resort to her charms, enticed a(nother) man, so that he slept with her, he! (i.e., the husband) shall slay that woman, but that man shall be set free."

[155] Cf. U. Cassuto, *Exodus*, 288. The failure of the Covenant Code to consider the case of rape is typical of its incompleteness (as is also the case with all ancient law collections). Cf., e.g., N.M. Sarna, *Exploring Exodus*, 168-171.

[156] Cf. Deut. 22:22-27.

This interest with the presumption of consent, or lack thereof, is abundantly paralleled in cuneiform law. The following are deemed cases of rape (where only the rapist is liable to a death penalty) based on the woman's lack of consent inferred from circumstantial evidence: LE §26; CH §155; MAL A §§12, 23b; and HL §197a. The following are deemed cases of adultery (where the woman and usually the man are both criminally liable) based on the woman's consent inferred from circumstantial evidence: LU §4; LE §28; CH §§129, 133b; MAL A §§13, 14, 15, 16, 23a, 23c; and HL §197b.

[157] Cf. D. Daube, "Covenanting under Duress" (1967) 352-59.

M. Malul stresses the importance of intention as a basic characteristic of symbolic actions having dispositive force (*Studies in Mesopotamian Legal Symbolism*, 27). There can be no intention if there is coercion.

Alternatively, cf. the stress on volition, particularly as expressed in the extant marriage contracts. Cf., e.g., Y. Muffs, *Studies in the Aramaic Legal Documents from Elephantine* (1973); *idem*, "Joy and Love as Metaphorical Expressions of Willingness and Spontaneity in Cuneiform, Ancient Hebrew, and Related Literatures" (1975) 1-36; *idem*, "Love and Joy as Metaphors of Volition in Hebrew and Related Literatures" (1979) 91-111; and M.T. Roth, *Babylonian Marriage Agreements: 7th - 3rd Centuries B.C.* (1989) 1.

[158] So also U. Cassuto, *Exodus*, 288. The alternative view of D.H. Weiss seems less likely ("A Note on אשר לא ארשה" [1962] 67-69). Weiss stresses that אֹרָשָׂה is a Pual perfect, rather than a Pual participle, hence "who had (never) been betrothed." According to Weiss the rationale for such a condition is that if the girl had ever been betrothed, even if the betrothal was later dissolved, the father would already have received a marriage present and so would incur no financial loss from this seduction.

"virgin [בְּתוּלָה]." It is doubtful, for example, that the text intends to stress her lack of previous sexual experience, since such a background would appear to be immaterial here. In any case, as argued by G.J. Wenham, the term בְּתוּלָה refers to a girl of marriageable age, not necessarily a *virgo intacta*.[159] Such a qualification in the present context may be intended to stress the woman's capacity to give consent or, perhaps, to differentiate this case from one of paedophilia (although biblical law gives little indication of how such a case might be viewed). Alternatively, and perhaps preferably, the identification of this woman as a בְּתוּלָה may be intended merely to distinguish this case from one involving a divorcée [גְּרוּשָׁה] or widow [אַלְמָנָה], for whom these stipulations would be inapplicable (i.e., such a marriage would not require a father's consent and the amount of the marriage present, if any was even required, would differ).[160]

The normal situation anticipated by this law is that any such act of "premarital" sex will be resolved by the man paying the marriage present [מֹהַר], which, if accepted, formalizes the relationship in marriage.[161] For our present purpose what is crucial to note is that the formation of the marriage, expressed in the dependent verbless clause לוֹ לְאִשָּׁה, "making her his wife," is not a third item in a list, contrary to a possible implication of the rendering of the RSV: "... lies with her, he shall give the marriage present for her, *and make her his wife* [italics added]." Instead, the girl is constituted a wife by

---

However, the perfect of statives and quasi-fientive verbs, such as אֵרַשׂ, is normally best rendered as a present tense, especially in the case of passives. So Waltke and O'Connor §30.5.3. Furthermore, as Weiss acknowledges, the LXX, Vulgate, and Targumim all agree with a present tense rendering for אֹרֵשָׂה in both Exod. 22:15 [ET 16] and Deut. 22:28, perhaps because of their appreciation of the complementarity between this law in Deut. 22:28f. and those which precede it (where the girl is betrothed).

[159] G.J. Wenham, "*betûlāh* 'A Girl of Marriageable Age'" (1972) 326-48. A. van Selms argues similarly for the Ugaritic term *ǵlmt*, noting, for example, the case of one lesser god, *gpn wugr*, who is called a son of (the divine) *ǵlmt* (*Marriage and Family Life in Ugaritic Literature* [1954] 38f.). Cf. also B. Landsberger, "Jungfräulichkeit: Ein Beitrag zum Thema 'Beilager und Eheschliessung'" (1968) 41-105, who stresses the evidence of the cognate Akkadian term *batultu* for a reference to age and not virginity as such; and M. Tsevat, *TDOT*, II, *s.v.* "בְּתוּלָה" 342f. In favour of "nubile," "marriageable," etc., rather than "virgin" as renderings of *batulu*, cf. also J.J. Finkelstein, "Sex Offences in Sumerian Laws," 356f.; and *CAD* B, *s.v. batulu*.

In favour of "virgin" for בְּתוּלָה and *batulu(m)*, contra Wenham, *et al.*, cf., e.g., T. Wadsworth, "Is There a Hebrew Word for Virgin? *Bethulah* in the Old Testament" (1980) 161-171; and especially C. Locher, *Die Ehre einer Frau in Israel* (1986). Likewise, M.T. Roth favours a reference to virginity among the range of meanings of *batulu* in the NB period ("Age at Marriage and the Household: A Study of Neo-Babylonian and Neo-Assyrian Household Forms" [1987] 742ff.). It is possible that the conflicting impression of these scholars may be the result of a confusion of reference with meaning — since in the ancient Near East a "marriageable" young woman would almost always be a virgin.

Alternatively, J.M. Sasson suggests that בְּתוּלָה means "virgin" in the sense that the womb of such a girl had been opened neither by birth nor by miscarriage (*Ruth*, 133).

[160] M. Burrows, for example, notes that a *terḥatum* was not normally required for marriage to a widow (*The Basis of Israelite Marriage*, 30). Cf. MAL §34. Cf. the treatment of this law in V. Korošec, "Die Ususehe nach assyrischem Recht" (1937) 1-12.

[161] The primary case may assume that the man in question is unmarried (cf. MAL A §55). For the more general case, cf. LE §§26-27 and MAL A §§55-56.

meeting two, and only two, indispensable requirements, namely sexual union and securing the formal consent of the bride's parents expressed in the payment and receipt of the marriage present: "... and lies with her, he shall give the marriage present for her, *making her his wife* [לְאִשָּׁה לוֹ]."

The subsidiary case in Exod. 22:16 [ET 17] considers the situation where the father of the girl refuses to give his daughter in marriage to the offending man. In such a case, the man must still pay "money equivalent to the marriage present for virgins." It seems plausible that in the main case the requirement for a marriage present (with its implied negotiations and receipt by the father) makes clear the consent of the girl's father and the subsequent legitimacy of the marriage, as well as providing indirectly for the financial well-being of the bride (as the marriage present [מהר] was customarily returned to brides in the dowry[162]). Whatever the precise justification for the payment in the subsidiary case (not identified as a marriage present [מהר] because there would be no marriage), it is clearly viewed as a penalty against the man for his sexual misconduct.[163]

Furthermore, if the qualifying phrase, "the marriage present for virgins," applies to the main case as well, in view of Shechem's desperate willingness to pay any price for Dinah and the readiness of Dinah's brothers to take advantage of his willingness, the intention of this text may have been to protect such a committed suitor from extortion.[164] The law stipulates that the marriage present [מֹהַר] will be no more (and no less) than the customary amount for a virgin.

Finally, the ability of the father to disallow the marriage in the subsidiary case (an ability presupposed also in the account of Shechem and Dinah in Genesis 34[165]) does not contradict the possibility that sexual union in certain contexts may have been viewed (at least by some biblical authors) as a covenant-forming oath-sign. This provision may be viewed merely as a corollary of a father's more general right to disallow any vow made by a dependant daughter (Num. 30:3-5).[166] On the other hand, the major case,

---

[162] Cf. footnote 126 above.

[163] E. Neufeld argues that the fine in the subsidiary case was intended as compensation for the father's financial loss (*Ancient Hebrew Marriage Laws*, 101, 103). So also M. Weinfeld, *Deuteronomy and the Deuteronomic School*, 284f. This explanation makes two assumptions which need justification. First, it assumes that such a daughter would now be unmarriageable, but cf. the readiness of David, for example, to marry the widowed Abigail, etc. Cf. also the apparent marriageability of the nonvirginal Ruth, Rahab, Bathsheba, etc. Second, Neufeld assumes that the father incurred a loss because, if his daughter had married, he would have been enriched by her husband's מהר. As mentioned earlier, however, in actual practice the מהר was not kept by the father, but was normally returned in the dowry.

[164] Given that such matters normally are made public only in the event of a pregnancy, one wonders whether this factor also contributed to Shechem's fervency. Gen. 34:26 makes clear that Dinah was already living with Shechem.

[165] Cf. F.C. Fensham, "Genesis 34 and Mari" (1975) 87-90.

[166] R. Yaron similarly appeals to Numbers 30 to explain why a lapse in the marital status of a woman following desertion, divorce, or widowhood does not re-establish the father's authority (*The Laws of Eshnunna* [1988] 220, n. 174). Hence she is free to contract

where the seducer marries the girl, may be compared to the normal requirement in Lev. 5:1-4 to keep even a rash oath (cf. Num. 30:2).[167]

Deuteronomy 22:28, 29
Deut. 22:28, 29 reads:

> "If a man meets a virgin/a woman of marriageable age who is not betrothed, and seizes her and lies with her, and they are found, then the man who lay with her shall give to the father of the young woman fifty shekels of silver, and she shall be his wife, because he has violated her; he may not put her away all his days."

28 כִּי־יִמְצָא אִישׁ נַעַר [נַעֲרָה] בְתוּלָה [נַעֲרָה] אֲשֶׁר לֹא־אֹרָשָׂה וּתְפָשָׂהּ וְשָׁכַב עִמָּהּ וְנִמְצָאוּ׃

29 וְנָתַן הָאִישׁ הַשֹּׁכֵב עִמָּהּ לַאֲבִי הַנַּעַר [הַנַּעֲרָה] חֲמִשִּׁים כָּסֶף וְלוֹ־תִהְיֶה לְאִשָּׁה תַּחַת אֲשֶׁר עִנָּהּ לֹא־יוּכַל שַׁלְּחָהּ כָּל־יָמָיו׃

Representative of a number of scholars, P.C. Craigie considers this law under the rubric: "The rape of a single woman."[168] The NIV shares a similar understanding, which it reinforces by the parallel construction of its translation of vss. 25 and 28, both using the verbs "meet" and "rapes":

> Deut. 22:25 [NIV]: "But if out in the country a man happens to meet [יִמְצָא] a girl pledged to be married and rapes her [וְהֶחֱזִיק־בָּהּ הָאִישׁ וְשָׁכַב עִמָּהּ], only the man who has done this shall die."
> Deut. 22:28 [NIV]: "If a man happens to meet [יִמְצָא] a virgin who is not pledged to be married and rapes her [וּתְפָשָׂהּ וְשָׁכַב עִמָּהּ] and they are discovered...."

From the context, there is no question that Deut. 22:25 deals with an act of rape, and all interpreters understand it as such. Accordingly, an idiomatic rendering of the hendiadys "he seizes her and lies with her [וְהֶחֱזִיק־בָּהּ הָאִישׁ וְשָׁכַב עִמָּהּ]" in that verse as "and rapes her" is perhaps justified.[169]

Contrary to Craigie and the NIV, however, it is not at all clear that Deut. 22:28-29 treats a case of rape rather than seduction or even premarital sex with mutual consent, as in the parallel case of Exod. 22:15, 16 [ET 16, 17]. The fact that this law employs vocabulary in vs. 28 different from that used in vs. 25 (תפש rather than החזיק) does not favour the assumption that the

---

her own second marriage (cf. LE §§29, 30, 59; CH §§137, 156, 172; and MAL A §§36, 45). For the similar Talmudic practice under such circumstances, cf. *m. Ketub.* 4:2.

[167] Cf. also Jer. 7:9; Ps. 15:4; 24:4; and Eccl. 5:4ff.

[168] *Deuteronomy*, 295. So also J. Morgenstern, "The Book of the Covenant, Part 2" (1930) 118ff.; G. von Rad, *Deuteronomy* (1966) 143; J. Ridderbos, *Deuteronomy* (1984) 227. M. Weinfeld observes that this is the typical view of rabbinic exegetes as well (*Deuteronomy and the Deuteronomic School*, 287, n. 2).

[169] The Hiphil of חזק typically means "seize," "take hold of," "overpower," etc., and is used elsewhere in quite general ways (e.g., cf. Ps. 35:2, "Take hold of shield and buckler," or Prov. 4:13, "Keep hold of instruction"), as well as in connection with various acts of physical violence including sexual violence (i.e., Judg. 19:25 and 2 Sam. 13:11). It is important to note, however, that in these last two examples חזק refers only to the seizure of the female victim, not to the sexual act itself. Judg. 19:25 makes this especially clear since the man who "seized" the Levite's concubine was not among those who sexually abused her.

context of rape in vss. 25-27 necessarily carries over to 28-29. Furthermore, while it is true that the verb תפש, "to lay hold of" or "to seize," can be used with reference to the detainment of persons (as in Deut. 21:19, or even Gen. 39:12, where Potiphar's wife "caught him by his garment [וַתִּתְפְּשֵׂהוּ בְּבִגְדוֹ], saying, 'Lie with me'") or acts of violence (as perhaps in Ps. 71:11), it can also be used in a quite general manner, as in Deut. 9:17, "So I took hold [תפש] of the two tables...," or Ezek. 14:5, "that I may lay hold [תפש] of the hearts of the house of Israel...."[170]

An extrabiblical parallel may support the possibility that the mention of "seizing" can be intended only to indicate the man's initiative, but it need not preclude the woman's consent. In HL §197a, a man "seizes a woman in the mountains, it is the man's crime and he will be killed." The apparent implication of the mountainous setting is that the screams for help of this woman could not be heard, and hence the case is one of rape. HL §197b, however, states, "But if he seizes her in (her) house, it is the woman's crime and the woman shall be killed." In this setting, with her apparent failure to cry for help, the law presumes that she gave her consent in spite of the use of the term "seize."[171]

Although a term for "seize" is not employed in MAL A §23b,c, a similar situation in which a woman did not intend to engage in extramarital relations and appears to have done so only under duress is envisaged (although there is some uncertainty about the meaning of *kî pîge* in line 30[172]). The facts of the case are sufficient to presume coercion in MAL A §23b if the woman immediately declares upon leaving the house that "she had been forced to have illicit relations [*nîkutūni*]." In MAL A §23c the woman neglects to make this critical declaration. Since this is the only difference from the earlier situation, which was deemed to be a case of rape, it must have been assumed that the man finally gained her consent (for which reason she did not later complain), and so the case is treated as one of adultery rather than rape.

Decisive evidence that Deut. 22:28-29 concerns a case of consenting premarital sex rather than rape appears in the expression, "and they are found [וְנִמְצָאוּ]."[173] It is notable that the same implication of consent attends the expression, "is found [יִמָּצֵא]," in Deut. 22:22 (rendering this a case of adultery rather than rape) and the Akkadian equivalent of this expression, the IV/1

---

[170] Cf. also Amos 2:15 and Jer. 2:8.

M. Weinfeld concludes, "The word ותפשה means 'held' and not necessarily 'attacked'" (*Deuteronomy and the Deuteronomic School*, 286); G.J. Wenham suggests "grab (impetuously)" (private communication).

[171] This presumption of consent is confirmed by the mention of "finding them" in the subsidiary case which immediately follows, "If the husband finds them, he may kill them, there shall be no punishment for him."

[172] It is unclear whether *kî pîge* in line 30 should be rendered "under threats" (cf. G.R. Driver and J.C. Miles, *The Assyrian Laws*, 467) or "under a pretext" (cf. R. Borger, *et al.*, *Rechtsbücher* [1982] 84).

[173] So also M. Weinfeld, *Deuteronomy and the Deuteronomic School*, 286; and A.D.H. Mayes, *Deuteronomy*, 312.

perfect of *ṣabātum*, in cuneiform law.[174]   Furthermore, as noted by A.D.H. Mayes, the verb "violate [עָנָה]" found in vs. 29 in the explanatory clause, "because he has violated her [תַּחַת אֲשֶׁר עִנָּהּ]," is used of a consenting woman earlier in the same chapter in vs. 24 and so does not require the assumption of rape, as often supposed.[175]   Mayes suggests rendering the expression: "because he had his way with her."[176]

Finally, given the likely concern for the well-being of the woman reflected in the denial of the guilty husband's right to divorce in vs. 29, the remedy of an enforced marriage to a rapist whom she may have bitterly hated appears contradictory and quite inexplicable.[177]   The clearest indication elsewhere regarding the biblical attitude toward the rape of an unbetrothed woman, namely 2 Samuel 13, suggests that marriage was possible if the couple were willing; otherwise, the implication of Tamar's scream in vs. 19 (cf. Deut. 22:24, 27; cf. also MAL A §23b and HL §197a) and the subsequent narrative indicate that such a rape merited the death penalty.[178]   In any case, although the rather severe MAL A §55 may permit marriage in the case of a rape, nowhere among cuneiform examples is marriage a *required* remedy for rape, as would be implied in Deut. 22:28f. on the view that this text concerns rape.[179]

---

[174] Cf., e.g., "if the wife of a man is found [*ittaṣbat*] lying with another man..." in CH §129. Cf. also LE §28 and MAL A §15.

Cf. also M.T. Roth, "'She will die by the iron dagger': Adultery and Neo-Babylonian Marriage" (1988) 192-7, for a discussion of the stipulation in certain Neo-Babylonian marriage documents, "Should ᶠPN be found with another man...." Roth considers that this expression implies both the woman's consent and also the fact that the adulterers are caught *in flagrante delicto* (much as in CH §§ 129, 131, 132; LE § 28; and MAL A §15).

Confirming the assumption of the woman's consent in 22:28f. and the relevance of the repetition of the expression "and they are found [וְנִמְצְאוּ]" in both 22:22 and 22:28, G.J. Wenham and J.G. McConville argue for an extensive intentional parallelism between the first three and the second three cases in Deut. 22:13-29, such that the law of adultery in 22:22 corresponds to the present law in 22:28f. ("Drafting Techniques in Some Deuteronomic Laws" [1980] 248-252).

[175] *Deuteronomy*, 313. So also M. Weinfeld, *Deuteronomy and the Deuteronomic School*, 286.

[176] *Deuteronomy*, 304. Note the similar sequence of verbs in Gen. 34:2, "and when Shechem the son of Hamor the Hivite, the prince of the land, saw her, he seized her [וַיִּקַּח אֹתָהּ] and lay with her [וַיִּשְׁכַּב אֹתָהּ] and humbled her [וַיְעַנֶּהָ]."

[177] Cf. M. Weinfeld, *Deuteronomy and the Deuteronomic School*, 286f.

Although biblical practice, as elsewhere in the ancient Near East, can hardly be said to stress the role of love as a motivation for marriage, or even the consent of the bride, there are a number of texts which reveal that such concerns may not have been totally disregarded. Cf., e.g., Gen. 24:5, 57ff.; 29:18; Exod. 2:21; Judg. 14:3, 7; 1 Sam. 18:20; 2 Sam. 13:13; Prov. 18:22; and Tob. 6:17. Cf. also M. Burrows, *The Basis of Israelite Marriage*, 24f.; T.L. Thompson, *The Historicity of the Patriarchal Narratives*, 251f.; and T. Jacobsen, *The Harps That Once... Sumerian Poetry in Translation* (1987) 10-15.

[178] The justice of Absalom's execution of Amnon is nowhere questioned and appears as an indictment against David's perversion of justice (advertised by Absalom in 2 Sam. 15:3f.) for having failed to deal with Amnon.

[179] The ensuing requirement in MAL A §55 that the wife of the rapist was now to be sexually abused (as a rigid, if not impractical, application of the *lex talionis*) has been called by J.J. Finkelstein "a piece of typically Assyrian moralistic 'calculated frightfulness'" ("Sex Offences in Sumerian Laws," 357).

Having argued that Deut. 22:28f. treats a case of premarital sex, rather than rape, we may observe several points of contrast between this law and the similar case in Exod. 22:15, 16 [ET 16, 17]. One obvious difference is the precise specification of the amount of the marriage present [מֹהַר], namely "fifty shekels of silver." Based on Exod. 22:15, 16 [ET 16, 17], W.H. Gispen, for example, assumes that this amount represented the normal marriage present for virgins.[180] This is possible, but not certain. As argued earlier, this figure may be exceptionally high in order to penalize the offender. At the same time, there may also be a secondary concern to compensate the parents, who are deprived somewhat of their customary right of refusal unlike the case in Exodus 22. In support of understanding the fifty shekel payment primarily as a penalty, G.J. Wenham and J.G. McConville note a chiastic literary structure in Deut. 22:13-29, whereby this fifty shekels paid to the girl's father and the prohibition of divorce find corresponding stipulations in the first case treated in vs. 19, where they are clearly intended as penalties.[181]

The apparent denial of the parents' right of refusal constitutes a second striking difference between the present law and that found in Exodus 22. A.D.H. Mayes suggests two possible explanations. First, it is thought that the Deuteronomic insistence on marriage may represent an innovation intended to protect the girl by ensuring that she would not be left unmarried. While possible, this insinuates that the girl needs protection from her own father's poor judgment, since Exodus 22 already insists on a marriage apart from his refusal. Second, Mayes suggests that the required marriage may be intended to prevent the girl's father from receiving a second marriage present.[182] It is

---

The apparently mandatory marriage to a rapist in SL §7 is a result of a mistranslation (*ANET*, 525f.). As appears from Finkelstein's transliteration of the text, the content of the girl's statement, if it was the girl's and not the offending man's, is not found in the text. Consequently, it is possible that the offending man or the girl merely reported to her parents what happened, and the text ought to be translated: "If (a man) deflowered the daughter of a free citizen in the street, and her father and her mother (did not know it), and she/he (then) tells her father and her mother, her father and her mother may give her to him as a wife."

On the other hand, in cases of cohabitation, where there is obvious consent on the part of the girl, but not as yet from her parents, cuneiform law requires this defect to be remedied by negotiating a marriage contract with her parents to formalize their consent. Apart from this remedy, no amount of time can regularize the marriage. Cf. LE §§27, 28, and CH §128. Cf. R. Westbrook, "Old Babylonian Marriage Law," II, 57f.

Cf. MAL A §56 and SL §8 for cases of solicitation (not merely consent) on the part of an unbetrothed girl.

Accordingly, K. van der Toorn argues that in Sumerian and Babylonian law a man had to marry a virgin if he seduced her, but only if the latter agreed (*Sin and Sanction in Israel and Mesopotamia* [1985] 161, n. 75). Cf. also B. Landsberger, "Jungfräulichkeit: Ein Beitrag zum Thema 'Beilager und Eheschliessung'," 50-52, cited by Van der Toorn.

[180] *Exodus*, 221. J.P. Hyatt, however, considers it more likely that it was not so high in the earlier period represented by the Covenant Code (*Exodus*, 241).

[181] "Drafting Techniques in Some Deuteronomic Laws" (1980) 250.

[182] Similarly, C.M. Carmichael suggests that under the influence of Genesis 34, Deuteronomy 22 is intended to close a loophole left by the provision in Exodus 22 (*Law*

unclear, however, why this would be deemed a problem given the examples cited elsewhere of widows and divorcees who commanded a second marriage present.[183]

C.M. Carmichael offers an alternative explanation for the denial of the parents' right of refusal in this law.[184] Given the concern expressed in Deut. 22:13-21 about marriage to a nonvirginal (or perhaps pregnant) bride, Deut. 22:28-29 may be intended to prevent this possibility by its insistence on marriage without exception.

A final possibility is that the explanation for the differing remedies in these laws is to be found in the degree of the girl's consent and (perhaps even on-going) abetment implied in the phrase "and they are found [וְנִמְצָאוּ]" in Deut. 22:28.[185] In other words, while Exodus 22 considers the case of the *seduction* of an unbetrothed nubile girl (a one-time occurrence perhaps requiring some assessment by her father of the degree of her reluctant consent), Deuteronomy considers the special case where there is unmistakable circumstantial evidence for consenting premarital sex.[186]

The last significant difference between Exod. 22:15, 16 [ET 16, 17] and Deut. 22:28, 29 concerns the revocation of the husband's right of divorce in the latter text (as also in Deut. 22:19b). The inequality of this punishment by contrast to Deut. 22:22, for example, where the girl is also punished, and the remarkable protection it affords to the wife suggest that this law "recognizes that an injury has been inflicted on the girl. This is entirely in accord with Deuteronomy's humanitarian ideals, particularly towards those who had no means of protecting themselves through the courts (Deut. 10:18, 24:17-22)."[187] This recognition of an injury to the girl need not contradict the earlier claim for her consent. Vs. 28a makes plain the man's initiative and so

---

and Narrative in the Bible [1985] 218-220). A father eager for financial gain is limited by Exodus 22 from jacking up the "bride price" beyond what was normal for virgins. Accordingly, he decides to collect the fine and double his gain by arranging another marriage. Deuteronomy 22 prevents this scenario by fixing the "bride price" and insisting on marriage.

[183] For example, R. Westbrook cites a case where a *terḫatum* was paid for a nonvirgin bride ("Old Babylonian Marriage Law," II, 155).

[184] *Law and Narrative in the Bible*, 220.

[185] Cf. M. Weinfeld, *Deuteronomy and the Deuteronomic School*, 286.

C.M. Carmichael, on the other hand, argues that the purpose of the qualifier, "and they are found," is merely to establish their guilt (*Law and Narrative in the Bible*, 220): "Without it, a woman in collusion with her father could exploit a man, especially under the existing law in Exod 22:16, 17)." It may be doubted, however, that in biblical times there would have been many girls or fathers who would have considered the potential damage to the daughter's reputation to be worth this financial gain. The case of Potiphar's wife, cited by Carmichael, differs significantly. The claim to have *rebuffed* the sexual advances of a youthful and handsome Joseph could only enhance her reputation and appearance of rectitude.

[186] With this evidence of the girl's complicity, there would be little point in a father so disregarding his daughter's implied wishes by forbidding a marriage. Cf. 1 Sam. 18:20 and 2 Sam. 13:13. Cf. also footnote 175 above.

[187] A. Phillips, "Another Look at Adultery" (1981) 9f., cf. also p. 12. Phillips accepts D.H. Weiss's proposal discussed above ("A Note on אשר לא ארשה" [1962] 67-69).

greater responsibility for what transpires: He "meets a virgin... seizes her and lies with her."[188]

Furthermore, if it is the case that in Exodus 22 the couple voluntarily reveal what has transpired, while in Deuteronomy "they are found," this difference may suggest a further explanation for the forfeiture of the husband's right of divorce in Deuteronomy 22. It may be that this law considers this man's marital intentions to be questionable, as in Deut. 22:19 where a husband who was looking for a way out of his marriage (but wanted to keep the marital property?) similarly forfeits his right of divorce.[189]   In Exodus 22, on the other hand, no such provision is necessary because it appears that this groom is quite ready to rectify his situation (much as was the case with Shechem). Not only are his honourable intentions implied by their self-revelation, but also the only impediment anticipated is that the bride's father might "utterly refuse" his request. As will be recalled, the stipulated customary "marriage present for virgins" may offer further testimony to the repentant groom's willingness, in that it may have been intended to protect him from extortion (cf. Gen. 34:11, 12).

Genesis 34 and 2 Samuel 13:16

The narratives of the premarital sexual intercourse of Shechem with Dinah in Genesis 34 and of Amnon with Tamar in 2 Samuel 13 are clear in their moral censure for these acts (cf. Gen. 34:5, 7, 31; and 2 Sam. 13:12f.). Both texts appear to exonerate the woman in question by stressing the forcible nature of the seduction ("he seized her [וַיִּקַּח אֹתָהּ] and lay with her [וַיִּשְׁכַּב אֹתָהּ]"[190] and humbled her [וַיְעַנֶּהָ]" in Gen. 34:2; and "he took hold of her... he would not listen to her; and being stronger than she, he forced her [וַיְעַנֶּהָ], and lay with her" in 2 Sam. 13:11, 14).

While both wrongs are finally redressed by the execution of the lover by the victim's brother, employing a deception, it is remarkable that the narrator leaves little doubt that the preferred remedy would have been the *urgent* regularizing of these relationships in marriage.[191]   Compare Gen. 34:4,

---

[188] As argued by J.J. Finkelstein, unmarried women (normally girls) in the ancient Near East almost never sought out sexual experiences on their own initiative ("Sex Offenses in Sumerian Laws," 368ff.). As a result, the law collections normally assume an element of coercion or persuasion on the part of the man in such cases (MAL A §56 and SL §8 are exceptions).

[189] In support of a parallel between the third and sixth cases presented in Deut. 22:13-29, cf. again the structural analysis of G.J. Wenham and J.G. McConville, "Drafting Techniques in Some Deuteronomic Laws" [1980] 248-252.

[190] Given the lack of any certain examples of שׁכב being used transitively (2 Sam. 13:14 and Ezek. 23:8 are both doubtful), perhaps אֹתָהּ should be repointed אִתָּהּ with *BHS*, following the LXX (and Syriac, Targum Pseudo-Jonathan, and Vulgate): μετ' αὐτῆς.

[191] Because of the inversion of love into hate in 2 Sam. 13:15 (perhaps a result of transferred guilt), it is perhaps too easy to dismiss the earlier mention of Amnon's "love" for Tamar in 13:1 as a euphemism for lust. In any case, the text implies that Tamar cared for Amnon, not only because of her ministration to him in his "sickness," as well as her willingness to feed him from her own hand the suggestive "heart-shaped cakes [הַלְּבִבוֹת]," but particularly because of her expressions of consent for marriage in 2 Sam. 13:13 and 13:16.

8, 11f.; 49:5-7; and especially Tamar's words to Amnon in 2 Sam. 13:16: "No, my brother, for this wrong in sending me away is greater than the other which you did to me." In other words, both texts imply that in the case of premarital sex the *in domum deductio* was expected to coincide with *copula carnalis*. Gen. 34:17, 26 makes explicit the fact that after intercourse Dinah remained in Shechem's home, even while negotiations were under way for the marriage.[192] On the other hand, Amnon's eviction of Tamar from his home was immediately understood as a decisi repudiation of any marital intention — in effect, redefining their act of intercourse as rape (in 2 Sam. 13:19 Tamar leaves expressing her grief and "crying aloud [וְזָעָקָה] as she went," the latter expression perhaps recalling the "crying out [צעק]" of the rape victim in Deut. 22:24, 27 and the "calling [קרא]" of Gen. 39:14f., 18).[193]

2.2.3 The obligatory nature of sexual union for the consummation of marriage

Cuneiform law makes plain a legal obligation on the part of the groom to consummate marriage once there has been inchoate marriage. Compare, for example, CH §159, where a groom has paid the *biblum* and *terḫatum*, but later has his eyes on another woman.[194] He announces to his father-in-law, "I will not take your daughter [*mâratka ul âḫḫaz*]," and accordingly forfeits the *biblum* and *terḫatum* as a penalty. One legal document from Sippar demonstrates this obligation in actual practice. *CT* 45, 86 is a court procedure concering a groom who refuses to consummate his marriage.[195] In the presence of witnesses, Aham-nirshi is questioned, "'Is this lady your wife?' He said, 'Hang me on a peg and dismember me! I will not do the taking [*ul âḫḫaz*]'" (lns. 18b-22). Accordingly, Aham-nirshi proceeds to bind up his bride's hem and cut it off in a recognized legal gesture for effecting a divorce,

---

While Genesis 34 nowhere explicitly mentions Dinah's love or consent, this consent may be inferred from the extraordinary emphasis in the narrative on Shechem's love and willingness to pay any price for her hand in marriage (cf. Gen. 34:3, 4, 8, 11, 12).

It is doubtful whether there would be the same expectation for the urgent regularizing of sexual relationships in marriage apart from such a context of consent and even love.

[192] Alternatively, M. Sternberg sees Dinah's detention as an offence, offering proof that her brothers were negotiating under duress and were justified to resort to "guile and violence" (*The Poetics of Biblical Narrative* [1985] 456ff., as pointed out to the writer by G.J. Wenham). As conceded by Sternberg, however, the text is not so clear in its moral assessment of the brothers' stratagem. In any case, at no point does the text state or imply that Dinah's residency in Shechem's home was either against her will or supportive of the brothers' charge that their sister was being treated like a harlot (whether by Judah, as Sternberg suggests, or by Shechem). Harlots were paid for their services, not domiciled. Furthermore, the contrast between Gen. 34:17, 26, and 2 Sam. 13:16, as well as the emphasis in Genesis 34 on Shechem's love for Dinah, does not favour Sternberg's view on this point.

[193] Cf. also S. Rattray, "Marriage Rules, Kinship Terms and Family Structure in the Bible" (1987) 537-544; and P. Trible, *Texts of Terror*, 37-63.

[194] This may be mentioned in order to stress the groom's culpability, rather than to suggest any defect in the girl which would warrant this change in plans.

[195] For a new edition of this text, cf. R. Westbrook, "Old Babylonian Marriage Law," I, 145-147.

providing evidence that a formal divorce was required for dissolving even an inchoate marriage.[196] The precise reference of the verb *aḫāzum*, "to take," is ambiguous in both of these examples. This verb may refer to the consummation of a marriage in general terms (perhaps referring to the acquisition of responsibility for and control over the bride), but it may also refer more particularly to sexual intercourse, as it appears to in CH §142.[197]

The Old Testament nowhere makes explicit the legal obligation, assuming one exists, of the groom to consummate a marriage in sexual union following betrothal. The celebrated case of Onan in Gen. 38:9 involves not a refusal to consummate a marriage in sexual intercourse, but a stratagem for avoiding impregnation. Genesis 38 does seem to imply an obligation on the part of Shua or Judah to consummate a marriage with the widowed Tamar, but it is arguable that this evidence would be applicable only to levirate betrothal, not to betrothal more generally.

Nevertheless, Deut. 20:7 indicates the high social priority which was placed on the consummation of marriage following betrothal.[198] After the conquest (during which all Israel was to fight), if Israel finds herself confronted by an enemy, the officers of the people were to exempt several categories of recruits, including men whose marriages were unconsummated: "... what man is there that has betrothed a wife and has not taken her? Let him go back to his house, lest he die in the battle and another man take her."[199] Alternatively, Deut. 28:30 lists among the curses for covenant breaking, "You shall betroth a wife, and another man shall lie[200] with her; you shall build a house, and you shall not dwell in it; you shall plant a vineyard, and you shall not use the fruit of it" — each threat reversing one of the three exemptions listed in Deut. 20:5-7.[201]

---

[196] Cf. J.J. Finkelstein, "Cutting the *sissiktu* in Divorce Proceedings" (1975-76) 236-240, at 240; and M. Malul, *Studies in Mesopotamian Legal Symbolism*, 203f. Cf. also Matt. 1:19.

[197] "If a woman hated her husband and [*šumma sinništum mussa izêrma*] she has declared, 'you may not *take* me [*ul tāḫḫazanni iqtabi*]', ..." The context and subsequent investigation of the wife makes plain that this was a full-fledged marriage, and so "take" cannot refer to the groom's acquisition of responsibility for and control over the bride from his father-in-law — this was already the case. Accordingly, most interpreters consider *tāḫḫazanni* a reference to the refusal of conjugal rights.

So also *CAD* A/1, s.v. *aḫāzu*, 1(b); and G.R. Driver and J.C. Miles, *The Babylonian Laws*, I, 299-301; II, 57, 223. Further possible examples of *aḫāzum* with a sexual reference are *CT* 8 37d, ln. 3 and especially *YOS* 8 51, ln. 7 (both of which are available in R. Westbrook, "Old Babylonian Marriage Law," I, 137-138, 309-311). A contrary view is expressed by R. Westbrook, *op. cit.*, II, 16-18.

[198] Cf. also Deut. 24:5.

[199] J.A. Thompson notes how this law expresses the humanitarian concern typical of Deuteronomy elsewhere (*Deuteronomy*, 221).

[200] Assuming the *qᵉrē*, יִשְׁכָּבֶנָּה, is to be preferred over the *kᵉtîb*, יִשְׁגָּלֶנָּה.

[201] It is unlikely that Joel 1:8 refers to a girl's mourning for her "bridegroom" (i.e., a betrothal situation). Cf. G.J. Wenham, "*bᵉtûlāh* 'A Girl of Marriageable Age'" (1972) 345.

2.2.4 Instances of synecdoche by which the consummation of marriage is effectively identified with sexual union

The evidence thus far considered for sexual union consummating marriage is further supported by examples of synecdoche both of the whole (expressions for marriage used to refer to sexual union in particular) and of the part (expressions for sexual union used to refer to marriage).

Specifically, it may be noted that while בּוֹא (G) + אֶל, "come to," in its sexual usage is not restricted to marital unions, in at least one case, Josh. 23:12, בּוֹא (G) + אֶל, "come to," appears to refer to the contraction of marriage as a whole by synecdoche: "For if you turn back, and join the remnant of these nations left here among you, and make marriages with them, so that you marry their women and they yours [וְהִתְחַתַּנְתֶּם בָּהֶם וּבָאתֶם בָּהֶם וְהֵם בָּכֶם]...."[202]

A similar extension of meaning from sexual union to the marriage it consummates may be observed with יָדַע, "know," in at least six texts where the expression יָדַע + לֹא, "not know," appears with reference to unmarried women. Although these examples merit more detailed consideration, it is enough to suggest here that the expressions, "who have not known a man," "whom no man had known," etc., may have less to do with a claim for technical virginity than with the more public and observable fact that such a woman had not yet experienced the consummation of a marriage. For example, Num. 31:17 records how the Israelite soldiers were to kill "every woman who has known a man." How were the Israelite soldiers to check for the requisite virginity? By impromptu medical examinations? By interviews? Would these women tell the truth about such a private matter, especially when their lives depended on their answer? Just as "the circumcised [περιτομή]" stands by synecdoche for "the Jews" in New Testament Greek (with no need for medical examinations), it seems likely that the concern in Num. 31:17 is with marital status, referred to in terms of this expression for sexual intercourse, not with technical virginity. Marital status, that is, whether a woman was currently married, a widow, or a divorcee, would be a matter of public record (perhaps evidenced in an item of dress such as a veil) and so would be readily ascertainable by the soldiers. Compare also Gen. 19:8; 24:16; Num. 31:35; Judg. 11:39; and Judg. 21:12.

Finally, Gen. 24:67 offers a possible example of synecdoche of the whole for the part involving the term לָקַח, "take": "Then Isaac brought her into the tent of his mother Sarah and took Rebekah, and she became his wife [וַיְבִאֶהָ יִצְחָק הָאֹהֱלָה שָׂרָה אִמּוֹ וַיִּקַּח אֶת־רִבְקָה וַתְּהִי־לוֹ לְאִשָּׁה]; and he loved her. So Isaac was comforted after his mother's death." Although לָקַח often means "marry" when it has a woman for its object,[203] in the context of this passage, especially following the mention of Rebekah's entrance into the family tent, it appears likely that "taking" Rebekah specifically refers to the act of sexual union. While Gen. 38:2f. distinguishes a marriage (וַיִּקָּחֶהָ, lit. "and he took her") from sexual union (וַיָּבֹא אֵלֶיהָ) and an ensuing pregnancy (וַתַּהַר) and

---

[202] As rendered by the RSV.
[203] Cf., e.g., Gen. 28:6; Judg. 14:3; etc. Even-Shoshan lists 52 examples.

birth (וַתֵּלֶד בֵּן), the following three texts are of interest because they appear to employ אִשָּׁה + לָקַח, "take a woman," to refer inclusively to marriage and sexual union (or to sexual union by synecdoche): Exod. 2:1f. ("and he took [to wife] a daughter of Levi and the woman conceived and bore a son."); Hos. 1:3 ("he took [to wife] Gomer the daughter of Diblaim and she conceived and bore him a son."); and possibly 1 Chron. 4:17f. ("Bithiah, the daughter of Pharaoh, whom Mered took [to wife], and she conceived and bore Miriam...").[204]

2.2.5 *E. Neufeld's view of "*בִּיאָה *Marriage" rejected*

From the evidence thus far considered, it is apparent that sexual union not only constitutes an important communicative gesture, but also serves a legal dispositive purpose, namely the consummation of marriage.[205] Recognition of this fact is not to imply complete agreement with E. Neufeld's understanding of בִּיאָה marriage (also called *usus* marriage from the analogous Roman practice). Neufeld supposes that בִּיאָה marriage, that is, marriage formed simply by cohabitation, was one of the earliest forms of marriage, of which traces remain in the Bible: Gen. 38:2; Deut. 22:13; and 2 Sam. 12:24. As further support, Neufeld notes that the Talmud offers its reluctant recognition of the validity of such a marriage.[206] The Talmudic evidence, however, may merely reflect the influence of later Roman practice, while none of the biblical examples is particularly convincing as evidence for the development posited by Neufeld.[207] Accordingly, S.F. Bigger concludes: "Neufeld's *Biah* formula was not an early marriage form, but, when used in connection with terms expressing marriage, it was the normal expression for the consummation [of marriage], and only in the case of the captive wife [and, we may add, perhaps also widows] was this sufficient without any negotiations or preliminaries."[208] Stating this conclusion differently, there is little evidence for any period that a man could marry a bride simply by cohabitation, if the bride in question was a dependent and the husband had

---

[204] The RSV transposes "took [to wife]" from the end of vs. 18. Whether or not the MT is emended to support this transposition, the sense demands that the expression "take to wife" be considered as referring to an event prior to the conception and birth.

[205] Cf. M. Malul, *Studies in Mesopotamian Legal Symbolism*, 22f.; and M.I. Gruber, *Nonverbal Communication, passim.*

[206] The legality of a בִּיאָה marriage is recognized in *b. Qidd.* 1a, but discouraged as immoral in *b. Qidd.* 12b and *b. Yebam.* 52a. Cf. also *b. Ketub.* 46a.

[207] Cf. P.E. Corbett, *The Roman Law of Marriage* (1930).

[208] "Hebrew Marriage and Family in the Old Testament Period," 84.

Cf. LU §8, which considers the case of a widow who has cohabited with a man without a marriage contract. The law does not call into question the validity of such a marriage, as it would, presumably, if the woman had been a dependent in her father's house and the marriage had lacked her parents' consent (as in LE §§27-28; CH §128). It merely demonstrates that in the absence of such a contract, a widow may be divorced without any compensation. Cf. also MAL A §34, where cohabitation of two years is required for a widow without a contract to assume the full rights of a wife with respect to divorce protection.

failed to gain the prior consent of her guardian.[209] This requirement for parental (or guardian) consent is explicit in Exod. 22:15-16 [ET 16-17] and is clear in Mesopotamian practice, for example, LE §§26, 27, and 28.[210]

2.2.6 Consequences of the inherently private nature of sexual union

Although sexual union was the means by which marriage was consummated in the Old Testament, as well as elsewhere in the ancient Near East, the inherently private nature of this act renders it unsuitable for some legal purposes. CH §§151-152, for example, considers the case of liability for prenuptial debts. Obviously a creditor cannot be privy to the precise moment of the *copula carnalis*, and so for pragmatic reasons the point at which the couple becomes liable for each other's debts starts when the woman "entered into the house of the man."[211]

As a result, there is a need for a degree of semiotic redundancy in the formation of marriage in order to give public evidence of the consummation of marriage. As modern couples may exchange rings, light a common candle, etc., giving public expression to the bond which will be privately expressed in sexual union, so also in the ancient world festivities, processions, pouring oil on the bride's head, symbolic acts involving clothes, the change of domicile, etc., served to give notice of the (impending) consummation of marriage. Nevertheless, it is clear that these additional ceremonies do not have the constitutive effect possessed by *copula carnalis*. For example, it would not be expected that if a wife were to remain in the domicile of her father, this would prohibit a valid marriage, as would be the case if she were to refuse *copula carnalis*.[212]

2.3 Sexual union meets the conditions expected of an oath-sign and, as such, resembles other covenant-ratifying oath-signs

Since sexual intercourse is the indispensable means for the consummation of marriage in the Old Testament, as elsewhere in the ancient Near East, can it also be viewed as an oath-sign for the ratification of the covenant of marriage? In that no text offers a theoretical discussion of sexual union in terms of covenant concepts, our discussion must necessarily proceed by way of probability and the accumulation of a weight of evidence. Before examining those texts which offer the most direct evidence for identifying

---

[209] The case of Judges 21 is extraordinary and complicated by the issue of kidnapping. Even here, however, parental consent was extracted *ex post facto*.

[210] Cf. also S. Greengus, "The Old Babylonian Marriage Contract," 521.

[211] Accordingly, this law is cited as the clearest evidence for *in domum deductio*, as argued by P. Koschaker. Cf. R. Westbrook, "Old Babylonian Marriage Law," II, 125-131.

The drafting of this law is less than felicitous given the discrepancy between CH §§151-152, ln. 37, which describes the transition point for liability for the husband's debts as when he "took that woman [*sinništam šu'āti iḫḫazu*]," while lns. 44-45, and especially lns. 54-55, use the woman's entrance into the house of the man as the transition point: "If the debt is incurred by them after that woman entered into the house of the man [*šumma ištu sinništum ši ana bît awīlim īrubu*]...."

[212] Cf. also R. Westbrook, "Old Babylonian Marriage Law," II, 131.

sexual union as a covenant-ratifying oath-sign, we shall first consider several important characteristics of sexual union which support this identification.

In the treaty between Muršiliš II of Ḫatti and Talmi-Šarruma of Aleppo, Muršiliš II enjoins his vassal, "May all of us together and our house be one [*gab-bi-ni ù bît-ni lu-ú ištēn*]. For this thing may the gods of the Ḫatti land and the gods of the Aleppo land be witness."[213] A similar commitment to being "one" is articulated in other treaties and implied in a great many alternative formulae, such as references to being "father" and "son," "brothers," "friends," etc.[214]

Corresponding to this characteristic stress on unity, some of the oath-signs discussed in Chapter 6 function merely by offering a solemn depiction of the covenant commitment to unity being undertaken. For example, it was argued that such was the case with eating together and giving one's hand in a handshake. With respect to the possible identification of sexual union as a similar oath-sign, it is self-evident that this act is ideally suited to depict the "one flesh" reality which is definitional of marriage in Gen. 2:24. In fact, this depiction is so clear that some scholars have identified the two becoming "one flesh" as a reference to the sexual act itself.[215] Furthermore, as in the case of giving one's hand in a hand shake, it is notable how many oath-signs involve physical contact or the use of the parts of the body to represent one's whole person on the principle of *pars pro toto*.[216] More particularly, at least two oath gestures involve the organs of generation: circumcision and placing

---

[213] E.F. Weidner, *Politische Dokumente aus Kleinasien* (1923) 86f., VI r. 9-10; cited as text #15 in P. Kalluveettil, *Declaration and Covenant*, 102.

[214] Other examples of "becoming one" mentioned in the treaties are found in the treaty between Muwatalliš and Sunassurah of Kizzuwatna, lns. 35-36, and in A.K. Grayson, *Assyrian Royal Inscriptions*, II, §459. Cf. further P. Kalluveettil, *Declaration and Covenant*, 93-106.

[215] E.g., cf. J. Skinner, *Genesis* (1930) 70; and H. Gunkel, according to C. Westermann, *Genesis 1-11*, 233.

Against limiting the reference of "one flesh" in Gen. 2:24 to the sexual act, cf. M. Gilbert, "'Une seule chair' (Gn 2,24)" (1978) 66-89.

[216] The giving of the hand represents the person, according to P. Kalluveettil, *Declaration and Covenant*, 21. M. Malul discusses how gestures involving the forehead and the head as a whole are similarly used to represent the person (*Studies in Mesopotamian Legal Symbolism*, 74, 176, 249ff.). Likewise, hair, fingernails, saliva, etc., in various gestures and ceremonies are identified by P. Koschaker as emblems of the person (so Malul, *op. cit.*, 115, n. 100).

Cf. also the claim of W.G.E. Watson that in Isa. 28:15 the parties metaphorically conclude a covenant with death by ceremonially facing each other and touching each other's chests (*Classical Hebrew Poetry*, 57). Related to this, according to Watson, is the manner in which covenants could be broken by fondling another's breasts as in Isa. 28:3dc. Cf. *CAD Ṣ*, 165f.

If Koschaker is correct that garments (undergarments), because of their proximity to the intimate parts of one's body, were a symbol of personality and could represent the owner, then it is all the more likely that those intimate parts themselves were symbolic of the person as a whole. In support of this understanding of garments, cf. also M. Malul, *Studies in Mesopotamian Legal Symbolism*, 114f., 152.

one's hands under another's "thigh" (Gen. 24:2, 9 and 47:29).[217] At the very least, these examples provide an associative context between the genitalia and oath taking.

Finally, recalling D.J. McCarthy's explanation for how a shared meal effects a covenant bond because only kinsmen eat together, a similar logic may well apply to sexual union.[218] Since sexual intercourse is characteristic of marriage and, further, since licit sexual acts take place only between husbands and wives, for a couple to willingly engage in sexual intercourse may simultaneously imply the recognition of each other as husband and wife. As an adjunct to McCarthy's explanation, it is possible that the covenant-forming effect of touching or of eating together may not be entirely arbitrary.[219] In any case, although it raises questions which exceed the scope of this study, it is possible that the posited union effected by sexual intercourse reflects and is reinforced by a deeper sociobiological reality of sexual imprinting and pair-bonding.[220]

2.4 The covenantal implication of referring to sexual union with the verb יֲדע, "know"

Not only does the symbolism of intercourse suggest that it may have functioned as a covenant-ratifying oath-sign, but also one of the prominent terms used to refer to intercourse, the term יֲדע, "know," may also point in the

---

[217] Cf. R.D. Freedman, "Put Your Hand Under My Thigh" (1976) 3ff.; M. Malul, "More on *paḥad yiṣḥāq* (Genesis xxiv 42,53) and the oath by the thigh" (1985) 192-200; and *idem*, "Touching the Sexual Organs as an Oath Ceremony in an Akkadian Letter" (1987) 491-2.

[218] *Treaty and Covenant*, 253ff., 266, 276. Cf. also P. Kalluveettil, *Declaration and Covenant*, 11.

[219] Cf., e.g., P. Farb, *Consuming Passions. The Anthropology of Eating* (1980).

[220] Cf. D. Morris, *The Naked Ape* (1967); *idem*, *Intimate Behavior* (1971).

For more technical studies in defence of the theory of (normally monogamous) pair-bonding in *homo sapiens*, cf. I. Eibl-Eibesfeldt, *Ethnology: The Biology of Behavior* (1975) 502; D.P. Barash, *Sociobiology and Behavior* (1977) 297, 360; L.A. Fairbanks, "Animal and human behavior: guidelines for generalization across species" (1977) 87-110; B.A. Hamburg, "The biosocial basis of sex differences" (1978) 155-213; and S.B. Hrdy, *The Woman That Never Evolved* (1981).

D. Morris, I. Eibl-Eibesfeldt, and S.B. Hrdy speculate that the extreme demands of rearing human children, due especially to their slow maturation by comparison to other primates, necessitated the permanent association of the parents (required to allow a more significant paternal investment in the offspring), which fostered the evolution of the "pair-bond." The similarity of human pair-bonding to that found in about 8,000 bird species, a few members of the dog family (coyotes, bat-eared foxes), and some other primates (the gibbons, or lesser apes, siamang, and marmoset) appears to be the result of convergence toward a similar solution to a similar problem, namely the special challenge of rearing offspring (cf. L.A. Fairbanks, *op. cit.*, 100). In each of these recognized pair-bonding species, the father contributes substantially to the care of the young.

Against the assumption of human adult male-female pair-bonding, based particularly on the sexual dimorphism of humans (a feature normally associated with non pair-bonding species), cf. E.O. Wilson, *Sociobiology: The New Synthesis* (1975); *idem*, *On Human Nature* (1978); and D. Symons, *The Evolution of Human Sexuality* (1979) 96-141.

M. Konner argues for an intermediate position: humans are pair-bonding, but imperfectly so (*The Tangled Wing: Biological Constraints on the Human Spirit* [1982] 261-290).

same direction. Whatever the precise historical explanation for the use of יָדַע,
"know," with reference to sexual union,[221] an association between the
covenantal use of this term and its sexual use (apparent, for example, in cases
of double entendre) may have fostered an ancient identification of sexual
union as a means of covenant recognition. Before presenting the evidence for
this association, it is necessary to review briefly the evidence for the
aforementioned covenantal usage.

As argued by H.B. Huffmon and S.B. Parker and since supported by
other scholars, there are a number of examples in the Old Testament where
יָדַע, "know," is used with personal objects in a non-cognitive and non-
experiential manner (apart from references to sexual union).[222] Huffmon
explains these relational uses as instances of a technical usage of "know"
drawn from treaty practice, in which the suzerain and vassal "recognize" each
other as covenant partners.[223] Huffmon offers as evidence of this background
a similar use of the Hittite verb šek- / šak-, meaning "(legally) recognize."
For example, in the treaty between Suppiluliumas and Ḫuqqanas, the suzerain
Suppiluliumas tells his vassal, "And you, Ḫuqqanas, know only the Sun [a
designation for the Hittite king] regarding lordship.... Moreover, another lord
... do not ... know!"[224]

---

[221] In spite of numerous attempts, the relevant facts for recovering the origin of the
sexual sense of "know" lie irrecoverably buried in hoary antiquity. Cf., e.g., G.J.
Botterweck, "יָדַע, yada'," TDOT, V, 448-481.

While it is possible that the range of usage for Hebrew יָדַע (paralleled by Ugaritic yd')
represents an independent development, it seems more likely that this remarkable range
reflects an early semantic borrowing, probably from Akkadian (where both idûm and
lamādum, "to know," may be used in a cognitive sense as well as a sexual one). It is not
clear, however, whether the Akkadian usage of idûm and lamādum itself may reflect a still
earlier semantic borrowing from Sumerian zu, which also means "to know" and can bear a
sexual sense, or whether the borrowing went the other way (as is now recognized to have
often been the case). It is also of interest that the Egyptian term rḫ can bear a sexual sense.

[222] H.B. Huffmon, "The Treaty Background of Hebrew yāda'" (1966) 31-37; H.B.
Huffmon and S.B. Parker, "A Further Note on the Treaty Background of Hebrew yāda'"
(1966) 36-38. In support, cf., e.g., F.M. Cross, Canaanite Myth and Hebrew Epic (1973)
269, 273; and A.D.H. Mayes, Deuteronomy, 202. Cf. also F.C. Fensham, "Covenant,
Alliance" (1980).

As an example of a simple "cognitive" use of the Qal of יָדַע with a personal object, i.e.,
"to know of, to be acquainted with," cf., e.g., Gen. 29:5, "Do you know Laban the son of
Nahor?" Cf. also Deut. 9:2; 22:2; 2 Sam. 22:44; Ps. 18:44 [ET 43]; Ezek. 28:19.

Related to this cognitive use is what might be termed an "analytic" use of יָדַע. Here the
knower is cognizant of the character of the individual, and hence יָדַע could be rendered, "to
know what an individual is like," "to understand." Cf., e.g., Exod. 32:22, "And Aaron said,
'Let not the anger of my lord burn hot; you know the people, that they are set on evil.'" Cf.
also 2 Sam. 3:25; 17:8; 2 Kgs. 9:11; Job 11:11; Ps. 139:1, 14; Jer. 9:23 [ET 24];12:3

The "experiential" use of the Qal of יָדַע with a personal object refers to cases where יָדַע
is used to indicate that the knower personally knows the other individual, hence "to know
personally." Cf., e.g., 1 Sam. 3:7, "Now Samuel did not yet know Yahweh, and the word of
Yahweh had not yet been revealed to him." Cf. also Exod. 33:13; Deut. 11:28; 13:3 [ET 2],
7 [ET 6], 14 [ET 13]; 28:33; 29:25 [ET 26]; 32:17; Judg. 2:10; Ruth 2:11; 1 Sam. 2:12;
10:11; Job 19:13; 42:11; Isa. 1:3; 29:15; 45:20; 55:5 (bis); Jer. 7:9f.; 19:4; 44:3; and Dan.
11:38.

[223] H.B. Huffmon, "The Treaty Background of Hebrew yāda'," 31.

[224] Huffmon suggests that the use of yāda' as "(legally) recognize" and a similar use of
idû in the Amarna tablets, not found in Akkadian more generally, may represent a calque

Since Huffmon's studies, under the strictures of modern lexical semantics, Biblical scholars have become considerably more sceptical about any claims for a technical usage.[225] Without insisting on Huffmon's posited restriction to formal covenantal contexts, a result of his assumption of a "technical" use, nevertheless, many of the non-cognitive, non-experiential examples of ידע discussed by Huffmon and others do appear to support his interpretation of these as meaning "to acknowledge (the authority of, the claims of, etc.)," "to recognize (legally, covenantally)," that is, "to recognize (or even to establish another as a covenant partner)."[226]

2.4.1 ידע, *"know," in covenantal contexts*

There are several examples of ידע, "know," where both the subject and the object are human, which appear to support the substance of Huffmon's understanding. Deut. 33:9 reads: "[Levi] who said of his father and mother, 'I regard them not'; he disowned his brothers and did not know his children [וְאֶת־בָּנָיו לֹא יָדָע]. For they observed thy word and kept thy covenant."[227] This example is instructive in that it both supports and improves Huffmon's thesis. It is supportive because Levi is blessed for his rrefusal to be bound by natural loyalties to his own children, that is, his refusal to "acknowledge" his own children, permitting him the requisite zeal to judge Israel for her idolatry in the incident of the golden calf.[228] As noted by D. Daube, the language here

---

from Hittite *šek-* / *šak-*, which normally means "know," but in the treaty texts can mean "legally recognize."

A. Goetze has challenged the assumption of direct borrowing from Hittite based on the fact that when *šek-* / *šak-* means "legally recognize," it is accompanied by the reflexive particle -*za*, usually attached to the first word in the sentence, while when it means "know," the particle -*za* is lacking ("Hittite *šek-* / *šak-* '(Legally) Recognize' in the Treaties" [1968-69] 7f.). While G.J. Botterweck concludes that this leaves Huffmon and Parker's analysis of ידע, "without foundation," this is far from the case (*s.v.* ידע in *TDOT*, V, 478). Goetze's argument concerns only the posited origin for this particular usage of Amarna Akkadian *idû* and Hebrew ידע. Goetze nowhere challenges and, in fact, appears to accept Huffmon's analysis of the usage itself in Hebrew, Akkadian, and Hittite. Even with respect to the origin of this usage, Goetze acknowledges that the Hebrew usage might still derive from Hittite, but insists that if it does, the borrowing is more complicated than at first thought. In support of Huffmon and Parker, however, since Hebrew and Akkadian both lack anything comparable to the separable particle -*za*, it is possible that a calque would depend simply on context to discriminate these usages.

[225] Cf., e.g., D.A. Carson, *Exegetical Fallacies* (1984) 45-48.

[226] E.W. Nicholson rejects Huffmon's proposal without citation (*God and His People* [1986] 80). Nicholson prefers the definition offered by Baumann, "know someone for one's own" or "choose and make someone one's own" (cf. E. Baumann, "*Yāda'* und seine Derivate. Ein sprachlich-exegetische Studie," 39). It is not clear, however, what Baumann means by "know someone for one's own" or "choose and make someone one's own" or that he intends anything different from Huffmon's definition (expressed, to be sure, without the tabooed adjective "covenantal").

S.E. Loewenstamm agrees that, apart from Huffmon's one-sided emphasis on the "mutual recognition of the partners to a treaty," his understanding of the covenantal usage of ידע is comparable to that of Baumann's ("A Didactic Ugaritic Drinkers' Burlesque" [1980] 374-375).

[227] This verse involves a minor *kᵉtîb-qᵉrē* problem with בְּנָיו as the *qᵉrē* for בְּנוֹ.

[228] Cf. A.D.H. Mayes, *Deuteronomy*, 403.

is formal and intended to express the legal severance of family relationships.[229]   On the other hand, improving Huffmon's thesis by extending his conclusions beyond a restriction to treaty contexts, the "acknowledgment" here is one not of treaty partners, but of family members. Similar in its import and vocabulary is Isa. 63:16: "For thou art our Father, though Abraham does not know us and Israel does not acknowledge us [כִּי אַבְרָהָם לֹא יְדָעָנוּ וְיִשְׂרָאֵל לֹא יַכִּירָנוּ]; thou, Yahweh, art our Father, our Redeemer from of old is thy name." Compare also Exod. 1:8.[230]

Turning to examples which support Huffmon and where God is the subject of ידע, Amos 3:2 offers what is perhaps the parade example of the posited covenantal usage of "know": "You only have I known [רַק אֶתְכֶם יָדַעְתִּי] of all the families of the earth; therefore I will punish you for all your iniquities." Not only would the assumed attributes of Yahweh, such as omniscience, appear to exclude any of the normal cognitive or experiential uses of ידע, "know," as unlikely for Amos 3:2, but also even apart from such assumptions these meanings appear inappropriate in the present context. Accordingly, W.H. Wolff translates the verb "selected."[231]   Similarly, D. Stuart offers "chosen" or "am I specially related to."[232]

While "select" or "choose" is a common rendering for this verse, one should not miss the fact that the "election [בחר]" of Israel in the Old Testament conception appears to be inextricably bound up with covenant recognition.[233]   In contrast to בחר, for example, which can mean "to choose" even when used with impersonal objects (cf., e.g., Gen. 13:11), ידע is never so used. Likewise, although בחר with a personal object can mean to "choose" or "select" for some task (cf., e.g., Exod. 17:9), ידע seems to require that the choosing result in a more enduring relationship.[234]   Accordingly, although Huffmon does not exclude the rendering of "choose," he observes that "'election' is subsidiary to the covenant" and so some variation of "recognize

---

[229] D. Daube, *Studies in Biblical Law*, 1947, 7f.; and *idem*, "Rechtsgedanken in den Erzählungen des Pentateuchs" (1961) 34.

[230] This verse could hardly refer to the new Pharaoh's lack of personal acquaintance with Joseph — such would be obvious and require no special comment since Joseph had long since died. The ensuing report of persecution shows that loyalty is what is at issue.

[231] W.H. Wolff, *Amos*, 174, 176f.

[232] *Hosea - Jonah*, 321f. J. Lindblom offers "care for," "be interested in, concerned in" (*Prophecy in Ancient Israel* [1962] 326). S.R. Driver offers "took notice of, deemed worthy of His self-revealing friendship and regard," as also in Gen. 18:19 and Deut. 34:10 (*Joel and Amos* [1915] and *idem*, *Deuteronomy* [1902] 425).

[233] Cf., e.g., G.E. Mendenhall, "Election," *IDB*, II, 79f. Those scholars who reject any pre-Deuteronomic reference to Yahweh's covenant with Israel (see footnote 59 in Chapter 8 below) explain Amos 3:2 as a reference to "election theology" (of J), rather than "covenant theology." Accepting a covenantal allusion in Amos 3:2, however, are H.L. Mays, *Amos* (1969) 56f.; H. McKeating, *The Books of Amos, Hosea and Micah* (1971) 26f.; D. Stuart, *Hosea - Jonah* (1987) 321f.; G.V. Smith, *Amos. A Commentary* (1989) 105; and F.I. Andersen and D.N. Freedman, *Amos* (1989) 381f.; among others.

[234] This is not to deny that בחר at times may also be used in this manner. Cf., e.g., Deut. 7:6; and Ps. 78:70.

(by covenant)" may be more adequate for ידע in those verses where the idea of election is in view.[235]

Other plausible examples where God is the subject of covenantal knowing include the following: Gen. 18:19; Exod. 33:12, 17; Deut. 9:24; 34:10; 2 Sam. 7:20; 1 Chron. 17:18; Ps. 144:3; Hos. 5:3; 13:5; Nah. 1:7; and especially Jer. 1:5, "Before I formed you in the womb I knew you [יְדַעְתִּיךָ], and before you were born I consecrated you [הִקְדַּשְׁתִּיךָ]; I appointed you [נְתַתִּיךָ] a prophet to the nations."

There are a number of examples where God is the object of this kind of knowing which may be helpful to note.[236] Jer. 22:16, for instance, says of the righteous king, "He judged the cause of the poor and needy; then it was well. Is not this to know me [הֲלוֹא־הִיא הַדַּעַת אֹתִי]? says Yahweh." It seems clear from such a text that "knowing" God is more than a matter of mere cognition! Similarly stressing the commitment of service implied in "knowing" God, David enjoins his son Solomon, "And you, Solomon my son, know the God of your father [וְאַתָּה שְׁלֹמֹה־בְנִי דַּע אֶת־אֱלֹהֵי אָבִיךָ], and serve him with a whole heart and with a willing mind; for Yahweh searches all hearts, and understands every plan and thought" (1 Chron. 28:9). Of note also is Hos. 6:6, which sets "the knowledge of God [וְדַעַת אֱלֹהִים]" in synonymous parallelism with "steadfast loyalty [חֶסֶד]": "For I desire steadfast loyalty and not sacrifice [כִּי חֶסֶד חָפַצְתִּי וְלֹא־זָבַח], the knowledge of God, rather than burnt offerings [וְדַעַת אֱלֹהִים מֵעֹלוֹת]." On the other hand, Prov. 2:5 seems to equate the "fear of Yahweh" with "knowing" God: "Then you will understand the fear of Yahweh and find the knowledge of God [וְדַעַת אֱלֹהִים]."[237] Other examples of the present use of ידע where God is the object include the following: Exod. 5:2; Job 18:21; 24:1; Ps. 36:11 [ET 10]; 79:6; 87:4; Prov. 3:6; 9:10; Isa. 19:21; 43:10; 45:4, 5; 53:11;[238] Jer. 2:8; 4:22; 9:2 [ET 3]; 9:5 [ET 6]; 10:25; 24:7; 31:34 (2x); Ezek. 38:16; Dan. 11:32; Hos. 2:22 [ET 20]; 4:1; 5:4; 6:3 (bis); 8:2; and 13:4.

---

[235] H.B. Huffmon, "The Treaty Background of Hebrew yāda'," 35.

Cf. also G.V. Smith, Amos, 105; and F.I. Andersen and D.N. Freedman, Amos, 381f. Andersen and Freedman argue for a covenantal implication for "know" in Amos 3:2, comparing Exod. 33:12, etc., as well as appealing to notions of intimacy (see M. Dahood on Ps. 1:6) and the use of "know" in marital contexts.

K. Cramer suggests that Amos 3:2 may presuppose the marriage metaphor. Accordingly, he renders the verse, "With you alone is my marriage bond" (Amos [1930] 32, 57, 60, as noted in TDNT, I, 698). It appears, however, that Cramer may have confused a particular usage of ידע with its meaning.

[236] Cf. also, "They shall not hurt or destroy in all my holy mountain; for the earth shall be full of the knowledge of Yahweh [דֵּעָה אֶת־יְהֹוָה] as the waters cover the sea" (Isa. 11:9).

[237] In this poetic verse, the "knowledge of God" is set in synonymous parallelism with the "fear of Yahweh." The popular misimpression of this latter expression, as if it meant "cowering dread," fails to take account of such remarkable passages as Exod. 20:20 (where Israel is told explicitly not to "fear" God in the sense of dread, but to "fear" him only in the sense of the reverent undivided attention which promotes obedience) or Ps. 130:4 [NIV], "But with you there is forgiveness, therefore you are feared."

[238] D.W. Thomas has suggested that the verb in question here is not derived from the common ידע meaning "to know," but from a homonym meaning "to be humiliated." So also R.N. Whybray, Isaiah 40-66, 180f. Against Thomas, cf. W. Johnstone, "yd' II, 'be humbled, humiliated'?" (1991). Cf. also J. Barr, Comparative Philology, 20.

2.4.2 יָדַע, "know," with a sexual reference

Apart from the above-mentioned covenantal use of יָדַע, "know," the only other non-cognitive and non-experiential examples of יָדַע used with personal objects are fourteen texts where יָדַע refers to sexual union. In other words, the only relational uses of יָדַע are either covenantal or sexual.

In eight of these examples the man is the subject and the woman is the object of "know," as in Gen. 4:1, "Now Adam knew Eve his wife [וְהָאָדָ֣ם יָדַ֔ע אֶת־חַוָּ֣ה אִשְׁתּ֑וֹ], and she conceived and bore Cain." Compare also Gen. 4:17, 25; 24:16; 38:26; Judg. 19:25; 1 Sam. 1:19; and 1 Kgs. 1:4. Four examples have the woman as the subject and the man as the object of the "knowing": Gen. 19:8, "Behold, I have two daughters who have not known a man [אֲשֶׁ֤ר לֹֽא־יָֽדְעוּ֙ אִ֔ישׁ]; let me bring them out to you, and you do to them as you please"; Num. 31:17; Judg. 11:39; and 21:12. Compare also the related Num. 31:35 and Judg. 21:11, which likewise describe unmarried enemy women who were spared as those who had not יָדְעוּ / יֹדַעַת + מִשְׁכַּב זָכָר, "known lying with a male." In the immediate context in both passages (i.e., Num. 31:17 and Judg. 21:12) the parallel expressions אִישׁ לְמִשְׁכַּב זָכָר + יֹדַעַת/יָדְעָה, "know a man by lying with a male," are encountered. Finally, there are two occurrences where יָדַע is used of homosexual intercourse: Gen. 19:5, "Bring them out to us, that we may know them [וְנֵדְעָ֖ה אֹתָ֑ם]" and the similar verse, Judg. 19:22.

In eleven of the fourteen cases discussed, it is likely that the sexual acts referred to by יָדַע are, in fact, marital unions. This is so even for quite general expressions such as "every woman who has known a man [וְכָל־אִשָּׁ֗ה יֹדַ֤עַת אִישׁ]" in Num. 31:17.

It is not difficult to explain the three remaining nonmarital cases as instances of irony or double entendre, where יָדַע was chosen for its covenantal associations. For example, in Gen. 19:5 when the Sodomites demand that Lot bring out his guests so that "we may know them [וְנֵדְעָ֖ה אֹתָ֑ם]," it is possible that they were making a mocking effort to obscure their perverted intention with words which could be understood in a quite different sense. Indeed, the Sodomites should have "known" these guests in the sense of "recognizing" them (covenantally) and so establishing them as covenant partners![239] The same explanation would account for the Gibeahite mob's request in Judg. 19:22, "Bring out the man who came into your house, that we may know him [וְנֵדָעֶ֑נּוּ]," which provides an obvious parallel to Gen. 19:5.[240] Judg. 19:25 continues the narrative, "So the man seized his [i.e., the other

---

[239] Cf. R. Boling (*Judges*, 276) and P. Trible (*Texts of Terror*, 73), both of whom note the ambiguity of the identical clause in Judg. 19:22.

[240] Cf. S. Niditch, "The 'Sodomite' Theme in Judges 19-20: Family, Community, and Social Disintegration" (1982) 365-378; R. Alter, *Putting Together Biblical Narrative* (1988); and H.-W. Jüngling, *Richter 19 — Ein Plädoyer für das Königtum* (1981).

man's[241]] concubine, and put her out to them; and they 'knew' her, and abused her [וַיֵּדְעוּ אוֹתָהּ וַיִּתְעַלְּלוּ־בָהּ] all night until the morning." When the narrator reports how the Gibeahites "knew" the concubine, he picks up this term from its earlier use by the Gibeahite mob, as if to underscore in bitter irony the heinousness of this atrocity.[242] Their brutal act was the antithesis of the kind of covenantal "knowing" which should have taken place. To avoid any misunderstanding, however, the narrator makes explicit that the Gibeahites' "knowing" consisted rather in "abusing her all night until the morning."

As a modern parallel to this ironic use of "know," one might imagine a gang of hoodlums demanding to "have a little fun" with some guest (an ironic use of a normally inoffensive phrase). Later, a newspaper account reports that the gang "had their fun" and in order to clarify the bitter sarcasm adds that "they abused her all night...." Our translation of Judg. 19:25 reflects this interpretation by its use of quotation marks around "knew." Naturally, because of the laconic nature of these texts, any such interpretation of Genesis 19 or Judges 19 can be no more than a suggestion. Nevertheless, if correct, it provides an interesting example of the possible interplay between the covenantal and sexual senses of ידע, "know."

2.4.3 The principal biblical texts which support an identification of sexual union as a covenant-ratifying oath sign

Apart from the possible ironic examples in Genesis 19 and Judges 19,[243] there are several key texts which clearly associate the two relational senses of ידע, "know," that is, the covenantal and the sexual senses, by means of double entendre. Of these texts, Hos. 2:22 [ET 20] and possibly Hos. 13:5 are crucial in that they consider Yahweh's covenantal relationship with Israel in terms of the metaphor of marriage and, in this context, appear to equate sexual union in the metaphor (referred to by ידע) with the ratifying oath of the covenant. If demonstrated, such a use offers significant evidence for the posited identification of sexual union in literal marriage as a covenant-ratifying oath-sign.

Hosea 2:22 [ET 20]

"I will betroth you to me in faithfulness; and you shall know Yahweh [וְאֵרַשְׂתִּיךְ לִי בֶּאֱמוּנָה וְיָדַעַתְּ אֶת־יְהוָה]" Hos. 2:22 [ET 20].

---

[241] This interpretation is supported by the extensive parallels between Genesis 19 and Judges 19, implying that it was the host, not the Levite, who negotiated with the Gibeahite mob. For additional arguments, cf. D.K. Stuart, *Old Testament Exegesis* (1984) 59f.

[242] So, e.g., P. Trible, *Texts of Terror*, 76.

[243] E.F. Campbell Jr. suggests that Ruth 3:3, "do not let yourself be known," may offer yet another example of sexual double entendre — although in this case, the primary sense of ידע is cognitive, not covenantal (*Ruth*, 131f.).

Cf. also the earlier discussion of Amos 3:2, according to the interpretations of K. Cramer, *Amos* (1930); and F.I. Andersen and D.N. Freedman, *Amos* (1989) 381f.

This passage provides critical evidence in that it uses "know" in an explicitly covenantal context (Hos. 2:20 [ET 18]) which alternatively describes Israel's promised restored relationship with God in terms of a marriage metaphor. According to most scholars, the variant reading found in a number of MSS, כִּי אֲנִי יהוה, "that I am Yahweh," is to be rejected as a tendentious alteration of the text.[244] The presence of such a reading, however, offers its own eloquent testimony to the unmistakable sexual allusion contained in the MT.

J.L. Mays notes that "the language of the sentence of consummation lends itself to a construction in terms of the marriage metaphor; 'to know' is one of the biblical terms for the sexual act."[245] Nevertheless, Mays appropriately doubts that Hosea would be promising here a literal eschatological *hieros gamos* between Yahweh and Israel. Indeed, if anything, it is arguable that the imagery behind Hos. 2:22 [ET 20] is intended as a polemic against the fertility cultus.[246] To defend his conviction Mays appears to impose on the reader a false dilemma: Does the rejection of a literal eschatological *hieros gamos* exclude the sexual meaning for ידע? It does so only if it is forgotten that Hosea is speaking metaphorically. Certainly the promise of 2:22a [ET 20a], "I will betroth you to me in faithfulness," ought not be pressed as if Israel were "really" going to marry Yahweh — though one need not deny that in terms of the metaphor אֲרַשׂ still literally means "betroth." Similarly, allowing "know" in 2:22 [ET 20] to include a marital-sexual allusion need not imply any literal eschatological sexual relation between Yahweh and Israel precisely because in the present context "know" is being used metaphorically.[247] Similarly, Mays' observation that Hosea elsewhere customarily uses "know" in a covenantal/theological sense, rather than in a sexual sense, carries little weight if the reader is prepared to allow a quite deliberate association of these senses in the present text by means of the marriage metaphor.

F.I. Andersen and D.N. Freedman assert that ידע, "know," cannot have a sexual connotation in Hos. 2:22 [ET 20] since here it is used of the bride Israel "knowing" Yahweh, but elsewhere in the Bible it is so used only with a male as the subject.[248] Here, however, Andersen and Freedman are merely repeating a frequently expressed misconception. One obvious counter-example *inter alia* is Judg. 11:39, where we read of Jephthah's daughter, who bewailed her virginity for two months upon the mountains: "she had never known a man."[249]

---

244 H.W. Wolff, "Erkenntnis Gottes im AT" (1955) 428ff. So also F.I. Andersen and D.N. Freedman, *Hosea*, 283; and G.A. Yee, *Composition and Tradition in the Book of Hosea* (1987) 88.
245 J.L. Mays, *Hosea*, 52.
246 O.J. Baab, "Marriage," *IBD* 3 (1962) 286.
247 Cf. H. McKeating, *Amos, Hosea, Micah*, 88.
248 *Hosea*, 284.
249 Cf. also Gen. 19:8; Num. 31:17, 35; and Judg. 21:12.

To insist with Mays and others that Hosea suddenly departs in vs. 22b [ET 20b] from the extended marital imagery which controls most, if not all, of 2:4-22a [ET 2-20a] is unpersuasive.[250] This is especially so since in their view Hosea accomplishes this imagined abrupt change in imagery by utilizing the second person *feminine* singular of ידע, "know," a term which is emphatically at home within a marital context and entirely to be expected following the promised betrothal "in faithfulness," in contrast to Israel's previous adultery.

Finally, as already suggested, to allow "know" in the present verse to include a sexual allusion does not imply that Hosea is necessarily abandoning his customary covenantal understanding of this verb.[251] Indeed, embedded as it is in the present marital imagery, the use of "know" within this verse offers an impressive confirmation of our hypothesis that as the marriage covenant-ratifying (and renewing) act sexual union is the means by which an individual "acknowledges" his or her spouse as covenant partner.

Hosea 13:5

"It was I who knew you [אֲנִי יְדַעְתִּיךָ] in the wilderness, in the land of drought" (Hos. 13:5). This verse offers an intriguing example of the usage under question. Unfortunately, however, the text of the MT is not beyond dispute. H.W. Wolff and J.L. Mays, for example, both prefer to emend the MT יְדַעְתִּיךָ, "I knew you," to רְעִיתִיךָ, "I pastured you," following the LXX, Targum, Syriac, and Vulgate.[252] Accordingly, the MT may be explained in terms of a ד - ר graphic confusion and dittography of the final *yôd* of the preceding אֲנִי. The LXX *et al.*, however, may be accounted for just as easily by the reverse errors, and the MT supported as a *lectio difficilior*.[253] The use of the emphatic pronoun אֲנִי, "I," may suggest a contrastive reference to the knowing mentioned previously in vs. 4, "I am Yahweh your God from the land of Egypt; you were to know no God but me [וֵאלֹהִים זוּלָתִי לֹא תֵדָע], and besides me there is no saviour."[254]

In support of the MT, H.B. Huffmon has advanced an important argument which had been previously overlooked.[255] Huffmon notes that ידע, "know," in this context offers a specific allusion to the covenant at Sinai, which is referred to as the place where God "knew" Israel in Deut. 9:24, "You have been rebellious against Yahweh from the day that I knew you

---

[250] Cf., e.g., H.W. Wolff, *Hosea*, 53.
[251] Cf. also D.K. Stuart, *Hosea - Jonah*, 60; and G.A. Yee, *Composition and Tradition in the Book of Hosea*, 88, although Yee considers 22b [ET 20b] to be an insertion by the final redactor.
[252] H.W. Wolff, *Hosea*, 220; and J.L. Mays, *Hosea*, 5. Cf. also W.R. Harper, *Amos and Hosea*, 397; and D.K. Stuart, *Hosea - Jonah*, 200 n. 5a, 203.
[253] In support of the MT, cf. C. van Leeuwen, *Hosea*, 258f.; and F.I. Andersen and D.N. Freedman, *Hosea*, 634. W. Nowack, *Die kleinen Propheten*, 3e Aufl. (1903) retains the MT and then adds to the beginning of v. 6: "I shepherded you" (based on the LXX).
[254] On this rendering of the Imperfect תֵדָע, cf. D.K. Stuart, *Hosea - Jonah*, 203.
[255] "The Treaty Background of Hebrew ידע" (1966) 31-7.

[מַמְרִים הֱיִיתֶם עִם־יְהוָה מִיּוֹם דַּעְתִּי אֶתְכֶם]." Compare also Amos 3:2 and Deut. 2:7.

As noted by F.I. Andersen and D.N. Freedman, Hos. 13:4-6 briefly alludes to the marriage metaphor developed in chapter 2, as it recalls the redemption from Egypt and subsequent wilderness wanderings under the figure of a trysting place.[256] Although the imagery is not blatant and lacks feminine gender references, the connections with Hosea 2 in vocabulary and subject matter are clear enough to recognize the allusion. In addition to the mention of "Egypt" and "wilderness" in Hos. 13:4f. (cf. 2:16f. [ET 14f.]), the repetition of the theme of the provisioning of Israel in 13:6 (cf. 2:7, 10, 11 [ET 5, 8, 9]) and the subsequent indictment that in their satiety Israel "forgot me" (cf. 2:15 [ET 13]), all offer points of contact.

In 2:16-17 [ET 14-15], Hosea identifies the period of the Exodus and wilderness wanderings as the point when Yahweh contracted his "marriage" with Israel. As Hos. 2:21f. [ET 19f.] promises a day when Yahweh's marriage will be renewed, when he will betroth Israel to himself forever, and when "you will know Yahweh" (employing the metaphor of the sexual consummation of the marriage covenant), so Hos. 13:5 recalls that already in the original marriage, "I knew you in the wilderness [אֲנִי יְדַעְתִּיךָ בַּמִּדְבָּר]."[257] In keeping with the same imagery, when Hos. 13:4 rehearses the central stipulation of the Sinaitic covenant, it does so in a manner which comports perfectly with the marital imagery.[258] As a wife owes her husband exclusive sexual fidelity, so "you [Israel] were to know no God but me [וֵאלֹהִים זוּלָתִי לֹא תֵדָע]."[259]

Hosea 5:3-4

3a"I know Ephraim [אֲנִי יָדַעְתִּי אֶפְרַיִם],
3band Israel is not hid from me [וְיִשְׂרָאֵל לֹא־נִכְחַד מִמֶּנִּי],

3cfor now, O Ephraim, you have played the harlot [כִּי עַתָּה הִזְנֵיתָ אֶפְרַיִם],
3dIsrael is defiled [נִטְמָא יִשְׂרָאֵל].

4aTheir deeds do not permit them [לֹא יִתְּנוּ מַעַלְלֵיהֶם]

---

256 *Hosea*, 634.

257 Could the fructifying effect of that "knowing" in the subsequent verses continue the implicit sexual allusion?

258 D.K. Stuart observes, "In effect the Sinai covenant's preamble (identification of Yahweh as the sovereign), prologue (recitation of his benevolence toward his people), and central stipulation (the first commandment) are all restated in this verse" (*Hosea - Jonah*, 203)

259 First made by Hosea, this identification of the formation of Yahweh's covenant with Israel at Sinai as a marriage was greatly elaborated in later Jewish speculation. The result of this speculation not only profoundly influenced the understanding of Yahweh's covenant, but also had a reciprocal effect on the traditional Jewish marriage ceremony (turning it in certain respects into an enacted parable of Sinai). Cf. T. Gaster, *Customs and Folkways of Jewish Life* (1955) 109-110, 126-128; and M.R. Wilson, "Marriage and Sinai: Two Covenants Compared," in *Our Father Abraham. Jewish Roots of the Christian Faith* (1989) 203-208.

4bto return to their God [לָשׁוּב אֶל־אֱלֹהֵיהֶם].

4cFor the spirit of harlotry is within them [כִּי רוּחַ זְנוּנִים בְּקִרְבָּם],
4dand they know not Yahweh [וְאֶת־יהוה לֹא יָדָעוּ]."

From the synonymous parallelism between 3a and 3b, it is apparent
that "know [ידע]" in the expression "I know [יָדַעְתִּי] Ephraim" bears its
customary cognitive sense (where Yahweh "understands" or "knows the
character" of an individual, as in Ps. 139:1). As F.I. Andersen and D.N.
Freedman point out, however, a closer analysis of these verses suggests that
there may be an intentional *inclusio* between this first mention of "know" in
3a and that in 4d, with the result: "I know Ephraim ... but they don't know
me."[260] Moreover, this *inclusio* frames repeated references to Israel's
idolatry expressed in terms of the metaphor of sexual infidelity (most obvious
in "you have played the harlot" and "the spirit of harlotry is within them," but
probably also intended by "Israel is defiled,"[261] and allowed by "their
deeds"[262]). Therefore, it appears likely that the second reference to "know"
and probably also the first offer an allusion to the sexual sense of "know" by
double entendre.

Jeremiah 31:34
In addition to the Hoseanic texts just considered, there is one final text, Jer.
31:34, which is less clear in its implication, but may provide further evidence
for an association between "know" as a reference to sexual union and its
covenantal use. Jer. 31:34 reads: "And no longer shall each man teach his
neighbour and each his brother, saying, 'Know Yahweh [דְּעוּ אֶת־יהוה],' for
they shall all know me [כִּי־כוּלָּם יֵדְעוּ אוֹתִי], from the least of them to the
greatest, says Yahweh; for I will forgive their iniquity, and I will remember
their sin no more." In the context, especially in view of the preceding verse
("But this is the covenant which I will make with the house of Israel after
those days, says Yahweh: I will put my law within them, and I will write it
upon their hearts; and I will be their God, and they shall be my people."), a
covenantal nuance to "know" seems plausible.[263] This passage is of special
interest, however, because Jer. 31:32 (if we are to follow the RSV rendering
of בָּעַלְתִּי as "I was a husband") may set this "knowing" within the context of
the marriage metaphor for the relationship between God and Israel. This
metaphor, which may have derived from Hosea, is used by Jeremiah in
chapter 3. While it must remain uncertain, it is possible that Jeremiah briefly
alludes to the marriage metaphor again in the present context. If so, a
reference to "knowing" in the context of the marriage metaphor suggests a

---

[260] *Hosea*, 391.
[261] Cf. Lev. 18:20; Num. 5:14, 29; Ezek. 18:6, 11, 15; 33:26; etc., as examples
elsewhere of טמא applied to adultery.
[262] מעלל is a sufficiently general term that it may refer to acts of sexual immorality, as
it does in Ps. 106:39.
[263] Cf. J.A. Thompson, *Jeremiah*, 581.

similar covenant-forming or renewing function for sexual union as for this recognition of Yahweh.

3. CONCLUSIONS

Chapters 6 and 7 have been concerned to answer the objection of J. Milgrom and M. Greenberg, who deny that literal marriage is a covenant based on the fact that a ratifying oath is indispensable for the existence of a "covenant [בְּרִית]" and marriage appears to lack any such oath. To prepare for a more adequate examination of the evidence in the present chapter, in Chapter 6 it was argued that covenant-ratifying oaths do not need to be self-maledictory, but that they often consist of *verba solemnia*, that is, a solemn declaration of the commitment being undertaken — solemn because the deity was implicitly invoked as a witness. Moreover, it was also noted that in the Old Testament, as well as elsewhere in the ancient Near East, oaths were frequently symbolic, that is, they consisted of "oath-signs," rather than being exclusively verbal.

In this chapter we began by considering a broad range of extrabiblical evidence (especially MAL A §41, the *eṭlu* tablet, the *ardat lilî* tablet, the marriage formulae from Elephantine and Murabbaʿat, and the implication of the corresponding divorce formulae), as well as biblical evidence (namely Gen. 2:23; Hos. 2:4, 17-19 [ET 2:2, 15-17]; Prov. 7:4f.; and Tob. 7:12), which demonstrates that throughout this period marriage was, in fact, typically formed with the use of *verba solemnia*.

Furthermore, since verbal oaths, such as *verba solemnia*, do not preclude the use of oath-signs, but instead typically supplement them, we examined the evidence for identifying sexual union as the expected covenant-ratifying oath-sign for marriage. To support this identification it was first necessary to exclude the once popular theory of "marriage by purchase," according to which the *terḥatum* / מֹהַר is held to be a "bride-price." The theory of "marriage by purchase" is antithetical to the view of marriage as a covenant not only because of its stress on the primacy of the relationship between a man and his father-in-law, rather than between a man and his wife, but also because of its expectation that the marriage-sale should be consummated not by the use of the object purchased (i.e., sexual union), but by its transfer (i.e., the *in domum deductio*), as in all sales transactions.

Accepting the present scholarly consensus which has rejected the theory of "marriage by purchase," we argued that payment and receipt of the *terḥatum* / מֹהַר is formative not of marriage, but merely of betrothal (also called "inchoate marriage"). Furthermore, we examined the evidence that *copula carnalis* does, in fact, consummate marriage (denied by the theory of "marriage by purchase"). In particular, supporting an analogy, suggested by R. Westbrook, between the two modes of adoption (i.e., adoption of foundlings vs. adoption of children who have natural parents) and the two corresponding modes of marriage, it was noted that in cases such as the marriage of a captive woman (Deut. 21:10-14), where there is no need to secure the parents' consent, the act of sexual union by itself is constitutive of marriage. A similar perspective of sexual union as constitutive of marriage is suggested by instances of synecdoche, by which sexual union is used to refer to marriage and vice versa.

Likewise, consistent with this predisposition to view sexual union as a marriage-forming act, Exod. 22:15, 16 [ET 16, 17]; Deut. 22:28f.; Genesis 34; and 2 Samuel 13 all encourage or insist on the formalizing of marriage following an act of "premarital" sex. This formalization consists simply of paying the marriage present, which, if accepted, constitutes an *ex post facto* approval of the union by the girl's parents and extinction of their parental authority.

Clearly, sexual union is the indispensable means for the consummation of marriage both in the Old Testament and elsewhere in the ancient Near East. While it is less certain, it seems probable that sexual union functioned in this manner precisely because it was viewed as an oath-sign. For example, Israel's covenant with Gibeon in Joshua 9 was considered irrevocable once Israel ratified it by the oath-sign of a shared meal, even though Gibeon secured this covenant through a blatant deception.[264] In an analogous manner, as was noted in our discussion of Genesis 29, Jacob's marriage with Leah appears to have been deemed valid and irrevocable, in spite of the underlying deception, once Jacob consummated the marriage through sexual union with Leah.

In any case, in support of this identification of sexual union, it was recalled how oath-signs, such as eating together or giving one's hand in a hand shake, often function by offering a solemn depiction of the covenant commitment to unity being undertaken. With respect to sexual union, it is clear that this act is ideally suited to depict the "one flesh" reality which is definitional of marriage in Gen. 2:24. Furthermore, it is notable that a number of oath-signs involve physical contact or the use of the parts of the body to represent one's whole person on the principle of *pars pro toto*, and two oath gestures involve the organs of generation (i.e., circumcision and placing one's hands under another's "thigh"). At the very least, such examples provide an associative context between the genitalia and oath taking.

---

[264] Cf. 2 Samuel 21 for the enduring consequences of this commitment which Saul attempted to revoke. Nevertheless, Josh. 9:14 makes plain that this meal was the decisive point of Israel's failure to consult the Lord, "So the men partook of their provisions, and did not ask direction from Yahweh." Cf. R.G. Boling and G.E. Wright, *Joshua*, 265.

CHAPTER EIGHT

MARRIAGE AS A COVENANT
ELSEWHERE IN THE OLD TESTAMENT

In the preceding chapters we established that Malachi identifies marriage as a covenant and that he grounds this identification in his interpretation of the Adam and Eve narrative. We also demonstrated that, in keeping with its identity as a covenant, marriage was apparently ratified by *verba solemnia*, as well as by the oath-sign of sexual union. We turn now to consider further corroborating evidence for an identification of marriage as a covenant elsewhere within the Old Testament.

Specifically, first we shall look at various indirect evidences that marriage was viewed as a sanction-sealed commitment between a husband and his wife. Second, we shall examine the other texts within the Old Testament which explicitly or implicitly identify marriage as a covenant. Finally, we shall consider the claimed indifference of the Old Testament to the husband's sexual fidelity, an indifference which has been thought to contradict the identification of marriage as a covenant.

With a view to this last objection, it will be of special interest throughout this chapter to determine, wherever possible, what was the precise nature of the sanction-sealed commitment undertaken by the husband and wife respectively. For example, if there were no oath other than the rather imprecise *verba solemnia*, "She is my wife and I am her husband from this day and forever,"[1] presumably the content of this commitment would be largely dependent on inherited cultural norms.[2] In a marriage bound only by such an oath a husband might be under no culturally defined obligation to be sexually faithful to his wife, while this might be the wife's principal obligation toward her husband. As an analogy, one might compare the disparity of obligations typical of suzerainty treaties, in which the vassal would be oath-bound to an exclusive loyalty to his suzerain without any hint that the suzerain should reciprocate by refraining from acquiring additional vassals.[3]

---

[1] So Cowley 15, line 4.

[2] So M.T. Roth, with respect to the declaration formula, "She will be my 'wife' [*lu aššatī šī*]," found in NB marriage documents ("'She will die by the iron dagger': Adultery and Neo-Babylonian Marriage," 190).

[3] Cf., e.g., Esarhaddon's Succession Treaty, ln. 129: you shall not "sw[ear an oa]th to any other king or any other lord" (S. Parpola and K. Watanabe, *Neo-Assyrian Treaties and Loyalty Oaths* [1988] 34).

Alternatively, if a marriage was ratified by the more demanding declaration formula of Gen. 2:23, as interpreted by Gen. 2:24 (or if the defining cultural norms for "I am her husband" included such texts as Genesis 2, Job 31, Proverbs 5, Malachi 2, etc.), and if sexual union was recognized as its inherently mutual oath-sign, then it may be expected that in such a marriage there would be a moral, though not necessarily legal, obligation of exclusive sexual fidelity on the part of the husband, no less than the wife. This obligation is regularly denied by scholars, however, mainly because of the failure to differentiate legality from ethical approval (a problem which has similarly vexed the scholarly discussion of polygyny — cf. Chapter 4, §6 above). The merits of this denial will be scrutinized here.

1. CONFIRMATORY (INDIRECT) EVIDENCE FOR THE EXISTENCE OF AN OATH, OR OATH-SIGN, IN MARRIAGE

Having posited the use of *verba solemnia* as a ratifying oath in marriage and having identified sexual union as a complementary ratifying oath-sign, we shall argue that marriage was not only a status regulated by custom (ethics) and family law, but also, at least in the minds of some biblical authors, a sanction-sealed commitment to which the deity was witness.

As has been discussed, the most direct evidence for this perspective is found in Mal. 2:14: "You ask, 'Why does he not?' Because Yahweh was witness between you and the wife of your youth [אֵשֶׁת ׀ וּבֵין בֵּינְךָ הֵעִיד יְהוָה נְעוּרֶיךָ], to whom you have been faithless, though she is your companion and your wife by covenant [בְרִיתֶךָ וְאֵשֶׁת חֲבֶרְתְּךָ וְהִיא]." Although Malachi nowhere mentions a ratifying oath in connection with marriage, the presence of such an oath, which would invoke the deity to act as a witness, is implied in his explicit identification of Yahweh as a "witness" between the husband and his wife.[4]

On the other hand, if marriage was understood more widely as a sanction-sealed commitment between husband and wife to which the deity was witness, even if other texts are less explicit than Malachi, four implications follow, for which we may seek evidence:

1) First, if a covenant existed between a husband and his wife, any offence against the marriage by either the husband or the wife may be

---

[4] There are only two other OT texts where God is acknowledged as a "witness *between* [עֵד/עוּד + בֵּין]" two parties; as in Malachi 2, in each case the declaration is made in an oath context. Cf. Gen. 31:50 and 1 Sam. 20:12, if the MT is emended with the Peshitta, as suggested by P.K. McCarter Jr., *1 Samuel*, 336. Cf. also Gen. 31:48, where in a covenant-ratifying oath context the "heap," perhaps acting as a representation of the deity, is acknowledged as "a witness between you and me." Cf. further Gen. 31:44 and Josh. 22:27.

Finally, cf. Judg. 11:10, which employs different vocabulary: "And the elders of Gilead said to Jephthah, 'Yahweh will be witness between us [בֵּינוֹתֵינוּ שֹׁמֵעַ יִהְיֶה יְהוָה]; we will surely do as you say."

Cf. our discussion in Chapter 7, §1.5 above in support of the assumption that the deity was considered to be a witness to marriage.

identified as sin (חטא, פשע, etc.), perfidy (מעל), or infidelity (בגד) against the other.

2) Second, if a covenant existed between a husband and his wife, because God is invoked in any covenant-ratifying oath to act as guarantor of the covenant, any marital offence by either the husband or the wife may be identified as sin (חטא, פשע, etc.) against God.

3) Third, if a covenant existed between a husband and his wife, because God is invoked in any ratifying oath to act as guarantor of the covenant, any marital infidelity ought to prompt God's judgment against the offending party.

4) Finally, if a covenant existed between a husband and his wife, because the deity is invoked in any ratifying oath, intermarriage with pagans ought to be prohibited because idolatry would necessarily ensue when a ratifying oath is sworn.

While these indirect evidences are not individually or even collectively sufficient to demonstrate the present thesis (since they readily admit alternative explanations), nevertheless, they are necessary conditions if marriage was considered an oath-ratified covenant. Moreover, if found to be the case, they would provide significant confirmatory support.

1.1 Marital offences may be identified as sin (חטא, פשע, etc.), perfidy (מעל), or infidelity (בגד) against one's spouse

As mentioned, if a covenant existed between a husband and his wife, then any offence against the marriage by either the husband or the wife may be identified as sin (חטא, פשע, etc.), perfidy (מעל), or infidelity (בגד) against the other, as these terms are employed elsewhere in analogous cases of covenant violation (e.g., 2 Kgs. 1:1; 18:14; etc.). Given the relatively few specific examples of adultery mentioned in the Old Testament, however, it is perhaps unsurprising that no biblical text identifies adultery, or any other marital offence, specifically as a sin (חטא) or act of rebellion (פשע) *against* one's spouse.[5] Nevertheless, some texts do describe adultery as "perfidy [מעל]" or "infidelity [בגד]" against one's spouse.

1.1.1 The significance of the use of מעל, "perfidy," for marital offences
Num. 5:12 and 27 describe a wife's adultery as an example of מעל, "perfidy," against her husband. Stressing the significance of these examples, J. Milgrom notes that these two verses represent the only occasions where מעל

---

[5] Some texts are ambiguous in that they pertain to the marriage analogy of Israel's relationship to Yahweh, describing Israel's spiritual "adultery" as פשע. Cf. Isa. 50:1 and 57:4. Cf. also Jer. 3:13. Alternatively Jer. 2:22 declares to adulterous Israel: the ineradicable "stain of your guilt [נכתם עונך] is still before me."

is used outside the sacral sphere of sancta and oath violations.[6] This observation makes very appealing the hypothesis that the reason that מעל, "perfidy," is applied to adultery is because it refers to a violation of the oath by which the marriage covenant was ratified. Further supporting the hypothesis of such an oath is the stipulation of a reparation/guilt offering [אָשָׁם] in Lev. 19:20-22 for adultery with a betrothed slave-girl. As Milgrom notes, the reparation offering is directly linked to perfidy [מעל] as the specific offering intended to redress sancta trespass or oath violations.[7]

Having drawn attention to these points, which naturally suggest that a covenant-ratifying oath was involved in marriage, nevertheless Milgrom rejects this inference for the following four reasons:

1) There is no explicit stipulation of an oath in any of the law codes or extant marriage contracts which have survived from the ancient Near East. This objection has already been answered in Chapter 6, §2.1.

2) The only explicit evidence in the Old Testament of an oath in marriage is Ezek. 16:8, which refers to an oath taken by Yahweh, the husband in this metaphor. According to Milgrom, however, "it should have been expected of the bride, Israel, for it is the bride, not the husband, who is subject to the laws of adultery."[8]

In large measure this objection was answered in Chapter 7, where we considered the evidence for an oath or oath-sign by both the husband and the wife. Even apart from that evidence, the fact that one chapter in Ezekiel mentions an oath by the husband hardly requires the conclusion that there could have been no corresponding oath by the wife. At the end of the present chapter we shall examine in more detail the widely-held assumption, shared by Milgrom, that the Old Testament obligates only wives and not husbands to sexual fidelity. Nevertheless, this has no bearing on the interpretation of Numbers 5 or its implication that adultery may represent an oath-violation, i.e. מעל, since the adultery in this chapter is by the wife.

3) In Num. 5:11ff. מעל, "perfidy," is used to refer to a wife's suspected adultery against her husband (vss. 12, 27). Everywhere else in the Old Testament, however, מעל is used of sancta or oath-violations committed against God. Hence Milgrom argues that in this passage מעל is "a literary metaphor and has no legal value."[9]

---

[6] *Cult and Conscience*, 133f. For examples of מעל with sancta violation, cf. Josh. 7:1; 2 Chron. 26:16, 18. For use with oath violation, cf. Num. 5:6-8; Lev. 26:40; and Ezek. 17:18-20. For מעל applied to adultery, cf. Num. 5:12, 27.

Cf. also Num. 31:16, where מעל is used for the Baal of Peor incident; Ezek. 20:27, where it is used of idolatry; and Ezra 10:2, 10, which so describes interfaith marriage.

Milgrom argues that these two categories of מעל, sancta trespass and oath violation, are essentially similar and were so considered throughout the ancient Near East (*op. cit.*, 21f.).

[7] Milgrom notes that מעל is found only with אָשָׁם in the sacrificial texts (*Cult and Conscience*, 16).

[8] *Ibid.*, 134.

[9] *Ibid.* Cf. especially note 486, where Milgrom suggests that the use of מעל in Numbers 5 probably derives from the analogy of Israel as an unfaithful wife whose מעל against Yahweh was literal. "Since *maal* denotes straying after other gods, it can also describe straying after other men."

Milgrom's assertion appears unconvincing. There is nothing in these texts to suggest the presence of "a literary metaphor" or an allusion to the prophetic marriage analogy. Given the limited corpus from which to reconstruct ancient Israel's jurisprudence, it is precarious to eliminate any data from consideration *ex hypothesi*. Rather, it seems likely that Milgrom has unnecessarily restricted the usage of מעל, "perfidy," and that מעל can be used of oath violations against persons other than God based on the evidence of Num. 5:12, 27. See Num. 5:6f., which is instructive in its awareness of such compound guilt and its significant conjoining of מעל, "perfidy," and אשם, "guilt": "Speak to the Israelites: When a man or woman commits any wrong toward a fellow man [כִּי יַעֲשׂוּ מִכָּל־חַטֹּאת הָאָדָם], thus breaking faith with Yahweh [= thus commiting perfidy against Yahweh; לִמְעֹל מַעַל בַּיהוָה], and that person realizes his guilt [וְאָשְׁמָה הַנֶּפֶשׁ הַהִוא], he shall confess the wrong that he has done. He shall make restitution in the principal amount [וְהֵשִׁיב אֶת־אֲשָׁמוֹ בְּרֹאשׁוֹ]...."[10]

Although מעל, "perfidy," is relatively well-attested outside of Num. 5:12, 27, in that the verb appears 35 times and the noun 29 times, one should not exaggerate the frequency of occurrence by failing to note that in 18 cases the verb מעל is employed with its cognate accusative (as in Num. 5:12, 27). Furthermore, it is notable that in most of its occurrences, including Num. 5:6, both the verb and the noun are accompanied by ביהוה,[11] "against Yahweh" / בִי,[12] "against me"/ ... באלהי, "against God"[13] to make explicit that the infidelity was committed against God. While this complementary prepositional phrase may be redundant, perhaps for emphasis, it is also possible that the phrase is required because מעל, "perfidy," can be committed against persons or entities other than God. This last option seems to be confirmed by Josh. 7:1 where מעל + ב + חרם, "commit perfidy against the ban," is found. Here ב, "against," marks an impersonal object, "the ban," in reference to which the specified מעל was committed.

Lastly, two examples of מעל, "perfidy," do not easily conform to the very restricted usage posited by Milgrom: Prov. 16:10 and Job 21:34.[14]

4) Finally, with respect to Lev. 19:20-22, Milgrom argues, "If the violation of the alleged betrothal oath is responsible for the penalty, why is the paramour liable at all — he did not take the oath!"[15] Rather than allowing Lev. 19:20-22 to overturn his view that the reparation offering [אָשָׁם] was limited to cases of מעל, that is, sancta and oath violations, Milgrom argues that adultery entails an oath violation after all — not the violation of a

---

[10] As rendered by the NJPS. In support, cf. J. Milgrom, *Cult and Conscience*, 17, 105 n. 388.

[11] Lev. 5:21 [ET 6:2]; Num. 5:6; Josh. 22:31; 1 Chron. 10:13; 2 Chron. 12:2; 26:16; 28:19, 22; and 30:7.

[12] Deut. 32:51; Lev. 26:40; Ezek. 14:13; 20:27; and 39:23, 26.

[13] Josh. 22:16; Ezra 10:2; Neh. 13:27; and 1 Chron. 5:25.

[14] Milgrom considers these both to refer to oath violation: "the king who commits *maal* with 'his mouth' by deviating from God's justice and the self-assumed authority of Job's friends to speak for God's theodicy" (*Cult and Conscience*, 20 n. 64).

[15] *Ibid.*, 134f.

betrothal vow, since the paramour was no party to this, but the violation of the Sinaitic oath by which all Israelites were obligated to adhere to the seventh commandment against adultery.

There are four main difficulties with Milgrom's explanation of Lev. 19:20-22.

a) Milgrom's assumption that the reparation offering [אָשָׁם] was restricted to cases of מַעַל, that is to sancta and oath violations, finds its strongest support in Lev. 5:14-24 [ET 6:5], the one text which addresses the purpose of the reparation offering in a general manner, but the limited evidence available to test this interpretation forbids certainty.[16] While the term אָשָׁם, bearing the meaning "reparation offering," appears about 34 times in the Old Testament, 11 of these are grouped within Lev. 5-7.[17] Of the remaining 23, the only instances which offer support for Milgrom's view are 4 verses in 1 Samuel 6, where the Philistines provide a reparation offering after they violated the sanctity of the ark. On the other hand, at least 13 examples occurring in four separate contexts call for explanation from Milgrom since they are not obviously related to oath or sancta violation.[18]

b) On Milgrom's view, any violation of any one of the commandments of the Decalogue ought to require an אָשָׁם, "a reparation offering," since every such violation will entail מַעַל, "perfidy," by reason of an oath violation (of the Sinaitic oath). One looks in vain, however, for examples of מַעַל applied to desecration of the Sabbath, dishonour to parents, murder, theft, covetousness,

---

[16] Perhaps the most decisive issue in establishing the meaning of the אָשָׁם offering is the contention of Milgrom that אָשָׁם in Lev. 5:6 and 7, as well as elsewhere, means "penalty" or "reparation," rather than "reparation offering." Cf. J. Milgrom, *Cult and Conscience*, §2, 3-7. For alternative explanations, however, cf., e.g., D. Kellermann, "אָשָׁם '*āshām*," *TDOT*, I, 431-434. Cf. also B.A. Levine, *In the Presence of the Lord* (1974) 91-101 [reviewed by J. Milgrom, *op. cit.*, Appendix D, 142f.].

[17] Lev. 5:15, 16, 18, 19, 25 [ET 6:6]; 6:10 [ET 17]; 7:1, 2, 5, 7, 37; 14:12, 13, 14, 17, 21, 24, 25 (2x), 28; 19:21, 22; Num. 6:12; 18:9; 1 Sam. 6:3, 4, 8, 17; Ezra 10:19; Isa. 53:10; Ezek. 40:39; 42:13; 44:29; and 46:20. For Isa. 53:10, cf. T.H. Gaster, "Sacrifices and Offerings, OT," *IDB*, IV, 152.

Some scholars would add 6 more occurrences of אָשָׁם with the meaning "reparation offering," or "guilt offering," to this list: Lev. 5:6, 7, 15, 24 [ET 6:5], 25 [ET 6:6] and 19:21.

If Lev. 5:6 and 7 are added, they would imply an essential identity between the אָשָׁם and the חַטָּאת offerings. The first occurrence of אָשָׁם in Lev. 5:15, 25 [ET 6:6] and 19:21 is identical to 5:6 and 7.

Alternatively, with J. Milgrom (*Cult and Conscience*, §2, 3-7), B.A. Levine (*Leviticus*, 28, 30), and G.J. Wenham (*Leviticus*, 104-112), אָשָׁם in these verses may bear a different sense, namely that of "penalty" or "reparation."

With respect to Lev. 5:24 [ET 6:5], cf. the RSV, which renders בְּיוֹם אַשְׁמָתוֹ, "on the day of his guilt offering." Alternatively, J. Milgrom renders the phrase, "as soon as he feels guilt" (*op. cit.*, 84).

[18] These are: nine examples found in Leviticus 14, as a required offering for persons who have been cleansed of a serious skin disease (*ibid.*, §45, 80-82); two (or three) examples in Leviticus 19, the text regarding sex with a promised female slave (*ibid.*, 129-137); one example in Numbers 6, the required offering for the Nazirite for his or her premature desanctification (*ibid.*, §39, 66-70); and one example in Ezra 10, where this offering is made after intermarriage with pagans (*ibid.*, §41, 71-73).

etc., or similarly, cases where a reparation offering is required for desecration of the Sabbath, dishonour to parents, murder, adultery, covetousness, etc.[19]

c) Furthermore, it is not clear that Lev. 19:20-22, in fact, depicts a case of adultery and hence concerns a violation of the seventh commandment. The operative term נאף, "commit adultery," is conspicuously absent,[20] and it is possible that this absence reflects the fact that the concern of this law is with a borderline case, one which superficially resembles adultery (hence the stipulation in vs. 20 that they not be put to death), but which entails an important difference with the result that adultery actually has not been committed, and so the usual sanction for adultery is inapplicable.[21] Perhaps that difference resides in the diminished capacity of a female slave to resist the sexual advances of the lover,[22] or perhaps it inheres in the fact that this woman was not yet betrothed (i.e., inchoately married), but only pledged (see below for a defence of this interpretation).[23]

d) Finally, it should be noted that text critical problems, and especially the presence of several *hapax legomena*, render the details of Lev. 19:20-22 uncertain.[24] For example, it is unclear whether the *hapax legomenon* בִּקֹּרֶת

---

[19] Achan's theft in Josh. 7:1 is better explained as a case of sancta trespass. For Lev. 19:20-22, often considered as a case of adultery, cf. the discussion below.

[20] Cf. Exod. 20:14 and Deut. 5:18. Cf. also Lev. 20:10.
The absence of נאף may not be decisive, however, since the term is similarly absent from Deut. 22:22, "If a man is found lying with the wife of another man [כִּי־יִמָּצֵא אִישׁ שֹׁכֵב עִם־אִשָּׁה בְעֻלַת־בַּעַל], both of them shall die, the man who lay with the woman, and the woman; so you shall purge the evil from Israel." Nevertheless, the more general language of Deut. 22:22 [שֹׁכֵב עִם] appears to have been dictated by the desire to establish more clearly the *legal* parallel which exists between adultery with a married woman, נאף, and the case of extramarital relations with a betrothed woman, which, contrary to KB, and *TWOT*, *s.v.*, is nowhere described as נאף, and may not be within the linguistic usage of נאף (cf. Deut. 22:23-24).

[21] Cf. Deut. 22:23f.

[22] On Milgrom's view this difference resides in the remaining slave-status of the woman, which denies her the legal status of a person (*Cult and Conscience*, 130 n. 463). It seems reasonable that the present law takes into account the diminished capacity of a slave to resist the sexual advances of a man (perhaps a member of her owner's household?). It is less clear why this law does not simply apply the death penalty to the offending man for raping a betrothed woman who was presumably an unwilling victim (cf. Deut. 22:25-27). While it can be no more than a suggestion, it is possible that this law would not exclude such a penalty, assuming that it could be established that a rape took place. It may be, however, that the controlling purpose of the law was simply to exclude the *joint* death penalty, which was normally required where there was circumstantial evidence for the woman's consent, precisely because of a female slave's diminished capacity to withhold consent.

[23] As will be argued below, the fact that this woman was pledged, but not betrothed, is indicated both by the lack of her redemption or manumission and by the use of the *hapax legomenon* נֶחֱרָפֶת, as opposed to the customary expression for betrothal, ארשׂ, as in Deuteronomy 22.

[24] The Samaritan Pentateuch adds *lw*, "to him" or "regarding him," after לֹא and reads יוּמְתוּ as a singular, yielding: *bqrt thyh lw l' ywmt*. The singular reading, "he will not die," may imply a resemblance of this case to rape, as in Deut. 22:25-27 (cf. LE §26; CH §130; HL §197), rather than to adultery, as in Deut. 22:23-24. In support of the singular reading of the Samaritan Pentateuch, a resemblance to rape may better account for the subsequent stress on the man's guilt and the lack of any punishment stipulated for the woman. On the other hand, it is unclear why the man should avoid execution "*because* she was not free."

refers to some additional penalty, perhaps a reprimand or more likely financial compensation, or whether it refers to an inquiry.[25]   More importantly, the key term נֶחֱרָפֶת in vs. 20 occurs nowhere else in Biblical Hebrew. Based on a cognate term חרופה found in Talmudic Hebrew, Milgrom argues for the meaning "betrothed."[26] This may also be favoured by the expected liability to the death penalty mentioned in vs. 20, implying at least a *de facto* resemblance to betrothal on the basis of Deut. 22:23f.[27] The fact that חרף is used in Leviticus 19, however, in preference to the customary term ארשׁ, "betrothed" (cf. Exod. 22:15 [ET 16]; Deut. 22:23ff.), suggests the possibility of a distinction in terms and does not favour Milgrom's interpretation. Based on the Akkadian *ḫarāpu*, "to be early, arrive early," E.A. Speiser and others argue for "assigned in advance," that is, a pledge toward betrothal and marriage in advance of redemption or manumission.[28]

Besides the term חרף, "pledged," three further considerations support this understanding of the slave's marital status as being less than betrothal. First, the text places considerable stress on the fact that the female slave was not yet redeemed or manumitted (vs. 20) — a point that could already be inferred from her designation as a שִׁפְחָה, "female slave." Although Milgrom adduces some ancient Near Eastern parallels for the betrothal and even marriage of an unmanumitted female slave to a man other than her owner, this situation must have been unusual in Israel or the text would not have needed to make this specification with such clarity.[29] Second, if betrothal normally affords a woman the same legal protection and responsibility in terms of rape and adultery as does marriage (cf. Deut. 22:23-27), then, as interpreted by Milgrom, Lev. 19:20-22 would suggest a similar clemency toward rape and adultery with a married slave. There is no evidence to support such a view. On the contrary, the brutal rape of the Levite's concubine in Judges 19, for example, is viewed with the utmost gravity, demanding a judicial response on the part of all Israel.[30] Third, a similar pre-

---

In addition to נֶחֱרָפֶת and בִּקֹרֶת, the noun חֻפְשָׁה and the verb חֻפְשָׁה are also *hapax legomena*. Their meaning is not in dispute, however, based on the related forms חֻפְשִׁית and חָפְשִׁי, supported by Akkadian and Ugaritic cognates.

[25] Cf., e.g., K. Elliger, *Leviticus* (1966) 260; Holladay, *s.v.*; KB, *s.v.*; E.A. Speiser, "Leviticus and the Critics," 33ff.; and J. Milgrom, *Cult and Conscience*, 129 n. 460.

[26] So J. Milgrom, *Cult and Conscience*, 129 n. 459. Cf. Jastrow, *s.v.*

[27] Cf. J. Milgrom, *Cult and Conscience*, 130; and G.J. Wenham, *Leviticus*, 271.

[28] E.A. Speiser, "Leviticus and the Critics," 34f. Cf. *CAD*, *s.v. ḫarāpu*, A. So also B. Maarsingh, *Leviticus* (1980) 169; and B.A. Levine, *Leviticus* (1989) 130.
S.M. Paul wonders if חרף may be related to the *ḫuruppatu* tokens of engagement in MAL A §42:17 and §43:20 (*Studies in the Book of the Covenant in the Light of Cuneiform and Biblical Law* [1970] 54 n. 3).

[29] J. Milgrom, *Cult and Conscience*, 131 n. 467.
Such a situation would seem inherently contradictory with the girl caught between a conflict of loyalties to her owner and to her husband, both designated as her בַּעַל. Moreover, if the woman was not yet engaged, that is, if the betrothal gift (brideprice) had not yet been fully paid, this fact would explain why she had not yet been "ransomed" (Lev. 19:20) — the requisite money had not yet been paid.

[30] Cf. also Gen. 49:4 and 2 Sam. 16:21ff.

betrothal status appears to be presupposed in cuneiform law.[31] In CH §156, for example, a man "chooses a bride [*kallatam iḫîrma*]" for his son, but before their marriage is consummated, the father lies with her himself. In such a case the father is required to pay a stiff fine and to return any dowry to the girl; she can then be married by the husband of her choice. Given that CH §130 stipulates a death penalty for a man who has sex with a betrothed girl, that is, an *aššat awīlum*, "the wife of a man" who has not yet known a man, it must be that the expression "choosing a bride [*kallatam iḫîrma*]" in CH §156 reflects an earlier stage in the process of marriage negotiation, at which point the bride-to-be is not yet accorded the legal status of an *aššat awīlum*.

To sum up, Lev. 19:20-22 should not be regarded as a case of intercourse with a betrothed slave-girl, but with a pledged pre-betrothed slave-girl; therefore, the offence attracts a lesser penalty and requires atonement with a reparation offering [אָשָׁם]. It does not disprove the view that marriage included an oath, the presence of which is indicated by the use of מעל, "perfidy," with reference to its breach in Num. 5:12, 27. This view finds further support in the use of בגד, "infidelity," with respect to marital offences, since בגד is an approximate synonym of מעל.

1.1.2 The significance of the use of בָּגַד, "act faithlessly," for marital offences
The verb בָּגַד, "to act faithlessly, treacherously," always in the Qal conjugation, appears 49 times in 39 verses in the Old Testament. In addition, there are five, or possibly six, occurrences of the cognate noun בֶּגֶד, "faithlessness"; the abstract noun בִּגְדוֹת, "faithlessness"; and the adjective בָּגוֹד, "faithless." There appears to be a scholarly consensus that these various forms of בגד refer not to improbity in general, but specifically to infidelity against some culturally expected or oath-imposed obligation. BDB, for example, suggests that the basic meaning of the root is "act or deal treacherously."[32]

Reflecting this basic meaning, it is not surprising to find בָּגַד frequently used to refer to infidelity against a covenant partner.[33] An example of this usage involving the violation of a secular covenant is found in Judg. 9:23:

F. Hauck supposes that the law of adultery was simply more lenient when applied to slaves (Lev. 19:20ff.), while it was more severe when applied to a priest's daughter (requiring burning, according to Lev. 21:9) ("μοιχεύω, κτλ.," *TDNT* 4, 730 n. 3). But he appears to be mistaken on both accounts. As argued here, Lev. 19:20ff. does not consider a case of adultery because the girl was not fully betrothed, and Lev. 21:9 is explicit that it pertains not to adultery (נאף), but to prostitution (זנה) — perhaps especially heinous in the case of priestly daughters because of the resemblance to cultic prostitution. Cf. also the penalty of burning in Gen. 38:24 and Lev. 20:14.

[31] Cf. also HL §§28-29. Cf. F. Mezger, "Promised but not engaged" (1944) 28-31.
[32] Cf. also KB, *s.v.* ("treulos handeln," "treulos verlassen"); S. Erlandsson, "בָּגַד, *bāghadh*," *TDOT*, I, 470-73 ("to act faithlessly [treacherously])"; and M.A. Klopfenstein, "בגד *bgd* treulos handeln," *THAT*, I, 261-4 .
[33] Cf. S. Erlandsson, "בָּגַד, *bāghadh*," 471-2.

"And God sent an evil spirit between Abimelech and the men of Shechem; and the men of Shechem dealt treacherously with Abimelech [וַיִּבְגְּדוּ בַעֲלֵי־ שְׁכֶם בַּאֲבִימֶלֶךְ]."[34] Most of the time, however, בָּגַד is used with reference to Israel's infidelity against Yahweh's covenant.[35] See, for example, Hos. 6:7: "But at [or, like?] Adam they transgressed the covenant; there they dealt faithlessly with me [וְהֵמָּה כְּאָדָם עָבְרוּ בְרִית שָׁם בָּגְדוּ בִי]." At times the infidelity is more particularly directed against fellow Israelites, as in Mal. 2:10: "Have we not all one father? Has not one God created us? Why then are we faithless to one another [מַדּוּעַ נִבְגַּד אִישׁ בְּאָחִיו], profaning the covenant of our fathers [לְחַלֵּל בְּרִית אֲבֹתֵינוּ]?"[36]

Consistent with this usage of בגד as a description of infidelity against one's covenant partner, בגד is frequently applied to marital offences, often in passages where the marriage analogy is employed for Israel's covenantal infidelity against Yahweh.[37] What is especially noteworthy is the fact that בגד is utilized not only to describe an unfaithful wife, whose infidelity typically consists of adultery or harlotry, but also to describe an unfaithful husband, whose infidelity also proves to be sexual, though at times may include other offences as well. For example, a wife's infidelity is termed בגד in Jer. 3:20: "Surely, as a faithless wife leaves her husband [אָכֵן בָּגְדָה אִשָּׁה מֵרֵעָהּ], so have you been faithless to me [כֵּן בְּגַדְתֶּם בִּי], O house of Israel, says Yahweh." Reflecting the same marriage analogy, Jer. 3:8 identifies a wife's adultery and harlotry as בגד: "She saw that for all the adulteries of that faithless one, Israel [אֲשֶׁר נִאֲפָה מְשֻׁבָה יִשְׂרָאֵל], I had sent her away with a decree of divorce; yet her false sister Judah did not fear [וְלֹא יָרְאָה בֹּגֵדָה יְהוּדָה אֲחוֹתָהּ], but she too went and played the harlot [וַתֵּלֶךְ וַתִּזֶן גַּם־הִיא]."[38]

In other verses, however, it is the husband who is guilty of committing infidelity [בגד]. What is particularly interesting is that several of these make explicit that the infidelity [בגד] in view is committed against [+ ב] one's wife and not merely against one's father-in-law, as some might suppose by extrapolating from the example of Laban's covenant with Jacob in Gen. 31:44 or from the evidence of many ancient Near Eastern marriage contracts.[39] So,

---

[34] For evidence that there was a covenant between Abimelech and the men of Shechem, cf. Judg. 9:3, 6 and the discussion of these texts in R.G. Boling, *Judges*, 171; and P. Kalluveettil, *Declaration and Covenant*, 62f., 209f.

[35] Cf., e.g., 1 Sam. 14:33; Ps. 25:3; 73:15; 78:57; 119:158; Isa. 24:16; 48:8; Jer. 3:7, 8, 10, 11, 20; 5:11; 12:1; Hos. 5:7; and Mal. 2:11.

[36] J.M.P. Smith observes that, "A covenant was regularly confirmed by an oath and thus given religious sanction; hence its violation is properly characterised as profanation; cf. Ps. 55:21 89:32. 35 [ET 31, 34]" (*Malachi*, 48).

[37] Cf. S. Erlandsson, "בָּגַד, *bāghadh*," 470.

As mentioned earlier, the obligations which are transgressed when there is "infidelity [בגד]" may be merely culturally expected, rather than specifically oath-imposed or covenantal. Cf., e.g., Lam. 1:2. The fact that these terms are so often used of violations of a covenant makes their appearance with marriage unsurprising on the view that marriage is a covenant.

[38] Cf. also Jer. 3:11 and Hos. 5:7.

[39] K. van der Toorn notes that Akkadian texts tend "to picture adultery as a breach of the good faith reigning among men" (*Sin and Sanction in Israel and Mesopotamia*, 17).

in Mal. 2:14, for instance, a husband is accused of committing infidelity against his wife because of his act of capricious divorce: "You ask, 'Why does he not?' Because Yahweh was witness to the covenant between you and the wife of your youth, to whom you have been faithless [אֲשֶׁר אַתָּה בָּגַדְתָּה בָּהּ], though she is your companion and your wife by covenant." Compare also Exod. 21:8 and Mal. 2:16.[40]

As we have already noted in Chapter 5, by its allusion to the creation account Mal. 2:15 reflects a yet more encompassing obligation of fidelity on the part of the husband to be "one" with his wife: "Did He not make [you/them] one, with a remnant of the spirit belonging to it? But you say, 'And what was the One seeking?' A godly seed! Therefore watch out for your lives and do not act faithlessly against the wife of your youth [וּבְאֵשֶׁת נְעוּרֶיךָ אַל־יִבְגֹּד]."

Jer. 9:1 [ET 2] similarly condemns adultery by a husband as infidelity [בגד], although it does not make explicit the object of the infidelity, whether it is the offended wife, the cuckolded husband, society at large, or God. Jer. 9:1 [ET 2] reads: "O that I had in the desert a wayfarers' lodging place, that I might leave my people and go away from them! For they are all adulterers [כִּי כֻלָּם מְנָאֲפִים], a company of treacherous men [עֲצֶרֶת בֹּגְדִים]." For our present purpose it is not necessary to decide whether the adultery in Jer. 9:1 [ET 2] is literal or metaphoric since on either view the prophet equates adultery [מנאף] with infidelity [בגד] through semantic parallelism, which is characteristic of the entire lament.[41]

One final example of interest is Prov. 23:27, 28: "For a harlot is a deep pit [כִּי־שׁוּחָה עֲמֻקָּה זוֹנָה]; an adventuress is a narrow well [וּבְאֵר צָרָה נָכְרִיָּה]. She lies in wait like a robber [אַף־הִיא כְּחֶתֶף תֶּאֱרֹב] and increases the faithless among men [וּבוֹגְדִים בְּאָדָם תּוֹסִף]." Unfortunately, however, because of its textual and lexical obscurities, Prov. 23:27f. cannot help advance the present discussion. The precise implication of וּבוֹגְדִים בְּאָדָם תּוֹסִף is unclear, prompting scholars to propose numerous emendations (or reinterpretations)

Cf., however, the discussion of marriage contracts in the previous chapter and R. Westbrook's summary: "marriage is a legal status and must be distinguished from the marriage contract which is incidental thereto" (Old Babylonian Marriage Law," I, ii).

[40] Cf. the fuller discussion of Exod. 21:8 in §3.4 below. Cf. Chapter 3 for a defence of our rendering of Mal. 2:16.

[41] W. McKane, among others, favours a figurative reference here and in Hos. 7:4, which is thought to be parallel (*Jeremiah*, I, 199). On the contrary, J.L. Mays and others note that Hosea usually uses "adultery," in contrast to "harlotry," for literal sexual unfaithfulness (*Hosea*, 105). Moreover, contrary to McKane, Jer. 2:20ff. and 3:1-5 differ significantly from Jer. 9:1 [ET 2] because, in keeping with the marriage metaphor elsewhere, their references to adultery are consistently in the feminine gender, not masculine plural as here. Cf. also Ezekiel 16 and 23. Furthermore, the mention of adultery in Jer. 9:1 [ET 2] constitutes the first in a (perhaps rhetorical or stereotypical) sequence of offences including falsehood, evil, untrustworthiness, slander, deception, oppression, etc. Since each of these successive offences appears to bear its literal sense, there is little reason to suppose otherwise for "adulterers."

of וּבוֹגְדִים, "the faithless."[42] Further, because of its epigrammatic nature, this text leaves unspecified the marital status of either the man or the woman (although the "harlot [זוֹנָה]" may typically have been unmarried, there are numerous exceptions). So, while it is possible that Prov. 23:27f. condemns extramarital sex with an unmarried woman as infidelity [בגד], it is far from certain.

1.2 Second, if a covenant existed between a husband and his wife, because God is invoked in any covenant-ratifying oath to act as guarantor of the covenant, any marital offence by either the husband or the wife may be identified as sin (חטא, פֶּשַׁע, etc.) against God.

Many biblical texts identify adultery as iniquitous, a sin against God, etc., which, correspondingly, brings shame and renders both of the participants unclean and guilty. If the converse of this were true, that is, if the Old Testament did not consider marital offences as sins against God, etc., such a perspective would contradict the view that marriage was a sanction-sealed covenant. It is unnecessary to suppose, however, that each particular condemnation was a conscious reflection of a covenantal view of marriage or even a reflection of the explicit prohibitions against adultery set forth in the Decalogue and elsewhere. Rather, the Old Testament appears to presuppose a general moral consciousness in man, shared even by pagans, which acknowledges adultery as a heinous wrong committed not only against the injured husband, but also against God. Hence, Gen. 20:6 records God's words to the pagan king Abimelech: "Then God said to him in the dream, 'Yes, I know that you have done this in the integrity of your heart, and it was I who kept you from sinning against me [מֵחֲטוֹ־לִי]; therefore I did not let you touch her.'" In response, Abimelech asked Abraham, "What have you done to us? And how have I sinned against you, that you have brought on me and my kingdom a great sin [חֲטָאָה גְדֹלָה]? You have done to me things that ought not to be done" (Gen. 20:9). Similarly, Abimelech addresses Isaac, "What is this you have done to us? One of the people might easily have lain with your wife, and you would have brought guilt [אָשָׁם] upon us'" (Gen. 26:10).

Supportive of these acknowledgments of adultery as a "great sin" on the lips of non-Israelites, an Akkadian text from Ugarit similarly condemns the adultery of Ammištamru's wife, the queen of Ugarit, saying she "sinned a great sin [ḫi-iṭ-ṭá ra-ba-a ti-iḫ-te-ṭì]" against her husband.[43] While this

---

[42] For a sampling of alternatives, cf. C.H. Toy, *Proverbs*, 437f.; and W. McKane, *Proverbs*, 391.

[43] *PRU* IV, 139. Cf. also W.L. Moran, "The Scandal of the 'Great Sin' at Ugarit" (1959) 280f. J.J. Rabinowitz notes that the same expression is attested in four Egyptian marriage contracts from about the ninth century B.C. ("The 'Great Sin' in Ancient Egyptian Marriage Contracts" [1959] 73).

Note, however, that the Akkadian expression "a great sin [*ḫitta rabā*]" also occurs in *PRU* III, 96ff.:13-17, where it refers to forging royal tablets. Hence, the phrase must simply refer to a serious offence, of which adultery was only an example. Cf. F.B. Knutson, "Literary Phrases and Formulae," *RSP*, II, 409-411.

particular text stresses adultery as an offence against the cuckolded husband, S.E. Loewenstamm has assembled a number of cuneiform religious texts which characterize adultery as a sin against the gods, deserving their punishment.[44] For example, a bilingual Sumero-Akkadian hymn to Ninurta lists adultery as one of many sins against Ninurta: "He who has intercourse with (another) man's wife, his guilt is grievous [*a-ran-šu kab-[tum-ma]*]."[45] Interestingly, one text echoes the tenth commandment: "A man who covets his neighbour's wife [*sá a-na al-ti tap-pi-šú iš-šu-ḫú [inē-šú]*]] will ... before his appointed day" ("The Šamaš Hymn," lns. 88-89).[46] Compare also Joseph's words in Gen. 39:9: "How then could I do such a wicked thing and sin against God [וְאֵיךְ אֶעֱשֶׂה הָרָעָה הַגְּדֹלָה הַזֹּאת וְחָטָאתִי לֵאלֹהִים]?"[47]

In the following examples adultery is characterized as "sin [חטא]," "iniquity [עון]," "evil [רעע]," or "an abomination [תוֹעֵבָה]": Lev. 18:29; Num. 5:15, 31; Deut. 22:22, 24; 2 Sam. 12:9, 13; Jer. 7:9f., 23:10; and Ezek. 22:11.[48] Similarly reflecting this moral assessment of adultery as an offence against God, the Old Testament considers that adultery defiles [טמא] both the man and the woman (and their land), whether or not they are caught. See, for example, Lev. 18:20, 25, 27; Num. 5:13f., 19f., 28f.; Ezek. 18:6, 11, 15; and 33:26.

1.3 Third, if a covenant existed between a husband and his wife, because God is invoked in any ratifying oath to act as guarantor of the covenant, any marital infidelity ought to prompt God's judgment against the offending party.

Many biblical texts indicate that marital infidelity and particularly adultery provoke God's direct judgment against the offenders, whether or not the adultery in question would have been justiciable within Israel's courts.[49] While this fact is consistent with the present view that marriage was a sanction-sealed covenant, once again, it is unlikely that these texts represent a conscious reflection of this fact. This is the case because, as in Mesopotamian practice, God is generally depicted as judging the guilty lover

---

[44] "The Laws of Adultery and Murder in Biblical and Mesopotamian Law," 146-53.

[45] W.G. Lambert, *Babylonian Wisdom Literature* (1960) 119, ln. 4.

[46] *Ibid.*, 130f. The broken text is thought to predict a premature death for the one who lusts.

[47] The citation of ancient Near Eastern parallels is not intended necessarily to imply an identity of outlook or jurisprudence with biblical practice. In the present case, for example, it appears that Joseph does share the outlook of LU §4, lns. 222-231, which considers it a mitigating circumstance if the woman entices the man into adultery. In such a case she is to be executed, while the man is allowed to go free. Of course, it is possible that while free of any criminal sanction, such a man might still be considered guilty before the gods.
Cf. also J.J. Finkelstein, who discusses the Mesopotamian predisposition to impute the burden of guilt for adultery to the married woman ("Sex Offences in Sumerian Laws," 366ff.). Cf. MAL A §§14, 16, and 22. Cf. also K. van der Toorn, *Sin and Sanction*, 17f.

[48] If Num. 5:6 may also be applied to the adulteress in Num. 5:11-31, then her offence may be further characterized as sin [חטאת] and infidelity [מעל] against God.

[49] Cf. Gen. 12:10-13:1; 20:1-8; 26:10; 39:9; 2 Sam. 12:13; and Wisdom of Solomon 3:16-19 (cf. 4:6).

who was not a party to the marriage vow.[50] So, for example, God closed the wombs of Abimelech's wife and his female slaves as a deterrent against committing adultery with Sarah. He also warned Abimelech in a dream that if Abimelech should go ahead and commit adultery with Sarah, God would kill Abimelech and his family (Gen. 20:7, 18). Although the book of Job rejects the simplistic views of suffering put forth by Job's "comforters," nevertheless in his oath of clearance in 31:9-12, Job himself acknowledges that the sin of adultery would rightfully incur both human and divine retribution. Other texts warn Israel that since adultery was one of the chief sins which prompted Yahweh's wrath against the Canaanites and for which Yahweh cast them out, Israel will incur a like judgment for her practice of adultery (Lev. 18:24; Jer. 5:7-9; 7:9-15; 23:10; 29:23; and Ezek. 33:26).[51]

1.4 Finally, if a covenant existed between a husband and his wife, because the deity is invoked in any ratifying oath, intermarriage with pagans ought to be prohibited because idolatry would necessarily ensue when a ratifying oath is sworn.

D.L. Magnetti argues that international parity treaties were prohibited for Israel because of the idolatry that would be a necessary consequence of swearing ratificatory oaths (Exod. 23:32; Deut. 7:2; and Judg. 2:2).[52] Although suzerains did not generally impose the worship of their gods on their unwilling vassals, the gods of both parties were invoked in parity treaties, and such an invocation carries an implicit acknowledgement of the reality of those gods and their ability to punish any would-be covenant breaker.[53]

If this is so, it would seem likely that the same concern would require an analogous prohibition of intermarriage with pagans if, as is being argued, marriage required the mutual swearing of ratifying oaths. As expected, there are several Old Testament prohibitions against intermarriage with pagans: Exod. 34:12-16; Deut. 7:2-4; Judg. 3:6; 1 Kgs. 11:2; Ezra 9:12; Neh. 10:31

---

[50] Cf., e.g., K. van der Toorn, *Sin and Sanction*, 17, 161 n. 80.

Similarly, S.E. Loewenstamm notes several cuneiform texts which assume that the offended gods will kill an adulterer ("The Laws of Adultery and Murder in Biblical and Mesopotamian Law," 146-53).

[51] Nathan's consolation of David after his repentance in 2 Sam. 12:13 implies that David's wrong was similarly deserving of a divinely-imposed death penalty: "Yahweh also has put away your sin; you shall not die." Because of the compound nature of David's offence (he was guilty of both adultery and murder), however, the text does not contribute unambiguously to the present argument.

[52] "The Oath in the Old Testament in the Light of Related Terms and in the Legal and Covenantal Context of the Ancient Near East" (1969) 85f.

On the importance of swearing one's oaths in the name of Yahweh, cf. Deut. 6:13; 10:20; Isa. 48:1; and Jer. 12:16.

[53] Cf. Gen. 31:53.

Cf. also G.E. Mendenhall, "Puppy and Lettuce in Northwest Semitic Covenant Making" (1954) 39; R. Frankena, "The Vassal Treaties of Esarhaddon and the Dating of Deuteronomy" (1965) 130; D.J. McCarthy, *Treaty and Covenant* (1981) 120; and P. Kalluveettil, *Declaration and Covenant*, 81 n. 301.

[ET 30]; and 13:25.[54] Of these, the most remarkable is found in Ezra 10:2, 10, where this offence is condemned as מעל, "perfidy," a term often used of oath violation.[55] As argued in an earlier chapter, these prohibitions are concerned to prohibit only interfaith marriage, not exogamous marriage as such. Moreover, the prohibitions assume that when a marriage is concluded with a pagan wife, idolatry will be an inevitable result. For example, Exod. 34:16 asserts that "their daughters will play the harlot after their gods and make your sons play the harlot after their gods." This confidence is puzzling if it assumes that Yahwistic husbands or wives will succumb in every case to a more resolute faith of their pagan spouses. On the other hand, it is entirely comprehensible if the mentioned idolatry is a necessary consequence of the very act of solemnizing such a marriage by means of bilateral oaths.

This brief review of the terminology associated with marriage breaking (i.e., "sin [חטא]," "transgression [פשע]," "perfidy [מעל]," "infidelity [בגד]," etc.) shows that the Old Testament regarded marriage as a mutual commitment probably sanction-sealed by an oath. This makes it likely that marriage was seen as a covenant, though this conclusion is not inevitable. We now turn to texts outside Malachi which render this conclusion certain by their explicit, or implicit, identification of marriage as a covenant.

2. TEXTS (OTHER THAN MALACHI 2:14) WHICH EXPLICITLY, OR IMPLICITLY, IDENTIFY MARRIAGE AS A COVENANT

We have already established a general conceptual and terminological compatibility between marriage and "covenant [בְּרִית]" (Chapter 6, §1.3 above), placing particular stress on the evidence for a covenant-ratifying oath in marriage in the form of *verba solemnia* and for sexual union as a complementary oath-sign (Chapter 7). Seeking to confirm the presence of such an oath, we began this chapter by considering various forms of indirect evidence that marriage was viewed as a sanction-sealed commitment to which the deity was witness. In particular, we noted the terminology of marital infidelity which is associated elsewhere with covenant or oath breaking (i.e., "sin [חטא]," "transgression [פשע]," etc., and especially "perfidy [מעל]" and "infidelity [בגד]").

Further evidence of this general conceptual and terminological compatibility between marriage and covenant, which serves to confirm the identification of marriage as a covenant, may be found in those texts which express Yahweh's relation to Israel in terms of the marriage analogy. Certainly other factors may also have played a significant role in this development, including a polemical interest in opposing the fertility cults, but

---

[54] Cf. also Numbers 25.
[55] An oath, such as is recorded in Neh. 13:25, however, may provide a sufficient explanation for terming this offence מעל.

it is likely that the recognition of marriage as a covenant may have been of special importance in fostering this development.[56]

2.1 The marriage analogy and especially Hosea 2:18-22 [ET 16-20]

Hosea appears to have been the first to describe Israel's infidelity as "adultery [נאף]" and to develop the marriage analogy so fully (cf., e.g., Hos. 2:4-25 [ET 2-23]). As a result of chronological priority, it is generally assumed that Hosea's use of the marriage analogy is the source of its reappearance in Isaiah (cf. Isa. 1:21; 54:5-8; 57:3-10; 61:10-11; 62:4-5); Jeremiah (cf. Jer. 2:2, 20; 3:1-5; 3:6-25; 13:27; 23:10; 31:32); Ezekiel (Ezekiel 16, 23); and perhaps also Proverbs (Proverbs 8).[57] Dependence on Hosea is not certain, however, and it is possible that some of these examples may represent an independent development.[58]

In the previous chapter (Chapter 7, §1.3) we examined Hos. 2:18-22 [ET 16-20] in an attempt to provide evidence for the use of marriage-forming *verba solemnia* in the biblical period. In that discussion evidence was offered

---

[56] O.J. Baab, for example, suggests that the marriage metaphor may have been a reflex of Israel's polemic against the fertility cults ("Marriage," 286).

Alternatively, W. Zimmerli considers that the marriage analogy may have been suggested by the popular OT figure of speech by which Zion, Egypt, Babylon, etc. were described as young women (*Ezekiel 1*, 335). Cf., e.g., Amos 5:2, where Israel is called "virgin Israel" (cf. also Jer. 4:31; 46:11, 24; and 50:42).

It is possible that the attribute of Yahweh as a "jealous God [אֵל קַנָּא]" in Exod. 20:5 and numerous other texts may also have contributed to this development, given the characteristic use of "jealousy" in marital contexts (cf., e.g., Num. 5:14; etc.). This is especially so because a text such as Exod. 34:14-16 appeals to Yahweh's character as a jealous God ("whose name is Jealous") as the basis for prohibiting "a covenant with the inhabitants of the land" and consequently intermarriage with these pagans because "they play the harlot after their gods," and they will "make your sons play the harlot after their gods." Cf. M. Greenberg for a discussion of harlotry (not specifically a marital offence) as descriptive of Israel's forbidden alliances with foreign powers (*Ezekiel 1-20*, 282f.). Cf. also examples where the harlotry refers instead to Israel's apostasy after other gods, as in Num. 25:1 and Judg. 2:17.

Though less clear than cases involving "adultery [נאף]," examples of "harlotry [זנה]" used figuratively may also have been suggestive of the marriage metaphor, if they do not presuppose it. Cf., e.g., Deut. 31:16.

[57] Cf. M. DeRoche, "Jeremiah 2:2-3 and Israel's Love for God during the Wilderness Wandering" (1983) 364-76; and C.V. Camp, *Wisdom and the Feminine in the Book of Proverbs*, 106-109, and especially 269-271.

[58] Although Malachi nowhere employs the marriage analogy itself (where Yahweh's covenant relationship to Israel is compared to a marriage), from this literary parallelism it is apparent that Malachi acknowledged a profound similarity between Israel's covenant with Yahweh and the marriage covenant. It is doubtful, however, that Malachi has "literalized" the earlier metaphor, against C.V. Camp, if this is intended to imply that the identification of marriage as a covenant was first suggested by the marriage analogy (*Wisdom and the Feminine in the Book of Proverbs*, 323 n. 8). To be sure, Malachi appears to offer the first of many "reverse applications" of the marriage analogy. In other words, while the marriage analogy was originally intended to elucidate Yahweh's relationship to Israel, it is now being reapplied to serve as a paradigm for marriage itself. Cf., e.g., Eph. 5:21-33 and especially the later rabbinic view of the marriage ceremony as a replica of the formation of God's covenant with Israel at Mt. Sinai. Cf. L. Ginzberg, *The Legends of the Jews* (1928) 6, 36 n. 200; T.H. Gaster, *Customs and Folkways of Jewish Life* (1955) 109f., 126-28; and M.R. Wilson, "Marriage and Sinai: Two Covenants Compared," in *Our Father Abraham* (1989) 203-208.

for an extensive parallelism between Yahweh's relationship with Israel (identified as a "covenant [בְּרִית]" in Hos. 8:1 and perhaps also 6:7) and the marital relationship between Hosea and Gomer, which is generally considered to have been the immediate impetus for Hosea's development of the marriage analogy.[59] Compare, for example, the manner in which Hos. 2:4 [ET 2] sets the formula for divorce in parallel with the formula for the dissolution of the covenant in Hos. 1:9, inviting an identification of a corresponding parallel between marriage and covenant.

While Hosea intercalates the promise of a new covenant in 2:20 [ET 18] between his two promises of an eschatological marriage to Yahweh (in vs. 18 [ET 16] and vs. 21f. [ET 19f.]), he does not explicitly identify the coming marriage as a covenant. Nevertheless, that identification seems probable given how Hosea parallels the marriage-forming *verba solemnia* in vs. 18 [ET 16], "My husband," with the theological covenant-making *verba solemnia* in vs. 25 [ET 23], "You are my people" and "Thou art my God."

What is implied in the marriage analogy is made explicit elsewhere. In addition to Mal. 2:14, there are five other texts which traditionally have been understood to identify marriage as a covenant: Prov. 2:17; Ezek. 16:8, 59, 60, and 62. Two other texts, Gen. 31:50 and Jer. 31:32, are also sometimes advanced as examples of an identification of marriage as a covenant, but these prove to be inadequate on closer examination. Finally, we shall add a new text, 1 Samuel 18-20, as corroborative evidence for the identification of marriage as a covenant — an implication of the carefully drawn analogy between David's marriage to Michal and his relationship to Jonathan (which is repeatedly termed a "covenant [בְּרִית]"). To these examples we now turn.

2.2 Proverbs 2:17

Prov. 2:16f. promises the young man that if he attains wisdom:

16a"You will be saved from the loose woman [לְהַצִּילְךָ מֵאִשָּׁה זָרָה],
16bfrom the adventuress with her smooth words [מִנָּכְרִיָּה אֲמָרֶיהָ הֶחֱלִיקָה],
17awho forsakes the companion of her youth [הַעֹזֶבֶת אַלּוּף נְעוּרֶיהָ]
17band forgets the covenant of her God [וְאֶת־בְּרִית אֱלֹהֶיהָ שָׁכֵחָה] ...."

Relying mainly on the context and the awareness of other biblical texts which identify marriage as a covenant, earlier commentators have generally

---

[59] Some scholars deny the relevance of Hos. 6:7, claiming that it refers to a political treaty, rather than to Yahweh's covenant with Israel. They also deny the authenticity of the reference to the covenant in Hos. 8:1, deeming it to be a later Deuteronomic addition. So, e.g., L. Perlitt, *Bundestheologie im Alten Testament* (1969) 141-144, 146-149. If this is so, then the marriage analogy as such offers no particular support for the identification of marriage as a covenant. Against the tendency to eliminate all pre-Deuteronomic references to covenant, cf. J. Day, "Pre-Deuteronomic Allusions to the Covenant in Hosea and Psalm LXXVIII" (1986) 1-12; and E.W. Nicholson, *God and His People* (1986) 179-188.

identified "the covenant of her God [וְאֶת־בְּרִית אֱלֹהֶיהָ]" as a reference to the marriage covenant.[60] There are two main alternative interpretations to this traditional view.

2.2.1 G. Boström's view that "the covenant of her god [אֱלֹהֶיהָ בְּרִית]" refers to a commitment to her pagan god

Defending the widely held view that זָרָה, "strange," and נָכְרִיָּה, "foreign," are intended as references to this woman's non-Israelite status, G. Boström argues that אֱלֹהֶיהָ, "her god," is most naturally interpreted as a reference to this foreign woman's pagan deity (cf., e.g., 2 Kgs. 19:37; 2 Chron. 32:21; Isa. 37:38; Dan. 1:2; and Jonah 1:5).[61] Boström supports his interpretation by the observation that יהוה, "Yahweh," is used consistently throughout Proverbs 1-9 (where it appears nineteen times); thus, a reference to אלהים, "god" or "God," is likely to be to a pagan deity.

Boström's interpretation, however, fails for five reasons: First, אלהים, "God," appears also in Prov. 2:5 (where it is in synonymous parallelism with יהוה, "Yahweh") and 3:4 (where it offers an unmistakable reference to the true God, so that its appearance in 2:17 as a reference to Israel's God is not without parallel within the corpus of Proverbs 1-9. Although אלהים, "God," appears only twice more in Proverbs 10-30, namely 25:2 and 30:9, in both cases the reference is once again to the true God. Second, since יהוה, "Yahweh," nowhere appears with a pronominal suffix, there is no lexical choice available for the precise expression וְאֶת־בְּרִית אֱלֹהֶיהָ, "the covenant of her God," and so there is no particular significance to the author's choice of אלהים instead of יהוה in such an expression. Third, it is unlikely that the orthodox author of Proverbs would condemn this woman for any offence against her pagan deity or that he would bother to brand her sexual immorality as such an offence, rather than emphasizing the wrong committed against the true God, or more likely the principles of wisdom. Fourth, while there is some evidence for the concept of a covenant between pagan deities and their followers, it is far too slight to make its appearance probable in the book of Proverbs.[62] Finally, it is not so clear that the terms זָרָה, "strange," and נָכְרִיָּה, "foreign," require the view that this woman is a non-Israelite, as

---

[60] Cf., e.g., J. Calvin, *The Twelve Minor Prophets, Vol. V, Zechariah and Malachi*, 553; F. Delitzsch, *Proverbs*, 82; and C.H. Toy, *Proverbs* (1899) 47.

Modern commentators who consider the covenant to be that of marriage include B. Gemser, "The Instructions of Onchsheshonqy and Biblical Wisdom Literature" (1960) 102-128; and R.B.Y . Scott, *Proverbs* (1965) 43.

[61] *Proverbiastudien: die Weisheit und das fremde Weib in Sprüche 1-9* (1935) 103ff. In support of זָרָה and נָכְרִיָּה as references to this woman's non-Israelite status, cf., e.g., J.G. Williams, *Women Recounted. Narrative Thinking and the God of Israel* (1982) 107-109.

[62] Cf., e.g., D.L. Magnetti, *The Oath in the Old Testament* (1969) 138; Z. Zevit, "A Phoenician Inscription and Biblical Covenant Theology" (1977) 110-118; K.A. Kitchen, "Egypt, Ugarit, Qatna, and Covenant" (1979) 453, 462; and D.J. McCarthy, *Treaty and Covenant* (1981) 31 n. 6.

K. van der Toorn summarizes the evidence, "Compared with the Mesopotamian documents, the Old Testament displays a striking preference for the covenantal concept to define the relation between God and his creatures" (*Sin and Sanction*, 49).

Boström and others suppose.[63] For example, it may be that this woman is termed a "strange" woman in order to emphasize that she is not the man's own legitimate wife.[64] Alternatively, L.A. Snijders has argued that these terms may stress the fact that this woman is a "social outsider," an Israelite woman who has become an outcast because of her behaviour.[65] Consequently, Snijders suggests rendering them as "loose," "unrestrained," or "unchaste," much as does the RSV ("You will be saved from *the loose* [זָרָה] woman, from *the adventuress* [מִנָּכְרִיָּה] with her smooth words").

2.2.2 The view that "the covenant of her God [בְּרִית אֱלֹהֶיהָ]" refers to the Sinaitic covenant

A. Cohen, among others, argues that "the covenant of her God [בְּרִית אֱלֹהֶיהָ]" refers to the Sinaitic covenant and notes that "the prohibition of adultery formed part of God's covenant with Israel (Exod. xx. 13)."[66] Although the seventh commandment is framed in conventionally androcentric terms, "You [masculine singular] shall not commit adultery [לֹא תִּנְאָף]," Cohen presupposes, reasonably enough, that this commandment applied no less to women.

D. Kidner's interpretation is similar, but he adds the observation that had the text intended to refer to the marriage covenant, the wording would have been closer to that found in Mal. 2:14.[67] In other words, Kidner

---

[63] Against Boström's view that personified Wisdom in Proverbs 1-9 is pitted against the "strange woman," who is literally a foreigner and devotee of Ishtar (or Canaanite Astarte), cf. R.N. Whybray, *Wisdom in Proverbs* (1965) 89-92; W. McKane, *Proverbs* (1970) 286, 312, 328-331; and C.V. Camp, *Wisdom and the Feminine in the Book of Proverbs* (1985) 25-28.

[64] So also P. Humbert, who argues that the author is mainly concerned to offer a polemic against adultery ("La femme étrangère du Livre des Proverbes" [1937] 40-64; and *idem*, "Les adjectifs 'Zâr' et 'Nokri' et la femme étrangère" [1939] 259-66).

Likewise, J. Huehnergard discusses a case of a will (Text 2) specifying that if the deceased's wife should later "go after a strange man [*amīli zayyāri*], let her put her clothes on a stool, and go where she will" ("Five Tablets From the Vicinity of Emar" [1983] 19, 30). Comparing Deut. 25:5, Huehnergard argues that "strange" means a man of another family. Cf. also K. van der Toorn, "Female Prostitution in Payment of Vows in Ancient Israel" (1989) 199.

Alternatively, F. Hauck and S. Schulz reject the identification of זָרָה as merely the wife of another, or a foreigner, much less an allegorical reference to the alien secular wisdom of Greece ("πόρνη κτλ.," in *TDNT* VI, 586). Rather, citing Egyptian Wisdom literature which "warns against wandering women from other places [Böhlig]," they suggest a reference to native Israelite women who are strangers to a particular locality and, as such, constitute a dangerous temptation to the local male population. Cf. "The Instruction of Ani," in *ANET*, 420.

Finally, G.A. Yee leaves undecided the precise identity of the אִשָּׁה זָרָה in Proverbs 1-9, but suggests that, analogous to lady Wisdom, a composite portrait of a single immoral woman stands behind the various designations of the אִשָּׁה זָרָה in Proverbs 1-9 ("'I Have Perfumed My Bed With Myrrh': The Foreign Woman (*'iššâ zārâ*) in Proverbs 1-9," 54).

[65] Cf. L.A. Snijders, "The Meaning of *zār* in the Old Testament" (1954) 1-154; and *idem*, "זוּר / זָר, *zûr / zār*," *TDOT*, IV, 56.

[66] A. Cohen, *Proverbs* (1946) 11f. So also H.W. Wolff, *Anthropology of the Old Testament* (1974) 168, citing E. Kutsch, *Verheissung und Gesetz* (1973) 134ff. Wolff nevertheless accepts the evidence of Mal. 2:14 and Ezek. 16:8, which he understands as references to the covenant of marriage.

[67] *Proverbs* (1964) 62.

considers that the text should have read "the husband of her covenant [וְאֶת־אִישׁ
בְּרִיתָהּ]" or perhaps "the covenant of her husband [וְאֶת־בְּרִית אִישָׁהּ]," rather than
"the covenant of her God [וְאֶת־בְּרִית אֱלֹהֶיהָ]."

W. McKane and others carry this interpretation further; they deny that
there is any reference to marriage in Prov. 2:17 because אַלּוּף, "the
companion," in vs.17a does not refer to the woman's husband.[68] McKane
renders the verse "who forsakes the *teacher* of her youth, and has forgotten
the covenant of her God."[69] McKane supports his understanding of אַלּוּף as
"teacher" based on Jer. 3:4 (suggesting that her "teacher" may have been her
father) and 13:21.

*2.2.3 The traditional view that "the covenant of her God [אֱלֹהֶיהָ בְּרִית]"
refers to her marriage covenant*
The following arguments may be advanced in support of the traditional
interpretation of Prov. 2:17:

1) Although the verb אלף I (appearing only in Job 15:5; 33:33; 35:11;
and Prov. 22:25) is recognized as meaning "to learn" or "to teach," McKane's
proposal to render the noun אַלּוּף as "teacher" is unconvincing.[70] While
McKane appeals to Jer. 3:4 as an example of אַלּוּף bearing this meaning, the
context does not favour the proposal. In the midst of an extended marriage
metaphor, it would be most unexpected for Israel, the harlot bride, to describe
Yahweh as her teacher! Rather, "My father" and "the friend of my youth"
appear to be intended as endearing appellations for a husband from a wife
who remains brazenly unrepentant.[71] Accordingly, W.L. Holladay, for
example, supports the traditional rendering of אַלּוּף in this text as "someone
trusted, confidant."[72] McKane also appeals to Jer. 13:21 in support of his
proposal, but against McKane both the text and the sense of this verse are
uncertain.[73] Apart from these two examples, no other occurrence of אַלּוּף

---

[68] *Proverbs*, 286. The rendering of the KJV is similar: "Which forsaketh the guide of
her youth." Cf. also B. Gemser, "The Instructions of Onchsheshonqy and Biblical Wisdom
Literature" (1960) 102-128.

C.H. Toy mentions that some commentators suggest that "the companion of her youth
[אַלּוּף נְעוּרֶיהָ]" in Prov. 2:17 refers to God (*Proverbs*, 46). The similar expression in Jer. 3:4
does appear to refer to God, but there it occurs within a metaphor of marriage. At the level
of the metaphor itself, with most commentators, the reference is to her husband. Specific
arguments in favour of this view are presented below.

[69] W. McKane, *Proverbs*, 213.

[70] KB, 57, adds Job 32:13, if the text is emended.

[71] Though unexampled elsewhere in the OT, for the use of "father" as an affectionate
epithet for a husband, cf. L.M. Muntingh, "Amorite Married and Family Life according to
the Mari Texts" (1974) 58-60; and J.B. White, *A Study of the Language of Love in the Song
of Songs and Ancient Egyptian Poetry* (1978) 95.

[72] *Jeremiah 1*, 115. Further supporting this marital interpretation of אַלּוּף נְעֻרַי in Jer.
3:4 is the similarity of its formation to that found in Joel 1:8; Mal. 2:15; and Prov. 2:17. Cf.
also Hos. 2:9, 17 [ET 7, 15]; and Ezek. 16:43.

[73] J. Bright, for example, despairs of offering any translation (*Jeremiah*, 93, 95).
Alternatively, W. Rudolph (*Jeremia*), A. Weiser (*Das Buch Jeremia*), and R.P. Carroll
(*Jeremiah*) maintain the traditional rendering of אַלֻּפִים as "friends." Given the ovine
context of the previous verse, however, perhaps אַלֻּפִים should be understood as bearing its

requires or supports McKane's suggested meaning (see Mic. 7:5; Ps. 55:14 [ET 13]; 144:14; Prov. 16:28; 17:9; and Sir. 38:25).[74]

2) Three considerations favour understanding "the companion of her youth [אַלּוּף נְעוּרֶיהָ]" in Prov. 2:17 as a reference to her husband. First, as seen above, the term אַלּוּף, "companion, is nowhere else used as an appellation for the deity. Although אַלּוּף does refer to God in Jer. 3:4, this is so only because of the marriage metaphor in that text. In terms of the metaphor "the companion of my youth [אַלּוּף נְעֻרָי]" is an endearing epithet used by a harlot (Israel) to refer to her husband (Yahweh). Second, the formation of אַלּוּף נְעוּרֶיהָ, "the companion of her youth," relating the companion to the woman's youth, finds a close parallel not only in Jer. 3:4, "the companion of my youth [אַלּוּף נְעֻרָי]," where it refers to a husband (in the metaphor), but also in Prov. 5:18, "the wife of your youth [אֵשֶׁת נְעוּרֶךָ]"; Isa. 54:6, "a wife of youth [אֵשֶׁת נְעוּרִים]"; Joel 1:8, "the bridegroom of her youth [בַּעַל נְעוּרֶיהָ]"; Mal. 2:15, "the wife of your youth [אֵשֶׁת נְעוּרֶיךָ]"; and especially Mal. 2:14: "Because Yahweh was witness to the covenant between you and the wife of your youth [אֵשֶׁת נְעוּרֶיךָ], to whom you have been faithless [אֲשֶׁר אַתָּה בָּגַדְתָּה בָּהּ], though she is your companion [וְהִיא חֲבֶרְתְּךָ] and your wife by covenant [וְאֵשֶׁת בְּרִיתֶךָ]."[75] Finally, given that Prov. 2:17 intends to describe a sexually immoral woman, it is not at all unexpected that such a woman would be described as one who "forsakes [עזב]" her husband. By contrast, compare Prov. 4:6, where the young man is enjoined not to "forsake [עזב]" wisdom, which is personified as a bride.[76] Compare also Deut. 31:16 and Hos. 4:10, where, perhaps in terms of the marriage metaphor, Israel is accused of committing "prostitution [זנה]," by which she has "forsaken [עזב]" the Lord.

3) Kidner's argument that Prov. 2:17 should have read "the husband of her covenant [וְאֶת־אִישׁ בְּרִיתָהּ]" or perhaps "the covenant of her husband [וְאֶת־בְּרִית אִישָׁהּ]," rather than "the covenant of her God [וְאֶת־בְּרִית אֱלֹהֶיהָ]," would be decisive were it not for the fact that there are several examples of inter-human covenants being identified simultaneously as covenants of God. Ezek. 17:16-20, for example, condemns Zedekiah for breaking his covenant with Nebuchadnezzar and assures him of Yahweh's impending judgment because of Zedekiah's perfidy and rebellious league with Pharaoh Psammetichus II.

---

first sense of "tamed," which KB recognizes for Jer. 11:19. Cf. W.L. Holladay, *Jeremiah 1*, 411, 414.

J.A. Thompson offers yet another proposal, understanding אֲלָפִים as an example of אַלּוּף II, meaning "tribal leader" (*Jeremiah*, 371).

[74] Though noting Gemser's proposal, KB offers *zutraulich*, *Vertrauter*, and *Rind* for אַלּוּף (I). The remaining forty-two occurrences of אַלּוּף (II) bear the meaning "tribal chief." C.H. Toy says simply of אַלּוּף, "the sense *guide, instructor*, is not found in the OT" (*Proverbs*, 46).

[75] Cf. also Hos. 2:9, 17 [ET 7, 15]; and Ezek. 16:43.

[76] For this personification, cf. C.V. Camp, *Wisdom and the Feminine in the Book of Proverbs, passim.*

For other examples of "forsake" used in marital contexts, cf. Isa. 54:6; 62:4.

Although vss. 16 and 18 state that the covenant and oath were with Nebuchadnezzar, vs. 19 concludes, "Therefore thus says Yahweh GOD: As I live, surely *my oath* which he despised [אָלָתִי אֲשֶׁר בָּזָה אִם־לֹא], and *my covenant* which he broke [וּבְרִיתִי אֲשֶׁר הֵפִיר], I will requite upon his head." Ezekiel considers this inter-human covenant (vassal-treaty) as sacrosanct, in spite of its extorted ratificatory oath (Ezek. 17:13), presumably because Yahweh's name was invoked (so 2 Chron. 36:13). Accordingly, Yahweh identifies the covenant and oath as his own and characterizes their breach as "treason against me [מַעֲלֹ־בִי]" (vs. 20)![77] A similar perspective is attested in Jer. 34:18 with respect to Zedekiah's covenant with the men of Jerusalem (called "my covenant [בְּרִתִי]" by Yahweh) and in 1 Sam. 20:8, where David refers to his covenant with Jonathan as "a covenant of Yahweh [בִּבְרִית יְהוָה]," again presumably because Yahweh was invoked as its guarantor.[78]

4) Against the view that "the covenant of her God [וְאֶת־בְּרִית אֱלֹהֶיהָ]" refers to the Sinaitic covenant is the appearance of the third feminine singular pronominal suffix on אֱלֹהֶיהָ, even if such a usage may not be impossible.[79] If the suffix applies to אֱלֹהִים, "she has forgotten the covenant with *her* God," the reference to "her God" seems unaccountably restrictive as a reference to the God of the Sinaitic covenant.[80] The God of Sinai was Israel's God, the God of "our fathers," or "your God."[81] Alternatively, if the suffix applies to בְּרִית, "she has forgotten *her* covenant with God," the reference to "*her* covenant" fails to take adequate account of the corporate identity of Israel as Yahweh's covenant partner at Sinai and applies an individualistic interpretation to that event which requires support.

5) To these arguments it may be added that in view of the concerns of Proverbs as wisdom literature, finding any reference to the Sinaitic covenant should be deemed unexpected. In general, Proverbs is not particularly alert to

---

[77] Cf. M. Tsevat, "The Neo-Assyrian and Neo-Babylonian Vassal Oaths and the Prophet Ezekiel" (1959) 199-204. So also C.T. Begg, "*Berit* in Ezekiel," 77, 79. More recent evidence of the imposition on vassals of an oath of allegiance by their own deity is provided by R. Frankena, "The Vassal Treaties of Esarhaddon and the Dating of the Deuteronomy" (1965) 131; and M. Cogan, *Imperialism and Religion: Assyria, Judah and Israel in the Eighth and Seventh Centuries B.C.E.* (1974) 46f.

Against this view is M. Greenberg, who argues that vss. 19-21 are concerned not with the vassal treaty of Nebuchadnezzar with Zedekiah, but with Yahweh's covenant with Israel, which Zedekiah was obligated to uphold and to which there is reference also in Ezek. 16:59 ("Ezekiel 17: A Holistic Interpretation," 152f.; and *idem, Ezekiel, 1-20*, 317-324). To maintain his view, Greenberg is forced to dismiss the evidence of 2 Chron. 36:13 as a reflex of the Chronicler's misunderstanding of Ezekiel 17.

[78] Cf., e.g., R.P. Gordon, *1 & 2 Samuel*, 166.

[79] Cf. "the law of his God [תּוֹרַת אֱלֹהָיו] is in his heart" in Ps. 37:31.

The LXX lacks the feminine pronoun, καὶ διαθήκην θείαν ἐπιλελησμένη, "and she has forgotten the covenant of God." Presumably this reading is the result of a graphic variant in the consonantal text of the *Vorlage* of the LXX, which read אלהים rather than אלהיה. With most commentators, the MT אֱלֹהֶיהָ is to be preferred as the *lectio difficilior*.

[80] By contrast, cf. Ps. 78:10 and 2 Chron. 34:32.

[81] Cf. the collective second person pronominal suffix in Lev. 2:13, referring to any Israelite who brings an offering, "You shall season all your cereal offerings with salt; you shall not let the salt of the covenant with *your* God [מֶלַח בְּרִית אֱלֹהֶיךָ] be lacking from your cereal offering; with all your offerings you shall offer salt."

historical or biblical-theological matters. For example, nowhere is there any mention of the patriarchs, Moses, the Exodus, Sinai / Horeb, David (apart from the ascription in 1:1), Zion / Jerusalem, the temple, etc. Furthermore, it is surely significant that 2:17 is the only text in Proverbs even to mention a "covenant [בְּרִית]." Such an exceptional use is best explained as the result of a secular use of "covenant [בְּרִית]," that is, as a reference to marriage, which is entirely appropriate in the context of 2:17, rather than to a theological construct (i.e., this woman's relation to the Sinaitic covenant).

6) Finally, building on the study of A. Robert, C.V. Camp notes the concentration of similar concerns and vocabulary between Prov. 2:16f. and Mal. 2:10-16 — although the perspective in Malachi is more radical than that in Proverbs since it is the husband who is faithless, rather than the wife.[82] Furthermore, there appears to have been a transformation from the "strange woman" in Proverbs, assuming she is thus designated because she is an adulteress, not because she is a non-Israelite, to the literal foreign woman in Mal. 2:11.[83]

Nevertheless, in terms of this resemblance, "forsakes the companion of her youth [הַעֹזֶבֶת אַלּוּף נְעוּרֶיהָ]" in Prov. 2:17 offers a parallel to "be faithless to the wife of his youth [וּבְאֵשֶׁת נְעוּרֶיךָ אַל־יִבְגֹּד]" in Mal. 2:16 (cf. also 2:14). Likewise אַלּוּף, "companion," in Prov. 2:17 finds a synonym in חֲבֶרְתְּךָ, "your companion," in Mal. 2:14. Similarly "forgets the covenant of her God [שָׁכֵחָה וְאֶת־בְּרִית אֱלֹהֶיהָ]" in Prov. 2:17 corresponds to "against whom you have been faithless, though she is ... your wife by covenant [אֲשֶׁר אַתָּה בָּגַדְתָּה בָּהּ ... אֵשֶׁת בְּרִיתֶךָ]" in Mal. 2:14.[84] Assuming the correctness of our previous exegesis of Mal. 2:14, where it was argued that the covenant in that text refers to the marriage relationship, this last correspondence confirms the identification of the covenant in Prov. 2:17 as a reference to marriage as well.

2.3 Ezekiel 16:8, 59, 60, and 62

וָאֶעֱבֹר עָלַיִךְ וָאֶרְאֵךְ וְהִנֵּה עִתֵּךְ עֵת דֹּדִים וָאֶפְרֹשׂ כְּנָפִי עָלַיִךְ וָאֲכַסֶּה עֶרְוָתֵךְ 8
וָאֶשָּׁבַע לָךְ וָאָבוֹא בִבְרִית אֹתָךְ נְאֻם אֲדֹנָי יְהוִה וַתִּהְיִי לִי:

"When I passed by you again and looked upon you, behold, you were at the age for love; and I spread my skirt over you, and covered your nakedness: yea, I plighted my troth to you and entered into a covenant with you, says Yahweh GOD, and you became mine."

In the context of an arraignment against Jerusalem for her wanton infidelity (so vs. 2), Ezekiel 16 offers an extended metaphor of Yahweh's

---

[82] C.V. Camp, *Wisdom and the Feminine in the Book of Proverbs*, 235-237, 269-271; and A. Robert, "Les attaches littéraires bibliques de Prov. I-IX," 505-25.

[83] This transformation need not have been particularly radical since it is likely that some allusion to foreign women, perhaps through double entendre, may underlie the immoral woman's twofold designation as נָכְרִיָּה and זָרָה. Alternatively, perhaps by her prohibited actions, this woman has in effect disavowed her Israelite heritage.

[84] Cf. C.V. Camp, *Wisdom and the Feminine in the Book of Proverbs*, 319 n. 5.

relationship with Jerusalem.[85] The text begins with an historical review of Yahweh's benefactions toward Jerusalem described first in terms of his rescue (and adoption[86]) of her as a foundling (vss. 3-7). This theme of benefaction continues in the second section, vss. 8-14, which describes Yahweh's marriage to Israel and his early lavish provisions for his wife-people. In the third section, vss. 15-43, the theme of undeserved benefaction from Yahweh changes to an indictment of the nymphomaniacal adultery of the wife-Jerusalem. In vss. 44-58, this indictment is continued with an invidious comparison between the wife-Jerusalem and her sisters Sodom and Samaria. The closing verses of the chapter, vss. 59-63, assure Jerusalem of judgment (vs. 59), but they also promise a new and eternal covenant with Jerusalem, which will be met on her part with remorse over her past ways.

Two main interpretative approaches attempt to correlate to historical reality this sequence of the rescue (adoption) of a foundling Jerusalem, Yahweh's marriage to her, and her subsequent infidelity. The first approach, represented by M. Greenberg among others, follows the Targum and considers Jerusalem a figure for the people of God as a whole.[87] Israel's birthplace was Canaan, where Yahweh revealed himself to Abraham and entered into covenant with him (Genesis 15). Israel's period of abandonment in Egypt, when she was "like an infant abandoned in the field, whose navel-cord was not cut," followed. Later God had mercy on Israel, delivering her out of Egypt and marrying her at Sinai, where he "entered into a covenant with you" (Ezek. 16:8).[88]

The alternative approach considers "Jerusalem" to represent the city by that name (i.e., its inhabitants) and the Davidic dynasty associated with it. On this view, the "rescue" corresponds to David's conquest of Jebus; the marriage corresponds to Yahweh's covenant with David (2 Samuel 7), which established the Davidic dynasty and Yahweh's choice of Jerusalem as the place where he would cause his name to dwell (where the temple was to be built).[89] This approach recognizes that the history of Jerusalem epitomizes the history of Israel; as such, to some degree the history of the Davidic covenant reflects or recapitulates the history of the Sinaitic covenant.

---

[85] This context of an arraignment is made explicit in the Targum of vs. 2, "Arraign ... and declare [וחוי ... אוכח]," a rendering offered also in 20:4 and 22:2, where the MT has some form of הודיע ... שפט. Cf. M. Greenberg, *Ezekiel 1-20*, 273. Cf. K. Nielsen, *Yahweh As Prosecutor and Judge* (1978). This legal setting is also discussed by W. Zimmerli, *Ezekiel I* (1979) 333ff.; and H.F. Fuhs, *Ezechiel 1-24* (1984) 80ff.

[86] Cf. CH §185. Cf. the detailed support offered by M. Malul, "Adoption of Foundlings in the Bible and Mesopotamian Documents. A Study of Some Legal Metaphors in Ezekiel 16:1-7" (1990) 97-126.

[87] *Ezekiel 1-20*, 273-306. Cf. also, e.g., C.F. Keil, *Ezekiel*, 195; A.B. Davidson and A.W. Streane, *The Book of the Prophet Ezekiel* (1916); and J.B. Taylor, *Ezekiel* (1969) 132ff.

[88] Kimchi, for example, relates Ezek. 16:8a, where Yahweh notices Jerusalem for a second time, to the vision of the burning bush when Yahweh announced his intention to deliver Israel (so according to S. Fisch, *Ezekiel* [1950] 86).

[89] Cf. also Ps. 132:13-17, cited by R.H. Alexander, "Ezekiel," 812.

Represented by W.H. Brownlee, among others, this view may do greater justice to the focus of the text on Jerusalem.[90]

Focusing our attention on Ezek. 16:8, there is considerable uncertainty about the precise symbolism intended by the expression, "I spread my skirt over you, and covered your nakedness." W.H. Brownlee, for example, doubts that a literal action was ever performed, even apart from the present metaphoric use, and suggests instead that the expression probably refers to sexual intercourse.[91] Accordingly, he suggests the translation, "I *opened* my robe to you...."[92]

While it is notoriously difficult to distinguish between symbolic actions and performable figures of speech (like "pulling one's leg" in English), three arguments favour the view that the mentioned covering was, in fact, typically performed, contrary to Brownlee's assumption. First, literal garments are known to have been used in various symbolic actions connected with marriage and divorce elsewhere in the ancient Near East, making reasonable the assumption of their use in Israelite marriage.[93] Moreover, there is an especially close parallel to the present text in early Arabic practice, where a widow could be acquired by a relative without the payment of a marriage present (*mahr*) simply by throwing his garment over her. It is likely, but not certain, that this action was also used more generally in the contraction of marriage.[94] Second, the fact that the common expression "to uncover the nakedness of [גלה ערות]" someone refers to (illicit) sexual intimacy makes it doubtful that the opposite expression "to cover the nakedness of [כסה ערות]" would also refer to sexual intimacy.[95] Finally, if the "covering" mentioned in Ezek. 16:8 refers to sexual union, the resulting order of sexual union preceding betrothal would be anomalous and, as such, would be unexpected as a description of divine activity.[96]

It seems more likely, then, that Ezekiel refers to a literal act of covering which was typically performed in the contraction of marriage, although, naturally, not in the present case because of the allegorical context.

---

[90] W.H. Brownlee, *Ezekiel 1-19*, 219-221, 226ff., and *passim*. So also H.-J. Kraus, *Worship in Israel* (1965) 179; J.W. Wevers, *Ezekiel* (1969) 94ff.; W. Eichrodt, *Ezekiel* (1970) 201ff.; W. Zimmerli, *Ezekiel 1*, 333-353; and R.H. Alexander, "Ezekiel" (1986) 810ff.

[91] *Ezekiel 1-19*, 225.

[92] Cf. also C.M. Carmichael, "'Treading' in the Book of Ruth" (1980) 258f.

[93] Cf. M. Malul, *Studies in Mesopotamian Legal Symbolism*, 179-208; and P.A. Kruger, "The Hem of the Garment in Marriage. The Meaning of the Symbolic Gesture in Ruth 3:9 and Ezekiel 16:8" (1984) 79-86; and especially A. Viberg, *Symbols of Law*, 136-144.

[94] Cf. W.R. Smith, who discusses the statement which refers to this practice in Ṭabari's commentary on the *Qur'ān* 4:19 (*Kinship and Marriage in Early Arabia*, 104f.). Cf. also D.R. Mace, *Hebrew Marriage*, 181-182; E. Neufeld, *Ancient Hebrew Marriage Laws*, 31f.; and M. Greenberg, *Ezekiel 1-20*, 277.

[95] Cf. W. Zimmerli, *Ezekiel 1*, 340. Cf. also Deut. 23:1 [ET 22:30]; 27:20.

[96] Brownlee's attempt to answer this objection by comparing David's capture of Jerusalem to a man passionately seizing a woman who acquiesces after a brief struggle is unconvincing (*Ezekiel 1-19*, 225).

It has been suggested that this action symbolized a claim of ownership,[97] or perhaps it constituted a pledge from the groom for the on-going provision of his bride with the necessities of life.[98] On the other hand, it has been suggested that the act of covering implies that the woman was now to be "covered" from all other men.[99] Alternatively, since the covering was accomplished with the use of one's own hem, it may have symbolized how the man and the woman would now be considered as one — being covered by the same clothes.[100] Finally, it is possible that the covering conveyed a promise of protection, especially in the light of Ruth 2:12.[101] In spite of this uncertainty about the precise symbolism, however, there appears little doubt that the gesture of covering in Ezek. 16:8 was intended as a marriage-forming act, especially given the support of Ruth 3:9.[102]

Following the gesture of covering, Yahweh says, "and I swore to you [וָאֶשָּׁבַע לָךְ] and I entered into a covenant with you [וָאָבוֹא בִּבְרִית אֹתָךְ]... and you became mine." While Mal. 2:14 implies the presence of an oath in marriage with its reference to Yahweh as "witness" to the covenant, and while Prov. 2:17 similarly implies a ratificatory oath which invoked the deity since it identifies the marriage covenant as a "covenant of God," no other biblical text is so explicit in identifying the presence of an oath in marriage as is Ezek. 16:8 (and vs. 59).[103]

M. Greenberg, however, among others, rejects an identification of the covenant and oath mentioned in vs. 8 (as also in vss. 59, 60, and 62) with

---

[97] M. Greenberg compares *m. Pe'a* 4:3, "If a poor man threw himself upon [the crop] and spread his cloak over it [in order to claim it], he is removed therefrom" (*Ezekiel 1-20*, 277).

[98] Traditionally the necessities were "food, oil, and clothing." Such a reference may find support in the subsequent mention of clothing in vss. 10-12 and perhaps also the use of nakedness in divorce — leaving the house with nothing. Cf. also the ironic reversal of symbolism in Isa. 4:1.

[99] Hence, illicit sexual relations can be described as "uncovering the edge of the father's garment," as in Deut. 23:1 [ET 22:30] and 27:20.

[100] This symbolism of unity may be favoured by the symbolic joining of clothes in marriage and in certain divorce rites, where the clothes are suddenly severed. For examples, cf. M. Malul, *Studies in Mesopotamian Legal Symbolism*, 152, 200 n. 197, 206f., 345.

[101] Cf. B. Green, "A Study of Field and Seed Symbolism in the Biblical Story of Ruth" (1980) 142, as cited by R.H. Hubbard Jr., *Ruth*, 212. Hubbard notes that the gesture may have simultaneously expressed both a promise of protection as well as a man's readiness for sexual consummation.
So also J.W. Wevers, *Ezekiel*, 96. J. Gray compares the custom of a kinsman putting part of his garment over a widow and cites J. Lewy, "Les textes paléo-assyriens et l'Ancien Testament" (1934) 31ff. (*Joshua, Judges, Ruth*, 392).

[102] Cf., e.g., A. Phillips, "Uncovering the Father's Skirt" (1980) 39; E.W. Davies, "Inheritance Rights and the Hebrew Levirate Marriage, Part 1" (1981) 143f.; and R.L. Hubbard Jr., *Ruth*, 212. In support Hubbard also mentions Deut. 23:1 [ET 22:30]; 27:20; and Mal. 2:16.

[103] C.T. Begg considers that Ezekiel's use of the marriage covenant as a figure for Yahweh's historic covenant with Israel (or David?) is yet another unique contribution of the prophet ("*Berit* in Ezekiel," 79f.).

marriage.[104] Although Greenberg accepts the likelihood of the use of *verba solemnia* in marriage (citing the evidence of Elephantine) and recognizes "and you became mine [וַתִּהְיִי לִי]" in vs. 8b as a declaration formula, he objects, "Nowhere but in Ezekiel is this [marriage] declaration called an oath."[105] Furthermore, Greenberg cites J. Milgrom (*Cult and Conscience*, pp. 133f.) for an alternative interpretation of Mal. 2:14 and Prov. 2:17, the two other key texts which traditionally have been thought to offer the clearest evidence for an identification of marriage as a covenant. Accordingly, Greenberg believes that the oath and covenant mentioned in vs. 8 are instances where the metaphor has given way to the underlying reality — they refer only to the Sinaitic covenant and not to marriage.

The following considerations may be advanced against Greenberg's interpretation:

1) It has already been argued that the proposed alternative interpretations for Mal. 2:14 and Prov. 2:17 are not convincing. Hence, marriage is identified elsewhere as a covenant; accordingly, there can be no presumptive objection to its similar identification in the present text.

2) Further, it has been demonstrated that *verba solemnia* do have an oath-like function, as is apparent in examples such as Gen. 2:23 and Exod. 24:3.[106] In fact, by failing to identify the oath function of *verba solemnia*, Greenberg is forced to suppose that the author of Ezek. 16:8 has (con)fused the record of Yahweh's oath to the patriarchs to grant the land of Canaan to their descendants (Gen. 26:3; Deut. 1:8, etc.) with the supposedly non-oath *verba solemnia* of mutual obligation connected with the Exodus and Sinaitic covenant (according to P and to Deuteronomy).[107] Greenberg also cites Ezek. 20:6 in support of his assumption of a fusion of the patriarchal and Exodus traditions. But any intentional allusion to the patriarchal period would be out of place in Ezek. 20:6, which is so explicit about its chronological setting: "On the day when I chose Israel, I swore to the seed of the house of Jacob, making myself known to them in the land of Egypt, I swore to them, saying, I am Yahweh your God. On that day I swore to them that I would bring them out of the land of Egypt into a land that I had searched out for them, a land flowing with milk and honey, the most glorious of all lands" (Ezek. 20:5-6). Moreover, even an unintended confusion of patriarchal and exodus traditions

---

[104] M. Greenberg, *Ezekiel 1-20*, 278. Cf. also, e.g., J. Herrmann, *Ezechiel* (1924) *ad loc.*; B.M. Vellas, *Israelite Marriage*, 24; M. Malul, "Adoption of Foundlings in the Bible and Mesopotamian Documents. A Study of Some Legal Metaphors in Ezekiel 16:1-7," 126 n. 112; and P. Kalluveettil, *Declaration and Covenant*, 79.

[105] *Ezekiel 1-20*, 278.

[106] "Moses came and told the people all the words of Yahweh and all the ordinances; and all the people answered with one voice, and said, 'All the words which Yahweh has spoken we will do.'" As D.J. McCarthy concedes concerning this text, any such "public commitment to follow Yahweh who has just presented Himself in all his power is *the equivalent of an oath* [italics mine]" (*Treaty and Covenant* [1981] 253). So also D.L. Magnetti, *The Oath in the Old Testament*, 128.

[107] *Ezekiel 1-20*, 278.

seems unnecessary, if Ezekiel understood, contrary to Greenberg, that Yahweh's sworn promise to give the land was renewed by its solemn oath-like reiteration in Exod. 6:2ff., for example.[108] In any case, it does not commend an interpretative theory to require confusion on the part of the ancient source in order to sustain it.

3) Greenberg's view that the marriage metaphor has suddenly given way to the underlying covenant reality in Ezek. 16:8 is unconvincing given the fact that the author so carefully maintains the metaphor throughout the whole of Ezekiel 16. At only three other points does Greenberg even suggest the possibility that the referent has similarly intruded into the metaphor, namely vss. 24 (cf. also 25, 31, 39), 41 and 59ff. On closer examination, each of these three possibilities proves doubtful.

a) Vss. 24f. reads: "you built yourself a vaulted chamber [גַּב], and made yourself a lofty place [רָמָה] in every square; at the head of every street you built your lofty place [רָמָתֵךְ] and prostituted your beauty, offering yourself to any passer-by, and multiplying your harlotry." If גַּב, "vaulted chamber," and רָמָה, "lofty place," are understood as synonyms for "high place [בָּמָה]," then the referent intrudes into the metaphor in vs. 24, as also in vss. 25, 31, 39, where these terms reappear. The posited identification for these difficult, perhaps quite general architectural terms, however, is far from certain.[109] For example, the LXX renders גַּב in vs. 24 as οἴκημα πορνικὸν, "house of prostitution, brothel," as it does also in vss. 31 and 39. On the other hand, the LXX renders רָמָה in vs. 24 as ἔκθεμα, "a public place," in vs. 25 as τὰ πορνεῖά σου, "your [places of] prostitution," and in vss. 31 and 39 as τὴν βάσιν σου, "your pedestal." In the end, Greenberg favours J. Herrmann's proposal that רָמָה means a "[harlot's] stand or booth."[110] It is likely that some such meaning is required and, if so, contrary to Greenberg's initial suggestion, the metaphor is maintained in these verses after all.

b) Ezek. 16:41 records the judgment: "And they shall burn your houses [וְשָׂרְפוּ בָתַּיִךְ בָּאֵשׁ] and execute judgments upon you in the sight of many women; I will make you stop playing the harlot, and you shall also give hire no more." Greenberg suggests that here, once again, the referent may have intruded into the metaphor since the houses of Jerusalem were in fact burned by Nebuchadnezzar's invading army, as 2 Kgs. 25:9 reports.

W. Zimmerli prefers to emend the MT with certain MSS and the Syriac to read "they will burn you with fire [וְשָׂרְפוּךְ בתוך האש]."[111] If this proposal were accepted, the metaphor would be maintained. Greenberg convincingly rejects this proposal, however, noting that the emendation yields

---

[108] Exod. 6:6 was also understood by the Rabbis to imply an oath. Cf. R. Tanhuma, *Wayera*, 2 (Midrashic commentary on the Pentateuch dating from the fourth century A.D.).

[109] Cf., e.g., the use of גַּב in Ezek. 43:13 with a proper altar for Yahweh.

[110] J. Herrmann, *Ezechiel* (1924) *ad loc.* Cf. also B. Lang, *Wisdom and the Book of Proverbs*, 99f. Lang cites the Akkadian term *ram*, "to settle down," and Ugaritic *rmm* "to erect a building," as possible cognates for רָמָה (*op. cit.*, 168 n. 17).

[111] *Ezekiel 1*, 330f.

unidiomatic Hebrew (elsewhere burning "with fire" is expressed by שׂרף + בְּ +
אֵשׁ, not שׂרף + בְּתוֹךְ + אֵשׁ).[112]

Nevertheless, the metaphor may not have been forgotten even in the
unemended text of Ezek. 16:41. After all, the verse is explicit that this
burning is to take place "in the sight of many women." It is doubtful that the
metaphor should have spoken of the burning of the harlot, rather than of her
houses, in spite of the evidence of Gen. 38:24 and Lev. 21:9. This is so
because Ezek. 16:40 has already specified that the harlot Jerusalem is to be
executed by stoning; this mode of execution finds support in other texts, for
example, Deut. 22:21 and perhaps 22:24.

If this harlot has filled the city with her brothels, as mentioned in vss.
24, 25, 31, and 39 (cf. the LXX οἴκημα πορνικὸν, "house of prostitution"), it
would seem entirely appropriate that such polluting structures would be
burned following her execution.[113]   Although no legal text specifies this
requirement regarding the burning of brothels (Deut. 13:17 [ET 16] may
provide an analogy, as perhaps also Judg. 14:15), Ezek. 23:47 appears to offer
a precise parallel: "And the host shall stone them [the harlots Oholah and
Oholibah] and dispatch them with their swords; they shall slay their sons and
their daughters, and burn up their houses."[114]

c) The only remaining example where Greenberg suggests that Ezekiel
may have forgotten his metaphor is Ezek. 16:59ff. Here Yahweh condemns
Jerusalem, who "despised the oath in breaking the covenant, yet I will
remember my covenant with you in the days of your youth, and I will
establish with you an everlasting covenant." If "covenant" and "oath" in
these verses, which parallel vs. 8, are not allowed to apply to marriage but are
deemed intrusions of the referent, then these are the only clear cases of such
intrusions in sixty-one verses (vss. 3-63). In the immediate context the
marriage metaphor is vividly maintained throughout vss. 59-63. This is
apparent in the mention of Jerusalem's anticipated shame over her past
misdeeds (vss. 61 and 63), the days of Jerusalem's youth, her sisters, etc., as
well as in the consistent use of feminine singular gender references
throughout. Accordingly, W.H. Brownlee, for example, does not hesitate to
identify the recalled "covenant with you in the days of your youth" as a
marriage covenant.[115]   Indeed, if vs. 8 is interpreted in a straightforward
manner as identifying marriage as a covenant which included a ratificatory
oath, then vss. 59ff. pose little problem in their similar reference to that
original marriage covenant and its subsequently violated oath, as well as in
their gracious promise of a future marriage covenant.

---

[112] M. Greenberg, *Ezekiel 1-20*, 288.

[113] Cf. Jer. 5:7 for the use of בַּיִת in reference to these "houses of prostitution." Cf. also,
perhaps, Josh. 6:22.

[114] It is easier to suppose that the burning of the harlot's house or brothel may have
been a standard penalty than to suppose that Ezekiel has committed the very same lapse in
this text as he is supposed to have in Ezekiel 16.

[115] *Ezekiel 1-19*, 251. The mention of "the days of your youth" favours this. Cf. the
earlier discussion of references to youth in marital contexts.

4) Finally, it has often been noted that Ezekiel's references to covenant [בְּרִית] cluster in Ezekiel 16 (6x) and 17:11-21 (6x), with only six other occurrences elsewhere (Ezek. 20:37; 30:5; 34:25; 37:26 [*bis*]; 44:7). Whether or not Ezekiel lacks a "well-defined covenant theology,"[116] it appears likely that the concentration of the use of this term in these two texts is due precisely to the influence of its secular uses — in Ezekiel 16, because of the reference to marriage; in Ezekiel 17, because of the reference to an international treaty.[117]

2.4 Two doubtful examples

2.4.1 Genesis 31:50

Although Gen. 31:50 is often adduced as evidence of the covenantal nature of marriage, J. Milgrom is correct in rejecting this claim.[118] While the text is explicit about the presence of a covenant (so 31:44) ratified with bilateral oaths, the covenant in question (apparently a combination of a marriage contract and a mutual non-aggression pact[119]) exists between Laban and Jacob, not between Jacob and his wives, as would be required for the covenant of marriage. Furthermore, as with many of the extrabiblical marriage contracts (which, as will be recalled, are ancillary to the marriage itself), the text leaves no doubt that this arrangement was concluded long after the formation of the marriage.[120]

2.4.2 Jeremiah 31:32

Jer. 31:31f. reads: "Behold, the days are coming, says Yahweh, when I will make a new covenant with the house of Israel and the house of Judah, not like the covenant which I made with their fathers when I took them by the hand to bring them out of the land of Egypt, my covenant which they broke [אֲשֶׁר־הֵמָּה הֵפֵרוּ אֶת־בְּרִיתִי], though I was their husband [וְאָנֹכִי בָּעַלְתִּי בָם], says Yahweh."

While the verb בָּעַל can mean "to be a master," the RSV has chosen to render the term with its alternative well-attested meaning "to be a husband":

---

[116] So, e.g., W. Zimmerli, *Ezekiel I*, 46; and C.T. Begg, "*Berit* in Ezekiel," 81.

[117] It should be noted that elsewhere Ezekiel finds little difficulty in reviewing Israel's history without explicit reference to any בְּרִית, as in chapter 23, or its future hope, as in 11:14-21; 36:1-38.

W. Eichrodt holds a view of Ezekiel 16 opposite to that being proposed here (*Ezekiel*, 206). On his view Ezekiel's understanding of Yahweh's divine covenant exercised a perceptible influence upon the narrative which resulted in the depiction of a marriage imposing a stronger tie upon the husband.

One final argument against interpreting Ezek. 16:8 as identifying literal marriage as a covenant is advanced by J. Milgrom, *Cult and Conscience*, 134. According to Milgrom, the mentioned oath "should have been expected of the bride, Israel, for it is the bride, not the husband, who is subject to the laws of adultery." This objection will be considered in more detail below in §3.

[118] J. Milgrom, *Cult and Conscience*, 134.

[119] Cf., e.g., M.G. Kline, "Genesis," 104f.

[120] It may be noted that the use of oaths and the protective clause prohibiting Jacob from taking additional wives (given that his wives have already borne children) are both features which also find ample parallels in the extrabiblical marriage contracts.

"though I was their husband." This interpretation has also been favoured by R.P. Carroll, among others.[121] If this rendering is accepted, this text would suggest that Jeremiah also viewed marriage as a covenant. The choice between these alternative renderings of בָּעַל, however, is not easy. Jeremiah 3 demonstrates the fact that the prophet was familiar with the marriage analogy (in 3:14 Jeremiah uses the same idiom, כִּי אָנֹכִי בָּעַלְתִּי בָכֶם, with the same ambiguity whether he intends "for I am your master [RSV]" or "for I am your husband [AV]"), and the use of this analogy in Hosea 2 to describe both the old covenant and a promised new covenant makes quite attractive the rendering of "husband" in the present text.[122]

Several considerations appear to favour the rendering "lord." First, if Jeremiah had meant to utilize the marriage analogy, it might be expected that, at least within the immediate context, he would have employed a feminine singular reference for Israel, "though I was *her* husband," rather than the masculine plural, "though I was *their* husband [וְאָנֹכִי בָּעַלְתִּי בָם]." Second, it appears that the term בעל does not require a marital reference to be at home within a covenant context. Compare, for example, the reference in Gen. 14:13 to Mamre, Eshcol, and Aner as "*lords* of the covenant of Abram [בַּעֲלֵי בְרִית־אַבְרָם]," usually rendered "covenant partners of Abram."[123] Finally, the rendering "though I was their lord" may seem tautological in view of the earlier assertions that Yahweh had made a covenant with his people and delivered them out of Egypt. The grammar of Jer. 31:32, however, with אָנֹכִי to be interpreted either as an intensive pronoun, "myself," or a nominative absolute, "as for me," stresses not the predicate, as in "though I was their *husband*," but the subject, "though *I myself* was their lord [or possibly "covenant partner"?]." In other words, it should not be expected that Jeremiah was introducing some new quality in Yahweh, namely his husband-like love, to highlight Israel's sin, but merely contrasting Israel's perfidy with the reminder that their covenant partner was no less than Yahweh, the very same one who had made the covenant in the first place and had redeemed his people.

---

[121] *Jeremiah*, 610. So also J. Coppens, "La nouvelle alliance en Jér 31.31-4," 14-15, as cited with approval by D.J. McCarthy, *Old Testament Covenant*, 33. Cf. also G.R. Dunstan, "The Marriage Covenant," 246; and S.-T. Sohn, "The Divine Election of Israel," 45f.

[122] In support of this appeal to Hosea 2, it is notable that the idea of a new covenant for the end time is found only in Jer. 31:31-34, Hos. 2:20 [ET 18], and Ezek. 36:24-32. As may be the case in Jeremiah 31, the promised new covenant is expressed in Hosea 2 in terms of the marriage metaphor. Cf. J.L. Mays, *Hosea* (1969) 50-52; and H.W. Wolff, *Hosea*, (1974) 51.

[123] Cf. C. Westermann, *Genesis 12-36*, 200. Cf. also "For many in Judah were bound by oath to him [כִּי־רַבִּים בִּיהוּדָה בַּעֲלֵי שְׁבוּעָה לוֹ]" in Neh. 6:18 and "Baal-berith [בַּעַל בְּרִית]" in Judg. 8:33; 9:4 [cf. 9:46].

2.5 1 Samuel 18-20 — a narrative analogy between David's covenant with Jonathan and David's (marriage) covenant with Michal

To the classic examples for the identification of marriage as a covenant considered above, we now add one further important line of evidence drawn from the narrative analogy between David's covenant with Jonathan and David's marriage to Michal in 1 Samuel 18-20. As was the case in the covenant between Zedekiah and Nebuchadnezzar in Ezekiel 17 and between Zedekiah and the people of Jerusalem in Jeremiah 34, the private covenant between David and Jonathan is similarly identified as Yahweh's own covenant in 1 Sam. 20:8 ("for you have brought your servant into a covenant of Yahweh with you [כִּי בִּבְרִית יְהֹוָה הֵבֵאתָ אֶת־עַבְדְּךָ עִמָּךְ]"). This identification presumably reflects the presence of a ratifying oath taken in the name of Yahweh (cf. 1 Sam. 20:23; 23:18).[124]

It has often been observed that the author of the "History of David's Rise" (approximately, 1 Samuel 15- 2 Samuel 8[125]) deliberately parallels and contrasts David's relationship to Jonathan with his relationship to Michal.[126] Jonathan and Michal were both children of Saul, and David's relationship to both helped to legitimise his claim to the throne.[127] Likewise, both of them appear to have initiated their relationship to David, with the text stressing to a remarkable degree their "love" for David.[128] Indeed, David enters into his covenant with Jonathan in 1 Sam. 18:1ff. precisely at the point where the reader expects David to marry a child of Saul, based on the promise of 1 Sam. 17:25 for the champion who would defeat Goliath. Just as this first act of valour appears to have gained Jonathan's affection, a second act of valour would gain the hand of Michal in 1 Sam. 18:25ff.

The vivid contrast between Jonathan and Michal, however, comes into focus in the artistic juxtaposition of their respective attempts to defend David against the murderous intentions of their father Saul in 1 Samuel 19-20. To be noted is the envelope structure of the narrative, also called "an incremental repetition," providing an A-B-A pattern, where the A sections help to interpret the B section, but also where the second A section offers a

---

[124] Cf. P. Kalluveettil, *Declaration and Covenant*, 12.

[125] With H.M. Wolf, "The Apology of Ḫattušiliš Compared with Other Political Self-Justifications of the Ancient Near East" (1967).

[126] A. Berlin writes, "This comparison cries out to be made" ("Characterization in Biblical Narrative: David's Wives" [1982] 70).

[127] See Chapter 6, §2.3.1 above, especially footnote 129.

1 Sam. 18:26 suggests David's own awareness of the potential political implications of his marriage to Michal. His desire to have Michal returned at the point of his accession to the throne at Hebron in 2 Sam. 3:13f. may, in part, have been similarly motivated. Cf. 1 Sam. 18:22f. Cf. J.D. Levenson and B. Halpern, "The Political Import of David's Marriage" (1980) 507-518; and A. Berlin, "Characterization in Biblical Narrative: David's Wives" (1982) 69-85.

[128] In the case of Jonathan, cf. 1 Sam. 18:1, 3; 20:17; 2 Sam. 1:26. In the case of Michal, cf. 1 Sam. 18:20, 28 (the Bible almost never mentions the girl's love as a motivation for marriage, but it may do so here in order to highlight this comparison with Jonathan).

significant development or resolution over the first A section.[129]   In the first A section, 1 Sam. 19:1-7, Jonathan successfully defends David before his father, who was intent on murdering David. In the B section, 1 Sam. 19:8-17, Michal aids David's escape from her father, but in the end protects herself from Saul's wrath by accusing David of having threatened uxoricide. While one may be tempted to sympathize with Michal, her false testimony appears to have provided Saul with the requisite circumstantial evidence that David had repudiated his marriage, allowing her to be given to another man.[130]   In addition, her deception appears to have confirmed her father in his estimate of David and further incited him against David — perhaps accounting for Jonathan's failure to assuage Saul in 1 Samuel 20, in contrast to his previous success in 1 Sam. 19:1-7. In any case, in 1 Sam. 26:19 David condemns exactly this sort of lie which had fed Saul's implacable enmity.[131]   In the second A section, 1 Samuel 20, Jonathan, in contrast to Michal, risks his life to defend David before his outraged father, but to no avail. Accordingly, in the end David laments Jonathan in 2 Sam. 1:26: "I am distressed for you, my brother Jonathan; very pleasant have you been to me; your love for me was more wonderful than the love of women [נִפְלְאַתָה אַהֲבָתְךָ לִי מֵאַהֲבַת נָשִׁים]." Exegetes who would find in this eulogy a veiled allusion to homosexuality have missed the point of 1 Samuel 18-20 and the covenant love and loyalty of Jonathan, which did, in fact, surpass that of Michal.[132]

For our present purpose, however, it is enough to notice that a text which is so deliberate in drawing extensive parallels between David's relationship to Jonathan and his marriage to Michal does so precisely by emphasizing that David was in a covenant [בְּרִית] with Jonathan (1 Sam. 18:3; 20:8; and 23:18). Indeed, the use of the exchange of clothing in the formation of Jonathan's covenant with David (1 Sam. 18:4) recalls the similar use of clothing in the formation of marriage in Ruth 3:9 and Ezek. 16:8.

In conclusion, there are texts scattered throughout the Old Testament which like Malachi identify marriage as a covenant, e.g., Hos. 2:18-22 [ET 16-20]; Prov. 2:17; Ezek. 16:8, 59, 60, and 62; and 1 Samuel 18-20. This supports our contention that in the Old Testament era marriage was seen as covenantal.

---

[129] Cf. the discussion of the A-B-A pattern in 1 Samuel 24-26 offered by R.P. Gordon, "David's Rise and Saul's Demise: Narrative Analogy in 1 Sam 24-26" (1980) 37-64. The same structure appears in 1 Samuel 13-15.

[130] 1 Sam. 25:44. Cf. Judg. 15:2.

[131] This justified, but unwitting curse of Michal recalls Saul's earlier unjustified and unwitting curse of Jonathan in 1 Sam. 14:24. 2 Sam. 6:20-23 appears to suggest that Michal's offence at David's dancing before the ark was motivated by her preference for her father to her husband. In vs. 23, it is significant that she is identified as "Michal, the daughter of Saul," rather than "Michal, the wife of David."

[132] Cf. also J.A. Thompson, "The Significance of the Verb *Love* in the David-Jonathan Narratives in I Samuel" (1974) 334-38; and P.R. Ackroyd, "The Verb Love — *'aheb* in the David-Jonathan Narratives; A Footnote" (1975) 213-214.

R.P. Gordon suggests that "brother" may also refer to the covenant relationship (cf. 1 Kgs. 9:13 and Amos 1:9) (*1 & 2 Samuel*, 212).

3. THE PROBLEM OF ADULTERY AND THE CLAIMED INDIFFERENCE OF THE OLD TESTAMENT TO A MAN'S SEXUAL FIDELITY

We now address one final problem with viewing marriage as a covenant, namely the alleged existence of a double standard in Israel whereby a wife had to be exclusively loyal to her husband, while a husband was allowed to indulge in extramarital sex with unattached women without censure. This view has wide scholarly currency.

Ezek. 16:8 refers to an oath taken by Yahweh, the husband in the marriage metaphor: "When I passed by you again and looked upon you, behold, you were at the age for love; and I spread my skirt over you, and covered your nakedness: yea, I plighted my troth to you and entered into a covenant with you [וָאֶשָּׁבַע לָךְ וָאָבוֹא בִבְרִית אֹתָךְ], says Yahweh God, and you became mine." According to J. Milgrom, however, "it should have been expected of the bride, Israel, for it is the bride, not the husband, who is subject to the laws of adultery."[133]

It has already been argued that there can be no fundamental objection to a husband binding himself in oath to his wife. Even if one accepts that there is a disparity of status and obligation in marriage which places the wife in an inferior position, the frequently attested analogy of ancient suzerains binding themselves by oath to their weaker partners would appear to offer sufficient support for the arrangement implied in Ezek. 16:8.[134] Furthermore, when one turns to the more direct evidence of oath taking within the covenant of marriage, such as Gen. 2:23 and the *verba solemnia* from the Elephantine marriage documents, the evidence is clearest precisely for a verbal oath on the part of the husband and less clear, though still likely, for an oath on the part of the wife.

Milgrom's objection, however, reflects the nearly unanimous view of scholars that within the Old Testament, as well as elsewhere in the ancient Near East, adultery [נאף] was restricted exclusively to an offence committed against a married man.[135] To express this in other terms, it would not be "adultery" if a married man had extramarital sex with an unmarried woman. This traditional view, which contrasts radically with modern usage, finds its most explicit support from the two texts which prohibit adultery with a "neighbour's wife," namely Lev. 20:10 and Jer. 29:23. While this may

---

[133] *Cult and Conscience*, 134.

[134] Cf. the example of Abba-AN of Yamkhad and Yarimlim of Alalaḫ discussed in Chapter 6, §2.3.3. For additional examples, cf. P. Kalluveettil, *Declaration and Covenant*, 87f. n. 329.

[135] Cf., e.g., J.J. Finkelstein, "Sex Offences in Sumerian Laws" (1966) 366 n. 34; and M.T. Roth, "'She will die by the iron dagger': Adultery and Neo-Babylonian Marriage" (1988) 186 n. 1.

T.S. Frymer-Kensky, however, argues that LU §11 refers to a case of an accusation of "adultery" against a man ("The Judicial Ordeal in the Ancient Near East" [1977] 145ff.). Other scholars challenge this interpretation. Cf., e.g., M.T. Roth, "'She will die by the iron dagger': Adultery and Neo-Babylonian Marriage" (1988) 194 n. 20.

appear to be a rather narrow base on which to construct the prevailing view, at least a dozen other texts reinforce the same point by condemning those who would "covet [חמד]," "lie carnally with [נתן + לְזָרַע שְׁכָבְתְּךָ]," "lie with [עִם שׁכב]," "violate [ענה]," "go into [אל + בא]," "neigh for [צהל]," "defile [טמא]," or "commit abomination with [אֶת + עָשָׂה תוֹעֵבָה]" "the wife of one's neighbour."[136] Furthermore, in spite of the presence of seventeen examples where a woman is said to commit adultery [נאף], there is not one indisputable example where the woman involved was clearly unmarried.[137]

In addition to these lexical arguments, B. Stade and others have argued that sexual intercourse by a married man with an unmarried and unbetrothed woman was considered morally inoffensive in the Old Testament, based on Gen. 38 and Judges 16, although it did entail a property violation according to Exod. 22:15f. [ET 16f.].[138] Similarly, E. Neufeld writes:

> "Hebrew law imposes no restraints on the husband in the sphere of extramarital intercourse, which was not regarded as adulterous. A man cannot sin against his own wife, as his wife has no proprietary rights as against him which he can infringe. Accordingly the adulterous conduct of a Hebrew man must refer exclusively to the case of a man having intercourse with another man's wife or betrothed, the offence being thus interference with that man's property. The husband was under no obligation whatsoever to his wife to refrain from extramarital intercourse, nor had the wife any ground for complaint, at all events as long as he did not deprive her of her necessary maintenance and her right to marital intercourse. This seems to be an implication of Ex. 21,10."[139]

Drawing out the implication of this understanding of adultery for an interpretation of marriage as a covenant, P.F. Palmer states, "In a society where ... adultery [was considered] a violation of the rights of the Hebrew male,... it would be unreal to speak of Jewish marriage as a covenant either of love or of fidelity."[140]

---

[136] Cf. Exod. 20:17; Lev. 18:20; Deut. 5:21; 22:22, 24; Job 31:9; Prov. 6:29; Jer. 5:8; Ezek. 18:6, 11, 15; 22:11; and 33:26.

[137] Lev. 20:10 (1x); Prov. 30:20; Isa. 57:3; Jer. 3:8, 9; 13:27; Ezek. 16:32, 38; 23:37 (2x), 43 (? cf. NIV), 45 (2x); Hos. 2:4 [ET 2]; 3:1; 4:13; and 4:14.

[138] B. Stade, *Biblische Theologie des Alten Testaments*, I, (1905) 199. Cf. also G.R. Driver and J.C. Miles, *The Assyrian Laws* (1935) 37ff.; M. Burrows, *The Basis of Israelite Marriage* (1938) 27; W. Lambert, "Morals in Ancient Mesopotamia" (1957) 195; F. Hauck, "μοιχεύω, κτλ.," *TDNT* 4 (1967) 730; J.J. Stamm and M.E. Andrew, *The Ten Commandments in Recent Research* (1967) 100; and B.S. Childs, *Exodus*, 422.

[139] *Ancient Hebrew Marriage Laws* (1944) 163.

[140] P.F. Palmer, "Christian Marriage: Contract or Covenant?" (1972) 621.

The view that a wife was considered the husband's property and the related theory of marriage by purchase (especially as articulated by P. Koschaker) can no longer be maintained. Cf. Chapter 7, §2.1 above.

Emphasizing the mandatory death penalty for adultery in Israelite law when the offenders are caught *in flagrante delicto*, A. Phillips argues that the concern of the law of adultery was not with protecting a husband's property because "a wife's position is not to be confused with that of a daughter. By her marriage the wife became an 'extension' of the husband himself (Gen. 2:24)..." ("Another Look at Adultery" [1981] 7, citing his earlier work, *Ancient Israel's Criminal Law*, 117ff.).

In response to this concluding objection to the identification of marriage in the Old Testament as a "covenant," it may be granted that in terms of its linguistic usage נאף (Qal or Piel), the specific term meaning "to commit adultery," and its cognate nominal forms נאפים, "adultery," and נאפופים, "marks of adultery," are nowhere used to refer to sexual relations between a married man and an unmarried woman. Likewise, the dozen or so other texts mentioned above, which prohibit extramarital sexual relations without employing נאף, invariably have in mind infidelity involving a married woman.

On the other hand, it is also the case that there are no indisputable examples of "adultery [נאף]" being committed by an unmarried man.[141] As a pragmatic matter, the fact is that it is doubtful that there would have been very many persons in the ancient world who were sexually mature and yet unmarried.[142] Although the Old Testament nowhere explicitly states the typical ages for marriage, the mention of the "age for (sexual) love" in Ezek. 16:8 may suggest that women generally married soon after puberty. In support of such an assumption, E.M. Yamauchi observes that in Egypt girls were married between the ages of twelve and fourteen, while boys were married between fourteen and twenty.[143] Likewise, MAL A §43 states that a boy had to be ten years of age before he could marry.[144] Consistent with this picture of an early age for marriage, the Talmud recommends that girls marry at puberty, that is, at twelve or twelve and a half (b. Yebam. 62b), while boys were recommended to marry between fourteen and eighteen.[145]

---

[141] The hypothetical adultery which was sought by Potiphar's wife with the apparently unmarried Joseph in Genesis 39 is not termed נאף and, in any case, was refused by Joseph.

[142] As a result, for example, it is often observed in connection with Jer. 16:2 that the OT does not even have a word for "bachelor."

[143] "Cultural Aspects of Marriage in the Ancient World" (1978) 241-243.

Yamauchi reports that while Greek girls were married as early as twelve, it was more common for them to be between fourteen and twenty, while boys normally married after their military service, that is, after twenty and often closer to thirty. On the other hand, in Rome at the time of Augustus the legal age for marriage was set at twelve for girls and fourteen for boys. Cf. also M.K. Hopkins, "The Age of Roman Girls at Marriage" (1964-5) 309-27; and J.L. Blevins, "The Age of Marriage in First-Century Palestine" (1980) 65-7.

[144] M.T. Roth suggests that in Neo-Babylonian times girls married at 14 to 20 years of age, while boys were typically 26 to 32 ("Age at Marriage and the Household: A Study of Neo-Babylonian and Neo-Assyrian Forms" [1987] 715-47).

This pattern of postponed marriage for men, if it was so, appears to have been due mainly to economic factors, in that most men did not marry until after their fathers' deaths in order to realize their inheritance. Cf. also M.T. Roth, Babylonian Marriage Agreements 7th - 3rd Centuries B.C., 9.

Roth's conclusions concerning matrimonial age, however, depend primarily on the indirect evidence of age as reflected in whether or not living parents are mentioned for the bride and groom in the extant marriage documents and assumed figures for longevity in ancient Mesopotamia.

[145] While the consent of older girls was required, if a girl was under twelve and a half, she could not refuse a marriage arranged by her father (b. Qidd. 2b).

From the discussion above, it appears that the modern reader must guard against reading back into the biblical text his cultural assumptions of a large population of

In addition to this assumption of early marriage in Israel, it appears that sexually nubile but as yet unbetrothed women would have been rendered virtually inaccessible not only by parental or sibling protection, but also by a combination of legal, religious, and cultural sanctions; fear of pregnancy, humiliation, and ostracism for any bastard offspring; etc.[146] Compare, for example, Amnon's complaint about Tamar in 2 Sam. 13:2-4 and the relatively demanding stratagem that was required even for a half-brother to be alone with her. Likewise, Tamar's emphatic disinterest in non-marital sexual intimacy, in spite of her apparent affection for Amnon, offers eloquent testimony to the deterring impact of those cultural and religious sanctions on at least one unmarried Israelite woman. If Tamar's views were at all representative, it should not be surprising that there are so few, if any, examples of "adultery" involving an unbetrothed woman.

3.1 Conventional androcentricity of legal discourse

Finally, the fact that many biblical texts expressly prohibit or condemn adultery with another man's wife does not necessarily imply that extramarital sex with another woman's husband would have been condoned. Given the conventional androcentricity of all ancient legal discourse, it is often difficult to decide whether the ancients would have construed any particular law as necessarily inapplicable to women (assuming that the appropriate gender changes are made). For example, although the Decalogue is consistently androcentric in its perspective (e.g., Exod. 20:17, "You shall not covet your neighbour's house; you shall not covet your neighbour's wife, etc."; note also how masculine forms abound, as in Exod. 20:13, "You shall not kill [לֹא תִּרְצָח]"), other biblical texts do not hesitate to apply these standards to women. See, for example, Deut. 13:7-10 [ET 6-9] (re. idolatry); Ezek. 16:38 and 23:44 (re. murder).[147]

"available" sexually active unmarried women. The fact that many of those accused of prostitution in the OT were actually married tells against such a presupposition.

[146] Cf. Genesis 34 and Absalom's concern to avenge the seduction/rape of Tamar.
Widows, who in other respects were perhaps the most legally "empowered" women in the ancient Near East in that they could marry without permission, acquire wealth, etc., were likewise expected to be sexually chaste. Cf. Jdt. 8:2-8 and 16:25. Cf. also R. Harris, "Independent Women in Ancient Mesopotamia?" (1989) 147.

[147] Cf. also CH §153 as an example of the criminal liability of a woman for the murder of her husband. Cf. further CH §151, where women are liable for their premarital debts (implying a degree of financial activity for women).
In spite of the fact that women do not enjoy a particularly high status in MA culture (cf. C. Saporetti, The Status of Women in the Middle Assyrian Period [1979]), it is instructive to note that women are liable to the laws against adultery (MAL A §§1, 2, 7, 8, 14, 15, 22, 23, 24), as well as lesser acts of sexual misconduct (MAL A §9). Furthermore, they are explicitly prohibited from blasphemy (MAL A §2), theft of temple property (MAL A §1), theft of a husband's property (MAL A §§3, 4), theft of private property (MAL A §5), assault (MAL A §§7, 8), murder (MAL A §10), and magic (MAL A §47).
On the other hand, women can own property, as widows, and the remarried widow can even acquire her husband's property if he enters her house (MAL A §35)!

It is possible, with A. Phillips, that the Deuteronomic law deliberately extended to women a number of provisions which were previously restricted to men (cf., e.g., Deut. 5:21; 7:3; 13:6-9; 15:12-17; 17:2-5; and 22:22).[148] For example, according to Phillips, the original prohibition against adultery did not include women at all; as a result, only the lover was to be put to death (citing Hos. 2:4 [ET 2] and Jer. 3:8 in support).[149] Whether or not Phillips' viewpoint is to be accepted, it appears that the author(s) of the Deuteronomic law and later editors of the Pentateuch did not consider it inconsistent to reinterpret earlier androcentric laws in this manner. One may compare also certain laws, such as Num. 5:6 and 6:2, which begin "when either a man or a woman...," but proceed to consider only the case involving the man. Seemingly, the legislator intends the subsequent androcentric case law to apply, with suitable gender modification, to a woman as well.

Cuneiform parallels may help caution against an overly facile assumption that an androcentric law would never be applied to women in actual practice. For example, one will from the vicinity of Emar reads, "I have established my daughter Unara as female and male," and proceeds to grant Unara the right to invoke her father's gods (and perhaps deceased ancestors), apparently involving "a kind of symbolic title to family property."[150] It should be noted that, in contrast to the situation with the daughters of Zelophehad in Numbers 27, Unara is granted this privilege in spite of the fact that the will mentions her three brothers. Another will says, "Now then, my wife Hebate is father and mother of my estate. Now then, I have established my daughter Al-ḫāṱi as female and male."[151] This second will also grants Al-ḫāṱi the right to call on her father's gods (and deceased ancestors?) and then proceeds to designate Al-ḫāṱi as the heir of her father's entire estate. While household authority and guardianship are normally restricted to fathers and inheritance rights are normally limited to sons, the legal fiction by which a wife is designated a "father" or a daughter is

---

Even MAL A §59, which limits the injuries a husband may inflict on his wife, presupposes there are limits. This law may be compared to MAL A §44, which limits the power of a creditor over the person of the debtor. Of interest also is MAL A §39, which protects women from cruelty if they are in the hands of their creditors, and MAL A §50, which protects pregnant women from assault by imposing a gradation of sanctions if there is a resulting miscarriage (perhaps to compensate the husband for deprivation of offspring, as argued by G.R. Driver and J.C. Miles, *The Assyrian Laws*, 107), but capital punishment if the woman dies (apparently on the principle of *lex talionis*, where the life of a male murderer is considered equal to that of his female victim).

[148] *Ancient Israel's Criminal Law* (1970) 15f., 110f. Cf. also *idem*, "Some Aspects of Family Law in Pre-Exilic Israel" (1973) 353; *idem*, "The Decalogue - Ancient Israel's Criminal Law" (1983) 6; and *idem*, "The Laws of Slavery: Exodus 21:2-11" (1984) 56.

[149] "Some Aspects of Family Law in Pre-Exilic Israel," 353.

[150] J. Huehnergard, "Five Tablets From the Vicinity of Emar" (1983) Text 1, lns. 6-7. Huehnergard suggests a comparison with Rachel's expropriation of the household gods in Gen. 31:34ff. and employs the above quotation from A.E. Draffkorn, "Ilāni/Elohim" (1957) 219 (*op. cit.*, 28).

[151] J. Huehnergard, "Five Tablets From the Vicinity of Emar," Text 2, lns. 5-10.

designated a "male" obviously allows these traditional norms to be applied across the gender boundary.[152]

In view of these and other similar examples of ancient Near Eastern circumvention of androcentric norms, one cannot assume without further proof that it was a legal innovation for the Jews at Elephantine to permit their women to initiate divorce, in spite of the androcentric wording of Deut. 24:1ff., or for Jesus of Nazareth to speak of men committing adultery against their wives, in spite of the androcentric wording of Lev. 20:10, etc.[153]

---

[152] Even if the written law seems relatively indifferent to the concerns of women, it is doubtful that those entrusted with dispensing justice were supposed to be. As noted by W. Lambert, in Mesopotamia justice was designed to aid most those who were without rights ("Morals," 192). Cf., e.g., LU lines 161-168; and J.J. Finkelstein, "Laws of Ur-Nammu," 68.

Cf. also J. Huehnergard, "Five Tablets From the Vicinity of Emar," Text 3, lns 3-5, where a wife is designated "father and mother of my estate."

Huehnergard also notes the Nuzi custom of adopting a woman so that she could acquire or inherit real estate (op. cit, 27 n. 23). Cf. also Z. Ben-Barak, "Inheritance by Daughters in the Ancient Near East" (1980) 22-33; and K. Grosz, "Daughters Adopted as Sons at Nuzi and Emar" (1987) 81-86.

The main conclusion to be drawn from these examples is that when the need or desire arose, women could, at least on certain occasions, assume the roles culturally expected of men.

[153] Cf. Mark 10:11 [and parallels in Luke 16:18 and Matt. 19:9], where Jesus asserts that adultery could be committed against a wife: καὶ λέγει αὐτοῖς, Ὃς ἂν ἀπολύσῃ τὴν γυναῖκα αὐτοῦ καὶ γαμήσῃ ἄλλην μοιχᾶται ἐπ᾿ αὐτήν ["And he said to them, 'Whoever divorces his wife and marries another, commits adultery against her.'"]

Admittedly, it is possible to translate ἐπ᾿ αὐτήν as "with her," i.e., with the second wife, rather than "against her," i.e., against the first wife. Even on this view, however, the adultery exists only because it is committed against the first wife. Cf., e.g., C.S. Mann, Mark (1986) 392.

Z.W. Falk notes that the Talmud recognizes the principle of the applicability of androcentric laws to women, with appropriate gender changes, even if it is inconsistent in its application (Introduction to Jewish Law of the Second Commonwealth II [1978] 261-263). Accordingly, b. B. Qam. 15a states, "Scripture made women equal to men in regard to every law in the Torah" (cf. also Sipre Numbers 2 and Deuteronomy 190). Hence, "women were never forced to sue through a guardian or representative" according to Falk. On the other hand, women were prohibited both from bearing witness and from judging (m. Nid. 6:4) and were not liable in tort (m. B. Qam. 8:4).

Certain other texts may seem to be androcentric and perhaps even supportive of a double standard in OT sexual ethics, but on closer examination prove not to be so. For example, the case of the Sōṭā in Num. 5:11-31 may seem to place a higher premium on the sexual fidelity of a wife than that of her husband — after all, where in the OT is there a special ordeal to determine the sexual fidelity of a husband for the sake of his jealous wife? However, such a question almost certainly misunderstands the intention of Num. 5:11-31. Based on the apparent effect of the ordeal, causing a miscarriage and infertility (cf. 5:22, 27f., though other suggestions include thrombophlebitis, false pregnancy, or dropsy — cf. G.J. Wenham, Numbers, 84), it seems likely that it was an unexpected pregnancy which prompted the husband's jealousy. If so, what is at issue is not marital harmony so much as paternity. In support of viewing Num. 5:11ff. as a "paternity rite," cf. A. Phillips, "Another Look at Adultery," 7f. A similar concern for the paternity of an unexpected pregnancy (occurring immediately after marriage) seems to be behind Deut. 22:13-21, a text which has often been misunderstood as reflecting a one-sided concern with a woman's premarital virginity. Cf. G.J. Wenham, "betûlāh 'A Girl of Marriageable Age'" (1972) 326-48; and A. Phillips, "Another Look at Adultery," 7f.

Of course, the view of B. Stade, E. Neufeld, *et al.*, regarding a husband's extramarital sex would be established if evidence could be found that the Old Testament does in fact approve, or at least disregard, instances of sex between a married man and an unmarried woman. On closer inspection, however, the texts cited by Stade and Neufeld prove to be unconvincing.

3.2 Genesis 38

For example, although Genesis 38 relates Judah's liaison with the disguised Tamar without moral censure — its interests lay elsewhere — it hardly endorses prostitution since Judah himself demanded Tamar's execution for her presumed guilt (so Gen. 38:24). E.J. Fisher thinks that "Tamar's penalty must be for adultery, not simple prostitution, since this alone carried the death penalty (Ezk 16:37-40)."[154] This is not so clear, however, because according to Deut. 22:22 adultery only carries a death penalty if the couple are caught *in flagrante delicto*; in addition, it is required that both guilty parties be executed (cf. also Lev. 20:10). Neither of these conditions is met in the case in Genesis 38.

Although it is possible that Judah was operating on legal principles other than those articulated within Deuteronomic or Priestly law, Tamar's situation appears to be remarkably consistent with Lev. 21:9 and especially Deut. 22:13-21.[155] Tamar was dwelling "in her father's house" (Gen. 38:11) at the time of her presumed act of prostitution. Furthermore, she is discovered by her pregnancy. Finally, Judah's right to press for her execution may stem from the fact that Tamar was not only Judah's daughter-in-law, she was also promised to Shelah (cf. Gen. 38:11).

In any case, Genesis 38 does not support the notion that a man's philandering was considered morally inoffensive to his wife, or that the only concern was with the aggrieved rights of the cuckolded husband. This is so because the text explicitly states that Judah's wife had died (so Gen. 38:12), presumably in order to stress Judah's personal eligibility and hence sin in failing to fulfil the obligation of levirate marriage toward his twice-widowed daughter-in-law.[156] Given that Judah acknowledges in Gen. 38:26 that his own guilt was greater than Tamar's and stresses his fault in driving Tamar to her stratagem, it may be pedantic to insist that the text further condemn Judah specifically for consorting with Tamar, particularly since the "prostitution" in question proved imaginary.

---

[154] "Cultic Prostitution in the Ancient Near East? A Reassessment" (1976) 232 n. 30.

[155] For the recognition that Tamar was being charged not with adultery, but with prostitution / fornication, cf. B.S. Jackson, "Reflections on Biblical Criminal Law," 60; and A. Phillips, "Another Look at Adultery," 24 n. 57.

[156] Cf. Deut. 25:5-10 and Ruth 4:1-12. Cf. also MAL A §§30, 31, 33 and HL §193, which agree that the father-in-law is next in line after any brothers to assume the obligation of the levirate.

3.3 Judges 16:1-3

Similarly, the example of Samson's involvement with the prostitute at Gaza, recorded in Judg. 16:1-3, fails to support the view of B. Stade, E. Neufeld, *et al.* As in the case of Judah, Judg. 15:6 makes clear that Samson was now a widower and so was incapable of committing adultery against his own wife. Furthermore, while it is true that the text reports Samson's relationship with the prostitute of Gaza without moral censure, this negative evidence is at best ambiguous. On a conventional reading, moral censure is implied throughout the Samson narrative.[157] Alternatively, it is possible to interpret Judg. 16:1-3 in the light of the often overlooked, but no less impressive literary and thematic parallels which exist between this text and Joshua 2, where the Israelite spies visit Rahab the harlot.[158] If, as is generally supposed, there was no sexual misconduct on the part of the spies in the latter text, in spite of its titillating language (בָּא + אֶל, "come [in] to"), it is possible that the same assumption should obtain for Samson at Gaza.

3.4 Exodus 21:7-11

The appeal to Exod. 21:7-11 as evidence that a husband was under no obligation to refrain from extramarital intercourse, as long as he did not deprive his wife of her necessary maintenance and intercourse, is likewise highly problematic. Even if it is supposed, with E. Neufeld, that the third case (21:10-11) requires a wife to accede to her husband's polygyny, so long as he does not "deprive the first one of her food, clothing and marital rights," it is not at all obvious that this stipulation would apply beyond the irregular circumstance envisioned by this law, namely a case where the wife in question was at the same time a slave. Furthermore, the acknowledgment of polygynous marriage under such a special circumstance is hardly to be equated with indifference toward extramarital intercourse.

On the other hand, an alternative interpretation of Exod. 21:7-11 is equally possible, and perhaps preferable. On this view, the text nowhere states or implies that the master had sexual relations with his female slave. Supported by the careful literary analysis of Exod. 21:2-11 offered by Y.

---

[157] Cf., e.g., L.R. Klein, *The Triumph of Irony in the Book of Judges* (1987).

[158] These parallels within the Deuteronomic History are rooted in the deeper analogy between Joshua, as the successor to Moses, and each of the subsequent judges of Israel, as well as in the on-going task under the judges to complete the conquest of Canaan, which had been begun under Joshua. Judg. 1:18, when emended with the LXX, asserts that Judah failed to take Gaza, demonstrating the later need for Samson to dispossess these Canaanites/Philistines.

In both texts, Israelites visit an enemy city where, in the nature of the case, the hostile Israelites cannot easily avail themselves of the hospitality of the city elders. This is the case not only because of their desire to maintain secrecy, but also because to benefit from the hospitality of the elders, eating together with them, etc., would result in a commitment of friendship that would prohibit their intended imminent attack. Cf. the discussion of the import of shared meals in Chapter 6, §2.3.3. Instead, they find a prostitute [אִשָּׁה זוֹנָה] with whom they choose to spend part of the night.

Zakovitch,[159] this approach considers the antecedent of שְׁלָשׁ־אֵלֶּה, "these three things," in vs. 11 to be the three preceding apodoses in vss. 8b, 9b, and 10b, rather than "her food, clothing and marital rights [שְׁאֵרָהּ כְּסוּתָהּ וְעֹנָתָהּ]."[160] Furthermore, this view considers the rendering "conjugal rights" for וְעֹנָתָהּ to be the least probable of the various alternative suggestions (including "oil" or "shelter") which have been advanced for this *hapax legomenon*.[161]

Finally, assuming the MT of יְעָדָהּ, "designated her," in vs. 8b is to be maintained, while other interpretations remain possible, it seems likely that this unusual expression was intended to refer either to betrothal (so the LXX

---

[159] Y. Zakovitch, *'For Three ... and for Four': The Pattern for the Numerical Sequence Three - Four in the Bible* (Hebrew) (1979). Cf. also B.S. Jackson, "Some Literary Features of the Mishpatim" (1987) 235-242; and G.C. Chirichigno, "Debt Slavery in the Ancient Near East and Israel: An Examination of the Biblical Manumission Laws in Exod 21:2-6, 7-11; Deut 15:12-18; Lev. 25:39-54" (1989) 174-175.

Chirichigno summarizes Zakovitch's view (*op. cit.*, 175): "In each law the fourth sub-section ... [here called the "Exception Case"] deals with an exceptional occurrence which does not fit in with the general principle – viz., the male slave chooses to remain with his master rather than going free in the seventh year, and the female slave goes out without payment when her lord does not fulfil his contractual obligations to her (i.e., Exod 21:8-10). Moreover, the fourth section ... of each law forms a chiastic structure with the two general principles in v. 2, 7 ... the male slave goes out free without payment in v. 2 as does the female slave in ... [vs. 11]; the female slave does not go out free in v. 7 as does the male slave who chooses to stay with his master in ... [vss. 5, 6]."

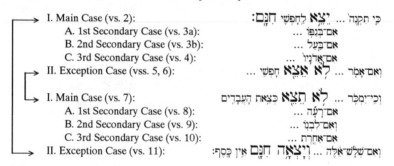

I. Main Case (vs. 2):	כִּי תִקְנֶה ... יֵצֵא לַחָפְשִׁי חִנָּם:
A. 1st Secondary Case (vs. 3a):	אִם־בְּגַפּוֹ ...
B. 2nd Secondary Case (vs. 3b):	אִם־בַּעַל ...
C. 3rd Secondary Case (vs. 4):	אִם־אֲדֹנָיו ...
II. Exception Case (vss. 5, 6):	וְאִם־אָמֹר ... לֹא אֵצֵא חָפְשִׁי ...
I. Main Case (vs. 7):	וְכִי־יִמְכֹּר ... לֹא תֵצֵא כְּצֵאת הָעֲבָדִים
A. 1st Secondary Case (vs. 8):	אִם־רָעָה ...
B. 2nd Secondary Case (vs. 9):	וְאִם־לִבְנוֹ ...
C. 3rd Secondary Case (vs. 10):	אִם־אַחֶרֶת ...
II. Exception Case (vs. 11):	וְאִם־שְׁלָשׁ־אֵלֶּה ... וְיָצְאָה חִנָּם אֵין כָּסֶף:

[160] So, e.g., Rashi, Ibn Ezra, Rashbam, A. Cohen, *The Soncino Chumash* (1947) 473; I. Mendelsohn, "Slavery in the OT," *IDB* IV, 384; Y. Zakovitch, *'For Three ... and for Four'*, 452; and G.C. Chirichigno, "Debt Slavery in the Ancient Near East and Israel," 226f.

[161] The view that וְעֹנָתָהּ is to be rendered "her marital rights" supposes, in general, that this term is related to עָנָה, "to ravish" [though Ibn Ezra relates it to עֵת, "time"]. This view receives its most direct support from the LXX, τὴν ὁμιλίαν αὐτῆς, "her cohabitation." Similar is R. North, "Flesh, Covering, a Response, Ex. xxi 10" (1955) 204-6,

A second interpretation of וְעֹנָתָהּ has been proposed by S.M. Paul, "Exod. 21:10: a Threefold Maintenance Clause" (1969) 48-53; and *idem*, *Studies in the Book of the Covenant in the Light of Cuneiform and Biblical Law* (1970) 56-61. Based on a number of Akkadian (and Sumerian) texts which stereotypically list *ipru*, *piššatu*, and *lubuštu*, "food, oil, and clothing," as the main necessities of life, Paul understands וְעֹנָתָהּ to be "her oil." Although these parallels are attractive, the lists are highly variable (cf., e.g., MAL A. §36, lns. 86-88; Eccl. 9:7-9; etc.), the meaning "oil" is otherwise unattested for the Hebrew term עֹנָה, and the etymology of עֹנָה, meaning "oil," is as yet unexplained.

Yet a third alternative, perhaps to be preferred, is offered by U. Cassuto, who argues for "her quarters" or "the conditions of her abode," based on Rashbam's suggested derivation from מָעוֹן, "refuge, home" (*Exodus*, 268). See now W. von Soden, "Zum hebräischen Wörterbuch" (1981) 159f.

and Vulgate) or to a pre-betrothal arrangement, i.e., a "promise" or "designation" (so Targum Onkelos and Pseudo-Jonathan).[162] As appears from the second subsidiary case in vs. 9, in contrast to the Nuzi practice of *adoptio in matrimonium*, in biblical law, according to S. Paul, "the girl is no longer considered a type of property that can be passed on from one husband to the next."[163] As the text makes clear, such a slave was to be treated by the master "according to the rights of daughters [כְּמִשְׁפַּט הַבָּנוֹת]."[164] Whatever other privileges may be intended, certainly "the rights of daughters" would prohibit promiscuous relations with the girl on the part of her owner.[165] As summarized by D. Patrick: "If the man purchases the woman for marriage with his son (vs. 9), he must treat her as a daughter within the household until she is married. Presumably this means that he is not to have sexual intercourse with her or treat her in a demeaning way."[166]

Accordingly, if any intended marriage with the female slave in Exod. 21:7-11 had not yet been consummated, as is being suggested here, then contrary to Neufeld, *et al.*, Exod. 21:7-11 can hardly be adduced as evidence that a husband was under no obligation to refrain from extramarital relations.[167]

3.5 Exodus 22:15-16 [ET 16-17] (and Deuteronomy 22:13-21)

Likewise, the appeal to Exod. 22:15-16 [ET 16-17] hardly warrants the conclusion that sexual intercourse with an unbetrothed virgin constitutes a mere property violation. To be sure the text requires the payment of a "marriage present [מֹהַר]," which is to be equal to the "marriage present for virgins [כְּמֹהַר הַבְּתוּלֹת]," in the event that the girl's father refuses his permission for the expected marriage. But what should not be overlooked is the more fundamental and normal requirement: "and [he shall] make her his wife."[168]

---

[162] So S.M. Paul, *Studies in the Book of the Covenant*, 54 n. 1.
For an analogous distinction in Hittite law between a girl who is "promised," *taranza*, and one who is "engaged" or "bound," *hamenkanza*, cf. F. Mezger, "Promised but not engaged" (1944) 28-31.
[163] S.M. Paul, *Studies in the Book of the Covenant*, 53
[164] S.M. Paul renders this phrase "as is the practice with free maidens" (*op. cit.*, 55).
[165] Cf. Lev. 18:8, 15 and 20:11, 12; Deut. 23:1 [ET 22:30]; 27:20; and Amos 2:7. Although the OT does not explicitly prohibit father-daughter incest, such a prohibition was no doubt assumed and is attested in cuneiform law (cf. Chapter 6, §2.1 above and CH §§154-156).
[166] D. Patrick, *Old Testament Law*, 71.
[167] Note that the use of אַחֶרֶת in the expression, "If he takes *another* [wife] to himself [אִם־אַחֶרֶת יִקַּח־לוֹ]," in 21:10 does not require the assumption of bigyny, as some suppose. While אַחֶרֶת could mean "another" in the sense of an "*additional*" wife, there are many examples of אַחֶרֶת similar to 21:10 which suggest that it may mean "another" in the sense of a "*different*" wife — that is, another wife instead of the female slave. Cf., e.g., Gen. 29:19; Deut. 24:2; Judg. 11:2; Jer. 3:1; etc. Cf. also W.C. Kaiser Jr., *Old Testament Ethics*, 184f.
[168] Cf. also the discussion of this text in Chapter 7, §2.2.2 above.

However one is to interpret Deut. 22:13-21, whether the underlying concern is with a wife's premarital virginity in general,[169] or whether the concern is more particularly with a honeymoon pregnancy which prompted a question of paternity,[170] the conclusion leaves little doubt that sexual promiscuity for an unbetrothed woman was no less morally reprehensible than for a married woman: "because she has wrought folly in Israel by playing the harlot in her father's house [כִּי־עָשְׂתָה נְבָלָה בְּיִשְׂרָאֵל לִזְנוֹת בֵּית אָבִיהָ]; so you shall purge the evil from the midst of you [וּבִעַרְתָּ הָרָע מִקִּרְבֶּךָ]" (Deut. 22:21).[171]

3.6 There are no texts which demonstrate that the extramarital sexual activity of men or the sexual activity of unmarried women was a matter of moral indifference

D. Patrick writes:

> "In the realm of extramarital sex, the double standard [where "a woman owed sexual fidelity to one man, but her husband did not owe her the same"] permitted a married man to have sexual intercourse with unattached women. Although prostitution ... was condemned in ancient Israel, it seems to have been *tolerated* [italics added] .... However, extramarital sexual relations generally, though they were *permitted* [italics added], were morally condemned."[172]

Similarly, P. Bird states that the harlot "was in every period a figure of disrepute and shame (Gen 34.31; Judg 11.1; 1 Kgs. 22.38; Isa 1.21; Jer 3.3; Ezek 16.30), at best merely ostracized, at worst (in circumstances involving infidelity and defilement) subjected to punishment of death (Gen 38.24; see also Lev 21.9). But the harlot was also *tolerated* [italics added] in every period by men who incurred no legal penalties – or even censure – for the enjoyment of her services (Gen 38.15ff.)."[173] S. Niditch and C.V. Camp make similar observations, especially with respect to Genesis 38. Rightly objecting to the double standard inherent in Judah's treatment of his supposed harlot daughter-in-law, Camp notes that harlots were "marginally *acceptable*

---

[169] Cf., e.g., M. Tsevat, *et al.*, "בְּתוּלָה *bethûlāh*," *TDOT* II, 342f.; and C. Locher, *Die Ehre einer Frau in Israel* (1986).

[170] Cf. G.J. Wenham, "*betûlāh* 'A Girl of Marriageable Age'" (1972) 326-48.

[171] H.G. Reventlow argues that the seduction of an unbetrothed woman was considered "shameful" and hence morally objectionable (*Gebot und Predigt im Dekalog*, 78f.). Cf. also B.S. Childs, *Exodus*, 422.

This text contradicts the assertion of B. Malina regarding the attitudes of both the OT and the NT: "in no case is pre-betrothal, non-commercial, non-cultic heterosexual intercourse (what is commonly called 'fornication' today) prohibited!" ("Does *Porneia* Mean Fornication?," 15). For a detailed refutation of Malina, cf. J. Jensen, "Does *Porneia* Mean Fornication? A Critique of Bruce Malina," (1978) 161-84.

[172] *Old Testament Law*, 55.

[173] P. Bird, "Images of Women in the Old Testament" (1974) 66f.

[italics added]" in Israel, particularly by those desiring their services, but only as long as they were no man's virgin daughter or wife![174]

Is it really the case that extramarital relations or prostitution were "tolerated," "permitted," or "acceptable" in Israel? In what sense are these terms intended when they are qualified by the mention of social and moral condemnation?[175] Any examination of the evidence is complicated by at least two factors: First, it is necessary to distinguish actual practice and attitudes held by the various members of a society from the views and ideals of its moralists (i.e., in the present case the biblical authors).[176] Second, there is the further need to distinguish criminal sanction from moral censure and to guard against the modern tendency to assume that the lack of criminal sanction necessarily indicates greater moral tolerance, if not approbation.

3.6.1 Genesis 38

In Genesis 38, for example, the "double standard," to which P. Bird, S. Niditch, C.V. Camp, and others object, pertains to what may be inferred of Judah's personal value system. It is doubtful, however, that the narrator shares Judah's viewpoint in this matter; the narrative is thoroughly disapproving of Judah and correspondingly sympathetic toward Tamar.

In addition to Judah's own explicit confession of Tamar's superior righteousness (Gen. 38:26), the narrative offers its own eloquent, if less direct, judgment against Judah through the device of narrative analogy. Twice before her encounter with Judah, Tamar is depicted as a tragic victim of the wickedness of Judah's sons: "But Er, Judah's first-born, was wicked in the sight of Yahweh; and Yahweh slew him" (Gen. 38:7); "And what he [Onan] did was displeasing in the sight of Yahweh, and he slew him also" (Gen. 38:10). The reader cannot fail to see a pattern developing, since Judah himself recognizes it: "Then Judah said to Tamar his daughter-in-law, 'Remain a widow in your father's house, till Shelah my son grows up' — for

---

[174] C.V. Camp, *Wisdom and the Feminine in the Book of Proverbs* (1985) 112-114; and S. Niditch, "The Wronged Woman Righted: An Analysis of Gen 38" (1979) 147.

[175] For an indication of the contempt in which harlots were held, cf., e.g., 1 Kgs. 22:38; Amos 7:17; and especially the extended harlot metaphor for folly in Proverbs 1-7.

It is notable that even in Mesopotamia, where cult prostitutes and common harlots (*ex officio* devotees of Ishtar) abounded, it appears that, at least among some thinkers, this practice was not entirely "acceptable." In the Babylonian *Counsels of Wisdom*, for example, a man is advised against marrying such a woman: "Do not marry a prostitute, whose husbands are legion, a temple harlot who is dedicated to a god, a courtesan whose favours are many...." W.G. Lambert briefly discusses this text, summarizing, "Here no distinction is made between different species of the kind, but all alike are condemned as unfit for marriage" ("Morals in Ancient Mesopotamia," 195).

[176] Cf. the OB document *RA* 69, 120ff., No. 8 (M. Anbar, "Textes de l'époque babylonienne ancienne" [1975] 109-136). Although Anbar considered the text to concern a husband and wife who agree not to refrain from sexual relations, R. Westbrook has argued that the text actually prohibits (by mutual oaths) a married man from engaging in sexual relations with a particular harlot ("The Enforcement of Morals in Mesopotamia" [1984] 753-756)!

Cf. also M.T. Roth, "'She will die by the iron dagger': Adultery and Neo-Babylonian Marriage," 193 n. 14.

he feared that he would die, like his brothers. So Tamar went and dwelt in her father's house" (Gen. 38:11). The irony is that while Judah sought to protect his family from incurring Yahweh's righteous judgment yet once more, his self-serving deception recalls that of his son Onan and establishes Judah himself as the third member in the pattern. The reader is prepared for the refrain, "And what Judah did was displeasing in the sight of Yahweh, and he slew him also." In effect Tamar saves Judah from the full extremity of his intended wrong by her deception, itself an ironic reversal and fitting retribution for Judah's earlier deception of Tamar.[177]

Finally, reinforcing the implicit moral indictment against Judah, in Gen. 38:20-23 Judah secures the help of his friend Hirah to pay his debt to the anonymous harlot (Tamar in disguise), perhaps out of a self-condemning shame.[178] This sense of shame is made explicit when Hirah, having failed his mission, returns and is instructed by Judah to give up further search and to allow the disguised Tamar to keep the valuable pledge left by Judah, "lest we be shamed [פֶּן נִהְיֶה לָבוּז]" (Gen. 38:23).[179]

3.6.2 1 Kings 3:16-28

Another text which is sometimes cited as demonstrating the toleration of prostitution in Israel is 1 Kgs. 3:16-28. Here it is mentioned in a matter-of-fact manner that it was two *prostitutes* [שְׁתַּיִם נָשִׁים זֹנוֹת] who came to stand before Solomon and benefit from his divinely inspired sagacity, as he determined the rightful mother of their surviving baby. Perhaps to the reader's surprise, nowhere does Solomon even question their livelihood, much less demand the exaction of any criminal penalty for their prostitution.

Such negative evidence, however, must be treated with particular caution in a text like this since it is clear that the interest of the narrator is almost exclusively directed toward the goal of exalting Solomon. For example, it has been noted that the two prostitutes are so insignificant as persons that "their names are not important enough to be preserved, stated, or

---

[177] "Poetic justice" or ironic reversals of this sort are a standard narrative device for intimating divine judgment within the OT. Cf., e.g., G.J. Wenham, *Numbers*, 84.

B. Lang says "Tamar, in the book of Genesis, was able to play the harlot without losing face" (*Wisdom and the Book of Proverbs* [1986] 98). Such a statement fails to take account of Tamar's extraordinary circumstance as one who had been wronged by Judah's refusal to provide his son Shelah as a husband or personally to assume the responsibility of the levirate.

[178] Cf. A. Brenner, *The Israelite Woman* (1985) 82.

[179] So the AV. The RSV "be laughed at" should not be misconstrued as if it merely implied the fear of a mild social embarrassment. Elsewhere בוז (cf. its probable by-form, בָּזָה) connotes notions of shame, disgrace, disdain, and contempt. Cf., e.g., M. Görg, "בָּזָה bāzāh," *TDOT*, II, 60-65.

In support of this emphasis on Judah's guilt, R. Alter has observed that the result of the intrusive placement of the Judah story within the Joseph narrative is that "we move in pointed contrast from a tale of exposure through sexual incontinence [Genesis 38] to a tale of seeming defeat and ultimate triumph through sexual continence — Joseph and Potiphar's wife [Genesis 39]" (*The Art of Biblical Narrative* [1981] 10; I am grateful to A. Lemaire for drawing my attention to Alter's discussion).

invented."[180] Perhaps more to the point, it is possible that their occupation as
harlots is mentioned precisely in order to stress not their guilt, but the
gracious condescension of this "wise king [who] would act on behalf of the
very lowest of his subjects."[181] Furthermore, the absence in the text of any
criminal sanction or, especially, any moral censure against prostitution may
be no more significant than the corresponding absence of any such sanction
or censure against kidnapping, deceit, or perjury, all of which are committed
in the same episode. Yet no scholar has suggested that kidnapping or perjury
was "tolerated" in Israel.

Nevertheless, it is possible that the fact that these two prostitutes lived
alone (stressed in 1 Kgs. 3:17f.), rather than in their father's house (cf. Gen.
38:11, 24; Lev. 21:9 and Deut. 22:21), or under a husband's authority (in
which case their harlotry would constitute adultery as well — cf. Ezekiel 16),
may have been an extenuating circumstance which allowed their prostitution
to be free from criminal sanction. In the ancient world the lack of such a
male patron or protector was likely to render a woman especially vulnerable
to the sexual advances of unprincipled men and, at the same time, to place her
in considerable financial hardship.[182] It is possible that the criminal law and
probable that the moral law (or at least public opinion) took into account such
mitigating factors.[183]

*3.6.3 There are no texts which demonstrate that the non-cultic, non-
commercial sexual activity of unmarried women was a matter of moral
indifference*
B. Malina asserts that, apart from ritualistic sexual acts and prostitution, the
willing sexual acts of an unmarried woman were viewed with moral
indifference in the Old Testament.[184] As we have observed, however, the
evidence simply does not support such a claim. In actuality, the fact that only
three Old Testament examples exist for consideration (i.e., Genesis 34,
Genesis 38, and 2 Samuel 13) may reflect the rarity of such acts in the ancient
world. We have already considered each of these texts above (cf. Chapter 7,
§2.2.2 and Chapter 8, §3.2); none appears to support Malina's contention.
Specifically, it should be noted that both Shechem's relationship with Dinah

---

[180] A. Brenner, *The Israelite Woman*, 81.

[181] S.J. DeVries, *1 Kings*, 61. With similar import, cf. the characterization of Jesus as a
"friend of ... 'sinners'" (Matt. 11:19).

[182] A similar awareness of the vulnerability of women when alone (in the open country,
rather than in the city where cries for help could be heard) radically affects the law of
adultery with betrothed women in Deut. 22:23-27.

[183] Prov. 6:30 may support the supposition that public opinion, if not moral norms, can
take such factors into account: "Men do not despise a thief if he stole to satisfy his soul
when he is hungry...."
   Prov. 7:14, 20 may provide more direct confirmation that financial destitution could be
a mitigating factor in judging prostitution, if the interpretation of K. van der Toorn is
accepted ("Female Prostitution in Payment of Vows in Ancient Israel," 199). Cf. also *b.
Ketub.* 44b, which suggests that the penalty prescribed in Deut. 22:21 could be waived in
the case of an orphan.

[184] "Does *Porneia* Mean Fornication?," 11 n. 2, 15.

in Genesis 34 and Amnon's forcible seduction of Tamar in 2 Samuel 13 are condemned in the strongest possible manner by the term נְבָלָה, "grievous folly," which significantly reappears in Deut. 22:21, a text which is also concerned with a woman's premarital sexual activity.[185] Dinah's brothers make clear their negative view of "premarital sex," even though Shechem loved Dinah (Gen. 34:3) and sought to remedy his offence with an earnest appeal for marriage. After killing Hamor, Shechem, and the men of Shechem because of Shechem's act, they justified their brutality by asking, "Should he treat our sister as a harlot [הַכְזוֹנָה יַעֲשֶׂה אֶת־אֲחוֹתֵנוּ]?" (Gen. 34:31).[186]

The key legal texts (e.g., Exod. 21:7-11; 22:15-16 [ET 16-17]; Lev. 19:20-22; Deut. 21:10-14; 22:13-21; 22:28-29) have been discussed previously and, similarly, were found nowhere to suggest an indifference to the sexual acts of unmarried women. Far from any such indifference, Exod. 22:15-16 [ET 16-17] and Deut. 22:28-29 require a marriage proposal to follow any act of "premarital sex." Failing this marital remedy, it is notable that Deut. 22:21 recalls the objection of Dinah's brothers in Gen. 34:31 by describing what may have been a single act of non-commercial sex with an unmarried girl as "prostitution [זנה]," as well as "grievous folly [נְבָלָה]," and "evil [רַע]," suggesting that Biblical Hebrew may not observe a terminological distinction between prostitution and fornication.[187]

3.7 Texts which encourage a husband's sexual fidelity regardless of the married state of the mistress

The modern categorical distinction between "illegal" and "immoral" does not apply easily to biblical practice, where criminal and moral norms were so thoroughly and deliberately intertwined. For example, A. Phillips notes that within the Covenant Code criminal and civil norms "which carry specific penalties to be enforced by the courts" (Exod. 21:12-22:19 [ET 20]) are juxtaposed with "humanitarian and cultic injunctions which envisage no legal action for their breach and specify no penalties" (22:20 [ET 21]-23:19).[188] Although observance of this second category of "law" depends on religious sanctions and moral suasion, rather than the threat of criminal sanction, it is no less obligatory and no less crucial for the proper functioning of the community of Israel.

The Decalogue itself offers a similar example of apodictic law which, at least in its present form, includes unenforceable injunctions alongside

---

[185] The traditional English rendering of נְבָלָה as "folly" cannot adequately convey the horror evoked by words or actions which are so termed in Hebrew and which are so regularly met with a death penalty (whether threatened or exacted by the wrath of God or by human courts). Cf. A. Phillips, "*Nebalah* - a term for serious disorderly and unruly conduct" (1975) 237-42.

[186] Notable is the fact that the brothers do not object to Shechem because he was an uncircumcised outsider. Cf. J. Jensen, "Does *Porneia* Mean Fornication? A Critique of Bruce Malina," 168.

[187] *Ibid.*, 166.

[188] "The Law of Slavery," 52.

criminal norms. Even in the case of a particular criminal law, such as the prohibition of adultery, the fact that adultery is punishable with death only when the couple is caught *in flagrante delicto* cannot be construed as implying that under other circumstances adultery would be "approved" or even "tolerated."[189]

Whatever legal apparatus there may have been to enforce a husband's sexual fidelity, it is clear that a *moral* obligation of sexual fidelity applied to the husband no less than to the wife — even where the extramarital relations would be with an unmarried woman.[190] This is the case even in Mesopotamian practice.[191] K. van der Toorn, for example, mentions the *Myth of the Guilty Slave Girl*, where "The goddess Inanna accuses the girl Amanamtagga, 'The-guilty-one', of having learned coitus and kissing from

---

[189] Given the limitations of the present study, it is not possible to consider in more detail the problematic evidence concerning the penal sanctions which attach to adultery (cf., e.g., Prov. 6:34f.) and their possible historical development or to enter into the larger debate concerning the claim that OT law (at least at some stage) was characterized by principles radically different from those presupposed in ancient Near Eastern law elsewhere. Specifically, it is claimed that while ancient Near Eastern law considered adultery to be an offence against the husband, who was consequently authorized to determine the punishment of his wife (with the law requiring equal treatment for the lover), biblical law considered adultery to be a sin against God and in every case where the couple was caught *in flagrante delicto* demanded the exaction of the death penalty and disallowed the husband the prerogative to commute the execution. This claim does not deny that other ancient Near Eastern societies likewise considered adultery as a sin against the deity. It merely asserts that this moral conviction did not inform their legal practice with the same consistency as is attested in the Bible.

Those who reject the radical distinctiveness of OT law, especially regarding adultery, include S.E. Loewenstamm, "The Laws of Adultery and Murder in Biblical and Mesopotamian Law" (1980 [originally published in Hebrew in 1962]) 146-53; *idem*, "The Laws of Adultery and Murder in the Bible. A reply to M. Weinfeld" (1980) 171-172; B.S. Jackson, "Reflections on Biblical Criminal Law" (1973) 8-38; H. McKeating, "Sanctions against Adultery in Ancient Israelite Society, with Some Reflections on Methodology in the Study of Old Testament Ethics" (1979) 57-72; *idem*, "A Response to Dr. Phillips" (1981) 25-26; and J.W. Welch, "Reflections on Postulates: Power and Ancient Laws - A Response to Moshe Greenberg" (1990) 113-119.

Those who support the radical distinctiveness of OT law, particularly regarding adultery, include M. Greenberg, "Some Postulates of Biblical Criminal Law" (1960) 5-28; *idem*, "Crimes and Punishments" in *IDB*, I, 737b; *idem*, "More Reflections on Biblical Criminal Law" (1986); *idem*, "Reply to the Comments of John Welch" (1990) 120-125; S.M. Paul, *Studies in the Book of the Covenant in the Light of Cuneiform and Biblical Law* (1970); A. Phillips, *Ancient Israel's Criminal Law: A New Approach to the Decalogue* (1970); *idem*, "Another Look at Adultery" (1981) 3-25; *idem*, "A Response to Dr. McKeating (*JSOT* 20 [1981] 25-26)" (1981) 142-143; *idem*, "The Decalogue - Ancient Israel's Criminal Law" (1983) 1-20; and H.J. Boecker, *Law and the Administration of Justice in the Old Testament and Ancient East* (1980) 113.

Cf. also M.T. Roth, "'She will die by the iron dagger': Adultery and Neo-Babylonian Marriage" (1988) 186-206. Cf. further LU §4; LE §28; CH §129; MAL A §13, 14, 15, 16, 23; and HL §§197, 198.

[190] With respect to the claim that "sexual relations between a man and an unmarried woman are taken up only in the case of rape or seduction of a virgin, where it is a civil, not moral crime," J. Jensen writes, "Such views are frequently expressed, but they do not appear to rest on a full consideration of the OT evidence. Some of Israel's laws can lead to a different conclusion; and there are further indications in the historical and wisdom traditions" ("Does *Porneia* Mean Fornication? A Critique of Bruce Malina," 165).

[191] Cf. footnote 176 above.

Dumuzi, her husband." Although the text nowhere hints of a legal charge against her husband of adultery with this single girl, nevertheless, "the act is referred to as an *ikkibu* (ÈM.GIG), a 'taboo'."[192] Other texts likewise stress the taboo violation or defilement which comes from sexual promiscuity. To these examples, Van der Toorn adds a reference to Babylonian behavioural omens which stress the detrimental effects of illicit sexual intercourse. Compare, for example, "If he is a fornicator (*nā'ik*): what he owns will decrease, he will become poor."[193]

With respect to the biblical data, perhaps the clearest examples of texts which appear to discourage sexual promiscuity on the part of husbands, even when it is committed with unmarried lovers, are: 1 Sam. 2:22; Job 31:1; Hos. 4:14; and especially Proverbs 5.[194]

3.7.1 1 Samuel 2:22
The least convincing of these examples is 1 Sam. 2:22, which records how Eli heard that his (married) sons "... lay with the women who ministered at the entrance to the tent of meeting [וְיִשְׁכְּבוּן אֶת־הַנָּשִׁים הַצֹּבְאוֹת פֶּתַח אֹהֶל מוֹעֵד]." Although the text does not explicitly identify these women as unmarried, this inference seems likely. First of all, husbands are nowhere mentioned or alluded to in the context. If the women were married, this omission would be surprising given the sexual nature of the offence. Second, the term "adultery [נאף]" nowhere appears. Third, when Eli reproves his sons, he says, "If a man sins against a man, God[195] will mediate for him; but if a man sins against Yahweh, who can intercede for him?" (1 Sam. 2:25). This statement may imply that Hophni and Phinehas had sinned only against God, not man, and so it may be surmised there were no offended husbands.[196] Finally, if the ministry of these women was modelled on that of Miriam, who appears to have been unmarried, this status may have been required of all such women.[197]

While Israel's complaint and the threatened divine judgment against Hophni and Phinehas for their promiscuity may demonstrate disapproval of

---

[192] *Sin and Sanction*, 17f. Against this rendering of *ikkibu*, cf. M.J. Geller, "Taboo in Mesopotamia (review of K. van der Toorn, *Sin and Sanction in Israel and Mesopotamia*)" (1990) 105-117.

[193] *CT* 51, 147, Rev. 21, as cited by K. van der Toorn, *Sin and Sanction*, 161 n. 80.

[194] Because harlots were frequently married, texts which condemn their use are less clear since they may merely reflect a condemnation of adultery. Cf., e.g., Jer. 5:7 and Ezek. 24:44, if emended with the LXX.

[195] "God" is understood by J.G. Baldwin as a possible reference to the "judges" (cf. Exod. 21:6; 22:8-9) (*1 and 2 Samuel*, 61).

[196] 2 Sam. 12:13 and Ps. 51:5 [ET 4] could be considered counter examples for this inference.

[197] Cf. Exod. 38:8 and the possibly relevant evidence for the concept of unmarried women being "married" to the deity attested elsewhere in the ancient Near East as well as in the NT (Luke 2:36; 1 Timothy 5:11). As R. Harris points out, when a *nadītum* entered a cloister, it was considered analogous to marriage ("The *Nadītu* Woman" ([1964] 105-135). For this reason a *biblum* was given. Cf. also R. Westbrook, "Old Babylonian Marriage Law," II, 304.

sexual promiscuity with unmarried women, there are a few difficulties with this text which diminish its utility. First, whatever the precise character of Hophni and Phinehas's offence, the exclusive interest of the text seems to be in condemning this wrong as an abuse of their priestly office, not as an offence against their marriages. Second, the clause, "and how they lay with the women who ministered at the entrance to the tent of meeting," is missing from two key witnesses, 4QSam[a] and LXX[B]. Accordingly, P.K. McCarter Jr. and R.W. Klein, for example, argue that it should be excised as a gloss from Exod. 38:8, inspired by a perceived link between the present situation and the Baal of Peor incident in Num. 25:6-15.[198] In support of the MT, however, the postulated connection with Num. 25:6-15 is not so strong as alleged. Further, it is notable that the MT is supported by LXX[L] and Josephus, *Antiquities* 5.339; accordingly, it is possible that the omission in 4QSam[a] and LXX[B] was merely the result of homoioarchton.[199] Finally, although it seems likely that these women are the same as those mentioned in Exod. 38:8, where "ministered [צבא]" also appears, there has been no scholarly consensus regarding the precise identity or function of these women. H.W. Hertzberg suggests that they "have the task of keeping the entrance clean; this was particularly important for what took place in the sanctuary."[200] J.P. Hyatt makes a similar suggestion and adds the possibility that they also repaired the tabernacle.[201] Alternatively, Hyatt and others have wondered whether they ministered by dancing and singing (perhaps following Miriam's example in Exod. 15:20) or functioned as prostitutes, perhaps accounting for their wealth.[202]

The suggestion of cultic prostitution in either Exod. 38:8 or 1 Sam. 2:22, however, seems unlikely. This is especially the case in Exod. 38:8, which explains that Bezalel made the copper laver and its pedestal "from the mirrors of the ministering women who ministered at the door of the tent of meeting." As J.I. Durham notes, "it is not likely that a reference associating the Laver with anything so antithetical to the P concept of cultic acceptability as cultic prostitution would have been included without some such explanation as that given in Num 17:1-5 [16:36-40], regarding the use upon the altar of the copper of the censers of Korah's company of rebels."[203] In any case, since צבא is also employed to describe the ministry of the Levites (Num. 4:23; 8:24), there is no need to assume a different sort of ministry for

---

[198] P.K. McCarter Jr., *1 Samuel* (1980) 81; and R.W. Klein, *1 Samuel* (1983) 22.

Taking the opposite view, J.P. Hyatt argues that Exod. 38:8 is a gloss deriving from 1 Sam. 2:22 (*Exodus* [1971] 330).

F.M. Cross Jr. compares the mention of "male cult prostitutes" in "houses" which "were in the house of the LORD, where the women wove hangings for the Asherah" in 2 Kgs. 23:7 (*Canaanite Myth and Hebrew Epic* [1973] 201-203).

[199] Cf. also R.P. Gordon, *1 & 2 Samuel*, 83.

[200] *I and II Samuel* (1964) 36.

[201] *Exodus* (1971) 330.

[202] Cf. G.H. Davies, *Exodus* (1967) 251; and R.A. Cole, *Exodus* (1973) 236. Cf. also Judg. 11:34; 21:21; and 1 Sam. 18:6.

[203] *Exodus*, 488.

these women in either Exod. 38:8 or 1 Sam. 2:22.[204] Moreover, the mention in 1 Sam. 2:22 of the ministry of the women "at the entrance of the tent of meeting" seems calculated to render Hophni and Phinehas all the more culpable for their offence, in a manner analogous to the priest's abuse of the offerings of the worshippers in vss. 13-17.[205] Further, the ability and willingness of Hophni and Phinehas to resort to force to commit their offence against the offerings mentioned in 1 Sam. 2:16 allow the possibility that they used similar force to have their way with these women. If so, this was not cultic prostitution, for which the women presumably would have willingly offered themselves.

3.7.2 Job 31:1

Job 31:1 reads, "I have made a covenant with my eyes; how then could I look upon a virgin [בְּרִית כָּרַתִּי לְעֵינָי וּמָה אֶתְבּוֹנֵן עַל־בְּתוּלָה]?" Although the covenant mentioned in this verse is clearly figurative and does not refer to the marriage covenant itself, the verse is revealing for the manner in which it extends the ethic of the tenth commandment (cf. Prov. 6:25). Whereas Exod. 20:17 and Deut. 5:21 prohibit coveting "your neighbour's wife [לֹא־תַחְמֹד אֵשֶׁת רֵעֶךָ]," Job 31:1 may avoid this restriction by its use of בְּתוּלָה, which probably means "a woman of marriageable age," but in any case refers mainly, though perhaps not exclusively, to unmarried women.[206]

Some scholars have suggested, however, that בְּתוּלָה may be a reference to "Virgin 'Anath [btlt 'nt]," or "the Queen of Heaven."[207] On this view Job 31:1 constitutes a disavowal of idolatry, a theme which is resumed in Job 31:26f. The main impetus for this view is the conviction that only idolatry would be of sufficient gravity to explain why this offence was chosen to head

---

[204] Cf. J.G. Baldwin, *1 and 2 Samuel* (1988) 60.

R.P. Gordon identifies these women as "female ancillary staff who performed menial duties in the pre-monarchical sanctuaries" (*1 & 2 Samuel*, 83). Though Gordon is cautious to avoid a more precise job description, it is unwarranted to assume that this service was necessarily "menial" given this use of צבא elsewhere.

[205] So, e.g., H.W. Hertzberg, *1 & 2 Samuel*, 36; and R.A. Cole, *Exodus*, 236.

[206] Cf. G.J. Wenham, "*bᵉtûlāh* 'A Girl of Marriageable Age'" (1972) 326-48. Wenham suggests that in the case of Job 31:1 the reference of בְּתוּלָה is to betrothed or married women exclusively (*op. cit.*, 345f.).

Apart from the uncertain case of Job 31:1, it is remarkable that among its fifty biblical occurrences the only verse where בְּתוּלָה clearly refers to a married woman is Joel 1:8. And here it is possible that בְּתוּלָה is employed in order to refer to a woman whose marriage was not yet consummated. Cf., e.g., H.W. Wolff, *Joel and Amos*, 29-31; and D. Stuart, *Hosea - Jonah*, 243. Cf. also Deut. 20:7.

[207] Cf., e.g., M.H. Pope, *Job* (1973) 228; A.R. Ceresko, *Job 29-31 in the Light of Northwest Semitic* (1980) 107-108; M. Tsevat, *et al.*, "בְּתוּלָה *bᵉthûlāh*," *TDOT* II, 341f.; and E.B. Smick, "Job" (1988) 992f.

Against this interpretation, cf. M.H. Pope, *Job*, 228f. (Pope, however, prefers A.S. Peake's unwarranted emendation of the text from בְּתוּלָה to נְבָלָה); S.R. Driver and G.B. Gray, *A Critical and Exegetical Commentary on the Book of Job* (2nd ed., 1950) 262f.; F.I. Andersen, *Job* (1976) 240f.; and most recently, N.C. Habel, *The Book of Job* (1985) 431f.

Though not interacting with this suggestion, in support of the traditional interpretation, cf. further É. Dhorme, *A Commentary on the Book of Job* (1984) 450; R. Gordis, *The Book of Job* (1978) 344f. and 542f.; and J.E. Hartley, *The Book of Job* (1988) 409.

the list of the disavowed sins which comprise chapter 31.[208]   Against this
proposal, however, is the fact that while "Virgin 'Anath [*btlt 'nt*]" is a well-
known epithet from the Ugaritic texts, nowhere is 'Anath referred to simply
as the "virgin [*btlt* = בְּתוּלָה]," as is required for Job 31:1. Furthermore, as
N.C. Habel notes, "in the pre-Israelite world of the patriarchal heroes where
the poet has located Job, a direct allusion to 'Anath as the rival of Yahweh
would be anachronistic."[209]

M. Tsevat argues against the traditional reference to lust in vs. 1,
claiming that this interpretation renders vss. 9-12 superfluous.[210] The precise
sin disavowed in vss. 9-12, however, involves overt adultery with a
neighbour's wife, not merely lust for a normally unmarried בְּתוּלָה.[211]

On the other hand, the more obvious reference to sexual purity may
not be so out of place in Job 31:1.[212] For example, there is a possible *inclusio*
between Job's eyes in vs. 1 and God's all-seeing vision in vs. 4.
Furthermore, from the wider context it is apparent that Job recognizes that
God's righteous judgment takes into account not merely overt acts, such as
adultery, but also the thoughts and intentions of the heart, such as the posited
lust in vs. 1. Compare, for example, Job's disavowal that he has rejoiced at
his wealth (vs. 25) or gloated at the ruin of his enemies (vs. 29 — cf. Prov.
24:17). Indeed, as R. Gordis has argued, the stress throughout Job 31 is on
the fact that Job has adhered to a standard of piety that goes well beyond such
palpable crimes as murder, theft, etc.[213] Here are almost exclusively
clandestine sins of the spirit representing a level of piety consistent with the
earlier reference in Job 1:5, where Job offered burnt offerings for his sons in
case they had "cursed God in their hearts."[214]

Finally, Sir. 9:5 offers a supportive parallel for the traditional
interpretation of Job 31:1, from which it may well derive: "At a virgin do not
look [בבתולה אל תתבונן], lest you be trapped into sin with her."[215] M. Tsevat
is unimpressed with this comparison, arguing that "it may be foolish to look

---

[208] Cf. E.B. Smick, "Job," 992.

[209] N. Habel, *The Book of Job*, 431f.

[210] M. Tsevat, *et al.*, "בְּתוּלָה *bethûlāh*," *TDOT* II, 341.

[211] Similarly, R. Gordis observes, "the sharp distinction in Semitic and biblical law
between the status of a virgin and that of a married woman rules out the combining of these
two themes on substantive grounds as well" (*The Book of Job*, 345).

[212] Cf., e.g., the *NAB*, which rearranges Job 31, placing vs. 1 with vs. 9. In defence of
this rearrangement of the text, cf. P.W. Skehan, *Studies in Israelite Poetry and Wisdom*
(1971) 116-120. As noted by M.H. Pope, however, this proposal founders on the self-
evident need for an introduction to vss. 2-4 (*Job*, 228). Moreover, as argued by E.B. Smick,
the present arrangement offers a semantic *inclusio* by which Job's eyes in vs. 1 find a
parallel in the mention of God's vision in vs. 4 ("Job," 992). Finally, as noted by R. Gordis,
the proposed rearrangement destroys the present double heptad structure of fourteen
possible offences (*The Book of Job*, 345).

[213] *The Book of Job*, 344f. and 542f. Only adultery appears as an exception, but it is
included because it too, in general, is carried on secretively. Cf. also J.E. Hartley, *The Book
of Job*, 407.

[214] So noted by N.C. Habel, *The Book of Job*, 431.

[215] As rendered by M. Pope from the Hebrew text of the Cairo Genizah (*Job*, 228).
On Sirach's dependency on Job 31:1, cf. R. Gordis, *The Book of Job*, 344; and P.W.
Skehan and A.A. Di Lella, *The Wisdom of Ben Sira* (1987) 219.

upon an (unmarried) maiden (this is the meaning of the quotation of this passage in Sir. 9:5, an item in a catalogue of women), but it is not sinful (Job 31:3)."[216] Tsevat's objection fails to be persuasive, however, because it assumes precisely what it needs to prove. Accordingly, the traditional view of Job 31:1 as a prohibition against lust is still to be preferred.

3.7.3 Hosea 4:14

Although D. Patrick considers that elsewhere in the Old Testament there obtains a "double standard," where a husband was under no obligation to sexual fidelity, he notes that "the prophet Hosea goes so far as to remove the double standard in an ironic twist: 'I will not punish your daughters when they play the harlot [לֹא־אֶפְקוֹד עַל־בְּנוֹתֵיכֶם כִּי תִזְנֶינָה], nor your brides when they commit adultery; for the men themselves go aside with harlots, and sacrifice with cult prostitutes, and a people without understanding shall come to ruin' (4:14).[217] The fathers and husbands would like God to punish their wayward women, but God will not because it is they who corrupt them." In a similar manner, D. Kidner contrasts Judah's hypocritical readiness to execute Tamar with Hos. 4:14 and states of the Hosea text that it "is in fact a landmark in moral history by its refusal to treat a man's sexual sins more leniently than a woman's."[218]

Some scholars, however, have questioned this interpretation of Hos. 4:14.[219] F.I. Andersen and D.N. Freedman, for example, consider it "inconceivable that the women could be exculpated, even if the men were primarily responsible."[220] As a result, they propose interpreting 14a either as a rhetorical question, "shall I not punish...?" (restoring an initial interrogative ה, lost by haplography), or as a positive assertion, "I will surely punish" (with the לֹא probably to be understood as an asseverative particle or perhaps to be corrected to the asseverative ל, with the א having arisen by dittography). If 14a is a rhetorical question, Hos. 4:14 still opposes a double standard by insisting on the punishment of the guilty men (14b) as well as the guilty women (14a).[221] On the asseverative view of Andersen and Freedman, however, vss. 13a-14a form a parenthesis, after which vs. 14b resumes the discourse about the priests which ended in vs. 12b. With vss. 13a-14a thus isolated, it is no longer so clear that the punishment of the guilty male priests

---

[216] M. Tsevat, et al., "בְּתוּלָה bethûlāh," TDOT II, 341.

[217] Old Testament Law, 55, quoting from the RSV.

[218] Love to the Loveless. The Message of Hosea (1981) 53.

[219] In support of the traditional rendering, cf., e.g., W.R. Harper, A Critical and Exegetical Commentary on Amos and Hosea (1905) 261; J.L. Mays, Hosea (1969) 75f.; and H.W. Wolff, Hosea (1974) 87-89.

[220] F.I. Andersen and D.N. Freedman, Hosea, 369. D. Stuart similarly wonders, "How would God punish 'land' and 'people' yet exempt the women?" (Hosea - Jonah, 83).

[221] Cf. D. Stuart, Hosea - Jonah, 71, 83f. On Stuart's view, most of the occurrences of זנה in Hosea are metaphoric, particularly when referring to Gomer. Against this, cf., e.g., I.H. Eybers, who objects that had Gomer been guilty only of idolatry, it is doubtful that the people, who were enmeshed in the same idolatry, would have noticed or comprehended this "prophetic sign" ("The Matrimonial Life of Hosea," 11-34, esp. 15). Stuart, however, acknowledges that in the present verse זנה is clearly literal.

in vs. 14b corresponds to the punishment threatened against the meretricious women.

Andersen and Freedman's proposal is problematic: it obliterates the frequently observed parallelism between vss. 13 and 14.[222] Furthermore, there is little evidence for the posited parenthetical character of vss. 13a-14a, and the proposal to emend לֹא in vs. 14a lacks textual support (LXX: καὶ οὐ μὴ ἐπισκέψωμαι; Vulgate: *non visitabo*; Targum: לָא אַסְעַר).

Finally, it should be noted that an allusion in vs. 14 to the disputed practice of *ius primae noctis* is possible, but unnecessary.[223] It is perhaps more likely that the prophet is condemning a widespread and quite general state of sexual immorality, fostered, to be sure, by the acceptance of cult prostitutes [הַקְּדֵשׁוֹת][224] and the people's defection from an orthodox faith in Yahweh.

3.7.4 *Proverbs 5:15-23*

Although Prov. 6:24-35 "admonishes the married man not to have intercourse with a harlot,"[225] since the harlot is depicted as married, it is possible, though perhaps doubtful, that this text is merely concerned to prohibit adultery against her cuckolded husband or to warn about the dire consequences of being caught.

On the other hand, Prov. 5:15-23 is indisputably concerned to promote a husband's fidelity to his own wife regardless of the married state of any potential lovers.[226] In a manner which resembles the awareness of God's omniscience in Job 31, Prov. 5:21 warns, "For a man's ways are before the eyes of Yahweh, and he watches all his paths." As a consequence, although a man's misdeeds may be beyond the pale of criminal sanction, "The iniquities of the wicked ensnare him, and he is caught in the toils of his sin. He dies for lack of discipline, and because of his great folly he is lost" (Prov. 5:22f.). In view of such a warning, the preceding verses require what criminal law cannot, namely an exclusive and absorbing love and fidelity from a husband for his wife.

"Drink water from your own cistern, flowing water from your own well [שְׁתֵה־מַיִם מִבּוֹרֶךָ וְנֹזְלִים מִתּוֹךְ בְּאֵרֶךָ]" (Prov. 5:15). With C.H. Toy, it is evident that the imagery of drinking from a cistern or well is intended to convey the ideas of sensual enjoyment, contentment, and satisfaction (cf. Isa.

---

[222] Cf. W.R. Harper, *Amos and Hosea*, 261.

[223] H.W. Wolff strongly favours such a reference (*Hosea*, 9f., 14 ["The Sex Cult"], 15f. and 86f.). J.L. Mays, however, is undecided (*Hosea*, 74f.).

Cf. also W.G. Lambert, "Morals in Ancient Mesopotamia" (1957-8) 195f.

[224] Perhaps of the sort envisioned by K. van der Toorn, "Female Prostitution in Payment of Vows in Ancient Israel," though cf. D. Stuart, *Hosea - Jonah*, 83f.

[225] So F. Hauck and S. Schulz, "πόρνη κτλ.," *TDNT*, VI, 586.

[226] Evident already in the Targum, which identifies the wife as the law in vs. 19, the attempt to transpose this text into an allegory for wisdom, etc. appears doubtful. So, e.g., C.H. Toy, *Proverbs*, 111. Even if such an allegory is intended, however, the implications for literal marriage must still hold true or the force of the allegory would be lost.

36:16) without any necessary allusion to procreation.[227] The text "introduces the wife not as child-bearer, but as source of pleasure."[228] As noted by R.B.Y. Scott, the fact that cisterns and wells were typically privately owned gives point to this metaphor for confining the satisfaction of sexual desire to one's own wife.[229] So that the lesson is not missed, W. McKane rather prosaically summarizes the verse, "Have sexual intercourse only with your wife."[230]

Assuming the presence of an unmarked interrogative in vs. 16, it appears that Prov. 5:16f. offers a figure for sexual infidelity.[231] The main interpretative question is whether the infidelity in view is that of the husband or of the wife: "Should your springs be scattered abroad, streams of water in the streets? [יָפוּצוּ מַעְיְנֹתֶיךָ חוּצָה בָּרְחֹבוֹת פַּלְגֵי־מָיִם] Let them be for yourself alone, and not for strangers with you [יִהְיוּ־לְךָ לְבַדֶּךָ וְאֵין לְזָרִים אִתָּךְ]" (Prov. 5:16f.). R.B.Y. Scott and others suggest that "your springs be scattered abroad" refers to a wife's promiscuity, which may be a response to her husband's infidelity. An advantage of this view is the manner in which it allows for a consistency of water references in vss. 15-18, allowing "cistern [בּוֹר]," "well [בְּאֵר]," "springs [מַעְיָנֹת]," "streams of water [פַּלְגֵי־מָיִם]," and "fountain [מָקוֹר]" all to refer to the wife. Retaliatory promiscuity, however, seems too modern a notion for such an ancient text.

Alternatively, it is possible that vss. 16f. refer to the husband's infidelity, whether "springs" and "streams of water" are intended as references to illicit sources of enjoyment (harlots and adulteresses — since they are "scattered abroad" or "in the streets")[232] or, as seems more likely based on vs. 17, to semen.[233] Favouring this line of interpretation, it is

---

[227] C.H. Toy, *Proverbs*, 112f.

Obviously, Proverbs 5 does not stand alone in the OT in its affirmation of erotic pleasure within marriage. Cf., e.g., Deut. 24:5; Cant. 4:1-16, and *passim*; and Eccl. 9:9. Cf. W.C. Kaiser Jr., *Toward Old Testament Ethics*, 192-195; and W. Neuer, *Man and Woman in Christian Perspective* (1990) 81-83. Naturally, the awareness of this aspect of marriage need not denigrate other less sensual aspects. Cf., e.g., Gen. 2:18, 24; Prov. 31:10-31; and Sir. 26:1-14; 36:23 [28].

[228] C.H. Toy, *Proverbs*, 113.

[229] R.B.Y. Scott, *Proverbs; Ecclesiastes*, 58.

Cf. Cant. 4:12, 15, for the underlying image of a fountain or well representing a woman. C.V. Camp argues that Prov. 5:15 alludes to Cant. 4:15 as a way to explain the incongruous juxtaposition of "flowing water [נֹזְלִים]" with a "well [בְּאֵר]" (*Wisdom and the Feminine in the Book of Proverbs*, 205f.).

[230] *Proverbs*, 318.

[231] An alternative interpretation of the MT is offered by the AV (and Vulgate) which takes vs. 16 as jussive: "Let thy fountains...," perhaps implying "from such a marriage, blessing streams out in the persons and influences of a true family" (so D. Kidner, *Proverbs*, 70).

Alternatively, as noted by W. McKane, if μὴ is read with the LXX[B], vs. 16 may be rendered either "lest [פֶּן] your springs be dispersed outside..." (with B. Gemser, *Sprüche Salomos* [1963]) or "Let not [אַל] your springs be dispersed outside..." (*Proverbs*, 318). Cf. *BHS*.

[232] So C.H. Toy, *Proverbs*, 113.

[233] Cf. G. Boström, *Proverbiastudien: die Weisheit und das fremde Weib in Sprüche 1-9* (1935); and W. McKane, *Proverbs*, 319.

notable that "springs [מַעְיְנֹת]" and "streams of water [פַּלְגֵי־מָיִם]" are both plural, while the images for the wife in vs. 15, "cistern [בּוֹר]" and "well [בְּאֵר]," are singular.[234] Accordingly, vs. 20 offers the literal meaning of vss. 16f., just as vss. 18f. give the literal meaning of vs. 15.[235] Compare also Sir. 26:19-21.

Turning to vs. 18, there is dispute about the reference of "your fountain [מְקוֹרְךָ]" in vs. 18a: "Let your fountain be blessed... [בָרוּךְ יְהִי־מְקוֹרְךָ]."[236] Most scholars appear to understand it as a reference to the wife comparable to the other water sources in vs. 15, "cistern [בּוֹר]" and "well [בְּאֵר]." If, however, "springs [מַעְיְנֹת]" and "streams of water [פַּלְגֵי־מָיִם]" in vs. 16 refer to the husband's semen and consequently vss. 16f. to his infidelity, then it is possible that "your fountain" continues this male imagery with a reference to the husband's own generative powers as the source of semen.[237]

Regardless of how vs. 18a is to be interpreted, vss. 18b and 19 are clear enough: "and rejoice in the wife of your youth [וּשְׂמַח מֵאֵשֶׁת נְעוּרֶךָ],[238] a lovely hind, a graceful doe [אַיֶּלֶת אֲהָבִים וְיַעֲלַת־חֵן]. Let her breasts fill you at all times with delight [דַּדֶּיהָ יְרַוֻּךָ בְכָל־עֵת],[239] be infatuated always with her

---

The older view of Aquila, Saadia, and Ibn Ezra, which finds a reference in vss. 16f. to descendants, has been defended more recently by A. Cohen (*Proverbs* [1946] 28), L.A. Snijders ("The Meaning of *zār* in the Old Testament: an exegetical study" [1954] 93), and H. Ringgren (*Sprüche/Prediger* [1962]). On this approach vs. 16 may be either interrogative, "Should your springs be dispersed outside?," or declarative, "(and so) your springs will be dispersed outside." Although the latter approach (Snijders and Ringgren) has the advantage that it does not require an unmarked interrogative, W. McKane considers it unlikely, noting that water from a cistern running to waste in the streets is normally to be avoided — a thought which is clearly inapplicable to descendants (*Proverbs*, 318).

[234] This is also the case with "fountain [מָקוֹר]" in vs. 18, although it is uncertain whether this refers to the wife or to the husband. Cf. below.

[235] Cf. C.H. Toy, *Proverbs*, 113.

[236] R.B.Y. Scott offers "be grateful for" as a paraphrase for "let it be blessed (by you)" (*Proverbs*, 58). This suggestion is rejected by C.V. Camp, *Wisdom and the Feminine in the Book of Proverbs*, 204 and 317 n. 15.

[237] Yet a third option has been suggested by C.V. Camp, that "your fountain" refers to "the relationship of the two," i.e., the man and the woman (*Wisdom and the Feminine in the Book of Proverbs*, 203f.) This certainly includes an allusion to their sexual pleasure (so Gemser and Toy) and may also imply offspring (McKane), but not necessarily.

[238] For "the wife of your youth," cf. Prov. 2:17; Isa. 54:6; and especially Mal. 2:14f. Cf. W.H. Wolff, *Joel and Amos*, 30.

[239] The RSV repointing of "her breasts [דַּדֶּיהָ]" as "her affection [דֹּדֶיהָ]," with the LXXℵ and LXXᴼ, ἡ δὲ φιλία, is possible (as it parallels "love" and is used with the same verb in 7:18) but unnecessary. As noted by D. Kidner, "the traditional rendering 'breasts' makes a rather more telling contrast with vs. 20 [which mentions the "bosom" of the adventuress], and should probably be retained" (*Proverbs*, 71). Cf. also C.H. Toy, *Proverbs*, 115. G.A. Yee notes a chiasm in vss. 19 and 20, with the A members having "her breasts [דַּדֶּיהָ]" // "the bosom of an adventuress [חֵק נָכְרִיָּה]" and the B members repeating תִּשְׁגֶּה ("'I Have Perfumed My Bed With Myrrh': The Foreign Woman ('*iššâ zārâ*) in Proverbs 1-9," 60). Cf. also Ezek. 23:3, where the fondling of breasts is used in a description of harlotry: "there their breasts [שְׁדֵיהֶן] were pressed and their virgin bosoms [דַּדֵּי בְּתוּלֵיהֶן] handled."

love [בְּאַהֲבָתָהּ תִּשְׁגֶּה תָמִיד]."[240] In the view of the author, such intoxicating[241] love for one's wife renders senseless any extramarital relations: "Why should you be infatuated, my son, with a loose woman and embrace the bosom of an adventuress [וְלָמָּה תִשְׁגֶּה בְנִי בְזָרָה וּתְחַבֵּק חֵק נָכְרִיָּה]?" (Prov. 5:20). Although it is an allegorical text, perhaps one may compare Prov. 4:5b-9 for its implication of a husband's devotion to his wife: "Get wisdom; get insight. Do not forsake her, and she will keep you; love her, and she will guard you.... Prize her highly, and she will exalt you; she will honour you if you embrace her. She will place on your head a fair garland; she will bestow on you a beautiful crown."[242]

Whatever other conclusions may be warranted from this remarkable paean to marital love, it is clear that the demand for a husband's sexual fidelity was certainly not too romantic an ideal for the ancient world to entertain.

4. SUMMARY

In this concluding chapter we began by considering various indirect evidences which would be not only consistent with, but also necessary for a view of marriage as a sanction-sealed commitment between a husband and his wife. In particular, it was noted that Yahweh is identified as a "witness between" husbands and wives and that marital offences are, in fact, identified as perfidy (מעל), a term frequently used of oath violation, and infidelity (בגד) against one's spouse.

Second, we examined the other texts within the Old Testament which like Mal. 2:14 explicitly or implicitly identify marriage as a covenant. The implication of the marriage metaphor, especially as articulated in Hos. 2:18-22 [ET 16-20], and the explicit evidences of Prov. 2:17, Ezek. 16:8, 59, 60, 62, and 1 Samuel 18-20 all proved to be convincing in their identification of marriage as a covenant.

Finally, we considered the claimed indifference of the Old Testament to a husband's sexual fidelity, an indifference which has been thought to

---

[240] A number of scholars propose to relocate Prov. 6:22 after 5:19. In support, cf. P.W. Skehan, *Studies in Israelite Poetry and Wisdom*, 1-8; R.B.Y. Scott, *Proverbs*, 58; and R.E. Murphy, *Wisdom Literature: Job, Proverbs, Ruth, Canticles, Ecclesiastes, Esther*, 59.

[241] שגה, which normally means "to stagger, go astray, to be lost," as in vs. 23, can at times be used of the effects of intoxication (as in 20:1 and Isa. 28:7). On this view, the verb may be rendered "be intoxicated" or "swoon" in vss. 19 and 20. Cf. A. Cohen, *Proverbs*, 29; R.B.Y. Scott, *Proverbs*, 55; and D. Kidner, *Proverbs*, 71. Alternatively, with W. McKane, שגה may have the meaning "wrapped in" (*Proverbs*, 313, 319).

[242] W. McKane argues that the scene is not of marriage but of a wealthy patroness embracing her protégé since "a bride does not protect her lover, she does not exalt him (tᵉrōmᵉmekkā), in the sense of securing his preferment, nor does she get honour for her lover (tᵉkabbēdᵉkā) when he embraces her" (*Proverbs*, 305f.). Cf. C.V. Camp, who rejects McKane's suggestion and defends the traditional view (*Wisdom and the Feminine in the Book of Proverbs*, 93-95). Cf. H. Ringgren, who suggests that vs. 9 includes a reference to wedding customs (*Word and Wisdom* [1947] 106). Cf. also G. Boström, *Proverbiastudien*, 162.

contradict the identification of marriage as a covenant, particularly if this covenant was ratified by the kind of declaration formula found in Gen. 2:23 (cf. also 2:24) and if sexual union was recognized as its inherently mutual oath-sign. After surveying the alleged examples of this indifference, it was determined that there are, in fact, no texts which condone a husband's sexual infidelity. On the contrary, it was demonstrated that a number of texts, including Job 31:1; Hos. 4:14; and particularly Prov. 5:15-23, make clear that, whether or not there was any *legal* obligation, there definitely was a *moral* obligation for exclusive sexual fidelity on the part of husbands.[243] This is consonant with the supposition that the Old Testament viewed marriage as a divinely protected covenant between husband and wife.

---

[243] Cf. also Gen. 2:24.

SUMMARY AND CONCLUSIONS

The purpose of the present study in Old Testament canonical ethics (Introduction §3.2) has been to explore Malachi's teaching concerning marriage as a covenant [בְּרִית] in Mal. 2:10-16, especially in the light of a growing number, if not the majority, of recent interpretations which deny this identification. Although other scholars have continued to support the traditional interpretation of marriage as a covenant, in general this conclusion has been upheld without sufficient attention to these recent challenges and, as noted in the Introduction, has yielded confusing and often contradictory results. Benefited by a vast scholarly literature devoted to the exploration of covenant concepts over the past half-century and further helped by a number of important recent studies on marriage elsewhere in the ancient Near East, this thesis has come to a variety of conclusions about the application of covenant concepts to marriage in the Old Testament. Only the most important of these will be summarized here.

We began our study by examining the historical and canonical context of Malachi and its literary structure in order to establish a proper interpretative framework within which to understand Mal. 2:10-16 (Chapter 1). After enumerating five principal arguments (Chapter 2, §1) in support of the traditional interpretation of Mal. 2:14, where Malachi identifies marriage as a "covenant [בְּרִית]," we attempted to answer the two main objections to this view arising from considerations internal to the book of Malachi:

1) Against those who argue that Malachi's reference to marriage is figurative, based especially on the sustained interests in cultic and priestly matters throughout the rest of his book (e.g., C.C. Torrey, I.G. Matthews, F.F. Hvidberg, A. Isaksson, J. Milgrom, G.S. Ogden, and others), it was argued that there is no reason to deem inappropriate a concern with literal marital offences in Mal. 2:10-16 in view of the example of Ezra, and to a lesser degree of Nehemiah, where these same concerns coexist. Moreover, consistent with his emphasis elsewhere, Malachi stresses the detrimental effects of these offences on the cult (they profane the sanctuary of Yahweh [2:11], they provoke Yahweh's rejection of their offerings [2:13], etc.). In doing so, he employs vocabulary and concepts similar to those found in Nehemiah's declamation regarding interfaith marriage (cf., e.g., Neh. 13:29). A previously undetected concentric literary structure for the book of Malachi also appears to favour a reference to literal marital offences in the 3rd disputation (2:10-16), since this section is balanced by the 4th disputation

(2:17-3:5 [or 3:6]), which offers a corroborating parallel in its treatment of literal marital and other ethical offences (Chapter 2).

2) Several arguments were advanced against those scholars (K. Marti, W. Nowack, E. Sellin, C. Locher, A.S. van der Woude, and others) who accept a reference to literal marriage in Malachi 2, but who hold that the covenant mentioned in 2:14, "your wife by covenant [וְאֵשֶׁת בְּרִיתֶךָ]," refers not to marriage, but to Yahweh's covenant with Israel as in Mal. 2:10 (thereby identifying the wife as a fellow-Jew). Perhaps the most significant of these arguments was the observation that this interpretation overlooks the opposing evidence of the four nominal syntagms of בְּרִית attested in Biblical Hebrew which parallel the disputed expression וְאֵשֶׁת בְּרִיתֶךָ, lit. "the wife of your covenant," including אַנְשֵׁי בְרִיתֶךָ, "the men of your covenant," in Obad. 7. In each case the mentioned covenant exists between the person(s) indicated by the *nomen regens* and the person referred to by the pronominal suffix or additional construct, exactly as is being argued for "your wife by covenant [וְאֵשֶׁת בְּרִיתֶךָ]" in Mal. 2:14 (Chapter 2).

Having established the plausibility that Mal. 2:14 identifies literal marriage as a "covenant [בְּרִית]" based on the grammar and context of the verse, we went on to consider in Chapters 3 and 4 two further difficulties for this view which arise from the wider context of this verse.

1) A reference to literal marriage in Malachi 2 has been challenged based on the contradiction between the unqualified condemnation of divorce in Mal. 2:16, as this verse is often interpreted, and its apparent toleration in Deuteronomy 24 (A. Isaksson and A.S. van der Woude). A closer examination of these texts, however, suggests that the perspectives of Malachi and Deuteronomy may not be so incompatible. Taking the initial כִּי clause as an unmarked conditional (favoured both by its fronted position and by the versional evidence) and identifying שַׁלַּח as an infinitive absolute, apparently unnoticed by others, we maintain the MT of Mal. 2:16 as the *lectio difficilior* and render it: "If one hates and divorces, says Yahweh, God of Israel, he covers his garment with violence, says Yahweh of hosts...."

Accordingly, while Malachi nowhere implies that such divorces were illegal, he does condemn divorce based on aversion [שׂנא] as ethically reprehensible and as an instance of infidelity [בגד], or covenant breaking (cf. 2:14), susceptible to divine judgment: "Therefore, take heed to yourselves!" Such a perspective offers significant support for the identification of literal marriage as a covenant in 2:14. Moreover, this moral assessment of divorce based on aversion is not in conflict with Deut. 24:1-4 since, with R. Westbrook, it appears likely that Deuteronomy presupposes a similar negative appraisal of divorce when based on aversion (i.e., the pairing in vs. 3 of the second case of divorce, which was motivated by hatred [שׂנא], with the case of the death of the husband may imply a favourable financial settlement for the offended wife) (Chapter 3).

2) Arising from the wider context of Mal. 2:14, a second objection to a reference to literal marriage in this verse has been raised by C.C. Torrey and A. Isaksson. These scholars argue that a reference to literal marriage in Mal. 2:10-16 is contradicted by the assumption that polygyny would have been freely tolerated by Malachi and his contemporaries. In response, it was argued that the traditional interpretation of Mal. 2:10-16, which assumes a causal relationship between the offences of mixed marriage and divorce (Jewish men had divorced their Jewish wives in order to marry Gentile women), is unnecessary. The text nowhere explicitly relates these two offences in a causal manner, and it may be preferable to explain their juxtaposition by another means. Specifically, it was suggested that Malachi intended the chiastic parallelism between 2:10-12 and 2:13-16 to underscore the similarity of the infidelity [בגד] against "the covenant of our fathers," which results from the sin of mixed marriage, to the infidelity [בגד] against a marriage covenant, which results from divorce based on mere aversion. In any case, it was argued that although polygyny was never illegal, monogamy is seen as the marital ideal in many texts (e.g., Gen. 4:19ff., Lev. 18:18, and Deut. 17:17) and that actual marital practice would have been monogamous with few, if any, exceptions especially in the post-exilic period (Chapter 4).

After thus defending the coherence of Malachi's theory of marriage and his identification of marriage as a "covenant [בְּרִית]" in 2:14 in terms of both its immediate and its wider context, we attempted to answer three more fundamental objections to this interpretation: 1) Malachi's identification of marriage as a covenant would be unprecedented and anachronistic in the post-exilic period (A. Isaksson and others); 2) marriage cannot be a covenant because it lacks a ratifying oath (J. Milgrom and M. Greenberg); and 3) marriage cannot be a covenant because of the double standard of the Old Testament, which demands only a wife's exclusive sexual loyalty (A. Isaksson, J. Milgrom, and P.F. Palmer).

1) In two ways we sought to answer the claim that the identification of literal marriage as a "covenant [בְּרִית]" in Mal. 2:14 would be unprecedented and anachronistic in the post-exilic period. First, we argued that from Malachi's own perspective his view of marriage was not unprecedented, but was consciously derived from, or at least supported by, the paradigmatic marriage of Adam and Eve (Gen. 2:24), to which he makes allusion in Mal. 2:15. While acknowledging the problematic character of this verse, it was argued that the MT is best maintained and rendered, "Did He not make [you/them] one [אֶחָד], with a remnant of the spirit belonging to it? And what was the One seeking? A godly seed! Therefore watch out for your lives and do not act faithlessly against the wife of your youth."

We stressed the grammatical and textual advantages of this interpretation (with its assumption of an unmarked rhetorical interrogative) and noted that an important confirmation for this rendering comes from the concluding admonition in 2:15b (cf. also 2:16b). Malachi warns any would-be unfaithful spouse that divorce constitutes an offence against one's own life. Only when 2:15a is rendered as suggested above ("Did He not make [you/them] one...?") is this equivalence between concern for one's life and fidelity to one's spouse explained: it is the result of the profound communion of life which God effects between a man and his wife as established in Gen. 2:24. Helping to confirm Malachi's indebtedness to Gen. 2:23f. is the fact that Genesis 2 invites an identification of the marriage of Adam and Eve as a covenant, especially based on the *verba solemnia* appearing in 2:23 (cf. also Chapter 5, §2.3 and §3.2.3). Notable also is the remarkable emphasis throughout Mal. 2:14-16 on the primacy of a husband's obligation of fidelity toward his wife, a viewpoint which is almost unparalleled apart from these two texts (Chapter 5).

We deferred to the last chapter a more encompassing answer to the objection that Malachi's view of marriage, if taken literally, would be unprecedented. There we argued that an explicit identification of marriage as a "covenant [בְּרִית]" is to be found also in Prov. 2:17 and Ezekiel 16. Furthermore, the same identification of marriage as a "covenant [בְּרִית]" appears to be implied in the marriage metaphor in Hos. 2:18-22 [ET: 16-20] as well as in 1 Samuel 18-20 (Chapter 8).

2) The second fundamental objection to the identification of marriage as a "covenant [בְּרִית]" in the Old Testament is based on the assumption that a ratifying oath is indispensable for the existence of a בְּרִית. According to J. Milgrom and M. Greenberg, marriage lacks such an oath and hence cannot be identified as a בְּרִית.

To respond to this objection it was necessary first to clarify the Old Testament view of "covenant [בְּרִית]." It was argued that a covenant is "an elected, as opposed to natural, relationship of obligation established under divine sanction." In terms of this understanding, it was agreed with Milgrom and Greenberg that a ratifying oath is the *sine qua non* of covenant because it invokes the deity to act against any subsequent breach of the covenant. Against Milgrom and Greenberg, however, it was emphasized that such oaths are not all overtly self-maledictory, nor are they exclusively verbal. In particular, many oaths function by a solemn positive declaration (i.e., *verba solemnia*) or symbolic depiction of the commitment being undertaken (such as the "oath-signs" of a shared meal or handshake) (Chapter 6).

In the case of marriage, the fact that *verba solemnia* did indeed function as the customary covenant-ratifying oath was demonstrated based on a broad range of extrabiblical evidence (e.g., MAL A §41, the *eṭlu* tablet, the *ardat lilî* tablet, the documentary marriage formulae from Elephantine and Murabba'at, and the implication of the corresponding divorce formulae), as well as biblical evidence (i.e., Gen. 2:23; Hos. 2:4, 17-19 [ET 2:2, 15-17]; Prov. 7:4f.; and Tob. 7:12). In the course of this search for an oath in the formation of marriage, it was necessary to oppose the tendency to confuse marriage as a "status," similar to adoption (pointed out by R. Westbrook), with the marriage contract, which whether oral or written was concerned with a variety of economic and other matters ancillary to the marriage itself (so also A.J. Skaist — see Chapter 6, §2.1 and Chapter 7, §2.1.1). With this distinction in mind, it appears that any rejection of the covenantal nature of marriage in the Old Testament (e.g., A. Isaksson), no less than any defence or elucidation of that covenantal nature (e.g., B. Glazier-McDonald), is methodologically flawed if it proceeds by way of a study of the extant marriage documents.

Furthermore, it was deemed likely that sexual union was understood as a complementary covenant-ratifying oath-sign, at least by some biblical authors. In support of this identification of the significance of sexual union, it was argued (contradicting the theory of "marriage by purchase") that sexual union is the indispensable means for the consummation of marriage both in the Old Testament and elsewhere in the ancient Near East. Moreover, it was recalled how oath-signs, such as a shared meal or handshake, often function by offering a solemn depiction of the covenant commitment to unity. With respect to sexual union, clearly this act is ideally suited to depict the "one flesh" reality which is definitional of marriage in Gen. 2:24, and its use as an oath-sign finds support in the use of the genitalia in other instances of oath taking (i.e., circumcision and placing one's hands under another's "thigh"). Finally, we examined several texts, especially Hos. 2:22 [ET 20] and 13:5, which associate the two relational senses of ידע, "know," namely covenantal and sexual, by means of double entendre. In an extended marriage metaphor Hos. 2:22 [ET 20] uses ידע, "know," to describe the point at which Israel will "acknowledge" Yahweh as her covenant partner. This fact appears to confirm our hypothesis that sexual union, as a marriage covenant-ratifying act, is the decisive means by which an individual "acknowledges" his or her spouse as covenant partner (Chapter 7).

3) Finally, we considered a third fundamental objection, namely that marriage cannot be a covenant because of the double standard of the Old Testament, which demands a wife's exclusive sexual loyalty while appearing to be indifferent to a husband's extramarital sexual behaviour (A. Isaksson, J. Milgrom, and P.F. Palmer). After examination of the alleged examples of this indifference, it was determined that there are, in fact, no texts which condone a husband's sexual infidelity. On the contrary, several texts including Job 31:1; Hos. 4:14; and especially Prov. 5:15-23 make clear that whether or not there was a *legal* obligation, there was definitely a *moral* obligation for exclusive sexual fidelity on the part of a husband. This comports with the view of this study that the Old Testament considered marriage as a divinely protected covenant between husband and wife.

BIBLIOGRAPHY

מקראות גדולות (Jerusalem: J. Weinfeld & Co., n.d.)
Aalders, G. Ch., *Obadja en Jona*, COT (Kampen: J.H. Kok, 1958)
Aberbach, M. and B. Grossfeld, *Targum Onkelos to Genesis: A Critical Analysis together with an English Translation of the Text* (New York: KTAV; University of Denver: Center for Judaic Studies, 1982)
Achtemeier, Elizabeth, *Nahum-Malachi*, Interpretation (Atlanta, GA: John Knox, 1986)
Ackroyd, Peter R., "The Verb Love — *'āhēb* in the David-Jonathan Narratives; A Footnote," *VT* 25 (1975) 213-214
———, "The History of Israel in the Exilic and Post-Exilic Periods," in *Tradition and Interpretation. Essays by Members of the Society for Old Testament Study*, G.W. Anderson, ed. (Oxford: Clarendon, 1979) 320-350
Aejmelaeus, Anneli, "Function and Interpretation of כי in Biblical Hebrew," *JBL* 105 (1986) 193-209
Ahlström, Gösta Werner, *Aspects of Syncretism in Israelite Religion*, E.J. Sharpe, trans. (Lund: C.W.K. Gleerup, 1963).
———, *Joel and the Temple Cult of Jerusalem*, SVT 21 (Leiden: E.J. Brill, 1971)
Albertz, M., and Claus Westermann, "רוּחַ *rûaḥ* Geist," in *THAT* 2 (München: Chr. Kaiser Verlag and Zürich: Theologischer Verlag, 1984) 726-52
Albright, William F., "The Hebrew Expression for 'Making a Covenant' in Pre-Israelite Documents," *BASOR* 121 (1951) 21-22
———, *Yahweh and the Gods of Canaan* (Garden City, NY: Doubleday, 1968)
Alden, Robert L., "Malachi," in *The Expositor's Bible Commentary*, 7, F.E. Gaebelein, ed. (Grand Rapids, MI: Zondervan, 1985) 701-725
Alexander, T. Desmond, David W. Baker, and Bruce K. Waltke, *Obadiah, Jonah, Micah. An Introduction and Commentary*, TOTC (Leicester, England and Downers Grove, IL: Inter-Varsity, 1988)
Alexander, Ralph H., "Ezekiel," in *The Expositor's Bible Commentary*, 6, F.E. Gaebelein, ed. (Grand Rapids, MI: Zondervan, 1986) 737-996
Allam, Schafik, "Ehe," *Lexicon der Ägyptologie*, Band 1, W. Helck and E. Otto, eds. (Wiesbaden: Otto Harrassowitz, 1975) 1162-81
———, *Some Pages from Everyday Life in Ancient Egypt*, Prism Archaeological Series, 1 (Guizeh, Egypt: Prism [Foreign Cultural Information Dept.], 1985)
Allen, Leslie C., *The Books of Joel, Obadiah, Jonah and Micah*, NICOT (Grand Rapids, MI: Eerdmans, 1976)
Allen, Leslie C., *Psalms 101-150*, WBC 21 (Waco, TX: Word, 1983)
Alt, A., "Ein phönikisches Staatswesen des frühen Altertums," *Forschungen und Fortschritte* 13 (1942) 207-209
Alter, Robert, *The Art of Biblical Narrative* (New York: Basic Books, 1981)
———, *Putting Together Biblical Narrative*, The Albert T. Bilgray Lecture, University of Arizona (Tucson, Arizona: The Bilgray Lectureship of Temple Emanu-El, 1988)
Altschul, David, see "מצודת דוד" included in מקראות גדולות
Althann, Robert, "Malachy 2,13-14 and UT 125,12-13," *Biblica* 58 (1977) 418-21
Al-Zeebari, Akram, *Texts in the Iraq Museum.Old Babylonian Letters, Part 1* [= *TIM* 1] (Baghdad, 1964)
Amram, David Werner, *The Jewish Law of Divorce According to Bible and Talmud with some reference to its development in Post-Talmudic Times* (Philadelphia, PA: E. Stern & Co., 1896 [reprint New York: Hermon 1968]).
Amsler, Samuel, André Lacocque and René Vuilleumier, *Aggée, Zacharie, Malachie*, Commentaire de l'Ancien Testament, XIc (Neuchatel and Paris: Delachaux & Niestlé Éditeurs, 1981)
Anbar, M., "Textes de l'époque babylonienne ancienne," *RA* 69 (1975) 109-136

Andersen, Francis I., "Israelite Kinship Terminology and Social Structure," *The Bible Translator* 20 (1969) 29-39
———, *The Hebrew Verbless Clause in the Pentateuch*, JBL Monograph Series, 14 (Nashville and New York: Abingdon, 1970)
———, *The Sentence in Biblical Hebrew*, Janua linguarum, Series practica 231 (The Hague: Mouton, 1974)
———, *Job, An Introduction and Commentary*, TOTC (London: Inter-Varsity, 1976)
Andersen, Francis I. and David N. Freedman, *Hosea. A New Translation with Introduction and Commentary*, AB 24 (Garden City, NY: Doubleday, 1980)
Andersen, Francis I., and David Noel Freedman, *Amos. A New Translation with Introduction and Commentary*, AB 24A (New York, London, Toronto, Sydney, Auckland: Doubleday, 1989)
Anderson, Arnold Albert, *The Book of Psalms*, 2 vols., NCB (London: Oliphants and Greenwood, SC: Attic, 1972)
———, "The Marriage of Ruth," *JSS* 23 (1978) 171-183
———, *2 Samuel*, WBC 11 (Dallas, TX: Word, 1989)
Anderson, Gary, *Sacrifices and Offerings in Ancient Israel. Studies in Their Social and Political Importance*, HSS 41 (Atlanta, Georgia: Scholars, 1987)
Andreasen, Niels-Erik, "Adam and Adapa: Two Anthropological Characters," *AUSS* 19 (1981) 179-194
"Art. IV - The General Assembly of 1842," *The Biblical Repertory and Princeton Review* 14:3 (1842) 472-523, at 518-520
Atkinson, David John, *To Have and to Hold: The Marriage Covenant and the Discipline of Divorce* (Grand Rapids, MI: Eerdmans, 1979)
Baab, Otto Justice, "Marriage," in *IDB* 3 (Nashville and New York: Abingdon, 1962) 278-287
"Baboon Bonding," *Discover* 11 (April, 1990) 20
Bailey, John A., "Initiation and the Primal Woman in Gilgamesh and Genesis 2-3," *JBL* 89 (1970) 137-150
Baker, David W. see A.T. Desmond, D.W. Baker, and B.K. Waltke, *Obadiah, Jonah, Micah*
Baldwin, Joyce G., *Haggai, Zechariah, Malachi: An Introduction and Commentary*, TOTC (Downers Grove, IL: Inter-Varsity, 1972)
———, "Malachi 1:11 and the Worship of the Nations in the OT," *TB* 23 (1972) 117-24
———, *1 and 2 Samuel. An Introduction and Commentary*, TOTC (Leicester, England and Downers Grove, IL: Inter-Varsity, 1988)
Baltzer, Klaus, *The Covenant Formulary in Old Testament, Jewish, and Early Christian Writings*, D.E. Green, trans. (Philadelphia, PA: Fortress, 1971 [from *Das Bundesformular*, WMANT 4, 2e Aufl., Neukirchen-Vluyn 1964; 1e Aufl. 1960])
Barash, D.P., *Sociobiology and Behavior* (New York: Elsevier North-Holland, 1977)
Barnes, William Emery, *Malachi with Notes and Introduction*, Cambridge Bible for Schools and Colleges, A.F. Kirkpatrick, ed. (Cambridge: University, 1917 [2nd ed. 1934, F.S. Marsh, ed.])
Barr, James, *The Semantics of Biblical Language* (Oxford: Oxford University, 1961)
———, "Some Semantic Notes on the Covenant," in *Beiträge zur alttestamentlichen Theologie. Fs für Walther Zimmerli zum 70. Geburtstag*, H. Donner, R. Hanhart, and R. Smend, eds. (Göttingen: Vandenhoeck & Ruprecht, 1977) 23-38
———, "Semitic Philology and the Interpretation of the Old Testament," in *Tradition and Interpretation. Essays by Members of the Society for Old Testament Study*, G.W. Anderson, ed. (Oxford: Clarendon, 1979) 31-64
———, *Comparative Philology and the Text of the Old Testament*, expanded edition (Winona Lake, IN: Eisenbrauns, 1987 [1st ed., Oxford: Oxford University Press, 1968])
Barth, Markus, *Ephesians. A New Translation with Introduction and Commentary*, 2 vols., AB 34, 34A (Garden City, NY: Doubleday, 1974)
Bauer, Hans, and Pontus Leander, *Historische Grammatik der hebräischen Sprache des Alten Testamentes* (Halle: Niemeyer, 1922 [reprinted 1965 by Georg Olms, Hildesheim])
Baumann, E., "*Yāda'* und seine Derivate. Ein sprachlich-exegetische Studie," *ZAW* 28 (1908) 22-41 and 110-143
Beckwith, Roger T., "The Unity and Diversity of God's Covenants," *TB* 38 (1987) 93-118
Beeston, A.F.L., "One Flesh," *VT* 36 (1986) 115-117

Begg, Christopher T., "*Berit* in Ezekiel," in *Proceedings of the Ninth World Congress of Jewish Studies, Jerusalem, August 4-12, 1985. Division A: The Period of the Bible* (Jerusalem: World Union of Jewish Studies, 1986) 77-84

Begrich, J., "*Berit*. Ein Beitrag zur Erfassung einer alttestamentlichen Denkform," *ZAW* 60 (1944) 1-11

Ben-Barak, Zafrira, "The legal background to the restoration of Michal to David," *Studies in Historical Books of the Old Testament*, SVT 30 (Leiden: E.J. Brill, 1979) 15-29

———, "Inheritance by Daughters in the Ancient Near East," *JSS* 25 (1980) 22-33

Benoit, Pierre, J.T. Milik, and Roland de Vaux, *Les Grottes de Murabba'ât*, DJD 2 (Oxford: Clarendon, 1961)

Benton Jr., W. Wilson, "Federal Theology: Review for Revision," in *Through Christ's Word. A Fs for Dr. Philip E. Hughes*, W.R. Godfrey and J.L. Boyd III, eds. (Phillipsburg, NJ: Presbyterian and Reformed, 1985) 180-204

Berg, Werner, "Der Sündenfall Abrahams und Saras nach Gen 16,1-6," *Biblische Notizen* 19 (1982) 7-14

Berlin, Adele, "Characterization in Biblical Narrative: David's Wives," *JSOT* 23 (1982) 69-85

Bewer, Julius A., see J.M.P. Smith, W.H. Ward, and J.A. Bewer, *A Critical and Exegetical Commentary on Micah, Zephaniah, Nahum, Habakkuk, Obadiah, and Joel*

Biale, Rachel, *Women and Jewish Law. An Exploration of Women's Issues in Halakhic Sources* (New York: Schocken Books, 1984)

Bickerman, E., "Couper une alliance," *Archives d'Histoire du Droit Oriental* 5 (1950-51) 133-56

Bigger, Stephen Frank, "Hebrew Marriage and Family in the Old Testament Period. A Perspective from the Standpoint of Social History and Social Anthropology," Ph.D. diss. (University of Manchester, 1974)

Bing, J.D., "Adapa and Immortality," *Ugarit-Forschungen* 16 (1984) 53-56

Bird, Phyllis, "Images of Women in the Old Testament," in *Religion and Sexism*, R.R. Ruether, ed. (New York City: Simon & Schuster, 1974) 41-88

Birnbaum, Solomon A., "The Kephar Bebhayu Marriage Deed," *JAOS* 78 (1958) 12-18

———, "The Bar Menasheh Marriage Deed," *Uitgaven van het Nederlands Historisch-Archaelogisch Instituut te Istanbul* 13 (1962) 1-26

Blank, Sheldon H., "The Curse, Blasphemy, the Spell, and the Oath," *HUCA* 23 (1950-51) 73-95

Blass, F., and A. Debrunner, *A Greek Grammar of the New Testament and Other Early Christian Literature*, trans. and revised by R.W. Funk (Chicago and London: University of Chicago, 1961)

Blau, Joshua, *On Polyphony in Biblical Hebrew*, Proceedings of the Israel Academy of Sciences and Humanities, VI/2 (Jerusalem: Ahva, Ltd., 1982)

Blenkinsopp, Joseph, *Ezra —Nehemiah, A Commentary*, OTL (Philadelphia: Westminster, 1988)

Blevins, James L., "The Age of Marriage in First-Century Palestine," *Biblical Illustrator* 7 (1980) 65-7

Blocher, Henri, *In the Beginning. The opening chapters of Genesis*, D.G. Preston, trans. (Leicester, England and Downers Grove, IL: Inter-Varsity, 1984)

Blommerde, Anton C.M., *Northwest Semitic Grammar and Job*, BibOr 22 (Rome: Biblical Institute, 1969)

Böcher, O., "Der Judeneid," *EvT* 30 (1970) 671-681

Boecker, Hans Jochen, "Bemerkungen zur formgeschichtlichen Terminologie des Buches Maleachi," *ZAW* 78 (1966) 78-80

———, "Anmerkungen zur Adoption im AT," *ZAW* 86 (1974) 86-89

———, *Law and the Administration of Justice in the Old Testament and Ancient East*, J. Moiser, trans. (Minneapolis, MN: Augsburg; London: SPCK, 1980)

Boling, Robert G., *Judges: A New Translation with Introduction and Commentary*, AB 6A (Garden City, NY: Doubleday, 1975)

Boling, Robert G., and G. Ernest Wright, *Joshua. A New Translation with Notes and Commentary*, AB 6 (Garden City, NY: Doubleday, 1982)

Borger, Rykle, "Zu den Asarhaddon Verträgen aus Nimrud," *Zeitschrift für Assyriologie* 54 (1961) 173-196

———, *Babylonisch-Assyrische Lesestücke*, 2 Bde, 2e Aufl., AnOr 54 (Rome: Biblical Institute, 1979)

Borger, Rykle, Heiner Lutzmann, Willem H. Ph. Römer, and Einar von Schüler, *Rechtsbücher*, Texte aus der Umwelt des Alten Testaments, I/1 (Gütersloh: Gerd Mohn, 1982)

Bossman O.F.M., David, "Ezra's Marriage Reform: Israel Redefined," *Biblical Theology Bulletin* 9 (1979) 32-38

Boström, Gustav, *Proverbiastudien: die Weisheit und das fremde Weib in Sprüche 1-9*, Lunds Universitets Årsskrift, N.F., Avd. I, Bd. 30, Nr. 3 (Lund: Gleerup, 1935)

Botterweck, G. Johannes, "Schelt- und Mahnrede gegen Mischehe und Ehescheidung. Auslegung von Malachias 2, 10-16," *Bibel und Leben* 1 (1960) 179-185

———, "יָדַע, *yāḏaʻ*," in *TDOT* 5 (Grand Rapids, MI: Eerdmans, 1986) 448-481

Botterweck, G. Johannes, and Helmer Ringgren, eds., *Theological Dictionary of the Old Testament* (Grand Rapids, MI: Eerdmans, 1977-)

Brandon, S.G.F., *Creation Legends of the Ancient Near East* (London: Hodder and Stoughton, 1963)

Bratsiotis, N.P., "בָּשָׂר, *bāśār*," in *TDOT* 2 (Grand Rapids, MI: Eerdmans, 1975) 317-332

Braun, Roddy L., *1 Chronicles*, WBC 14 (Waco, TX: Word, 1986)

Brauner, Ronald A., "'To Grasp the Hem' and 1 Samuel 15:27," *JANESCU* 6 (1974) 35-38

Bravmann, M.M., "Concerning the Phrase 'and shall cleave to his wife'," *Le Muséon* 85 (1972) 269-74

———, "The Original Meaning of 'A Man Leaves His Father and Mother' (Gen 2.24)," *Le Muséon* 88 (1975) 449-553

———, *Studies in Semitic Philology* (Leiden: E.J. Brill, 1977)

Breneman, J. Mervin, "Nuzi Marriage Tablets," Ph.D. diss. (Brandeis University, Waltham, MA, 1971)

Brenner, Athalya, *The Israelite Woman: Social Role and Literary Type in Biblical Narrative*, The Biblical Seminar (Sheffield, England: JSOT Press, 1985)

Brichto, Herbert Chanan, *The Problem of 'Curse' in the Hebrew Bible*, JBL Monograph Series, 13 (Philadelphia: Society of Biblical Literature, 1963 [reprinted 1968]).

———, "The Case of the Śōṭā and a Reconsideration of Biblical 'Law'," *HUCA* 46 (1975) 55-70

Bright, John, *Jeremiah. A New Translation with Introduction and Commentary*, AB 21 (Garden City, NY: Doubleday, 1965)

———, *A History of Israel*, 3rd ed. (Philadelphia: Westminster, 1981 [1st ed. 1959; 2nd ed. 1972])

Brinkman, John A., Miguel Civil, Ignace J. Gelb, A. Leo Oppenheim, and Erica Reiner, eds., *The Assyrian Dictionary of the Oriental Institute of the University of Chicago* (Chicago, IL: Oriental Institute; and Glückstadt, Germany: J.J. Augustin, 1956-)

Brockelmann, Carl, *Grundriss der vergleichenden Grammatik der semitischen Sprachen*, 2 Bde. (Berlin: Reuter und Reichard, 1908-1913 [reprinted 1961 Hildesheim: Olms])

———, *Lexicon syriacum*, 2nd ed. (Halle: Max Niemeyer, 1928 [reprinted 1965, Hildesheim: Olms])

———, *Hebräische Syntax* (Neukirchen-Vluyn: Neukirchener Verlag, 1956)

Brockington, Leonard Herbert, "Malachi," in *Peake's Commentary on the Bible*, Matthew Black and H.H. Rowley, eds. (London: Nelson, 1962) 656-658

———, *The Hebrew Text of the Old Testament*, The readings adopted by the translators of the new English Bible (Oxford, Cambridge, London: Oxford University Press, 1973)

Brown, Francis, Samuel Rolles Driver, and Charles A. Briggs, *A Hebrew and English Lexicon of the Old Testament* (Oxford: Clarendon, 1907 [repr. 1962, 1966])

Brownlee, William H., *Ezekiel 1-19*, WBC 28 (Waco, TX: Word, 1986)

Brueggemann, Walter, "David and His Theologian," *CBQ* 30 (1968) 156-81

———, "Of the Same Flesh and Bone (Gn 2,23a)," *CBQ* 32 (1970) 532-42

———, *Genesis*, Interpretation (Atlanta, GA: John Knox, 1982)

Bruno, D. Arvid, *Das Buch der Zwölf. Eine rhythmische und textkritische Untersuchung* (Stockholm: Almqvist & Wiksell, 1957)

Budd, Philip J., *Numbers*, WBC 5 (Waco, TX: Word, 1984)

Budde, K., "Zum Text der drei letzten kleinen Propheten," *ZAW* 26 (1906) 1-28

Bullinger, E.W., *Figures of Speech Used in the Bible: Explained and Illustrated* (London: Messrs. Eyre and Spottiswoode, 1898 [reprinted 1968 Grand Rapids, MI: Baker])

Bulmerincq, Alexander von, *Der Prophet Maleachi, Band 1: Einleitung in das Buch des Propheten Maleachi* (Dorpat: Acta et Commentationes, Univ. Dorpat, 1926)

———, "Die Mischehen im B. Maleachi," in *Oriental Studies published in commemoration of the fortieth anniversary (1883-1923) of Paul Haupt as Director of the Oriental*

Seminary of the Johns Hopkins University, Baltimore, MD, C. Adler and A. Ember, eds. (Baltimore, MD: Johns Hopkins, 1926) 31-42

——, *Der Prophet Maleachi, Band 2: Kommentar zum Buche des Propheten Maleachi* (Tartu: Kommissionsverlag von J.G. Krüger, 1932)

Burke, David G., "Gesture," in *ISBE* 2 (Grand Rapids, MI: Eerdmans, 1986) 449-457

Burrows, Millar, "The Complaint of Laban's Daughters," *JAOS* 57 (1937) 259-276

——, *The Basis of Israelite Marriage*, American Oriental Series 15 (New Haven, CN: American Oriental Society, 1938)

Buss, Martin J., review of L. Perlitt, *Bundestheologie im Alten Testament (WMANT 36)*, *JBL* 90 (1971) 210-212

Callison, Walter L., "Divorce, the Law, and Jesus," *Your Church* (May, 1986) 18-23

Calvin, John, *The Twelve Minor Prophets, Vol. V, Zechariah and Malachi*, J. Owen, trans. (Edinburgh: T. & T. Clark, 1849)

——, *Commentaries on the First Book of Moses called Genesis, Vol. 1*, J. King, trans. and ed. (Grand Rapids, MI: Baker, 1979 reprint [orig. published in Latin, 1554])

——, *Commentaries on the Four Last Books of Moses Arranged in the Form of a Harmony*, vol. 3, C.W. Bingham, trans. (Grand Rapids, MI: Baker, reprint 1979)

Camp, Claudia V., *Wisdom and the Feminine in the Book of Proverbs*, Bible and Literature Series, 11 (Sheffield: Almond, 1985)

Campbell Jr., Edward F., *Ruth. A New Translation with Introduction, Notes and Commentary*, AB 7 (Garden City, NY: Doubleday, 1975)

Campbell, Robert C., "Teachings of the Old Testament concerning Divorce," *Foundations* 6 (1963) 174-178

Cardascia, Guillaume, *Les lois assyriennes. Introduction, traduction, commentaire*, Litt. Anc. du Proche-Orient, 2 (Paris: Éditions du Cerf, 1969)

Carmichael, Calum M., *The Laws of Deuteronomy* (Ithaca, NY: Cornell University, 1974)

——, *Women, Law, and the Genesis Traditions* (Edinburgh: Edinburgh University, 1979)

——, "'Treading' in the Book of Ruth," *ZAW* 92 (1980) 248-66

——, *Law and Narrative in the Bible. The Evidence of the Deuteronomic Laws and the Decalogue* (Ithaca and London: Cornell University, 1985)

Carroll, Robert P., *Jeremiah. A Commentary*, OTL 8 (London: SCM Ltd., 1986)

Carson, D.A., *Exegetical Fallacies* (Grand Rapids, MI: Baker, 1984)

Carson, D.A. and H.G.M. Williamson, eds., *It is Written: Scripture Citing Scripture. Essays in Honour of Barnabas Lindars* (Cambridge: University Press, 1988)

Cashdan, Eli, "Malachi," in *The Twelve Prophets*, Soncino Books of the Bible, A. Cohen, ed. (London, Jerusalem, New York: Soncino, 1948) 335-356

Cassuto, Umberto, *A Commentary on the Book of Genesis. Part I: From Adam to Noah, Genesis I-VI 8*, I. Abrahams, trans. (Jerusalem: Magnes, The Hebrew University, 1961)

——, *A Commentary on the Book of Exodus*, I. Abrahams, trans. (Jerusalem: Magnes, The Hebrew University, 1967)

——, "Second Chapter of the Book of Hosea," in U. Cassuto, *Biblical and Oriental Studies, I: Bible* (Jerusalem: Magnes, 1973) 101-140

Cathcart, Kevin J., and Robert P. Gordon, *The Targum of the Minor Prophets: Translated, with a Critical Introduction, Apparatus, and Notes*, The Aramaic Bible, 14 (Wilmington, DE: Michael Glazier, 1989)

Cazelles, Henri, "חבר, *chābhar*," in *TDOT* 4 (Grand Rapids, MI: Eerdmans, 1980) 193-197

Ceresko, Anthony R., *Job 29-31 in the Light of Northwest Semitic. A Translation and Philological Commentary*, BibOr 36 (Rome: Biblical Institute, 1980)

Charles, R.H., ed., *The Apocrypha and Pseudepigrapha of the Old Testament in English* (Oxford: Clarendon, 1913)

Charlesworth, James H., *Jesus Within Judaism. New Light from Exciting Archaeological Discoveries*, The Anchor Bible Reference Library (New York, London, Toronto, Sydney, Auckland: Doubleday, 1988)

Chary O.F.M., Théophane, *Aggée - Zacharie - Malachie*, Sources Bibliques (Paris: J. Gabalda et Cie, 1969)

Childs, Brevard S., *The Book of Exodus: A Critical, Theological Commentary*, OTL (Philadelphia, PA: Westminster, 1974)

——, *Introduction to the Old Testament as Scripture* (Philadelphia, PA: Fortress, 1979)

Chirichigno, Gregory Conrad, "Debt Slavery in the Ancient Near East and Israel: An Examination of the Biblical Manumission Laws in Exod 21:2-6, 7-11; Deut 15:12-18; Lev. 25:39-54," Ph.D. diss. (Council for National Academic Awards, 1989)

Çig, M., H. Kizilyay, F.R. Kraus, *Altbabylonische Rechtsurkunden aus Nippur* (Istanbul, 1952)

Clark, W. Malcolm, "The Flood and the Structure of the Pre-Patriarchal History," *ZAW* 83 (1971) 204-10

Clay, Albert Tobias, *Babylonian Records in the Library of J. Pierpont Morgan*, Part 4 (New Haven: Yale University, 1923)

Clements, Ronald E., *Abraham and David. Genesis 15 and its Meaning for Israelite Tradition*, SBT II/5 (Geneva, AL: Allenson-Breckinridge and London: SCM, 1967) ·

Clines, David J.A., "The Theology of the Flood Narrative," *Faith and Thought* 100 (1972-3) 128-42

——, *The Theme of the Pentateuch*, JSOTSup 10 (Sheffield, England: University of Sheffield, 1978)

——, *Ezra, Nehemiah, Esther*, NCB (Grand Rapids, MI: Eerdmans; and London: Marshall, Morgan & Scott , 1984)

——, *What Does Eve Do to Help? and Other Readerly Questions to the Old Testament*, JSOTSup 94 (Sheffield: Sheffield Academic, 1990)

Coats, George W., *Genesis with an Introduction to Narrative Literature*, The Forms of Old Testament Literature, 1 (Grand Rapids, MI: Eerdmans, 1983)

Cody O.S.B., Aelred, "Jethro Accepts a Covenant with the Israelites," *Biblica* 49 (1968) 153-166

Cogan, Morton, *Imperialism and Religion: Assyria, Judah and Israel in the Eighth and Seventh Centuries B.C.E.*, SBLMS 19 (Missoula, Montana: Scholars, 1974)

Cogan, Mordechai, and Hayim Tadmor, *II Kings. A New Translation with Introduction and Commentary*, AB 11 (Garden City, NY: Doubleday, 1988)

Coggins, R.J., *Haggai, Zechariah, Malachi*, Old Testament Guides (Sheffield: JSOT Press, 1987)

Cohen, Abraham, *Proverbs. Hebrew Text and English Translation with an Introduction and Commentary*, Soncino Books of the Bible, A. Cohen, ed. (London: Soncino, 1946)

——, *The Soncino Chumash. The Five Books of Moses with Haphtaroth. Hebrew text and English translation with an exposition based on the classical Jewish commentaries*, Soncino Books of the Bible, A. Cohen, ed. (London: Soncino, 1947)

——, "Zephaniah," in *The Twelve Prophets. Hebrew Text & English Translation with Introductions and Commentary*, Soncino Books of the Bible, A. Cohen, ed. (London: Soncino, 1948)

Cohen, Chaim, "Studies in Extra-Biblical Hebrew Inscriptions I. The Semantic Range and Usage of the terms אָמָה and שִׁפְחָה," *Shnaton* 5-6 (1978-79 [published 1982]) xxv-liii

Cohen, Shaye J.D., "Conversion to Judaism in Historical Perspective: From Biblical Israel to Post-Biblical Judaism," *Conservative Judaism* 36 (1983) 31-45

——, "From the Bible to the Talmud: The Prohibition of Intermarriage," *Hebrew Annual Review, Vol. 7. Biblical and Other Studies in Honor of Robert Gordis*, Columbus: Department of Judaic and Near Eastern Languages and Literatures, The Ohio State University, R. Ahroni, ed. (1984) 23-39

——, "The Origins of the Matrilineal Principle in Rabbinic Law," *Judaism* 34 (1985) 5-13

Cole, R. Alan, *Exodus. An Introduction and Commentary*, TOTC (London and Downers Grove, IL: Inter-Varsity, 1973)

Collins, John J., "The Message of Malachi," *The Bible Today* 22 (1984) 209-15

Corbett, P.E., *The Roman Law of Marriage* (Oxford: Clarendon, 1930)

Cotterell, Peter, and Max Turner, *Linguistics and Biblical Interpretation* (Downers Grove, IL: InterVarsity, 1989)

Cowles, Henry, *The Minor Prophets; with Notes, Critical, Explanatory, and Practical, designed for both pastors and people* (New York: D. Appleton, 1867)

Cowley, A.E., *Aramaic Papyri of the Fifth Century B.C. Edited with Translation and Notes* (Oxford: Clarendon, 1923 [reprinted 1967])

Craigie, Peter C., *The Book of Deuteronomy*, NICOT (Grand Rapids, MI: Eerdmans, 1976)

——, *Psalms 1-50*, WBC 19 (Waco, TX: Word, 1983)

——, *Twelve Prophets. Vol. 2*, The Daily Study Bible Series, J.C.L. Gibson, ed. (Philadelphia, PA: Westminster, 1985)

Cramer, Karl, *Amos*, BWANT, 51 (Stuttgart: W. Kohlhammer, 1930)

Cresson, Bruce C., "The Condemnation of Edom," in *The Use of the Old Testament in the New. W.F. Stinespring Fs*, J.M. Efird, ed. (Durham, NC: Duke University, 1972) 125-48

Cross Jr., Frank Moore, *Canaanite Myth and Hebrew Epic. Essays in the History of the Religion of Israel* (Cambridge, MA: Harvard University, 1973)
———, "אל, *'ēl*," in *TDOT* 1 (Grand Rapids, MI: Eerdmans, 1977) 242-261
Cross Jr., Frank Moore, and Richard J. Saley, "Phoenician Incantations on a Plaque of the Seventh Century B.C. from Arslan Tash in Upper Syria," *BASOR* 197 (1970) 42-49
Crown, A.D., "Aposiopesis in the Old Testament and the Hebrew Conditional Oath," *Abr-Nahrain* 4 (1963-64) 96-111
Cuneiform Texts from Babylonian Tablets, etc., in the British Museum (London: British Museum, Department of Egyptian and Assyrian Antiquities, 1896-)
Cuq, E., *Études sur le droit babylonien, les lois assyriennes et les lois hittites* (Paris: Geuthner, 1929)
Curtis, Edward Lewis, and Albert Alonzo Madsen, *A Critical and Exegetical Commentary on the Books of Chronicles*, ICC (Edinburgh: T. & T. Clark and New York: Charles Scribner's Sons, 1910)
Dahlberg, Bruce T., "On recognizing the unity of Genesis," *Theology Digest* 24 (1976) 360-67
Dahood, Mitchell, *Psalms I: 1-50, Introduction, Translation, and Notes*, AB 16 (Garden City, NY: Doubleday, 1965)
———, "Hebrew-Ugaritic Lexicography IV," *Biblica* 47 (1966) 403-419
———, "The Phoenician Contribution to Biblical Wisdom Literature," in *The Role of the Phoenicians in the Interaction of Mediterranean Civilizations. Papers presented to the Archaeological Symposium at the American University of Beyrouth, March, 1967*, W.A. Ward, ed. (Beirut: American University of Beirut, 1968) 123-53
———, *Psalms II: 51-100, Introduction, Translation, and Notes*, AB 17 (Garden City, NY: Doubleday, 1968)
———, *Psalms III: 101-150, Introduction, Translation, and Notes, with an Appendix, The Grammar of the Psalter*, AB 17A (Garden City, NY: Doubleday, 1970)
Dahood, Mitchell, and Tadeusz Penar, "Ugaritic-Hebrew Parallel Pairs," in *RSP* 1 (Rome: Biblical Institute, 1972) 71-382
Dalley, Stephanie, "Old Babylonian Dowries," *Iraq* 42 (1980) 53-74
Daube, David, *Studies in Biblical Law* (Cambridge: University, 1947)
———, "Terms for Divorce," in *The New Testament and Rabbinic Judaism*, D. Daube, ed. (London: Athlone, 1956 [reprint by Arno, New York, 1973]) 366
———, "Rechtsgedanken in den Erzählungen des Pentateuchs," in *Von Ugarit nach Qumran. Beiträge zur alttestamentlichen und altorientalischen Forschung Otto Eissfeldt zum 1. September 1957 dargebracht von Freunden und Schülern*, W.F. Albright, W. Baumgartner, J. Lindblom, J. Pedersen, and H.H. Rowley, eds., BZAW, 77 (Berlin: W. de Gruyter, 1961) 32-41
———, "Covenanting under Duress," *The Irish Jurist* 2 (1967) 352-59
Daube, David, and Reuven Yaron, "Jacob's Reception by Laban," *JSS* 1 (1956) 60-62
David, Martin, *Die Adoption im altbabylonischen Recht*, Leipziger rechtswissenschaftliche Studien 23 (Leipzig: Th. Weicher, 1927)
———, *Vorm en wezen van de huwelijkssluiting naar de oud-oostersche rechtsopvatting; openbare les gehouden bij den aanvang van zijn lessen als privaat-docent in de oostersche rechtsgeschiedenis en de grieksch-egyptische papyrologie aan de Rijks-Universiteit te Leiden op Woensdag 31 Januari 1934* (Leiden: E.J. Brill, 1934)
Davidson, A.B., and A.W. Streane, *The Book of the Prophet Ezekiel*, Cambridge Bible for Schools and Colleges (Cambridge: Cambridge University, 1916)
Davies, Eryl W., "Inheritance Rights and the Hebrew Levirate Marriage, Part 1," *VT* 31 (1981) 138-144
———, "Inheritance Rights and the Hebrew Levirate Marriage, Part 2," *VT* 31 (1981) 257-268
Davies, G.H., *Exodus*, Torch Bible Commentary (London: SCM, 1967)
Day, John, "Pre-Deuteronomic Allusions to the Covenant in Hosea and Psalm LXXVIII," *VT* 36 (1986) 1-12
De Boer, P.A.H., *Fatherhood and Motherhood in Israelite and Judean Piety* (Leiden: E.J. Brill, 1974)
Deden, D., *De kleine profeten*, BOT (Roermond-Maaseik: Romen & Zonen, 1953)
Deissler, Alfons, *Zwölf Propheten*, Die Neue Echter Bibel, 4 (Stuttgart: Echter, 1981)
Deissler, Alfons, and M. Delcor, *Les petits prophètes, II, Michée-Malachi*, La Sainte Bible, Pirot-Clamer 8 (Paris: Letouzey & Ané, 1964)
Delaughter, Thomas J., *Malachi: Messenger of Divine Love* (New Orleans: Insight, 1976)

Delitzsch, Franz, *Proverbs, Ecclesiastes, Song of Solomon*, J. Martin, trans., in Carl Friedrich Keil and F. Delitzsch, Commentary on the Old Testament (Edinburgh: T. & T. Clark, 1875 [reprinted 1982 by Eerdmans, Grand Rapids, MI])

Deller, K., "*šmn bll* (Hosea 12,2). Additional Evidence," *Biblica* 46 (1965) 349-52

Dentan, Robert C., and Willard L. Sperry, "The Book of Malachi," in *The Interpreter's Bible*, 6, G.A. Buttrick, ed. (New York and Nashville: Abingdon; London: Nelson, 1956) 1115-1144

DeRoche, Michael, "Jeremiah 2:2-3 and Israel's Love for God during the Wilderness Wandering," *CBQ* 45 (1983) 364-76

Deutsch, Richard R., see Ogden, Graham S., and Richard R. Deutsch

Dever, William G., "Asherah, Consort of Yahweh? New Evidence from Kuntillet 'Ajrûd," *BASOR* 255 (1984) 21-37

DeVries, Simon J., *1 Kings*, WBC 12 (Waco, TX: Waco Books, 1985)

Dhorme, Édouard, *A Commentary on the Book of Job*, with a Prefatory Note by H.H. Rowley; with a Preface by Francis I. Andersen, H. Knight, trans. (Nashville, Camden, New York: Thomas Nelson, 1984)

Dillmann, A., *Die Genesis*, 6e Aufl., Kurzgefasstes exegetisches Handbuch (Leipzig: Hirzel, 1892)

Dodd, C.H., *According to the Scriptures. The Substructure of New Testament Theology* (Digswell Place, Welwyn, Herts: James Nisbet, 1952)

Dommershausen, Werner, "חלל *chālal* II," in *TDOT* 4 (Grand Rapids, MI: Eerdmans, 1980) 417-421

Donner, Herbert, "Adoption oder Legitimation?" *Oriens Antiquus* 8 (1969) 87-119

Doughty, Charles Montagu, *Travels in Arabia Deserta*, 2 vols. (Cambridge: Cambridge University Press, 1888)

Draffkorn, Anne E., "Ilāni/Elohim," *JBL* 76 (1957) 216-224

Driver, Godfrey Rolles, "'I was [am] no prophet, neither was [am] I a prophet's son.' (RV)," *ExpTim* 67 (1955-56) 91-92

Driver, Godfrey Rolles, and John C. Miles, *The Assyrian Laws. Edited with translation and commentary* (Oxford: Clarendon, 1935)

Driver, Godfrey Rolles, and John C. Miles, *The Babylonian Laws*, 2 vols., (Oxford: Clarendon, vol. 1, 1952, vol. 2, 1955)

Driver, Samuel Rolles, *Notes on the Hebrew Text and the Topography of the Books of Samuel* (Oxford: Oxford University Press, 1890)

———, *A Treatise on the Use of Tenses in Hebrew and Some Other Syntactical Questions*, 3rd ed. (Oxford: Clarendon, 1892 [1st ed. 1874])

———, *A Critical and Exegetical Commentary on Deuteronomy*, 3rd ed., ICC (Edinburgh: T. & T. Clark, 1902)

———, *The Book of Genesis with Introduction and Notes*, 3rd ed. (London: Methuen, 1904)

———, *The Minor Prophets: Nahum, Habakkuk, Zephaniah, Haggai, Zechariah, Malachi. Introductions, Revised Version with Notes, Index, and Map* The Century Bible (Edinburgh and London: T.C. and E.J. Jack; New York: Oxford, 1906)

Driver, Samuel Rolles, and George Buchanan Gray, *A Critical and Exegetical Commentary on the Book of Job Together with a New Translation*, 2 vols., ICC (Edinburgh: T. & T. Clark, 1921 [2nd ed., 1950])

Driver, Samuel Rolles, and H.C.O. Lanchester, *The Books of Joel and Amos*, The Cambridge Bible for Schools and Colleges (Cambridge: University Press, 1915 [1st ed. 1897])

Duhm, Bernhard, *Die zwölf Propheten in den Versmassen der Urschrift übersetzt* (Tübingen: J.C.B. Mohr [P. Siebeck], 1910)

———, *Anmerkungen zu den zwölf Propheten* Sonderabdruck aus der *ZAW* 31: 1-43; 81-110; 161-204 (Giessen: Rickeische, 1911)

Dumbrell, William J., "Malachi and the Ezra-Nehemiah Reforms," *The Reformed Theological Review* 35 (1976) 42-52

Dunstan, Gordon R., "The Marriage Covenant," *Theology* 78 (1975) 244-52

Dupont-Sommer, A., *The Essene Writings From Qumran*, G. Vermes, trans. (Oxford: Basil Blackwell, 1961 [reprinted 1973 by Peter Smith, Gloucester, MA])

Durham, John I., *Exodus*, WBC 3 (Waco, TX: Word, 1987)

Dwight, Sereno Edwards, *The Hebrew Wife* (New York: Leavitt, 1836)

Dyrness, William, *Themes in Old Testament Theology* (Downers Grove, IL: InterVarsity, 1979)

Ebeling, Erich, *Die akkadische Gebetsserie "Handerhebung" von neuem gesammelt und herausgegeben* (Berlin: Akademie Verlag, 1953)

——, ed., *Keilschrifttexte aus Assur juristischen Inhalts*, Wissenschaftliche Veröffentlichungen der Deutschen Orient-Gesellschaft 50 (Leipzig: J.C. Hinrichs, 1927)

Ehrlich, Arnold Bogumil, *Randglossen zur hebräischen Bibel. Textkritisches, Sprachliches und Sachliches*, 7 Bde (Leipzig: Hinrichs, 1908-1914 [reprint Hildesheim 1968])

Eibl-Eibesfeldt, I., *Ethnology: The Biology of Behavior* (New York: Holt, Rinehart and Winston, 1975)

Eichrodt, Walther, *Theology of the Old Testament*, 2 vols., P.R. Ackroyd, trans. (London: SCM, 1961)

——, *Ezekiel. A Commentary*, C. Quin, trans., OTL (Philadelphia: Westminster, 1970)

——, "Prophet and Covenant," in *Proclamation and Presence. Old Testament essays in honour of G. Henton Davies*, J.I. Durham and J.R. Porter, eds. (London and Richmond: John Knox, 1970) 167-188

Eissfeldt, Otto, *The Old Testament: An Introduction*, P.R. Ackroyd, trans. (New York: Harper & Row, 1965)

——, "Renaming in the Old Testament," in *Words and Meanings. Essays presented to David Winton Thomas on his retirement from the Regius Professorship of Hebrew in the University of Cambridge, 1968*, P.R. Ackroyd and B. Lindars, eds. (Cambridge: University Press, 1968) 69-79

Elliger, Karl, *Das Buch der zwölf kleinen Propheten. II. Die Propheten Nahum, Habakuk, Zephanja, Haggai, Zacharja, Maleachi*, ATD 25/2 (Göttingen: Vandenhoeck & Ruprecht, 1950 [8e Aufl. 1981])

——, *Leviticus*, HAT (Tübingen: J.C.B. Mohr [Paul Siebeck], 1966)

——, *Deuterojesaja. 1. Teilband: Jesaja 40,1-45,7*, BKAT XI/1 (Neukirchen-Vluyn: Neukirchener Verlag, 1978)

Elliger, Karl, and W. Rudolph, eds., *Biblia Hebraica Stuttgartensia* (Stuttgart: Deutsche Bibelgesellschaft, 1983)

Emerton, J.A., "New Light on Israelite Religion: the Implications of the Inscriptions from Kuntillet 'Ajrud," *ZAW* 94 (1982) 2-20

Epstein, Louis M., *The Jewish Marriage Contract. A Study in the Status of the Woman in Jewish Law* (New York: Jewish Theological Seminary of America, 1927)

——, *Marriage Laws in Bible and Talmud*, HSS 12 (Cambridge, MA: Harvard University [reprinted 1968], 1942)

Erlandsson, Seth, "אָחַר *'acher*," in *TDOT* 1 (Grand Rapids, MI: Eerdmans, 1977) 201-203

——, "בָּגַד *bāghadh*," in *TDOT* 1 (Grand Rapids, MI: Eerdmans, 1977) 470-473

——, "זָנָה *zānāh*," in *TDOT* 4 (Grand Rapids, MI: Eerdmans, 1980) 99-104

Even-Shoshan, Abraham, ed., *A New Concordance of the Old Testament Using the Hebrew and Aramaic Text*, Intro. by John H. Sailhamer (Grand Rapids, MI: Baker and Ridgefield, 1984 [Jerusalem: Kiryat Sepher, 1983])

Ewald, Georg Heinrich August von, *Commentary on the Prophets of the Old Testament, 5: Commentary on the Books of Haggái, Zakharya, Mal'uki, Yona, Barûkh, Daniel, with Translation*, J.F. Smith, trans. (Edinburgh and London: Williams and Norgate, 1881)

——, *Ausführliches Lehrbuch der hebräischen Sprache des alten Bundes*, 8 ed. (Leipzig: Hinrichs, 1870)

Eybers, I.H., "The Matrimonial Life of Hosea," *Die Ou-Testamentiese Werkgemeenskap in Suid-Afrika* 7 (1964-65) 11-34

Fairbairn, Patrick, *The Christian Treasury* (Edinburgh: Johnson, Hunter & Co., 1847)

Fairbanks, L.A., "Animal and human behavior: guidelines for generalization across species," in *Ethnological Psychiatry: Psychopathology in the Context of Evolution Biology*, M.T. McGuire and L.A. Fairbanks, eds. (New York: Grune & Stratton, 1977) 87-110

Falk, Ze'ev W., "Gestures Expressing Affirmation," *JSS* 4 (1959) 268-269

——, *Hebrew Law in Biblical Times. An Introduction* (Jerusalem: Wahrmann Books, 1964)

——, *Introduction to Jewish Law of the Second Commonwealth*, Arbeiten zur Geschichte des antiken Judentums und des Urchristentums, 11 (Leiden: E.J. Brill, vol. 1, 1972; vol. 2, 1978)

Falkenstein, Adam, *Die neusumerischen Gerichtsurkunden*, 1 Teil, Bayerische Akademie der Wissenschaften, Philosophisch-historische Klasse, Abhandlungen - Neue Folge Heft 39 (München: Beck, 1956)

Farb, Peter, *Consuming Passions: The Anthropology of Eating* (New York: Washington Square, 1980)

Fausset, A.R., "Malachi," in *A Commentary, Critical and Explanatory on the Old and New Testaments*, vol. 1, R. Jamieson, A.R. Fausset, and D. Brown, eds. (Hartford: S.S. Scranton, 1887)

Feigin, Samuel I., "The Captives in Cuneiform Inscription," *AJSL* 50 (1934) 217-245

Feinberg, Charles Lee, *The Major Messages of the Minor Prophets. Habakkuk: Problems of Faith; Zephaniah: The Day of the Lord; Haggai: Rebuilding the Temple; Malachi: Formal Worship* (New York: American Board of Missions to the Jews, 1951)

Feldman, David M., *Marital Relations, Birth Control, and Abortion in Jewish Law* (New York: Schocken Books, 1974)

Fensham, Frank Charles, "The Treaty between Solomon and Hiram and the Alalakh Tablets," *JBL* 79 (1960) 59-60

———, "Salt as Curse in the Old Testament and the Ancient Near East," *BA* 25 (1962) 48-50

———, "The Treaty Between Israel and the Gibeonites," *BA* 27 (1964 [reprinted in *The Biblical Archaeologist Reader* 3, E.F. Campbell Jr. and D.N. Freedman, eds., Garden City, NY: Doubleday, 1970, 121-126]) 96-100

———, "The Covenant-Idea in the Book of Hosea," *Die Ou-Testamentiese Werkgemeenskap in Suid-Afrika* 7 (1964-65) 35-49

———, "The Treaty between the Israelites and Tyrians," in *Congress Volume, Rome*, SVT 17 (Leiden: E.J. Brill, 1969) 71-87

———, "The Covenant as Giving Expression to the Relationship between Old Testament and New Testament," *TB* 22 (1971) 82-94

———, "Father and Son as Terminology for Treaty and Covenant," in *Near Eastern Studies in Honor of William Foxwell Albright*, H. Goedicke, ed. (Baltimore, MD: Johns Hopkins, 1971) 121-135

———, "Genesis 34 and Mari," *JNSL* 4 (1975) 87-90

———, "Covenant, Alliance," in *The Illustrated Bible Dictionary*, rev. ed., 1, J.D. Douglas, *et al.*, eds. (Wheaton, IL: Tyndale House, 1980) 326-331

———, *The Books of Ezra and Nehemiah*, NICOT (Grand Rapids, MI: Eerdmans, 1982)

———, *Exodus*, 3de druk, POT (Nijkerk: G.F. Callenbach, 1984)

———, "Oath," in *ISBE* 3 (Grand Rapids, MI: Eerdmans, 1986) 572-574

Finkelstein, Jacob Joel, "Ammisaduqa's Edict and the Babylonian Law Codes," *JCS* 15 (1961) 103-104

———, "Sex Offences in Sumerian Laws," *JAOS* 86 (1966) 355-72

———, "Cutting the *sissiktu* in Divorce Proceedings," *Die Welt des Orients* 8 (1975-76) 236-40

Fisch, Solomon, *Ezekiel. Hebrew Text & English Translation with an Introduction and Commentary*, Soncino Books of the Bible, A. Cohen, ed. (London: Soncino, 1950)

Fischer, James A., "Notes on the Literary Form and Message of Malachi," *CBQ* 34 (1972) 315-20

Fishbane, Michael, "Accusations of Adultery: A Study of Law and Scribal Practice in Numbers 5:11-31," *HUCA* 45 (1974) 24-45

———, *Biblical Interpretation in Ancient Israel* (Oxford: Clarendon, 1985)

Fisher, Eugene J., "Cultic Prostitution in the Ancient Near East? A Reassessment," *Biblical Theology Bulletin* 6 (1976) 225-236

Fisher, Loren R., F. Brent Knutson, and Donn F. Morgan, eds., *Ras Shamra Parallels: Texts From Ugarit and the Hebrew Bible*, 1, AnOr 49 (Rome: Biblical Institute, 1972)

Fisher, Loren R., Duane E. Smith, and Stan Rummel, eds., *Ras Shamra Parallels: Texts From Ugarit and the Hebrew Bible*, 2, AnOr 50 (Rome: Biblical Institute, 1975)

Fitzmyer, Joseph A., "A Re-Study of an Elephantine Aramaic Marriage Contract (AP 15)," in *Near Eastern Studies in Honor of William F. Albright*, H. Goedicke, ed. (Baltimore, MD and London: Johns Hopkins, 1971 [= *A Wandering Aramaean. Collected Aramaic Essays*, Missoula, Montana, 1979, 243-71]) 137-68

Fohrer, Georg, "Altes Testament - 'Amphiktyonie' und 'Bund'?" *TLZ* 91 (1966 [= G. Fohrer, *Studien zur alttestamentlichen Theologie und Geschichte*, 84-119]) 801-16, 893-904

———, *Introduction to the Old Testament*, D. Green, trans. (London: S.P.C.K., 1968)

Fokkelman, Jan P., *Narrative Art and Poetry in the Book of Samuel. Vol. 1: King David (2 Sam. 9-20 and 1 Kings 1-2)* (Assen, The Netherlands: Van Gorcum, 1981)

Fourie, L.C.H., "Die betekenis van die verbond as sleutel vir Maleagi," M.Th. diss. (University of Stellenbosch, 1982)

Fraine, J. de, *Genesis uit de grondtekst vertaald en uitgelegd*, BOT Deel 1 / Boek 1 (Roermond and Maaseik: J.J. Romen & Zonen Uitgevers, 1963)

France, Richard Thomas, *Jesus and the Old Testament* (Downers Grove, IL: InterVarsity, 1971)

Frankena, Rintje, "The Vassal Treaties of Esarhaddon and the Dating of Deuteronomy," *OTS* 14 (1965) 122-154

Freedman, R. David, "'Put Your Hand Under My Thigh' — The Patriarchal Oath," *BAR* 2:2 (1976) 3-4

Frey, Hellmuth, *Das Buch der Kirche in der Weltwende: Die kleinen nachexilischen Propheten*, Die Botschaft des Alten Testaments 24, 5e Aufl. (Stuttgart: Calwer, 1963)

Friedman, M.A., "The Minimum *Mohar* Payment as Reflected in the Geniza Documents: Marriage Gift or Endowment Pledge?" *Proceedings of the American Academy for Jewish Research* 43 (1976) 15-48

———, "Israel's Response in Hosea 2:17b: 'You Are My Husband'," *JBL* 99 (1980) 199-204

———, *Jewish Marriage in Palestine. A Cairo Geniza Study*, 2 vols. (Tel-Aviv: Tel Aviv University, The Chaim Rosenberg School of Jewish Studies and 'Moreshet' Project for the Study of Eastern Jewry; and New York: The Jewish Theological Seminary of America, 1980-81)

Frymer-Kensky, Tikva S., "The Atrahasis Epic and its Significance for our Understanding of Genesis 1-9," *BA* 40 (1977) 147-155

———, "The Strange Case of the Suspected Sotah (Numbers v 11-31)," *VT* 34 (1984) 11-26

———, "The Judicial Ordeal in the Ancient Near East," Ph.D. diss. (Yale, 1977)

Fuhs, H.F., *Ezechiel 1-24*, Die Neue Echter Bibel (Würzburg: Echter, 1984)

Fuller, Daniel P., *Gospel and Law: Contrast or Continuum?* (Grand Rapids, MI: Eerdmans, 1980)

Fuller, Russell, "Does Yahweh Hate Divorce? Malachi 2:16 and Text of Malachi at Qumran," a paper read at the Annual Meeting of the New England Section of the Society of Biblical Literature, Cambridge, MA, March 25, 1988 (1988)

———, "untitled paper on Malachi 2:10-16," (c/o Wellesley College, Wellesley, MA 02181, n.d.) 1-12.

———, "Text-Critical Problems in Malachi 2:10-16," *JBL* 110 (1991) 47-57. See also Fuller's forthcoming treatment of 4QXII[a] in DJD.

Funk, Robert W., *A Beginning-Intermediate Grammar of Hellenistic Greek*, Sources for Biblical Study, 2 (Missoula, Montana: Scholars, 1973)

Gadd, Cyril John, "Tablets from Kirkuk," *RA* 23 (1926) 49-161

———, "The Harran Inscriptions of Nabonidus," *Anatolian Studies* 8 (1958) 35-92

Gage, Warren Austin, *The Gospel of Genesis. Studies in Protology and Eschatology*, Foreword by Bruce K. Waltke (Winona Lake, IN: Carpenter Books, 1984)

Gaster, Theodor H., *Customs and Folkways of Jewish Life* (New York: William Sloane Associates, 1955)

———, "Sacrifices and Offerings, OT," in *IDB* 4 (Nashville and New York: Abingdon, 1962) 147-159

———, *The Dead Sea Scriptures in English Translation with Introduction and Notes*, 3rd ed. (Garden City, NY: Anchor / Doubleday, 1976)

Gelb, Ignace Jay, review of D.J. Wiseman, *The Vassal-Treaties of Esarhaddon*, *BO* 19 (1962) 161-162

Geller, Markham J., "The Elephantine Papyri and Hosea 2,3: Evidence for the Form of the Early Jewish Divorce Writ," *JSJ* 8 (1977) 139-148

———, "Taboo in Mesopotamia (review of K. van der Toorn, *Sin and Sanction in Israel and Mesopotamia*)" *JCS* 42 (1990) 105-117

Gemser, Berend, "The Importance of the Motive Clause in Old Testament Law," in *Congress Volume, Copenhagen, 1953*, SVT 1 (Leiden: E.J. Brill, 1953) 50-66

———, "The *rîb*- or Controversy-Pattern in Hebrew Mentality," in *Wisdom in Israel and the Ancient Near East. Presented to Harold Henry Rowley by the Editorial Board of Vetus Testamentum in celebration of his 65th birthday, 24 March 1955*, M. Noth and D.W. Thomas, eds., SVT 3 (Leiden: E.J. Brill, 1955) 120-137

———, "The Instructions of Onchsheshonqy and Biblical Wisdom Literature," *Congress Volume, Oxford, 1959*, SVT 7 (Leiden: E.J. Brill, 1960) 102-128

———, *Sprüche Salomos*, 2e Aufl., HAT 16 (Tübingen: J.C.B. Mohr, 1963)

Gerstenberger, Erhard, review of Dennis J. McCarthy, *Treaty and Covenant*, Rome: Biblical Institute, 1963 (AnBib, Vol. 21), *JBL* 83 (1964) 198-99

———, "Covenant and Commandment," *JBL* 84 (1965) 38-51

——, *Wesen und Herkunft des Apodiktischen Rechts*, WMANT 20 (Neukirchen-Vluyn: Neukirchener Verlag, 1965)

——, "תעב *t'b* pi. verabscheuen," in *THAT* 2 (München: Chr. Kaiser Verlag; Zürich: Theologischer Verlag, 1984) 1051-1055

Gesenius, Wilhelm, *Hebrew Grammar*, rev. by E. Kautzsch, 2nd English ed., A.E. Cowley, ed. and tr. (Oxford: Clarendon, 1910)

——, *Gesenius' Hebrew and Chaldee Lexicon*, S.P. Tregelles, trans. (Grand Rapids, MI: Eerdmans, 1949 [German orig., 1835])

Gibson, John C.L., *Textbook of Syrian Semitic Inscriptions. Vol II: Aramaic Inscriptions including inscriptions in the dialect of Zenjirli* (Oxford: Clarendon, 1975)

Gilbert, Maurice, "'Une seule chair' (Gn 2,24)," *Nouvelle Revue Théologique* 100 (1978) 66-89

Ginsberg, H. Louis, "Studies in Hosea 1-3," in *Yehezkel Kaufmann Jubilee Volume*, M. Haran, ed. (Jerusalem: Magnes, 1960)

Ginzberg, L., *The Legends of the Jews* (Philadelphia: Jewish Publication Society, 1928)

Girdlestone, Roger Baker, *Synonyms of the Old Testament: Their Bearing on Christian Doctrine* (Grand Rapids, MI: Eerdmans, n.d.; reprint of 1897 ed.)

Gispen, W.H., *Genesis vertaald en verklaard*, COT (Kampen: J.H. Kok, 1974)

——, *Exodus*, E.M. van der Maas, trans., Bible Student's Commentary (Grand Rapids, MI: Zondervan and St. Catharines, Ont.: Paideia, 1982)

Glazier-McDonald, Beth, "Malachi 2:12: *'ēr wᵉ'ōneh* - Another Look," *JBL* 105 (1986) 295-298

——, "Intermarriage, Divorce, and the *bat 'ēl nēkār*: Insights into Mal 2:10-16," *JBL* 106 (1987) 603-611

——, *Malachi: The Divine Messenger*, SBLDS, 98 (Atlanta, GA: Scholars, 1987)

Goetze, Albrecht, "Hittite *šek-* / *šak-* '(Legally) Recognize' in the Treaties," *JCS* 22 (1968-69) 7-8

Gordis, Robert, "Hosea's Marriage and Message: A New Approach," *HUCA* 25 (1954) 9-35

——, *The Book of Job. Commentary, New Translation and Special Studies* (New York City: The Jewish Theological Seminary of America, 1978)

Gordon, Cyrus H., "Nuzi Tablets Relating to Women," in *Miscellanea Orientalia dedicata Antonio Deimel annos LXX complenti*, AnOr 12 (Rome: Biblical Institute, 1935) 163-84

——, "Hosea 2:4-5 in the Light of New Semitic Inscriptions," *ZAW* 54 [N.F. 13] (1936) 277-280

——, "The Story of Jacob and Laban in the Light of the Nuzi Tablets," *BASOR* 66 (1937) 25-27

——, *Ugaritic Textbook*, AnOr 38 (Rome: Biblical Institute, 1965 [Supplement, 1967])

——, "His Name is 'One'," *JNES* 29 (1970) 198-199

——, "*Erēbu* Marriage," in *Studies on the Civilization and Culture of Nuzi and the Hurrians in Honor of Ernest R. Lacheman*, M.A. Morrison and D.I. Owen, eds. (Winona Lake, IN: Eisenbrauns, 1981) 155-160

Gordon, Robert Patterson, "David's Rise and Saul's Demise: Narrative Analogy in 1 Samuel 24-26 (Tyndale OT Lecture 1979)," *TB* 31 (1980) 37-64

——, *1 and 2 Samuel*, Old Testament Guides (Sheffield: JSOT Press, 1984)

——, *1 & 2 Samuel. A Commentary* (Exeter: Paternoster, 1986)

Görg, M., "בּוּז *bāzāh*," in *TDOT* 1 (Grand Rapids, MI: Eerdmans, 1977) 60-65

Goslinga, C.J., *Het Tweede Boek Samuël*, COT (Kampen: J.H. Kok, 1962)

Goss, Karl, "Die literarische Verwandschaft Jeremias mit Hosea," Ph.D. diss. (Berlin, 1930)

——, "Hoseas Einfluss auf Jeremias Anschauungen," *Neue kirchliche Zeitschrift* 42 (1931) 241-265; 327-343

Gowan, Donald E., "Prophets, Deuteronomy and Syncretistic Cult in Israel," in *Essays in Divinity VI: Transitions in Biblical Scholarship*, J.C. Rylaarsdam, ed. (Chicago, IL: University of Chicago, 1968) 93-112

Graetz, H., *Emendationes in plerosque Sacrae Scripturae V.T. libros ex relicto defuncti auctoris manuscripto*, 3 Lieff., G. Bacher, ed. (Vratislaviae, 1892-94)

Granqvist, Hilma, *Marriage Conditions in a Palestinian Village* I-II. Societas Scientarum Fennica, Commentationes Humanarum Litterarum, III,8, and VI,8 (Helsingfors: Centraltryckeriet, 1931,1935)

Gray, John, *Joshua, Judges, and Ruth*, NCB (Grand Rapids, MI: Eerdmans, and Basingstoke: Marshall Morgan & Scott, 1986)

Grayson, Albert Kirk, *Assyrian Royal Inscriptions*, 2 vols., Records of the Ancient Near East, H. Goedicke, ed. (Wiesbaden: Otto Harrassowitz, vol. 1 1972, vol. 2 1976)

Green, B., "A Study of Field and Seed Symbolism in the Biblical Story of Ruth," Ph.D. diss. (Graduate Theological Union, 1980)

Greenberg, Moshe, "The Hebrew Oath Particle, *hay / hê*," *JBL* 76 (1957) 34-39

——, "Some Postulates of Biblical Criminal Law," in *Yehezkel Kaufmann Jubilee Volume*, M. Haran, ed. (Jerusalem: Magnes, 1960) 5-28

——, "Crimes and Punishments," in *IDB* 1 (Nashville and New York: Abingdon, 1962) 733-744

——, *Ezekiel 1-20. A New Translation with Introduction and Commentary*, AB 22 (Garden City, NY: Doubleday, 1983)

——, "Ezekiel 17: A Holistic Interpretation," *JAOS* 103 (1983) 149-154

——, "More Reflections on Biblical Criminal Law," in *Studies in Bible 1986: Scripta Hierosolymitana* 31, S. Japhet, ed. (Jerusalem: Magnes, 1986)

——, "Reply to the Comments of John Welch," in *Religion and Law. Biblical-Judaic and Islamic Perspectives*, E.B. Firmage, B.G. Weiss, and J.W. Welch, eds. (Winona Lake, IN: Eisenbrauns, 1990) 120-125

Greenfield, Jonas C., "Aramaic Studies and the Bible," *Congress Volume, Vienna, 1980*, SVT 32 (Leiden: E.J. Brill, 1981) 110-130

Greengus, Samuel, "The Aramaic Marriage Contracts in the Light of the Ancient Near East and the Later Jewish Materials," M.A. diss. (University of Chicago, 1959)

——, "Old Babylonian Marriage Ceremonies and Rites," *JCS* 20 (1966) 55-72

——, "The Old Babylonian Marriage Contract," *JAOS* 89 (1969) 505-32

——, "A Textbook Case of Adultery in Ancient Mesopotamia," *HUCA* 40-41 (1969-70) 33-44

——, "Law in the OT," in *IDBSup* (Nashville, TN: Abingdon, 1976) 532-537

——, *Old Babylonian Tablets from Ishchali and Vicinity*, Nederlands Historisch-Archaelogisch Instituut te Instanbul (Leiden: Nederlands Instituut voor het Nabije Oosten, 1979)

Greenstein, E.L., "'To Grasp the Hem' in Ugaritic Literature," *VT* 32 (1982) 217-218

Grelot, Pierre, *Man and Wife in Scripture* (New York: Herder and Herder, 1964)

——, "The Institution of Marriage: Its Evolution in the Old Testament," *Concilium* 55 (1970) 39-50

Gressmann, H., "Mythische Reste in der Paradieserzählung," *Archiv für Religionswissenschaft*, 10 (1907) 345-367

Griffith, F.L., "The Millingen Papyrus," *Zeitschrift für ägyptische Sprache und Altertumskunde* 34 (1896) 35-51

Grintz, Jehoshua M., "The Treaty of Joshua with the Gibeonites," *JAOS* 86 (1966) 113-126

Grosz, Katarzyna, "Daughters Adopted as Sons at Nuzi and Emar," in *La Femme dans le proche-orient antique, Compte Rendu de la XXXIVeme Rencontre Assyriologique Internationale (Paris, 7-10 Juillet 1986)*, J.-M. Durand, ed. (Paris: Editions Recherche sur les Civilisations, 1987) 81-86

——, "Some Aspects of the Position of Women in Nuzi," in *Women's Earliest Records From Ancient Egypt and Western Asia. Proceedings of the Conference on Women in the Ancient Near East, Providence Rhode Island, November 5-7, 1987*, B.S. Lesko, ed., Brown Judaic Studies 166 (Atlanta, Georgia: Scholars, 1989) 167-180 (responses on pp. 181-189)

Gruber, Mayer I., *Aspects of Nonverbal Communication In the Ancient Near East*, 2 vols., Studia Pohl 12/1 and 12/2 (Rome: Biblical Institute, 1980)

Gunkel, Hermann, *Genesis übersetzt und erklärt*, 9e Aufl., HKAT I/1 (Göttingen: Vandenhoeck und Ruprecht [1st ed.: 1902], 1977 [= 3rd ed.: 1910])

Ha, John, *Genesis 15: A Theological Compendium of Pentateuchal History* (Berlin: Walter de Gruyter, 1989)

Habel, Norman C., *The Book of Job. A Commentary*, OTL (Philadelphia: Westminster and London: SCM Ltd., 1985)

Halbe, J., *Das Privilegrecht Jahwes. Ex. 34, 10-26: Gestalt und Wesen, Herkunft und Wirken in vordeuteronomischer Zeit*, FRLANT, 114 (Göttingen: Vandenhoeck & Ruprecht, 1975)

Hallo, William W., "The Origins of the Sacrificial Cult: New Evidence from Mesopotamia and Israel," in *Ancient Israelite Religion. Essays in Honor of Frank Moore Cross*, P.D. Miller Jr., P.D. Hanson, and S.D. McBride, eds. (Philadelphia: Fortress, 1987) 3-13

Hamburg, B.A., "The biosocial basis of sex differences," in *Human Evolution: Biosocial Perspectives*, S.L. Washburn and E.R. McCown, eds. (Menlow Park, CA: Benjamin/Cummings, 1978) 155-213

Hamilton, Victor P., *The Book of Genesis, Chapters 1-17*, NICOT (Grand Rapids, MI: Eerdmans, 1990)

Hammond, Philip C., *The Nabataeans — Their History, Culture and Archaeology*, Studies in Mediterranean Archaeology 27 (Gothenburg, Sweden: Paul Astroms, 1973)

Harper, Robert Francis, *Assyrian and Babylonian Letters*, 14 vols. (Chicago: University Press, 1892-1914)

Harper, William Rainey, *A Critical and Exegetical Commentary on Amos and Hosea*, ICC (Edinburgh: T. & T. Clark, 1905)

Harris, R. Laird, Gleason L. Archer Jr., and Bruce K. Waltke, eds., *Theological Wordbook of the Old Testament* (Chicago: Moody, 1980)

Harris, Rivkah, "The *Nadītu* Woman," in *Studies presented to A. Leo Oppenheim, June 7, 1964*, R.D. Biggs and J.A. Brinkman, eds. (Chicago: Oriental Institute, University of Chicago Press, 1964) 105-35

———, "The Case of Three Babylonian Marriage Contracts," *JNES* 33 (1974) 363-365

———, "Independent Women in Ancient Mesopotamia?" in *Women's Earliest Records From Ancient Egypt and Western Asia. Proceedings of the Conference on Women in the Ancient Near East, Brown University, Providence Rhode Island November 5-7, 1987*, B.S. Lesko, ed., Brown Judaic Studies 166 (Atlanta, Georgia: Scholars, 1989) 145-156

Harrison, Roland Kenneth, *Introduction to the Old Testament* (Grand Rapids, MI: Eerdmans, 1969)

———, *Leviticus. An Introduction and Commentary*, TOTC (Downers Grove, IL: Inter-Varsity, 1980)

Hartley, John E., *The Book of Job*, NICOT (Grand Rapids, MI: Eerdmans, 1988)

Hasel, Gerhard F., *Old Testament Theology: Basic Issues in the Current Debate*, 2nd ed. (Grand Rapids, MI: Eerdmans, 1975)

———, "Linguistic Considerations Regarding the Translation of Isaiah's Shear-Jashub : A Reassessment," *AUSS* 9 (1971) 36-46

———, "Semantic Values of Derivatives of the Hebrew root *š'r*," *AUSS* 11 (1973) 152-69

———, "Remnant," in *IDBSup* (Nashville, TN: Abingdon, 1976) 736-38

———, *The Remnant. The History and Theology of the Remnant Idea from Genesis to Isaiah*, 3rd. ed., Andrews University Monographs, 5 (Berrien Springs: Andrews University, 1980)

———, "The Meaning of the Animal Rite in Genesis 15," *JSOT* 19 (1981) 61-78

Hauck, Friedrich, "μοιχεύω, κτλ.," in *TDNT* 4 (Grand Rapids, MI: Eerdmans, 1967) 729-735

Hauck, Friedrich, and Siegfried Schulz, "πόρνη, κτλ.," in *TDNT* 6 (Grand Rapids, MI: Eerdmans, 1968) 579-595

Hauser, Alan Jon, "Linguistic and Thematic Links between Genesis 4:1-16 and Genesis 2-3," *JETS* 23 (1980) 297-305

———, "Genesis 2-3: The Theme of Intimacy and Alienation," in *Art and Meaning: Rhetoric in Biblical Literature*, D.J.A. Clines, D.M. Gunn, and A.J. Hauser, eds., JSOTSup 19 (Sheffield: JSOT Press, 1982) 20-36

Hawthorne, G.F., "Name," in *ISBE* 3 (Grand Rapids, MI: Eerdmans, 1986) 480-483

Heidel, Alexander, *The Gilgamesh Epic and Old Testament Parallels*, 2nd ed. (Chicago: University of Chicago, 1949)

———, *The Babylonian Genesis. The Story of Creation*, 2nd ed. (Chicago: University of Chicago, 1951)

Henderson, Ebenezer, *The Twelve Minor Prophets. Translated from the original Hebrew with a critical and exegetical commentary*, 2nd ed. (Hamilton, Adams and Co., 1858 [reprinted by Baker, 1980])

Hendricks, Hans Jurgens, "Juridical Aspects of the Marriage Metaphor in Hosea and Jeremiah," D.Lit. diss. (University of Stellenbosch, South Africa, n.d. [1974?])

Herrmann, Johannes, *Ezechiel*, KAT XI (Leipzig and Erlangen: A. Deichert, 1924)

Hertz, J.H., "Foreword," in *The Babylonian Talmud. Seder Nashim*, 4 vols., I. Epstein, ed. 1 (London: Soncino, 1936) xiii-xxvi

Hertzberg, Hans Wilhem, *I and II Samuel. A Commentary*, J.S. Bowden, trans., OTL (Philadelphia: Westminster, 1964)

Heth, William A., and Gordon J. Wenham, *Jesus and Divorce. Towards an Evangelical Understanding of New Testament Teaching* (London, Sydney, Auckland, Toronto: Hodder and Stoughton, 1984)

Hieronymus (Jerome), "Commentariorum in Malachiam Prophetam," in *S. Hieronymi Presbyteri Opera, Pars I, Opera Exegetica 6 in the Corpus Christianorum series* (Turnholti: Typographi Brepols Editores Pontificii, 1970)

Hillers, Delbert Roy, *Treaty-Curses and the Old Testament Prophets*, BibOr 16 (Rome: Biblical Institute, 1964)

———, *Covenant: The History of a Biblical Idea*, Seminars in the History of Ideas (Baltimore, MD: Johns Hopkins, 1969)

———, *Lamentations. Introduction, Translation and Notes*, AB 7A (Garden City, New York: Doubleday, 1972)

Hitzig, Ferdinand, and Heinrich Steiner, *Die zwölf kleinen Propheten*, 4e Aufl., Kurzgefasstes exegetisches Handbuch, HAT (Leipzig: Hirzel, 1881)

Hoehner, Harold W., "A Response to Divorce and Remarriage [a paper read by William A. Heth]," in *Applying the Scriptures. Papers from ICBI Summit III*, K.S. Kantzer, ed. (Grand Rapids, MI: Zondervan, 1987) 240-246

Hoftijzer, J., "Review: the Nominal Clause Reconsidered," *VT* 23 (1973) 446-510

Holladay, William L., *A Concise Hebrew and Aramaic Lexicon of the Old Testament. Based upon the lexical work of Ludwig Koehler and Walter Baumgartner* (Grand Rapids, MI: Eerdmans; and Leiden: E.J. Brill, 1971)

———, *Jeremiah 1. A Commentary on the Book of the Prophet Jeremiah, Chapters 1 — 25*, Hermeneia (Philadelphia: Fortress, 1986)

Holst, Robert, "Polygamy and the Bible," *International Review of Missions* (London Edinburgh Geneva) 56 (1967) 205-213

Holtzmann, Oskar, "Der Prophet Maleachi und der Ursprung des Pharisäerbundes," *Archiv für Religionswissenschaft* 29 (1931) 1-21

Hooke, Samuel Henry, ed., *Myth and Ritual. Essays on the myth and ritual of the Hebrews in relation to the culture pattern of the ancient East* (London: Oxford University Press, 1933)

———, *Myth, Ritual and Kingship. Essays on the Theory and Practice of Kingship in the Ancient Near East and in Israel* (Oxford: Clarendon, 1958)

Hoonacker, A. van, *Les douze petits prophètes, traduits et commentés*, Études Bibliques (Paris: Librairie Victor Lecoffre, J. Gabalda et Cie, 1908)

Hopkins, M.K., "The Age of Roman Girls at Marriage," *Population Studies* 18 (1964-5) 309-27

Horst, Friedrich, "Nahum bis Maleachi," in *Die zwölf kleinen Propheten*, T.H. Robinson and F. Horst, ed., HAT, 3e Aufl. (Tübingen: J.C.B. Mohr [Paul Siebeck], 1964 [1e Aufl. 1938])

House, Paul R., *The Unity of the Twelve*, Bible and Literature Series, 27, JSOTSup 97 (Sheffield: Almond [Sheffield Academic], 1990)

Hrdy, S.B., *The Woman That Never Evolved* (Boston: Harvard University, 1981)

Hubbard Jr., Robert L., *The Book of Ruth*, NICOT (Grand Rapids, MI: Eerdmans, 1988)

Huehnergard, John, *An Introduction to Old Babylonian Akkadian* (New York: Columbia University, 1982)

———, "Five Tablets From the Vicinity of Emar," *RA* 77 (1983) 11-43

Huffmon, Herbert B., "The Covenant Lawsuit in the Prophets," *JBL* 78 (1959) 285-95

———, "The Exodus, Sinai and the Credo," *CBQ* 27 (1965) 101-113

———, "The Treaty Background of Hebrew *yāda'*," *BASOR* 181 (1966) 31-37

Huffmon, Herbert B., and S.B. Parker, "A Further Note on the Treaty Background of Hebrew *yāda'*," *BASOR* 184 (1966) 36-38

Hugenberger, Gordon P., "Michal," in *ISBE* 3 (Grand Rapids, MI: Eerdmans, 1986) 348

———, "Rib," in *ISBE* 4 (Grand Rapids, MI: Eerdmans, 1988) 183-185

———, "Women in Church Office: Hermeneutics or Exegesis? A Survey of Approaches to 1 Timothy 2:8-15," *JETS* 35 (1992) 341-360

———, "Marriage as a Covenant: A study of biblical law and ethics governing marriage developed from the perspective of Malachi," Ph.D. dissertation (C.N.A.A., The Cheltenham & Gloucester College of Higher Education (The College of St. Paul & St. Mary) and The Oxford Centre for Postgraduate Hebrew Studies, 1991)

Hughes, John H., and Frederick C. Prussner, *Old Testament Theology, its History and Development* (Atlanta, GA: John Knox, 1985)

Humbert, Paul, "Mythe de création et mythe paradisiaque dans le second chapitre de la Genèse," *Revue d'histoire et de philosophie religieuses* 16 (1936) 445-461

——, "La femme étrangère du Livre des Proverbes," *Revue des Études Sémitiques* 6 (1937) 40-64

——, "Les adjectifs 'Zâr' et 'Nokri' et la femme étrangère," in *Mélanges Syriens offerts à M. René Dussaud I*, Bibliothèque Archéologique et Historique, tome 30 (Paris: Geuthner, 1939 [= *Opuscles d'un hébraïsant. Mémoires de l'Université de Neuchâtel*, 26, 1958, 111-118]) 259-66

——, "Études sur le récit du paradis et de la chute dans la Genèse," *Mémoires de l'Univ. de Neuchâtel* 14 (1940) 1-193

——, "Étendre la main," *VT* 12 (1962) 383-395

Hurvitz, Avi, "The Evidence of Language in Dating the Priestly Code; A Linguistic Study in Technical Idioms and Terminology," *RB* 81 (1974) 24-56

——, *A Linguistic Study of the Relationship between the Priestly Source and the Book of Ezekiel: A New Approach to an Old Problem*, Cahiers de la Revue Biblique, 20 (Paris: J. Gabalda et Cie, 1982)

——, "The Language of the Priestly Source and its Historical Setting - the Case for an Early Date," *Proceedings of the Eighth World Congress of Jewish Studies, Jerusalem, August 16-21, 1981. Panel Sessions: Bible Studies and Hebrew Language* (Jerusalem: World Union of Jewish Studies and The Perry Foundation for Biblical Research, 1983) 83-94

Hvidberg, Flemming Friis, "The Canaanitic Background of Gen I-III," *VT* 10 (1960) 285-94

——, *Weeping and Laughter in the Old Testament. A Study of Canaanite-Israelite Religion*, N. Haislund, trans. (Leiden: E.J. Brill; and København: Nyt Nordisk Forlag, Arnold Busck, 1962)

Hyatt, J. Philip, *Exodus*, NCB (Grand Rapids, MI: Eerdmans; and London: Marshall, Morgan & Scott, 1971)

Isaac, Erich, "Circumcision as Covenant Rite," *Anthropos* 59 (1964) 444-456

Isaksson, Abel, *Marriage and Ministry in the New Temple: A Study With Special Reference to Mt. 19:1 - 12 and 1 Cor. 11:3-16*, N. Tomkinson and J. Gray, trans., Acta Seminarii Neotestamentici Upsaliensis 24 (Lund: Gleerup / Copenhagen: Munsgaard, 1965)

Isopescul, Octavian, *Der Prophet Malachias. Einleitung, Übersetzung und Auslegung* (Czernowitz: K.K. Hof und Staatsdruckerei in Wien, 1908)

Jackson, Bernard S., "The Problem of Exodus XXI 22-25 (*Ius Talionis*)," *VT* 23 (1973) 271-304

——, "Reflections on Biblical Criminal Law," *JJS* 24 (1973) 8-38

——, "Some Literary Features of the Mishpatim," in *Wünschet Jerusalem Frieden. Collected Communications to the XIIth Congress of the International Organization for the Study of the Old Testament, Jerusalem 1986* (Frankfurt am Main, Bern, New York, Paris: Verlag Peter Lang, 1987) 235-242

Jacobsen, Thorkild, *The Sumerian King List* (Chicago: University of Chicago, 1939)

——, "The Eridu Genesis," *JBL* 100 (1981) 513-529

——, *The Harps That Once... Sumerian Poetry in Translation* (New Haven and London: Yale University Press, 1987)

Jagendorf, Zvi, "'In the morning, behold, it was Leah': Genesis and the Reversal of Sexual Knowledge," *Prooftexts: A Journal of Jewish Literary History* 4 (1984) 187-192

Jakobson, Vladimir A., "Studies in Neo-Assyrian Law (I. Matrimonial Law; 2. Legal Practice)," *Altorientalische Forschungen* 1 (1974) 115-121

James, Edwin Oliver, *Myths and Rites in the Ancient Near East. An Archaeological and Documentary Study* (London: Thames and Hudson, 1958)

Japhet, Sara, "Law and 'the Law' in Ezra-Nehemiah," in *Proceedings of the Ninth World Congress of Jewish Studies, 1985 Panel Sessions: Bible Studies and Ancient Near East* (Jerusalem: World Union of Jewish Studies, 1988) 66-98

Jastrow, Marcus, *A Dictionary of the Targumim, the Talmud Babli and Yerushalmi, and the Midrashic Literature* (New York: Traditional Inc., 1903)

Jenni, Ernst, and Claus Westermann, eds., *Theologisches Handwörterbuch zum Alten Testament*, 2 Bde (München: Chr. Kaiser Verlag und Zürich: Theologischer Verlag, 1971, 1984)

Jensen, Joseph, "Does *Porneia* Mean Fornication? A Critique of Bruce Malina," *NovT* 20 (1978) 161-84

Jepsen, Alfred, "*Ama^h* und *Schiphcha^h*," *VT* 8 (1958) 293-97

——, "Berith. Ein Beitrag zur Theologie der Exilszeit," in *Verbannung und Heimkehr. Beiträge zur Geschichte und Theologie Israels im 6. und 5. Jahrhundert v. Chr. Fs für Wilhelm Rudolph,* A. Kuschke, ed. (Tübingen: J.C.B. Mohr [Paul Siebeck], 1961) 161-179

Jeremias, Alfred, *The Old Testament in the Light of the Ancient East,* 2 vols., C.H.W. Johns, ed., C.L. Beaumont, trans. (New York: Putnam's Sons, 1911)

Job, John B., *The Covenant of Marriage,* The eighth annual lecture sponsored by the association of Conservative Evangelicals in Methodism. Presented at Wroxham Road Methodist Church, Norwich, 1 July, 1981 (n.p., 1981)

Jobling, David K., *The Sense of Biblical Narrative: Three Structural Analyses in the Old Testament (1 Samuel 13-31; Numbers 11-12; 1 Kings 17-18),* JSOTSup 7 (Sheffield, England: JSOT Press, 1978)

Johnstone, William, "*yd'* II, 'be humbled, humiliated'?" *VT* 41 (1991) 49-62

Jones, Alexander, ed., *The Jerusalem Bible* (Garden City, NY: Doubleday; London: Darton, Longman & Todd, Ltd., 1966)

Jones, Douglas Rawlinson, *Haggai, Zechariah, Malachi. Introduction and Commentary,* Torch Bible Commentaries (London: SCM Ltd., 1962)

Jones, Gwilym H., *1 and 2 Kings,* 2 vols., NCB (Grand Rapids, MI: Eerdmans and London: Marshall, Morgan & Scott, 1984)

Joüon, Paul, *Grammaire de l'hébreu biblique,* 2nd ed. (Rome: Biblical Institute, 1923)

Jüngling, Hans-Winfried, *Richter 19 — Ein Plädoyer für das Königtum. Stilistische Analyse der Tendenzerzählung Ri 19, 1-30a; 21,25,* AnBib 84 (Rome: Biblical Institute, 1981)

Junker, Hubert, *Das Buch Deuteronomium übersetzt und erklärt,* Die Heilige Schrift des Alten Testamentes II/2 (Bonn: Peter Hanstein, 1933)

——, *Die zwölf kleinen Propheten. II Häfte: Nahum, Habakuk, Sophonias, Aggäus, Zacharias, Malachias,* Die Heilige Schrift des Alten Testamentes VIII/3/II (Bonn: Peter Hanstein, 1938)

Kaiser Jr., Walter C., *Toward an Old Testament Theology* (Grand Rapids, MI: Zondervan, 1978)

——, *Toward Old Testament Ethics* (Grand Rapids, MI: Zondervan, 1983)

——, *Malachi. God's Unchanging Love* (Grand Rapids, MI: Baker, 1984)

Kaiser, Otto, *Isaiah 13-39, A Commentary,* R.A. Wilson, trans., OTL (Philadelphia: Westminster, 1974)

Kalluveettil C.M.I., Paul, *Declaration and Covenant. A Comprehensive Review of Covenant Formulae from the Old Testament and the Ancient Near East,* AnBib 88 (Rome: Biblical Institute 1982)

Kaufman, Stephen A., "The Structure of the Deuteronomic Law," *Maarav* 1/2 (1978-79) 105-158

Keel, Othmar, *The Symbolism of the Biblical World. Ancient Near Eastern Iconography and the Book of Psalms,* T.J. Hallett, trans. (New York: Seabury, 1978)

Keil, Carl Friedrich, *Biblical Commentary on the Prophecies of Ezekiel,* 3 vols. in 1, J. Martin, trans., in Carl Friedrich Keil and F. Delitzsch, Commentary on the Old Testament (Edinburgh: T. & T. Clark, 1876 [Reprinted Grand Rapids MI: Eerdmans, 1982])

Keil, Carl Friedrich, and Franz Delitzsch, *The Pentateuch,* 3 vols. J. Martin, trans., in Carl Friedrich Keil and F. Delitzsch, Commentary on the Old Testament (Edinburgh: T. & T. Clark, 1878 [Reprinted Grand Rapids MI: Eerdmans, 1981])

Keil, Carl Friedrich, and Franz Delitzsch, *The Twelve Minor Prophets,* 2 vols., J. Martin, trans., in Carl Friedrich Keil and F. Delitzsch, Commentary on the Old Testament (Edinburgh: T. & T. Clark, 1868 [reprinted Grand Rapids, MI: Eerdmans, 1954])

Keller, C.A., "אלה *'ālā* Verfluchung," *THAT* 1 (München: Chr. Kaiser Verlag, Zürich: Theologischer Verlag, 1984) 149-152

——, "שבע *sb'* ni. schwören," *THAT* 2 (München: Chr. Kaiser Verlag, Zürich: Theologischer Verlag, 1984) 855-863

Kellermann, Diether, "אשם *'asham,*" in *TDOT* 1 (Grand Rapids, MI: Eerdmans, 1977) 429-437

Kellermann, Ulrich, "Erwägungen zum Esragesetz," *ZAW* 80 (1968) 373-85

Kelley, Page H., *Layman's Bible Book Commentary, Micah, Nahum, Habakkuk, Zephaniah, Haggai, Zechariah, Malachi* (Nashville, TN: Broadman, 1984)

Kennedy, James M., "Peasants in Revolt: Political Allegory in Genesis 2-3," *JSOT* 47 (1990) 3-14

Khanjian, John, "Wisdom," in *RSP* 2 (Rome: Biblical Institute, 1975) 371-400

Kidner, Derek, *Proverbs. An Introduction and Commentary*, TOTC (Downers Grove, IL: InterVarsity, 1964)

——, "Genesis 2:5,6: wet or dry?" *TB* 17 (1966) 109-114

——, *Genesis. An Introduction and Commentary*, TOTC (Downers Grove, IL: Inter-Varsity, 1967)

——, *Ezra and Nehemiah. An Introduction and Commentary*, TOTC (Leicester, England: InterVarsity, 1979)

——, *Love to the Loveless. The Message of Hosea*, The Bible Speaks Today (Downers Grove, IL: InterVarsity, 1981)

Kikawada, Isaac M., "Literary Convention of the Primaeval History," *Annual of Japanese Biblical Institute* 1 (1975) 3-21

Kikawada, Isaac M., and Arthur Quinn, *Before Abraham Was. The Unity of Genesis 1-11* (Nashville: Abingdon, 1985)

Kirkpatrick, Alexander Francis, *The Doctrine of the Prophets. The Warburtonian Lectures for 1886-1890*, 3rd ed. (London: MacMillan, 1907 [1st ed. 1892])

Kitchen, Kenneth A., *Ancient Orient and Old Testament* (Downers Grove, IL and Leicester: InterVarsity, 1966)

——, *The Bible in Its World. The Bible and Archaeology Today* (Exeter: Paternoster; and Downers Grove, IL: InterVarsity, 1977)

——, "Egypt, Ugarit, Qatna and Covenant," in *Ugarit-Forschungen* 11 (Kevelaer: Verlag Butzon & Bercker; and Neukirchen-Vluyn: Neukirchener Verlag, 1979) 453-464

——, "Law, Treaty, Covenant and Deuteronomy," a paper read on 13 July 1988, Old Testament Study Group of Tyndale Fellowship Cambridge, England (1988)

Klein, Ralph W., *Textual Criticism of the Old Testament From the Septuagint to Qumran*, Old Testament Guides to Biblical Scholarship (Philadelphia: Fortress, 1974)

——, *1 Samuel*, WBC 10 (Waco, TX: Word, 1983)

Klíma, Josef, "Marriage and Family in Ancient Mesopotamia," *New Orient* (Prague) 5 (1966) 99-103

Kline, Meredith G., "The Two Tables of the Covenant," *WTJ* 22 (1959/60) 133-146

——, "Divine Kingship and Genesis 6:1-4," *WTJ* 24 (1961/1962) 187-204

——, *Treaty of the Great King. The Covenant Structure of Deuteronomy: Studies and Commentary* (Grand Rapids, MI: Eerdmans, 1963)

——, "Abram's Amen," *WTJ* 31 (1968) 1-11

——, *By Oath Consigned. A Reinterpretation of the Covenant Signs of Circumcision and Baptism* (Grand Rapids, MI: Eerdmans, 1968)

——, "Genesis," in *The New Bible Commentary*, 3rd rev. ed., D. Guthrie, ed. (Downers Grove, IL: Inter-Varsity, 1970) 79-114

——, *The Structure of Biblical Authority*, 2nd ed. (Grand Rapids, MI: Eerdmans, 1975)

——, "*Lex Talionis* and the Human Fetus," *JETS* 20 (1977) 193-201

——, *Images of the Spirit*, Baker Biblical Monograph (Grand Rapids, MI: Baker, 1980)

——, *Kingdom Prologue* (South Hamilton, MA: M.G. Kline, 1981-85)

Kline, Meredith M., "The Holy Spirit as Covenant Witness," Th.M. diss. (Westminster Theological Seminary, 1972)

Klopfenstein, M.A., *Die Lüge nach dem AT* (Zürich: Gotthelf Verlag, 1964)

——, "בגד *bgd* treulos handeln," *THAT* 1 (München: Chr. Kaiser, Zürich: Theologischer Verlag, 1984) 261-264

Knudtzon, Jörgen Alexander, Otto Weber, and Erich Ebeling, *Die El-Amarna-Tafeln*, 2 Bde, Vorderasiatische Bibliothek, 2 (Leipzig: Hinrichs, 1915)

Knutson, F. Brent, "Literary Genres in *PRU IV*," in *RSP* 2 (Rome: Biblical Institute, 1975) 153-214

——, "Literary Phrases and Formulae," in *RSP* 2 (Rome: Biblical Institute, 1975) 401-422

——, "Political and Foreign Affairs," in *RSP* 2 (Rome: Biblical Institute, 1975) 109-129

Kodell O.S.B., Jerome, *Lamentations, Haggai, Zechariah, Malachi, Obadiah, Joel, Second Zechariah, Baruch*, Old Testament Message, A Biblical-Theological Commentary, 14 (Wilmington, DE: Michael Glazier, 1982)

Koehler, Ludwig, and Walter Baumgartner, *Supplementum ad Lexicon in Veteris Testamenti Libros* (Leiden: E.J. Brill, 1958)

Koehler, Ludwig, and Walter Baumgartner, *Hebräisches und aramäisches Lexicon zum Alten Testament*, 3e Aufl. (Leiden: E.J. Brill, 1967, 1974, 1983, 1990)

Koffmahn, E., *Die Doppelurkunden aus der Wüste Juda* (Leiden: E.J. Brill, 1968)

Köhler, August, *Die Weissagungen Maleachis*, Die nachexilischen Propheten (Erlangen: Deichert, 1865)

Köhler, Ludwig, "Problems in the Study of the Language of the Old Testament," *JSS* 1 (1956) 3-24

König, Eduard, *Historisch-comparative Syntax der hebräischen Sprache*, Schlussteil des historisch-kritischen Lehrgebäudes des Hebräischen (Leipzig: Hinrichs, 1897)

———, *Stilistik, Rhetorik, Poetik in Bezug auf die biblische Litteratur* (Leipzig: T. Weicher, 1900).

Konner, Melvin, *The Tangled Wing: Biological Constraints on the Human Spirit* (New York: Holt, Rinehart and Winston, 1982)

Korošec, Viktor, *Hethitische Staatsverträge: Ein Beitrag zur ihrer juristischen Wertung*, Leipziger rechtswissenschaftliche Studien, Heft 60 (Leipzig: T. Weicher, 1931)

———, "Die Ususehe nach assyrischem Recht," *Orientalia* NS 6 (1937) 1-12

———, "Ehe," in *RLA* II (Berlin and Leipzig: Walter de Gruyter, 1938) 281-299

Koschaker, P., *Rechtsvergleichende Studien zur Gesetzgebung Hammurapis, Königs von Babylon* (Leipzig: Veit, 1917)

———, "Quellenkritische Untersuchungen zu den altassyrischen Gesetzen," *Mitteilungen der Vorderasiatischen Gesellschaft* 26 (1921) 1-84

———, *Neue keilschriftliche Rechtsurkunden aus der El-Amarna Zeit* (Leipzig: Hirzel, 1928 [= *Abhandlungen der Sächsischen Akademie der Wissenschaften, Philo-Hist. Klasse* 39/5, 1929])

———, "Fratriarchat, Hausgemeinschaft und Mutterrecht in Keilschriftrechten," *Zeitschrift für Assyriologie* 41 (1933) 1-89

———, "Eheschliessung und Kauf nach altem Recht, mit besonderer Berücksichtigung der älteren Keilschriftrechte," *Archiv Orientální* 18 (1950) 210-296

———, "Zur Interpretation der Art. 59 des Codex Bilalama," *JCS* 5 (1951) 104-122

Kraeling, E., *The Brooklyn Museum Aramaic Papyri. New Documents of the Fifth Century B.C. from the Jewish Colony of Elephantine* (New Haven, CN: Yale, 1953 [reprinted New York, 1969])

Kraetzschmar, Richard, *Die Bundesvorstellung im Alten Testament in ihrer geschichtlichen Entwicklung, untersucht und dargestellt* (Marburg: N.G. Elwert, 1896)

Kraus, Hans-Joachim, *Worship in Israel* (Richmond: John Knox, 1965)

———, "Der lebendige Gott," *EvT* 27 (1967 [reprinted in his *Biblisch-theologische Aufsätze*, 1972, 1-36]) 169-200

Kroeze, J.H., *Het Boek Job*, COT (Kampen: J.H. Kok, 1961)

Kruger, Paul A., "The Hem of the Garment in Marriage. The Meaning of the Symbolic Gesture in Ruth 3:9 and Ezekiel 16:8," *JNSL* 12 (1984) 79-86

Kruse-Blinkenberg, L., "The Pesitta [*sic*] of the Book of Malachi," *Studia Theologica* 20 (1966) 95-119

———, "The Book of Malachi according to Codex Syro-Hexaplaris Ambrosianus," *Studia Theologica* 21 (1967) 62-82

Kuhl, Curt, "Neue Dokumente zum Verständnis von Hosea 2, 4-15," *ZAW* 52 (1934) 102-109

———, *The Prophets of Israel*, 2nd ed. (Edinburgh: Oliver & Boyd, 1963)

Külling, S.R., *Zur Datierung der "Genesis-P-Stücke," namentlich des Kapitels Genesis 17* (Kampen: J.H. Kok, 1964)

Kunstmann, Walter G., *Die babylonische Gebetsbeschwörung*, Leipziger semitische Studien NF 2 (Leipzig: J.C. Hinrichs, 1932)

Kutsch, Ernst, "Gesetz und Gnade. Probleme des alttestamentlichen Bundesbegriff," *ZAW* 79 (1967) 18-35

———, "Sehen und Bestimmen. Die Etymologie von ברית," in *Archäologie und Altes Testament. Festschrift für Kurt Galling*, A. Kuschke and E. Kutsch, eds. (Tübingen: J.C.B. Mohr [Paul Siebeck], 1970) 165-178

———, *Verheissung und Gesetz. Untersuchungen zum sogennanten 'Bund' im Alten Testament*, BZAW 131 (Berlin: Walter de Gruyter, 1973)

———, "ברית *bᵉrît* Verpflichtung," *THAT* 1 (München: Chr. Kaiser, Zürich: Theologischer Verlag, 1984) 339-352

Lackenbacher, S., "Note sur l'ardat-lilî," *RA* 65 (1971) 119-154

Laetsch, Theodore, *Bible Commentary. The Minor Prophets* (St. Louis, MO: Concordia, 1956)

Lambdin, Thomas O., *Introduction to Biblical Hebrew* (New York: Charles Scribner's Sons and London: Darton, Longman and Todd, 1971)

Lambert, W.G., *Babylonian Wisdom Literature* (Oxford: Clarendon, 1960)

———, "A New Look at the Babylonian Background of Genesis," *JTS* 16 (1965) 287-300

———, "Trees, snakes and gods in ancient Syria and Anatolia," *Bulletin of the School of Oriental and African Studies*, University of London 48 (1985) 435-451

———, "Old Testament Mythology in its Ancient Near Eastern Context," in *Congress Volume Jerusalem 1986*, SVT 40 (Leiden: E.J. Brill, 1988)

———, "Devotion: The Language of Religion and Love" in *Figurative Language in the Ancient Near East*, M. Mindlin, M.J. Geller, and J.E. Wansbrough, eds. (London: University of London, 1987) 25-39.

Lambert, W.G., and A.R. Millard, *Atra-ḫasīs: The Babylonian Story of the Flood with the Sumerian Flood Story by Miguel Civil* (Oxford: Oxford University, 1969)

Lambert, W.G., and Simon B. Parker, *Enuma Eliš. The Babylonian Epic of Creation. The Cuneiform Text* (Birmingham, England: W.G. Lambert, on sale by Blackwell's, Oxford, 1966)

Lamsa, George M., *The Holy Bible From the Ancient Eastern Text* (Philadelphia, PA: A.J. Holman, 1933)

Landsberger, Benno, *Die Serie ana ittišu*, MSL, 1 (Roma: Biblical Institute, 1937)

———, "Jungfräulichkeit: Ein Beitrag zum Thema 'Beilager und Eheschliessung' (mit einem Anhang: Neue Lesungen und Deutungen im Gesetzbuch von Eshnunna)," in *Symbolae Iuridicae et Historicae Martino David dedicatae*, vol. 2, J.A. Ankum, R. Feenstra, and W.F. Leemans, eds., Iura Orientis Antiqui (Leiden: E.J. Brill, 1968) 41-105

Lang, Bernhard, *Wisdom and the Book of Proverbs: an Israelite Goddess redefined* (New York: Pilgrim, 1986)

Latham, James E., *The Religious Symbolism of Salt*, Théologie Historique 64 (Paris: Éditions Beauchesne, 1982)

Lawlor, J.I., *The Nabataeans in Historical Perspective* (Grand Rapids, MI: Baker, 1974)

Leeuwen, C. van, *Hosea*, 3e druk, POT (Nijkerk: G.F. Callenbach, 1984 [1 druk, 1978])

Leggett, Donald A., *The Levirate and Goel Institutions in the Old Testament with Special Attention to the Book of Ruth* (Cherry Hill, New Jersey: Mack, 1974)

Lehmann, Manfred R., "Biblical Oaths," *ZAW* 81 (1969) 74-92

Lemaire, A., and J. M. Durand, *Les inscriptions araméennes de Sfiré et l'Assyrie de Shamshi-Ilu*, Hautes études orientales, 20 (Geneva and Paris: Librairie Droz, 1984)

Lemaire, A., "Populations et territoires de la Palestine à l'époque perse," *Transeuphratène* 3 (1990) 31-74

Lemche, Niels Peter, "The 'Hebrew Slave.' Comments on the Slave Law Ex. xxi 2-11," *VT* 25 (1975) 129-144

Levenson, Jon D. and Baruch Halpern, "The Political Import of David's Marriage," *JBL* 99 (1980) 507-518

Levin, M.Z., "A Protest Against Rape in the Story of Deborah," *Beth Mikra* [Hebrew] 25 (1979) 83-84

Levine, Baruch A., *In the Presence of the Lord* (Leiden: E.J. Brill, 1974)

———, *Leviticus. The Traditional Hebrew Text with the New JPS Translation*, The JPS Torah Commentary (Philadelphia, New York, Jerusalem: Jewish Publication Society, 1989)

Levine, Etan, "On Intra-familial Institutions of the Bible," *Biblica* 57 (1976) 554-559

Levy, Jacob, *Neuhebräisches und chaldäisches Wörterbuch über die Talmudim und Midraschim*, 2 Bde. (Leipzig: Brockhaus, 1878)

Lewy, Julius, "Les textes paléo-assyriens et l'Ancien Testament," *Revue de l'histoire des religions* 110 (1934) 29ff.

———, "On some institutions of the Old Assyrian Empire," *HUCA* 27 (1956) 1-79

Lillback, P.A., "Covenant," in *New Dictionary of Theology*, S.B. Ferguson, D.F. Wright, and J.I. Packer, eds. (Downers Grove, IL and Leicester, England: InterVarsity, 1988) 173-176

Limburg, James, "The Root *ryb* and the Prophetic Lawsuit Speeches," *JBL* 88 (1969) 291ff

Lindblom, Johannes, *Prophecy in Ancient Israel* (Philadelphia, PA: Fortress, 1962)

Lipiński, E., "Malachi, Book of," in *Encyclopaedia Judaica* 11 (Jerusalem, Israel: Keter; and NY: Macmillan, 1971) 812-816

———, "The Wife's Right to Divorce in the Light of an Ancient Near Eastern Tradition," *Jewish Law Annual*, 4, B.S. Jackson, ed. (Leiden: E.J. Brill, 1981) 9-27

Locher, Clemens, "Altes und Neues zu Maleachi 2,10-16," in *Mélanges Dominique Barthélemy; études bibliques offertes à l'occasion de son 60e anniversaire*, P. Casetti, et al., eds., Orbis biblicus et orientalis 38 (Freiburg Schweiz: Universitätsverlag; and Göttingen: Vandenhoeck & Ruprecht, 1981) 241-271

——, *Die Ehre einer Frau in Israel. Exegetische und rechtsvergleichende Studien zu Deuteronomium 22,13-21*, Orbis biblicus et orientalis 70 (Freiburg Schweiz: Universitätsverlag; and Göttingen: Vandenhoeck & Ruprecht, 1986)

Loewenstamm, Samuel E., "Exodus XXI 22-25," *VT* 27 (1977) 352-60

——, *Comparative Studies in Biblical and Ancient Oriental Literatures*, AOAT 204 (Kevelaer: Verlag Butzon & Bercker; and Neukirchen-Vluyn: Neukirchener Verlag, 1980)

Lohfink, Norbert, "Gen 2-3 as 'historical etiology'," *Theology Digest* 13 (1965) 11-17

——, *Die Landverheissung als Eid: Eine Studie zu Gn. 15*, Stuttgarter Bibel-Studien 28 (Stuttgart: Verlag Katholisches Bibelwerk, 1967)

——, "Dt 26,17-19 und die Bundesformel," *Zeitschrift für katholische Theologie* 91 (1969) 517-53

Lohfink, Norbert, and Jan Bergman, "אֶחָד *'echādh*," in *TDOT* 1 (Grand Rapids, MI: Eerdmans, 1977) 193-201

Loretz, O., "Berît — Band, Bund," *VT* 16 (1966) 239-41

Lowe, W.H., "Malachi," in *A Bible Commentary for English Readers by Various Authors, 5, Jeremiah to Malachi*, C.J. Ellicott, ed. (London, Paris, New York and Melbourne: Cassell, n.d.) 597-609

Luck, William F., *Divorce and Remarriage. Recovering the Biblical View* (San Francisco, CA: Harper & Row, 1987)

Lüddeckens, E., *Ägyptische Eheverträge*, Ägyptologische Abhandlungen 1 (Wiesbaden: O. Harrassowitz, 1960)

Luther, Martin, *Die Bibel nach der deutschen Übersetzung d. Martin Luthers* (Berlin: Evangelisch Haupt-Bibelgesellschaft, 1962)

——, *Luther's Works, vol. 18: Lectures on the Minor Prophets I: Hosea, Joel, Amos, Obadiah, Micah, Nahum, Zephaniah, Haggai, Malachi*, H.C. Oswald, ed. (the Wittenberg Text), R.J. Dinda, trans. (St. Louis, MO: Concordia, 1975)

Lyons, John, *Semantics*, 2 vol. (Cambridge: Cambridge University, 1977)

Lys, Daniel, "Rûach," in his, *Le Souffle dans l'Ancien Testament. Enquête anthropologique à travers l'histoire théologique d'Israël* (Paris: Presses Universitaires de France, 1962) 19ff.

Maarsingh, B., *Het Huwelijk in Het Oude Testament* (Baarn: Bosch & Keuning, 1963)

——, *Leviticus*, 2de druk, POT (Nijkerk: G.F. Callenbach, 1980)

Mace, David R., *Hebrew Marriage: A Sociological Study* (London: Epworth, 1953)

Magnetti, Donald Louis, "The Oath in the Old Testament in the Light of Related Terms and in the Legal and Covenantal Context of the Ancient Near East," Ph.D. diss. (The Johns Hopkins University, 1969)

Malamat, Abraham, "Organs of Statecraft in the Israelite Monarchy," *BA* 28 (1965 [= *The Biblical Archaeologist Reader 3*, E.F. Campbell Jr. and D.N. Freedman, eds., Garden City, NY: Doubleday, 1970, pp. 163-198]) 34-65

——, "The Twilight of Judah in the Egyptian-Babylonian Maelstrom," in *Congress Volume, Edinburgh*, SVT 28 (Leiden: E.J. Brill, 1975) 123-45

Malina, Bruce, "Does *Porneia* Mean Fornication?" *NovT* 14 (1972) 10-17

Malinowski, B., *Crime and Custom in Savage Society* (London, 1926)

Malul, Meir, "More on *paḥad yiṣḥāq* (Genesis xxiv 42,53) and the oath by the thigh," *VT* 35 (1985) 192-200

——, "*sissiktu* and *sikku* — Their Meaning and Function," *BO* 43 (1986) 20-36

——, "Touching the Sexual Organs as an Oath Ceremony in an Akkadian Letter," *VT* 37 (1987) 491-2

——, *Studies in Mesopotamian Legal Symbolism*, AOAT 221 (Kevelaer: Verlag Butzon & Bercker; and Neukirchen-Vluyn: Neukirchener Verlag, 1988)

——, "Adoption of Foundlings in the Bible and Mesopotamian Documents. A Study of Some Legal Metaphors in Ezekiel 16:1-7," *JSOT* 46 (1990) 97-126

Mann, C.S., *Mark. A New Translation with Introduction and Commentary*, AB 27 (Garden City, NY: Doubleday, 1986)

Marks, Herbert, "The Twelve Prophets," in *The Literary Guide to the Bible*, R. Alter and F. Kermode, eds. (Cambridge, MA: Harvard University and Glasgow: William Collins Sons & Co., 1987) 207-233

Marshall, I. Howard, "Some Observations on the Covenant in the New Testament," in *Jesus, the Saviour. Studies in New Testament Theology*, I.H. Marshall, ed. (Downers Grove, IL: InterVarsity, 1990) 275-289

Marshall, J.T., "The Theology of Malachi," *ExpTim* 7 (1896) 16-19, 73-75, 125-127

Marti, Karl, *Das Dodekapropheton*, Kurzer Hand-Commentar zum Alten Testament, XIII (Tübingen: J.C.B. Mohr [Paul Siebeck], 1904)

Martin, James D., "The Forensic Background to Jeremiah III 1," *VT* 19 (1969) 82-92

Mason, Rex A., *The Books of Haggai, Zechariah, and Malachi*, CBC (Cambridge: University, 1977)

Matthews, I.G., "Tammuz Worship in the Book of Malachi," *Journal of the Palestine Oriental Society* (1931) 42-50

———, "Haggai, Malachi," in *An American Commentary on the Old Testament, The Minor Prophets*, 2 (Philadelphia: American Baptist Publication Society (The Judson), 1935)

Mawhinney, Allen, "God as Father: Two Popular Theories Reconsidered," *JETS* 31:2 (1988) 181-189

Mayes, A.D.H., *Deuteronomy*, NCB (Greenwood, S.C.: Attic Press, 1979)

Mays, James Luther, *Hosea, A Commentary*, OTL (London: SCM Ltd and Philadelphia: Westminster, 1969)

———, *Amos, A Commentary*, OTL (London: SCM Press Ltd and Philadelphia: Westminster, 1969)

McCarter Jr., P. Kyle, "The Apology of David," *JBL* 99 (1980) 489-504

———, *I Samuel. A New Translation with Introduction, Notes and Commentary,* AB 8 (Garden City, NY: Doubleday, 1980)

———, *II Samuel. A New Translation with Introduction, Notes and Commentary*, AB 9 (Garden City, NY: Doubleday, 1984)

McCarthy, Dennis J., *Old Testament Covenant: A Survey of Current Opinions* (Oxford: Basil Blackwell, 1972)

———, "Hosea XII 2: Covenant by Oil," *VT* 14 (1964 [= "Hosea XII 2: Covenant by Oil," *Institution and Narrative: Collected Essays*, AnBib 108, Rome: Biblical Institute, 1985, 14-20]) 215-221

———, "Three Covenants in Genesis," *CBQ* 26 (1964 [= *Institution and Narrative: Collected Essays*, 1985, 3-13]) 179-89

———, "Notes on the Love of God in Deuteronomy and the Father-Son Relationship Between Yahweh and Israel," *CBQ* 27 (1965) 144-147

———, "*berît* in Old Testament History and Theology," *Biblica* 53 (1972) 110-121

———, "*Berît* and Covenant in the Deuteronomistic History," in *Studies in the Religion of Ancient Israel*, SVT 23 (Leiden: E.J. Brill, 1972 [reprinted in *Institution and Narrative: Collected Essays*, AnBib 108, Rome: Biblical Institute, 1985, 21-41]) 65-85

———, "The Uses of *wehinnēh* in Biblical Hebrew," *Biblica* 61 (1980 [reprinted in *Institution and Narrative: Collected Essays*, AnBib 108, Rome: Biblical Institute, 1985, 237-49]) 330-342

———, *Treaty and Covenant: A Study in Form in the Ancient Oriental Documents and in the Old Testament*, AnBib 21a (Rome: Biblical Institute, 1981 [1st ed, 1963])

———, *Institution and Narrative: Collected Essays*, AnBib 108 (Rome: Biblical Institute, 1985)

McComiskey, Thomas Edward, "The Status of the Secondary Wife: Its Development in Ancient Near Eastern Law. A Study and Comprehensive Index," Ph.D. diss. (Brandeis University, 1965)

———, *The Covenants of Promise. A Theology of the Old Testament Covenants* (Grand Rapids, MI: Baker, 1985)

McConville, J. Gordon, "Priests and Levites in Ezekiel. A Crux in the Interpretation of Israel's History," *TB* 34 (1983) 3-31

———, *Law and Theology in Deuteronomy*, JSOTSup 33 (Sheffield, England: JSOT Press, 1984)

McCree, W.T., "The Covenant Meal in the Old Testament," *JBL* 45 (1926) 120-128

McFadyen, John Edgar, "Malachi," in *The Abingdon Bible Commentary*, F.C. Eiselen, E. Lewis, and D.G. Downey, eds. (New York: Abingdon, 1929)

McKane, William, *Proverbs. A New Approach*, OTL (London: SCM Ltd., 1970)

———, *A Critical and Exegetical Commentary on Jeremiah Vol. 1, Introduction and Commentary on Jeremiah I-XXV*, ICC (Edinburgh: T. & T. Clark, 1985)

McKay, J.W., "Man's Love for God and the Father/Teacher – Son/Pupil Relationship," *VT* 22 (1972) 426-435

McKeating, Henry, *The Books of Amos, Hosea and Micah*, CBC (Cambridge: Cambridge University Press, 1971)

——, "Sanctions against Adultery in Ancient Israelite Society, with Some Reflections on Methodology in the Study of Old Testament Ethics," *JSOT* 11 (1979) 57-72

——, "A Response to Dr Phillips," *JSOT* 20 (1981) 25-26

McKenzie, Steven L., and Howard N. Wallace, "Covenant Themes in Malachi," *CBQ* 45 (1983) 549-563

Mendelsohn, Isaac, "The Conditional Sale into Slavery of Free-born Daughters in Nuzi and the Law of Ex. 21:7-11," *JAOS* 55 (1935) 190-95

——, *Slavery in the Ancient Near East* (Oxford: Oxford University, 1949)

——, "Samuel's Denunciation of Kingship in the Light of the Akkadian Documents from Ugarit," *BASOR* 143 (1956) 17-22

——, "On Marriage in Alalakh," in *Essays on Jewish Life and Thought presented in honor of Salo Wittmayer Baron*, J.L. Blau, A. Hertzberg, Ph. Friedman, and I. Mendelsohn, eds. (New York: Columbia University, 1959) 351-57

——, "Slavery in the OT," in *IDB* 4 (Nashville and New York: Abingdon, 1962) 383-391

Mendenhall, George E., "Puppy and Lettuce in Northwest-Semitic Covenant Making," *BASOR* 133 (1954) 26-30

——, "Ancient Oriental and Biblical Law," *BA* 17 (1954 [reprinted in *The Biblical Archaeology Reader, 3*, Edward F. Campbell Jr. and David Noel Freedman, eds, Garden City, NY: Doubleday, 1970, 3-24]) 26-46

——, "Covenant Forms in Israelite Tradition," *BA* 17 (1954 [reprinted in *The Biblical Archaeology Reader, 3*, Edward F. Campbell Jr. and David Noel Freedman, eds, Garden City, NY: Doubleday, 1970, 25-53]) 50-76

——, *Law and Covenant in Israel and the Ancient Near East* (Pittsburgh, PA: The Biblical Colloquium [reprinted from *The Biblical Archaeologist* 17, 1954, 26-46, 49-76], 1955)

——, "Covenant," in *IDB* 1 (Nashville and New York: Abingdon, 1962) 714-723

——, "Election," in *IDB* 2 (Nashville and New York: Abingdon, 1962) 76-82

——, *The Tenth Generation: The Origins of the Biblical Tradition* (Baltimore, MD: Johns Hopkins, 1973)

Mettinger, Tryggve N.D., *King and Messiah: The Civil and Sacral Legitimation of the Israelite Kings*, Coniectanea biblica, Old Testament Series 8 (Lund: C.W.K. Gleerup, 1976)

Meyer, Ed., *Die Israeliten und ihre Nachbarstämme* (Halle: Max Niemeyer, 1906)

Meyer, Rudolph, *Hebräische Grammatik*, 3 Aufl., Sammlung Göschen Band 5765 (Berlin: Walter de Gruyter, 1966-72)

Meyers, Carol L., and Eric M. Meyers, *Haggai, Zechariah 1-8. A New Translation with Introduction and Commentary*, AB 25B (Garden City, NY: Doubleday, 1987)

Meyers, Eric M., "Priestly language in the book of Malachi," *Hebrew Annual Review*, Biblical and Other Studies. Tenth Anniversary Volume (The Ohio State University, Department of Judaic and Near Eastern Languages and Literatures, 1986) 10 (1986) 225-237

Mezger, Fritz, "Promised but not engaged," *JAOS* 64 (1944) 28-31

Milgrom, Jacob, *Cult and Conscience: The Asham and the Priestly Doctrine of Repentance*, Studies in Judaism in Late Antiquity 18 (Leiden: E.J. Brill, 1976)

Millard, Alan R., "A New Babylonian 'Genesis' Story," *TB* 18 (1967) 3-18

——, "Covenant and Communion in First Corinthians," in *Apostolic History and the Gospel. Biblical and Historical Essays Presented to F.F. Bruce on his 60th Birthday*, W.W. Gasque and R.P. Martin, eds. (Grand Rapids: Eerdmans, 1970) 242-248

Mitchell, Hinckley G., "The Omission of the Interrogative Particle," in *Old Testament and Semitic Studies in memory of William Rainey Harper*, vol. 1, R.F. Harper, F. Brown, and G.F. Moore, eds. (Chicago: University of Chicago, 1908) 115-129

Mitchell, Hinckley G., John Merlin Powis Smith, and Julius A. Bewer, *A Critical and Exegetical Commentary on Haggai, Zechariah, Malachi and Jonah*, ICC (Edinburgh: T. & T. Clark, 1912)

Moor, Johannes Cornelis de, *De Profeet Maleachi* (Amsterdam: Kirberger & Kesper, 1903)

Moore, George Foot, *A Critical and Exegetical Commentary on Judges*, ICC (Edinburgh: T. & T. Clark, 1895)

——, *Judaism in the First Centuries of the Christian Era* (Cambridge, MA: Harvard University, 1927)

Moore, Thomas V., *A Commentary on Haggai and Malachi: A New Translation with Notes* (New York: Robert Carter & Bros., 1856 [reprinted 1960 in The Geneva Series Commentary by Banner of Truth Trust, London])

Moran, William L., "The Use of the Canaanite Infinitive Absolute as a Finite Verb in the Amarna Letters from Byblos," *JCS* 4 (1950) 169-172
——, "The Scandal of the 'Great Sin' at Ugarit," *JNES* 18 (1959) 280-1
——, "The Ancient Near Eastern Background of the Love of God in Deuteronomy," *CBQ* 25 (1963) 77-87
——, *The Amarna Letters* (Baltimore, MD and London: Johns Hopkins, 1992)
Morgenstern, Julian, "Beena Marriage (Matriarchat) in Ancient Israel and its Historical Implications," *ZAW* 47 (1929) 91-110
——, "The Book of the Covenant, Part 2," *HUCA* 7 (1930) 19-258
——, "Additional Notes on Beena Marriage (Matriarchat) in Ancient Israel," *ZAW* 49 (1931) 46-58
——, "Jerusalem - 485 B.C.," *HUCA* 28 (1957) 15-47
——, "David and Jonathan," *JBL* 78 (1959) 322-325
Morris, Desmond, *The Naked Ape* (New York: McGraw-Hill, 1967)
——, *Intimate Behavior* (New York: Random House, 1971)
Moule, C.F.D., "The Judgment Theme in the Sacraments," in *The Background of the New Testament and Its Eschatology (Festschrift for Charles Harold Dodd)*, W.D. Davies and D. Daube, eds. (Cambridge: University Press, 1956) 464-481
Mowinckel, Sigmund Olaf Plytt, *The Psalms in Israel's Worship*, 2 vols., D.R. Ap-Thomas, trans. (New York and Nashville: Abingdon and Oxford: B. Blackwell, 1962)
Muffs, Yohanan, "Studies in Biblical Law, IV: The Antiquity of P," Lectures at the Jewish Theological Seminary of America New York (New York: mimeographed by the Jewish Theological Seminary of America, 1965)
——, *Studies in the Aramaic Legal Documents from Elephantine*, 2nd. ed., Studia et Documenta ad Iura Orientalis Antiqui Pertinentia 8 (Leiden: E.J. Brill, and New York: Ktav, 1973 [1st ed. 1969])
——, "Joy and Love as Metaphorical Expressions of Willingness and Spontaneity in Cuneiform, Ancient Hebrew, and Related Literatures," in *Christianity, Judaism and Other Greco-Roman Cults, Studies for Morton Smith at Sixty, Part 3: Judaism Before 70*, J. Neusner, ed., Studies in Judaism in Late Antiquity 12 (Leiden: E.J. Brill, 1975) 1-36
——, "Love and Joy as Metaphors of Volition in Hebrew and Related Literatures, Part II: The Joy of Giving," *JANESCU* 11 (1979) 91-111
Muntingh, L.M., "Married Life in Israel according to the Book of Hosea," *Die Ou-Testamentiese Werkgemeenskap in Suid-Afrika* 7-8 (1964-65) 77-84
——, "Amorite Married and Family Life according to the Mari Texts," *JNSL* 3 (1974) 50-70
Muraoka, Takamitsu, *Emphatic Words and Structures in Biblical Hebrew* (Jerusalem: Magnes and Leiden: E.J. Brill, 1985)
Murdock, George Peter, *Social Structure* (London and New York: Macmillan, 1949)
Murphy, Roland E., *Wisdom Literature: Job, Proverbs, Ruth, Canticles, Ecclesiastes, Esther*, The Forms of The Old Testament Literature, 13 (Grand Rapids, MI: Eerdmans, 1981)
Murray, John, *The Covenant of Grace. A Biblico-Theological Study* (London: Tyndale, 1954 [reprinted 1988 by Presbyterian and Reformed, Phillipsburg, NJ])
——, *Principles of Conduct. Aspects of Biblical Ethics* (Grand Rapids, MI: Eerdmans; and London: Tyndale, 1957)
——, *Divorce* (Phillipsburg, NJ: Presbyterian and Reformed, 1961)
Myers, Jacob M., *Ezra, Nehemiah*, AB 14 (Garden City, NY: Doubleday, 1965)
——, *II Chronicles. Introduction, Translation, and Notes*, AB 13 (Garden City, NY: Doubleday, 1965 [2nd ed. 1979])
——, *The World of the Restoration*, Backgrounds to the Bible Series (Englewood Cliffs, NJ: Prentice-Hall, 1968)
Naylor, Peter John, "The Language of Covenant. A Structural Analysis of the Semantic Field of ברית in Biblical Hebrew, with Particular Reference to the Book of Genesis," D.Phil. diss. (Oxford University, 1980)
Neil, W., "Malachi," in *IDB* 3 (Nashville and New York: Abingdon, 1962) 228-232
Neuer, Werner, *Man and Woman in Christian Perspective*, G.J. Wenham, trans. (London, Sydney, Aukland, Toronto: Hodder & Stoughton, 1990)
Neufeld, E., *Ancient Hebrew Marriage Laws — With special references to General Semitic Laws and Customs* (London, New York, Toronto: Longmans, Green & Co., 1944)

Neusner, Jacob, translator, *The Talmud of Babylonia, An American Translation. Volume XXID: Tractate Bava Mesia Chapters 7-10,* Brown Judaic Studies 216 (Atlanta, GA: Scholars Press, 1990)

Newcome, William, *An Attempt towards a metrical arrangement, and an explanation of the Twelve Minor Prophets* (London: J.J. Johnson, C.G.J. and J. Robinson, 1785)

Newman, Murray L., Review of E. Kutsch, *Verheissung und Gesetz, JBL* 94 (1975) 117-120

Nicholson, Ernest W., *God and His People. Covenant and Theology in the Old Testament* (Oxford: Clarendon, 1986)

———, "The Origin of the Tradition in Exodus XXIV 9-11," *VT* 26 (1976) 148-160

Nida, Eugene A., "The Implications of Contemporary Linguistics for Biblical Scholarship," *JBL* 91 (1972) 73-89

Niditch, Susan, "The Wronged Woman Righted: An Analysis of Genesis 38," *HTR* 72 (1979) 143-49

———, "The 'Sodomite' Theme in Judges 19-20: Family, Community, and Social Disintegration," *CBQ* 44 (1982) 365-378

Nielsen, Eduard, *Shechem: A Traditio-Historical Investigation,* 2nd ed. (Copenhagen: G.E.C. Gad, 1959 [1st ed., 1955])

Nielsen, Kirsten, *Yahweh As Prosecutor and Judge. An Investigation of the Prophetic Lawsuit (Rîb-pattern),* F. Cryer, trans., JSOTS 9 (Sheffield, England: JSOT Press, 1978)

Nöldeke, Theodor, *Compendius Syriac Grammar,* J.A. Crichton, trans. (London: Williams & Norgate, 1904)

North, Robert, "Flesh, Covering, a Response, Ex. xxi 10," *VT* 5 (1955) 204-6

Noth, Martin, *Das System der zwölf Stämme Israels,* BWANT IV:1 (Stuttgart, Berlin: Kohlhammer, 1930)

———, *The History of Israel,* 2nd ed., P.R. Ackroyd, trans. (New York and London: Harper & Row, 1960 [1st ed. 1958])

———, "Old Testament Covenant Making in the Light of a Text from Mari," in his *The Laws in the Pentateuch and Other Studies,* D.R. Ap-Thomas, trans. (Edinburgh and London: Oliver & Boyd, 1966) 108-117

Nötscher, F., *Zwölfprophetenbuch,* Echter Bibel, 2e Aufl. (Würzburg: Echter, 1957)

Nowack, Wilhelm, *Die kleinen Propheten,* Göttinger HKAT III/4, 3e Aufl. (Göttingen: Vandenhoeck & Ruprecht, 1922 [1e Aufl., 1897; 2e Aufl., 1903])

O'Brien, Julia M., "Torah and Prophets: Malachi and the Date of the Priestly Code," a paper read at the Annual Meeting of the Society of Biblical Literature in Chicago November 20, 1988 (1988)

———, *Priest and Levite in Malachi,* SBLDS 121 (Atlanta, GA: Scholars, 1990)

O'Connor, M., "Northwest Semitic Designations for Elective Social Affinities," *The JANESCU* 18 (1986) 67-80

Oduyoye, Modupe, *The Sons of the Gods and the Daughters of Men: An Afro-Asiatic Interpretation of Genesis 1-11* (Maryknoll, NY: Orbis, 1984)

Ogden, Graham S., "The Use of Figurative Language in Malachi 2:10-16," *Bible Translator* 39 (1988) 223-230

Ogden, Graham S., and Richard R. Deutsch, *A Promise of Hope —A Call to Obedience. A Commentary on the Books of Joel and Malachi,* International Theological Commentary (Grand Rapids, MI: Eerdmans; and Edinburgh: Handsel, 1987)

Orelli, Conrad von, *The Twelve Minor Prophets,* J.S. Banks, trans. (Edinburgh: T. & T. Clark, 1893 [reprinted 1977 by Klock & Klock, Minneapolis, MN])

———, *Die zwölf kleinen Propheten,* 3e Aufl., kurzgefaßter Kommentar zu den heiligen Schriften Alten und Neuen Testamentes zowie zu den Apokryphen [SZKK], A. Altes Testament, 5. Abteilung, 2 Hälfte, H. Strack and O. Zöckler, eds. (München: C.H. Beck, 1908 [1e Aufl., 1888])

Oswalt, John N., *The Book of Isaiah: Chapters 1-39,* NICOT (Grand Rapids, MI: Eerdmans, 1986)

Packard, Joseph, "The Book of Malachi," in *Commentary on the Holy Scriptures, Critical, Doctrinal and Homiletical: Minor Prophets,* J.P. Lange, ed. (New York: Scribner, Armstrong & Co., 1876 [reprinted Grand Rapids, MI: Zondervan, n.d.])

Palmer, Paul F., "Christian Marriage: Contract or Covenant?" *Theological Studies* 33 (1972) 617-665

Parker, B., "The Numrud Tablets, 1952 — Business Documents," *Iraq* 16 (1954) 29-58

Parker, Simon B., "The Marriage Blessing in Israelite and Ugaritic Literature," *JBL* 95 (1976) 23-30

Parpola, Simo, and Kazuko Watanabe, eds., *Neo-Assyrian Treaties and Loyalty Oaths*, State Archives of Assyria 2 (Helsinki: Helsinki University, 1988)

Patai, Raphael, *Sex and Family in the Bible and in the Middle East* (Garden City, NY: Doubleday, 1959)

———, *The Hebrew Goddess* (New York: Ktav, 1967)

Patterson, Richard D., "Old Babylonian Parataxis as Exhibited in the Royal Letters of the Middle Old Babylonian Period and in the Code of Hammurapi," Ph.D. diss. (University of California, Los Angeles, 1970)

Paul, Shalom M., "Exod. 21:10: a Threefold Maintenance Clause," *JNES* 28 (1969) 48-53

———, *Studies in the Book of the Covenant in the Light of Cuneiform and Biblical Law*, SVT 18 (Leiden: E.J. Brill, 1970)

———, "Adoption Formulae: A Study of Cuneiform and Biblical Legal Clauses," *Maarav* 2:2 (1979-1980 [revision of an earlier Hebrew article by the same name published in *H.L. Ginsberg Volume, Eretz-Israel*, 14, Jerusalem: Israel Exploration Society and The Jewish Theological Seminary of America, 1978, 31-36]) 173-85

Payne, J. Barton, "rûah," in *TWOT* 2 (Chicago: Moody, 1980) 386f

Peake, A.S, *Job*, The Century Bible (London: T.C. & E.C. Jack, 1904)

Pedersen, Johannes, *Der Eid bei den Semiten in seinem Verhältnis zu verwandten Erscheinungen, sowie die Stellung des Eides im Islam*, Studien zur Geschichte und Kultur des islamischen Orients, 3 (Zwanglose Beihefte zu der Zeitschrift "Der Islam") (Strassburg: Trubner, 1914)

———, *Israel, Its Life and Culture*, I-II, rev. ed. (London: Oxford University Press, 1959 [1st ed., Copenhagen: S.L. Møller, 1946-1947])

Perlitt, Lothar, *Bundestheologie im Alten Testament*, WMANT 36 (Neukirchen-Vluyn: Neukirchener Verlag, 1969)

Perowne, T.T., *Malachi, with Notes and Introduction*, The Cambridge Bible for Schools and Colleges (Cambridge: University, 1890)

Pestman, P.W., *Marriage and Matrimonial Property in Ancient Egypt*, Papyrologica Lugduno-Batava 9 (Leiden: E.J. Brill, 1961)

Pfeiffer, E., "Die Disputationsworte im Buche Maleachi," *EvT* 19 (1959) 546-68

Pfeiffer, Robert H., *Introduction to the Old Testament* (New York: Harper & Bros., 1948)

Pfeiffer, Robert H., and E.A. Speiser, *100 New Selected Nuzi Texts, transliterated by Robert H. Pfeiffer, with translations and commentary by E.A. Speiser*, AASOR 16 (New Haven: Yale University, 1935-36)

Phillips, Anthony C.J., *Ancient Israel's Criminal Law: A New Approach to the Decalogue* (Oxford: Clarendon and New York: Schocken, 1970)

———, *Deuteronomy*, CBC (Cambridge: Cambridge University, 1973)

———, "*Nebalah* — a term for serious disorderly and unruly conduct," *VT* 25 (1973) 237-242

———, "Some Aspects of Family Law in Pre-Exilic Israel," *VT* 23 (1973) 349-361

———, "Uncovering the Father's Skirt," *VT* 30 (1980) 38-43

———, "Another Example of Family Law," *VT* 30 (1980) 240-245.

———, "Another Look at Adultery," *JSOT* 20 (1981) 3-25

———, "A Response to Dr. McKeating (JSOT 20 [1981] 25-26)," *JSOT* 22 (1981) 142-143

———, "The Decalogue - Ancient Israel's Criminal Law," *JJS* 34 (1983) 1-20

———, *Lower than the Angels. Questions raised by Genesis 1-11. Foreword by Stuart Blanch* (London: The Bible Reading Fellowship, 1983)

———, "The Laws of Slavery: Exodus 21:2-11," *JSOT* 30 (1984) 51-66

———, "The Book of Ruth — Deception and Shame," *JJS* 37 (1986) 1-17

Pinches, T.G., "Babylonian Contract-Tablets with Historical References," *Records of the Past* NS 4 (1890)

———, "Notes," *Journal of the Transactions of the Victoria Institute* 26 (1892-93) 21-23

Plautz, Werner, "Die Frau in Familie und Ehe. Ein Beitrag zum Problem ihrer Stellung im Alten Testament," Ph.D. diss. (Kiel, 1959)

———, "Monogamie und Polygynie im Alten Testament," *ZAW* 75 (1963) 3-27

———, "Die Form der Eheschliessung im Alten Testament," *ZAW* 76 (1964) 298-318

Pococke, Edward, "A Commentary on the Prophecy of Malachi," in *Theological Works*, vol. 1, L. Twells, ed. (London, 1740) 105-206

Poebel, Arno, *Babylonian Legal and Business Documents from the time of the first dynasty of Babylon chiefly from Nippur*, The Babylonian Expedition of the University of

Pennsylvania, Series A, vol. 6, part 2, H.V. Hilprecht, ed. (Philadelphia: Department of Archaeology, University of Pennsylvania, 1909)

Poole, Matthew, *Annotations upon the Holy Bible*, 1 (Glasgow: John Kirk and Robert Williamson, 1803)

Pope, Marvin H., "Oaths," in *IDB* 3 (Nashville and New York: Abingdon, 1962) 575-577

——, *Job. A New Translation with Introduction and Commentary*, 3rd ed., AB 15 (Garden City, NY: Doubleday, 1973)

——, *Song of Songs. A New Translation with Introduction and Commentary*, AB 7C (Garden City, NY: Doubleday, 1977)

Porten, Bezalel, *Archives from Elephantine* (Berkeley and Los Angeles: University of California, 1968)

Porten, Bezalel, and Ada Yardeni, *Textbook of Aramaic Documents From Ancient Egypt, Volume 2: Contracts*, The Hebrew University Department of the History of the Jewish People. Texts and Studies for Students (Jerusalem: Hebrew University, 1989)

Porter, Stanley E., "The Pauline Concept of Original Sin, in the Light of Rabbinic Background," *TB* 41 (1990) 3-30

Postgate, J.N., *Fifty Neo-Assyrian Legal Documents* (Warminster, England: Aris & Phillips, Ltd., 1976)

Praag, A. van, *Droit matrimonial assyro-babylonien*, Allard Pierson Stichting, Archaeologische-Historische Bijdragen, XII (Amsterdam: Noord-Hollandsche, 1945)

Pressel, Wilhelm, *Commentar zu den Schriften der Propheten Haggai, Sacharja, und Maleachi* (Gotha: Schloessmann, 1870)

Price, J.M., "The Oath in Court Procedure in Early Babylonia and the Old Testament," *JAOS* 49 (1929) 22-29

Priest, John F., "The Covenant of Brothers," *JBL* 84 (1965) 400-406

Pritchard, James B., ed., *Ancient Near Eastern Pictures* (Princeton, NJ: Princeton University, 1969)

——, ed., *Ancient Near Eastern Texts Relating to the Old Testament* (Princeton, NJ: Princeton University, 1969)

Procksch, Otto, *Die Genesis übersetzt und erklärt*, 2-3 Aufl., KAT (Leipzig: A. Diechertsche Verlagsbuchhandlung; and Erlangen: Dr. Werner Scholl, 1924)

——, *Die kleinen prophetischen Schriften nach dem Exil*, Erläuterungen zum Alten Testament, 2e Aufl., Teil VI (Stuttgart: Calwer, 1929 [1e Aufl., 1916])

Propp, William H., "The Origins of Infant Circumcision in Israel," *Hebrew Annual Review* 11 (1987) 355-370

Prussner, Frederick C., "The Covenant of David and the Problem of Unity in Old Testament Theology," in *Transitions in Biblical Scholarship*, J.C. Rylaarsdam, ed. (Chicago and London: University of Chicago Press, 1968) 17-41

Pusey, Edward Bouverie, *The Minor Prophets with a Commentary. Explanatory and Practical and Introductions to the Several Books*, Vol 2: Micah, Nahum, Habakkuk, Zephaniah, Haggai, Zechariah and Malachi (New York: Funk & Wagnalls; and London: Walter Smith, 1885 [1st ed., London: Parker, Deighton, Bell & Co., 1860])

Qimron, Elisha, *The Hebrew of the Dead Sea Scrolls*, HSS 29 (Atlanta, Georgia: Scholars, 1986)

Rabinowitz, Jacob J., "Marriage Contracts in Ancient Egypt in the Light of Jewish Sources," *HTR* 46 (1953) 91-7

——, *Jewish Law. Its Influence on the Development of Legal Institutions* (New York: Bloch, 1956)

——, "The 'Great Sin' in Ancient Egyptian Marriage Contracts," *JNES* 18 (1959) 73

Rad, Gerhard von, *Old Testament Theology*, D.M.G. Stalker, trans. (New York: Harper & Row, 1962-65 [*Theologie des Alten Testaments*, 1957, 1960])

——, *Deuteronomy. A Commentary*, D. Barton, trans., OTL (Philadelphia: Westminster, 1966)

——, *Genesis. A Commentary*, revised ed., J.H. Marks, trans., OTL (Philadelphia: Westminster, 1972)

Radday, Yehuda T., and Moshe A. Pollatschek, "Vocabulary Richness in Post-Exilic Prophetic Books," *ZAW* 92 (1980) 333-46

Radday, Yehuda T., and Dieter Wickmann, "The Unity of Zechariah Examined in the light of Statistical Linguistics," *ZAW* 87 (1975) 30-55

Rahlfs, Alfred, ed., *Septuaginta id est Vetus Testamentum graece iuxta LXX interpretes* (Stuttgart: Württembergische Bibelanstalt, 1935)

Rattray, Susan, "Marriage Rules, Kinship Terms and Family Structure in the Bible," in *Society of Biblical Literature 1987 Seminar Papers* (Atlanta, GA: Scholars, 1987) 537-544

Rawlinson, George, *Ezra and Nehemiah: Their Lives and Times* (New York: Randolf, 1890)

Reckendorf, H., *Arabische Syntax* (Heidelberg: Winter, 1921 [reprinted 1973 by A.P.A., Amsterdam])

Reinke, Laur., *Der Prophet Maleachi* (Giessen: Ferber'sche Universitätsbuchhandlung, 1856)

Reiser, Werner, "Die Verwandtschaftsformel in Gen. 2,23," *Theologische Zeitschrift* 16 (1960) 1-4

Rendsburg, Gary A., "Late Biblical Hebrew and the Date of P," *JANESCU* 12 (1980) 65-80

———, "A New Look at the Pentateuchal HW ?," *Biblica* 63 (1982) 351-369

———, *The Redaction of Genesis* (Winona Lake, IN: Eisenbrauns, 1986)

Rendtorff, Rolf, "Maleachibuch," in *RGG³* IV, K. Galling, ed. (Tübingen: J.C.B. Mohr [Paul Siebeck], 1957-65) 628f

———, *The Old Testament. An Introduction*, J. Bowden, trans. (London: SCM Ltd., 1985)

Renger, J., "Who are all those People?" *Orientalia* 42 (1973) 259-273

Renker, Alwin, *Die Tora bei Maleachi: Ein Beitrag zur Bedeutungsgeschichte von tôrā im Alten Testament*, Freiburger Theologische Studien 112 (Freiburg, Basel, Wien: Herder, 1979)

Reventlow, Henning Graf, *Gebot und Predigt im Dekalog* (Gütersloh: Gerd Mohn, 1962)

———, *Problems of Old Testament Theology in the Twentieth Century* (Philadelphia, PA: Fortress, 1985)

Richter, W., "Urgeschichte und Hoftheologie," *Biblische Zeitschrift* 10 (1966) 96-105

Ridderbos, Jan, *Het Godswoord der Profeten, Vol. IV: Van Ezechiel tot Maleachi* (Kampen: J.H. Kok, 1941)

———, *Deuteronomy*, E.M. van der Maas, trans., Bible Student's Commentary (Grand Rapids, MI: Zondervan and St. Catharines, Ont.: Paideia, 1984)

———, *De kleine profeten. Opnieuw uit den grondtekst vertaald en verklaard; IIIde Deel: Haggai, Zacharia, Maleachi*, Korte Verklaring der Heilige Schrift met nieuwe Vertaling, 3de druk (Kampen: J.H. Kok, N.V., 1968)

Riessler, Paul, *Die kleinen Propheten oder das Zwölfprophetenbuch nach dem Urtext übersetzt und erklärt* (Rottenburg a.N.: Badaer, 1911)

Ringgren, Helmer, *Word and Wisdom: Studies in the Hypostatization of Divine Qualities and Functions in the Ancient Near East* (Lund: Hakan Ohlssons Boktryckeri, 1947)

———, *Sprüche/Prediger*, ATD 16/1 (Göttingen: Vandenhoeck & Ruprecht, 1962)

———, *Israelite Religion*, D. Green, trans. (London: S.P.C.K. and Philadelphia, PA: Fortress, 1966)

———, "חָיָה chāyāh," in *TDOT* 4 (Grand Rapids, MI: Eerdmans, 1980) 324-344

Rivkin, Ellis, "Aaron, Aaronides," in *IDBSup* (Nashville, TN: Abingdon, 1976) 1-3

Robert, A., "Les attaches littéraires bibliques de Prov. I-IX," *RB* 43 (1934) 42-68, 172-204, 374-84

———, "Les attaches littéraires bibliques de Prov. I-IX," *RB* 44 (1935) 344-65; 505-25

Robinson, G.L., *The Twelve Minor Prophets* (Grand Rapids, MI: Baker, 1952)

Robinson, Theodore H., and Friedrich Horst, *Die zwölf kleinen Propheten*, Bd 2, 3e Aufl., HAT 1/14 (Tübingen: J.C.B. Mohr [Paul Siebeck], 1964 [1 Aufl., 1938])

Rogerson, John, *The Supernatural in the Old Testament* (Guildford and London: Lutterworth, 1976)

Rooy, Herculaas Frederik van, "Conditional Sentences in Biblical Hebrew," in *Proceedings of the Ninth World Congress of Jewish Studies, Jerusalem, August 4-12, 1985 Division D, Vol. 1: Hebrew and Jewish Languages* (Jerusalem: Magnes, 1986)

Rosenberg, Joel W., "The Garden Story Forward and Backward: The Non-Narrative Dimension of Gen. 2-3," *Prooftexts: A Journal of Jewish Literary History* 1 (1981) 1-27

———, *King and Kin. Political Allegory in the Hebrew Bible* (Bloomington and Indianapolis: Indiana University, 1986)

Ross, James F., "Meal," in *IDB* 3 (Nashville and New York: Abingdon, 1962) 315

———, "Salt," in *IDB* 4 (Nashville and New York: Abingdon, 1962) 167

Roth, Martha T., "Age at Marriage and the Household: A Study of Neo-Babylonian and Neo-Assyrian Forms," *Comparative Studies in Society and History* (Cambridge University) 29 (1987) 715-47

——, "'She will die by the iron dagger': Adultery and Neo-Babylonian Marriage," *Journal of the Economic and Social History of the Orient* 31 (1988) 186-206

——, *Babylonian Marriage Agreements: 7th - 3rd Centuries B.C.*, AOAT 222 (Kevelaer: Verlag Butzon & Bercker; and Neukirchen-Vluyn: Neukirchener Verlag, 1989)

——, "Marriage and Matrimonial Prestations in First Millennium B.C. Babylonia," in *Women's Earliest Records From Ancient Egypt and Western Asia. Proceedings of the Conference on Women in the Ancient Near East, Brown University, Providence Rhode Island, November 5-7, 1987*, B.S. Lesko, ed., Brown Judaic Studies 166 (Atlanta, Georgia: Scholars, 1989) 245-255 (responses on pp. 256-260)

Rowley, Harold Henry, "The Chronological Order of Ezra and Nehemiah," in *Ignace Goldziher Memorial Volume*, S. Löwinger and J. Somogyi, eds. (Budapest, 1948 [reprinted in *The Servant of the Lord and Other Essays on the Old Testament*, 2nd. ed., Oxford: Blackwell; and Naperville, IL: Allenson, 1965, 135-168]) 117-149

——, "The Marriage of Hosea," *Bulletin of the John Rylands Library* 39 (1956-7 [reprinted in *Men of God: Studies in Old Testament History and Prophecy*, London: Nelson, 1963, 66-97]) 200-233

Rudolph, Wilhelm, *Chronikbücher*, HAT (Tübingen: Mohr, 1955)

——, *Hosea*, KAT 13/1 (Gütersloh: Gerd Mohn, 1966)

——, *Jeremia*, 3e Aufl., HAT 12 (Tübingen: J.C.B. Mohr [Paul Siebeck], 1968)

——, *Haggai, Sacharja 1-8, Sacharja 9-14, Maleachi, mit einer Zeittafel von Alfred Jepsen*, KAT XIII/4 (Gütersloh: Gerd Mohn and Neukirchen: Neukirchener Verlag, 1976)

——, "Zu Malachi 2:10-16," *ZAW* 93 (1981) 85-90

Rummel, Stan, ed., *Ras Shamra Parallels: The Texts From Ugarit and the Hebrew Bible*, vol. 3, AnOr 51 (Rome: Biblical Institute, 1981)

Sabottka, Liudger, *Zephanja: Versuch einer Neuübersetzung mit philologischen Kommentar*, BibOr 25 (Rome: Biblical Institute, 1972)

Sanders, Henry A., and Carl Schmidt, *The Minor Prophets in the Freer Collection and The Berlin Fragment of Genesis* (New York and London: Macmillan, 1927)

Saporetti, Claudio, *The Status of Women in the Middle Assyrian Period*, Monographs on the Ancient Near East, vol. 2, fasc. 1 (Malibu, CA: Undena Publications, 1979)

Sarna, Nahum M., *Exploring Exodus. The Heritage of Biblical Israel* (New York: Schocken Books, 1986)

——, *Genesis. The Traditional Hebrew Text with the New JPS Translation*, The JPS Torah Commentary (Philadelphia, New York, Jerusalem: Jewish Publication Society, 1989)

Sasson, Jack M., *Ruth: A New Translation with a Philological Commentary and a Formalist-Folklorist Interpretation*, Johns Hopkins Near Eastern Studies (Baltimore, MD: Johns Hopkins, 1979)

Sauer, G., "אֶחָד *'æḥād* einer," *THAT* 1 (München: Chr. Kaiser; and Zürich: Theologischer Verlag, 1984) 104-107

Saurin, Jacques, *Kurtzer Entwurff [sic] der Christlichen Theologie und Sitten-Lehre* [= abregé de theologie et morale chretienne, dt.] (1723)

Scharbert, Josef, "'Fluchen' und 'Segnen' im Alten Testament," *Biblica* 39 (1958) 1-26

——, "Ehe und Eheschliessung in der Rechtssprache des Pentateuchs und beim Chronisten," in *Studien zum Pentateuch (Fs. Walter Kornfeld)*, G. Braulik, ed. (Wien, Freiburg, Basel: Herder, 1977) 213-225

——, "בָּרַךְ, *brk*," in *TDOT* 1 (Grand Rapids, MI: Eerdmans, 1977) 279-308

——, "אָלָה, *'ālāh*," in *TDOT* 1 (Grand Rapids, MI: Eerdmans, 1978) 261-266

Schmidt, Werner H., *Introduction to the Old Testament*, M.J. O'Connell, trans. (London: SCM, 1984)

Schoors, A., "The Particle כִּי," *Remembering All the Way*, OTS 21 (Leiden: E.J. Brill, 1981) 240-276

Schorr, Moses, *Urkunden des altbabylonischen Zivil- und Prozessrechts*, Vorderasiatische Bibliothek 5 (Leipzig: J.C. Hinrichs, 1913)

Schreiner, Stefan, "Mischehen-Ehebruch-Ehescheidung. Betrachtungen zu Mal 2,10-16," *ZAW* 91 (1979) 207-228

Schumpp, P. Meinrad, *Das Buch der zwölf Propheten*, Herders Bibelkommentar X/2 (Die Heilige Schrift für das Leben erklärt) E. Kalt, ed. (Freiburg: Herder, 1950)

Scott, R.B.Y., *Proverbs. Ecclesiastes. Introduction, Translation, and Notes*, 2nd. ed., AB 18 (New York, London, Toronto, Sydney, Auckland: Doubleday, 1965)

Scott, Thomas, *The Holy Bible containing the Old and New Testaments, according to the Authorized Version; with Explanatory Notes, Practical Observations, and Copious*

Marginal References, Vol. 4 (Boston: Samuel T. Armstrong, and Crocker and Brewster, 1832 [reprint of the 1st ed., 1788-1792])

Segal, Moshe, "לבנית פסוקי השבועה והנדר בעברית," *Leshonenu* 1 (1929) 215-227

Sellin, Ernst, *Das Zwölfprophetenbuch. Zweite Hälfte: Nahum-Maleachi*, KAT XII (Leipzig: A. Diechertsche Verlagsbuchhandlung; Erlangen: Dr. Werner Scholl, 1922 [2e and 3e Aufl., 1930])

Selman, Martin J., "Published and Unpublished Fifteenth Century B.C. Cuneiform Documents and Their Bearing on the Patriarchal Narratives of the Old Testament," Ph.D. diss. (University of Wales, 1975).

Selms, Adriaan van, *Marriage and Family Life in Ugaritic Literature* (London: Luzac and Co., Ltd., 1954)

———, "The Inner Cohesion of the Book of Malachi," in *Studies in Old Testament Prophecy*, W.C. van Wyk, ed., OTWSA (Potchefstroom: Pro Rege, 1975) 27-40

———, *Genesis deel I*, 4e druk, POT (Nijkerk: G.F. Callenbach, 1984 [1 druk, 1967])

Shea, William H., "Adam in Ancient Mesopotamian Traditions," *AUSS* 15 (1977) 27-41

———, "A Comparison of Narrative Elements in Ancient Mesopotamian Creation-Flood Stories with Genesis 1-9," *Origins* 11 (1984) 9-29

Sievers, Eduard, *Metrische Studien, I, Studie zur hebräischen Metrik*, Abhandlungen der philologisch-historischen Classe der königlich Sächsischen Gesellschaft der Wissenschaften, 21 (Leipzig: B.G. Teubner, 1901)

———, *Alttestamentliche Miscellen, 4, Zu Maleachi*, Abhandlungen der philologisch-historischen Classe der königlich Sächsischen Gesellschaft der Wissenschaften, 57 (Leipzig: B.G. Teubner, 1905)

Silbermann, A.M., and M. Rosenbaum, *Chumash with Targum Onkelos, Haphtaroth and Rashi's Commentary: Bereshith, translated into English and Annotated* (Jerusalem: The Silbermann Family, 1934)

Silva, Moisés, *Biblical Words and Their Meaning: An Introduction to Lexical Semantics* (Grand Rapids, MI: Zondervan, 1983)

Skaist, Aaron J., "Studies in Ancient Mesopotamian Family Law Pertaining to Marriage and Divorce," Ph.D. diss. (University of Pennsylvania, 1963)

Skehan, Patrick W., *Studies in Israelite Poetry and Wisdom*, Catholic Biblical Quarterly Monograph Series, 1 (Washington, D.C.: Catholic Biblical Association, 1971)

Skehan, Patrick W., and Alexander A. Di Lella, *The Wisdom of Ben Sira. A New Translation with Notes by Patrick W. Skehan. Introduction and Commentary by Alexander A. DiLella*, AB 39 (New York: Doubleday, 1987)

Skinner, John, *Prophecy and Religion. Studies in the Life of Jeremiah*, 2nd ed. (Cambridge: Cambridge University, 1922)

———, *A Critical and Exegetical Commentary on Genesis*, 2nd. ed., ICC (Edinburgh: T. & T. Clark Ltd., 1930 [1st ed. 1910])

Smend, Rudolf, *Die Bundesformel*, Theologische Studien 68 (Zürich: EVZ-Verlag, 1963)

———, *Die Mitte des Alten Testaments*, Theologische Studien 101 (Zürich: EVZ-Verlag, 1970)

———, "Essen und Trinken — ein Stück Weltlichkeit des AT," in *Beiträge zur alttestamentlischen Theologie. Fs für Walther Zimmerli zum 70. Geburtstag*, H. Donner, R. Hanhart, and R. Smend, eds. (Göttingen: Vandenhoeck & Ruprecht, 1977) 446-459

Smick, Elmer B., "כָּרַת (*kārat*) cut off a part of the body, etc.," in *TWOT* 1 (Chicago: Moody, 1980) 456-457

———, "בְּרִית (*bᵉrit*) covenant," in *TWOT* 1 (Chicago: Moody, 1980) 128-130

———, "Job," in *The Expositor's Bible Commentary*, 4, F.E. Gaebelein, ed. (Grand Rapids, MI: Zondervan, 1988) 843-1060

Smit, G., *De kleine profeten, III: Habakuk, Haggai, Zacharia, Maleachi*, Texte und Untersuchungen (Den Haag: Wolters, 1934)

Smith, George Adam, *The Book of the Twelve Prophets Commonly Called the Minor in Two Volumes — Volume 2: Zephaniah, Nahum, Habakkuk, Obadiah, Haggai, Zechariah, Malachi, Joel, Jonah*, 2nd ed. (New York and London: Harper & Brothers, 1929 [1st ed. 1899])

Smith, Gary V., "Malachi," in *ISBE* 3 (Grand Rapids, MI: Eerdmans, 1986) 226-28

———, *Amos. A Commentary*, The Library of Biblical Interpretation (Grand Rapids, MI: Zondervan, 1989)

Smith, Henry Preserved, *A Critical and Exegetical Commentary on the Books of Samuel*, ICC (Edinburgh: T. & T. Clark, 1899 [reprinted 1977])

Smith, John Merlin Powis: see H.G. Mitchell, J.M. Powis Smith, and J.A. Bewer, *A Critical and Exegetical Commentary on Haggai, Zechariah, Malachi and Jonah*

Smith, John Merlin Powis, "A Note on Malachi 2:15a," *AJSL* 28 (1911/12) 204-206

——, "The Syntax and Meaning of Genesis 1:1-3," *AJSL* 44 (1928) 108-115

——, "The Use of Divine Names as Superlatives," *AJSL* 45 (1929) 212-213

Smith, John Merlin Powis, William Hayes Ward, and Julius A. Bewer, *A Critical and Exegetical Commentary on Micah, Zephaniah, Nahum, Habakkuk, Obadiah and Joel*, ICC (Edinburgh: T. & T. Clark, 1911 [reprinted 1974])

Smith, Morton, "Jewish religious life in the Persian period," in *The Cambridge History of Judaism. Vol 1: Introduction; The Persian Period*, W.D. Davies and L. Finkelstein, eds. (Cambridge, London, and New York: Cambridge University, 1984) 219-278

Smith, Ralph L., *Micah-Malachi*, WBC 32 (Waco, TX: Word, 1984)

——, "The Shape of Theology in the Book of Malachi," *Southwestern Journal of Theology* 30 (1987) 22-27

Smith, R. Payne, *A Compendious Syriac Dictionary*, J.P. Smith, ed. (Oxford: Clarendon, 1903)

Smith, Sidney, "The Age of Ashurbanipal," in *Cambridge Ancient History, III: The Assyrian Empire*, J.B. Bury, S.A. Cook, and F.E. Adcock, eds. (Cambridge, London, New York, and Melbourne: Cambridge University Press, 1929 [1st edition 1925]) 89-112 ("Assyrian Law" on pp. 104-108)

Smith, William Robertson, *Kinship and Marriage in Early Arabia*, 2nd ed. (Cambridge and London: Cambridge University, 1903 [reprinted 1963 by Beacon, Boston])

——, *Lectures on the Religion of the Semites: The Fundamental Institutions*, 3rd ed. (London and New York: Macmillan, 1927)

Snijders, Lambertus A., "The Meaning of *zār* in the Old Testament," *OTS* 10 (1954) 1-154

——, "זר/זור, *zûr/zār*," in *TDOT* 4 (Grand Rapids, MI: Eerdmans, 1980) 52-58

Snyman, S.D., "Antiteses in die boek Maleagi," Ph.D. diss. (University of Pretoria, South Africa, 1985)

——, "Antitheses in Malachi 1,2-5," *ZAW* 98 (1986 [orig. published as "Chiasmes in Mal. 1:2-5," *Skrif en Kerk*, 1984, 17-22]) 436-38

Soden, Wolfram von, "Die Unterweltsvision eines assyrischen Kronprinzen," *Zeitschrift für Assyriologie und verwandte Gebiete* 43 (1936) 1-31

——, *Akkadisches Handwörterbuch*, 2e Aufl., 3 Bde (Wiesbaden: Otto Harrassowitz, 1959-1985)

——, *Grundriss der Akkadischen Grammatik, samt Ergänzungsheft zum Grundriss der Akkadischen Grammatik*, AnOr 33 and 47 (Rome: Biblical Institute, 1969)

——, "Zum hebräischen Wörterbuch," in *Ugarit-Forschungen* 13 (Kevelaer: Verlag Butzon & Bercker; and Neukirchen-Vluyn: Neukirchener Verlag, 1981) 157-164

Soggin, J. Alberto, "Akkadisch TAR *berîti* und hebräisch *krt bryt*," *VT* 18 (1968) 210-215

——, *Introduction to the Old Testament From Its Origins to the Closing of the Alexandrian Canon*, 3rd ed., J. Bowden, trans., OTL (Philadelphia: Westminster, 1989)

Sohn, Seock-Tae, "The Divine Election of Israel," Ph.D. diss. (New York University, 1986)

Sonsino, R., "Characteristics of Biblical Law," *Judaism* 33 (1984) 202-209

Speiser, Ephraim Avigdor, *New Kirkuk Documents Relating to Family Laws*, AASOR 10 (New Haven: Yale University, 1930)

——, "Ethnic Movements in the Near East in the Second Millennium," AASOR 13 (New Haven: Yale University, 1933) 13-54

——, *100 New Selected Nuzi Texts*, see Robert H. Pfeiffer and E.A. Speiser

——, "'I Know Not the Day of My Death' [Gen 27:2]," *JBL* 74 (1955) 252-256

——, "Leviticus and the Critics," in *Yehezkel Kaufmann Jubilee Volume*, M. Haran, ed. (Jerusalem: Magnes, 1960) 29-45

——, *Genesis. Introduction, Translation, and Notes*, AB 1 (Garden City, NY: Doubleday, 1964 [3rd ed. 1979])

Sperber, Alexander, *The Bible in Aramaic, III: The Latter Prophets according to Targum Jonathan*, The Bible in Aramaic (Leiden: E.J. Brill, 1962)

Sperber, J., "Der Personenwechsel," *Zeitschrift für Assyriologie und verwandte Gebiete* 32 (1918/19) 23-33

Spoer, Hans H., "Some New Considerations towards the Dating of the Book of Malachi," *Jewish Quarterly Review* 20 (1908) 167-86

Stade, Bernhard, *Lehrbuch der hebräischen Grammatik* (Leipzig: Vogel, 1879)

——, *Biblische Theologie des Alten Testaments* 1 (Tübingen: J.C.B. Mohr, 1905)

Stamm, Johann Jakob, and Maurice Edward Andrew, *The Ten Commandments in Recent Research*, Studies in Biblical Theology, 2nd. series, 2 (London: SCM Ltd.; and Nashville, TN: Alec R. Allenson, 1967)

Sternberg, Meir, *The Poetics of Biblical Narrative: Ideological Literature and the Drama of Reading*, Indiana Literary Biblical Series (Bloomington, IN: Indiana University Press, 1985)

Strack, H.L., and P. Billerbeck, *Kommentar zum Neuen Testament aus Talmud und Midrasch*, 6 Bde (München: Beck, 1923-1961)

Strassmaier, Johann Nepomucen, *Die babylonischen Inschriften im Museum zu Liverpool, nebst anderen aus der Zeit von Nebukadnezzar bis Darius*, Actes du sixième congrès international des Orientalistes tenu en 1883 à Leide, II, Section Sémitique (1) (Leipzig, J.C. Hinrichs, 1885)

Stuart, Douglas K., *Hosea - Jonah*, WBC 31 (Waco, TX: Word, 1987)

———, *Old Testament Exegesis: A Primer for Students and Pastors*, 2nd ed. (Philadelphia, PA: Westminster, 1984)

Stuhlmueller, Carroll, "Malachi," in *The Jerome Biblical Commentary*, R.E. Brown, J.A. Fitzmyer, and R.E. Murphy, eds. (London: Geoffrey Chapman, 1970) 398-401

———, "Sacrifice among the Nations," *The Bible Today* 22 (1984) 223-25

Swetnam, James, "Malachi 1,11: An Interpretation," *CBQ* 31 (1969) 200-209

Symons, Donald, *The Evolution of Human Sexuality* (New York and Oxford: Oxford University, 1979)

Tadmor, Hayim, "Treaty and Oath in the Ancient Near East: An Historian's Approach," in *Humanizing America's Iconic Book: Society of Biblical Literature Centennial Addresses 1980*, SBL Centennial Publications, Scholars Press, G.M. Tucker and D.A. Knight, eds., Society of Biblical Literature Biblical Scholarship in North America, 6 (Chico, CA: Scholars Press, 1982) 127-152

Taylor, John B., *Ezekiel. An Introduction and Commentary*, TOTC (Downers Grove, IL: Inter-Varsity, 1969)

Teubal, Savina J., *Sarah the Priestess. The First Matriarch of Genesis* (Athens, Ohio; Chicago; London: Swallow, 1984)

The Holy Bible. An American Translation (New Haven, Missouri: Leader, 1976)

The Holy Bible. New International Version (Grand Rapids, MI: Zondervan, 1978; London, Sydney, Auckland, Toronto: Hodder and Stoughton, 1979)

The Holy Bible. The Revised Version (Oxford and London: Oxford University; and New York: Thomas Y. Crowell, 1885)

The Holy Bible containing the Old and New Testaments. Newly Edited by the American Revision Committee, A.D. 1901, Standard Edition (New York: Thomas Nelson & Sons, 1901)

The Holy Scriptures according to the Masoretic Text (Philadelphia, PA: Jewish Publication Society of America, 1917)

The New American Bible (Nashville, Camden, and New York: Thomas Nelson, 1970)

The Old Testament in Syriac According to the Peshitta Version, Prepared by the Peshitta Institute, Leiden, Part 3, fasc. 4 (Leiden: E.J. Brill, 1980)

Thiselton, Anthony C., "Semantics and New Testament Interpretation," in *New Testament Interpretation*, I.H. Marshall, ed. (Exeter: Paternoster; and Grand Rapids, MI: Eerdmans, 1977) 75-104

Thomas, D. Winton, "The Root *yd'* in Hebrew," *JTS* 35 (1934) 298-306

Thompson, John Arthur, *Deuteronomy. An Introduction and Commentary*, TOTC (Downers Grove, IL: InterVarsity, 1974)

———, "The Significance of the Verb *Love* in the David-Jonathan Narratives in I Samuel," *VT* 24 (1974) 334-38

———, "Covenant (OT)," in *ISBE* 1 (Grand Rapids, MI: Eerdmans, 1979) 790-793

———, *The Book of Jeremiah*, NICOT (Grand Rapids, MI: Eerdmans, 1980)

Thompson, Thomas L., *The Historicity of the Patriarchal Narratives. The Quest for the Historical Abraham*, BZAW 133 (Berlin and New York: Walter de Gruyter, 1974)

Tigay, Jeffrey H., "Israelite Religion: The Onomastic and Epigraphic Evidence," in *Ancient Israelite Religion. Essays in Honor of Frank Moore Cross*, P.D. Miller Jr., P.D. Hanson, and S.D. McBride, eds. (Philadelphia: Fortress, 1987) 157-194

Toorn, Karel van der, *Sin and Sanction in Israel and Mesopotamia: a comparative study*, Studia Semitica Neerlandica, 22 (Assen: Van Gorcum, 1985)

———, "Ordeal Procedures in the Psalms and the Passover Meal," *VT* 38 (1988) 427-445

———, "Female Prostitution in Payment of Vows in Ancient Israel," *JBL* 108 (1989) 193-205

Torczyner, Harry, *Lachish I. The Lachish Letters* (Oxford and London: Oxford University, 1938)

Torrance, James B., "Covenant or Contract? A Study of the Theological Background of Worship in Seventeeth-Century Scotland," *Scottish Journal of Theology* 23 (1970) 51-76

Torrey, Charles Cutler, "The Edomites in Southern Judah," *JBL* 17 (1898) 16-20

———, "The Prophecy of 'Malachi'," *JBL* 17 (1898) 1-15

Tosato, Angelo, *Il matrimonio nel Giudaismo antico e nel Nuovo Testamento* (Rome: Biblical Institute, 1976)

———, "Il ripudio: delitto e pena (Mal 2,10-16)," *Biblica* 59 (1978) 548-553

———, *Il matrimonio israelitico. Una theoria generale*, AnBib 100 (Rome: Biblical Institute, 1982)

———, "The Law of Leviticus 18:18: A Reexamination," *CBQ* 46 (1984) 199-214

Toy, Crawford H., *A Critical and Exegetical Commentary on the Book of Proverbs*, ICC (Edinburgh: T. & T. Clark, 1899)

Trible, Phyllis, *God and the Rhetoric of Sexuality*, Overtures to Biblical Theology (Philadelphia, PA: Fortress, 1978)

———, *Texts of Terror: Literary-Feminist Readings of Biblical Narratives*, Overtures to Biblical Theology (Philadelphia: Fortress, 1984)

Trumbull, H.C., *The Covenant of Salt, as Based on the significance and Symbolism of Salt in Primitive Thought* (New York: Scribner, 1899)

Tsevat, Matitiahu, "Marriage and Monarchical Legitimacy in Ugarit and in Israel," *JSS* 3 (1958) 237-243

———, "The Neo-Assyrian and Neo-Babylonian Vassal Oaths and the Prophet Ezekiel," *JBL* 78 (1959) 199-204

———, "Studies in the Book of Samuel," *HUCA* 34 (1963) 71-82

Tsevat, Matitiahu, Jan Bergman, and Helmer Ringgren, "בְּתוּלָה *bᵉthûlāh*," in *TDOT* 1 (Grand Rapids, MI: Eerdmans, 1977) 338-343

Tucker, Gene M., "Covenant Forms and Contract Forms," *VT* 15 (1965) 487-503

———, "Prophetic Superscriptions and the Growth of a Canon," in *Canon and Authority. Essays in Old Testament Religion and Theology*, G.W. Coats and B.O. Long, eds. (Philadelphia: Fortress, 1977) 56-70

Tur-Sinai [Torczyner], N.H., *The Book of Job*, rev. ed. (Jerusalem: Kiryat-Sefer, 1967)

Ulrich Jr., Eugene Charles, *The Qumran Text of Samuel and Josephus* (Missoula, MT: Scholars, 1978)

Van Seters, John, "The Problem of Childlessness in Near Eastern Law and the Patriarchs of Israel," *JBL* 87 (1968) 401-8

———, "Jacob's Marriages and Ancient Near East Customs: a re-examination," *HTR* 62 (1969) 377-95

———, *Abraham in History and Tradition* (New Haven: Yale University, 1975)

Vannoy, J. Robert, *Covenant Renewal at Gilgal. A Study of 1 Samuel 11:14-12:25* (Cherry Hill, NJ: Mack, 1978)

Vaux O.P., Roland de, *Ancient Israel, Vol. 1, Social Institutions* (New York: McGraw-Hill, 1961 [orig. published as *Les Institutions de L'Ancien Testament*, 1, Paris: Les Éditions du Cerf, 1958])

Vawter, Bruce, "The Biblical Theology of Divorce," *Proceedings of the Catholic Theological Society of America* 22 (1967) 223-43

———, *On Genesis: A New Reading* (Garden City, NY: Doubleday, 1977)

Veenhof, K.R., review of E. Kutsch, *Salbung als Rechtsakt im Alten Testament und im alten Orient*, *BO* 23 (1966) 308-13

Vellas, Basil M., *Israelite Marriage*, J.S. Koulouras, trans. (Athens: n.p., 1956)

Verhoef, Pieter Adriaan, "Some Notes on Malachi 1:11," in *Biblical Essays, Proceedings of the Ninth Meeting of Die Ou-Testamentiese Werkgemeenskap in Suid-Afrika, held at the University of Stellenbosch, July 1966* (Potchefstroom: Pro Rege, 1967 [reprint in *Nederduits Gereformeerde Teologiese Tydskrif*, 21, 1980, 21-30]) 163-72

———, *Maleachi*, COT 19 (Kampen: J.H. Kok, 1972)

———, *The Books of Haggai and Malachi*, NICOT (Grand Rapids, MI: Eerdmans, 1987)

Viberg, Åke, *Symbols of Law. A Contextual Analysis of Legal Symbolic Acts in the Old Testament*, Coniectanea Biblica, Old Testament Series, 34 (Stockholm: Almqvist and Wiksell International, 1992)

Vollmer, J., "עָשָׂה 'śh machen, tun," *THAT* 2 (München: Chr. Kaiser Verlag, Zürich: Theologischer Verlag, 1984) 359-370

Volterra, Edoardo, review of Emil G. Kraeling, *The Brooklyn Museum Aramaic Papyri*, Yale University Press, 1953, *Iura* 6 (1955) 349-360

Vriezen, Theodorus Christaan, *Onderzoek naar de paradijsvoorstelling bij de oude semietische volken. Diss. Utrecht* (Wageningen: H. Veenman, 1937)

———, *An Outline of Old Testament Theology* (Newton, MA: Charles T. Brantford, 1958)

———, "Eid," in *Biblische-historisches Handwörterbuch*, Bd. 1, B. Reicke and L. Rost, eds. (Göttingen: Vanderhoeck & Ruprecht, 1962-66) 374-76

———, "The Exegesis of Exodus 24:9-11," *OTS* 17 (1972) 100-133

———, "How to Understand Malachi 1:11," in *Grace upon Grace: Essays in Honor of Lester J. Kuyper*, J.I. Cook, ed. (Grand Rapids, MI: Eerdmans, 1975) 128-36

Vuilleumier, René, see Samuel Amsler, André Lacocque and René Vuilleumier, *Aggée, Zacharie, Malachie*

Wadsworth, T., "Is There a Hebrew Word for Virgin? Bethulah in the Old Testament," *Restoration Quarterly* 23 (1980) 161-171

Wallis, Gerhard, "Wesen und Struktur der Botschaft Maleachis," in *Das ferne und nahe Wort: Fs Leonard Rost*, F. Maass, ed., BZAW 105 (Berlin: A. Töpelmann, 1967) 229-237

———, "אָהַב, 'āhabh," in *TDOT* 1 (Grand Rapids, MI: Eerdmans, 1978) 99-118

———, "דָּבַק, dābhaq," in *TDOT* 3 (Grand Rapids, MI: Eerdmans, 1978) 79-84

Waltke, Bruce K., and M. O'Connor, *An Introduction to Biblical Hebrew Syntax* (Winona Lake, IN: Eisenbrauns, 1990)

Walton, John H., *Ancient Israelite Literature in its Cultural Context. A Survey of Parallels Between Biblical and Ancient Near Eastern Literature* (Grand Rapids, MI: Zondervan, 1989)

Ward, William A., "Reflections on some Egyptian terms presumed to mean 'harem, harem-woman, concubine'," *Berytus* 31 (1983) 67-74

Watson, Wilfred G.E., *Classical Hebrew Poetry. A Guide to Its Techniques*, JSOTSup 26 (Sheffield, England: JSOT Press, 1984, 1986)

Watt, W. Montgomery, *Muhammad, Prophet and Statesman* (London: Oxford University, 1964)

Watts, John D.W., *Obadiah. A Critical Exegetical Commentary* (Grand Rapids, MI: Eerdmans, 1969 [reprinted 1981 by Winona Lake, IN: Alpha Publications])

———, *Isaiah 1-33*, WBC 24 (Waco, TX: Word, 1985)

———, *Isaiah 34-66*, WBC 25 (Waco, TX: Word, 1987)

Weber, Robertus, *et al.*, eds., *Biblia Sacra Iuxta Vulgatam Versionem* (Stuttgart: Deutsche Bibelgesellschaft, 1983)

Weidner, E.F., *Politische Dokumente aus Kleinasien. Die Staatsverträge in akkadischer Sprache aus dem Archiv von Boghazkoi. Boghazkoi Studien* 8-9 (Leipzig, 1923)

Weinfeld, Moshe, "Deuteronomy — The Present State of Inquiry," *JBL* 86 (1967) 249-262

———, "The Covenant of Grant in the Old Testament and in the Ancient Near East," *JAOS* 90 (1970) 184-203

———, *Deuteronomy and the Deuteronomic School* (Oxford: Clarendon, 1972)

———, "Bᵉrît — Covenant vs. Obligation," *Biblica* 56 (1975) 120-128

———, "Covenant, Davidic," in *IDBSup* (Nashville, TN: Abingdon, 1976) 188-192

———, "The Loyalty Oath in the Ancient Near East," in *Ugarit-Forschungen* 8 (1976) 379-414

———, "בְּרִית bᵉrîth," in *TDOT* 2 (Grand Rapids, MI: Eerdmans, 1977) 253-279

———, "Social and Cultic Institutions in the Priestly Source against their Ancient Near Eastern Background," in *Proceedings of the Eighth World Congress of Jewish Studies, Jerusalem, August 16-21, 1981. Panel Sessions: Bible Studies and Hebrew Language* (Jerusalem: World Union of Jewish Studies and The Perry Foundation for Biblical Research, 1983) 95-129

Weiser, Artur, *Das Buch Jeremia*, ATD 20/21 (Göttingen: Vandenhoeck & Ruprecht, 1969)

Weiss, David Halivni, "A Note on אשר לא ארשה," *JBL* 81 (1962) 67-69

———, "The Use of qnh in Connection with Marriage," *HTR* 57 (1964) 244-248

Welch, Adam Cleghorn, *Post-Exilic Judaism*, The Baird Lecture for 1934 (Edinburgh: Blackwood, 1935)

Welch, John W., "Reflections on Postulates: Power and Ancient Laws - A Response to Moshe Greenberg," in *Religion and Law. Biblical-Judaic and Islamic Perspectives*,

E.B. Firmage, B.G. Weiss, and J.W. Welch, eds. (Winona Lake, IN: Eisenbrauns, 1990) 113-119

Wellhausen, Julius, *Skizzen und Vorarbeiten. Die kleinen Propheten übersetzt, mit Noten,* 5e Aufl. (Berlin: Georg Reimer, 1892 [4e Aufl. reprinted by W. De Gruyter, Berlin, 1963])

Wendland, Ernst, "Linear and Concentric Patterns in Malachi," *The Bible Translator* 36 (1985) 108-121

Wenham, Gordon J., "Legal Forms in the Book of the Covenant," *TB* 22 (1971) 95-102

——, "*betûlāh* 'A Girl of Marriageable Age'," *VT* 22 (1972) 326-48

——, *The Book of Leviticus,* NICOT (Grand Rapids, MI: Eerdmans, 1979)

——, "The Restoration of Marriage Reconsidered," *JJS* 30 (1979) 36-40

——, *Numbers. An Introduction and Commentary,* TOTC (Leicester, England and Downers Grove, IL: Inter-Varsity, 1981)

——, "The Symbolism of the Animal Rite in Genesis 15: A Response to G.F. Hasel, *JSOT* 19 (1981) 61-78," *JSOT* 22 (1982) 134-137

——, "Sanctuary Symbolism in the Garden of Eden," in *Proceedings of the Ninth World Congress of Jewish Studies, Jerusalem, August 4-12, 1985. Division A: The Period of the Bible* (Jerusalem: World Union of Jewish Studies, 1986) 19-25

——, *Genesis 1-15,* WBC 1 (Waco, TX: Word, 1987)

Wenham, Gordon J., and J.G. McConville, "Drafting Techniques in Some Deuteronomic Laws," *VT* 30 (1980) 248-252

Westbrook, Raymond, "Old Babylonian Marriage Law," Ph.D. diss. (Yale University, 1982)

——, "The Enforcement of Morals in Mesopotamia," *JAOS* 104 (1984) 753-756

——, "Biblical and Cuneiform Law Codes," *RB* 92 (1985) 247-264

——, "*Lex talionis* and Exodus 21:22-25," *RB* 93 (1986) 52-69

——, "The Prohibition on Restoration of Marriage in Deuteronomy 24:1-4," in *Studies in Bible 1986: Scripta Hierosolymitana* 31, S. Japhet, ed. (Jerusalem: Magnes, 1986) 387-405

Westbrook, Raymond, *et al.,* "Responses to Prof. Roth's Paper," in *Women's Earliest Records From Ancient Egypt and Western Asia. Proceedings of the Conference on Women in the Ancient Near East, Brown University, Providence Rhode Island, November 5-7, 1987,* B.S. Lesko, ed., Brown Judaic Studies 166 (Atlanta, Georgia: Scholars, 1989) 256-260

Westcott, Richard S., "The Concept of *berît* with Regard to Marriage in the Old Testament," Th.M. diss. (Dallas Theological Seminary, 1985)

Westermann, Claus, *Genesis 1-11: A Commentary,* J.J. Scullion, trans. (London: SPCK and Minneapolis: Augsburg, 1984)

——, *Genesis 12-36: A Commentary,* J.J. Scullion, trans. (Minneapolis: Augsburg, 1985)

——, *Genesis 37-50: A Commentary,* J.J. Scullion, trans. (Minneapolis: Augsburg, 1986)

Westermann, Claus, and R. Albertz, "רוּחַ *rûaḥ* Geist," *THAT* 2 (München: Chr. Kaiser Verlag, Zürich: Theologischer Verlag, 1984) 726-753

Wevers, John William, *Ezekiel,* NCB (London: Thomas Nelson and Sons Ltd., 1969)

Whitaker, Richard E., ed., *The Eerdmans Analytical Concordance to the Revised Standard Version of The Bible* (Grand Rapids, MI: Eerdmans, 1988)

White, Hugh C., "The Divine Oath in Genesis," *JBL* 92 (1973) 165-179

White, John Bradley, *A Study of the Language of Love in the Song of Songs and Ancient Egyptian Poetry,* SBLDS 38 (Missoula, MT: Scholars, 1978)

Whybray, R.N., *Wisdom in Proverbs,* Studies in Biblical Theology 45 (London: SCM, 1965)

Widengren, Geo., "The Persian Period," in *Israelite and Judean History,* J.H. Hayes and J.M. Miller, eds. (Philadelphia: Westminster, 1977) 489-538

Wierzbicka, Anna, *Lexicography and Conceptual Analysis* (Ann Arbor: Karoma, 1985)

Wifall Jr., Walter R., "Bone of my Bones and Flesh of my Flesh - The Politics of the Yahwist," *Currents in Theology and Missions* 10 (1983) 176-183

Wildberger, Hans, *Jesaja.I. Teilband: Jesaja 1-12,* BKAT X/1 (Neukirchen-Vluyn: Neukirchener Verlag, 1972)

——, *Jesaja. 2. Teilband: Jesaja 13-27,* BKAT X/2 (Neukirchen-Vluyn: Neukirchener Verlag, 1978)

——, *Jesaja. 3. Teilband: Jesaja 28-39; Das Buch, der Prophet und seine Botschaft,* BKAT X/3 (Neukirchen-Vluyn: Neukirchener Verlag, 1982)

——, "שאר *s'r* übrig sein," *THAT* 2 (München: Chr. Kaiser, Zürich: Theologischer Verlag, 1984) 844-55

Williams, James G., *Women Recounted: Narrative Thinking and the God of Israel*, Bible and Literature Series, 6 (Sheffield: Almond, 1982)

Williams, Ronald J., *Hebrew Syntax: An Outline*, 2nd ed. (Toronto and Buffalo: University of Toronto, 1976)

Williamson, H.G.M., *Ezra, Nehemiah*, WBC 16 (Waco, TX: Word, 1985)

Wilson, Edward O., *Sociobiology: The New Synthesis* (Cambridge, MA: Harvard University, 1975)

——, *On Human Nature* (Cambridge, MA: Harvard University, 1978)

Wilson, John A., "The Oath in Ancient Egypt," *JNES* 7 (1948) 129-156

Wilson, Marvin R., *Our Father Abraham. Jewish Roots of the Christian Faith* (Grand Rapids, MI: Eerdmans; and Dayton, OH: Center for Judaic-Christian Studies, 1989)

Wilson, Robert W., "Sociology of the Old Testament," in *Harper's Bible Dictionary*, P.J. Achtemeier, *et al.*, eds. (San Francisco: Harper and Row, 1985) 968-973

Winckler, Hugo, "Maleachi," in *Altorientalische Forschungen, II Reihe, Band III* (Leipzig: Eduard E. Pfeiffer, 1899) 531-539

Wiseman, Donald J., *The Alalakh Tablets*, Occasional Publications of the British Institute of Archaeology at Ankara, No. 2 (London: British Institute of Archaeology at Ankara, 1953)

——, "Supplementary Copies of Alalakh Tablets," *JCS* 8 (1954) 1-30

——, "Abban and Alalaḫ," *JCS* 12 (1958) 124-129

——, *The Vassal-Treaties of Esarhaddon, Iraq*, 20, Part 1 (London: British School of Archaeology in Iraq, 1958)

——, "The Laws of Hammurabi Again," *JSS* 8 (1962) 161-72

——, "'Is it Peace?' — Covenant and Diplomacy," *VT* 32 (1982) 311-326

Wolf, Herbert, *Haggai and Malachi: Rededication and Renewal*, Everyman's Bible Commentary (Chicago: Moody, 1976)

——, "The Apology of Ḫattušiliš Compared with Other Political Self-Justifications of the Ancient Near East," Ph.D. diss. (Brandeis University, 1967)

Wolff, Hans Walter, "Erkenntnis Gottes im AT," *EvT* 15 (1955) 426-431

——, "The Kerygma of the Yahwist," *Interpretation* 20 (1966) 131-58 [orig. published in *EvT* 24, 1964, 73-97]

——, *Anthropology of the Old Testament*, M. Kohl, trans. (Philadelphia, PA: Fortress and London: SCM Ltd., 1974)

——, *Hosea. A Commentary on the Book of the Prophet Hosea*, Hermeneia (Philadelphia: Fortress, 1974)

——, *Joel, Amos. A Commentary on the Books of the Prophets Joel and Amos*, Hermeneia, W. Janzen, S.D. McBride Jr., and C.D. Muenchow, trans. (Philadelphia: Fortress, 1977)

——, *Obadiah and Jonah. A Commentary*, M. Kohl, trans. (London: SPCK; and Minneapolis: Augsburg, 1986)

Woude, Adam Simon van der, "1 Reg. 20 $_{34}$," *ZAW* 76 (1964) 188-190

——, *Haggai, Maleachi*, POT (Nijkerk: G.F. Callenbach, 1982)

——, "Malachi's Struggle for a Pure Community. Reflections on Malachi 2:10-16," in *Tradition and Re-interpretation in Jewish and Early Christian Literature. Essays in Honour of Jürgen C.H. Lebram*, J.W. van Henten, H.J. de Jonge, P.T. van Rooden, and J.W. Wesselius, eds., Studia Post-Biblica 36 (Leiden: E.J. Brill, 1986) 65-71

Woudstra, Marten H., "The Everlasting Covenant in Ezekiel 16:59-63," *Calvin Theological Journal* 6 (1971) 22-48

Wright, Christopher J.H., *An Eye for An Eye* (Downers Grove, IL: InterVarsity, 1983)

Wright, G.E., "The Lawsuit of God. A Form-Critical Study of Deuteronomy 32," in *Israel's Prophetic Heritage*, B.W. Anderson and W. Harelson, eds. (New York and London: Harper, 1962) 26-67

Würthwein, Ernst, *The Text of the Old Testament*, E.F. Rhodes, trans. (Grand Rapids, MI: Eerdmans, 1979)

Yadin, Yigael, "Expedition D - The Cave of the Letters," *IEJ* 12 (1962) 244-245

Yamauchi, Edwin M., "Ezra, Nehemiah," in *The Expositor's Bible Commentary*, 4, F.E. Gaebelein, ed. (Grand Rapids, MI: Zondervan, 1988) 565-771

——, "Cultural Aspects of Marriage in the Ancient World," *Bibliotheca Sacra* 135 (1978) 241-252

——, "The reverse order of Ezra/Nehemiah reconsidered," *Themelios* 5 (1980) 7-13

Yaron, Reuven, "On Divorce in Old Testament Times," *Revue Internationale des Droits de l'Antiquité*, 3rd series 4 (1957) 117-128
——, "Aramaic Marriage Contracts from Elephantine," *JSS* 3 (1958) 1-39
——, "Aramaic Marriage Contracts: Corrigenda and Addenda," *JSS* 5 (1960) 66-70
——, *Introduction to the Law of the Aramaic Papyri* (Oxford: Clarendon, 1961)
——, "Matrimonial Mishaps at Eshnunna," *JSS* 8 (1963) 1-16
——, "The Restoration of Marriage," *JJS* 17 (1966) 1-11
——, *The Laws of Eshnunna*, 2nd ed. (Leiden: E.J. Brill; and Jerusalem: Magnes, The Hebrew University, 1988)
Yee, Gale A., *Composition and Tradition in the Book of Hosea: A Redaction Critical Investigation*, SBLDS 102 (Atlanta, GA: Scholars, 1987)
——, "I Have Perfumed My Bed With Myrrh': The Foreign Woman (*'iššâ zārâ*) in Proverbs 1-9," *JSOT* 43 (1989) 53-68
Young, Dwight Wayne, "A Ghost Word in the Testament of Jacob (Gen 49:5)?" *JBL* 100 (1981) 335-342
Youngblood, Ronald F., "תָּעַב abhor, etc.," in *TWOT* 2 (Chicago: Moody, 1980) 976-977
Zakovitch, Yair, *'For Three ... and for Four': The Pattern for the Numerical Sequence Three - Four in the Bible* [Hebrew] (Jerusalem: Makor, 1979)
——, "The Woman's Rights in the Biblical Law of Divorce," *The Jewish Law Annual*, 4, B.S. Jackson, ed. (Leiden: E.J. Brill, 1981) 28-46
Zeitlin, Solomon, "The Origin of the Kethubah: A Study in the Institution of Marriage," *Jewish Quarterly Review* N.S. 24 (1933-34) 1-7
Zevit, Ziony, "A Phoenician Inscription and Biblical Covenant Theology," *IEJ* 27 (1977) 110-118
——, "Converging Lines of Evidence Bearing on the Date of P," *ZAW* (1982) 481-511
Ziegler, Joseph, "Die Liebe Gottes bei den Propheten," *Alttestamentliche Abhandlungen* 11 (1930) 73-77
——, ed., *Duodecim Prophetae. Septuaginta, Vetus Testamentum Graecum, Auctoritate Academiae Scientiarum Gottingensis editum*, 13 (Göttingen: Vandenhoeck & Ruprecht, 1984)
Zimmerli, Walther, *Ezekiel I. A Commentary on the Book of the Prophet Ezekiel, Chapters 1-24*, Hermeneia, R.E. Clements, trans. (Philadelphia: Fortress, 1979)
——, *Ezekiel 2. A Commentary on the Book of the Prophet Ezekiel Chapters 25-48*, J.D. Martin, trans., Hermeneia (Philadelphia: Fortress, 1983)

INDEX OF SOURCES

1. BIBLE

2. CUNEIFORM LEGAL CORPORA

3. OTHER ANCIENT SOURCES

INDEX OF TERMS

AKKADIAN

ARABIC

ARAMAIC

EGYPTIAN

HEBREW

HITTITE

LATIN

PHOENICIAN

SUMERIAN

UGARITIC

INDEX OF AUTHORS

INDEX OF SUBJECTS

Gordon P. Hugenberger (Ph.D., C.N.A.A., College of St. Paul and St. Mary/ The Oxford Centre for Post-Graduate Hebrew Study) is senior minister of Park Street Church, Boston. He also teaches Old Testament at Gordon-Conwell Theological Seminary.